# THE LETTERS OF
# CHARLES DICKENS

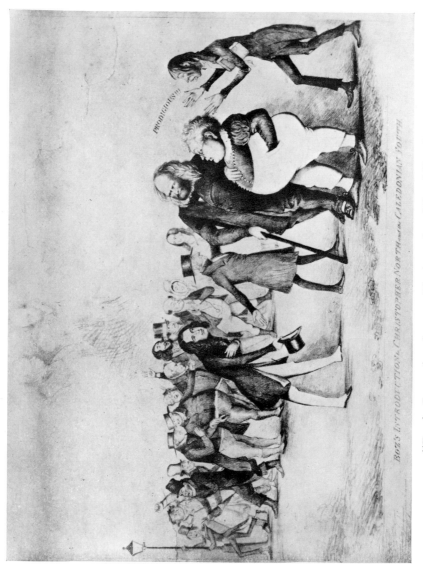

PRODIGIOUS!!

*BOZ'S INTRODUCTION to CHRISTOPHER NORTH—the CALEDONIAN YOUTH*

"Boz's Introduction to Christopher North", 1841

THE PILGRIM EDITION

# The Letters of
# Charles Dickens

Volume Two
1840–1841

EDITED BY
Madeline House & Graham Storey

ASSOCIATE EDITOR
Kathleen Tillotson

CLARENDON PRESS · OXFORD
1969

*Oxford University Press, Ely House, London W.1*

GLASGOW NEW YORK TORONTO MELBOURNE WELLINGTON
CAPE TOWN SALISBURY IBADAN NAIROBI LUSAKA ADDIS ABABA
BOMBAY CALCUTTA MADRAS KARACHI LAHORE DACCA
KUALA LUMPUR SINGAPORE HONG KONG TOKYO

Printed and bound in Great Britain by Butler & Tanner Ltd, Frome and London

# CONTENTS

# ILLUSTRATIONS

# PREFACE

Since the publication of our first volume in 1965, new letters have continued to flow in. The total of letters known to us has risen by 802 (from 11,956 to 12,758), and the total that we have transcribed from the originals or photographs by 591 (from 8038 to 8629). The present volume contains 706 letters (including extracts and mentions), of which 250 are published for the first time. The texts of 471 are given from the originals or photographs. Of the rest, 80 are extracts from letters to Forster of which the manuscripts have presumably been destroyed.

The volume begins with Dickens's preparations for *Master Humphrey's Clock*, includes the first public dinner given in his honour and his tour of the Highlands, and ends on the eve of his departure for America.

The year 1841 is unique in Dickens's correspondence, in being the only year in which the letters he received have survived in some bulk. These escaped his later holocausts through being deposited, before he left for America, with his solicitor, Thomas Mitton, with whom they remained, forgotten—at least by Dickens himself. An account is given in Volume I, p. xx, of how in 1879, the year after Mitton's death, Georgina Hogarth went through the box containing the letters and burnt "*piles*" of them— many from his parents and other relations about their money difficulties. But she spared a large number of letters from Dickens's friends. These are for the most part so intimately connected with Dickens's side of the correspondence, and so often supply annotation, that we have chosen to quote from them extensively in our footnotes, rather than isolate them (complete) in an Appendix. We have omitted only such parts as seem irrelevant or repetitive. Out of the 136 letters to Dickens of this period known to us,[1] there are only eight[2] for which no place has been found.

The years 1840–41 were a period in which Dickens's social life was rapidly expanding and he made or consolidated some of the most important friendships of his life. Maclise and Macready both became firmer friends; through Forster he met and won the affection of Landor; Lord Jeffrey became his fervent admirer; Miss Burdett Coutts took him up socially, thus beginning their long association; Samuel Rogers not only invited him

---

[1] 124 are in the Henry E. Huntington Library, and a dozen scattered elsewhere. Six were published in the New York *Tribune* of 7 Oct 1883.

[2] Two invitations from Ainsworth; a note from Stanfield and another from John Allen (on Lady Holland's behalf) concerning dinner engagements; an excuse from Maclise for not seeing Dickens; a note from John Elliotson, enclosing a pamphlet on phrenology, and another from Southwood Smith, making an appointment; an apology from Cattermole for troubling Dickens with a message to Coutts's Bank about payment for illustrations.

to his breakfasts but made friends of him and Catherine at Broadstairs; he was entertained by the widowed Lady Holland; the doors of Gore House opened to him; he exchanged long letters with Washington Irving in anticipation of his visit to America.

No letters from Forster remained in the Mitton collection after it had passed through Georgina Hogarth's hands. But there must have been scores. Forster's importance to Dickens was now paramount. While still playing his indispensable role in the lives of Landor, Macready and Bulwer, he was Dickens's boon companion and his representative in complicated publishing negotiations with both Richard Bentley and Chapman & Hall. He read the proofs of *Master Humphrey's Clock*, and was frequently given *carte blanche* to make deletions and minor alterations. And it was on his suggestion that Dickens decided that Nell was to die.

The complete manuscripts of *The Old Curiosity Shop* and *Barnaby Rudge* are preserved in the Victoria & Albert Museum, together with corrected galley proofs of Chapters 40–66 of the first and Chapter 18 of the second. The corrected galley proofs of Chapters 29–31 and 37 of *The Old Curiosity Shop* are in the J. F. Dexter collection, now owned by Mrs A. M. Stern. These are the earliest full manuscripts and the first proofs of Dickens's novels to have survived.[1] To clarify his many references to them, we have drawn on them frequently.

With their numerous alterations and cancellations, the proofs afford evidence of the difficulties Dickens experienced in writing for the first time in weekly numbers each containing only twelve printed pages, instead of in monthly parts of 32 pages—which gave him room to advance his story at leisure. It seems unthinkable that he would have embarked on weekly publication, even for the sake of novelty,[2] had he realized that *Master Humphrey's Clock* would develop into two full-length novels (to be written in less than twenty months), instead of continuing as the weekly miscellany he had thought would relieve him from constant pressure—but which, "glorious" as was the sale of the first number,[3] so quickly proved unacceptable to readers and critics alike.[4] *The Old Curiosity Shop*, with sales reaching 100,000 copies, saved the situation, and fully justified the experiment with weekly numbers. But in the following year, when the sales of *Barnaby Rudge* shrank from 70,000 to 30,000, Dickens faced the possibility that he was overwriting.

His letters make little of the strain the two novels put upon him, but

---

[1] Although Dickens apparently became aware of the value of his manuscripts while writing *Nicholas Nickleby* (see Vol. I, p. 437), all but six chapters of it are lost.

[2] See *To* Cattermole, 13 Jan 40.          [3] See *To* William Hall, ?7 Apr 40.

[4] "All this nonsense about the giants [in *Master Humphrey's Clock*, No. 1]", protested the *Monthly Review*, May 40, "is only to usher in one of the weakest and most unfortunate tales—the vilest attempt at pathos—the veriest abortion in the shape of an endeavour to create interest or afford amusement that ever was perpetrated. How Dickens, with his talents and experience, could have suffered such a *thing* to go forth under the sanction of his name is to us a matter of unfeigned marvel."

they show how immense was his relief on winning from Chapman & Hall a year of subsidized freedom.[1] The promise of another novel in 1843, this time in monthly parts, pleased everyone. "We are not sorry that Mr Dickens has discontinued the weekly form of publication", wrote Forster in the *Examiner*, 4 Dec 41. "If it did not impair his powers, it interfered with their right enjoyment. The reader was as much vexed as comforted, by these brief snatches of a story". However, Forster was "not without suspicion" that Dickens's writing in such short instalments "had its advantages too": the opportunities for "mere self-indulgence . . . were extremely rare"; his "tendency to exaggerate" was less; and the two books were "less padded out with useless epithet in matters of reflection."

*The Old Curiosity Shop* was a landmark in Dickens's reputation. But certain legends have grown up around its reception which the letters and related material do not support. Many recent writers have concentrated disproportionately on Nell, in the apparent belief that it was she who was responsible for the vast contemporary success of a novel whose "particular ingredient", according to George Ford, was "tears".[2] Much also has been written about the change in English sensibility since the 1840s—some of it arising from the questionable view that, on reading of Nell's death, most of Dickens's readers wept.

For the response of the public in general, little evidence has been collected. But since 1897, when F. G. Kitton cited Daniel O'Connell, Lord Jeffrey and W. C. Macready as three who were overcome with grief,[3] one writer after another has produced instances to support a generalization about the grief of the majority. Kitton's three names are usually repeated, but others added. The snowball has included Forster, Landor and Thomas Hood ("all at one in weeping");[4] Carlyle ("completely overcome");[5] Edward FitzGerald, Sydney Smith and Poe.

There is indeed evidence for the tears of two of these readers, Jeffrey and Macready.[6] But none has been found to support the inclusion of Carlyle and Sydney Smith (whose admiration of Dickens's pathos was kept for Chuffey).[7] Hood, moreover, wrote his *Athenæum* review of *The Old Curiosity Shop*,[8] in which he devoted only two out of 23 paragraphs to Nell, three months before her death—which he did not foresee. The response of the others was mixed. O'Connell flung away the book after reading of

---

[1] See letters of early Sep 41.
[2] *Dickens and his Readers*, Princeton, 1955, p. 38.
[3] *The Novels of CD*, p. 66.
[4] Arthur Waugh, *A Hundred Years of Publishing*, 1930, p. 49.
[5] Una Pope-Hennessy, *CD, 1812–1870*, 1945, p. 149; see also Edgar Johnson, *CD, his Tragedy and Triumph*, 1953, 1, 304.
[6] See *To* Macready, 22 Jan 41, *fn*, and *To* Forster, 18 Mar 41, *fn*.
[7] *The Letters of Sydney Smith*, ed. Nowell C. Smith, 1953, II, 776.
[8] *Athenæum*, 7 Nov 40.

Nell's death, but with indignation, not tears: "It was obvious", the editor of his *Correspondence*, W. J. Fitzpatrick, reports him as saying, "that the author had not sufficient talent to maintain Nell's adventures with interest to the end and bring them to a happy issue, so he killed her to get rid of the difficulty,"[1] FitzGerald "made a short extract of Nelly's wanderings" for a friend's little girl, but cut out "Boz's sham pathos".[2] Poe's main criticism of *The Old Curiosity Shop* was that Nell's death, though "of the highest order of literary excellence", left "too painful an impression, and should therefore have been avoided."[3]

That the majority of Dickens's readers felt affection for Nell and were deeply interested in her wanderings cannot be doubted. Crabb Robinson, moreover, thought the "pathetic parts" of the book "among the best things" Dickens had written.[4] Two examples of the reaction of the general public to Nell's death can be given. Basil Hall's family shed copious tears when the chapters were read aloud.[5] On the other hand, a response as indignant as O'Connell's and illustrative of Poe's is described in a letter to Forster from a Mrs Jane Greene, of Dublin, written after publication of the first volume of the *Life*. Her uncle, she says:

> like Mr Landor, was so *enchanted* with Little Nell that anyone might have supposed she was a *real living* child in whose sad fate he was deeply interested. One evening while silently reading . . . he suddenly sprung from his chair, flung the book violently on the ground, and exclaimed "The Villain! The Rascal!! The bloodthirsty scoundrel!!!" His astonished brother thought he had *gone mad*, and enquired aghast of whom he was speaking? "Dickens, he roared, he would *commit murder*! He killed my little Nell—He killed my sweet little child"![6]

[1] *Correspondence of Daniel O'Connell*, 1888, II, 112–13.

[2] *Letters of Edward FitzGerald*, ed. [W. A. Wright], 1894, I, 174. FitzGerald's inclusion clearly springs from the following by Una Pope-Hennessy (*CD, 1812–1870*, p. 149): "In Trinity College, Cambridge, there is a small exercise-book entitled '*Little Nell's Wanderings*—such a tale of their wanderings that few can read it without being moved to tears'. Edward FitzGerald . . . had extracted the adventures of Little Nell from the body of *The Old Curiosity Shop* . . ." But the Trinity College MS (in a copyist's hand) has no title, and the words "such a tale . . . tears" do not appear in it. Dame Una has undoubtedly fused a title invented by Charles Ganz for his edition of the Trinity College MS (1933) with an unattached quotation by Ganz from an unspecified source. In fact, pathos—whether sham or otherwise—is singularly lacking in FitzGerald's telling of Nell's story. The death of the schoolmaster's favourite pupil (whom she never meets) is merely reported to her; and her own death is told thus: "And on Christmas day—the 2nd Christmas day of their abode in the Village—Nell died; and while the Holly was fresh in the windows, & the Sun shone clear into the room, there she lay with a smile on her lips as she used to do when asleep in her little bed room in the Old Curiosity Shop.| Finis."

[3] *Graham's Magazine*, May 1841 (reprinted in *The Dickens Critics*, ed. G. H. Ford and Lauriat Lane, Jr, New York, 1961).

[4] *H. Crabb Robinson on Books and their Writers*, ed. E. J. Morley, 1938, II, 590.

[5] See *To* Hall, 19 Feb 41, *fn*.

[6] MS University of California, Los Angeles. Endorsed by Forster: "Kept for its comicality!"

A different argument against Nell's death was advanced in the *Metro-politan Magazine*, March 1841:

> The heroine, little Nelly, for whom every reader must have become so deeply interested, demands and deserves a better fate than to die so prematurely. The author should always bear in mind the vast extent of the number of his readers, and think how many of these there be who are, not at all, or only slightly, imbued with religious principles. Moral, mere moral justice would have awarded a happier fate to the poor girl.

But a periodical "imbued with religious principles"—the High Church *Christian Remembrancer* (Dec 42)—was equally displeased:

> . . . we do object most strongly to the way in which [Nell's] dying and her death are worked up . . . through several numbers, and with minute touches; and yet, if we except her haunting the old church, not a single christian feature is introduced. The whole matter is one tissue of fantastic sentiment, as though the growth of flowers by one's grave, and the fresh country air passing over it, and the games of children near it, could abate by one particle the venom of death's sting, or cheat the grave of any the smallest element of his victory. . . . to work up an elaborate picture of dying and death, without the only ingredient that can make the undisguised reality other than "an uncouth hideous thing" . . . is not dealing fairly by us. . . . Furthermore, we have great doubts as to the propriety of this incessant working up our feelings by pictures of consumption. . . . The subject is, to half the families of England, too fraught with painful reality to be thus introduced in a work of amusement, and amid dreamy sentiment.

That Dickens himself came to believe—as he said in his speech at Edinburgh in June 1841—that it was the "deaths of some imaginary beings"[1] that had endeared him to his readers is probably attributable to the response of Macready, Jeffrey, and Forster (who felt Nell's death as "a kind of discipline of feeling and emotion" which would do him "lasting good");[2] to Landor's comparisons with Shakespeare;[3] to the letters he had apparently received from "the remote wilds of America";[4] and to the particular effort he had put into the writing of the death chapters.

The speeches made at Edinburgh in his honour gave no support to that belief.[5] But at the Boston dinner on 1 February 1842 it gained partial support. Though the great majority of the speakers alluded solely to characters in *Pickwick*, *Oliver Twist* and *Nicholas Nickleby* (particularly *Pickwick*), the president of the dinner, Josiah Quincy, Jr, did refer briefly to the emotion bereaved parents might feel on reading of the school-master's little scholar and Nell; in the nineteenth speech of the evening

---

[1] *Caledonian Mercury*, 26 June 41.        [2] See *To* Forster, ?17 Jan 41 *fn.*
[3] See *H. Crabb Robinson on Books and their Writers*, ed. E. J. Morley, II, 593, and John Forster, *Life of Landor*, 1876, I, 449.
[4] See *To* L. G. Clark, 28 Sep 41 and *fn.*        [5] See *To* Forster, 26 June 41, *fn.*

J. C. Park, rather maudlin, spoke of the "hundreds of mothers" in Boston alone who blessed "with tears of happiness and consolation" the man who "painted to life their own lost and loved one in the saint-like death of little Nell"; and in the twentieth speech George Minns declared that he also knew of instances of parents consoled by the "beautiful sentiments" with which Dickens concluded his account of Nell's death.[1]

Forster's comment, in the *Life*,[2] on *The Old Curiosity Shop*'s reception and "extraordinary success"—"in America most especially"—reads thus: "The pathetic vein it had opened was perhaps mainly the cause of this, but opinion at home continued still to turn on the old characteristics"— humour, the discernment of good, and, finally, the "luxuriant" yet properly controlled "enjoyment and fun".

The letters show that Dickens's state of mind during the writing of the bulk of the book was itself buoyant and cheerful. Moreover, they provide no evidence that his thoughts, during the first 70 chapters, ever turned to his dead sister-in-law, Mary Hogarth.[3] Nell's creation had been haphazard; her death had been no part of a plan until Forster suggested it; it was as "the child" that she had pursued him all night after he had written the chapter first foreshadowing her death;[4] and she was no more than "the poor child" a few days before he began to "murder" her.[5] Mary is only known to have been in his mind when he embarked on the chapter leading up to the discovery of Nell's death. "Old wounds", he wrote to Forster, "bleed afresh when I only think of the way of doing it: . . . Dear Mary died yesterday when I think of this sad story."[6] He had refused several invitations, he continued, because: "I am afraid of disturbing the state I have been trying to get into, and having to fetch it all back again." That "state" was plainly connected with his grief for Mary, but the suggestion here that it was deliberately induced is evidence against an emotional obsession.

It is worth noting how unsentimental his attitude was to the death of an actual child, Macready's daughter, six weeks before he wrote Chapters 71 and 72. Forster's "display of grief" irritated him.[7]

Work on the dating of undated letters has been lighter for this volume than it was for Volume I[8]—though by no means negligible. A considerable number of letters could not have been dated with any sort of confidence if

---

[1] W. G. Wilkins, *CD in America*, 1911, pp. 80 and 81, quoting from the *Boston Advertiser*.

[2] Ed. J. W. T. Ley, 1928, p. 151.

[3] George Ford (*Dickens and his Readers*, p. 64) enlists Dickens's deep distress at having to give up Mary's grave for her brother as evidence of his emotional state of mind while writing *The Old Curiosity Shop*. But he misdates by a year. George Hogarth died in October 1841, nine months after the completion of the book.

[4] *To* Forster, 3 Nov 40.                                    [5] *To* Macready, ?6 Jan 41.

[6] *To* Forster, ?8 Jan 41.                    [7] See *To* Maclise, 27 Nov 40, and *fn.*

[8] See I, xxiii–xxvi.

Devonshire Terrace
Friday Eighteenth December

Dear Miss Coutts.

I cannot thank you
sufficiently for your great kindness,
and am most happy to avail
myself of it.

I have kept the order
for this evening, and beg to return
you the other.

I beg my compliments to
Miss Meredith, and assure you
that I am always with great
sincerity.     Faithfully yours

Charles Dickens

Miss Coutts.

Letter to Miss Coutts, 18 December [1840]

Devonshire Terrace.

Twenty Seventh December 1841.

My Dear Sir.

Some time ago, you sent me
an interesting book of which you are
the author. I forgot to thank you for
it; and I take shame to myself for
having done so. Accept this tardy
acknowledgment, and believe me

Faithfully Yours
Charles Dickens

Robert Owen Esquire.

Letter to Robert Owen, 27 December 1841

a study had not once again been made of the developments in Dickens's signature and handwriting.[1] Out of the 471 letters of which we have seen the originals, 93 are dated with no more than the day of the week—the subject-matter frequently providing no clues to the month or even year of writing. In another 75 letters, the day of the week, date of the month, and the month itself are given, and only the year omitted; but even here the handwriting is often needed to determine the correct year. A letter to Beard, for instance, dated "Devonshire Terrace, Saturday 25th. April",[2] is placed by the Nonesuch editor in 1846, in which year 25 April was indeed a Saturday. But so it was in 1840; and the handwriting makes that year certain. In fact, for dating purposes, an eye must be kept on the handwriting whenever the original is available; for Dickens himself from time to time misdated his letters—for instance at the beginning of a new year.[3]

The signature, when present, is always the most helpful guide, and the formation of the C of "Charles" the most helpful part of it. There are a number of minor variants and occasional regressions, but the general development is clear. At the beginning of 1840 it was very similar to signatures of November and December 1839.[4] During the spring and summer the stroke backwards within the now egg-shaped C was pointed, not looped. In late-summer and autumn this backwards stroke on its return protruded slightly to the right of the C (now no longer a closed egg-shape), across the base of the next few letters. In winter 1840-1 it began the gradual droop and elongation to the right which brought it to the signature of December 1841 shown in this volume, plate 3. (See also Vol. I, plate 2, no. 10.)

Unfortunately many letters do not contain full signatures: some are notes in the third person; others are signed "Boz", or simply with initials (which vary only slightly). The dating of such letters had to depend on the handwriting of the text itself. As with the letters in Volume I, Dickens's writing of his address proved helpful: for instance, the e of "Terrace" (round in early 1840, a small Greek e for the later part of the year) in most of 1841 dropped well below the line, while a correspondingly long-tailed e appeared in "Esquire" in the subscription, and sometimes at the end of paragraphs. For this long final e see plate 3.

But the most interesting change in Dickens's handwriting was one which clearly resulted from his printers' misreading his manuscript. The tail of his initial y had before July 1841 become vestigial (see plate 2). By August he had changed both his y and Y to a new bold form (see plate 3). So —though the old short-tailed y continued to make occasional appearances—it is usually possible to tell at a glance whether a letter is pre- or post-August 1841.

[1] A study which will in fact be essential throughout the edition; for even in the later years there will be occasional undated notes to friends among the great mass of dated letters. [2] See p. 62.
[3] For his misdating also in moments of stress, see To Macready, 21 Feb 40, and To Forster, ?17 Jan 41. [4] See Vol. I, plate 2, no. 8, and plate 7.

For the undated letters of which we have not been able to see the originals (27 of them to Forster, quoted in the *Life*) we have had to assign conjectural dates on the evidence available in other, dated, letters.

Once more there has been difficulty in determining whether Dickens intended capital or small initial letters for many words beginning with *a*, *c*, *m*, *n*, *o*, and *s*. In general, we have judged each ambiguous letter on its own merit, though deciding to print capitals in such combinations as "Infant Children" and "Lord Chamberlain" in the letter to T. J. Thompson of 13 February 1840, where both *c*s in fact look small, and "Old Brompton" in the letter to Maclise of 27 May 1841, where Dickens seems to have written "old". We also print "America" with a capital though the initial *a* is often tiny. Where Dickens refers to *Master Humphrey's Clock* by the last word in the title only, we have made it a rule to give the word as "Clock" even though there may be occasions when he intended "clock", as a joke.

For other details of our policy with regard to texts, see the Preface to Volume I, section 6.

Our references to Forster's *Life* are always, unless otherwise stated, to J. W. T. Ley's annotated edition of 1928; but they include the books and chapters into which the 1876 edition and later reprints were divided, for the guidance of owners of all other editions except the first, which is divided into chapters only. Our texts, however, follow the first edition, 1872–4.

It seems certain that Dickens's long descriptive letters to Forster, such as those from the Highlands in July 1841, were originally broken up into more paragraphs than they are given in the *Life*, and that the dots Forster has inserted in the text often mark the end of a paragraph. But since these dots may cover omissions as well, it has seemed safest not to speculate on their meaning, but to follow the paragraphing in the *Life* exactly.

The letters to Dickens from his friends, on which we draw in footnotes, are sometimes curiously punctuated, and apostrophes are frequently missing. We follow the manuscript except on a very few occasions when a change such as a full-stop for comma makes for easier reading.

When referring to illustrations to *Master Humphrey's Clock*, we give the titles supplied by Thomas Hatton in "A Bibliographical List of the Original Illustrations to the Works of Charles Dickens" (*Retrospectus and Prospectus*, The Nonesuch Dickens, 1937). The illustrations to the first edition, all woodcuts inset in the text, have no titles. Titles—not, however, of Dickens's choosing—were added for the Library Edition, 1861; and various later editions have provided their own. Hatton's is nearest to a standard list.

MADELINE HOUSE
GRAHAM STOREY

# ACKNOWLEDGMENTS

Our acknowledgments must once again begin with an expression of gratitude to the Pilgrim Trustees for the generous grant which has made this edition possible.

We must next thank Mr Christopher C. Dickens, owner of the copyright in Dickens's letters since the death of his grandfather Mr H. C. Dickens, for our continued permission to use unpublished material.

In our first volume we made acknowledgment to all those who had helped since our work on the edition began. Many others have most kindly assisted us since that volume went to press; and we have had further support from those who were closest to our work in earlier years.

First, we owe especial thanks to Professor Kathleen Tillotson for the invaluable help and advice she has generously given us at every stage of this volume. We are most grateful to Sir Rupert Hart-Davis for his continued interest in the edition which owes its birth to him, for his reading of our proofs and his warming encouragement. Once again we gratefully acknowledge the help of Mr W. J. Carlton, particularly in the identification of a number of minor characters. We are much indebted to Professor K. J. Fielding for his work on the Huntington Library's collection of letters to Dickens. We also wish to thank Professor Edgar Johnson for his help on notes concerning Sir Walter Scott and for much useful information about Dickens letters in America; Dr A. N. L. Munby for his many reports on letters advertised in catalogues; Professor Philip Collins for his response to appeals for information; and Mrs Zoë Girling, an Associate Editor in the early days of the edition, for her further help on texts. Finally we must express our gratitude to Mr James Thornton for his index and for much help and advice. Full acknowledgment to Mr Noel Peyrouton, whose sudden death has deprived us of one of our most indefatigable helpers, will be made in our third volume of which he was an Associate Editor.

We acknowledge with gratitude the permission granted by Her Gracious Majesty the Queen to quote from manuscripts in the Royal Archives at Windsor Castle.

For their continued help we are greatly indebted to many libraries and collections in England and America, and in particular to the Pierpont Morgan Library, New York; the Henry W. and Albert A. Berg Collection, New York Public Library; the Fales Collection, New York University Library; and the Victoria & Albert Museum. To the Free Library of Philadelphia (home of the Benoliel Collection) and the Miriam Lutcher Stark Library, University of Texas, we are especially grateful for up-to-date reports on their many recent acquisitions. Our debt to the Henry E. Huntington Library is particularly great in this volume, of which their long series of letters to Dickens from his friends is a major feature. Finally we must express our gratitude to the Trustees of Dickens House, London, for the loan of a microfilm of their whole collection of letters, and to Miss Doris Minards and Miss M. E. Pillers for untiringly reporting to us every letter which comes to their notice.

For permission to publish the letters they have recently made available to us, we gratefully thank the authorities of the following institutions:

Abbot Hall Art Gallery, Kendal; Armidale Folk Museum and City Council, New South Wales; the Australian National University; the Municipal Libraries & Victoria Art Gallery, Bath; Bedford College, University of London; University Library, Bergen; the British Theatre Museum; Claremont College, South California; Connecticut Historical Society; the Imperial College of Science and Technology; Johns Hopkins University; Knox College, Illinois; Milwaukee Public Library; the National Széchényi Library, Budapest; the Society of Antiquaries, Newcastle-upon-Tyne; the Royal Institution, London; the Royal Shakespeare Theatre; the Shakespeare Birthplace Trust; Southeast Missouri State College; Stanford University Libraries; the Swedenborg Society; the Governors of the Wakefield Charities; West Suffolk Record Office.

A major collection of letters from Dickens to Count D'Orsay has recently come to light in the possession of the Duc de Gramont and the Comte de Gramont, to both of whom we wish to express our most grateful thanks for permission to publish them. We must also state our great indebtedness to Dr Claire-Éliane Engel, who will be drawing on the letters in a forthcoming book on D'Orsay yet generously waived her right to prior publication of the earlier ones, and provided us with photographs of the whole collection.

We are also extremely grateful to the following owners who have most kindly allowed us to see original letters or have sent us photographs:

Mrs Gladys Ahern; the Albion Hotel, Broadstairs; Mr David Anderson; Dr Peter Beattie; Mrs M. Bell; Mr Alfred C. Berol; Mr William D. Blatner; Mr J. H. Bolton; the British Transport Hotels and Mr P. Long; Mr R. M. R. Church; Messrs Clark & Smith; Mrs J. R. Cohen; Mr Ralph Crawford; the Earl of Cromer; Mr Robert Cutler; Mrs Richard Heath Dabney; Mr Cedric Dickens; Documents and Autographs Ltd; Mr Laurence H. Eldridge; Mr Edwin A. Elsbach; Mr E. R. Ennion; Mr R. V. Forward; Mr Edward V. E. Fremantle; Professor Helena M. Gamer; Mr R. A. Gilbert; Miss L. E. Godden; Mr George D. Gopen; Mr Eric Dickens Hawksley; Mr James H. Heineman; Sir John Heygate, Bart; Major M. F. Hobbs; Professor Robert D. Horn; Major Sir Joslan Ingilby, Bart; Mrs K. M. Jonas; Mr Lewis P. Kinsey, Jr; Mr D. E. D. Lawson; Mr J. H. Locker-Lampson; Miss Margaret M. Low; Miss Mary Elspeth Milford; Dr A. Murray; Miss B. M. McLeavy; Mrs E. B. McLucie; Mr W. S. G. Macmillan; Mrs Robert Nuttall; Mr James M. Osborn;

Professor Ronald Paulson; Miss Janet Phillips; Messrs Phillips, Son & Neale, Ltd; Mr T. A. G. Pocock; Dr Gordon Ray; Mr R. E. D. Rawlins; Mr Harry Secombe; Mr St John G. A. Sechiari; Mr Laurence Senelick; Mrs John Silcock; Mrs Sheila Sokolov-Grant; Mrs Jessie Stewart; Mr D. Cleghorn Thomson; the Times Bookshop; Mrs Elaine Waley; Miss Ward; Mrs R. E. Yeats-Brown.

We are particularly grateful to Dr E. G. Millar for his kindness in allowing us to see his excellent collection before it passed to the Brotherton Library.

Among those who have assisted us in other ways, we owe especial thanks to Mr Alan Bell for his help on problems connected with Dickens's visit to Edinburgh, as well as for his many reports on letters advertised in catalogues; also to Miss Nina Burgis for some valuable material and her careful reading of our proofs. Mr Edwin G. Sanford, to whom we were already indebted for much assistance on American sale catalogues, has put us still further in his debt by continuing the help Mr Peyrouton gave on questions concerning Dickens's first visit to America. For several extremely helpful suggestions we are indebted to Miss Ruth Mateer[1] and Mr John Harvey.[2]

For other help of many varying kinds we must express our grateful thanks to the following:

Miss Jennifer Aylmer; Professor James J. Barnes; Mr John C. Broderick; Dr LaFayette Butler; Mr John Archer Carter, Jr; Mr John A. V. Chapple; Professor C. L. Cline; Mr Charles Cudworth; Dickinson College, Pennsylvania; Mrs E. Duncan-Jones; Dr J. S. Elce; Mr Malcolm Genet; Mr John W. Gibson; Mr Robin Gilmour; Mr Mark Girouard; Mr John Greaves; Mr W. L. Hanchant; Professor J. P. Hardy; the Historical Manuscripts Commission and Miss Claire Bush; Mr John House; Mr R. W. Ketton-Cremer; Lady Pansy Lamb; Mr Samuel A. Lamson; Miss Jane Langton; Professor Anne Lohrli; Mr David Magee; Dr I. A. H. Munro; the Map Room of the National Library of Scotland; the National Maritime Museum, Greenwich; Dr H. G. Nicholas; Dr Eleanor Nicholes; Mr Richard Ormond; Professor Edgar Rosenberg; Miss E. J. Rowley; Mrs Audrey Scott; Miss A. H. Scott-Elliot; Miss Eirene Skilbeck; Mr W. Slatcher; Dr Michael Slater; Professor Harry Stone; Dr Stanley Wells; Professor Edward M. Wilson.

Finally we must thank, for their help in research, transcription and checking, Dr Rachel O'Higgins, Mrs Arthur Goodman, Mrs Else Eton, Mr Anthony Laude and Mr Frank Robinson.

[1] Especially with regard to the link between Hugh, in *Barnaby Rudge,* and Orson (see p. 338*n*).
[2] Particularly concerning the probable influence of Hood's review of *The Old Curiosity Shop* on its final text (see p. 221*n*).

# BIOGRAPHICAL TABLE

## 1840–1841

| | | |
|---|---|---|
| 1840 | 10 Feb | *Sketches of Young Couples* published. |
| | 29 Feb–4 Mar | At Bath with Forster, to see Landor. |
| | 3–?7 Apr | At Birmingham, visiting Stratford and Lichfield with Catherine and Forster. |
| | 4 Apr | *Master Humphrey's Clock* No. 1 published. |
| | 25 Apr–6 Feb 41 | *The Old Curiosity Shop* published in 40 weekly numbers of *Master Humphrey's Clock*; uninterruptedly from No. 12 (20 June). |
| | 1–?28 June | At Broadstairs, with Catherine and the children. |
| | ?29–30 June | At Chatham, Rochester and Cobham with Forster and Maclise. |
| | 27 July–4 Aug | Visits his parents at Alphington, Devon. |
| | 30 Aug–?10/11 Oct | At Broadstairs, with Catherine and the children. |
| | 15 Oct | *Master Humphrey's Clock*, Vol. I, published. |
| 1841 | 13 Feb–27 Nov | *Barnaby Rudge* published in 42 weekly numbers of *Master Humphrey's Clock*. |
| | 8 Feb | Walter Landor Dickens born. |
| | 24 Feb–3 Mar | At Brighton, with Catherine. |
| | ?12/15 Apr | *Master Humphrey's Clock*, Vol. II, published. |
| | 29 May | Invited to stand as Liberal MP for Reading, but declines. |
| | 19 June | Leaves for Scotland with Catherine. |
| | 22 June–4 July | In Edinburgh. |
| | 25 June | Dinner in Edinburgh in his honour. |

| | | |
|---|---|---|
| 1841 | 29 June | Receives Freedom of the City of Edinburgh. |
| | 4–16 July | Tour of Scotland with Catherine and Angus Fletcher. |
| | 18 July | Returns to London. |
| | 1 Aug–2 Oct | At Broadstairs, with Catherine and the children. |
| | 9 Aug | *The Pic Nic Papers* published. |
| | 19 Sep | Tells Forster of his decision to go to America. |
| | 2–5 Oct | At Rochester, Cobham and Gravesend with Forster. |
| | 8 Oct | Operated on for fistula. |
| | 24 Oct | Death of Catherine's brother, George Thomson Hogarth. |
| | 6–20 Nov | Convalesces at Windsor. |
| | 4 Dec | Publication of final weekly number (No. 88) of *Master Humphrey's Clock*. |
| | 15 Dec | *Master Humphrey's Clock*, Vol. III published. |
| | 15 Dec | Publication of *The Old Curiosity Shop* and *Barnaby Rudge*, each in one volume. |

# ABBREVIATIONS AND SYMBOLS

| | |
|---|---|
| CD | Used throughout this edition in all references to Charles Dickens and for his name in titles of books and articles. |
| *D* | *The Dickensian; a Magazine for Dickens Lovers*, The Dickens Fellowship, 1905–. |
| *DAB* | *Dictionary of American Biography*. |
| *DNB* | *Dictionary of National Biography*. |
| F, 1872–4 | John Forster, *The Life of Charles Dickens*, 3 vols, 1872–4. |
| F | John Forster, *The Life of Charles Dickens*, edited by J. W. T. Ley, 1928. Our references are to this edition unless otherwise stated. |
| FC | The Forster Collection, Victoria & Albert Museum, London. |
| Macready, *Diaries* | *The Diaries of William Charles Macready 1833-51*, edited by William Toynbee, 2 vols, 1912. |
| MDGH | *The Letters of Charles Dickens*, edited by his Sister-in-law and his Eldest Daughter. Vols I & II, 1880. Vol. III, 1882. |
| MDGH, 1882 | *The Letters of Charles Dickens*, edited by his Sister-in-law and his Eldest Daughter, 2 vols, 1882. |
| MDGH, 1893 | *The Letters of Charles Dickens*, edited by his Sister-in-law and his Eldest Daughter, 1 vol., 1893. |
| N | *The Letters of Charles Dickens*, edited by Walter Dexter, 3 vols, Nonesuch Press, 1938. |
| *OED* | *Oxford English Dictionary*. |
| *To* | "*To*" before a correspondent's name denotes a letter from Dickens. |
| [ ] | Square brackets in letter-headings enclose conjectural dates. In the text they denote words conjecturally supplied and breaks caused by damage to the MS. In footnotes they indicate editorial interpolations. |
| ⋆ | Asterisks in letter-headings denote letters which we believe to be hitherto unpublished. (Extracts from some of these have, however, appeared in Edgar Johnson, *Charles Dickens, his Tragedy & Triumph*, 2 vols, 1953, and in sale-catalogues.) |
| † | Daggers in letter-headings denote letters of which we believe part to be hitherto unpublished. |

# THE LETTERS
## 1840 – 1841

*To* MESSRS BRADBURY & EVANS,[1] 2 JANUARY 1840

MS Dickens House.

1 Devonshire Terrace | Thursday Night January 2nd. 1840
My Dear Sirs.

I determined not to thank you for the Turkey until it was *quite gone*, in order that you might have a becoming idea of its astonishing capabilities.

The last remnant of that blessed bird made its appearance at breakfast yesterday—I repeat it, yesterday—the other portions having furnished forth seven grills, one boil, and a cold lunch or two.

Accept my warm thanks (in which Mrs. Dickens begs to join) for your annual recollection of us, which we value very highly as one of the pleasant circumstances of a pleasant season—and couple with them my hearty wishes for many happy years to both of you and both of yours—and of good health and good work and good feeling to all of us.

Always Faithfully Yours

Messrs. Bradbury and Evans.       CHARLES DICKENS


*To* JOHN FORSTER,[2] [3 JANUARY 1840]

MS Victoria & Albert Museum (FC). *Date:* clearly the day before CD's visit to Upcott of 4 Jan (see *fn*). His Diary entry for 9 Jan records correcting proofs of *Sketches of Young Couples*.

Devonshire Terrace. | Friday Afternoon

My Dear Forster.

Recollecting on consideration that the servants have been up very late indeed for a great many nights—and moreover that I have not yet finished the Couples[3] and have to wait on Mr. Upcott[4] tomorrow—I have

---

[1] See Vol. I, p. 397*n*.

[2] John Forster (1812–76; *DNB*): see Vol. I, p. 239*n*. "This Forster", wrote Carlyle, 31 Oct 41, "is a most noisy man, but really rather a good fellow (as one gradually finds), and with some substance in his tumultuary brains" (*Letters of T. Carlyle to J. S. Mill, John Sterling and R. Browning*, ed. A. Carlyle, 1923, p. 250).

[3] *Sketches of Young Couples*, "By the author of 'Sketches of Young Gentlemen'", illustrated by Browne, was published by Chapman & Hall on 10 Feb 40. No doubt both were

anonymous because CD had agreed with Bentley not to write anything for another publisher (except *Pickwick*, *Nickleby*, the projected one-volume annual publication, and his contribution to *The Pic Nic Papers*) until *Barnaby* was completed (see Vol. I, pp. 650 and 674). "Sketches" were so common at the time that CD's hand was not recognized. The *Mirror* reviewer, 7 Mar 40, wrote of *Sketches of Young Couples*: "A right whimsical review, indeed, does this quizzical brochure make, of all the married couples in the United Kingdom. . . .

determined to resist the Pantomime[1] and to come straight home like a good boy—for which resolution blame Christmas and the New Year; not me.

I shall expect to see you at 2 on Sunday. Meanwhile and always

Believe me | Faithfully Yours

CHARLES DICKENS

## *To* W. C. MACREADY,[2] [?JANUARY 1840]

Extract in Sotheby's catalogue, July 1929; *MS* 1 p.; dated Devonshire Terrace, Saturday morning. *Date:* possibly early 1840: in Oct 39 CD had discussed Burnett's future with Macready (see Vol. 1, p. 592), and by 18 Jan 40 Burnett, having refused other engagements, was in Bath (see *To* Mrs CD, 1 Mar, *fn*).

*Saying that he wants to* come over to [Macready] and ask a question about Burnett who being in a cleft stick requires [CD's] advice.

one and all are cleverly touched by the satirically-pointed pen of the shrewd sketcher." CD received £200 for the book. He had received £125 for *Sketches of Young Gentlemen* (published 10 Feb 38).

[4] William Upcott (1779–1845; *DNB*): see Vol. 1, p. 594*n*. A letter to the *Dickensian* in 1924 reported the sale, "about 1910", of a copy of *Pickwick* presented by CD to Upcott, with the following in CD's hand pasted into it: "January 4th, 1830 [*clearly a mistake for 1840*], 102 Upper Street, Islington. Being the date of my first visit to this most extraordinary antiquarian mansion, whereto I mean to return at the earliest possible opportunity to refresh myself with a few dusty draughts from its exhaustless well. CHARLES DICKENS'' (*D*, July 1924, xx, 159). A copy of Chapman & Hall's "new edition" of *Sketches by Boz*, 1839, inscribed by CD to Upcott, was sold at Sotheby's in 1930. See also CD's Diary entry for 17 June 41 (Appx, p. 463).

[1] Perhaps the Drury Lane pantomime, which the *Examiner* described on 29 Dec 39 as "introduced by a satirical burlesque on *Jack Sheppard*, which we have not yet seen, but of which we hear excellent accounts". A review of the burlesque was promised for the following week but did not

materialize. Possibly Forster, on CD's crying off, decided not to go either.

[2] William Charles Macready (1793–1873; *DNB*): see Vol. 1. p. 279*n*. At the Haymarket under Benjamin Webster until 7 Dec 41, except for a brief spell at Drury Lane 22 Jan–8 Mar 40 and a short provincial tour in Spring 41. In Dec 39 had hoped to be appointed Licenser of Plays, give up the stage, and retire with this family to the country (*Diaries*, II, 37); but the post went elsewhere. During 1839 a subscription list had been opened for a testimonial to him, in recognition of his "exertions to elevate the National Drama" (*To* Miss Coutts, 28 Feb 43); the original list was in CD's hand, "for the use of John Forster Esq" (Walter T. Spencer catalogue, n.d., in Eastgate House, Rochester); but on the failure of Hammersley's Bank, Sep 40, the testimonial was postponed till June 43 (see Vol. III). Though he continued to make enemies on the stage (and aroused the jealousy of Knowles and Talfourd when he preferred Bulwer's plays), he also inspired devotion: "I worshipped Macready both as an actor and a man", said Mrs Keeley (of her engagement at Drury Lane Dec 41); "He was one of the kindest and most courteous gentlemen I have ever known" (W. Goodman, *The Keeleys*, 1895, p. 85).

## *To* CHARLES MOLLOY,[1] JANUARY [1840]

Extract in P. J. Dobell & Son catalogue, New Series No. 1 (1913); *MS* 2 pp.; from Devonshire Terrace. *Date:* Jan (1840) according to catalogue; presumably shortly before *To* Molloy, 9 Jan, on the same subject.

I am very much and very truly obliged to you for the interest you have taken in that annoying matter. If anything could have obliged me more than your frank and friendly communication to me in the first instance, it would have been this.

I am still very uneasy and nervous lest any gentleman unknown should be signing my name for his own convenience[2]—and I think the best thing I can do will be to tell either Sir Edmund Antrobus[3] or Mr. Marjoribanks[4] what I have heard and beg them to look out carefully for me.

## *To* CHARLES MOLLOY, [9 JANUARY 1840]

MS Brotherton Library, Leeds. *Date:* PM 9 Jan 40 (Thursday). *Address:* Charles Molloy Esquire | 8 New Square | Lincolns Inn.

1 Devonshire Terrace, York Gate. | Thursday Morning.
My Dear Sir

I am much obliged to you, and think you are right. We will let the matter rest where it is.

Faithfully Yours

Charles Molloy Esquire.　　　　　　　　CHARLES DICKENS

## *To* THOMAS MITTON,[5] [?9 JANUARY 1840]

MS Winifred A. Myers (Autographs) Ltd. *Date:* Handwriting suggests early 1840. The parcel was perhaps the "proofs of Young Couples" which CD spent the whole of Thurs 9 Jan correcting, and the enclosed cheque perhaps the £19 to the Britannia Life Insurance Co. shown in his Account Book (MS Messrs Coutts) as paid on 18 Jan (the amount of the next premium, paid 8 Aug 40, was £18.17.6—i.e. "something less" than the cheque sent in Jan). Apparently Mitton did not dine with CD as suggested: see next. *Address:* Mr. Thomas Mitton | Charles Molloy Esqre | 8 New Square | Lincolns Inn.

Devonshire Terrace | Thursday Morning.
My Dear Mitton

I have received a parcel from Bradbury's people this morning which

---

[1] Charles Molloy (?1796–1852): see Vol. 1, p. 35*n*.

[2] For the report that had caused CD's fear, see *To* Molloy, 28 Dec 39; 1, 623–624.

[3] Sir Edmund Antrobus, Bart (1792–1870), partner in Coutts's Bank since 1816.

[4] Edward Marjoribanks (1776–1868): see Vol. 1, p. 527*n*. Partner in Coutts's Bank since 1797.

[5] Thomas Mitton (1812–78): see Vol. 1, p. 35*n*. In partnership with Charles Smithson; but purchased the practice late 1841 (see *To* Mitton, 29 Oct 41), and continued as CD's solicitor, alone.

will oblige me (most unwillingly) to stay at home all day. Our engagement therefore must stand over.

I haven't my banker's book at home and consequently don't know exactly what the Insurance money is. But I think the amount is something less than that of the inclosed cheque.

I shall expect to see you to dine here tomorrow. Will you call in before you wait upon the prig next door,[1] that I may shew you what I propose to do.

> Always Faithfully Yours
>
> CD.

## *To* JOHN FORSTER, [?10 JANUARY 1840]

Extract in F, ii, vi, 143. *Date:* according to Forster, "a few days" before next; but CD had not thought of the two possible titles until 9 Jan and did not dine out that day (see Diary, p. 461). Letter must surely have been written between his "considering new work in all possible ways" on the 9th (*ibid*) and starting work on the 11th: i.e. on the same day as next.

I will dine with you. I intended to spend the evening in strict meditation (as I did last night); but perhaps I had better go out, lest all work and no play should make me a dull boy. *I* have a list of titles too, but the final title I have determined on—or something very near it. I have a notion of this old file in the queer house, opening the book by an account of himself, and, among other peculiarities, of his affection for an old quaint queer-cased clock; showing how that when they have sat alone together in the long evenings, he has got accustomed to its voice, and come to consider it as the voice of a friend; how its striking, in the night, has seemed like an assurance to him that it was still a cheerful watcher at his chamber-door; and how its very face has seemed to have something of welcome in its dusty features, and to relax from its grimness when he has looked at it from his chimney-corner. Then I mean to tell how that he has kept odd manuscripts in the old, deep, dark, silent closet where the weights are; and taken them from thence to read (mixing up his enjoyments with some notion of his clock); and how, when the club came to be formed, they, by reason of their punctuality and his regard for this dumb servant, took their name from it. And thus I shall call the book either *Old Humphrey's Clock,*[2] or *Master Humphrey's Clock*; beginning with a woodcut of old Humphrey and his clock, and explaining the why and wherefore. All Humphrey's own papers will be dated then From my clock-side, and I have divers thoughts about the best means of introducing the others. I thought about this all day yester-

---

[1] Edmund Sharp, solicitor, lived at 2 Devonshire Terrace. Possibly a pun: both "prig" and "sharp" are slang for "cheat".

[2] CD possibly rejected this title on remembering or being reminded that George Mogridge (1787–1854; *DNB*) had used "Old Humphrey" as his pen-name in the Religious Tract Society's *Weekly Visitor* (1833–7) and in 1839 published *Old Humphrey's Addresses* and *Old Humphrey's Observations.*

day and all last night till I went to bed. I am sure I can make a good thing of this opening, which I have thoroughly warmed up to in consequence.


## *To* JOHN FORSTER, [10 JANUARY 1840]

MS Victoria & Albert Museum (FC). *Date:* clearly Fri 10 Jan, the day after he entered in his Diary: "Qy. Title | Old Humphrey's Clock | Master Humphrey's Clock" (see Appx, p. 461). He started work on the book on Sat 11th (*To* Cattermole, 13 Jan). *Address:* John Forster Esquire.

Devonshire Terrace | Friday.

My Dear Forster

Coutts's people had made a mistake in not entering the bill in my book for this year, and I was fearful that it might fall due before we had provided for it. I find now, that the day is the *14th*.[1]

I am thinking awfully,[2] but not writing, as I intend (Please God) to start tomorrow. I incline rather more to *Master* Humphrey's Clock than old Humphrey's—if so be that there is no danger of the pensive confounding "master" with a boy.

Faithfully CD.


## *To* THOMAS HUMPHREYS,[3] [JANUARY 1840]

Mention by Dr Charles Rogers in *Daily News* letter reprinted in *Notes & Queries*, 30 July 70, and quoted by H. Burnett Watson in "The Story of Dotheboys Hall", *Monthly Chronicle of North Country Lore and Legend*, 1 (1887), 294–6. *Date:* probably soon after finally deciding on the title *Master Humphrey's Clock*.

*Telling him that his clock*[4] *had suggested the title of the new book.*[5]

[1] On 14 Jan "Jno Forster's Note £50", deleted, appears on the credit side of CD's account (MS Messrs Coutts).

[2] Used in its slang intensive sense since 1830 (*OED*).

[3] Thomas Humphreys (1787–1868), clock-maker at Barnard Castle from 1815. Had given CD information about the Yorkshire schools while he was staying in Barnard Castle Feb. 38.

[4] William Humphreys (*b.* 1812), son of Thomas, made a clock which stood in a niche on the right of the shop-door 1829–38 and must have been seen by CD. William took it with him to Old Hartlepool in Summer 1838, and Thomas made a new clock which was over his shop-door 1840–57 when he sent it to William and made himself yet another. This last clock was sold by private contract in Newcastle 1876

as the original "Master Humphreys' Clock" and with it CD's "letter of thanks written to Thomas Humphreys in 1839 [*but see below*] . . . concerning the time-piece and his visit to Barnard Castle. The sale was commented on in the local papers at the time, and in the *New York Times*; but the authenticity of the clock was immediately denied by Master Humphreys himself" (*Monthly Chronicle of North Country Lore and Legend*, 1, 391). Clearly the letter "concerning the time-piece" (i.e., presumably, CD's letter about his choice of title) could not have been written before Jan 1840; but an 1839 letter to Humphreys might have thanked him for his help and accompanied a copy of *Nickleby* (see below). Whether in fact CD had any particular clock in mind is uncertain; but there seems no doubt that

*To* MESSRS LONGMAN & CO.,[1] [JANUARY 1840]

Mention in next. *Date:* shortly before the 11th.

*To* MESSRS LONGMAN & CO., 11 JANUARY 1840*

MS Free Library of Philadelphia.

1 Devonshire Terrace | Saturday 11th. January 1840

Dear Sirs.

I am obliged to you for your letter and am in the very best humour I assure you—in proof of which let me say that I am now quite sure you had no intention to annoy or do me an injustice, and that if I shewed you any want of courtesy (which, even under a mistaken impression, was not my intention) I am very sorry for it.

I had not the remotest idea that you intended to "knock me down with poor Jack". But I thought—and I was not alone in thinking—that you were twisting a paragraph for poor Jack's purposes;[2] it always annoys and irritates me greatly to be dragged into print in connection with matters with which I have no concern;[3] and I was the more annoyed that *you* should do this, as I had congratulated myself very much previously, on having such people as you in the same field. Your reply to my note assures me that I did not calculate upon your fairness and integrity without good reason.

Very truly Yours

Messrs. Longman and Company.                    CHARLES DICKENS

---

the clock-shop inspired his new title. See also *To* Alexander, 3 Dec 41 and *fn*.

[5] Humphreys told Dr Rogers (who visited him 1864): "I have a letter from [CD] stating this, and a copy of [*Nickleby*] inscribed with his own hand. For some years we corresponded" (*Notes & Queries*, 30 July 70).

[1] Of Paternoster Row, publishers since 1724. The firm's imprint was now Longman, Orme, and Co. They were Marryat's chief publishers: see next. CD was on friendly terms with both Thomas Longman (1804–79; *DNB*), partner since 1832 and head of the firm from 1842, and William Longman (1813–77; *DNB*), partner since 1839.

[2] Longmans, in their advertisement of the first monthly part of Marryat's

*Poor Jack* (*Morning Chronicle*, 8 Jan), had quoted from the *Examiner* review of 29 Dec 39: "Poor Jack will take a rank of his own, to which he is well entitled, quite apart from those shoals of trash which we owe to Pickwick and Nicholas Nickleby". The full context shows the reviewer to have been pointing out that *Poor Jack* was "an imitation of the admirable writings of Mr Dickens" solely "in the manner of publication" (monthly parts), and was in no other way like the "shoals of trash" which had followed *Pickwick* and *Nickleby*.

[3] For CD's annoyance when Mrs Trollope's *Michael Armstrong* was advertised by Colburn as uniform with *Pickwick* and *Nickleby*, see Vol. 1, pp. 506–7 and 640.

## *To* WILLIAM UPCOTT, [?JANUARY 1840]*

*MS Berg Collection. Date:* Signature suggests early 1840; probably not long after CD's visit to Upcott of 4 Jan.

1 Devonshire Terrace | Saturday Afternoon

My Dear Sir

Thank you a thousand times for your kind recollection of me, and useful inclosure.

I wish I could send you some autographs. A great many of the kind you wish come here sometimes, but I find on enquiry that my lady wife has been bestowing them upon her friends.

Always believe me | Faithfully Yours

William Upcott Esquire                                        CHARLES DICKENS

## *To* GEORGE CATTERMOLE,[1] 13 JANUARY 1840

*MS Free Library of Philadelphia.*

1 Devonshire Terrace | Monday January 13th. 1840

My Dear Cattermole.

I am going to propound a mightily grave matter to you. My new periodical work appears—or I should rather say the first No. does—on Saturday the 28th. of March;[2] and as it has to be sent to America[3] and Germany[4] and must therefore be considerably in advance, it is now in hand—I having in fact begun it on Saturday last. Instead of being published in *monthly* parts at a *shilling* each, only, it will be published in *weekly* parts at three pence *and* monthly parts at a shilling—my object being to baffle the imitators[5] and make it as novel as possible. The plan is a new one—I mean the plan of the fiction—and it will comprehend a great variety of tales. The title is, "*Master Humphrey's Clock*".

[1] George Cattermole (1800–68; *DNB*): see Vol. 1, p. 277*n*.

[2] In fact No. 1 appeared on 4 Apr.

[3] For the arrangement under which Lea & Blanchard, of Philadelphia, published *Master Humphrey* simultaneously in America, see 22 Nov 39; 1, 604. They paid CD £2.10 per No. for advance sheets.

[4] Cf. *To* Diezmann, 10 Mar 40. Until 1840 CD's main German publishers had been J. J. Weber and C. B. Lorck (both of Leipzig) and Georg Westermann and F. Vieweg (both of Brunswick). Two translations of *Master Humphrey* appeared 1840–1, by E. A. Moriarty for Lorck, and by O. von Czarnowski for Vieweg. *Old Curiosity Shop* and *Barnaby* both won higher praise from German critics than had been given to *Oliver* or *Nickleby*. See E. N. Gummer, *Dickens' Works in Germany*, Oxford, 1940, pp. 7–8 and 29–31.

[5] In *Pickwick* (less by design than by the accident of its origin as letterpress to Seymour's plates) CD had been a pioneer in monthly-part fiction. It was a form imitated by Lever, Ainsworth, Thackeray, Surtees, Trollope and many others during the next 30 years. In initiating weekly numbers CD was original again; but whether he would have made the experiment, even to "baffle the imitators" (in which he succeeded), if he had known that *Master Humphrey's Clock* would develop into two full-length novels, is uncertain. Again accident seems to have played a part.

Now, among other improvements, I have turned my attention to the illustrations, meaning to have wood-cuts dropped into the text, and no separate plates.[1] I want to know whether you would object to make me a little sketch *for* a wood-cut[2]—in indian ink would be quite sufficient—about the size of the inclosed scrap: the subject an old quaint room with antique Elizabethian[3] furniture, and in the chimney-corner an extraordinary old clock—*the* clock belonging to Master Humphrey in fact—and no figures. This I should drop into the text at the head of my opening page.[4]

I want to know besides—as Chapman and Hall[5] are my partners in the matter there need be no delicacy about my asking or your answering the question—what would be your charge for such a thing, and whether (if the work answers our expectations) you would like to repeat the joke at regular intervals, and if so, on what terms. I should tell you that I intend asking Maclise to join me likewise,[6] and that the copying the drawing on wood,[7] and the cutting, will be done in first-rate style.[8] We are justified

[1] This was no novelty. Various cheap periodicals had done the same; and CD no doubt chose this illustrative plan because it was suitable for a miscellany. For the use CD made of his freedom to choose where on the page an illustration should be "dropped" to give point to the text, see Joan Stevens, "Woodcuts dropped into the Text", *Studies in Bibliography*, Virginia, xx (1966), 113–134). As index of the impact the illustrations made, Professor Stevens points out that the scenes or images in *Old Curiosity Shop* that Forster particularly recalls (F, II, vii, 152) are all scenes accompanied by illustrations. (Cf. Hood in his *Athenæum* review, 7 Nov 40: see *To Hood*, ?Feb or Mar 41, *fn*).

[2] CD would probably have known and admired Cattermole's drawings of buildings and scenery in Scott's novels, as engraved for Leitch Ritchie's *Scott and Scotland*, 1835; and it was doubtless because of his skill in antiquarian and architectural subjects that he made this request. For CD's original idea of including in *Master Humphrey* papers on such subjects as "London as it was many years ago" and "as it is now", and travel tales along the lines of Irving's *Alhambra*, see Vol. 1, p. 564. When what he had envisaged as miscellany developed into *Old Curiosity Shop* and *Barnaby*, he went out of his way to arrange architectural subjects for Cattermole—such as the gateway put in

"expressly" for him (see ?7 Aug), and the outside of Varden's house.

[3] Thus in MS.

[4] The room Cattermole drew for the headpiece to No. 1 was Elizabethan, but hardly "quaint"; and the clock was central—not in a chimney-corner.

[5] See Vol. 1, p. 128*n*.

[6] 21 of the *Master Humphrey* illustrations are signed by Cattermole; nine, unsigned (one of them a frontispiece), are shown by letters to have been his; seven others, also unsigned, are clearly his on style; two more ("Tony Weller and grandson at the Housekeeper's" and "Master Humphrey's room deserted") seem his—though attributed by Thomas Hatton (*A Bibliographical List of the Original Illustrations to the Works of CD*, 1937) to Browne. Maclise and Samuel Williams (see 31 Mar 40, *fn*) provided one illustration each. But the main illustrator, although not mentioned here, was Browne: 128 illustrations are signed by him; four others, unsigned, are in his style. Hatton (*op. cit.*), mistakenly attributes two illustrations signed by Browne ("Nell and the stoker" and "Mrs Rudge's cottage") to Cattermole.

[7] For a time Browne copied Cattermole's drawings on to the wood (see ?21 Jan). But in Feb 41, Cattermole was himself furnished with a block (see 9 Feb)—probably not for the first time.

[8] 74 of the woodcuts were engraved

by past experience in supposing that the sale would be enormous, and the popularity very great; and when I explain to you the notion I have in my head, I think you will see that it opens a vast number of very good subjects.

I want to talk the matter over with you, and wish you would fix your own time and place—either here, or at your house, or at the Athenæum, though this would be the best place, because I have my papers about me. If you could take a chop with me, for instance, on Tuesday or Wednesday, I could tell you more in two minutes than in twenty letters, albeit I have endeavoured to make this as business-like and stupid as need be.

Of course all these tremendous arrangements are as yet a profound secret, or there would be fifty Humphreys in the field.[1] So write me a line like a worthy gentleman, and convey my best remembrances to your worthy lady.

Believe me always, My Dear Cattermole
Faithfully Yours

George Cattermole Esquire                           CHARLES DICKENS


## To JOHN FORSTER, [?15 JANUARY 1840]

Extract in F, II, viii, 158. *Date:* according to Forster, the day after CD's attendance as juryman at the inquest on a baby "alleged to have been murdered by its mother" (F, II, viii, 157). The inquest was almost certainly that held on 14 Jan at Marylebone Workhouse on the newly-born child of Eliza Burgess.[2]

by Charles Gray (see 13 Oct 40, *fn*); five by Vasey; five by Samuel Williams. 88 were signed by Ebenezer Landells, though 30 of them were in fact cut by the Brothers Dalziel: the proofs are preserved in a scrapbook of their work 1839–47 in the BM. (For this information we are indebted to Mr John Harvey.) Only one illustration, "Leaving the Old Curiosity Shop", lacks the engraver's signature.

[1] Cf. *Richard III*, V, iv, 11: "I think there be six Richmonds in the field".

[2] CD describes serving on a coroner's jury, soon after his move to Devonshire Terrace, in "The Uncommercial Traveller", *All the Year Round*, IX (1863), 279–80—later reprinted as "Some Recollections of Mortality". All the facts fit the inquest on Eliza Burgess's baby, held before Thomas Wakley (see *To* Thompson, 13 Feb, *fn*) on 14 Jan. The mother was a domestic servant aged 25, and the baby discovered dead in her employer's house in Edgware Road. Through CD's exertions, which Wakley encouraged (see CD's article), the jury brought in a verdict of "Found dead", and the mother was sent to trial for concealment of birth, not murder. CD's article continues: "I caused some extra care to be taken of her in the prison, and counsel to be retained for her defence when she was tried at the Old Bailey; and her sentence was lenient, and her history and conduct proved that it was right." Eliza Burgess was tried on 9 Mar, defended by Richard Doane, found guilty of the concealment, but with a strong recommendation to mercy. On a former employer's offering to take her back pending her admittance to the Magdalen Asylum, she was released until the next session. See W. J. Carlton, "Dickens in the Jury Box", *D*, LII (1956), 65–9.

Whether it was the poor baby, or its poor mother,[1] or the coffin,[2] or my fellow-jurymen,[3] or what not, I can't say, but last night I had a most violent attack of sickness and indigestion which not only prevented me from sleeping, but even from lying down. Accordingly Kate and I sat up through the dreary watches.[4]


## To FREDERICK YATES,[5] [?15 JANUARY 1840]

MS Dickens House. *Date:* Handwriting points to Winter 1839–40; Forster in the *Examiner*, 29 Dec 39, announced his intention "to take an early opportunity" of reviewing the Adelphi Pantomime (see *fn*); 15 Jan was the first Wednesday after the 29th on which CD was free to accompany him.

1 Devonshire Terrace | Wednesday Afternoon

My Dear Sir

Forster and I—he for purposes of business, I suppose, and I for pleasure

[1] Forster quotes from "Some Recollections of Mortality" (with slight alterations) CD's description of the mother after the verdict: "The poor desolate creature dropped upon her knees before us with protestations that we were right (protestations among the most affecting that I have ever heard in my life), and was carried away insensible" (F, II, viii, 157).

[2] In "Some Recollections of Mortality", CD describes going to view the body—which was stretched "in the midst of a perfect Panorama of coffins of all sizes", not itself in a coffin but on a clean white cloth on the box in which its mother had first put it, "with a surgical instrument or so at hand" (it had been opened and neatly sewn up again).

[3] By whom CD was "unanimously received . . . as a brother of the utmost conceivable insignificance". Among them were "a broker who had lately cheated [him] fearfully in the matter of a pair of card-tables", but "was for the utmost rigour of the law", and an undertaker who gave him his card as "an inhabitant that was newly come into the parish, and was likely to have a young family" ("Some Recollections of Mortality").

[4] Possibly in replying to this letter Forster suggested a visit to the Adelphi that night: see next.

[5] Frederick Henry Yates (1797–1842; *DNB*), actor-manager of great versatility. Father of Edmund Yates (later friend of CD's). His early parts ranged from Richard III and Shylock to Falstaff and Jaques. Bought the Adelphi in 1825 with Daniel Terry; managed it jointly with Charles Mathews 1825–35; then alone from 1836. Specialized in comic and eccentric parts there, and was clearly at home with dramatizations of CD. For CD's proposal to dramatize *Oliver* for him, see Vol. I, p. 388 and *n.* He produced *The Peregrinations of Pickwick*, in which he played Mr Pickwick, Oct 36 and Apr 37; *Oliver Twist*, Feb 39 (Fagin, with Mrs Yates as Nancy); and *Barnaby Rudge*, Dec 41 (Sir John Chester and also Miss Miggs for a few nights only, with Mrs Yates as Dolly Varden). For his productions of *Nickleby*, see *To* Mrs CD, 1 Mar 40, *fn*; and of *Old Curiosity Shop*, *To* Mitton, 9 Nov 40 and *fn*. In Buckstone's *Jack Sheppard*, Oct 39, he played three parts —Gay, Abraham Mendez and Sam, the one-eyed sailor. He died after breaking a blood-vessel in Dublin 1842. William Oxberry appreciated the particular talent that drew him to CD's characters: "Give Mr. Yates an excrescence upon nature and he is at home" (*Dramatic Biography*, 1826–7, v, 119).

—have just designed a visit to you to-night.[1] Have you an untaken box which you have no better means of bestowing than on such vagrants as we?

Faithfully Yours<br>
CHARLES DICKENS

Frederick Yates Esquire

## *To* H. G. ADAMS,[2] 18 JANUARY 1840†

MS Benoliel Collection.

Private                     1 Devonshire Terrace | York Gate, Regents Park.
Saturday Jany. 18th. 1840

Dear Sir.

The pressure of other engagements will, I am compelled to say, prevent me from contributing a paper to your new local Magazine.[3] But I beg you to set me down as a subscriber to it, and foremost among those whose best wishes are enlisted in your cause. It will afford me real pleasure to hear of your success for I have many happy recollections connected with Kent, and am scarcely less interested in it than if I had been a Kentish man bred and born, and had resided in the County all my life.

---

[1] To see J. B. Buckstone's adaptation of Ainsworth's *Jack Sheppard* and the pantomime *Harlequin and Mother Red Cap; or, Merlin and the Fairy Snowdrop* which followed it. Forster had said of the pantomime on 29 Dec: "we hear that the tricks are excellent"; but no proper review followed. *Jack Sheppard*, which had been on at the Adelphi since 28 Oct 39, had been noticed in the *Examiner* on 3 Nov as follows: "Our readers will excuse us, for a very obvious reason [*the disapproval Forster had just expressed of Ainsworth's book and its adaptations*], from saying more of the adaptation of *Jack Sheppard* at this Theatre, than that Mrs Keeley, Mr Yates, and Mr Bedford, display much misplaced power, and that the scenic effects are really most surprisingly good." The Adelphi *Jack Sheppard* must in fact have been highly enjoyable, and Mrs Keeley delightful as Jack himself (see Walter Goodman, *The Keeleys*, 1895, pp. 4f.) But "the press took up a severely moral tone, and so much pressure was brought to bear upon the Lord Chamberlain that by-and-bye all plays upon the subject were interdicted" (H. B. Baker, *The London Stage*, 1889, II, 94). For earlier use of the exploits of Jack Sheppard (1702–24; *DNB*), see S. M. Ellis's "Epilogue. Jack Sheppard in Literature and Drama" in Horace Bleackley, *Jack Sheppard*, 1933.

[2] Henry Gardiner Adams (?1811–81), at one time a Canterbury chemist; now living at the Parsonage House, Chatham (*To* Overs, 16 Feb 40); apothecary dispenser to the Rochester, Chatham and Strood Dispensary in 1847. Wrote books on birds, insects and flowers, religious verse, and a biography of Dr Livingstone. Edited *God's Image in Ebony*, 1854, an anthology demonstrating the mental powers of negroes. As Secretary of the Mechanics' Institute, Chatham, was frequently in touch with CD during the 1860s.

[3] The *Kentish Coronal*, Simpkin & Marshall, 1841, "consisting of original contributions in prose and poetry, by persons connected with the County of Kent". It contained "The Trysting Tree" by J. A. Overs (see *To* Overs, 21 Jan 41 and *fn*). Among other contributors were Richard Johns and Charles Mackay. Though called in the Preface "the first volume of this little miscellany", no further volumes have been traced.

*a*I beg you to excuse, and to attribute to constant occupation, so long a delay in answering your note, and am Dear Sir*a*

H. G. Adams Esquire

Faithfully Yours

CHARLES DICKENS

## *To* GEORGE CATTERMOLE, [?21 JANUARY 1840]

MS Free Library of Philadelphia. *Date:* probably eight days rather than one after CD's request of 13 Jan for a sketch of an "old quaint room".

Devonshire Terrace | Tuesday Afternoon

My Dear Cattermole

I think the drawing[1] *most famous*, and so do the publishers, to whom I sent it to-day. If Browne[2] should suggest anything for the future which may enable him to do you justice in copying (on which point he is very anxious) I will communicate it to you. It has occurred to me that perhaps you will like to see his copy on the block *before* it is cut,[3] and I have there-fore told Chapman and Hall to forward it to you.

In future, I will take care that you have the No. to *choose* your subject from. I ought to have done so, perhaps, in this case; but I was very anxious that you should do the room.

Perhaps the shortest plan will be for me to send you *as inclosed*, regularly, but if you prefer keeping account with the Publishers they will be happy to enter upon it when, where, and how you please.

George Cattermole Esquire

Faithfully Yours always

CHARLES DICKENS

## *To* JOHN FORSTER, [JANUARY 1840]

Extract in F, II, vi, 143. *Date:* On 29 Jan CD had a rough proof of No. 1 to send to Macready (see next); he would presumably have finished writing the No. not many days before.

I have finished the first number, but have not been able to do more in the space than lead up to the Giants, who are just on the scene.[4]

*aa* Not previously published.

[1] "Master Humphrey's room".

[2] Hablot Knight Browne, "Phiz" (1815–82; *DNB*): see Vol. I, p. 163*n*. Provided 132 of the 173 illustrations to *Master Humphrey*, and two of the three frontispieces. Since the success of *Pickwick*, had been in great demand as an illustrator (e.g., in 1840–1, by Lever and Mrs Trollope, among others). He had one painting in the RA exhibition 1841—*A Grave Hint*.

[3] It was cut by Samuel Williams.

[4] Gog is about to address Magog as the 1st No. ends.

## *To* W. C. MACREADY, [29 JANUARY 1840]*

MS Morgan Library. *Date:* Macready recorded under date 29 Jan 40: "Dickens sent me a parcel—the pamphlet relating to *Glencoe,* and the proof sheets of his first number of his new work—*Master Humphrey's Clock*" (*Diaries,* II, 43).

Devonshire Terrace. | Wednesday Morning

My Dear Macready.

I inclose you the Pamphlet about Glencoe.[1] I have not read it, and don't know whether it possesses any interest or no.

I also inclose you (sub rosa) the rough draft of the first Number of my new Work, being anxious to hear what you think *of the idea.*[2] The blanks that you see are for Wood-cuts, and the part of which I want to know your opinion is the first article.[3] You come fresh upon it, and I shall be greatly interested to know how it strikes you. When you have had time to look at it, send it back to me.—Of course I shall be proud to extend my confidence to the Ladies.

Always My Dear Macready | Faithfully Yours

W. C. Macready Esquire                                    CHARLES DICKENS

## *To* THOMAS MITTON, [29 JANUARY 1840]*

MS Mrs A. M. Stern. *Date:* CD's birthday, 7 Feb, fell on a Friday in 1840; reference to Bentley and *Barnaby* makes that year certain.

Devonshire Terrace. | Wednesday Morning.

My Dear Mitton.

I saw Cruikshank[4] (who has—of course—quarrelled with Bentley)[5] in

---

[1] Possibly *Authentic Narrative of the Massacre of Glencoe, Contained in a Report of the Commission Given by His Majesty* . . ., 1818, or *The Massacre of Glencoe. In a letter from a Gentleman in Edinburgh to his friend in London* . . ., 1819; but it could have been any one of several others. CD had from the beginning interested himself in Macready's producing Talfourd's *Glencoe:* see Vol. I, pp. 611 and 615–16.

[2] For CD's outline of the idea and how he hoped to work it out, see the notes enclosed in *To* Forster, 14 July 39; I, 563–5.

[3] Occupying six pages in which Master Humphrey introduced himself, his house, room, and clock in ruminative, leisurely prose. CD clearly hoped for assurance that the excellence of the writing compensated for the article's slow pace and lack of incident. Mac-

ready read the No. to his wife and sister the same day, and they were all "much affected and amused by it"; but when he re-read it on publication he "had a questioning feeling of whether or not it was too good for so wide a circulation" (*Diaries,* II, 43 and 56). Thackeray, after reading it on publication, wrote: "The new Boz is dull but somehow gives one a very pleasing impression of the man: a noble tender-hearted creature, who sympathizes with all the human race" (*Letters and Private Papers of W. M. Thackeray,* ed. G. N. Ray, 1945–6, I, 438).

[4] George Cruikshank (1792–1878; *DNB*): see Vol. I, p. 82*n.* See also 7 Nov 40, *fn.*

[5] Richard Bentley (1794–1871; *DNB*): see Vol. I, p. 164*n.* Cruikshank disliked the terms of his agreement as illustrator of *Bentley's Miscel-*

the street the other day, and he told me that Bentley had told Ainsworth[1] that if I did the New Work instead of Barnaby,[2] he *intended to publish all the letters I had ever written him*!!![3] I think this looks like desperation, and that the Sharks of Bedford Row are likely to bring it to a Compensation Question 'afore long. What do *you* think?

Hold yourself disengaged for the Evening of Friday Week, which is my birthday,[4] and of which further particulars will be expressed in future bills. I should like to see you soon, if you can manage to get up here. I suppose you have no news of Adlington's Entire,[5] or I should have heard.

Don't leave the inclosed about, 'till the First of Next Month.

Always Faithfully Yours

Thomas Mitton Esquire                                                 CD.

*lany*, and was believed to have done deliberately inferior illustrations to Ainsworth's *Guy Fawkes* (*Miscellany*, Jan 40–Dec 41) to obtain his release from it (see Blanchard Jerrold, *The Life of George Cruikshank*, 1882, I, 249n). On 11 Mar he wrote to Ainsworth of a visit paid him by Bentley, who had expressed "considerable displeasure at the plates for the *Guy* and *Stanley Thorn*" and announced his intention of employing another artist for the *Miscellany* besides Cruikshank; whereupon Cruikshank declined having anything more to do with it, and some heated words followed. "I shall be very glad if I can be really quit of him", Cruikshank ended (S. M. Ellis, *W. H. Ainsworth and his Friends*, 1911, I, 403–4). Barham commiserated with Bentley on "the temper Cruikshank continues in" on 4 Sep (MS Berg); and the quarrel went on through 1841. In Feb 42 Cruikshank used his new position as illustrator of *Ainsworth's Magazine* to attack Bentley in an address, "A Few Words to the Public about Richard Bentley" (printed on the verso of the table of Contents for the first No.)—but nevertheless continued as one of the *Miscellany* illustrators until Autumn 1843.

[1] William Harrison Ainsworth (1805–1882; *DNB*): see Vol. I, p. 115n. Editor of *Bentley's Miscellany* from Feb 39 (see Vol. I, p. 498n) to Dec 41, the enormous popularity of his *Jack Sheppard* (*Miscellany*, Jan 39–Feb 40) helping to raise the 1840 sales (by 8/900) to *c*. 8500—though they dropped to 5000 in 1841 (R. A. Gettmann, *A Victorian Publisher*, Cambridge, 1960,

p. 143). For attacks on *Jack Sheppard*, associating *Oliver* with it, see *To* Horne, ?Feb 40 and *fn*. The book and its stage adaptations aroused so much hostility that Ainsworth declined nomination to the Athenæum Club in the belief that he would be blackballed by the "Anti-Jack-Sheppardites". His friendship with CD and Forster had been in abeyance since Apr 39, but was renewed Dec 40, shortly after the dinner celebrating publication of his *The Tower of London* (see *To* Ainsworth, 18 Dec and *fn*).

[2] Thus violating his Agreement with Bentley of 27 Feb 39 (see *To* Forster, 3 Jan, *fn*).

[3] A threat he did not carry out, though later his son George had the letters set up in proof for possible publication (see Vol. I, p. 495n). Bentley made a similar threat to Bulwer on 12 Mar 40, on Bulwer's refusing him permission to reprint three novels which had appeared in Bentley's Standard Novels series unless he undertook to publish no book by Rosina Bulwer (MSS Lytton Papers).

[4] It was also the first night of Leigh Hunt's *A Legend of Florence*, at Covent Garden, under Madame Vestris's management. On 6 Feb Forster wrote to Hunt: "Strange, and not an unlucky omen—that tomorrow is Dickens' birthday! He and I would have had a box together, but for this, for a party was invited to him long ago, and nothing but your play would have kept me from it" (Maggs Bros catalogue No. 427, Autumn 1922).

[5] I.e. Messrs Adlington, Gregory,

## *To* JOHN FORSTER, [?30 JANUARY 1840]

MS Victoria & Albert Museum (FC). *Date:* Handwriting suggests early 1840; but letter cannot refer to No. 1, which CD began on a Saturday (11 Jan). Probably refers to No. 2, begun about a fortnight later; Forster's "news", then, may have contained further details of Bentley's threats (see last). *Address:* John Forster Esquire.

Thursday.[1]

Dear Forster

I was thinking all yesterday, and have begun at Master Humphrey to-day. Your news however has suddenly pulled me up and awakened my ferocity. I am going down to Mitton's and shall be with you—most probably as soon as Henry.[2]

Faithfully
CD.

## *To* JOHN FORSTER, [?JANUARY 1840]

MS Victoria & Albert Museum (FC). *Date:* Handwriting suggests early 1840.

Devonshire Terrace. | Friday Night

My Dear Forster.

I shall order the "Wan" at a quarter past Ten, and shall (I hope) assuredly be at home by the half hour. Whoever is here first, let him rush to the Study Fire.

Faithfully Yours
CD

Oh Bisery, bisery!

Faulkner & Follett, of Bedford Row, Bentley's solicitors—"Adlington's Entire" as if an advertisement of "entire beer" (a blend of ale, beer and twopenny: *OED*). Bentley must by now have realized that a break with CD was inevitable. However on 8 Feb his solicitors wrote one more letter to Smithson & Mitton. It read: "Observing in the papers the announcement of a new work by Mr Dickens which it is intended should be brought out in the course of next month we must beg to be informed whether Mr Dickens is now prepared with the manuscript of 'Barnaby Rudge' which he has pledged himself should be the first work to be published by him" (MS Mr C. C. Dickens). Smithson replied on 11 Feb that he had deferred answering because Mitton was out of London, and ended: "However, I am quite satisfied that we have not any specific instructions from Mr. Charles Dickens upon the subject of his alleged agreement with Mr. Bentley" (MS Mr C. C. Dickens). Bentley's next known move was once more to advertise *Barnaby*: see *To* Macready, 21 Feb and *fn*.

[1] Written at bottom of page and overlooked by the editor of N, who therefore gives letter as referring to *Master Humphrey* No. 1.

[2] Forster's man-servant, who had clearly just brought the "news" from Forster.

## *To* RICHARD MONCKTON MILNES,[1] [1 FEBRUARY 1840]

MS Trinity College, Cambridge. *Date:* the Saturday before CD's 28th birthday (Fri 7 Feb).

1 Devonshire Terrace | Saturday Morning

My Dear Mr. Milnes

I never went out to breakfast in my life, and am afraid to try how one feels under such circumstances; but I will be with you next Friday at eleven o'Clock for purposes of small talk—that being the day which did itself the honor of presenting me to the world twenty eight years ago.

I really would immortalize myself if I were you by presenting that national anthem to Catnac[2] of the Seven Dials.[3] It is a capital notion. Perhaps you have heard that song in the streets about the Queen's marriage, whereof the burden is—

> (Her Majesty being supposed to sing it)
> So let 'em say, whatee'r[4] they may,
> Or do whatee'r they can;
> Prince Hallbert he vill[5] alvays be
> My own dear Fancy Man.

There is also another prose composition in the form of a catechism. This is performed by two gentlemen and opens thus.

*Question.* Vell Mr. Bull Sir what is your private opinions with respectin' to German Sassages—fresh as imported Sir from Saxe Humbug and Go-to-her?[6]

*Answer* (in a melancholy growl) My opinion is Sir as they comes wery dear.

*Question.* Supposin' Mr. Bull as these here foreign sassages wos to cost the country a matter o' thirty thousand pound per annewum, who do you think ought to stand that 'ere wast and enormous expenditer?

*Answer.* Them as awails theirselves o' the sassages aforesaid. (a laugh in the crowd)

---

[1] Richard Monckton Milnes, first Baron Houghton (1809–85; *DNB*): see Vol. 1, p. 508*n*. An habitué of Gore House at this time, and friend of Carlyle (whom he teased). In July 40 published *Poetry for the People* (see *To Milnes*, 10 Mar 41 and *fn*): "The greatest poet in the House of Commons came here ... and we drove together ... to Newgate to see Courvoisier killed", wrote Thackeray on 7 July (*Letters and Private Papers of W. M. Thackeray*, ed. G. N. Ray, 1, 454). In 1841, after the condemnation of Newman's *Tract XC*, published *One Tract More*, a defence of the Tractarians which was highly thought of. Re-elected Conservative MP for Pontefract unopposed in July 41, but was greatly disappointed on being given no office by Peel. See later vols.

[2] Mis-spelt by CD. James Catnach (1792–1841; *DNB*), printer, ballad-monger and broadsheet distributor, of Monmouth Court, Seven Dials; produced at least one set of verses on Queen Victoria's marriage to Prince Albert.

[3] Cf. "Seven Dials" in *Sketches by Boz*: "Seven Dials! the region of song and poetry— ... hallowed by the names of Catnach and of Pitts—names that will entwine themselves with coster-mongers, and barrel-organs, when penny magazines shall have superseded penny yards of song".

[4] Apostrophe thus in MS.

[5] Written with initial "w" changed to "v".

[6] Prince Albert's father was Duke of Saxe-Coburg-Gotha.

*Question.* Then in your opinion Mr. Bull they're a wery dear commodity? *Answer.* I consider Sir as they would be uncommon dear at any price, and what I says is, let us rewert to the good wholesome home-made, dairy-fed native sassages—the Cambridge sassages of right down English Manafacter[1]—the Protestant Sassages[2] as our forefather and Marshal Blue Cur[3] fought and bled for (Great applause)

  (Both sing)
  Oh *didn't* the Prince look as sveet as new honey
  Ven Melbourne said, Johnny should get the full money;
  And *isn't* his Missis vith Joe rayther vild,
  Now they're almost too poor for to vet-nurse the child![4]

— — —

I return the letter which is a very extraordinary and a very sad one.
      Always believe me | Faithfully Yours
Richard Milnes Esquire         CHARLES DICKENS

---

## *To* T. N. TALFOURD,[5] 4 FEBRUARY [1840]

Text in N, I, 247, checked from MS Sotheby's, 15 Dec 1964. *Date:* 4 Feb was Tuesday in 1840.

    I Devonshire Terrace, York Gate | Tuesday 4th. February.
My Dear Talfourd.
 Many thanks for the little book,[6] which I hope will prove among the most interesting I shall ever leave to those for whom I work.

---

[1] The Queen's cousin, Prince George of Cambridge (1819–1904; *DNB*), had been regarded by some—but certainly not by himself—as a possible husband for her. In 1847 he made a morganatic marriage with Louisa Fairbrother (Mrs Fitzgeorge), an actress whom he first met in 1840.

[2] Doubts had been cast upon Prince Albert's Protestantism, since two members of his family had married Roman Catholics.

[3] The part Field-Marshal von Blücher had played in the defeat of Napoleon—and particularly his intervention at Waterloo—had made him extremely popular in England.

[4] The subject of the song was Prince Albert's Annuity Bill, debated in the Commons on 27 Jan 40. Lord John Russell proposed that the Prince should have the £50,000 a year usually paid to a Consort; Joseph Hume, radical critic of Government expenditure, proposed £21,000—including among his objections to the larger sum "the danger of placing a young man down in London with so much money in his pocket". The figure decided upon was £30,000. For CD's enjoyment of a popular ballad on the announcement that the Queen was expecting a child, see Mrs E. E. Christian, "Reminiscences of CD", *Englishwoman's Domestic Magazine*, x (1871), 340.

[5] Thomas Noon Talfourd (1795–1854; *DNB*): see Vol. I, p. 290n. After their association over *Glencoe*, CD's friendship with Talfourd seems to some extent to have cooled, perhaps partly through the influence of Macready (whose diary in 1841 shows particular irritation at Talfourd's envy of Bulwer) or of Forster (who was outraged by the "contemptible figure" he cut when a second reading of his Copyright Bill

As you will come fresh upon the subject, I am curious to see how the idea of the first No. of my projected work, strikes you. I inclose you the proof (a secret yet, of course) which, when you have had time to look at, please return to me. It is the first article that I want you most to read. The blanks are for Wood Cuts.

Macready certainly is most singularly warm upon *the*[1] subject.[2] I saw him at dinner the other evening,[3] and he took me aside and dwelt upon what he felt he could do with his part[4] (which it seemed he had been going over that day) in a manner which for him is most extraordinary.

                                    Faithfully Yours always
Mr. Serjeant Talfourd | &c &c.                CHARLES DICKENS


## *To* UNKNOWN CORRESPONDENT, 4 FEBRUARY 1840*

MS Berg Collection.

                    1 Devonshire Terrace | York Gate, Regents Park, London
                                                4th. February 1840.

Mr. Charles Dickens presents his compliments to his fair correspondent unknown, & begs to inform her that Mr. Mantalini's companion in the cellar is certainly *not* his wife, and that her appreciation of the lady's character is perfectly correct and just.[5]

---

was defeated 5 Feb 41: MS Lytton Papers). In Talfourd's own journal-entry for 6 Jan 42, summing up the previous years, he showed much bitterness, recording his "increasing distaste" for the Whigs; his lack of Govt briefs; his decreased income for 1841 (£1000 less than for 1840); that his Copyright Bill had been "thrown out [*in fact modified*] in one night by Macaulay"; and that his "extravagant eulogies" of Macready had brought him only ill-will elsewhere—and now "Mr. Macready will never act one of my Plays" (quoted by Vera Watson, "The Journals of Thomas Noon Talfourd", *Times Literary Supplement*, 8 Feb 1957). Nevertheless, he had much "to be thankful for—wife—children—a good name—and much, very much love after all misunderstandings and mistakes" (*ibid*). See later vols.

[6] Presumably Talfourd's *Three Speeches Delivered in the House of Commons in Favour of a Measure for an*

*Extension of Copyright*, published early Feb 40. A copy inscribed "Charles Dickens, Esq., from his admirer and friend, T. N. Talfourd" was in the Gad's Hill library at CD's death (*Catalogue of the Library of CD*, ed. J. H. Stonehouse, 1935, p. 108).

[1] Underlined twice.

[2] His production of *Glencoe*.

[3] Macready, Rogers, the Cattermoles, Maclise and Forster dined with CD on 23 Jan.

[4] Halbert Macdonald. After the first night, 23 May, Macready recorded: "I did all I could do—all that the very short period allowed for preparation allowed me to do" (*Diaries*, II, 61).

[5] The following year, CD was asked the same question again: see *To* Miss Myers, 30 Nov 41. He had also been asked it before: see *To* Dr J. H. Hutton, ?Oct 39; I, 590 (and *fn* on the change he made in later editions of *Nickleby*, Ch. 64).

## *To* RICHARD MONCKTON MILNES, [?7 FEBRUARY 1840]*

MS Berg Collection. *Date:* Handwriting suggests early 1840. Perhaps Fri 7 Feb, the day fixed in *To* Milnes, 1 Feb, for CD's visit; Milnes had possibly given him the choice of Friday or Saturday. *Address:* Richard Milnes Esquire MP. | &c &c | 26 Pall Mall.

1 Devonshire Terrace | Friday Morning

My Dear Sir

I am very much annoyed that an unexpected arrival from the country obliges me to postpone the pleasure of seeing you, until tomorrow.

In haste | Believe me

Always Faithfully Yours

Richard Milnes Esquire                                   CHARLES DICKENS


## *To* JOHN OVERS,[1] [?7 FEBRUARY 1840]†

MS Berg Collection. *Date:* Signature suggests Feb 40; CD was perhaps referring to Ainsworth's note of 4 Feb: see *fn.*

Devonshire Terrace. | Friday Afternoon

Dear Mr. Overs.

I have been much occupied—not with business, I am sorry to say, but with pleasure—[2]during the past week, but have nevertheless sat down to alter your story. I find it, however, almost an impossible job without having you at my elbow, for I cannot cut it down to anything like the limits that will give you a fair chance of seeing it in Print without having all the story at my fingers' ends as I go on—[a]the referring backwards and forwards, being a most grievous trial to me and by no means the best course for you. If you can be with me at *12 exactly* next Sunday, I can spare an hour and a half, and I have no doubt that will be quite sufficient for our purpose.[a]

I regret to say that I have no occupation for anybody, such as you describe. I never copy,[3] correct but very little, and that invariably as I write. But I fancy that I see something in Mr. Ainsworth's note which may be worth your keeping in view.[4] What it is, I will explain to you when we meet.

[1] John Overs (1808–44): see Vol. 1, p. 504*n.*

[2] "pleasure—" is written in above 4 words heavily cancelled, apparently "what you call pleasure—".

[a][a] Not previously published.

[3] I.e. he did not copy whole chapters: cf. *To* Lester, 19 July 40.

[4] In a letter to Overs of 4 Feb Ainsworth, while praising one of his stories, had suggested that he should choose subjects from his own walk of life: "For instance, in my last work—*Jack Shep-* *pard*—what immense value the knowledge of your business would have been to me in the delineation of such a character as Wood. Believe me, a plain, homely story, depicting in the nervous, natural language which you have at command, the struggles, adventures, loves, hatreds (if you please) of a young carpenter would be worth a hundred high-flown, historical romances. . . . Write, in fact, your own life. . . . In this you could not fail" (quoted in S. M. Ellis, *W. H. Ainsworth and his Friends,*

*a*I beg that you will not mention any slight pains I may be at in your behalf (which are in truth so many pleasures to me) or rate slight services so very highly. I most sincerely wish that I saw any clearly-defined and certain way of assisting you in your design. It would afford me nearly as much pleasure as it would yield you, and whether we hit our mark or fall short of it, believe me that my interest in you will remain the same.

Very faithfully Yours

Mr. J. A. Overs.                                    CHARLES DICKENS*a*


## *To* R. H. HORNE,[1] [?FEBRUARY 1840]

MS Comtesse de Suzannet. *Date:* Handwriting suggests Feb 40, in which month Ainsworth's *Jack Sheppard* had terminated in the *Miscellany*. For the coupling of *Oliver* and *Jack Sheppard* in print in Jan and Feb 40, see *fn.*

At Forster's | Saturday Night

My Dear Horne.

I am by some jolter-headed enemies most unjustly and untruly charged with having written a book after Mr. Ainsworth's fashion.[2] Unto these jolter-heads and their intensely concentrated humbug, I shall take an early

---

I, 392). No such story by Overs is known, but Ainsworth's advice may have led him to include "The Carpenter", a profile, in his *Evenings of a Working Man*, 1844.

*aa* Not previously published.

[1] Richard Henry (or Hengist) Horne (1803–84; *DNB*): see Vol. I, p. 500*n*. Published in 1840 a tragedy, *Gregory VII*, with a prefatory "Essay on Tragic Influence"; and in 1841 *The History of Napoleon*, 2 vols, and *Poems of Chaucer Modernized* (in CD's library at his death), his collaborators including Wordsworth, Leigh Hunt, Monckton Milnes, Thomas Powell, and Elizabeth Barrett (with whom he corresponded regularly 1839–46, though they did not meet until 1851). She greatly admired his tragedies; projected with him a joint play, to be called "Psyche Apocalypté"; and her "Cry of the Children", 1843, was inspired by his Report as an Asst Commissioner to inquire into the Employment of Children.

[2] Several recent reviews of *Jack Sheppard* had linked it with *Oliver*— partly, no doubt, because both had been serialized in *Bentley's Miscellany*, illustrated by Cruikshank, had crime for their subject, and had been advertised together by Bentley (see Vol. I, p. 617*n*). *Dearden's Miscellany* (Jan 40, III, 66) had coupled CD and Ainsworth as of "the gallows-school of novelists" —though ranking CD as much the superior writer. An article in the *Monthly Chronicle* (Jan 40, v, 36), "Novel Writing and Newspaper Criticism", had attacked *Jack Sheppard* as pandering to one extreme of taste, that for the lowest society, and had added that "even Boz himself" was not entirely unaffected by the fashion. But what must have most annoyed CD was a passage in the final chapter of *Catherine*, Thackeray's parody of the Newgate novel, in the February *Fraser's* (xxi, 211): CD's power was "so amazing", it read, that the reader was led "breathless to watch all the crimes of Fagin, tenderly to deplore the errors of Nancy, to have for Bill Sikes a kind of pity and admiration, and an absolute love for the society of the Dodger. . . . And what came of *Oliver Twist*? The public wanted something more extravagant still, more sympathy for thieves, and so *Jack Sheppard* makes his appearance."

opportunity of temperately replying.[1] If this opportunity had presented itself and I had made this vindication, I could have no objection to set my hand to what I know to be true concerning the late lamented John Sheppard,[2] but I feel a great repugnance to do so now, lest it should seem an ungenerous and unmanly way of disavowing any sympathy with that school, and a means of shielding myself.

Believe me that I concur heart and hand and shall be ready to do so at all needful times with pen and purse, in your great object,[3] and that I sincerely regret being with-held by this consideration of delicacy from being among the Pioneers. I hope I shall shew not unworthily in the van, yet.

Faithfully Yours

CHARLES DICKENS

[1] CD answered the charges in his Preface to *Oliver* of Apr 41 (see *To* Forster, 17 June 40, *fn*). "I wished to show in little Oliver", he wrote, "the principle of Good surviving through every adverse circumstance, and triumphing at last". In spite of their satire *The Beggar's Opera* and *Paul Clifford* had made a thief's life alluring. But "what manner of life is that which is described in [*Oliver's*] pages, as the everyday existence of a Thief? What charms has it for the young and ill-disposed, what allurements for the most jolter-headed of juveniles?" In one of its "Literary Recipes" (for "A Startling Romance") *Punch* (Aug 41, I, 39) mocked at the invincible innocence of Oliver: "Take a small boy, charity, factory, carpenter's apprentice, or otherwise, ... stew him well down in vice— garnish largely with oaths and flash songs— ... Serve up with a couple of murders—and season with a hanging match. | N.B. Alter the ingredients to a beadle and a workhouse—the scenes may be the same, but the whole flavour of vice will be lost, and the boy will turn out a perfect pattern.—Strongly recommended for weak stomachs."

[2] I.e. to sign a Petition drawn up by Horne: see below.

[3] The ending of the patent theatres monopoly. Sir Robert Walpole's Licensing Act of 1737 had become an anachronism: 73 new theatres had sprung up since that date (see H. B. Baker, *History of the London Stage*, 1904, x–xiii), privileged to open only in the summer months, when Covent Garden and Drury Lane were closed, and to perform only "Burlettas" (i.e. everything except serious drama). When Bunn at Drury Lane resorted mainly to opera to make the theatre pay and even descended to Van Amburgh's performing lions (see *To* Macready, 26 Jan 39 and *n*; 1, 497), and Madame Vestris at Covent Garden (late 1839) put on light pieces from the Olympic, the absurdity of the monopoly became clearer than ever. A Committee of Enquiry had been set up in 1832 as a result of Bulwer's efforts, and now Horne was collecting signatures for a Petition "that every theatre should be permitted to enact the best dramas it could obtain" (*Letters of Elizabeth Barrett Browning Addressed to R. H. Horne*, ed. S. R. T. Mayer, 1877, 1, 43 and 44*n*). Presumably the Petition mentioned—as one shocking result of the monopoly—the spate of adaptations of *Jack Sheppard* running at various non-patent theatres (the Adelphi, Surrey, City of London, Victoria, Pavilion, Queen's and Sadler's Wells) during the last months: hence CD's "consideration of delicacy". The Bill abolishing the monopoly was not passed until 1843.

## *To* T. J. THOMPSON,[1] [?9 FEBRUARY 1840]*

Facsimile in unidentified catalogue. *Date:* Handwriting suggests early 1840.
Possibly the Monday morning engagement was for 10 Feb, to see the Queen's
wedding procession from Thompson's chambers, 63 Pall Mall.

Devonshire Terrace | Sunday.

My Dear Thompson.

Maclise[2] and I, coming from the place where you were *not* last night,
and going in to the Piazza to supper, then and there encountered Forster
who learning how we were engaged tomorrow Morning[3] enquired (with
much humility and prostration of spirit) whether I thought you would give
him house-room. I ventured to make answer that I thought you would—
and write to inform you of the heavy responsibility which I have herein
contracted.

I am confined at home with the worst cold you can conceive, and am all
alone. You are *such* a gentleman of England and live at home so *much* at
ease[4], or I should ask you to come in and take your wine in my sanctum
——?

Faithfully Yours always

T. J. Thompson Esquire                                     CHARLES DICKENS

---

[1] Thomas James Thompson (1812–1881): see Vol. 1, p. 416*n*. A widower and man of leisure, with a son of six and daughter of five who apparently lived with his sister Mrs Smithson (see *To* Smithson, ?9 June 41, *fn*).

[2] Daniel Maclise (?1806–70; *DNB*): see Vol. 1, p. 201*n*. Elected RA 10 Feb 40; elected to the RA Council 10 Dec 40; on the Arranging Committee Apr 41. In 1840 became one of the "trio" with CD and Forster. CD clearly delighted in his company; but Maclise's relations with Forster seem at this date to have been the more affectionate: a number of his letters to Forster (MSS V & A) begin or close with "My dear" or "Mon cher". His portrait of CD, painted Summer 1839, was among the four pictures he exhibited in the 1840 RA Exhibition.

[3] It is possible that the following undated letter to CD from Maclise, although kept among CD's 1841 correspondence, refers to this engagement—Maclise not realizing that Thompson's chambers were on the route of the wedding procession, but expecting to see it from his club: "Don't laugh—I beg of you send the enclosed acceptance of Thompson's invitation to the post for me—*with* his *Christian* name—I give up his being a Jew after yesterday— | I am ashamed to appear ignorant of it —and on looking over Blue Book I find him designated amid a column of others of the same uncommon name | Captain Thompson 7 Sloane St. I suppose tis he—Take care your hand when you prefix the letters is not recognized— none of your forcible J F D C [*initials written bold, and the "C" with an attempt at CD's flourish*] failed in the C.—I am very very C.D. this morning and my picture appears to me the map of disgust from right to left but what is that to me. | Ever yours | Danl. Maclise | the laughing gas lighted eyes of [?Maxalls] Mistress illuminated the margin of my dreams last night. | I'll never forgive you if you tell Thompson as Forster would" (MS Huntington).

[4] From the 17th century ballad, "You gentlemen of England, that live at home at ease", often adapted.

## *To* W. S. LANDOR,[1] [11 FEBRUARY 1840]

Extract in F, II, viii, 155. *Date:* "the 11th of February, the day after the royal nuptials", according to Forster.

Society is unhinged here, by her majesty's marriage, and I am sorry to add that I have fallen hopelessly in love with the Queen,[2] and wander up and down with vague and dismal thoughts of running away to some uninhabited island with a maid of honor, to be entrapped by conspiracy for that purpose. Can you suggest any particular young person, serving in such a capacity, who would suit me? It is too much perhaps to ask you to join the band of noble youths (Forster is in it, and Maclise) who are to assist me in this great enterprise, but a man of your energy would be invaluable. I have my eye upon Lady . . . ,[3] principally because she is very beautiful and has no strong brothers. Upon this, and other points of the scheme, however, we will confer more at large when we meet; and meanwhile burn this document, that no suspicion may arise or rumour get abroad.[4]

[1] Walter Savage Landor (1775–1864; *DNB*), author of *Imaginary Conversations*; CD's original for Boythorn. Lived 1838–58 in Bath, having left his family in Florence. Had known Forster since May 36, first as a sympathetic reviewer of his work in the *Examiner* and *New Monthly*; later as friend and literary adviser. Forster had especially urged him to write plays, and in Nov 38 Landor sent him *Andrea of Hungary* and *Giovanna of Naples*. For Bentley's delays over printing the plays, see Vol. I, p. 531. Landor and CD had exchanged messages before they ever met. In a letter to Forster, Apr 39, Landor wrote: "Tell [Dickens] he has drawn from me more tears and more smiles than are remaining to me for all the rest of the world, real or ideal" (Forster, *W. S. Landor*, 1869, II, 395). At about the same date, CD, through Forster, urged Landor to write Bentley "a contemptuous letter" about the delays in advertising and printing his two plays (R. H. Super, *W. S. Landor*, 1957, p. 304, quoting Nicoll and Wise, *Literary Anecdotes of the Nineteenth Century*, 1895–6, I, 207–8). Their first meeting was at Lady Blessington's in Jan 40, through Forster—future biographer of both. In a letter postmarked 10 Feb 40 Landor wrote to G. P. R. James: "In town I made a new acquaintance in a [?really] popular, and what is much better, truly extraordinary man—the author of Nicholas Nickleby. He comes

on Saturday [*in fact Saturday fortnight*] to spend a few days with me at Bath, and on Monday I have invited my elite of beauty [*the Paynters: see* To *Landor, 26 July, and fn*] to meet him— How I wish you could too! . . . Dickens is really a good as well as a delightful man. It is rarely that two such persons meet, as you and he—nor in any other society could I easily be the least of three" (MS Virginia Historical Society). In London or at Bath CD gave Landor copies of *Pickwick* and *Nickleby*, inscribed "From his warm admirer Charles Dickens". For Landor's inscription to CD of copies of *Andrea* and *Giovanna* and accompanying letter, see 26 July, *fn*.

[2] This joke may be based on the attempts made by various madmen to enter Buckingham Palace or Windsor Castle; on 29 Nov 39, for instance, a certain John Stockledge had demanded to be admitted to the Castle "as the King of England", and explained that "he was like all other men who wanted wives; he was looking after one" (*Morning Chronicle*, 2 Dec 39). For the Boy Jones's attempts see *To* Smedley, 1 Apr 41 and *fn*.

[3] Perhaps Lady Fanny Cowper: see p. 28.

[4] "Poor puzzled Mr. Landor" sent this letter on to Forster, asking: "What on earth does it all mean?" (F, II, viii, 155).

## *To* JOHN FORSTER, [12 FEBRUARY 1840]

Extract in F, II, viii, 156. *Date:* 12 Feb 40 according to Forster.

I am utterly lost in misery, and can do nothing. I have been reading *Oliver, Pickwick,* and *Nickleby* to get my thoughts together for the new effort, but all in vain:

> My heart is at Windsor,[1]
> My heart isn't here;
> My heart is at Windsor,
> A following my dear.[2]

I saw the Responsibilities this morning, and burst into tears. The presence of my wife aggravates me. I loathe my parents. I detest my house. I begin to have thoughts of the Serpentine, of the regent's-canal, of the razors upstairs, of the chemist's down the street, of poisoning myself at Mrs. ——'s table, of hanging myself upon the pear-tree in the garden, of abstaining from food and starving myself to death, of being bled for my cold and tearing off the bandage, of falling under the feet of cab-horses in the New-road, of murdering Chapman and Hall and becoming great in story (SHE must hear something of me then—perhaps sign the warrant: or is that a fable?), of turning Chartist,[3] of heading some bloody assault upon the palace and saving Her by my single hand——of being anything but what I have been, and doing anything but what I have done. Your distracted friend, C.D.[4]

## *To* GEORGE CATTERMOLE, [?12 FEBRUARY 1840]

MS Comtesse de Suzannet. *Date:* Since No. 1 of *Master Humphrey* was presumably finished not long before 29 Jan when CD sent Macready a proof, and No. 3 was finished by 28 Feb (*To* Chapman & Hall, that day), Wed 12 Feb seems the probable date for his sending Cattermole "the greater portion" of No. 2.

Devonshire Terrace | Wednesday Morning

My Dear Cattermole.

This (that I sen[d][5] you now) is the greater portion of No. 2. I am writing such things as occur to me without much regarding, for the present, the

---

[1] Where the Queen was spending her few days of honeymoon.

[2] A parody of Burns's: "My heart's in the Highlands, my heart is not here; | My heart's in the Highlands a-chasing the deer."

[3] Reports of the Chartist trials at Monmouth, and of further minor outbreaks and arrests in London and the North, had filled the newspapers in Jan.

[4] "This incoherence", says Forster, closed with a "wild derangement of asterisks in every shape and form": i.e. it closed, presumably, like the letters to Thompson and Maclise written next day, with a pattern of crosses representing kisses.

[5] MS reads "sent".

order in which they will appear,[1] and thus you will receive in the course of the week another Story.[2] When you have looked over the two, perhaps I shall see or hear from you?

> In haste, believe me
> Always Faithfully Yours

George Cattermole Esquire                    CHARLES DICKENS


## *To* T. J. THOMPSON, [13 FEBRUARY 1840]†

MS Benoliel Collection. *Date:* clearly the Thursday after the Queen's wedding.

> Devonshire Terrace. | Thursday Morning.

My Dear Thompson

*ᵃ*I called to enquire after the bill[3] yesterday, but it was not made out. When I have it, I will not fail to call a settlement of the same.*ᵃ*

Maclise and I are raving with love for the Queen—with a hopeless passion whose extent no tongue can tell, nor mind of man conceive. On Tuesday we sallied down to Windsor, prowled about the Castle, saw the Corridor and their private rooms—nay, the very bedchamber (which we know from having been there twice) lighted up with such a ruddy, homely, brilliant glow[4]—bespeaking so much bliss and happiness—that I, your humble servant, lay down in the mud at the top of the long walk and refused all comfort—to the immeasurable astonishment of a few straggling passengers who had survived the drunkenness of the previous night. After perpetrating sundry other extravagances we returned home at Midnight in a Post Chaise, and now we wear marriage medals next our hearts and go about with pockets full of portraits which we weep over in secret. Forster was with us at Windsor and (for the joke's sake) counterfeits a passion too, but *he does not love her.*[5]

Don't mention this unhappy attachment. I am very wretched, and

[1] See next, *To* Thompson, in which CD says he has "on hand" three Nos of *Master Humphrey.*

[2] No. 2 contained the story told by Magog to Gog. The next story CD wrote was probably "Mr. Pickwick's Tale", which was originally intended for No. 3 but moved to Nos 5 and 6 (*To* Forster, ?8 Mar and *fn*).

*ᵃᵃ* Not previously published.

[3] Possibly for some celebration of the Queen's wedding in which Thompson shared: cf. ?9 Feb, *fn.*

[4] Cf. Charles Greville's ill-natured journal-entry, 13 Feb 40: "It was much remarked too that [the Queen] and P[rince] A[lbert] were up very early on Tuesday morning walking about, which

is very contrary to her former habits. Strange that a bridal night should be so short; and I told Lady Palmerston that this was not the way to provide us with a Prince of Wales" (*The Greville Memoirs*, ed. Lytton Strachey and Roger Fulford, 1938, IV, 241). But see the fuller picture painted by Elizabeth Longford (*Victoria R.I.*, 1964, pp. 143–4, 150).

[5] Underlined twice. Maclise's "love" may have been all the warmer for his knowing that the Queen admired his work. The following entries in her Journal show how strong her interest was.—On 4 May 38: "At ½ p. 1 I went to the Exhibition of the Royal Academy . . . there are some beautiful pictures by

think of leaving my home. My wife makes me miserable,[1] and when I hear the voices of my Infant Children, I burst into tears. I fear it is too late to ask you to take this house, now that you have made such arrangements of comfort in Pall Mall;[2] but if you will, you shall have it very cheap —furniture at a low valuation—money not being so much an object, as escaping from the family. For God's sake turn this matter over in your mind, and please to ask Captain Kincaide[3] what he asks—his lowest terms, in short, for ready money—for that Post of Gentleman at Arms. I must be near her, and I see no better way than that - - for the present.

I have on hand three Numbers of Master Humphrey's Clock, and the two first chapters of Barnaby.[4] Would you like to buy them? Writing any more in my present state of mind, is out of the question. They are written in a pretty fair hand and when I am in the Serpentine may be considered curious. Name your own terms.

I know you don't like trouble, but I have ventured, notwithstanding, to make you an Executor of my will. There won't be a great deal to do, as there is no money. There is a little bequest having reference to *her*[5] which you might like to execute. I have heard on the Lord Chamberlain's authority, that she reads my books and is very fond of them[6] - - I think she

---

Landseer— . . . some wonderfully clever ones by McLise. Lord Melbourne told me . . . that Landseer said of McLise: 'He is beating us all; his imagination, grouping, and drawing is wonderful; he must soften his colouring perhaps a little.' " On 6 May 38: "Spoke of another picture by Landseer . . . of others . . . by McLise etc.; his (Mc-Lise's) of the Merry Xmas . . . Lord Melbourne thinks would be a good picture for a dining-room." On 2 Feb 39, she talked with Melbourne of Maclise's affair with Lady Sykes (see *To* Maclise, 2 June 40, *fn*). On 9 Feb 39: "Saw, and bought, two *beautiful* pictures by McLise; the one is taken from the Burletta of Midas . . .; the other is from 'Gil Blas, Chapitre 2, livre 1; His adventure with the Parasite'. . . . At 25 m. p. 12 came Lord Melbourne. . . . I found him looking at the 2 Pictures, and asked him how he liked them; . . . 'What can be cleverer', he said, and admired them much." On 14 Feb 39: "Lord M. looked at the 2 pictures by McLise and liked the one of Gil Blas best; he thinks Apollo's legs too thick in the other; and he said: 'Not like the expression of peasant girls; rather improper', which made me laugh" (MSS The Royal Archives,

Windsor Castle). For Queen Victoria's commissioning "secret pictures" from Maclise as birthday presents for Prince Albert, see *To* C. C. Felton, 1 Sep 43.

[1] "Wretched" cancelled; "miserable" added over caret.

[2] Thompson lived at 63 Pall Mall, near the Athenæum and Reform Clubs of both of which he was a member, until his second marriage, to Christiana Weller, in 1845.

[3] Mis-spelt by CD. John Kincaid (1787–1862; *DNB*), retired Army Captain; had served in the Peninsular campaigns and at Waterloo, and was now one of the Queen's Gentlemen-in-Waiting. Author of *Adventures in the Rifle Brigade*, 1830, and *Random Shots of a Rifleman*, 1835.

[4] CD had made an abortive start on *Barnaby* Jan 39; had worked on it again more hopefully in Oct and Nov; but by mid-Dec—when he informed Bentley that the MS of the completed book would not be forthcoming on 1 Jan 40 (the date fixed in the Agreement of 27 Feb 39) and declared "war to the knife" (see Vol. 1, pp. 616–19)—he had clearly given up again, with only two chapters written.

[5] Underlined twice.

[6] Perhaps a joke: but the Queen had

will be sorry when I am gone. I should wish to be embalmed, and to be kept (if practicable) on the top of the Triumphal Arch at Buckingham Palace[1] when she is in town, and on the north-east turrets of the Round Tower when she is at Windsor *x x x x                                    x

x x x x x x

x                                                                                    x

x x x x x x x x x x x x x x x x x x*

From your distracted and blighted friend

C.D.

*(Don't shew this to Mr. Wakley,[2] if it ever comes to that)*

## *To* DANIEL MACLISE, [13 FEBRUARY 1840]*

MS Berg Collection. *Date:* obviously same day as last.

### V. R.[3]

Devonshire Terrace | Thursday Afternoon

My Dear Maclise[4]

I send you a copy of Pickwick and the two little books.[5] Let the authorship of the last-named trifles remain in the bosom of your family.

in fact read *Oliver* a year before and found it "excessively interesting" (Diary entry, 30 Dec 38: *The Girlhood of Queen Victoria*, ed. Viscount Esher, 1912, II, 86). On 1 Jan 39 she recorded: "Talked of my getting on in *Oliver Twist*; of the descriptions of 'squalid vice' in it; of the accounts of starvation in the Workhouses and Schools, Mr. Dickens gives in his books . . . told [Melbourne] Mamma admonished me for reading light books"; on 3 Jan: "liked it so much and wished [Melbourne] would read it"; and on 7 Apr: " 'It's all among Workhouses, and Coffin Makers, and Pickpockets,' he said; 'I don't like that low debasing style'. . . . We defended Oliver very much, but in vain" (*op. cit.*, II, 89, 91, 144). At their meeting in Mar 70 the Queen asked for a set of CD's works and gave him an autographed copy of her *Journal of our Life in the Highlands*.

[1] The Marble Arch, then in front of the Palace (moved in 1851).

*aa* Not previously published.

*bb* Written at the top of p. 1, above the address.

[2] Thomas Wakley (1795–1862; *DNB*), surgeon and medical reformer; coroner for West Middlesex since 1839.

Founded the *Lancet* 1823 to report medical lectures and hospital cases and to expose nepotism and inefficiency in hospital administration, and met with fierce opposition; pressed for reform of the Royal College of Surgeons, and was finally ejected from the College theatre. Turned to politics: as MP for Finsbury 1835–52, was an ardent supporter of liberal causes. CD had served on a jury under him in Jan 40 (see *To* Forster, ?15 Jan, *fn*).

[3] Written large and bold.

[4] This letter was at one time in the hands of Walter T. Spencer of New Oxford Street, who apparently took it seriously and in 1909 sent a copy to CD's son Henry. Henry replied, on 7 Dec: "You have strangely misread the letter . . . I cannot understand how anyone could imagine the letter to be other than a joke. . . . At the date of this letter, (which was years before his separation from my mother) the deepest affection existed between them. Read the letter again and you will see how completely you were 'taken in' " (MS Berg).

[5] No doubt the recently published *Sketches of Young Couples* and its earlier, also anonymous, companion *Sketches of Young Gentlemen.*

The last aggravating word has touched that tender chord in my heart which you understand so well. Have you heard from Forster this morning? I have, but oh what a mockery it is. *He does not love her.*[1]

I have seen my wife—spoken to her—been in her society. I burst into tears on hearing the voices of my infant children. I loathe my parents. I hate my house. I love nobody here but the Raven,[2] and I only love him because he seems to have no feeling in common with anybody. What is to be done. Heavens my friend, what is to be done!

What if I murder Chapman and Hall. This thought has occurred to me several times. If I did this she would hear of me; perhaps sign the warrant for my execution with her own dear hand. What if I murder myself. Mr. Wakley is a beast—a coarse unsympathizing coroner—and would not understand such feelings as mine. I feel that, and lay down my razor as the thought occurs to me. Is there no sentimental coroner? I have heard of Mr. Baker[3] but I don't know how his mind is constituted. I have also heard of Mr. Higgs,[4] but the name is not promising. I think there is one named Grubb.[5] Perhaps *he* has high feeling and could comprehend me. The Serpentine is in his district, but then the Humane Society[6] steps in. They might disfigure me with drags—perhaps save me and expect me at the next Anniversary Dinner to walk round Free-Mason's Hall with a bible under my arm. She would never love me after *that*. —All is difficulty and darkness.

What is to be done? Would any alliance with the Chartists serve us? They have no doubt in contemplation attacks upon the palace, and being plain men would very likely resign *her* to us with great cheerfulness. Let us then toss—the best out of three—and the loser to poison himself. Is this feasible?

I dreamt of Lady Fanny Cowper[7] all night, but I didn't love her, sleeping, nor do I now that I am awake although I did but a few days back. I feel tenderly towards your sister[8] because she knows our secret. With the great exception that I need not name, she is now the only woman on Earth that I do not shrink from in horror. Here is a state of mind!

How are you to-day. It will be some consolation to me to receive a detail of your sufferings. On Saturday Morning I shall call upon you. Conceive

[1] Underlined twice.
[2] Grip.
[3] Coroner for Middlesex.
[4] Thomas Higgs, coroner for the Duchy of Lancaster.
[5] Perhaps CD meant J. H. Gell—Coroner for the City of Westminster.
[6] Its principal depot (erected 1794 by Decimus Burton on ground given by George III) was on the Serpentine (north side)—a favourite spot for suicides.
[7] Lady Frances Elizabeth Cowper (1820–80), the Queen's favourite Maid of Honour; married Lord Jocelyn 1841 and became a Lady of the Bedchamber. Daughter of Lord Melbourne's sister, who, after Lord Cowper's death 1837, had married Palmerston 1839. She looks indeed lovely in the portrait by Chalon engraved in *Heath's Book of Beauty. 1839*, facing p. 129.
[8] Isabella, Maclise's unmarried elder sister, who lived with him devotedly until her death in 1865.

my misery until then! Tonight—tomorrow—all tories[1]—nothing but slight and insult upon her generous head[2]—Gracious Powers where will this end!

I am utterly miserable and unfitted for my calling. What the upshot will be, I don't know, but something tremendous I am sure.—I feel that I am wandering.

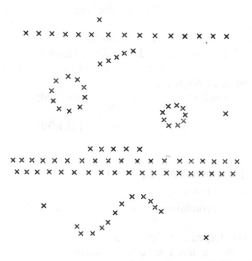

Daniel Maclise Esquire

Your distracted friend
CHARLES DICKENS

[1] I.e., presumably, nothing but Tory company that night and next day. On 13 Feb CD and Catherine dined with a Mrs Rolls (Macready, *Diaries*, II, 45), his fellow guests including Abel Rous Dottin, Conservative MP for Southampton, and a Walpole—probably Spencer Horatio Walpole (1806–98; *DNB*), Conservative MP from 1846 and later Home Secretary.

[2] Two incidents in 1839 had made Tory hostility to the Queen acute. In March the Court scandal concerning the Tory Lady Flora Hastings had become public; accusations that she was with child—the Queen being "one of the first, if not the first, to entertain false suspicions" (Elizabeth Longford, *Victoria R.I.*, p. 123)—were discovered to be unfounded; and when she died, 5 July, from a diseased liver, there was great public indignation and the *Spectator*, *Age* and *Morning Post* attacked the Queen unceasingly. With Melbourne's return to power after the "Bedchamber" crisis of May, Tory feeling was further embittered. Public insult was for a time so common that one entry in the Queen's Journal recorded that she and Melbourne had ridden in Rotten Row "*without* one *hiss*" (*op. cit.*, p. 122). The Tory leaders had their revenge when, on the Queen's marriage, they forced the reduction of Prince Albert's allowance from the customary £50,000 a year to £30,000, and refused to give him the precedence she demanded for him. "Poor dear Albert, how cruelly are they ill-using that dearest Angel!", she wrote in her Journal, 2 Feb 40; "Monsters! you Tories shall be punished. Revenge, revenge!" (*op. cit.*, p. 137).

## *To* THOMAS MITTON, [?13 FEBRUARY 1840]

MS Huntington Library. *Date:* Watermark 1839; handwriting suggests early 1840; perhaps 13 Feb, referring to Mrs Rolls's dinner that night (see last, *fn*). Mitton, who had been away from London earlier in the week, had perhaps now received the letter of 8 Feb from Bentley's solicitors (see *To* Mitton, 29 Jan, *fn*) and wished to report on it to CD. *Address:* Thomas Mitton Esquire | Southampton Buildings | Chancery Lane.

Devonshire Terrace. | Thursday Morning.

My Dear Mitton.

I am obliged to attend a dinner party to-day, and another (I grieve to say it) tomorrow. All the morning to-day and tomorrow I shall most probably be at home, but if the matter you write of may rest until Saturday, I can be with you then at 12 o'Clock.

Let me know in one line if this will do.—If not, make your own appointment.

Faithfully Yours always

CD.

## *To* JOHN OVERS, 16 FEBRUARY 1840

MS Free Library of Philadelphia.

1 Devonshire Terrace, York Gate | February 16th. 1840.

Dear Mr. Overs.

I have read your Legend of Canterbury with great interest and pleasure. It would have been a most creditable performance to anybody—it is strikingly and remarkably so to you, who write under so many disadvantages —and if I had the controul of any Magazine, I would publish it immediately.

It has occurred to me that as this Story possesses a local as well as a general interest, it would be excellently adapted to a Kentish Magazine. Now although there is no such thing in existence (that I know of) at this moment, I have reason to believe that there soon will be, as a gentleman who has such a periodical in contemplation wrote to me about it a few weeks since.[1] I strongly recommend you to write to this gentleman yourself—to mention me in any way you please—and to say that you will be happy to send him your tale for perusal, if he will permit you. His address is "H. G. Adams Esquire—J Bryant Esquire's Parsonage House— Chatham". I think it will be an acquisition to him, and that you will be mutually obliged to each other.[2]

I don't know what the resources of this local Magazine may afford—very little, I dare say—but the gentleman of whom I speak, cannot be offended by your asking the question and I have no doubt will return you a straight forward answer. I would lose no time, but write to him immediately, and I again empower you to make the fullest use of my poor recommendation.

Very faithfully Yours

Mr. J. A. Overs.                                        CHARLES DICKENS

[1] See *To* Adams, 18 Jan.                    [2] "The Legend of Canterbury" did not appear in the *Kentish Coronal*.

## *To* W. C. MACREADY, [21] FEBRUARY 1840*

MS Morgan Library. *Date:* Letter misdated by a week, no doubt through exasperation. Bentley's advertisement of *Barnaby* "was repeated" on 21 Feb (see *fn*).

Friday Night 28th. Feby/40

My Dear Macready.

The advertisement was repeated today in the Times and Herald;[1] and the dog's solicitors (God forgive me for libelling his good animals) doggedly inform us that they mean to repeat it. The contradiction, therefore,—from my solicitors—appears in the Evening papers tomorrow, the respectable Sunday Papers, and all the Morning Papers on Monday.[2] This done, he means, as he tells us, to advertize the agreements—and that done, I don't know what happens.[3]

If I have any news, I shall be able to tell it you on Sunday.[4] It would be a very bad return for your kind and affectionate interest, if I made any shew of apology for wearying you with these details.

For to-day, the Vagabond has stopped my clock—and he knows that as well as I. I shall try to sleep it off and go to work tomorrow; and if I do, with any success, he may go to — but I won't anticipate, having no doubt his ultimate destination is already arranged.

Always My Dear Macready | Your faithful friend

W. C. Macready Esquire                       CHARLES DICKENS

---

[1] The following advertisement appeared in *The Times* and *Morning Herald* on 21 Feb: "Preparing for publication, in 3 vols. post 8vo, BARNABY RUDGE; A Story of the Great Riots. By CHARLES DICKENS, Esq., Author of 'The Pickwick Papers', 'Oliver Twist', and 'Nicholas Nickleby'. Richard Bentley, New Burlington-street." A similar advertisement had appeared in the *Morning Chronicle*, 14 Dec 39, headed "Mr. Dickens's New Work" (for CD's protest, see *To* Smithson & Mitton, 16 Dec 39; I, 616–18).

[2] The contradiction reads: "BARNABY RUDGE.—It appearing that Mr. Bentley, of New Burlington-street, Publisher, continues to advertise a Book under this title, as being a work of Mr. Charles Dickens, now preparing for publication, we are authorised to inform the public (with the view of preventing any disappointment or misunderstanding) that

Mr. Bentley's Solicitors have twice had notice in writing from us, that Mr. Dickens is not at present engaged upon such work. SMITHSON and MITTON, 23, Southampton-buildings, 22nd. February, 1840" (*Standard*, 22 Feb). It appeared in the *Examiner* on 23 Feb, *The Times* and *Morning Chronicle* on 24 Feb, and the *Morning Herald* on 25 Feb.

[3] Bentley was apparently intending to give an account of the dispute in the *Miscellany* (see Edgar Johnson, *CD, his Tragedy and Triumph*, 1953, I, 251), but did not do so; and it was left to George Bentley to publish the details of his father's dealings with CD in a letter to *The Times*, 7 Dec 71, after the publication of Forster's *Life*.

[4] When they were probably, as on numerous other Sundays, expecting to dine together.

## *To* W. C. MACREADY, [?23 FEBRUARY 1840]*

MS Morgan Library. *Date:* There is a discrepancy between CD's "Sunday" (if correct, clearly Sun 23 Feb) and entry under 23 Feb in Macready's *Diaries* (II, 45). Almost certainly CD's date is right and the *Diaries* entry refers to Sat 22 Feb, not the 23rd. See *fn.*

1 Devonshire Terrace | Sunday Morning.

My Dear Macready

I fear I may not have sufficiently expressed to you yesterday,[1] my sense of your most kind and friendly interest in the matter of Bentley. Nor can I express it now, although I desire to do so. Like most men who are sensitive to irritation and annoyance, I am at least equally alive to their reverse; and I do assure you that the few words which passed between us yesterday brace me up even against the Court of Chancery,[2] and give me a

---

[1] It seems probable that between CD's letters to Macready of 21 and ?23 Feb what happened was as follows. On the afternoon of Sat 22 Feb (not 23 Feb, as given in *Diaries*, II, 45) Macready, having just seen, he recorded, CD's advertisement in the *Examiner* (no doubt the Saturday, "country edition") "walked out with Edward [*his brother*] and called on Dickens". He took with him, in case CD was out, the following note:

"York Gate, Saturday | My dear Dickens | I shall see you tomorrow [*cf. mention in* To *Macready, 21 Feb, of meeting arranged for Sunday*], and therefore will not bother you much now. I only wish to urge on you my objection to see you before the public:—and my annoyance at your exposure to so much disgust & suffering, [ ?over something] which won't interfere with you seriously in any way.—*Cannot* mediation do something?—I cannot give up the hope, until it is proved unavailing. | Sincerely & always | Yours WM" (MS preserved among CD's letters to Macready in the Morgan Library; clearly not delivered because CD was at home). Macready's diary entry continues thus: "Urged on him the necessity of arranging the quarrel with Bartley [*clearly a misreading of Bentley*], and dissuaded him from answering any attack that B—— might make upon him next week. He showed me a letter he had prepared, but I requested him not to send it. He is quite in the wrong. He makes a contract, which he considers advantageous at the time, but subsequently finding his talent more lucrative than he had supposed, he refused to fulfil the contract" (*Diaries*, II, 45–6).

Bentley's solicitors duly published the following notice (unanswered by CD): "BARNABY RUDGE.—An advertisement having appeared, signed by Messrs. Smithson and Mitton, Southampton-buildings, announcing that Mr. Charles Dickens is not at present engaged upon the work under the above title, it is necessary, in justice to Mr. Bentley, to state, that, by an agreement under the hand of Mr. Charles Dickens, dated in February last, Mr. Dickens agreed to write the above work for Mr. Bentley, to be completed and delivered to him by the first day of January then next; and also engaged not to commence or write any other work until the same should be completed except 'Nicholas Nickleby', which is completed, and an annual publication in one volume, which has been abandoned, and a book to be published by Mr. Colburn, and edited by Mr. Dickens, which has [not] been published; and that, up to this time, Mr. Dickens has not expressed his intention to refuse to perform his agreement, by writing the work in question. ADLINGTON, GREGORY, FAULKNER, and FOLLETT, Bedford-row. I certify the facts above stated to be true, JOHN S. GREGORY, Bedford-row. Feb. 24, 1840" (*Morning Herald*, 25 Feb). This was repeated in *The Times*, 26 Feb, and the *Examiner*, 1 Mar.

feeling of true pleasure which I can scarcely separate from the subject that give[s]¹ it birth.

I am exceedingly anxious that you should understand that I do not reject your good offices from any obstinate or wrong-headed feeling, but simply because I *know* the hopelessness of any mediation just now, and know this man as well as anybody living. The law, bad as it is, is more true and more to be trusted than such a hound as he, and *unless* he gives me the opening for a negociation, I must trust myself to its tender mercies, and submit to its vexations with what philosophy I may. If I were a builder or a stone-mason I might fulfil my contract with him, but write for him I really cannot unless I am forced and have no outlet for escape.

If the question should resolve itself into one of compensation (which I devoutly hope it may) then I shall not scruple to avail myself of your friendly mediation. Mean time believe me that if it had been used and had been attended with the most triumphant success, it could scarcely have made me happier than the proffer of it has already.

      I am always My Dear Macready | Faithfully Yours
W. C. Macready Esquire         CHARLES DICKENS

## *To* JOHN BROWNLOW,² 26 FEBRUARY 1840*

MS³ Thomas Coram Foundation for Children.

     1 Devonshire Terrace, York Gate | February 26th. 1840.
Sir
 I am much indebted to you for your obliging note. We *have* removed

² Clearly on 23 Feb CD had not yet received the opinion of his Counsel, James Bacon (see *To* Mitton, ?27 Feb). But Bentley had been advised on 12 Feb by his Counsel, Sutton Sharpe, that he could not expect to obtain an injunction in Chancery restraining CD from publishing any new work before *Barnaby*, and that his only recourse would be to a Court of Law for damages (MS Berg). Chapman & Hall apparently held the first two chapters of *Barnaby* (referred to in *To* Thompson, 13 Feb); for on 11 Mar—still fearing that the case might be taken to Court—they wrote to Smithson & Mitton that they had spoken to Forster of "returning the MS" (doubtless to protect themselves); that Forster (no doubt also wanting protection) "thought it ought in case he was examined as a witness, to be accompanied by a letter stating [Chapman & Hall's] reasons for declining the work"; that they had

written the letter (perhaps with reasons purporting to be that they respected Bentley's claim); that Mitton had previously urged that correspondence was "better avoided", and they now agreed with Smithson & Mitton that the letter should not be sent (MS Mr C. C. Dickens). It seems almost certain that they never seriously meant to "decline" *Barnaby*. But it was probably wise not to have the two chapters of MS in their keeping if the case came to Court. Without them, they would feel reasonably safe, since *Master Humphrey* at this date was still seen not as a "new work" but as a weekly miscellany. In fact, Bentley took no legal action, but negotiated instead (see *To* Mitton, 2 June 40, *fn*).

¹ MS reads "give".
² John Brownlow (*d.* 1873), a foundling himself; employed in the Secretary's office of the Foundling Hospital 1814, became Treasurer's Clerk 1828,

*have* forgotten to give notice at the Foundling,[1] and the chapel[2] being too far for us (which we greatly regret, as we miss it very much) shall be glad if you will have the goodness to hold the Pew at your disposal.

Yours very truly

Mr. Brownlow                                            CHARLES DICKENS


## *To* JOHN FORSTER, [?27 FEBRUARY 1840]

MS Victoria & Albert Museum (FC). *Date:* probably two days before 29 Feb when they left for Bath to see Landor; handwriting supports.

Devonshire Terrace | Thursday Morning

My Dear Forster

I waxed rather stupid yesterday and consequently must keep close to-day. Will you dine with us tomorrow at *a quarter before 4*? If so, we can go to Southampton Buildings in a body, calling for Mac as we go.[3]

You write to Landor I suppose? Mitton has taken places, but at what

and was Secretary 1849–72. Author of several works on the Foundling Hospital. He had written to CD as "Collector of Pew Rents" (R. H. Nichols & F. A. Wray, *History of the Foundling Hospital*, 1935, pp. 277–8).

[3] Preserved in a copy of the Christmas Numbers of *All the Year Round*, inscribed "CHARLES DICKENS To the Foundling Hospital | December, 1868".

[1] Incorporated 1739, through the efforts of Thomas Coram (?1668–1751; *DNB*), as "The Hospital for the Maintenance and Education of Exposed and Deserted Young Children". The Hospital, in Bloomsbury Fields, completed in 1747, was renamed the Thomas Coram Foundation for Children in 1953.

[2] A very popular place of worship in the 1840s. Handel presented its first organ. CD is said to have been "a regular attendant" while living in Doughty Street (Nichols & Wray, *op. cit.*, p. 285). With W. H. Wills, he wrote an article on the Hospital for *Household Words* (19 Mar 53, VII, 49–53).

[3] The purpose of their visit to Mitton in Southampton Buildings was presumably to obtain particulars of their journey. According to F, II, vii, 145, both Catherine and Maclise accompanied CD and Forster to Bath. But *To*

Catherine, 1 Mar 40, shows that she certainly did not; and the omission of Maclise's "regards" at the end of that letter suggests that he did not either. It was almost certainly while CD and Forster were at Bath that Maclise wrote a 6-page letter (endorsed by Forster "The Queen's marriage | 1840"), beginning "My dear friends and fellow sufferers" (MS Forster Collection, V & A). It described his prostration when they had gone; he had hardly enough fortitude to wait till Thursday [the day of their return from Bath]: "You ought not", he wrote, "to have left a too sensitive being alone—without the sustaining consolation which had hitherto made our sympathy a bond between us—when we were the true 'Tria juncta in you know'." It seemed to him but yesterday that they had been to the theatre together: "we had braved the dreadful feelings conjured up by an actual contemplation of that Divine object which had united us eternally in one cause—we had seen HER we had seen him—we had seen her touch him—talk to him look at him—beat time with him—we had heard him shouted for . . ." This was probably at Drury Lane, on Wed 26 Feb, when the Queen and Prince Albert heard John Barnett's opera *The Mountain Sylph*.

hour the Coach starts, this Deponent knoweth not,—though he verily believes it is 10 from the Railroad.

Faithfully Always<br>CD.

## *To* THOMAS MITTON, [?27 FEBRUARY 1840]*

*MS Mrs Percy W. Valentine. Date:* probably the Thursday after 23 Feb, when CD had not yet received Bacon's opinion (see *To* Macready, 23 Feb, *fn*).

1 Devonshire Terrace, York Gate.<br>Thursday Morning | (I should say, afternoon)

My Dear Mitton

Nothing can be clearer or more satisfactory than Bacon's[1] opinion.[2] We may put our hands in our pockets and wait for the Dragon's approach with perfect philosophy.

I have not received the message you refer to. I will call tomorrow or next day, and do the needful.[3]

Faithfully Yours always

Thomas Mitton Esquire.                                CHARLES DICKENS

## *To* MESSRS CHAPMAN & HALL, 28 FEBRUARY [1840]*

*MS New York Public Library. Date:* Handwriting shows this must refer to the journey to Bath of 29 Feb 40.

Devonshire Terrace. | Friday Afternoon 28th. Feby.

Dear Sirs.

Herewith I send you No. 3. I meant to have seen you to-day; but having to finish it, could not get out.

I mark on the other side,[4] such subjects in it as occur to me for illustration.—You will see that the story is not finished, but runs into No. 4.[5]

I go to Bath tomorrow morning and return on Wednesday Night by Mail. You are not likely to have any occasion to write to me, but if you have, Mrs. Dickens will give you the address.

Accept my blessing, each partner on one knee (the left) to render it the more impressive—and believe me

Always Faithfully Yours

Messrs. Chapman & Hall.                                CHARLES DICKENS

[1] James Bacon (1798–1895; *DNB*), Chancery counsel and later Judge. Barrister 1827; QC 1846; Chief Judge in Bankruptcy 1869–83; the last Vice-Chancellor 1870. Retired from the Bench 1886, aged 88. He advised Smithson & Mitton on several of CD's Agreements from 1837 onwards.

[2] Not traced, but presumably similar to that given by Sutton Sharpe to Bentley: see *To* Macready, ?23 Feb, *fn*.

[3] I.e., presumably, pay for the coach tickets to Bath: see next.

[4] Clearly of a folded sheet. The back page has not survived.

[5] This was before the changes he outlined to Chapman & Hall and to Cattermole on 9 Mar.

## *To* MRS CHARLES DICKENS, 1 MARCH 1840

MS British Museum.

35 Saint James's Square, Bath.[1] | March 1st. 1840.

My Dearest Kate

We reached here in safety last night, after a very pleasant ride, during a great part of which (the day being so very fine) we came outside; stopping to lunch vigorously at two o'Clock, and arriving here shortly before 8. We were alone at dinner, and although desperately learned and frequently first-person-singular-ish, we were much better than I had expected.[2] Indeed I was not bored—for which I am very thankful and devout this morning.

We sleep at the York House—the largest hotel here—where the beds are very good and very warm. Of course I *arranged* both the room and my luggage before going to bed, and had everything very tidy.

The first thing I did on arriving, was to look at a play-bill, wherein Rob Roy[3] was announced for last night, and Somnabula[4] for tomorrow, but no mention of Burnett in either,[5] the tenor being one *Mr. T. Bishop*![6] Upon my life I begin to think that Burnett has been writing deceitful

---

[1] Landor's lodgings; the house in which CD first thought of Nell. For Landor's later declaration that he had "never in his life regretted anything so much" as having failed to buy the house and burn it to the ground, so that "no meaner association should ever desecrate the birthplace of Nell", see Forster, *W. S. Landor*, II, 459, repeated in F, II, vii, 145*n*. CD confirmed the story in *To* Forster, 9 May 69.

[2] Cf. Crabb Robinson of his first meeting with Landor (1830): "He was . . . a *leonine* man, and with a fierceness of tone well suited to his name; his decisions being confident, and on all subjects, whether of taste or life, unqualified . . . But why should I trouble myself to describe him? He is painted by a master hand in Dickens's novel, 'Bleak House', now in course of publication . . . The combination of superficial ferocity and inherent tenderness, so admirably portrayed in 'Bleak House', still at first strikes every stranger" (*Diary, Reminiscences, and Correspondence*, ed. Thomas Sadler, 1869, II, 481–2).

[3] *Rob Roy Macgregor; or, Auld Lang Syne!*, an opera based on Scott's novel, with libretto by Isaac Pocock, music by John Davy. Misread "Drob Droy" in *Mr. & Mrs. CD*, ed. Walter Dexter, 1935, as a result of CD's curious "R"s.

[4] Thus in MS. Bellini's opera *La Sonnambula*.

[5] During the season 18 Jan–13 June 40 CD's brother-in-law Henry Burnett was the leading tenor at the Theatre Royal, Bath, and performed 40 times in 15 different works, among them *Der Freischütz*, *The Maid of Palaiseau* (English adaptation of *La Gazza Ladra*), *The Love Spell* (English version of *L'Elisir D'Amore*), *Fra Diavolo*, and the English comic opera *Love in a Village* (Bickerstaffe and Arne). He was described in the preliminary announcement as "of Braham's St. James's Theatre, and Nobilities Concerts". Clearly the tenor rôles in *Rob Roy* and *La Sonnambula* were not in his repertoire; and on the night of CD's arrival, Sat 29 Feb, he was singing in a concert at the Pump Room.

[6] Unidentified except as a tenor who had first appeared at the Theatre Royal, Bath, 21 Feb 40, and shared the tenor rôles with Burnett during the season. Underlining and exclamation-mark may perhaps be explained by bishops being anathema to the Nonconformist Burnett.

letters—has never been here at all—and is hiding himself in some remote corner, whence he steals out now and then, and issues to the Post Office for his letters.—I communicated this suspicion to Forster this morning, and amused him mightily with it. Seriously, it is odd enough that there is no mention of him in the Posters on the walls; and as for excitement—oh dear you can't think how calm the place is. It seems as if there were no Burnett here.[1] I shall make it my business to investigate the truth tomorrow, and shall report it when I come home, which will be on Thursday Morning about Six or half past. You must have one of the servants up *by six,* and perhaps you will have a fire lighted in our bedroom in order that I may warm myself and get a cup of coffee.

You may suppose that having been on a Coach all day yesterday, I have no great News, though I hope to bring back amusing intelligence of one kind or another.[2] Meantime I look forward to Wednesday Night with great eagerness, and am charmed to think that besides to-day only Monday and Tuesday stand between. God bless you my love. Kiss the darling babs and write a *long* letter (and don't forget to put it in the post, which you must if you wish it to reach me) as soon as you receive this.

Always yours truly & affectionately
CHARLES DICKENS

Forster's best regards—Landor's ditto. I see Yates announces another portion of Nickleby.[3] *Unless* you have already written for a box, I would rather you didn't go, until I return.

## *To* WILLIAM UPCOTT, 6 MARCH 1840*

MS University of Texas.

Devonshire Terrace. | Friday 6th. March 1840.

My Dear Sir

I hope the inclosed will *do*.[4] If not, tell me and I'll try another form.

---

[1] Burnett later told the Rev. James Griffin that he had been offered engagements in London, Edinburgh, Dublin and Bath, and had chosen Bath so as to be able to attend Argyle Independent Chapel of which the Rev. William Jay (1769–1853; *DNB*) was pastor. He had taken lodgings with members of the congregation (J. Griffin, *Memories of the Past*, 1883, p. 170). His decision to give up the stage was made soon afterwards.

[2] Such as, perhaps, their amusement at a picture Landor had recently bought and described as "a fine Rubens—a lion". According to Rose Paynter, "as they walked back to their hotel, at midnight, the usually quiet streets of Bath rang with their inextinguishable laughter, with which were mingled 'Roars for the lion!'" (*Letters of W. S. Landor, Private and Public*, ed. S. Wheeler, 1899, p. 37 and *n*).

[3] For Yates's earlier production of Edward Stirling's adaptation of *Nickleby* (19 Nov 38), when only eight parts of the book had appeared, see Vol. 1, pp. 459–60 and 463–4. Stirling's *The Fortunes of Smike; or, a Sequel to Nicholas Nickleby* was first performed at the Adelphi on 2 Mar 40, again with Yates as Mantalini and Mrs Keeley as Smike. Buckstone played Newman Noggs.

[4] Probably his autograph for Upcott's collection.

I am in haste to answer your note as I have just come back from Bath and fear you may think me neglectful.

Faithfully Yours

William Upcott Esquire                    CHARLES DICKENS

## *To* H. K. BROWNE, [?6 or 7 MARCH 1840]

Facsimile in F. G. Kitton, *CD and his Illustrators*, 1899, facing p. 72. *Date:* CD's comments are written at the foot of Browne's sketch for "Master Humphrey and his companion",[1] which on 9 Mar CD sent on to Chapman & Hall, Browne having presumably made the small changes requested without delay.

Master Humphrey *admirable*.[2] Could his stick (with a crooked top) be near his chair? I misdoubt the deaf gentleman's pipe and wish he could have a better o[ne].[3]

## *To* JOHN OVERS, 7 MARCH 1840

MS Free Library of Philadelphia.

1 Devonshire Terrace | 7th. March 1840.

Dear Mr. Overs.

I think Mr. Adams a very unconscionable person, a very obtrusive one, and extraordinarily self-sufficient. His enquiry whether you can make out a relationship with Kent is ridiculous in the last degree (coming as it does after his acceptance of the story) and his cool confession of having copied a part of my note to you is "something more",—and I would fain hope not a necessary ingredient in the Kentish character.

If he *paid* you, I would cheerfully give *you* (not him) the permission he seeks.[4] As he does not, I beg you to with-hold it and to say that you have not the inclination to make any such request to me,—as your note assures me you have not. I have a nervous dread and horror of being supposed to direct the judgements of people who can judge very well for themselves, or of seeming to patronize—both of which I should certainly appear to do if I yielded this permission.

Nevertheless if it would do you any tangible service, you should have it. As it can do no such thing, but would on the contrary place you in a position with reference to this gentleman in which you have no right to stand, I know you will agree with me that it should not be given.

I will read your paper[5] in the course of next week, and communicate with you when I have done so.

Faithfully Yours

Mr. J. A. Overs                             CHARLES DICKENS

[1] The headpiece to No. 3.
[2] Underlined twice.
[3] There is no stick in the original sketch; but Browne added one and made the pipe longer and the grotesque figures on its bowl clearer.

[4] Presumably permission to quote from *To* Overs, 16 Feb, when publishing the story.
[5] See *To* Overs, 12 Apr.

### *To* MRS A. T. THOMSON,[1] 8 MARCH [1840]†

MS Huntington Library. *Date:* 8 Mar was Sunday in 1840; handwriting supports that year.

1 Devonshire Terrace | Sunday 8th. March

My Dear Madam

I should have answered your letter immediately, but that I have been on a short visit to Bath whence I have only just returned.

Sir Edward Bulwer[2] has already applied to me with reference to the subject in which you so kindly interest yourself,[3] and I have already arranged with Mr. Forster—a mutual friend of ours who communicated with me on Bulwer's behalf—for promoting it with my slight assistance.[4] I have not seen Sir Edward himself lately, but he understands this, I have no doubt.[5]

*a* In all that you say so well concerning poor Mrs. Landon[6] and her unfortunate daughter[7] I most cordially and heartily concur.*a* Let me thank

[1] Katherine Thomson, *née* Byerley (1797–1862; *DNB*), author of numerous historical biographies and novels. Had known L.E.L. (see below) since 1826: see her account of her in *Recollections of Literary Characters*, 1854, and their correspondence in Laman Blanchard's *Life and Literary Remains of L. E. Landon*, 2 vols, 1841. Her husband, Anthony Todd Thomson (1778–1849; *DNB*), physician, had attended L.E.L. in London.

[2] Sir Edward George Earle Lytton Bulwer (1803–73; *DNB*): see Vol. 1, p. 337*n*.

[3] An appeal on behalf of the widowed mother of Letitia Landon. Cf. Macready's *Diaries*, II, 46, entry for 28 Feb 40: "A note . . . from Bulwer, asking me to subscribe to an annuity for the destitute mother of L.E.L."

[4] The payment of £10 to Forster shown in CD's accounts on 28 Feb 40 may well have been his contribution to the Landon fund.

[5] Bulwer had been a close friend of L.E.L.'s since 1827, and had given her away on her marriage to George Maclean in 1838 (see below).

*aa* Given in N, 1, 206 from catalogue source. Letter otherwise unpublished.

[6] Catherine Jane Landon, *née* Bishop (*d.* 1854); widowed 1824 and mainly dependent on her two children, Letitia and Whittington, an ill-paid curate until he became Secretary of the Literary Fund 1837 (see Vol. 1, p. 510 and *n*).

[7] Letitia Elizabeth Landon, Mrs Maclean (1802–38; *DNB*). Perhaps the subject of last paragraph of *To* Forster, ?3 Jan 39 (1, 489), though not named. A writer from earliest childhood, in her teens had charmed William Jerdan, and soon became one of the chief contributors to his *Literary Gazette*. Published 5 vols of verse 1821–9; contributed regularly to annuals; wrote several novels and one unacted tragedy. The impression she made on Henry Crabb Robinson in 1826 was of "a starling— . . . with a gay good-humoured face" (*Diary, Reminiscences, and Correspondence*, ed. T. Sadler, 1869, II, 329). Later, when trying to live down the scandalous rumours about her relations with Maginn, her "hectic, hysterical high-spirits", when in company, were disapprovingly noted by H. F. Chorley: there was a "certain audacious brightness in her talk; but it was . . . smart, not sound" (*Autobiography, Memoir, and Letters*, compiled by H. G. Hewlett, 1873, I, 252). Soon after her engagement (?1834 or 35) to Forster, the malicious rumours were revived (possibly, it seems, by Rosina Bulwer); and Forster (then aged 22—ten years her junior and inevitably out of his depth) faced her with them. Hurt and indignant, she broke off the engagement (see her letter to Bulwer, quoted in Michael Sadleir, *Bulwer and his Wife*, new edn, 1933, pp. 425–6). Her marriage in 1838 to

you for your note and especially for your kind expressions towards myself, and beg you to believe me

Dear Madam | Faithfully Yours

Mrs. Thomson.                                           CHARLES DICKENS

## *To* JOHN FORSTER, [?8 MARCH 1840]

Extract in F, II, vii, 145. *Date:* 4 Mar according to Forster; but unless CD changed his plans he and Forster did not reach London until early in the morning of the 5th (see *To* Catherine, 1 Mar). Probably CD was writing on the day before the 9th, when he announced the changes in *Master Humphrey* to Chapman & Hall and Cattermole.

If you can manage to give me a call in the course of the day or evening, I wish you would. I am laboriously turning over in my mind how I can best effect the improvement we spoke of last night, which I will certainly make by hook or by crook, and which I would like you to see *before* it goes finally to the printer's. I have determined not to put that witch-story into number 3,[1] for I am by no means satisfied of the effect of its contrast with Humphrey. I think of lengthening Humphrey, finishing the description of the society,[2] and closing with the little child-story, which is SURE to be effective, especially after the old man's quiet way.[3]

## *To* MESSRS CHAPMAN & HALL, [9 MARCH 1840]*

MS Morgan Library. *Date:* clearly the same day as next.

Devonshire Terrace | Monday Morning

Dear Sirs

The inclosed Sketch[4] arrived yesterday afternoon. Will Mr. Chapman take *the pipe* under his especial care?

George Maclean, Governor of Cape Coast Castle, seems to have been an act of desperation. For her death six months later, see Vol. I, p. 488*n*. Many people, including her brother Whittington, were convinced that the cause was not suicide as generally believed, but that she was murdered by Maclean's African mistress. The question was still discussed in 1847: see William Howitt, *Homes and Haunts of the Most Eminent British Poets*, 1847, II, 125–44 (Howitt thought her murder unlikely). Nor did Forster forget her: in Geraldine Jewsbury's *Half Sisters* he found "a young girl wonderfully like Miss Landon in manner and appearance", he wrote to Leigh Hunt, 16 Sep 48 (MS BM).

[1] Called "Mr. Pickwick's Tale", it comes in Nos 5 and 6.

[2] No. 3 contains the account of Master Humphrey's meeting and friendship with the deaf gentleman, and descriptions of the other two members of the society, Jack Redburn and Owen Miles.

[3] In fact (presumably as a result of discussion when Forster called) No. 3 closed with "A Confession Found in a Prison in the Time of Charles the Second" ("I was a lieutenant": see next). No. 4 opened with "the little child-story"—the genesis of *Old Curiosity Shop*.

[4] "Master Humphrey and his companion" (see *To* Browne, ?6 or 7 Mar).

I should like to see the said Mr. Chapman tomorrow morning or to-day, if he can conveniently call upon me. I have it in contemplation to alter the contents of the third Number, and to throw the witch story over to 4, 5, or 6—putting the story which Mr. Chapman calls "I was a lieutenant" into No. 3, and lengthening Master Humphrey so as to finish if possible the Sketch of the Society in the same No. I feel that this will be a great improvement. I am also trying by some slight alteration in No. 1 to connect the stories more immediately with the clock,[1] and to give the work a less discursive appearance.[2]—In short I am beginning to be stimulated by finding myself in March, and am rising with the occasion.

Faithfully Yours always

Messrs. Chapman and Hall.          CHARLES DICKENS

## *To* GEORGE CATTERMOLE, 9 MARCH 1840

MS Huntington Library.

1 Devonshire Terrace. | Monday March 9th. 1840.

My Dear Cattermole.

I have been induced on looking over the works of the Clock, to make a slight alteration in their disposal, by virtue of which the story about John Podgers[3] will stand over for some little time, and that short tale will occupy its place which you have already by you, and which treats of the assassination of a young gentleman under circumstances of peculiar aggravation.[4] I shall be greatly obliged to you if you will turn your attention to this last morsel as the feature of *No. 3*, and still more so if you can stretch a point with regard to time (which is of the last importance just now) and make a subject out of it, rather than find one in it.[5] I would neither have made this alteration nor have troubled you about it, but for weighty and cogent

[1] CD's original idea (as outlined in *To* Forster, ?10 Jan) had been that the collection of MSS kept in the clock was Master Humphrey's own, and that when later the club was formed it took its name from the clock. In the published text it is the members of the club who with their own hands place MSS in the clock and thus "link [their] enjoyments" with it. Whether this slight alteration was in fact made by CD at this stage cannot be known, since the proofs of *Master Humphrey* No. 1 have not survived.

[2] In this he did not succeed. Reviewing *Master Humphrey*, Vol. 1, in the *Athenæum*, 7 Nov 40, Thomas Hood wrote: "The main fault of the work is in its construction . . . some of the figures, however ornamental, tend seriously to complicate and embarrass the movements of the machine. We allude to Master Humphrey and his leash of friends. . . . The truth is, the Author is rather too partial to one of the most unmanageable things in life or literature, a Club." (For Hood's admiration of Nell, however, and of other characters in *Old Curiosity Shop*, see *To* Hood, ?Feb or Mar 41, *fn*.)

[3] The "witch-story" (see *To* Forster, ?8 Mar).

[4] The subject of the "new No. 3 tale" (see postscript and *To* Forster, ?8 Mar, *fn*) is the murder of a four-year-old boy by his uncle.

[5] Cattermole's subject, "The arrest", is the story's climax—the scenting of the child's grave, beneath a chair on which the murderer sits, by two bloodhounds.

reasons which I feel very strongly, and into the composition of which caprice or fastidiousness has no part.[1]

I should tell you perhaps with reference to Chapman and Hall that they will never trouble you (as they never trouble me) but when there is real and pressing occasion, and that their representations in this respect, unlike those of most men of business, are to be relied upon.

I cannot tell you how admirably I think Master Humphrey's room[2] comes out, or what glowing accounts I hear of the second design[3] you have done. I had *not the faintest anticipation* of anything so good,—taking into account the material and the dispatch.

With best regards at home, believe me dear Cattermole
Heartily Yours
CHARLES DICKENS

The new No. 3 tale begins "I held a Lieutenant's commission in His Majesty's Army, and served abroad in the Campaigns of 1677 and 1678." It has at present no title.

## *To* JOHN FORSTER, [?9 MARCH 1840]

Extract in F, II, vii, 145–6. *Date:* This came "hard upon" letter of ?8 Mar according to Forster.

What do you think of the following double title for the beginning of that little tale? "PERSONAL ADVENTURES OF MASTER HUMPHREY: *The Old Curiosity Shop.*" I have thought of *Master Humphrey's Tale, Master Humphrey's Narrative, A Passage in Master Humphrey's Life*—but I don't think any does as well as this. I have also thought of *The Old Curiosity Dealer and the Child* instead of *The Old Curiosity Shop.* Perpend. Topping[4] waits.[5]

[1] CD's decision that the "child-story" should come first in No. 4 instead of last in No. 3, and his reference to "weighty and cogent reasons", suggest that he now had thoughts of running it through several numbers; but "little tale" and the titles suggested for it in *To* Forster, ?9 Mar, show that he was still thinking of a story rather than a novel. Eight years later, in his Preface to the First Cheap Edn of *Old Curiosity Shop*, he wrote that already, before publication of the opening chapter of *Old Curiosity Shop* in No. 4 (on 25 Apr), he had "been made uneasy by the desultory character" of *Master Humphrey*, and believed that his readers shared this feeling (as they certainly did). The drop in sales (see *To* Overs, 12 Apr, *fn*) brought home to him what he had been half-aware of as early as 9 Mar.

[2] The headpiece to No. 1. Cf. *To* Cattermole, 13 and ?21 Jan.
[3] The headpiece to No. 2, "Master Graham's body".
[4] William Topping, first engaged as CD's groom 2 Mar 39 (see Vol. 1, p. 640); described in *To* Mitton, ?31 May 40 as taken on "again".
[5] Forster, after quoting from this and CD's previous letter to him, points out how gradually *Old Curiosity Shop* took form, "with less direct consciousness of design on his own part than I can remember in any other instance of all his career"; and yet it was the story which, more than any other of his works, made "the bond between himself and his readers one of personal attachment" (F, II, vii, 146).

## *To* J. A. DIEZMANN,[1] 10 MARCH 1840

MS Berg Collection. *Address:* Dr. A. Diezman | Leipzig.

1 Devonshire Terrace, York Gate,
Regents Park London, 10th. March 1840.

My Dear Sir.

I will not attempt to tell you how much gratified I have been by the receipt of your *first* English letter; nor can I describe to you with what delight and gratification I learn that I am held in such high esteem by your great countrymen, whose favorable appreciation is flattering indeed.[2]

To you who have undertaken the laborious (and often, I fear, very irksome) task of clothing me in the German garb, I owe a long arrear of thanks. I wish you would come to England, and afford me an opportunity of slightly reducing the account.

It is with great regret that I have to inform you in reply to the request contained in your pleasant communication, that my publishers have already made such arrangements[3] and are in possession of such stipulations relative to the proof sheets of my new works, that I have no power to send them out of England. If I had, I need not tell you what pleasure it would afford me to promote your views.

I am too sensible of the trouble you must have already had with my writings, to impose upon you a long letter. I will only add, therefore, that I am my Dear Sir

With great sincerity | Faithfully Yours

Dr. A. Diezman.[4]                                CHARLES DICKENS

[1] Dr Johann August Diezmann (1805–69), scholar and translator. Lived most of his life in Leipzig. Published books on Goethe and Schiller, several dictionaries, and numerous translations of English and French writers, including—besides CD—Sterne, Marryat, Bulwer, Ainsworth, Dumas and Hugo. *Nickleby* (of which he translated five of the seven serial Parts), 1838–9, was the first book published by Georg Westermann of Brunswick; his translations of *Sketches*, 1838–9, and of *Oliver*, 1839, the second and tenth. He later translated *A Christmas Carol*. For details of the *Nickleby* translation see Comte de Suzannet in *D*, XXVIII (1931–2), 60–2.

[2] For the numerous German translations of CD's early works, from *Sketches* onwards, see E. N. Gummer, *Dickens' Works in Germany*, pp. 7–9.

Gummer records an especially strong critical interest in CD in 1839 when translations of *Sketches*, *Oliver* and *Nickleby* were appearing. As against an average of seven articles a year 1840–8, he had found 23 on him in 1839—some criticizing him for looseness of composition and (in *Oliver*) over-emphasis on the dark side of life, but few failing to mention his great popularity with German readers (*op. cit.*, pp. 28–9).

[3] For the two authorized translations of *Master Humphrey*, 1840–1, see *To Cattermole*, 13 Jan, *fn*. *Old Curiosity Shop* also appeared throughout 1841 (obviously pirated) in the *British Museum*, Bielefeld, a German weekly magazine printed in English (Gummer, *op. cit.*, p. 29).

[4] Mis-spelt thus in MS.

## *To* W. H. HARRISON,[1] 14 MARCH 1840*

MS Free Library of Philadelphia.

1 Devonshire Terrace, York Gate | 14th. March 1840.

My Dear Sir

Many thanks for your note. I was already aware of the circumstance, as I presided at the club[2] last Wednesday.

The long-talked of book *proceeds*, and only awaits the Illustrations, and a few sheets from the Printer.[3]

Faithfully Yours

W. H. Harrison Esquire                          CHARLES DICKENS


## *To* JOHN MILLER,[4] 15 MARCH [1840]*

MS Mr Harry Secombe. *Date:* 15 Mar was Sunday in 1840; handwriting supports that year.

1 Devonshire Terrace, York Gate.
Sunday Morning March 15th.

Mr. Charles Dickens presents his compliments to Mr. Miller, and begs to inform him that he has sent to Messrs. Chapman and Hall a note which he received last night from Messrs. Lea and Blanchard; and that if Mr. Miller will have the goodness to treat with those gentlemen on the subject to which it refers, he will find them prepared to treat with him.[5]


## *To* J. P. HARLEY,[6] 16 MARCH [1840]

Photograph, John Rylands Library. *Address:* Prepaid | J. P. Harley Esquire | 14 Upper Gower Street. *Date:* PM 16 Mar 40.

1 Devonshire Terrace, York Gate | Monday 16th. March.

My Dear Harley.

If you know no reason
Why good wine in season
Should ever be forgot

—dine with me, not on the fifth of November, as this commencement

[1] William Henry Harrison (?1792–1874): see Vol. 1, p. 374*n*.

[2] Probably the Literary Fund Club: Harrison was for some years Registrar of the Literary Fund (see Vol. 1, p. 283*n*).

[3] Clearly CD was still expecting to publish Harrison's "Wild Beasts and Authors" in *The Pic Nic Papers*. Why it did not appear there is not known. For CD's "Mem" to write to him about it, see Diary entry for 31 Dec 40 (Appx, p. 462).

[4] Lea & Blanchard's London agent since 1817; authorized to select English books suitable for American reprinting and to make arrangements with publishers and authors; acted also on behalf of American writers publishing in England, such as Irving and Fenimore Cooper (see *Oliver Twist*, ed. K. Tillotson, Oxford, 1966, p. 373 and *n*).

[5] Miller's previous dealings had been with Bentley.

[6] John Pritt Harley (1786–1858;

would seem to imply, but next Sunday at Six o'Clock *sharp,* when we will renew that former acquaintance which we used to have together.

It is so long since I have seen you, that I expect to find you greatly changed, and am filled with sad anticipations.

Faithfully Yours always

J. P. Harley Esquire                                CHARLES DICKENS


## *To* EBENEZER LANDELLS,[1] [?20 MARCH 1840]*

MS Mrs S. S. Clephan. *Date:* Presumably refers to the first drawing of Nell to appear in *Master Humphrey*—Cattermole's headpiece ("The Shop") to No. 4, which Landells engraved. Since on Mon 9 Mar CD gave Cattermole instructions, with some urgency, for his illustration to No. 3, this was probably written on the Friday of the following week (20th). On 25 Mar CD gave Chapman instructions for the second illustration to No. 4.

Devonshire Terrace | Friday Morning

My Dear Sir.

I sent the drawing back to Mr. Chapman, for I was more than doubtful of the child's face, and the subject is one of the last importance to the work.

I presume he has taken it back to Mr. Cattermole this morning (that was my wish)—and I have no doubt you will hear from him in the course of the day.

Believe me | Faithfully Yours

E. Landells Esquire                                 CHARLES DICKENS


## *To* THOMAS BEARD,[2] 22 MARCH [1840]

MS Comtesse de Suzannet. *Date:* endorsed, in contemporary hand, "March — 1841"; but subject and signature could fit only 1840, in which year 22 Mar was Sunday. *Address:* Thomas Beard Esquire | 42 Portman Place | Edgeware Road.

Devonshire Terrace | Sunday Morning March 22nd.

My Dear Beard

I have been very anxious to see you for some time, for I have been ill at ease about Master Humphrey, in the one respect of connecting you with

*DNB*): see Vol. 1, p. 167*n*. He was still at Covent Garden (under Charles Mathews and Madame Vestris, who succeeded Macready as lessees Sep 39–Apr 42), playing mainly in contemporary comedies and farces. For CD's comparison of his acting with Keeley's, see *To* Keeley, ?29 Dec 41, *fn.*

[1] Ebenezer Landells (1808–60; *DNB*), wood-engraver; pupil of Thomas Bewick, and teacher of many leading draughtsmen, including Birket Foster 1841–6. Engraved Seymour's design for "The Tuggs's at Ramsgate", 1836. Ostensibly the engraver of more than half the illustrations to *Master Humphrey*, though 30 of them were cut by the Brothers Dalziel (see *To* Cattermole, 13 Jan, *fn*). Joint-projector with Henry Mayhew of *Punch*, for which he acted for a time virtually as art editor as well as engraver. Worked for the *Illustrated London News* and other illustrated periodicals.

[2] Thomas Beard (1807–91): see Vol. 1, p. 3*n*.

that labour, which, as you know I anxiously desire, I will say very little about.

It has been for weeks quite clear to us that I must write it *all*,[1] if we are to hope for that great success which we expect. Now if I do this, the office which I had assigned to you of managing the correspondence, correcting proofs and so forth, vanishes into air,[2] because there will be no proofs but my own and nobody to write to or transact business with, but me.

Although I have seen this for a pretty long time, I have refrained from telling you, in the hope that I should yet see some way of being useful to you and establishing a new link between us. *Do not for a moment believe that I have lost this hope even in connection with the Clock*—on the contrary I have a great many possibilities and probabilities in my brain which a little time and experience may arrange into something tangible—but I am anxious that you should know that this alteration has in the outset disarranged my plans and scattered them completely.

I wish you would call upon me one morning in the week—on Tuesday if you can—about one [o'] Clock[3] or so, when we can talk a little upon this matter—and also about the *when* to ask your friend Mr. Blackburn[4] to dinner (who has been kind enough to send me a very interesting Calcutta newspaper) and also about a certain misty notion I have begun to form of some queer old farm house distant about 20 miles from town,[5] and of goings down and comings up all *through the Summer*!!!!!!!!!!!!!!!

Faithfully Yours always

Thomas Beard Esquire                                      CHARLES DICKENS


## *To* EDWARD CHAPMAN,[6] 25 MARCH [1840]*

MS Berg Collection. *Date:* 25 March was Wednesday in 1840; signature supports that year.

Devonshire Terrace | Wednesday 25th. March

My Dear Sir

The best plan will be for Mr. Browne to read the number, and take or make any subject that he fancies. It should have the girl in it, that's all.[7]

Faithfully Yours

Edward Chapman Esquire                                    CHARLES DICKENS

---

[1] For CD's original plans for *Master Humphrey*, see Vol. 1, pp. 563–4.

[2] Whether this would have been a full-time or only a part-time job is uncertain. Beard was still on the staff of the *Morning Chronicle* (which he had joined 1834) at the end of 1842.

[3] MS reads "or Clock".

[4] Almost certainly John Blackburn, sub-editor of the *Englishman*, Calcutta, and author of *The Overland Traveller*,

*or Guide to Persons Proceeding to Europe via the Red Sea, from India*, Calcutta, 1838.

[5] Cf. "some queer cabin at Cobham in Kent" (*To* Beard, 1 June 40).

[6] Edward Chapman (1804–80): see Vol. 1, p. 128*n*.

[7] Clearly refers to the second illustration to No. 4 (published 25 Apr), in which Nell—already drawn by Cattermole in the headpiece to No. 4—

## *To* T. P. GRINSTED,[1] 25 MARCH 1840

MS Berg Collection. *Address:* Prepaid | Mr. T. P. Grinsted | &c &c | 3 Glos'ter Terrace | Brighton.

1 Devonshire Terrace, York Gate
Regents Park London | 25th. March 1840.

Dear Sir.

I have to thank you—which I do with great heartiness—for your letter, and through you to thank those gentlemen who remembered me in their flowing cups last Thursday.[2]

Do me the favor to convey to the Nickleby Club,[3] the warmest expression of my gratitude and interest in their proceedings. I trust they may continue to hold me, and I them, in pleasant and cheerful recollection for very many years, and long connect their recreations with a name which is naturally associated in my mind with favorite and familiar thoughts.

Faithfully Yours
CHARLES DICKENS

Mr. T. P. Grinsted
&c &c

## *To* MESSRS CHAPMAN & HALL, [?27 MARCH 1840]

MS Benoliel Collection. *Date:* Presumably refers to progress with the Agreement for *Master Humphrey*, signed 31 Mar (see *fn*); and to the Wellers' first appearance in the later part of No. 6, which CD would have been writing towards the end of March.

1 Devonshire Terrace. | Friday

Dr. Sirs

I should like to have a line reporting progress,[4] either to-day or to-morrow. I am very busy upon the Wellers, father and Son.

Faithfully Yours
CHARLES DICKENS

Messrs. Chapman and Hall

---

appeared again. (She made no further appearance until No. 10, published 6 June.) In fact the illustration, "Nell in bed", was done not by Browne but by Samuel Williams, a wood-engraver who had not illustrated CD before (see *To* Williams, 31 Mar).

[1] Thomas Peter Grinsted (1808–57), son of a farmer, employed for many years by Curtis & Son, Brighton, and as corrector for the press by William Clowes, the London printer. Contributed a series of six articles to *Bentley's Miscellany* (then owned and edited by Ainsworth): "The Theatres of London. Their History—Past and Present" (xxxv and xxxvi, 1854); also "Old Actors— A Reverie at the Garrick Club",

"Charles Young", and "Madame Vestris" (XL, 1856). Author of *Relics of Genius: Visits to the Last Homes of Poets, Painters and Players*, 1859. Ainsworth recommended his work to the Literary Fund in Oct 61, and his widow's application for relief was successful (MS Royal Literary Fund).

[2] Cf. *Henry V*, IV, iii, 55.

[3] Presumably in Brighton, but not traced.

[4] On 20 Mar one clause in the Agreement was still not settled. The original draft (MS Mr C. C. Dickens), prepared by William Chapman (elder brother of Edward and the firm's solicitor: see 3 Aug 41 and *fn*), reveals the successive stages in the negotiations. On 3 Mar

## To JAMES HOGGINS,[1] 27 MARCH 1840*

MS Berg Collection. *Address:* James Hoggins Esquire | Literary and Philosophical Society | Newcastle.

1 Devonshire Terrace | York Gate Regents Park London
27th. March 1840.

Mr. Charles Dickens presents his compliments to Mr. Hoggins, and begs to inform him, in reply to his enquiry, that his Works comprise three volumes of Sketches, the Pickwick Papers, Oliver Twist, and Nicholas Nickleby.

## To THOMAS MITTON, [?MARCH 1840]*

MS Historical Society of Pennsylvania. *Date:* Signature suggests Mar 1840.

Devonshire Terrace | Friday Morning
Dear Tom
I'll come down[2] by the Rail as you recommend.
In haste | Faithfully Yours
Thomas Mitton Esquire                          CHARLES DICKENS

## To SAMUEL WILLIAMS,[3] [31 MARCH 1840]*

MS Mrs Elaine Waley. *Date:* presumably the Tuesday after 25 Mar when CD gave Chapman instructions for the second illustration to No. 4. Accompanying wrapper (see *To* Chapman & Hall, ?3 Apr) supports 31 Mar.

Devonshire Terrace | Tuesday Evg.
Mr. Charles Dickens sends his compts. to Mr. Williams, and greatly regrets having been obliged to be from home this morning at the time he called.

Smithson & Mitton endorsed Chapman's draft (in accordance with Instructions drawn up by James Bacon on 25 Feb: MS Mr C. C. Dickens): "We have perused the Document and subject to the alterations made by us in red ink do approve this on behalf of Mr. Dickens". On 13 Mar it was endorsed by William Chapman: "Subject to the alterations in blue ink I have no objection to the alterations made in red ink—on behalf of Messrs. Chapman & Hall." On 20 Mar Chapman wrote to Smithson & Mitton: "The clause you contend for is so opposed to all my notions of what is right, not only abstractedly [*thus*], but as fairly arising out of the proposals made by Mr Dickens himself & assented to by my clients, that as a matter of business to be settled by us professionally *I* never could agree to it. The question must be decided by the parties themselves. I shall forward your letter to Messrs. Chapman & Hall & request them to settle the point as they think proper" (MS Mr C. C. Dickens). Which clause Chapman was objecting to, the corrected draft makes clear; for among Smithson & Mitton's additions in red ink only one clause is cancelled by Chapman—with a later "stet" beside it (Chapman & Hall evidently having accepted it). For the disputed clause, see the Agreement, Appx, p. 467 and *fn.*

[1] James Hoggins, porter and later a sub-librarian of the Newcastle Literary and Philosophical Society.
[2] Mitton was living at Sipson, Middlesex, 1838–41.
[3] Samuel Williams (1788–1853;

The object being to shew the child in the midst of a crowd of uncongenial and ancient things, Mr. Dickens scarcely *feels* the very pretty drawing inclosed, as carrying out his idea: the room being to all appearance an exceedingly comfortable one pair,[1] and the sleeper being in a very enviable condition. If the composition would admit of a few grim, ugly articles seen through a doorway beyond, for instance, and giving a notion of great gloom outside the little room and surrounding the chamber, it would be much better. The figure on the bed is not sufficiently *childish*, and would perhaps look better without a cap, and with the hair floating over the pillow. The last paragraph of the paper (which perhaps Mr. Williams has) expresses Mr. Dickens's idea better than he can convey it in any other words.[2]

As Mr. Dickens hopes to communicate with Mr. Williams on very many future occasions, he will not weary him with any apology for these remarks just now.[3]

## *To* JOHN FORSTER, [MARCH 1840]

Extract in F, II, viii, 156. *Date:* Mar 40 according to Forster.

I find it will be positively necessary to go, for five days in the week at least, on a perfect regimen of diet and exercise,[4] and am anxious therefore not to delay treating for a horse.

*DNB*), draughtsman and wood engraver—"at the head of this art", excelling "in light and shade . . . and great variety of touch", according to an article in the *London and Westminster Review*, XXXI (1838), 275. Books he illustrated included Hone's *Every-Day Book*, 1825–7; Lady Charlotte Guest's *Mabinogion*, 1838; Lockhart's *Spanish Ballads*, 1840; and the Abbotsford edn of Scott, 1842. Mary Howitt (while he was working on William Howitt's *Rural Life in England*, 1838) described him as "not apt in originating ideas"; but he had produced "under William's eye . . . some of the very best designs that have appeared in wood since Bewick" (*The Friendships of Mary Russell Mitford*, ed. A. G. L'Estrange, 1882, II, 28). F. G. Kitton believed that his illustration "Nell in bed" was copied on wood from a drawing "undoubtedly supplied by Cattermole" (*CD and his Illustrators*, 1899, p. 123); but this is disproved both by CD's letter and by the signature "S. Williams del et sc".

[1] I.e. first-floor room (see OED).

[2] The sepia drawing made by Williams after receiving this letter—and closely followed in the published woodcut, "Nell in bed"—is in the possession of Mrs Elaine Waley. It shows Nell asleep (capless, with flowing hair), surrounded by "gaunt suits of mail with their ghostly silent air" and "faces all awry, grinning from wood and stone", as described in the last paragraph of CD's "paper" (the *Old Curiosity Shop* section of No. 4)—itself a summary of a passage earlier in the No. (p. 40) and probably added by CD so that the picture of Nell "alone in the midst of all this lumber and decay" would be what remained in the reader's mind. (It did, e.g., in Hood's and Forster's: see *To* Cattermole, 13 Jan 40, *fn*.)

[3] The idea of employing Williams for the second illustration to No. 4 seems to to have been Chapman's: CD had been expecting that Browne would do it (see *To* Chapman, 25 Mar). The aim may have been to bring in a second illustrator with experience of antiquarian subjects; but this became unnecessary

## *To* MESSRS CHAPMAN & HALL, [?3 APRIL 1840]*

MS Mrs Elaine Waley. *Date:* written on inside of wrapper which almost certainly enclosed Williams's drawing "Nell in bed" (see *To* Williams, 31 Mar, *fn*); "off" therefore meant off to Birmingham 3 Apr. *Address:* Messrs. Chapman & Hall | 186 Strand; signed CHARLES DICKENS.

All right
In great speed
Off![1]

## *To* [WILLIAM HALL, ?7 APRIL 1840]*

MS Private. *Date:* CD dined with Chapman and Hall on 21 Apr 40 ("Easter Tuesday"): see *To* Forster, that day. He was probably writing on 7 Apr (the Tuesday after publication of *Master Humphrey* No. 1 when its prospects seemed at their brightest),[2] having returned from Birmingham earlier that day.[3] *Address:* presumably to Hall, since letter mentions Chapman.

Devonshire Terrace | Tuesday Afternoon.

My Dear Sir

Easter Tuesday is a very good day for dining out. I don't think that if I went through the almanack, I could find a better.

The Clock goes gloriously indeed. What will the wiseacres say to weekly issues *now*? And what will they say to any of those ten thousand things we shall do together to make 'em wink, and stagger in their shoes? Thank God for this great hit. I always had a quiet confidence in it, but I never expected *this*, at first.

I hope to put Mr. Chapman at rest (pro tem at least, for he will be an

when the original plan for *Master Humphrey* was dropped and *Old Curiosity Shop* developed into a full-scale novel. Good as his illustration had been, Williams was not employed to illustrate CD again.

[4] "Some ailments which dated from an earlier period in his life", says Forster, "made themselves felt in the spring of the year, as I remember, and increased horse exercise was strongly recommended to him" (F, II, viii, 156). Cf. *To* Beard, 12 Oct 41, on his operation for fistula, "a disease caused by working over much which has been gathering it seems for years".

[1] Written large. On 3 Apr CD (with, presumably, Catherine) went off to Birmingham, according to his "rule"

(only, so far, observed for *Nickleby*) of being out of London on publication-day of the first No. of a book.

[2] Forster had joined him at Birmingham on the 4th, "with news of the sale of the whole sixty thousand copies to which the first working had been limited, and of orders already in hand for ten thousand more!" (F, II, viii, 158).

[3] "The excitement of the success somewhat lengthened our holiday", says Forster—but probably only by one day (on which they visited Stratford and Lichfield), extending their week-end until the Tuesday. They had run short of money and had to employ Alfred Dickens, who had joined them from Tamworth, to pawn their gold watches (F, *ibid*).

unquiet spirit always, and a thorn in my side, I know) tomorrow.[1] The result I hope to send him on Thursday Morning.

Commend me to him though he *does* wear me to a shadow, and believe me always

Faithfully Yours<br>
CHARLES DICKENS

*To* AUGUSTUS DE MORGAN[2] and MRS DE MORGAN,[3]
12 APRIL 1840

Text from S. E. De Morgan, *Memoir of Augustus De Morgan*, 1882, p. 266n.

1 Devonshire Terrace, York Gate, April 12, 1840.

Mr. Charles Dickens sends his compliments both to the gentleman and the lady who do him the honour to differ upon an illustrated point in *Nicholas Nickleby*, and begs to inform them that the lady sitting down is intended for Mrs. Kenwigs, and the lady standing up for the designing Miss Petowker. But Mr. Dickens begs the gentleman and lady unknown to take especial notice that neither of their portraitures is quite correct, Mrs. Kenwigs being constitutionally slim and delicate and of a slight figure (quite unimpaired by her frequent confinements), and Miss Petowker a young female of some personal attractions, set off by various stage effects and professional captivations.[4]

[1] Under the Agreement of 31 Mar, CD was to furnish Chapman & Hall with the MS of each No. "at least thirty days" before the day of publication. He was probably hoping on the following day to send Chapman No. 6—published 9 May. This would be 30 days in advance, but—for a book he had begun nearly three months earlier—was not so good as it seemed. Remembering last minute rushes over *Nickleby*, Chapman had qualms with some reason. By 5 June CD was only a fortnight in advance.

[2] Augustus De Morgan (1806–71; *DNB*); first Professor of Mathematics, University College, London, 1828–31 and 1836–66, resigning twice on matters of principle. Fellow of the Astronomical Society from 1828; active member of the Society for the Diffusion of Useful Knowledge 1828–46; tried to promote decimal coinage. Met CD through Charles Knight at Broadstairs in the 1850s (see S. E. De Morgan, *Memoir*, p. 265) and contributed a note on Ed-

mund Waller to *Household Words* (24 Oct 57, XVI, 402).

[3] Sophia Elizabeth De Morgan (1809-1892), daughter of William Frend (1757–1841; *DNB*), the reformer. Supported women's higher education, female emancipation, workhouse reform, anti-vivisection. At the same time a conscientious and devoted mother: see her "nursery Journal" kept 1842 when her eldest son, William, was three (A. M. W. Stirling, *William De Morgan and his Wife*, 1922, pp. 38–50). Helped to found The Ladies' College, Bedford Square (now Bedford College) 1849. Wrote books on mesmerism and contributed "A Plea for Playgrounds" to *Household Words* (30 Jan 58, XVII, 160). As a committee member of the Playground and General Recreation Society, attended the anniversary dinner 1 June 58, when CD was in the chair.

[4] See Browne's illustration to *Nickleby*, Ch. 16. Mrs De Morgan recounts the difference of opinion which led up to this letter. De Morgan

## *To* WILLIAM H. SOTHAM,[1] 12 APRIL 1840

MS Historical Society of Pennsylvania.

1 Devonshire Terrace, York Gate | Regents Park London
12th. April 1840.

Sir.

Let me thank you for your letter, and the obliging terms in which it is couched. I fear I am rather behind-hand in my reply, but constant occupation makes me too often an indifferent correspondent. It shall never make me unmindful of your hospitable offer if I visit America, or of that English Farmer's-home[2] to which you welcome me (in anticipation) with so much kindness.

Pray assure the proprietors of the Knickerbocker[3] that I have not

believed that the "stout lady" was Miss Petowker, and Mrs De Morgan that she was Mrs Kenwigs. "The dispute ran so high that ... Mr. De Morgan sent a letter to the author from 'a lady and gentleman who, being husband and wife, seldom agreed about anything, though they were in one mind in admiration of the novel,' entreating the author to adjudicate the question." The reply, she adds, "was according to my husband's impression, so he was triumphant and I crestfallen" (S. E. De Morgan, *Memoir*, pp. 265–6n).

[1] William Henry Sotham (1801–84), breeder of Hereford cattle. English by birth; son of an Oxfordshire farmer, owner of 200 acres. On leaving school 1815, worked on the farm, principally handling and marketing sheep. In America from 1832, cattle farming. During 1840–3 imported Herefords into America from England, beginning with 21 cows and heifers and a bull. Contributed to the *Cultivator* (Albany, N.Y.), and wrote a history of the Herefords for the *Chicago Drover's Journal*, 1881 (reprinted 1902; see below).

[2] At Northleach, Glos., the home of William Hewer, an old friend of Sotham's, whom Sotham had just visited to buy the third consignment of cattle that he took to America. According to an account—lacking dates—by Sotham (reprinted in T. L. Miller, *History of Hereford Cattle ... with which is Incorporated a History of the Herefords in America by Wm. H. Sotham*, Chillicothe, Missouri, 1902),

he was accompanied to Northleach by Capt. Elisha Morgan of Connecticut, on whose ship, the *Philadelphia*, he had crossed the Atlantic; and while at Northleach Morgan invited him and Hewer to meet CD at dinner in London on board his ship, the *Hendrik Hudson* —at which dinner, says Sotham, CD invited them both to dine with him the following day. Clearly, in recounting this, Sotham has confused visits of 1840 and 1841: the *Hendrik Hudson's* maiden voyage from New York was not until July 41; she was in London from Sep 41 (when—according to the Boston *Evening Mercantile Journal*, 11 Oct 41— thousands visited her) till her return journey Jan 42. With his own voyage approaching, CD would have been interested to see the ship, and his accepting an invitation from Morgan (presumably after his convalescence at Windsor 6–20 Nov 41) seems quite possible. According to Sotham, Morgan at one time believed that CD would be his passenger on the *Hendrick Hudson*. For Capt. Morgan (Silas Jonas Jorgan in "A Message from the Sea", *All the Year Round*, Christmas No., 1860), see later vols. (We are indebted to Mr Edwin G. Sanford of the Boston Public Library for information used in this note.)

[3] For the *Knickerbocker Magazine*, see Vol. I, p. 431n. Sotham was a contributor. His "Fox-Chase of Old England" had appeared in the *Knickerbocker*, Aug 38, XII, 133–8.

forgotten my promise, though appearances are certainly against me. I fear I shall find it more difficult to redeem than ever, engaged as I am just now, but as I do not despair myself, I would not have them do so, either. To Mr. Clark, I beg you to convey my best remembrances with the assurance that I will take *an early opportunity* of writing to him through the Knickerbocker Agents.[1]

I cannot charge you with any commission for New York, but this is my residence and if you can call here before you sail, I shall be quite as happy to see you, as you are good enough to say you will be to see me.

Believe me | Very truly Yours

Mr. William Sotham.                                        CHARLES DICKENS

## *To* JOHN OVERS, 12 APRIL [1840]

MS Free Library of Philadelphia. *Date:* 12 Apr was Sunday in 1840; signature supports that year.

1 Devonshire Terrace | Sunday Evening 12th. April

Dear Mr. Overs.

I am much obliged to you for your note, and all your good wishes. The probability of such a feeling as you mention[2] occurred to me more than once while I had my plan under consideration; but as I have no reason to suppose it of extensive growth (but quite the contrary)[3] and as I think it scarcely fair or reasonable, seeing that no man is compelled to trust one against his will, I shall leave it to its course.[4]

I dare say you think me very unkind for not having given your paper[5] an earlier perusal. I have, however, been so closely occupied that I have not had time to look at it until within these few days. I would certainly recommend you to *offer* it somewhere, though I don't think it tells so well as your other story, except in the one respect of being very compact and close, and in that essential quality a great improvement. The idea of the nightcap is a good one and capable of much, I think; but it is not very natural though it may be true. Neither do I think that the closing passage about the woman produces its effect, for this one reason.—You cannot interest your readers in any character unless you have first made them hate, or like him. This is an utterly insignificant fellow; so much so that one feels disposed to doubt whether the child is really his or some gentleman's

[1] In fact CD wrote to Clark himself: see 14 Apr.

[2] No doubt disappointment in his readers on finding that *Master Humphrey* had opened as a miscellany, not a continuous story.

[3] CD was wrong. After the huge sales of No. 1, there was a strong reaction: "The falling off in sales for the second number was alarming; by the third week it was disastrous" (Arthur Waugh,

*A Hundred Years of Publishing*, 1930, p. 48). But the beginning of *Old Curiosity Shop* in No. 4, and the decision to let it run without interruption from No. 12 (20 June), more than restored the original success.

[4] Presumably Overs had suggested that CD should make his intentions for *Master Humphrey* clearer.

[5] The paper (unidentified) which CD had acknowledged on 7 Mar.

unknown—indeed I incline to the latter opinion from all you say about him, and do not sympathize with the feeling of the scene as much as I ought, in consequence.

Offer it somewhere by all means, and God speed you. Its acceptance in any quarter would scarcely please you more than me.

Faithfully Yours

Mr. J. A. Overs.                                          CHARLES DICKENS

## *To* RICHARD MONCKTON MILNES, [?12 APRIL 1840]*

MS Trinity College, Cambridge. *Date:* probably 12 Apr; CD was at Lord Northampton's on the 11th (Macready, *Diaries*, II, 57); handwriting supports.

Private

Devonshire Terrace | Sunday Morning

My Dear Milnes.

Pray do not suppose that my difference with Bentley is a question of money. It is with me a matter of strong feeling, upon which I take my stand with the certainty of a great present loss. It involves besides (which is worse to me) the postponement of a story I had sketched out with great care, which I am very anxious to write, and upon which my thoughts have been actively employed for a long time.[1]

I neither require nor expect any sympathy from the class (of which I am one) whose pens are their support. But I am resolved at whatever sacrifice of peace or pocket to shew this fellow that he cannot count on always doing as he pleases with them, and as I can certainly and surely defeat him, be his legal weapons what they may, I am determined to do so.

As there were bystanders last night when we spoke on this subject at Lord Northampton's,[2] I did not pursue it. But as I should greatly regret your receiving or diffusing a false impression with reference to it, I am anxious to convey to you the assurance with which this note sets out.

Always believe me | Faithfully Yours

Richard M Milnes Esquire                                  CHARLES DICKENS

---

[1] This is disingenuous—implying that the postponement of *Barnaby* was Bentley's fault.

[2] Spencer Joshua Alwyne Compton (1790–1851; *DNB*), 2nd Marquis of Northampton; Tory MP 1812–20, often associating himself with liberal causes. President of the Royal Society 1838–48; trustee of the British Museum and the National Gallery. Among those who attended the soirées at his house in Piccadilly were numerous painters and writers. On 11 Apr Macready noted that Maclise, Etty, Pickersgill, Stanfield, Wilkie, Jerdan and Hook were present (*Diaries*, II, 57).

## *To* [LEWIS GAYLORD CLARK],[1] 14 APRIL 1840†

MS Berg Collection. *Address:* clearly to the Editor of the *Knickerbocker*; and since in answer to a letter from Clark, probably addressed to him by name.

1 Devonshire Terrace, York Gate Regents Park London
14th. April 1840.

My Dear Sir

I am about to write you a very short letter, lest I should despair, in the multitude of my avocations, and write none at all.

Firstly—believe me, that I have not forgotten the promise to the Knickerbocker—that I cannot venture to say when I can redeem my pledge—but that I *will* redeem it, please Heaven, and strive for an early opportunity.[2] You may suppose that I am very much engaged with Master Humphrey's Clock.

[a]Secondly—commend me heartily to Mr. Washington Irving,[3] who I am

---

[1] Lewis Gaylord Clark (1808–73; *DAB*): see Vol. I, p. 469*n*. Co-owner and editor of the *Knickerbocker Magazine*, New York. Twin brother of the poet Willis Gaylord Clark. For CD's meeting him in New York, see Vol. III.

[2] On the strength of this, a foreword to the *Knickerbocker*, June 40 (XV, 540), in listing past and future contributors to the magazine, included CD's name. But he never fulfilled his promise.

[aa] Under the heading "International Copy-right Law: Mr. Dickens" in the June 40 *Knickerbocker*, L. G. Clark quoted this paragraph from CD's letter in the following passage: "We must believe that the present Congress will not adjourn, without passing the International Copy-right Law, so imperiously demanded, on every ground of justice and common sense. The necessity of this measure was *first* advocated in the KNICKERBOCKER, and it has been urged by us . . . up to the present moment. It is within our personal knowledge, that many of the most distinguished members of the American Congress, including Mr. Webster and Mr. Clay, will enforce the passage of this bill, with all the strength of their eminent talents. We cannot forbear illustrating this matter with a passage from a recent letter to the Editor, from Mr. Dickens: ['*Commend me heartily*' to '*Literature of their own*' *follows*]. Passing the question of justice to our own writers, let us look at the

foregoing fact. Here is an author, whose delightful productions entertain and amuse millions of readers in this country; for his works are perused in every state and territory, and doubtless in every country and town, in the whole Union, . . . and yet for this wide diffusion of the liveliest enjoyment, what does our literary benefactor receive? Nothing—literally NOTHING! [*But see p. 56, fn.*] We hope in our next number to be enabled to register the passage of this act of simple *justice* to native and foreign authors." This hope was not realized, but strong pressure for the bill continued. Many people considered that public indignation at CD's intervention in 1842 delayed it still further; but by its use of this letter, the *Knickerbocker* may be said to have brought him into the fray and encouraged his later outspokenness.

[3] Washington Irving (1783–1859; *DAB*) had published relatively little since his return to America after 17 years in England and on the Continent; but his fame rested secure on his earlier books (for CD's admiration of them, see *To* Irving, 21 Apr 41 and *fns*). He was now living at "Sunnyside", near Tarrytown on the Hudson, with his nieces; and was closely associated with Clark's *Knickerbocker*, to which he contributed many of the sketches collected in *Wolfert's Roost*, 1855, and *Biographies and Miscellaneous Papers*, 1867. For his and CD's later relations, see Vol. III.

rejoiced to hear from you has lent his powerful aid to the international copyright question.[1] It is one of immense importance to me, for at this moment I have received[2] from the American Editions of my works—fifty pounds.[3] It is of immense importance to the Americans likewise if they desire (and if they do not, what people on earth should) ever to have a Literature of their own.[a4]

Thirdly—accept my thanks for your kind communications, and a hasty but sincere assurance of the pleasure they afford me, and of the truth with which I am

Faithfully Yours<br>
CHARLES DICKENS

## *To* MISS AYRTON,[5] 14 APRIL 1840

Text from N, I, 255.

1 Devonshire Terrace | 14th April 1840

My dear Miss Ayrton,

Kate tells me that you want a small specimen of my writing. Here it is, under my hand. There is a certain *seal* required of the receiver in such cases, which I shall not fail to demand of you when I see you next.

Believe me | Faithfully yours<br>
[CHARLES DICKENS]

[1] In the *Knickerbocker*, Jan 40 (xv, 78–9), Irving had associated himself with "those who pray most earnestly to Congress for this act of international equity . . . due, not merely to foreign authors, . . . but to our own native authors, who are implicated in the effects of the wrong done by our present laws". As an instance of the wrong, he cited the recent treatment of a "work of merit" by an American: publishers refused it even at the author's cost, "alleging that it was not worth their while to trouble themselves about native works, of doubtful success, while they could pick and choose among the successful works daily poured out by the British press, *for which they had nothing to pay for copy-right*". A number of the arguments against the bill, Irving ended, were "so sordid and selfish . . . as almost to be insulting to those to whom they are addressed".

[2] Misquoted in the June *Knickerbocker* (xv, 529), as "I have never received".

[3] According to H. C. Lea and the Lea & Blanchard records, he had received £50 for *Pickwick* and a further £50 for part of the MS of *Oliver* (see Vol. I, p. 322n). For *Master Humphrey* he received from Lea & Blanchard £2.10 per No. for advance sheets. After two Nos had appeared in America, the *Knickerbocker* (June 40, xv, 533) commended Lea & Blanchard's edition "as the earliest, best, and most correctly executed, and the only one that is accompanied by the original illustrations". For American piracies of CD's books, see Vol. III.

[4] A point he repeated in his first public speech in America (at Boston, 1 Feb 42): see *Speeches*, ed. K. J. Fielding, Oxford, 1960, p. 21; and see Vol. III.

[5] One of William Ayrton's daughters (see Vol. I, pp. 205n and 690). Possibly became Katey's godmother: see Macready's entry for the day of the christening, 25 Aug 40. He mentions that the two godmothers were at the christening itself; then lists those present at a celebratory dinner with CD the same evening—among whom only two were women, Miss Ayrton and Fanny Burnett.

### *To* MRS C. B. WILSON,[1] 14 APRIL 1840

MS John Rylands Library.

1 Devonshire Terrace, York Gate. | 14th. April 1840.

Dear Mrs. Wilson

Accept my best thanks for your charming volume,[2]—and trust me, that the Elegiac Stanzas in particular have lost none of their interest or beauty in my eyes, but that they are, and will always be, together with your kind feeling at that time, fresh in my recollection.

Faithfully Yours

Mrs. Cornwell Baron-Wilson.  CHARLES DICKENS

### *To* THOMAS HILL,[3] 14 APRIL 1840*

MS Private.

1 Devonshire Terrace | April 14th. 1840.

My Dear Mr. Hill.

Thank you for your kind note, which has truly gratified me. The Clock thank God is going nobly, and I hope I may venture to predict that its future proceedings will not lessen it by any means in your good opinion.

Believe me always | Faithfully Yours

Thomas Hill Esquire  CHARLES DICKENS

### *To* ANGUS FLETCHER,[4] 14 APRIL 1840

Extract in Winifred A. Myers Ltd catalogue, Feb 1953; *MS* 2 pp.; dated Devonshire Terrace, 14 Apr 40.

I wish I could say *certainly* that I will come to Edinburgh . . . but I *can* say that I mean to come.

*Invites Fletcher to come South and* to stop here—you observe that?— here. . . . Reform the poor-laws by all means, but if you wait until you have done that, I suspect you'll find me with bleared eyes and a white beard. . . . The clock is doing *wonders*. It is rather sharp work, but so long as it is a triumph I don't care for that a rush. I hope the Edinburgh people like

---

[1] Margaret Harries (1797–1846; *DNB*), wife of Cornwell Baron Wilson: see Vol. I, p. 266*n*.

[2] *A Volume of Lyrics*, 1840, which included the "Elegiac Stanzas" on Mary Hogarth originally published in *Bentley's Miscellany*, July 37, II, 16.

[3] Thomas Hill (1760–1840; *DNB*): see Vol. I, p. 329*n*.

[4] Angus Fletcher (1799–1862): see Vol. I, p. 514*n*. For his bust of CD 1839—his last RA exhibit—see Vol. I,

p. 574 and *n*. According to Forster, he gave up the profession of sculptor soon afterwards, being "too fitful and wayward to concentrate on a settled pursuit"; and this was part of his appeal to CD, for whom his absurdities, "always the genuine though whimsical outgrowth of the life he led, had a curious charm" (F, II, x, 180). For his Highland ancestry, see *To* Forster, 9 July 41 and *fn*.

it ? Number 3 I rather take to myself. Kate and I [ ?wished we][1] were at Edinburgh when the pictures were exhibiting[2] . . . she sends all manner of kind remembrances.

## To THE COUNTESS OF BLESSINGTON,[3] [16] APRIL 1840*

MS Benoliel Collection. *Date:* 15 Apr 40 was Wednesday; presumably CD was writing on 16 Apr (date of PM; year illegible); 1840 confirmed by signature. *Address:* The | Countess of Blessington | Gore House | Kensington.

1 Devonshire Terrace, York Gate
Thursday 15th. April 1840.

Dear Lady Blessington.

Forster communicated to me the substance of your note,[4] yesterday, and was proceeding to back it by various friendly influences, when I stopped him with the assurance that a request of yours needed no such assistance, and said that I would immediately write to you myself and explain to you my exact situation.

[1] Catalogue reads "Kate and I were". But CD's first visit to Edinburgh was in June 41.

[2] Presumably refers to the 14th Annual Exhibition of the Royal Scottish Academy, which was the subject of seven reviews in the *Scotsman* 12 Feb–28 Mar 40.

[3] Marguerite, Countess of Blessington (1789–1849; *DNB*), hostess and author; *née* Power; *b.* in Co. Tipperary. When 15, forced by her father into an unhappy marriage with Capt. Maurice Farmer, but left him after three months (he died 1817); lived quietly in the house of another army officer, Capt. Thomas Jenkins, 1809–1816, reading widely. On marrying the wealthy Earl of Blessington 1818, found herself cold-shouldered—as a nobody with a doubtful past—in London society, but attracted to her house in St James's Square many politicians and writers. She and Lord Blessington, now joined by Count D'Orsay (see 2 June 41), lived in Italy 1822–8, meeting Byron 1823. After Blessington's death in Paris, she returned to London 1830, living first in great style, on an income of only £2000 p.a., in Seamore Place 1830–6; then, as an "economy", at Gore House 1836–49. Owing to scandalous rumours about her relations with D'Orsay and libellous taunts in the gutter-press, she was ostracized by the great London host-esses, yet conducted a brilliant salon of her own in defiance of them, always commanding "the best male society", as Bulwer noted (MS Lytton Papers). Bulwer and Landor were both close friends of hers; among her other frequent guests were Disraeli, Milnes, Marryat, Fonblanque—who may have first introduced Forster (*c.* 1837); and in 1838 Louis Napoleon. To supplement her income, she had turned to authorship, publishing *Conversations with Lord Byron*, 1834 (reprinted from the *New Monthly*, July 32–Dec 33); several society *romans à clef*; and—most successful of all—*The Idler in Italy*, 3 vols, 1839–40, and *The Idler in France*, 1841. Her *Works* were published in Philadelphia, 1838. Her charm and intelligence struck all her friends; also her kindness and generosity. Bulwer (who knew her better than anyone) was convinced that in her relations with D'Orsay there had been "no criminal connection. . . .—Nor indeed any love of that kind. . . . She was confessedly of very cold temperament, but very affectionate to friends—& most true to them" (MS Lytton Papers). No doubt Bulwer's view of her relations with D'Orsay was accepted unquestioningly by CD, Forster and other friends.

[4] Clearly asking him to persuade CD to write for one of her Annuals (see below).

I have (as I think Forster told you) a kind of tacit understanding with my publishers at present, which binds me not to write except for my Clock. It is one which I could, at a word, induce them very cheerfully to relinquish, but the truth is that my thoughts are so constantly and continually occupied with the very difficult game I am playing now, (which I would never have undertaken but with very high stakes before me) that I *have not leisure* to turn them to any other occupation, however slight. I have been for a long time past engaged at times in getting together a little book of voluntary contributions for the benefit of Macrone's (the publisher's) widow, and I assure you that I am so much occupied at this moment that I cannot even write a short story to complete it, and am keeping it back, to my own unspeakable annoyance and the poor lady's great anxiety.

I have always had an objection to write, and therefore have never yet written, in an Annual. But I assure you most unaffectedly that I could not have resisted *your* appeal,[1] and would have cheerfully responded to it, had I been less firmly bound and less constantly beset than I am at this moment. Let me hope that next year I shall be able to devote a few mornings to proving to you how very sincere I am in what I say.[2]

I intended to ride over to Kensington this morning and tell you this and a great deal more to the same purpose, by word of mouth. But not knowing when I should be likely to find you at home, and fearing that any delay on my part might induce you to suppose that I was unmindful of or indifferent to your wish, I have written this note instead.

Believe me always | Faithfully Yours

The | Countess of Blessington.                    CHARLES DICKENS

## *To* DANIEL MACLISE, [?16 APRIL 1840]*

MS Private. *Date:* Presumably refers to the same dinner party as next. *Address:* Daniel Maclise Esquire.

Devonshire Terrace. | Thursday.

My Dear Maclise

What is Bankes's[3] address? I promised to let him know what time we dine next Sunday—and don't know where he lives.[4]

[1] Lady Blessington was editor of Heath's *Book of Beauty* 1834–50, and of the *Keepsake* 1841–50, so could have been asking CD for a contribution to either. Illustrated Annuals, which had been so immensely popular in England for the past 15 years, had by 1832 come to depend on snob-appeal (of the 33 contributors to the *Keepsake* of 1834, for instance, 19 had titles); and her rank had doubtless influenced Heath's choice of Lady Blessington to follow L. E. L. as editor of the *Book of Beauty*. But because there were genuine writers among the friends whom she persuaded

to write for her (e.g. Bulwer, Talfourd, Marryat, Procter and Landor—who contributed two "Imaginary Conversations" to her first *Book of Beauty*), the standard of her Annuals was considerably higher than that of her competitors.

[2] She approached him again the following year: see 2 June 41.

[3] I.e. P. W. Banks (1805–50), Maclise's brother-in-law: see Vol. I, p. 160*n*. His name is similarly mis-spelt in letters in Vol. I.

[4] He moved frequently; in 1839–40 lived at 4 Serjeant's Inn.

Do you feel vagabondishly disposed for this evening?—I have a confused idea of Astley's[1] or some such place, and in case you were in the same plight would call upon you, or be glad to see you here, about 7 o'Clock or so.

Faithfully Yours always

CD.[2]

Or, I am now going out Willesden-wards to ride and walk. How do you say about that? We might be public house-ish.


## To DANIEL MACLISE, [?18 APRIL 1840]*

MS Colonel Richard Gimbel. *Date:* Handwriting points to first half of 1840. Possibly Banks was to have dined with CD on 19 Apr, the only Sunday in this period for which Macready records a dinner invitation from CD (*Diaries,* II, 58).

Devonshire Terrace | Saturday Night

My Dear Maclise.

I found a note from Bankes to-night, pleading another engagement for tomorrow, the sd. engagement having reference to some avocations in behalf of a friend. *As you know the why and wherefore,* of this note coming now, better than anybody, I have no hesitation in saying that I hope you have nothing better to do than to join our party, which is a pleasant one— Talfourd, Lord Nugent,[3] Macready, Dr. Elliotson, and the rest all friends. Do come, and give me a new reason for enjoying it. We were saying this morning that a dinner here without you, seemed an absurdity.

Faithfully Ever

CD.

Send me round a line.

---

[1] Astley's Amphitheatre, in Westminster Bridge Road; founded 1774 by Philip Astley (1742-1814); immensely popular for its exhibitions of trick horsemanship, elaborate spectacles and clowning. The present manager was Andrew Ducrow (mentioned in *To* Catherine Hogarth, 18 Dec 35; I, 109)— who went mad from shock when the house was burnt down for the third time 1841. Rebuilt, Astley's finally came under the management of the Sanger brothers; it closed 1893. CD, who had already devoted one of his *Sketches* to Astley's (*Evening Chronicle,* 9 May 35), takes the Nubbles family and Barbara there in *Old Curiosity Shop,* Ch. 39 (written in Sep 40).

[2] At the bottom of the page CD has drawn a pointing hand, and from its index finger a line running up to the postscript, written across the top of the page.

[3] George Nugent Grenville, Baron Nugent of Carlanstown (1788-1850; *DNB*), Whig-radical politician and man of letters. MP for Aylesbury 1812-32 and again 1847-8. High Commissioner, Ionian Islands 1832-5. Published *Memorials of John Hampden,* 1832. Probably he and CD first met at the dinner in Macready's honour on 20 July 39, when Nugent sat on Macready's right and CD was one of the speakers.

## *To* JOHN FORSTER, [?20 APRIL 1840]

MS Victoria & Albert Museum (FC). *Date:* Mr Weller appears in Nos 6, 7 and 9—of which No. 6 seems ruled out by *To* Hall, ?7 Apr, and No. 9 by *To* Forster, ?early May ("We are to be heard of at the Eel Pie House"). CD would probably have been correcting proofs of No. 7 on Mon 20 Apr; weather supports.

Devonshire Terrace | Monday Morning

My Dear Forster

I inclose the proofs, with no further alteration than one or two letters illustrative of Mr. Weller's pronunciation.

Kate and I have been saying this morning, what a pleasant trip it wod. be in this fine weather,[1] to go down per steamer to Gravesend, dine there, and return in the Evening—Do you feel this at all?

Faithfully Always
CD.

## *To* JOHN FORSTER, 21 APRIL [1840]

MS Victoria & Albert Museum (FC). *Date:* 21 Apr was Tuesday in 1840; signature supports that year.

Devonshire Terrace. | Tuesday Morning April 21st.

My Dear Forster

I did not know that Kate had promised Fanny[2] we would call for *her* to day. As our places are all taken, get you to C & H's per cab.[3]

I must send my letter to Alphington *tonight*, for an imperative epistle[4] has arrived, demanding (as though the writer were majestic in his virtue) my opinion upon the "vital questions" already propounded.

! ! ! ! ! ! ! ! ! ! ! !

Faithfully Yours
CHARLES DICKENS

## *To* THOMAS BEARD, [24 APRIL 1840]

MS Dickens House. *Date:* clearly the day before next; handwriting supports. Watermark 1839. *Address:* Wait | Thomas Beard Esquire | 42 Portman Place | Edgeware Road.

Devonshire Terrace. | Friday Morning.

My Dear Beard.

Will you dine with us on Sunday—alone? I have made a purchase of port which I should like you to taste. It is *rayther* uncommon.

---

[1] On Fri 24 Apr Sir C. J. F. Bunbury wrote from London of his enjoyment of that week's "delicious weather" (*Life, Letters and Journals*, ed. F. J. Bunbury, [1894], I, 185).

[2] CD's sister, Fanny Burnett (1810–

1848): see Vol. I, p. 4*n*. Her husband, Henry, was away—singing at Bath (see *To* Mrs CD, 1 Mar, *fn*).

[3] For dinner: see *To* Hall, ?7 Apr.

[4] Clearly from his father.

I am riding, at present, a poney which is something too slight for me. A friend of Topping's has a cob (warranted sound) rising six year old, and price £20—described as a good trotter and everything about him "in a concatenation accordingly".[1] He is in an awfully rough state at this minute, but curry-combable of course. I should like to know what you say about him. If Topping brought him up to you at about 10 or 11 tomorrow morning, would you give me your opinion—inspect and try?[2]

Faithfully Always<br>CHARLES DICKENS

Thomas Beard Esquire

I don't care about his being "demnition fast"[3] as long as he can *keep on.*

## *To* THOMAS BEARD, 25 APRIL [1840]

MS Dickens House. *Date:* 25 Apr was Saturday in 1840; handwriting supports that year. *Address:* (With a quadruped) | Thomas Beard Esquire | 42 Portman Place | Edgeware Road.

Devonshire Terrace | Saturday 25th. April

My Dear Beard

Behold the little horse. As I have only taken one observation of him from a staircase window, while Topping industriously trotted him out of sight, pray don't spare him on my account.

We dine at 6 tomorrow, as I have to write and to take exercise, first. If I call for you at 4 will you come Willesden-wards in the phaeton?

The beer is in a high state of perfection. The port is—but we will not anticipate.

Faithfully Ever<br>CD.

## *To* JOHN FORSTER, [?28 APRIL 1840]

MS Victoria & Albert Museum (FC). *Date:* Probably the note from Lady Holland contained the invitation refused in next; handwriting supports.

[              ]⁴ | Tuesday Morning.

My Dear Forster.

Your letter found me—my pen blushes to the feather, and my ink turns red as I write it—in bed.

I have said 'yes' to Bulwer, and must therefore say 'no' to Lady Holland

---

[1] Goldsmith, *She Stoops to Conquer*, Act I. CD's favourite quotation.

[2] Beard seems to have advised against the cob; for no payment of £20 appears in CD's accounts until many months later. But by ?31 May he had a horse (see *To* Mitton, that day); and payments in his accounts of £2, or something over, for "Stable"—ten times in 1840 the first on 20 May) and 15 times in

both 1841 and the second half of 1842— suggest that he was hiring as well.

[3] As Mr Mantalini would have said.

[4] The letter occupied 1⅓ sides of a single sheet of paper. A paragraph starting about 7 lines from the bottom of p. 1 and running over by one line on to p. 2 has been cut away; the address at the head of the letter went with it.

from whom I found a note last night with a bidding for to-day.[1] The
Monday affair had best, I think, stand over.

[                           ][2]

Heres[3] a day!

Faithfully Ever

CD.

## *To* LADY HOLLAND,[4] 28 APRIL [1840]*

Text from transcript by Walter Dexter. *Date:* 28 Apr was Tuesday in
1840; reference to Pickwick and the Wellers confirms that year.

1, Devonshire Terrace, York Gate | Tuesday 28th. April

Dear Lady Holland,

Your kind note (dated the 25th.) only reached me *last night,* and as I
was at Rochester yesterday[5] I did not see it until this morning.

I am exceedingly sorry to say that to-day I am engaged, and that the
engagement is not one which I can postpone upon so short a notice.

Pray do not suppose that in sending you the Clock, I intended to impose
upon you the penalty of acknowledging its receipt. It never occurred to me
that any answer was required.

I am almost vain enough to believe that you will be glad to hear of Mr.
Pickwick, who, with Mr. Weller and his father, are about to return to
public life under Master Humphrey's auspices.[6]

Yours faithfully and obliged

The Lady Holland.                                    CHARLES DICKENS

[1] The engagement with Bulwer was not in fact for Tues 28 Apr. In a letter to Forster of 26 Apr 40 Bulwer had written: "Will you allow me to say Thursday next instead of Wednesday [*the day he had suggested in an earlier letter*]—for our reunion—on which latter day I shall be delighted to see Dickens, Maclise & Horne for whom I enclose notes" (MS Lytton Papers). Clearly there had been some uncertainty about the day.

[2] See *fn* 4, p. 62.

[3] Thus in MS.

[4] Elizabeth Vassall Fox (1770–1845; *DNB*), wife of the 3rd Baron Holland: see Vol. I, p. 412*n*. CD had first visited Holland House in Aug 38. On Lord Holland's death 22 Oct 40—which Disraeli saw as "not unimportant. It breaks up an old clique of pure Whiggery" (letter to his sister, quoted in Sotheby's catalogue, 18 July 1967)—Lady Holland wrote in the Holland House "Dinner Book": "This wretched day closes all the happiness, refinement and hospitality within the walls of Holland House" (quoted in *Elizabeth, Lady Holland to her Son, 1821–1845,* ed. Lord Ilchester, 1946, p. 189). She moved to her "Nutshell" in South Street, left her by her mother, and in 1841 only twice returned to Holland House; other visiting was curtailed by her fear of the railway. The defeat of the Whigs in Aug 41 greatly upset her. Writing to her son on 15 June 41, she mentioned CD's coming visit to Scotland and that he was to be "honoured by a public dinner", and commented on *Master Humphrey*: "His present work, which is in progress still, is very intriguing; & even you who dislike his Pick Wick style might approve this, tho' occasionally he relapses into *slang,* which is to me as well as to you offensive" (*op. cit.,* p. 193).

[5] Possibly searching for the "queer old farm house" of *To* Beard, 22 Mar, or the "queer cabin" of *To* Beard, 1 June.

## *To* DANIEL MACLISE, [?30 APRIL 1840]*

MS Private. *Date:* before Nov 40 on salutation "Maclise" (not "Mac" as later). Catherine was present at the RA private view Fri 1 May[1] (Macready, *Diaries*, II, 59), but CD was not. Possibly "the inclosed" was the ticket he could not make use of.

Devonshire Terrace | Thursday Morning

My Dear Maclise

Kate is very much obliged to you, but will not interfere with the chance of your bestowing the inclosed elsewhere.

Faithfully always

Daniel Maclise Esquire      CHARLES DICKENS

## *To* EDWARD MOXON,[2] 5 MAY 1840*

MS the Executors of the late Miss E. H. Gray.

1 Devonshire Terrace | York Gate Regents Park.
5th. May 1840.

My Dear Sir.

Let me thank you cordially, for your beautiful and interesting present,[3] for which, believe me, I am truly obliged to you.

Faithfully Yours

Edward Moxon Esquire      CHARLES DICKENS

## *To* JOHN OVERS, 5 MAY 1840

MS Morgan Library.

Devonshire Terrace | May 5th. 1840.

Dear Mr. Overs.

I don't think you could have done better than you have done. You do not tell me whether the odd fellow carries his eccentricity so far, as to *pay*.

A part of his original plan: see Vol. I, p. 563. Mr Pickwick appears in No. 5 of *Master Humphrey*, published 2 May, and the Wellers in No. 6.

[1] At which Maclise's 1839 portrait of CD was first exhibited.

[2] Edward Moxon (1801–1858; *DNB*), publisher. Worked for Longman's before setting up on his own in 1830 with £500 lent by Samuel Rogers. Intimate friend of Lamb, whose adopted daughter he married 1833. Published Lamb, Rogers, and most of the major poets who were his contemporaries, including Wordsworth, Shelley, Tennyson and Browning; also several volumes of mainly derivative verse by himself.

Prosecuted for blasphemy June 1841 after his publication of Shelley; ably defended by his friend Talfourd (whose speech of 23 June he published); found guilty, but not punished. Worked with Talfourd on changing the copyright law (H. G. Merriam, *Edward Moxon, Publisher of Poets*, New York, 1939, p. 153). Forster was among his wide range of literary friends. See later vols.

[3] Perhaps Massinger and Ford's *Dramatic Works*, ed. Hartley Coleridge, published by Moxon in Mar 40 (in the inventory of his books made by CD before leaving for Italy 1844, and still in his library at his death).

I should like to know that. If he does, he sustains his character to perfection.

Mr. Adams's letter I return herewith. He appears to be a very nice man indeed.[1]

If you can spare time to let me know the result of your proceedings, when any result comes of them, I shall be interested to know how you get on.

And I am always very truly Yours

Mr. Overs.                                                      CHARLES DICKENS


## *To* JOHN FORSTER, [?EARLY MAY 1840]

MS Victoria & Albert Museum (FC). *Date:* clearly 1840 on handwriting. No. 9 of *Master Humphrey* was published 30 May. Possibly this letter and *To* Hunt, 12 May, refer to the same visit to Eel Pie House. *Address:* John Forster Esquire | 58 Lincolns Inn Fields.

My Dear Forster

We are *a*to be heard of at the Eel Pie House, Twickenham,*a*[2] where we shall dine at half after five or thereabouts, and where we will take care of you if you come.

Faithfully Always

CD.

*b*I remain dissatisfied until you have seen (and read) *No. 9b*[3].


## *To* EDWIN LANDSEER,[4] 11 MAY 1840*

MS Victoria & Albert Museum.

1 Devonshire Terrace | May 11th. 1840.

My Dear Sir.

Allan[5] is going to dine with us on Friday at 6, which is the only day he has to spare before going north'ards; and therefore this short notice. If you have no better engagement, will you make one of our little party?

Very faithfully Yours

Edwin Landseer Esquire.                          CHARLES DICKENS

[1] Cf. *To* Overs, 7 Mar.

*aa* Quoted in F, II, i, 93.

[2] On "Eel-pie Island"—an island of seven acres in the Thames off Twickenham—then a popular resort for Londoners. In *Nickleby*, Ch. 52, Morleena Kenwigs goes there by steamer from Westminster Bridge, "to make merry upon a cold collation, bottled-beer, shrub, and shrimps, and to dance in the open air to the music of a locomotive band".

*bb* Misquoted and misapplied by Forster thus: "The third number [of *Nickleby*] introduced the school; and 'I remain dissatisfied until you have seen and read number three', was his way of announcing to me his own satisfaction with that first handling of Dotheboys-hall" (F, II, iv, 124).

[3] Which he had probably just finished. It contained "Mr Weller's Watch" and *Old Curiosity Shop*, Ch. 5 —devoted to Quilp.

[4] Edwin Henry Landseer (1802–73; *DNB*), animal painter. See Vol. III.

[5] William Allan (1782–1850; *DNB*), historical painter. Studied at Trustees'

## *To* LEIGH HUNT,[1] 12 MAY 1840

MS British Museum.

1 Devonshire Terrace | Tuesday May 12th. 1840.

My Dear Hunt.

A crowd of thanks, treading on each others' heels and tripping one another up most pleasantly—a crowd of thanks, I say, for that Rustic Walk which I have just taken with you, and for the dinner,[2] and for the no-mention of the bill, or of the little squat doll-looking tumbler which you knocked over with your elbow when you were talking so merrily, and broke.[3] As to the apostrophe[4] I wouldn't lay a hand upon it for the world; and shew me the printer who dares to mar it!

I should have been exceedingly glad to shake hands with your son;[5] but when he called, I was on a rustic walk with Maclise, and was doing all that you did—only not so well—and eating lamb chops, and drinking beer, and laughing like a coal-heaver,—and all this at the Eel Pie House on Twickenham Island, which teaches one geography on the practical method, and

---

Academy, Edinburgh, with Wilkie. Spent 1805–14 in Russia, painting scenes of Russian life; on his return painted scenes from Scottish history, inspired by Scott's novels. RA 1835; President of the Royal Scottish Academy 1838; succeeded Wilkie as Limner to the Queen in Scotland 1841; knighted 1842. A sketch he made of CD at the Edinburgh dinner, 25 June 41, is reproduced in the *Review of English Literature*, II (1961), facing p. 51. He had two pictures in the RA 1840: *Prince Charles Edward in Adversity* and *The Orphan and his Bird*.

[1] James Henry Leigh Hunt (1784–1859; *DNB*): see Vol. I, p. 341*n*.

[2] Hunt had clearly sent CD a MS copy of his poem extolling the pleasures of a country walk and dinner in an "old-fashioned inn-room", which appeared in two Parts ("The Walk" and "The Dinner") in the *Monthly Magazine*, Sep and Oct 42 (XCVI, 233–40 and 343–6): see *To* Hunt, 20 Oct 42. It was written, according to Hunt's introductory note, in "intentionally unelevated" blank verse—"it is literally *sermo pedestris*—poetry *on foot*".

[3] Neither the bill nor the tumbler appear in the published poem.

[4] Probably the opening lines of "The Dinner":

"Blessings be thine, and a less hard old sofa,
    Thou poor apartment, rich in pleasant memories,
Old-fashioned inn-room! may no insincere
    Heart enter thee, nor any sigh remember,
    Except for tenderness; . . .
O rester of the tired, welcome's embracer,
    Promptest apparitor of meal on table,
    Encloser of sweet after-dinner talk, . . .
*Reader.* Truly, a high apostrophe, and deserved!"

[5] Presumably Thornton Leigh Hunt (1810–73; *DNB*), Hunt's eldest son, a journalist, for whom CD wrote a testimonial on 10 July 40 (*To* the Committee of the Western Literary Institute). Through Laman Blanchard's influence appointed political editor of the *Constitutional* 1836; edited the *North Cheshire Reformer* and the Glasgow *Argus*; returned to London 1840 and wrote for the *Globe* and the *Morning Chronicle*. Contributed regularly to the *Spectator* for 20 years. For his establishing the *Leader* with G. H. Lewes, his liaison with Lewes's wife and the consequent break-up of Lewes's marriage, see later vols.

illustrates that problem about the tract of country "entirely surrounded by water", rendering it intelligible and pleasant to the meanest capacity.

Good God how well I know that room! Don't you remember a queer, cool, odd kind of smell it has, suggestive of porter and even pipes at an enormous distance? Don't you remember the tea-board, and the sand, and the press on the landing outside full of clean linen intensely white? Don't you recollect the little pile of clean spittoons in one nook near the fireplace, looking like a collection of petrified three-cornered hats once worn by the dead-and-gone old codgers who used to sit and smoke there? The very sound of the bell—flat like a sheep-bell as if it had caught its tones from listening to it in its idle, shady, drowsy time of rest—the jingling wire more noisy than the bell—I have it in my ears. And closing my eyes, I'm down stairs in the bar where the soda water comes out of the window seat on which the landlady sits o' fine evenings, where the lemons hang in a grove each in its own particular net, where "the cheese" is kept, with great store of biscuits hard by in a wicker basket—where those wonderful bottles are, that hold cordials. You know 'em? great masses of grapes painted on 'em in green, blue, and yellow, and the semblance of an extraordinary knot of ribbon supporting the emblem of a label, whereon is the name of the compound? On one of these is "Lovitch". Great Heaven what is Lovitch? Has it any connection with peppermint, or is it another name for nectar? Tell me my heart, can *this* be Love-itch.[1]

Oh Hunt I'm *so* lazy, and all along o' you! The sun is in my eyes, the hum of the fields in my ears, the dust upon my feet—and a boy, redolent of the steam engine and sweltering in warm ink is slumbering in the passage, waiting for "Copy".

Tell your son I can shake hands with him though he comes without a letter in his palm. And believe me always

Heartily Yours, in *the* faith,

Leigh Hunt Esquire                     CHARLES DICKENS

### *To* CLARKSON STANFIELD,[2] [15 MAY 1840]*

MS Mr C. W. Bliss. *Date:* Handwriting points to first half of 1840; the invitation was doubtless for Fri 15 May (see *To* Landseer, 11 May).

Devonshire Terrace | Friday Morning

My Dear Stanfield

This is an invitation to-dinner, *for to-day*. If the shortness of the notice hasn't taken your breath away, respire 'till you have sent a word of answer.

---

[1] Cf. "Tell me my Heart if this be love", the refrain of George Lyttelton's "When Delia . . .". CD probably knew it in J. F. Burrowes's setting (*Six English Ballads*, [?1806]).

[2] Clarkson Stanfield, RA (1793–1867; *DNB*): see Vol. 1, p. 553n. After a long stay in Italy 1839, exhibited seven paintings in the RA 1840 and three the following year, most of them Italian seascapes. His *Castello D'Ischia, from the Mole*, 1841, was engraved by E. Goodall for the Art Union, 1844, and therefore became well-known; "a little

It is a little party I have made up for old Allan Scotchman and painter, before he goes home'ards. I still want a twelfth. Be that twelfth, and count upon the "tarnal" gratitude of

Yours always Faithfully

Clarkson Stanfield Esquire                                    Boz

## *To* W. HERING,[1] 16 MAY [1840]

Text from N, I, 257. *Date:* 16 May was Saturday in 1840.

1 Devonshire Terrace | Saturday 16th May

My dear Sir

I am exceedingly sorry that I cannot oblige you in the matter of the enclosed, for I have no interest at the "Chronicle",[2] and have deemed it best under all circumstances (situated as I am) not to make any.

I hope I need not say how readily I would have complied with your request had it been in my power, or how much I regret the not being able to do so.

Believe me | Faithfully yours<br>[CHARLES DICKENS]

## *To* W. C. MACREADY, 16 MAY 1840*

MS Morgan Library.

Devonshire Terrace | Saturday May 16th. 1840.

My Dear Macready.

Is the Glencoe day fixed?[3] I trouble you with the enquiry, because I am anxious to take our Box without delay. It is odd enough that I have dreamt of that Tragedy for the last two nights—two first nights I have had in my sleep; and very indifferently it was done too.

It has occurred to me, whether, as that book was sent about by Moxon, it would not be a good thing to keep the name of the play out of the bill, until the actual night, in order that it might not be identified with Collinson too soon.[4] Very possibly this has occurred to you; very possibly it is

more invention in the sky, a little less muddiness in the rocks, and a little more savageness in the sea, would have made it an impressive picture", wrote Ruskin in *Modern Painters*; "it just misses the sublime, yet is a fine work" (*The Works of John Ruskin*, ed. E. T. Cook and A. Wedderburn, 1903, III, 227). Completed a series of ten pictures at Bowood for the Marquess of Lansdowne 1840, and almost at once began a series of Venetian subjects at

Trentham for the Duchess of Sutherland. He also illustrated his friend Marryat's *Poor Jack*, 1840.

[1] Name given editorially in N, but not in text. Possibly William Hering, surgeon, of 14 Foley Place.

[2] CD had resigned from the *Morning Chronicle* reporting staff in Nov 36.

[3] Talfourd's tragedy, *Glencoe; or, the Fate of the Macdonalds*, was first performed on 23 May 40.

[4] The authorship of *Glencoe* was still

impracticable, but I don't mind troubling you with the idea, as it has occurred to me very often and seems on better acquaintance to be the more prudent and advisable.

Always My Dear Macready | Faithfully Yours

W. C. Macready Esquire                    CHARLES DICKENS


## *To* UNKNOWN CORRESPONDENT, [?16 MAY 1840]

Mention in next.

*Accepting a dinner invitation.*


## *To* W. C. MACREADY, [?16 MAY 1840]*

MS Morgan Library. *Date:* Signature points unmistakably to 1840, in which year the only "Thursday the 28th" was in May. CD could scarcely have been writing on Sat 23 May, day of the first production of *Glencoe;* nor on Sat 9 May, when he spent the evening with Macready at Babbage's (*Diaries,* II, 59). Probable date therefore 16 May—Macready's invitation having crossed letter written earlier in the day.

Devonshire Terrace. | Saturday Afternoon.

My Dear Macready.

I am very sorry to say that having a cousin from France[1] staying with us, we have a small family circle here tomorrow, and cannot get quit of it—which I assure you we would gladly do, to dine in Clarence Terrace.[2]

I wrote and despatched, two minutes before your note arrived, an acceptance of a dinner invitation for Thursday the 28th. I am now going to write another note to put it off.

Always faithfully Yours

W. C. Macready Esquire                    CHARLES DICKENS

known only to a handful of people. Macready first read the tragedy (in a copy privately printed by Moxon and given him by CD) in the belief that it was by a Mr Collinson. On his announcing on 12 Dec 39 that he intended to act it, Talfourd revealed his authorship. But it was agreed that the secret should be closely guarded; that the play should be billed as "by Mr. Collinson", and not until Macready's speech after the first performance should Talfourd's authorship be made public. Since Moxon had now "sent about" copies of the anonymous privately printed edition, CD presumably felt that advance billing of the play as "by Mr. Collinson" would mislead its readers improperly. (Collinson had dined with CD 1 Jan 40: see Diary entry, Appx, p. 461. See also *To* Fred Dickens, 26 Sep 41.)

[1] Unidentified—unless Martha Ball: see *To* Maclise, 22 July and *fn.*

[2] Macready had moved from Elstree to 5 Clarence Terrace that spring: see *Diaries,* II, 53 and 57.

## *To* T. N. TALFOURD, 17 MAY [1840]

Summary in Sotheby's catalogue, 19 July 1907; *MS* 2 pp.; dated Devonshire Terrace 17 May—clearly 1840 (see *To* Talfourd, 22 May and *fns*).

*Saying that Macready is about to bring out "Collinson's" tragedy; men-*
*tioning the bubble and speculation in the Sunday papers;*[1] *adding that he is*
*anxious about Talfourd, has dreamt of the production twice already, but is*
*confident.*

## *To* JOHN FORSTER, [?MAY 1840]

Extract in F, II, vii, 146–7. *Date:* "after the first half dozen chapters",
according to Forster (F, II, vii, 146); probably refers to Dick Swiveller's and
Fred Trent's conversation over "the rosy" in No. 10 (Ch. 7), published
6 June. Forster had no doubt seen it in proof—probably in the third week
of May.

I am very glad indeed that you think so well of the *Curiosity Shop*, and
especially that what may be got out of Dick strikes you. I *mean* to make
much of him. I feel the story extremely myself, which I take to be a good
sign; and am already warmly interested in it. I shall run it on now for four
whole numbers together, to give it a fair chance.[2]

## *To* T. N. TALFOURD, [22 MAY 1840]

Text in N, I, 258 checked from MS Sotheby's, 8 Dec 1964. *Date:* clearly
Fri 22 May, "*the* day *before*" the first night of *Glencoe*. *Address:* Mr Serjeant
Talfourd | &c &c.

At your chambers<br>Friday Morning (the day before)

My Dear Talfourd.

Macready called on me this morning and begged me to come straightway to you, and urge upon you the propriety of abusing Moxon to the
utmost extent of your powers, and impressing upon him a due sense of the

---

[1] The *Observer*, 17 May, for instance,
announcing *Glencoe*, said of it: "A certain degree of mystery is attempted to
be kept up as usual, but we believe nobody doubts that it is by Sir E. L
Bulwer."

[2] He had presumably just finished
writing No. 11 (Chs 8 and 9, published
13 June), which contained a short
"Master Humphrey" interpolation.
From No. 12 onwards, *Old Curiosity
Shop* continued uninterrupted, not only
for four Nos, "to give it a fair chance",
but in fact to the end. At about this
time he also decided to put an end to
rumours that *Master Humphrey* would
contain contributions by other writers
besides himself, and wrote the following
announcement (printed on the inside

cover of No. 9, published 30 May):
"Mr. Dickens begs to inform all those
ladies and gentlemen who have tend-
ered him contributions for this work,
and all those, who may now or at any
future time have it in contemplation
to do so, that he cannot avail himself of
their obliging offers, as it is written
solely by himself, and cannot possibly
include any production from other
hands. | This announcement will serve
for a final answer to all correspondents,
and will render any private communica-
tions unnecessary. | 1840" (text checked
from MS Sotheby's; endorsed in unknown hands: "Top of the first page
No. 9"; "May 19"; and "[May 30,
1840]").

gross and unwarrantable violation of your confidence, of which he has been guilty.

Not content with telling Tom Hill, Wordsworth, Browning,[1] and Heaven knows who besides, this traitorous publisher told (yesterday) Knowles,[2] who straightway repairs to the Box office of the Theatre and takes a place for Saturday "to see his friend Talfourd's play". "Mr. Talfourd's play!" cries the box-keeper[3] "You don't say it's Mr. Talfourd's! Why, it has been kept the closest secret here, and nobody had the least idea of the Author's name!" Knowles replies "oh yes, he knows it from the publisher who is his publisher too", and in case the man *should* keep the secret, dashes round to Webster,[4] and there blurts it out again. It ran of course like wildfire through the Theatre, and by last night was generally known to the company.

I really cannot tell you how disgusted I am with the envy and ill-nature of Knowles, who must have known of course that you would not have concealed your name but for some sufficient reason. I am equally disgusted with the coarse and vulgar babbling of Moxon, who I think has behaved most culpably and improperly. This last-named person you *can* take to account for his conduct—and I hope you will.[5]

Macready is still very anxious (as no doubt you will be also) that every effort should be made to prevent the spreading of this disclosure and keep it quiet; the chances in our favor being strengthened by the shortness of the time that will yet intervene before the play is presented. He is also exceedingly anxious for you to state in your preface *the exact circumstances under*

---

[1] Whom CD had perhaps met for the first time in Macready's dressing-room 26 June 37 (*Diaries*, I, 401).

[2] James Sheridan Knowles (1784–1862; *DNB*), dramatist and actor; son of a first cousin of Sheridan. After acting in Ireland, and running a school first in Belfast and afterwards in Glasgow, made his reputation as a dramatist with four five-act plays—the tragedy *Virginius* (1820), *William Tell* (1825), and the comedies *The Hunchback* (1832) and *The Love Chase* (1837). *Virginius* and *William Tell*, with Macready triumphing in the title roles, had raised hopes of a renaissance of the "legitimate drama"; and in Horne's *A New Spirit of the Age*, 1844, Knowles is described as "at the head of the acted Dramatists of the age"—though mainly because he personified the age in his "truly domestic feeling" and through his "stage influence as an actor". He continued acting until 1843, and wrote eight more plays 1837–43—several of them produced by Mme Vestris at

Covent Garden 1839–41. He and Macready had been scarcely on speaking terms since Jan 39, each accusing the other of ingratitude; but *Virginius* remained in Macready's repertory throughout his career. CD had acquired *The Hunchback* in 1832; and Knowles gave him *Love*, 1839, inscribed "from his admiring friend, J. S. Knowles" (*Catalogue of the Library of CD*, ed. J. H. Stonehouse, 1935, pp. 69 and 92).

[3] MS reads "box-box-keeper".

[4] Benjamin Nottingham Webster (1797–1882; *DNB*), actor and dramatist; lessee of the Haymarket since 1837. He played MacIan in *Glencoe*. For his relations with Macready, see *To* Macready, 2 Dec 41, *fn*.

[5] Macready recorded in his diary for 22 May both his own call on CD in the morning and a return call by CD "to tell me that Talfourd would write to Moxon immediately about the breach of confidence in regard to his play" (*Diaries*, II, 61).

*which the play was put into his hands*,[1] as he naturally feels himself in a very awkward position with reference to Webster, who is, of course, not over-flattered to find that a matter kept so scrupulously from him has been confided to Knowles (with whom nobody trusts anything) and by him belched out to his own boxkeeper.[2] I promised, to put him at his ease on these points, that I would see you immediately, and so went to Guildhall. Finding the court shut up, and you absent from here, I have scribbled down the substance of what I had to say to you.—I need only add that so far as my share in the presentation of the play goes, [you][3] cannot state anything which will not be pleasant to [me; so][4] freely use my name if you think proper.

I am more confident than ever. I[?was at the][5] Rehearsal yesterday, and cannot keep away to day [          ][5] possibly be done tomorrow, and what will become [of Master][5] Humphrey's Clock, I don't know—it's your fault, that's [my ?view].[6]

Always My Dear Talfourd | Faithfully Yours<br>CHARLES DICKENS

## *To* WILLIAM BRYDEN,[7] 23 MAY [1840]*

MS Berg Collection. *Date:* 23 May was Saturday in 1840; handwriting supports that year.

1 Devonshire Terrace | Saturday Morning May 23rd.

My Dear Sir

I am much obliged to you for your note. I greatly regret having been

[1] The exact circumstances were given not in the Preface but in an "Advertisement to the Second Edition", dated 25 May 40. There Talfourd explained his anxiety not to be charged again with obtaining "an unfair advantage . . . by the previous distribution of the Play", as he had been with *Ion*; the secrecy and postponed publication ensured that *Glencoe* "should take its fair chance for success or failure, at the hands of an audience wholly without bias." He gave these details because this was a time when plays "superior to [*Glencoe*] in many of the essentials" had recently been published—but not produced, because of the dearth of "competent actors" and of theatres licensed to perform them. For R. H. Horne's views on the superiority at this time of the Un-acted Drama over the Acted, and on Macready's frequent misjudgements, see "Sheridan Knowles and William Macready" in *A New Spirit of the Age*, 1844. Horne somewhat cynically re-

marks that Macready, through con-stantly encouraging serious but un-skilled dramatists to "write another,—write another", where the chances of production were minimal, "wasted the time of more men of genius and talent than any other individual on record."

[2] In his speech at the end of the first performance, Macready told the "Col-linson" story, stressing—clearly with the aim of placating Webster—that it was "sometime after" he had decided to act the play and Webster had "accepted it unhesitatingly" that he himself learnt the identity of its author (*Diaries*, II, 61).

[3] A piece torn out of the last page of the MS has removed words from 6 lines. A short word missing here; "you" seems nearly certain.

[4] About 6 letters missing.

[5] About 9 letters missing.

[6] Parts of "my" are visible; a short word followed.

[7] Unidentified. But cf. Macready *to* Bulwer, 15 June 40: "Will you, if you

compelled to trouble you in the matter; but you will see that my doing so was unavoidable.

I think with you—not only that the conduct of these Cuffs[1] is most unjustifiable, but that it is paltry and mean in the extreme. It is as bad as the dinner they gave us, and no known language could express anything worse than that.

Faithfully Yours

William Bryden Esquire                    CHARLES DICKENS

## *To* W. C. MACREADY, 24 MAY [1840]*

MS Morgan Library. *Date:* obviously the morning after the first night of *Glencoe.*

Devonshire Terrace | Sunday Morning May 24th.

My Dear Macready.

Talfourd, armed with his proposed preface,[2] will call with his carriage—first for me to-day, and then for you.[3] I arranged on our joint behalf that we would be ready for him at half past Six.

I inclose you the letters he received from Knowles and Moxon.[4] Will you put them in your pocket, so that he may have them back?

The Messenger waits to know how Mrs. Macready[5] is after the anxieties and delights of last night. I should think *you* must be rather the worse to-day. I have seen you play ever since I was | *that* high, but I never saw you make such a gallant stand as you did last night, or carry anything through

can, give me your interest for a very worthy person, whom I found in every way deserving,—and for whom I retain the kindest feelings—I mean Bryden" (*Bulwer and Macready*, ed. C. H. Shattuck, University of Illinois Press, 1958, p. 151). The names "Bryden" and "Brydone" are chaotically confused in the index to Macready's *Diaries*; but Brydone is identified by Shattuck as Macready's sometime business manager, dismissed for incompetence early in 1842.

[1] A pejorative term for "old men". They have not been identified; nor has the subject of this letter.

[2] See *To* Talfourd, 22 May and *fn.*

[3] To take them both to dinner with Rogers: see Macready, *Diaries*, II, 62. Macready lists as Rogers's other guests Lord and Lady Seymour, Mrs Norton, Lady Dufferin, Lord Denman, Luttrell and Poole. Doubtless it was to this dinner party that the following letter to

CD from Maclise refers: "You dine with the Anti Floriculturist—The careless gay lusty and ruthless devastator of feminine blossoms—the blight of budding beauty, and Azrael of virgin promise—very well—take care of yourself thats all— | That he may not have The Heavenly Norton on one side of him and the blessed Seymour on t'other (for this is too much to bear) [*sketch here of three heads close together—Rogers between the two sisters*] is my prayer— | No one knows how wretched I was all yesterday for love of Mary [?*Marion Ely*]. I am ill to-day. Consequent upon Medicine—and my mind is more at ease about her—but I shall relapse again—'burn when night is near'— | I hope Mrs. Dickens is getting on well. I wish Charlie had that cravat off" (MS Huntington).

[4] Clearly letters of apology: see 22 May.

[5] See 13 Nov 40, *fn.*

so triumphantly and manfully by the force of your own great gifts.[1] If I felt the agitation of an anxious author yesterday, I assure you that I feel the gratitude and admiration of a successful one this morning.[2]

Always Dear Macready | Faithfully Yours

W. C. Macready Esquire                          CHARLES DICKENS

## *To* MRS CHARLES SMITHSON,[3] 27 MAY 1840†

MS Benoliel Collection. *Address:* Immediate | Mrs Smithson | Southampton Buildings.

Wedy. | 27th. May/40

My Dear Mrs. Smithson

In the hope and belief that an extra knife and fork will not pierce your heart, and in the assurance that you will be glad to see him, I am going to bring Maclise with me today, *a*with whom I have been walking this afternoon and was in a manner pledged to dine.*a*

Forgive the penitent and weeping

BOZ.

## *To* GEORGE BRIGHTWEN,[4] 28 MAY 1840

Facsimile in American Art Association catalogue, Apr 1929.

1 Devonshire Terrace, York Gate | Regents Park London
May 28th. 1840.

Sir.

In reply to your letter, I beg to inform you that the portrait originally published in Nicholas Nickleby, and since published separately by Messrs. Chapman and Hall is considered the best likeness that has been engraved

---

[1] Although Talfourd had composed *Glencoe*, he said (in the Advertisement to the Second Edition), "chiefly for the purpose of embodying the feelings which the grandest scenery in the Highlands of Scotland had awakened" on a visit in 1838, and with no distinct intention of ever having it acted, he "almost unconsciously blended with the image of its hero the figure, the attitudes, and the tones" of Macready. William Archer describes it as "a gloomy and stilted production", which "took no permanent place on the stage" (*W. C. Macready*, 1890, p. 126). But it was well received by most of the audience.

[2] In recognition of all the trouble CD had taken over the play, Talfourd in his Advertisement paid tribute to "my friend, Mr. Charles Dickens,—whose generous devotion to my interests amidst his own triumphant labours I am most happy thus to boast".

[3] Elizabeth Dorothy Smithson (*b.* ?1811), *née* Thompson. Sister of T. J. Thompson.

*aa* Not previously published.

[4] George Brightwen (1820–83), later senior clerk in Overend, Gurney & Co, and husband of Eliza Brightwen (1830–1906; *DNB*), the naturalist.

of its author.[1] You can order it of any bookseller. There is another published with the signature of "*Boz*",[2] which I am told is not so good.

Faithfully Yours

George Brightwen Esquire                          CHARLES DICKENS[3]

### *To* JOHN FORSTER, [?LATE MAY 1840]

Extract in F, II, vii, 147. *Date:* Ch. 8, describing Dick's behaviour at the
Wackles's party (No. 11, published 13 June), was probably in proof before
1 June, when CD left London (on 5 June he had finished writing No. 12).

Dick's behaviour in the matter of Miss Wackles will, I hope, give you
satisfaction. I cannot yet discover that his aunt has any belief in him, or is
in the least degree likely to send him a remittance, so that he will probably
continue to be the sport of destiny.[4]

### *To* JOHN FORSTER, [LATE MAY 1840]

Extract in F, II, viii, 158. *Date:* May 40 according to Forster; during the
week before CD and family left for Broadstairs.

I don't know of a word of news in all London,[5] but there will be plenty
next week, for I am going away, and I hope you'll send me an account of it.
I am doubtful whether it will be a murder, a fire, a vast robbery, or the
escape of Gould,[6] but it will be something remarkable no doubt.[7]

---

[1] For the great demand for prints of William Finden's engraving, see Vol. I p. 599*n*.

[2] Presumably a lithograph of the crayon drawing by Samuel Laurence signed "Boz", which was exhibited at the RA 1838 and now belonged to CD himself (see Vol. I, p. 395*n*). For an engraving of it by Edward Stodart, see F. G. Kitton, *CD by Pen and Pencil*, 1890, I, frontispiece.

[3] A crude forgery of this letter was on sale in Brighton in 1956.

[4] This and next may well be different parts of the same letter. The reason for CD's writing rather than speaking about No. 11 would then be that Forster was out of London (see *fn* to next).

[5] Forster was himself away from London at the time (F, II, viii, 158).

[6] Richard Gould, *alias* Arthur Nicholson, had been tried at the Central Criminal Court, 14 Apr 40, for the murder of John Templeman on 17 Mar at Islington—and acquitted. Recommitted on 13 May, on a charge of burglary at Templeman's house, he was found guilty and sentenced. He was transported 22 June 40.

[7] Forster tacks on here, as if part of the same letter, CD's "almost" blaming himself for the "poor girl who leaped off the Monument", and the finding of the skeleton in a London sewer, while he was at Broadstairs 1839—part of *To* Forster, 18 Sep 39 (Vol. I, p. 582).

## *To* W. C. MACREADY, [?MAY 1840]*

MS Tenri University Library, Japan. *Date:* Signature suggests May 1840.

Devonshire Terrace. | Thursday Morning

My Dear Macready.

The orders I want, are for tonight.[1] The ravenous demand is four *in two two's*. Forgive me this time, and I'll never do so any more.

Kate sends her love, and enquiries after Miss Macready.[2]

Always | Faithfully Yours

W. C. Macready Esquire                                   CHARLES DICKENS


## *To* HENRY GILPIN,[3] 30 MAY 1840

MS Rosenbach Foundation.

1 Devonshire Terrace | York Gate Regents Park.
May 30th. 1840.

Dear Sir

I seize a moment before leaving town for a few weeks, to acknowledge the receipt of your note, dated the day before yesterday. I should be most happy to promote your object, but I fear it is not in my power to do so. The *worthiness* of your work, no one, I imagine, can question for a moment.

Dear Sir | Very truly Yours

Henry Gilpin Esquire                                     CHARLES DICKENS


## *To* THOMAS MITTON, [?31 MAY 1840]*

MS Huntington Library. *Date:* shortly before CD's June visit to Broadstairs on evidence of signature.

Devonshire Terrace | Sunday.

My Dear Mitton

I have taken Topping on again. As you said you would look at the advertisements for "grass", I have told him to call upon you on Tuesday morning, and see whether you know of any place to which he can take the noble animal. If you have not seen anything that will suit, will you appoint a time with him when he may call again?

I shall write you very soon from Broadstairs. Any letter addressed to

---

[1] For *Glencoe* again, almost certainly.
[2] Letitia Margaret Macready (1794–1858): see Vol. I, p. 572*n*.
[3] Perhaps Henry Gilpin (*b.* Bristol 1816), auctioneer and estate agent; son of James Gilpin and brother of Charles Gilpin (1815–74). Author of *The Massacre of the Bards, and Other Poems*, 1839. Like his brother Charles, the abolitionist, to whom CD wrote in Mar and Apr 46 and Nov 49, he was a member of the Society of Friends.

me there, will find me. Our house is next to Barnes's[1] Library and everybody in the place will know all about us.

Think well about coming to the sea breeze.

Always your faithful friend
CHARLES DICKENS

## *To* THOMAS BEARD, 1 JUNE 1840

MS Comtesse de Susannet. *Address:* Thomas Beard Esquire | 42 Portman Place | Edgeware Road | London.

37 Albion Street Broadstairs.
Monday Night June 1st. 1840

My Dear Beard.

With that tremendous energy which characterizes the proceedings of this establishment, we thought of coming here one day last week, and accordingly came this very morning. We have been in the house two hours, and the dining-parlor closet already displays a good array of bottles, duly arranged by the writer hereof—the Spirits labelled "Gin", "Brandy", "Hollands" in autograph character—and the wine tasted and approved. The castors already boast mushroom ketchup, harvey,[2] cayenne, and such like condiments; the writing table is set forth with a neatness peculiar to your estimable friend; and the furniture in all the rooms has been entirely re-arranged by the same extraordinary character. The sea is rolling away, like nothing but the sea, in front of the house, and there are two pretty little spare bedrooms waiting to be occupied.

We mean to stay here a Month, and to return, please God, for another Month in the beginning of September. For occasional manly sports in July and August, I shall endeavour to find some queer cabin at Cobham in Kent.

Meantime verbum sap. Every Saturday Morning at 9 o'Clock[3] there is a Ramsgate steamer leaving London Bridge Wharf, which, being boarded off this place by a boat belonging to it, will deposit you in the family's arms. On Monday Mornings you can leave here either at 8 or 9, and be in town, as you please, at about $\frac{1}{2}$ past 3 or $\frac{1}{2}$ past 4.

Therefore, as I am very tired and just now going to bed preparatory to close work tomorrow, I merely forward you these instructions, expecting by return of post a becoming assurance of your duty and submission.

My Dear Beard | Heartily Yours
Thomas Beard Esquire                           CHARLES DICKENS

---

[1] "Barnes, David, library & reading rooms, house agent & bath proprietor, Albion street" (*P.O. Directory of the Six Home Counties*, 1845).

[2] Harvey's Sauce.
[3] MS reads "OC'lock".

## *To* THOMAS MITTON, 2 JUNE 1840*

MS Mrs A. M. Stern.

Broadstairs | Tuesday June 2nd. 1840.

My Dear Mitton

We arrived here in famous time yesterday, and with no miseries of any kind. The house is beautifully situated, very clean, and very commodious. The place quiet, fresh, and beautiful. I hope you will reconsider the visit I proposed to you, and determine to make it before we leave.

I shall expect to hear from you before long. I shall be anxious to know what Forster and Jerdan[1] do, and I hope and trust they may be able to arrange that matter and set it at rest for ever. You have heard from Forster, I dare say, of Jerdan's admission that it was intended to include a settlement of the Barnaby question? That's a great point, I know you will think, as I do.[2]

We had a heavy shower here this morning, though a very short one. For the rest, as I look for news to those whom I have left behind me in "old england",[3] I can only commend myself as being now and ever

Your faithful friend

CHARLES DICKENS

Thomas Mitton Esquire

Nothing *yet* from Alphington.[4]

## *To* JOHN FORSTER, [2 JUNE 1840]

Extract in F, II, viii, 159. *Date:* Tues 2 June according to Forster. *From* Broadstairs.

*Before* I tasted bit or drop yesterday, I set out my writing-table with extreme taste and neatness, and improved the disposition of the furniture generally.[5]

---

[1] William Jerdan (1782–1869; *DNB*): see Vol. I, p. 207n. Had welcomed *Master Humphrey* No. 1 in a short, enthusiastic notice in his *Literary Gazette*, 4 Apr 40.

[2] CD was represented by Forster and Bentley by Jerdan in the negotiations for the final Agreement with Bentley, which had opened with a note from Jerdan on 20 May (F, II, viii, 158). For Jerdan's report to Bentley 19 June, see *To* Mitton, 18 June, *fn*.

[3] Apparently a small "e" intended.

[4] But see *To* Mitton, 14 June.

[5] This was his "invariable habit upon entering any new abode, whether to stay in it for days or for years" (F, II, viii, 159).

## *To* DANIEL MACLISE, 2 JUNE 1840

MS Free Library of Philadelphia.

Broadstairs | Tuesday June 2nd. 1840.

My Dear Maclise.

My foot is in the house,
My bath is on the sea,
And before I take a souse
Here's a single note to thee.[1]

It merely says that the sea is in a state of extraordinary sublimity, that this place is, as the Guide Book most justly observes, "unsurpassed for the salubrity and purity of the refreshing breezes which are wafted on the ocean's pinions from far distant climes"—that we are all right after the perils and voyages of yesterday—that the sea is a rowling away in front of the window at which I indite this epistle—and that everything is as fresh and glorious as fine weather and a splendid coast can make it. Bear these recommendations in mind, and shunning Talfourdian pledges and Elyian blandishments,[2] come to the bower which is shaded for you[3] in the one pair front, where no chair or table has four legs of the same length, and where no drawers will open till you have pulled the pegs off, and then they keep open and won't shut again.

### COME![4]

I can no more.[5]

Always Faithfully Yours
CHARLES DICKENS

[1] A parody of verses written by Byron to Thomas Moore, first published in the *Traveller*, 8 Jan 1821: "My boat is on the shore, | And my bark is on the sea; | But, before I go, Tom Moore, | Here's a double health to thee!"

[2] Omitted in MDGH, I, 33; restored but misread "Egian" in N, I, 261. The first of a number of references to Maclise's present devotion to Marion Ely, Mrs Talfourd's niece, a grand-daughter of John Towill Rutt. Crabb Robinson, after dining at Talfourd's 6 June 40, noted in his diary: "[Maclise] sat next Miss Ely and was whispering to or ogling her all the time" (MS Dr Williams Library). Maclise had earlier had a notorious affair with Disraeli's mistress, Lady Sykes (who was simultaneously conducting an affair with the 65-year-old Lord Lyndhurst). Sykes surprised her in bed with Maclise 1837 and sued him the following year (see

B. R. Jerman, *The Young Disraeli*, 1960, pp. 280-2). Even the Queen knew of the scandal, but took it calmly. On 2 Feb 39 she entered in her Journal: "Talked of McLise having run away with Lady Sykes; Lord M. said: 'They're a bad set; they're grand-daughters of Elmore, the horse-dealer; . . . old Elmore traficked [*thus*] with his daughters as much as he did with his horses'" (MS The Royal Archives, Windsor Castle).

[3] From "Will you come to the bower I have shaded for you?"—a song attributed to Moore. For 33 allusions to Moore's songs and poems in CD's novels, see D. O'Sullivan, "CD and Thomas Moore", *Studies*, Dublin, XXXVII (1948), 169–78; ten are in *Old Curiosity Shop*.

[4] In huge capitals.

[5] Maclise repeats the phrase in a letter to Forster, [8 Aug 41], which he ends:

## *To* LADY DENMAN,[1] 4 JUNE 1840*

MS Mr John Schroder.

Broadstairs | Thursday June 4th. 1840.

Mr. Charles Dickens would have had the utmost pleasure in waiting on Lady Denman on Saturday evening but he is unfortunately absent from town for a month, and cannot avail himself of her kind invitation.

## *To* MESSRS CHAPMAN & HALL, 5 JUNE 1840†

MS Berg Collection. *Address:* Messrs. Chapman & Hall.

Broadstairs. | Friday June 5th. 1840.

Dr. Sirs.

Behold No. XII[2] which I think will be found a good 'un. No. XIII will finish the part[3] at rather a good point, I expect.[4] I will write you more at large when I send the subjects for it,[5] which *I hope* will be by the Post from here, on Sunday Night.

Always Faithfully Yours

Messrs. Chapman and Hall.                         CHARLES DICKENS

[a]I shall expect to hear from you on Sunday. (*Sunday*)[a]

## *To* JOHN FORSTER, [?EARLY JUNE 1840]

Extract in F, II, vii, 147. *Date:* placed by Forster after extract of ?late May about *Master Humphrey* No. 11; probably refers to No. 13 (see *fn*)—the first chapter of which CD would have finished a few days after 5 June (see *To* Chapman & Hall, that day).

I was obliged to cramp most dreadfully what I thought a pretty idea in the last chapter. I hadn't room to turn.[6]

"I fall back, as Dickens would say quite exhausted and can no more" (MS Forster Collection, V & A). Cf. *To* Maclise, 28 June 39 (I, 557).

[1] *Née* Theodosia Vevers, wife of Thomas Denman, first Lord Denman, Lord Chief Justice (see *To* Forster, 12 Apr 41, *fn*).

[2] *Old Curiosity Shop*, Chs 9 and 10 (published 20 June).

[3] I.e. the "monthly part", containing the text of the previous four or five (in June, five) weekly numbers, collected, and stitched in a greenish-blue wrapper.

[4] No. 13 (*Old Curiosity Shop*, Chs 11 and 12) ended with Nell and her grandfather setting out on their wanderings. The story then continued, without

"Master Humphrey" interruptions, to its end.

[5] Browne illustrated "Quilp and Brass smoking" in Ch. 11. "Leaving the Old Curiosity Shop", in Ch. 12 (probably by Cattermole, but unsigned), came on the last page of the No. (and of the monthly part), emphasizing a turning point in the story.

[aa] Not previously published; written on outside of the letter above the address. The bracketed "Sunday" is underlined twice and written with extreme care and clarity.

[6] Forster introduces this with: "His difficulties were the quickly recurring times of publication, the confined space in each number that yet had to contri-

## *To* H. G. ADAMS, 9 JUNE 1840*

MS Dr A. N. L. Munby.

Broadstairs | 9th. June 1840.

Dear Sir

Let me thank you in few words for your letter, and express (with the very soul of wit whose name is brevity)[1] my hope that the Kentish Coronal will not wither yet.

I am so constantly and closely occupied, that I am obliged to reduce even my letters to this standard. Can I give you a more emphatic answer to your request?

Very truly Yours

H. G. Adams Esquire                                  CHARLES DICKENS

## *To* ROBERT KNOX,[2] 9 JUNE 1840*

MS Huntington Library.

Broadstairs. | June 9th. 1840.

Dear Sir

I have to acknowledge the receipt of your letter (which has been forwarded to me), and should have had very great pleasure in attending the dinner on the 20th.[3] but that I am staying here at present for a few weeks, and cannot spare the time which would be occupied in travelling to and fro.

Faithfully Yours

Robert Knox Esquire                                  CHARLES DICKENS

## *To* JOHN FORSTER, [?12 JUNE 1840]

Extract in F, II, viii, 158. *Date:* The "heroic speeches" of Edward Oxford (see *fn*) were reported in the papers on 12 June. *From* Broadstairs.

It's a great pity they couldn't suffocate that boy, Master Oxford,[4] and say no more about it. To have put him quietly between two feather-beds

bute its individual effect, and (from the suddenness with which he had begun) the impossibility of getting in advance." CD was almost certainly referring to his difficulties while writing an early No. of *Old Curiosity Shop*—possibly No. 13 (Chs 11 and 12, published 27 June), his second after abandoning the "Master Humphrey" interpolations. The "pretty idea" would then have been Kit's touching invitation to Nell and her grandfather to make their home in the Nubbles's cottage (Ch. 11).

[1] Cf. *Hamlet*, II, i, 90.

[2] Probably Robert Knox (1808–59),

journalist, on staff of the *Morning Herald*. Editor of the *Morning Herald* 1846–57. Registrar to the Mixed Commission, Cape of Good Hope, 1858.

[3] Probably of the Newspaper Press Benevolent Association, held that day.

[4] Edward Oxford, a London pot-boy aged 17, who shot at the Queen and Prince Albert while they were driving up Constitution Hill on 10 June. He was arrested immediately, brought to trial on 9 July, and found guilty but insane the following day. In his letter on capital punishment to the *Daily News*, 9 Mar 46, CD classed Oxford with those

would have stopped his heroic speeches,[1] and dulled the sound of his glory very much. As it is, she will have to run the gauntlet of many a fool and madman, some of whom may perchance be better shots and use other than Brummagem firearms.[2]

## *To* JOHN DICKENS, [14 JUNE 1840]

Mention in next.

## *To* THOMAS MITTON, 14 JUNE [1840]

MS Huntington Library. *Date:* 14 June was Sunday in 1840; handwriting supports that year.

Broadstairs | Sunday 14th. June

My Dear Mitton

When I came home last evening from an afternoon's excursion, I found the inclosed from my father, which had arrived by the Day Mail. This morning I wrote and despatched the reply of which I send you the Rough Draught. Keep them both safe, please, till I return.

You can shew them, of course, to Forster. If you can spare time, I should like to see a line or so of your handwriting by return.

[Sm]ithson[3] is at Ramsgate, and [?comes he]re[3] today.

Always Faithfully Yours

CD.

Brilliant Weather!

who committed or attempted murder with no other object than to gain "the distinction of being in danger of death at the hangman's hands". These, the death penalty encouraged. There was "no proved pretence whatever for regarding him as mad; other than that he was . . . brimful of conceit, and a desire to become, even at the cost of the gallows (the only cost within his reach) the talk of the town."

[1] On his arrest he was said to have expressed regret at not having killed "the pair of them", and to have stated "I do not think that a country like this should be governed by a Queen"

(*Morning Chronicle*, 12 June). In his lodgings was found a copy of the rules of "Young England", a secret society; but at the trial his counsel urged that these were all written by Oxford himself. The attack aroused great public excitement and the Queen's popularity rose.

[2] Oxford's pistols were "evidently of Birmingham make, and made more for show than effect" (*Morning Chronicle*, 11 June).

[3] A tear at fold of paper has removed first two letters of what was plainly "Smithson" and about eight letters at the beginning of next line.

## *To* THOMAS MITTON, 16 JUNE 1840

MS Huntington Library. *Address* (envelope, MS Comtesse de Suzannet): Thomas Mitton Esquire | 23 Southampton Buildings | Chancery Lane | London. PM 17 June [1840].[1]

Broadstairs | June 16th. 1840.

Dear Tom.

I am sorry to hear about that eye of yours, and think sea water would be the thing to cure it. We are flourishing exceedingly, and as brown as berries. I am up every morning at 7, and usually finish work for the day, before 2. I hope on Friday Night next, to have gained a number.[2] It takes a long time doing, I can tell you.

With regard to your difference with Smithson[3] (respecting which you do me a great injustice if you suppose I am not the person most interested, next after yourself) we must have a long talk upon the subject when I come back. Meanwhile there are two or three points which perhaps I don't clearly understand. They are these:—

As you have drawn the £600 quarterly, and may therefore be presumed to elect at the beginning of the year, would it not have been better to have urged this matter *prospectively* rather than fall back upon the second year, which had expired? And when he talked about dissolving the partnership, would it not have been better to have expressed the utmost astonishment at such a reply to your just demand, than for one moment to have entertained or hinted at the subject of *terms*? You seem to me to have made a mistake here, for a man like him would immediately think that a dissolution was your real object, and run his head against that one idea for evermore. Was there any intemperance or heat in the discussion, on either side or on both; and when he made this apparently monstrous tirade about an apology, had he any excuse in the *manner* and not the matter of your demand?

These latter questions only relate to the particular conversation. What I want to know upon the main point, is this:

Does your receiving these quarterly sums, affect your right to claim for the third of the profits during the time over which those receipts extend? Or, did you want to know the state of the accounts, in order that you might, upon seeing them, decide whether you would continue to take your share, or the guaranteed amount? If this were your object, did you state it to him plainly, and did he merely evade it by saying it was not convenient, and so forth?

In any case, it seems to me that you—making the demand in a straightforward and gentlemanly manner—have an undoubted right to know at the close of every year, the exact state of the accounts down to the uttermost farthing, or it is no partnership at all, and you might as well (or

---

[1] Final figure of year not clear, but intense black stamp confirms 1840.

[2] If he achieved this, he apparently wrote No. 15 in three days: see next.

[3] With whom Mitton had been in partnership since early 1838 (see Vol. I, p. 35*n*).

better) be managing the business. And I think that this is a claim so clear and plain that, if you referred it to a friend, I for one would readily prefer it on your behalf and insist upon it besides.[1]

I wish you would decide me on these doubts, and tell me how you met and what you said. I have made a great many erasures and mistakes in this short space,[2] but I have nearly written my head off this morning and am dismally stupid. Don't leave this about, as there are ladies in the neighbourhood, and always believe me

Your faithful friend
CHARLES DICKENS

## *To* JOHN FORSTER, [17 JUNE 1840]

Extracts in F, II, vii, 147 and F, II, viii, 159*n. Date:* 17 June according to Forster. *From* Broadstairs.

It's now four o'clock and I have been at work since half-past eight. I have really dried myself up into a condition which would almost justify me in pitching off the cliff, head first—but I must get richer before I indulge in a crowning luxury. Number 15,[3] which I began to-day, I anticipate great things from. There is a description of getting gradually out of town, and passing through neighbourhoods of distinct and various characters, with which, if I had read it as anybody else's writing, I think I should have been very much struck. The child and the old man are on their journey of course, and the subject is a very pretty one.

*Pondering on what might be done to help off the unsold stock of* Oliver[4] *when he had regained the copyright from Bentley, CD suggests:*

Would it not be best to print new title-pages to the copies in sheets and publish them as a new edition, with an interesting Preface?[5] I am talking

---

[1] For further advice given by CD on this subject, see *To* Mitton, 18 Nov 40.

[2] Only two words are cancelled and in three places a word added over a caret.

[3] *Old Curiosity Shop*, Chs 15 and 16 (published 11 July). In Ch. 16 Nell and her grandfather fall in with Codlin and Short.

[4] The 1002 copies to be handed over by Bentley on the signing of the final Agreement of 2 July 40: see *To* Mitton, 18 June, *fn*, and Appx, p. 473. They were clearly what was left of the edition Bentley had published in Mar 40 (advertised on the 21st in the *Athenæum's* "List of New Books"), perhaps timing it to appear just before publication of *Master Humphrey* No. 1 in order to annoy CD. For the 1840 edition, see *Oliver Twist*, ed. Kathleen Tillotson, Oxford, 1966, pp. xxvii, li, and Kath-

leen Tillotson, "*Oliver Twist* in Three Volumes", *The Library*, June 1963, xviii, 127–30. Bentley had sunk some money in it, probably thinking that by producing another edition he would place himself in a better bargaining position, and "hoping for quick returns before Dickens, in his 'war to the knife', recaptured the copyright" (*The Library*, xviii, 127).

[5] CD may have had this in mind as early as Feb 40 (see *To* Horne, Feb 40); but the Preface was not written until the following year (*To* Forster, 8 Mar 41). The edition, of which the text is a re-issue of 1840 sheets, appeared on 15 May 41. For the edition advertised by Chapman & Hall between 1 Aug 40 and 30 Jan 41, of which no copy is known, see *Oliver Twist*, ed. Kathleen Tillotson, pp. xxvii, lii. The Preface was not

about all this as though the treaty were concluded, but I hope and trust that in effect it is, for negotiation and delay are worse to me than drawn daggers.

## *To* THOMAS MITTON, 18 JUNE 1840

Text from N, I, 263. *Address* (envelope, MS Dickens House)*:* Thomas Mitton Esquire | 23 Southampton Buildgs. | Chancery Lane | London. PM Ramsgate 18 June 40.

Broadstairs | 18th June 1840

My dear Mitton,

Nothing can be plainer than your case,[1] I am delighted to find that it is so—almost as much pleased to find that there is more than a chance of seeing you here.

Let the Miscellany papers go.[2] They are of no great worth, and when one has the Devil on one's shoulders, it is best to shake him off, though he has one's cloak on.

Faithfully yours always
[CHARLES DICKENS]

in fact successful in helping off the stock, 600 copies being still on hand in May 44.

[1] In his difference with Smithson: see 16 June.

[2] Neither CD nor Jerdan thought it worth disputing the copyright in the five papers written for the *Miscellany* ("Public Life of Mr. Tulrumble", Jan 37; "The Pantomime of Life", Mar 37; "Some Particulars concerning a Lion", May 37; and the two "Mudfog Association" papers, Oct 37 and Sep 38). On 19 June Jerdan wrote to Bentley, concerning the various matters to be settled: "I have agreed on your part, which you may either ratify, or reject *altogether*, that you will assign your interest in the Copy-right of Oliver Twist to Mr. Dickens for £1500—the same to be a final settlement of all claims & concerns between you and him. | That you will not publish or advertize the same hereafter in any other manner than you have hitherto done in the Miscellany; and that if ever Mr. Dickens may publish a Collection of his Writings he shall be at liberty to include the three or four slight papers he has contributed to the Miscellany (a matter of very small importance). | You are to give Cruikshanks plates, and shd. you ever require

any impressions for the Miscellany they are to be at yr. command. | The fifteen hundred pounds are to be paid down on signing the Agreement. | I have also settled that on your handing over the 1002 Copies of Oliver Twist, their being compared & found right (say within a week after the deed is signed) you will receive £750 in full of all demands. | The whole amount £2250" (MS Berg). On a Saturday (probably 27 June) Jerdan wrote to Bentley again, saying: "I return the Agreement, altogether approved except that the giving up the past deed to be cancelled is a sine qua non. | Without its Surrender it seems the present arrangement wd. be worth nothing; and as all things between you are finally settled, I do not see any use or purpose of keeping the past papers. The Grimaldi as I supposed, is declined; & on the contrary a hint thrown out that you had better give C.D. £50 for his future chance in it. *I* wd. leave it entirely except you may wish Dickens to give up any claim" (MS Berg). By the final Agreement of 2 July, which Mitton was now preparing, Bentley retained the copyright of the *Miscellany* papers, but relinquished the copyrights of *Oliver* and the anticipated *Barnaby*. See Appx, pp. 471-5.

## *To* JOHN BLACK,[1] 21 JUNE 1840*

MS Mr H. J. O. Harris.

Broadstairs, Kent. | Sunday June 21st. 1840.

My Dear Sir

If you have no objection to the insertion of the accompanying letter in Tuesday's Chronicle, I should *very much like* to see it there.[2]

I have marked this letter "immediate" as I am staying at this place until the beginning of next week, and fear it might otherwise come to you a day after the fair.[3]

Believe me My Dear Sir | Faithfully Yours
CHARLES DICKENS

John Black Esquire

## *To* THE EDITOR OF THE MORNING CHRONICLE, [?21 JUNE 1840]

Text from *Morning Chronicle*, 23 June 40; signed "Manlius". *Date:* Presumably this was the letter enclosed in *To* Black, 21 June.[4]

Sir

At the risk of giving some offence to the members of a profession which is accounted (and justly so, when its duties are becomingly exercised) a

[1] John Black (1783–1855; *DNB*), editor of the *Morning Chronicle*: see Vol. I, p. 83*n*.

[2] See next.

[3] After the event, too late (*OED*).

[4] The arguments for CD's authorship of this and *To* the editor of the *Morning Chronicle*, 26 June, both signed "Manlius", seem conclusive:—

1. It is extremely improbable that Black would have rejected a letter sent by CD with such a strongly-expressed wish to see it published.

2. This was the only letter published in the *Chronicle* on Tues 23 June.

3. Both letters were written from Kent (see 26 June) where CD was then staying.

4. CD had a strong interest in Courvoisier and had witnessed his execution.

5. In his letter on capital punishment published in the *Daily News*, 28 Feb 46, he wrote of his "particular detestation of that murderer; not only for the cruel deed he had done, but for his slow and subtle treachery, and for his wicked defence".

6. "The License of Counsel" (the *Chronicle's* heading to the two letters) was precisely what he attacked in Bardell *v.* Pickwick, and commented on, as an abuse not yet remedied, in the Preface to the Cheap Edition of *Pickwick*, 1847. Courvoisier's counsel, Phillips, who was notorious for his pleadings in *crim. con.* cases and as "a great practical patron of the brow-beating system" (James Grant, *Portraits of Public Characters*, 1841, I, 212), may well have been one of the lawyers CD had particularly in mind in creating Buzfuz.

7. The rhythm and choice of words, as well as the attitude and method, have the stamp of CD's other public letters.

He may have written anonymously simply because he wished to give a representative, 'plain man's' view, rather than flourish his own authorship. But another possible motive may have been a wish to keep Easthope (proprietor of the *Chronicle*) in the dark—this being his first contribution to the paper since his haughty withdrawal from it in 1836 (see Vol. I, pp. 195–7).

highly honourable one, I beg to propose to you, and through you to the public mind, a few questions which have been suggested to me in the reports of the late trial of Courvoisier for the murder of Lord William Russell.[1]

Firstly, Was Mr. Phillips,[2] the counsel for the prisoner, justified, knowing as he did his client's guilt from his own confession to himself,[3] in seeking to cast the guilt of a foreknowledge of the murder, if not of the murder itself, upon the prisoner's female fellow servant,[4] a witness on the trial?

Secondly, Was Mr. Phillips justified in distinctly and solemnly stating his conviction that the stolen articles found in the prisoner's box had been placed there by the police for purposes best known to themselves, when he

[1] Lord William Russell, aged 73, uncle of Lord John Russell, had been murdered in his bed in the early morning of 6 May. His throat had been cut with a carving-knife, and the money and personal jewellery by his bedside, besides some silver plate, stolen. His valet, François Benjamin Courvoisier, a Swiss aged 23, was tried for his murder at the Old Bailey 18–20 June, found guilty, and publicly executed on 6 July. The trial aroused intense excitement, and a vast crowd—estimated by some at 40,000—watched the execution. It included Thackeray, who recorded his disgust at the scene in "Going to See a Man Hanged" (*Fraser's*, Aug 40, XXII, 150–8), and CD himself—who on a sudden impulse hired a room facing the gallows—with Maclise and Henry Burnett (see Burnett's reminiscences, quoted in Kitton, *CD by Pen and Pencil*, II, 142–3). The second of CD's letters to the *Daily News* advocating the abolition of capital punishment, published 28 Feb 46, contains his horrified account of the experience, which clearly affected his description of the public executions in *Barnaby*. For a recent account of the Courvoisier trial, see Yseult Bridges, *Two Studies in Crime*, 1959.

[2] Charles Phillips (1787–1859; *DNB*), an Irishman and Roman Catholic; entered the Middle Temple 1807; called to the Irish bar 1812 and to the English 1821; soon leader at the Old Bailey. His florid style of oratory, though criticized by many, was often highly successful with juries; but his defence of Courvoisier caused considerable controversy and much damaged his reputation. Said to have refused silk. Appointed Commissioner of the Bankruptcy Court, Liverpool, 1842; Commissioner of the Insolvent Debtors' Court, London, 1846. A miscellaneous writer in his moments of leisure, he published (besides speeches) poems, biography, and a pamphlet against the death penalty, *Vacation Thoughts on Capital Punishment*, 1857. His daughter Bertha elopes to the U.S.A. with Augustus Dickens *c.* 1859.

[3] CD is incorrect here. On the last day of the trial, before the sitting began, Courvoisier told Phillips (who up to that time had believed in his innocence) that the Prosecution had discovered evidence of his having deposited the stolen plate in Leicester Place immediately after the murder. But "he did not, as was generally supposed and asserted at the time, avow that he had committed the murder, although doubtless what he did own was very stringent evidence of the fact; and the communication was certainly made, not for the purpose of admitting his guilt, but merely to prepare his counsel to deal with the evidence" (Serjeant Ballantine, *Some Experiences of a Barrister's Life*, 1882, I, 91). In view of this admission by Courvoisier, Phillips was later strongly criticized for the vehemence of his final speech for the Defence. After his conviction, Courvoisier made three separate confessions of his guilt, and was reported to have insisted "that the idea was first suggested to him by reading and seeing the performance of 'Jack Sheppard'" (*Morning Chronicle*, 25 June)—though this was later denied.

[4] Sarah Mancer, the housemaid.

well knew at the time he made this statement that the prisoner had stolen and secreted them with his own hands?[1]

Thirdly, Was Mr. Phillips justified in stigmatising the men who, in the discharge of their duty, had been actively and vigilantly employed in tracing the guilty man through all the mazes of his crime, as "inquisitorial ruffians" and "miscreant blood-hounds",[2] and in applying to them other wild-flowers of speech of the like nature, which are easily grown, but have a very rank and foul smell in the nostrils of honest men?

Fourthly, Was Mr. Phillips justified when he found he could not weaken the force of that most important and remarkable circumstance deposed to by the landlady of the hotel in Leicester-place,[3] so critically and providentially made known—was he justified, unable to shake this woman's evidence in any degree, in casting disgraceful aspersions on her character; thus seeking to render the discharge of that sacred duty to society which she had come there to perform, not matter of consolatory reflection to her, but a most painful and degrading circumstance?

Whether Mr. Phillips was justified in appealing so frequently and solemnly to his God[4] in behalf of a man whose hands he knew were reeking with venerable blood, most savagely, barbarously, and inhumanly shed—whether he was justified in doing this, and in plainly stating that the jury, in finding him guilty, endangered their eternal salvation,[5] is a question in which I have no right or wish to interfere, but which I leave between that gentleman and his own conscience.

For myself, sir, I am a plain man, and perhaps unable to balance the advantages of continuing that license which is extended to counsel, against the disadvantage of restricting and confining it within more limited bounds. But the impression made upon me (and if it be made upon me, I have a right to assume it is made on many other practical men also), by the perusal of these proceedings, is—firstly, that I never would stretch out my hand to arrest a murderer, with these pains and penalties before me; and, secondly,

[1] CD is again incorrect. It was not the stolen articles but Courvoisier's own blood-stained gloves, shirt-front and handkerchief (found in his box after the first search had failed to reveal them) that Phillips alleged the police had planted. This was not proved: but after the trial an Inspector was severely reprimanded for negligence, and two constables were dismissed.

[2] Phrases used by Phillips of Police-Sergeant Baldwin. He charged the police with conspiracy to produce false evidence for the sake of the £400 reward offered for the murderer's conviction.

[3] Charlotte Piolaine, wife of the proprietor of the Hotel Dieppe, whose last-minute evidence that Courvoisier had deposited with her a parcel of silver plate stolen from Lord William made his conviction virtually certain. Phillips's attempts to blacken both her and the hotel were unsuccessful.

[4] In the last 15 sentences of his final speech, Phillips invoked God six times and Heaven once.

[5] Phillips, speaking to them, he said, as "a friend and fellow-Christian", warned them of the consequences of speaking the word "Guilty" lightly: "It will pursue you in your noon-day walks and in your secret retirements—it will meet you in your daily avocations, haunt your dying bed, and plead against you in condemnation before the judgment seat of your God. So beware what you do!" (Morning Post, 22 June).

that no earthly consideration should induce me to permit my wife or daughter to give evidence at the Old Bailey, if any effort of mine could shield her from such a trial.

I am, sir, your faithful servant,<br>MANLIUS.[1]

## *To* W. SCROPE,[2] 22 JUNE 1840*

MS Private.

Broadstairs, Kent | Monday June 22nd. 1840.

My Dear Sir.

Your note and inclosure have been forwarded to me here, where I am staying until the end of the month. If you should see Lady Shelley,[3] may I trust to your kindness to spare her the trouble of any formal communication from me, and to say that I hope to have the pleasure of availing myself of her kind Invitation on my return to town?

My Dear Sir | Very truly Yours

W. Scrope Esqre.
CHARLES DICKENS

## *To* GEORGE CHAPMAN,[4] 25 JUNE 1840

Extract in Sotheby's catalogue, March 1923; *MS* 1½ pp.; dated Broadstairs, 25 June 40.

Every day since I have been here (except on Mondays when in common with other vagabonds I usually make holiday) I have been at my desk for many hours ... my country escapes must be limited for the present to quiet places near at hand, where I can take root and put out my *leaves* without interruption,

[1] Perhaps CD's latinization of "manly"—though he might have had in mind Manlius Torquatus, traditional embodiment of Roman piety and stern justice; twice Dictator and three times Consul, mid-4th century B.C.

[2] Probably William Scrope (1772–1852; *DNB*), amateur artist and sportsman. Exhibited at the RA and British Institution, of which he became director. Published *The Art of Deer-Stalking*, 1838, and *Days and Nights of Salmon Fishing in the Tweed*, 1843, with plates after Landseer, Wilkie, &c. Became a friend of Scott, who called him "one of the very best amateur painters I ever saw" (J. G. Lockhart, *Life of Sir Walter Scott*, Edinburgh, 1902–3, VIII, 205).

[3] No doubt Frances (1787–1873), *née* Winckley, wife of Sir John Shelley, sixth Bart, London hostess and intimate friend of the Duke of Wellington (see *Diary of Frances Lady Shelley, 1787–1817*, ed. R. Edgcumbe, 1912). Samuel Rogers and Monckton Milnes were among those who attended her morning parties at Lonsdale House, Fulham.

[4] Probably George Chapman (1807–1885), fourth son of Thomas Chapman (1771–1833) and younger brother of Edward Chapman of Chapman & Hall. Like his eldest brother, Thomas, a land agent: on his joining the firm of T. Chapman & W. Webb, land agents, 3 Arundel St., Strand, *c.* 1841–2, it became T. Chapman, W. Webb & Geo. Chapman, and later George & Thomas Chapman.

## *To* THE EDITOR OF THE MORNING CHRONICLE, 26 JUNE 1840

Text from *Morning Chronicle*, 29 June 1840; signed "Manlius".[1]

Friday, 26th June.

Sir,

As I addressed my last letter to you from Kent, at a distance of nearly eighty miles from London, where I still am, and as I did not see your paper of Thursday until noon to-day, I need offer no apology to you for not returning an earlier reply to the "Templar".[2]

It strongly occurs to me, sir, as I have no doubt it has occurred to many of your readers, that this "Templar" is a very young one of that order of Knights Templars who first make their giants and then kill them. For the "Templar", assuming that I mean to do what I do not, girds up his loins to attack his own assumption (whose weak points none, of course, know better than he), and having pierced it with several small wounds, concludes that he has vanquished me. I regret to awaken the Templar from his agreeable delusion, but I beg to say that his assumption and my questions are identified in no one respect.

The plain state of the case, and the plain drift and purport of my letter which you printed in your Tuesday's paper, was this:—Mr. Phillips being counsel for a murderer, and having received from that murderer's lips a confession of his guilt,[3] does not confine himself to defending that man, and endeavouring to show by argument or inference that he may not have been guilty of the crime, but attacks with violent language the witnesses for the prosecution, *whose evidence he knows is true*, and plainly imputes his crime to them. I ask, was this necessarily part and parcel of Mr. Phillips's duty to his wretched client? I know it was his bounden duty to defend one side, but did the discharge of that duty of necessity include a most foul attack upon the other? Could he not argue that his client was guiltless of the murder without attempting to show that the witnesses against his client were guilty of it, and of other crimes almost as bad, themselves? Is there any man of common sense and reason (not a logician as the "Templar" is),[4] who can fail to see this broad and manifest distinction? And have Lord ERSKINE's remarks on PAINE's trial[5]—which I cannot but think that the "Templar" quotes rather as a proof of his legal reading than for any useful purpose—the remotest influence upon or application to it?

The "Templar" speaks of the "startling equivocation" of the landlady

---

[1] For the arguments for CD's authorship of this letter, see *To* the Editor of the *Morning Chronicle*, ?21 June, *fn.*

[2] For the letter to the *Morning Chronicle* signed "A Templar", which appeared on Thurs 25 June in reply to CD's letter of ?21 June, see Appx, p. 491.

[3] CD's mistake: see ?21 June, *fn.*

[4] Cf. the "Templar's" letter, paragraph 7.

[5] The "Templar" quotes a passage from Lord Erskine's speech, in the prosecution of Thomas Paine for criminal libel (1792), asserting the duty of an advocate to defend, undeterred by "what he may think of the charge or of the defence".

of the hotel in Leicester-place. I could wish with you[1] that he had pointed out in what it consisted. Will he say that it related to a point of fact respecting which the truth was likely to be elicited by such questions as "who slept with her when her husband was away?" or that it gave Mr. Phillips the faintest glimmering of a right to raise the insinuation that she was an adulteress and a strumpet?

Upon this last point, sir, I shall take leave to make a remark which will kindle the ire of a great many Templars, I have no doubt; but as I appeal from Templars to those who employ them, and to those by whose opinion, strongly and properly expressed, their too free flights may be at last restrained, I shall venture upon it notwithstanding. It is, that in cross-examination of all kinds, but especially in the cross-examination of women, counsel do most abominably and shamefully abuse the licence they enjoy. Every man—not being a Templar or other party concerned —who has watched a criminal trial, or who has sat upon a jury at the Old Bailey, knows that a counsel cross-examining a female in a desperate case invariably begins with a reckless assault upon her character; and that when he has bullied her into a state of extreme confusion, and shamed her modesty into tears, he triumphantly calls upon the jury to observe her "equivocation" and embarrassment.

All the questions which I propounded in my former letter I repeat; and I beg, emphatically and earnestly, to call the calm attention of your readers to them once again. I recognise the right of any counsel to take a brief from any man, however great his crime, and, keeping within due bounds, to do his best to save him; but I deny his right to defeat the ends of truth and justice by wantonly scattering aspersions upon innocent people, which may fasten a serious imputation upon them for the remainder of their lives—as those so profusely showered by Mr. Phillips would have done in this instance, in the not impossible case of Courvoisier having been acquitted. In so doing, I maintain that he far oversteps his duty, and renders his office, not a public protection, but a public nuisance.

I am, sir, your faithful servant,

MANLIUS.

## *To* MRS MARJORIBANKS,[2] 26 JUNE [1840]*

MS Free Library of Philadelphia. *Date:* 26 June was Friday in 1840; handwriting supports that year.

Broadstairs, Kent. | Friday 26th. June.

Dear Mrs. Marjoribanks.

I should have had real pleasure in availing myself of your kind invitation

---

[1] An editorial footnote to these words in paragraph 7 of the "Templar's" letter reads: "We wish our correspondent had pointed out the startling equivocation."

[2] *Née* Georgiana Lautour; married Edward Marjoribanks in 1808.

for last Thursday, but that I have been staying here since the beginning of the month, and do not return to town until its close. Your note was only forwarded to me this morning, or I need scarcely say I should have answered it immediately.

I beg to be remembered to Mr. Marjoribanks and your daughters,[1] and am

Very faithfully Yours
CHARLES DICKENS

Mrs. Marjoribanks.


## *To* THOMAS MITTON, [?LATE JUNE 1840]

Extract in unidentified catalogue; from Broadstairs; signed initials. *Date:* perhaps referring to the smoking chimney (see 4 July) and written shortly before CD's return to London at the end of June.

Will you see after the subject matter enclosed, and if any alteration must be made, direct Topping accordingly; I should like the neighbourly scamp in question (who is of course a Jew) to know that I appreciate the neighbourly manner in which he has made his communication.[2]


## *To* W. C. MACREADY, [?30 JUNE 1840]

Mention in Macready, *Diaries*, II, 67. *Date:* Macready recorded its receipt on 30 June.

*A very humorous card of* inquiry[3] *from Dickens, Maclise and Forster.*[4]


## *To* THOMAS BEARD, 1 JULY [1840]

MS Dickens House. *Date:* PM 1 July 40. *Address:* Thomas Beard Esquire | 42 Portman Place | Edgeware Road.

1 Devonshire Terrace | Wednesday 1st. July

My Dear Beard.

If you have nothing better to do, will you come and dine with us next Sunday? The hour is Six, but if you are for a walk beforehand, I am your man.

Faithfully Always
CHARLES DICKENS

Thomas Beard Esquire

---

[1] There were eight daughters living on Marjoribanks's death in 1868.

[2] For CD's two neighbours see *To* Forster, ?9 or 10 July, *fn.*

[3] No doubt concerning the health of Mrs Macready and their third son and fifth child, born 27 June.

[4] Who with CD (on his way back to London) had just spent two days in Chatham, Rochester and Cobham (F, II, viii, 159).

## *To* THOMAS MITTON, [?EARLY JULY 1840]*

MS Morgan Library. *Date:* Signature suggests late May to early July 40; probably July since at end of May Forster was away from London and in June CD was at Broadstairs. *Address: Wait* | Thomas Mitton Esquire | Southampton Buildings.

At Forster's | Wednesday Morng.

My Dear Mitton

You *will*[1] receive a note from me appointing one oClock tomorrow for me to call on you. But having come out unexpectedly, I am now here, if you have time to come over.

Faithfully
CHARLES DICKENS

## *To* MESSRS CHAPMAN & HALL, 2 JULY 1840†

MS (copy in clerk's hand)[2] Mr C. C. Dickens.

1, Devonshire Terrace, | Thursday July 2nd. 1840.

My dear Sirs,

The terms upon which you advance the Money to day for the purchase of the Copyright and Stock of Oliver on my behalf,[3] are understood between us to be these:—

That this £2,250 is to be deducted from the purchase Money of a Work by me, entitled "Barnaby Rudge", of which two Chapters are now in your hands,[4] and of which the whole is to be written within some convenient time to be agreed upon between us. But if it should not be written (which God forbid) within five years,[5] you are to have a lien to this amount on the property belonging to me that is now and will be then in your hands, namely, my Shares in the Stock and Copyright of "Sketches by Boz", "The Pickwick Papers", "Nicholas Nickleby", "Oliver Twist", and "Master Humphrey's Clock", in which we do not include my Share of the Current profits of the last named Work, which I still remain at liberty to draw at the times stated in our Agreement.[6]

Your purchase of Barnaby Rudge is made upon the following terms. It is to consist of matter sufficient for ten monthly numbers of the size of "Pickwick" and "Nickleby" which you are, however, at liberty to divide

[1] Underlined twice.
[2] Two copies are extant.
[3] Under the Agreement with Bentley signed that day (see Appx, p. 471), CD paid him £2250, advanced by Chapman & Hall—£1500 of it for the copyright of *Oliver* and for release from the Agreement to write *Barnaby*, £750 for the unsold stock of 1002 copies of *Oliver* and the plates (see *To* Mitton, 18 June, *fn*, letter from Jerdan to Bentley).

[4] See *To* Thompson, 13 Feb 40, *fn*, and *To* Forster, 22 Jan 41, *fn*.
[5] A liberal margin; but after his previous failure to write the book for Bentley, CD was wary. In fact he finished *Barnaby* in the course of the following year.
[6] Under his Agreement for *Master Humphrey* of 31 Mar 40 (Appx, p. 464), CD was to receive £50 for each weekly No. and half the profits.

and publish in fifteen smaller numbers if you think fit.—The terms for the purchase of this edition in numbers, and for the Copyright of the whole book, for six months after the publication of the last number, are £3,000. At the expiration of the six Months, the whole Copyright reverts to me.[1]

*a*I had nearly omitted to mention, that as a security to you, my life is to be insured in the sum of Fifteen hundred Pounds. The remainder of the money you advance, being for the purchase of the Stock which you will have on hand, need not (as I take it) be included in the Policy.[2]—

Dear Sirs | Faithfully yours

Messrs. Chapman & Hall.                          CHARLES DICKENS*a*

## *To* T. N. TALFOURD, [?2 JULY 1840]

Text from City Book Auctions catalogue No. 551; *MS* 1 p.; n.d. *Date:* probably 2 July 40, enclosing last.

My Dear Talfourd.

Enclosed with this are two letters—one which I received from Chapman and Hall last night, and one which I propose to send as an answer thereto this evening. I consulted with Forster this morning about the letter, and he quite acquiesced in its propriety, but I cannot prevail upon myself to send it without first asking your advice. I went to your chambers an hour or two ago but you were not there. May I tax your friendship by asking you to return the enclosed to me when you have [read] them, with one line telling me whether you think I have done right or not? I shall be guided entirely by your opinion.

Always Faithfully Yours<br>[CHARLES DICKENS]

## *To* EDWARD CHAPMAN, [?2 JULY 1840]

Mention in *To* Chapman & Hall, ?3 Aug 41.

*A private letter of thanks for the ready and kind way in which the firm had advanced the £2250.*

---

[1] For the Agreement for *Barnaby* which embodies these terms—treating it as a monthly serial like *Pickwick* and *Nickleby*, not as part of *Master Humphrey's Clock*—see Appx, pp. 475-7.

*aa* Not previously published.

[2] Delighted both to be free from Bentley and by the ready way in which Chapman & Hall had advanced the £2250 (see next), CD, though knowing this letter was a security only in equity, apparently thought that his relations with the firm were friendly enough for

them not to take the step they were entitled to of putting it into law (see *To* Chapman & Hall, ?3 Aug 41). But William Chapman, the firm's solicitor, thought otherwise, and on 25 July 40 wrote to Smithson & Mitton: " 'Barnaby Rudge' etc | I forward two drafts one relative to 'Barnaby Rudge' and the other the proposed Security for the £2250 advanced to Mr. Dickens—The expence of the latter is I understand to be borne solely by Mr. Dickens—of the former to be that each party pays his

## *To* MISS BURDETT COUTTS,[1] 4 JULY 1840*

MS Morgan Library.

Devonshire Terrace | Saturday 4th. July 1840.

Mr. Charles Dickens has great pleasure in accepting Miss Coutts's kind Invitation for Wednesday the Fifteenth.

## *To* THOMAS MITTON, 4 JULY [1840]

MS Huntington Library. *Date:* paper watermarked 1840; handwriting supports that year.

Devonshire Terrace | 4th. July

My Dear Mitton

I sent over to the District Surveyor this morning, who said "he had nothing to do with my chimneys"[2] and declined the honor of coming over, intimating that I might go and see him. To this I returned (per Topping) a reply that I should find it inconvenient to Carry the chimney and that I wanted him to survey it and say if it was right or wrong—whereunto he rejoined that "he had nothing to do with my chimnies"[2] once more, and there the matter ended.

Blast the chimney, what's to be done?

Faithfully always
CD.

## *To* EDWARD MARJORIBANKS, 6 JULY 1840†

MS Morgan Library.

1 Devonshire Terrace, York Gate | 6th. July 1840.

[a]My Dear Sir.

A kind of impossible possibility occurred to me this morning, and filled me with a shadowy dread. I have determined to apply to you to solve my doubts.[a] Miss Coutts's card for the fifteenth has solemn mention of a Royal Duke and Duchess[3]—*are* gentlemen expected to wear court-dresses in consequence?

Forgiving my troubling you. I have already appeared in that very extraordinary costume and am prepared for the worst; [b]but I have no confidence

own Solicitor" (MS Mr C. C. Dickens). The Agreement for *Barnaby* was presumably signed not long after; but Chapman's proposed Security for the £2250 was superseded by negotiations on 10 Nov (see *To* Macready, 6 Nov 40, *fn*).

[1] Angela Georgina Burdett Coutts (1814–1906; *DNB*): see Vol. I, p. 559*n*.
[2] Thus in MS.
[aa, bb] Not previously published.
[3] Probably Prince Adolphus and Princess Augusta, Duke and Duchess of Cambridge, with whom Miss Coutts was on cordial terms.

in my legs, and should be glad to hear that the etiquette went in favor of trowsers.

My Dear Sir Believe me

Faithfully Yours

Edward Marjoribanks Esquire                          CHARLES DICKENS[b]

## To W. C. MACREADY, 7 JULY 1840*

MS Morgan Library.

Devonshire Terrace. | July 7th. 1840.

My Dear Macready.

I want a couple of orders for Glencoe for a man with a letter of introduction—a mutual admirer of yours and mine—from Liverpool[1]—any early night except to-night. If you are at home can you return them to me by bearer? If not will you send them down to me?

Faithfully Yours

CHARLES DICKENS

## To J. S. DALTON,[2] 8 JULY 1840*

MS Mr Roger W. Barrett.

Devonshire Terrace. | Wednesday 8th. July 1840.

Dear Sir.

I send you a couple of orders for Saturday to the new Tragedy at the Haymarket. If you have leisure and inclination to go, I think I can answer for your being much pleased.

Very truly Yours

J. S. Dalton Esquire.                                CHARLES DICKENS

## To MESSRS BRADBURY & EVANS, 8 JULY 1840*

MS Mr James H. Heineman.

1 Devonshire Terrace. | 8th. July 1840.

My Dear Sirs

There are no alterations to make in No. 16.[3] Mr. Chapman must have misunderstood me. Go on with it as soon as you please.

Faithfully Yours

CHARLES DICKENS

Messrs. Bradbury and Evans.

---

[1] J. S. Dalton: see next.
[2] Probably John Stuart Dalton (?1796–1868), schoolmaster, of Birken-head; Librarian, Liverpool Free Public Library, 1852 to his death.
[3] Chs 17 and 18, published 18 July.

## *To* JOHN FORSTER, [8 JULY 1840]

Extract in F, II, viii, 160*n*. *Date:* 8 July 40 according to Forster.

Accept from me, as a slight memorial of your attached companion, the poor keepsake which accompanies this. My heart is not an eloquent one on matters which touch it most, but suppose this claret jug[1] the urn in which it lies, and believe that its warmest and truest blood is yours. This was the object of my fruitless search, and your curiosity, on Friday. At first I scarcely knew what trifle (you will deem it valuable, I know, for the giver's sake) to send you; but I thought it would be pleasant to connect it with our jovial moments, and to let it add, to the wine we shall drink from it together, a flavor which the choicest vintage could never impart. Take it from my hand—filled to the brim and running over with truth and earnestness. I have just taken one parting look at it, and it seems the most elegant thing in the world to me, for I lose sight of the vase in the crowd of welcome associations that are clustering and wreathing themselves about it.

## *To* EDWARD GOULBURN,[2] 8 JULY 1840

Mention in Sotheby's catalogue, Feb 1919; *MS* 1 p.; dated Devonshire Terrace, 8 July 40.

## *To* THOMAS MITTON, [?8 JULY 1840]*

MS Morgan Library. *Date:* watermark 1840; handwriting supports. Last paragraph almost certainly refers to the smoking chimney mentioned in *To Mitton*, 4 July; the party at "little Hall's" is more likely to have taken place on 7 July, celebrating the signing of the Agreement of 2 July, than on 1 July, the day before it.

Devonshire Terrace | Wednesday Morning

My Dear Mitton.

By the time I was up this morning (having been kept abed by some very doubtful wine of little Hall's) Macready had gone out, and was busily rehearsing at the Theatre. Name another night.

I think as the Smithsons will be here, I won't come out tonight. I'll write or see you tomorrow morning, which will be more to the purpose.

Topping waits to know what news you have—you must have *some*, I think.

Always Faithfully
CD.

---

[1] Described by Forster as "an antique silver-mounted jug of great beauty of form and workmanship" (F, II, viii, 159). The gift commemorated not only the part Forster had played in the recent negotiations between Chapman & Hall and Bentley but also (says Forster) "the gladness of his own escape from the last of the agreements that had hampered the opening of his career, and the better future which was now before him" (*op. cit.*, p. 160).

[2] Edward Goulburn (1787–1868; *DNB*), Serjeant-at-law: see Vol. 1, p. 607*n*.

## *To* JOHN FORSTER, [?9 or 10 JULY 1840]

Extract in F, II, viii, 157. *Date:* Since this records the end of the chimney dispute, clearly later than Sat 4 July. The visit to Hall "the other night" was on a Tuesday (see *To* Mitton, ?8 July), and CD clearly writing soon after.

I shall give you my latest report of the chimney in the form of an address from Topping, made to me on our way from little Hall's at Norwood the other night, where he and Chapman and I had been walking all day, while Topping drove Kate, Mrs. Hall, and her sisters, to Dulwich. Topping had been regaled upon the premises, and was just drunk enough to be confidential. "Beggin' your pardon, sir, but the genelman next door sir, seems to be gettin' quite comfortable and pleasant about the chim'ley."— "I don't think he is, Topping."—"Yes he is sir I think. He comes out in the yard this morning and says, *Coachman* he says" (observe the vision of a great large fat man called up by the word) "*is that your raven* he says, *Coachman? or is it Mr. Dickens's raven?* he says. My master's sir, I says. *Well*, he says, *It's a fine bird. I think the chimley 'ill do now Coachman,— now the jint's taken off the pipe* he says. I hope it will sir, I says; my master's a genelman as wouldn't annoy no genelman if he could help it, I'm sure; and my missis is so afraid of havin' a bit o' fire that o' Sundays our little bit o' weal or wot not, goes to the baker's a purpose.—*Damn the chimley, Coachman*, he says, *it's a smokin' now.*—It a'nt a smokin your way sir, I says; *Well* he says *no more it is, Coachman, and as long as it smokes anybody else's way, it's all right and I'm agreeable.*" Of course I shall now have the man from the other side upon me, and very likely with an action of nuisance for smoking into his conservatory.[1]

## *To* THE COMMITTEE OF THE WESTERN LITERARY INSTITUTION,[2] 10 JULY 1840

MS Berg Collection. *Address:* To | The Committee of | The Western Literary Institution.

1 Devonshire Terrace | York Gate Regents Park.
July 10th. 1840.

Gentlemen.

I beg to recommend to you, Mr. Thornton Hunt, who is a candidate for the situation of librarian to your valuable Institution.

I venture to commend this gentleman to your notice most warmly and earnestly; not because I have a great esteem and regard for his father, but

---

[1] CD's immediate neighbours were Edmund Sharp at 2 Devonshire Terrace (see *To* Mitton, ?9 Jan, *fn*) and Henry Loder, Surgeon, at Church House, New Road, Marylebone. Which had complained is not known.

[2] The Western Literary and Scientific Institution for the Diffusion of Useful Knowledge amongst Persons Engaged in Commercial and Professional Pursuits; founded 1837. Its address was 47 Leicester Square 1839–45. One of its Vice-Presidents was Samuel Rogers.

because of his own personal character and qualifications. Besides possessing abilities which would qualify him for a much higher station than that which he seeks to fill, he is a person of the highest honor and integrity: most punctual and exact in the discharge of any duties he undertakes, and a truly zealous and conscientious man.

I am happy to bear this testimony to the character of Mr. Thornton Hunt; and I offer no apology, gentlemen, for obtruding it on you, being quite certain that if you elect him, you will never require any.[1]

I am Gentlemen | Your faithful Servant<br>CHARLES DICKENS

To | The Committee of | The Western Literary Institution.

## *To* LEIGH HUNT, 10 JULY 1840

MS Brotherton Library, Leeds.

1 Devonshire Terrace | 10th. July 1840.

My Dear Hunt.

I send you the testimonial.[2] If it's too long, or too short, or too little, or too much, send it back again, and I'll write another.

I send herewith an imaginary old shoe which please to throw after your son—instantly if he is at home, and if not, directly on his return.

Faithfully Yours<br>CHARLES DICKENS

Leigh Hunt Esquire.

P.S. I fancied there was the slightest possible peculiarity in your speech last night—just an elaborate show of distinctness—a remarkably correct delivery—an exquisite appreciation of the beauty of the language, with the faintest smack of wine running through it—This was mere fancy, I suppose?[3]

## *To* JOHN OVERS, 13 JULY 1840

MS Morgan Library. *Address:* Mr. J. A. Overs | Messrs. Springweiler & Co. | 2 Duke Street | West Smithfield.[4]

Devonshire Terrace | 13th. July 1840.

Dear Mr. Overs.

Frazer's[5] flourish about payment was meant for my eye, I think; and it strongly occurs to me that you will have to write to him again.[6]

---

[1] Whether Hunt was appointed is not known.

[2] See last. Hunt had probably asked for it the night before, at the party the letter implies.

[3] An enormous question-mark.

[4] Springweiler & Thomson, medicine chest and dressing case manufacturers.

[5] Mis-spelt by CD. James Fraser (d. 1841; *DNB*), proprietor of *Fraser's Magazine*.

[6] No contribution by Overs to *Fraser's Magazine* is known.

I have been greatly interested by your account of the Moral World,[1] though I cannot make up my mind whether I shall pursue the subject or leave it alone. Several grave questions have arisen in my mind respecting the very doubtful propriety of noticing it at all, when the great object of its Citizens is plainly notoriety.[2]

I will send you your paper very soon. Meantime, thank you for your letter.[3]

Yours very truly

Mr. Overs.                                               CHARLES DICKENS

## *To* DANIEL MACLISE, 15 JULY [1840]*

MS Benoliel Collection. *Date:* 15 July was Wednesday in 1840; handwriting and "Maclise" in salutation support that year. *Address:* Wait | Daniel Maclise Esquire.

Devonshire Terrace | Wedy. 15th. July

My Dear Maclise.

My better half is going out to dinner to day, and I am going out at night,[4] but I shall not want to come home to dress, before Nine or half past. Shall you and I, taking advantage of the beautiful day, walk somewhere, and dine? If so, I'll call for you—or rather you call here, for it's in the way to all foreign parts—at any hour you please. Name it, that's all, and I'll be ready.

Faithfully Ever<br>CD.

[1] The *New Moral World* (the Socialist weekly journal conducted by Robert Owen and his disciples 1834–45) published a long article entitled "Boz's Sketches" on 18 July. Perhaps Overs knew that this was coming and suspected that CD might wish to reply to it. "Who can more ably develop the vital truth, that circumstances make, or mar, the man, than the inimitable Dickens?", the article asked; "The society which he so clearly depicts, cries aloud for change". It directed attention to those of his sketches which most clearly demonstrated "the existence of evils that Socialism has it in contemplation to remove"; and urged "the gouty old aristocrat" to go through "a few touching pictures of Boz" and then open his heart to "an impartial consideration of what the philanthropical Owen would live and die to render effectual".

[2] Earlier in the year Henry Phillpotts, Bishop of Exeter, had suddenly attracted public attention to the Owenites by a virulent attack on them in the Lords (24 Jan), following it with a motion (3 Feb) praying that "steps be taken to prevent the diffusion of blasphemous and immoral doctrines". Owen replied with a "Manifesto" in the *New Moral World*, 15 Feb (of which 50,000 copies were said to have been sold), and a pamphlet, *The Catechism of the New Moral World*. Numerous pamphlets attacking him and his principles followed; and in June a mob at Burslem, Staffs, was incited to set on him when he attempted to lecture. For CD's one letter to him, see 27 Dec 41.

[3] Which probably thanked CD for a copy of Stow's *Survey of London*, 1633, with inscription dated 1 July 40. It is now in the Huntington Library.

[4] To Miss Coutts's: see 4 July.

## *To* MISS ROGERS,[1] 16 JULY [1840]*

MS Professor E. S. Pearson. *Date:* 16 July was Thursday in 1840; hand-writing supports that year.

Devonshire Terrace. | Thursday 16th. July.

Dear Miss Rogers.

I sat in a draught at a party last night,—before an open window and door all the evening—and have such a raging pain to day in every tooth in my head, that I am enduring a perfect martyrdom. I really believe nobody ever had such a complication and concentration of this most abominable torture as I am suffering at this moment.

Will you pity me for not being able to come to you to-day, and pity the cause also? If anything will do me good, I think that will. And pray believe me

Faithfully Yours
CHARLES DICKENS


## *To* CHARLES EDWARDS LESTER,[2] 19 JULY 1840

MS Berg Collection.

Devonshire Terrace. | Sunday July 19th. 1840.

Dear Sir.

As I have not the complete MS of Oliver[3] (I wish I had, as it would one

---

[1] Sarah Rogers (?1773–1855), Samuel Rogers's only unmarried sister, with whom he was on close and affectionate terms. She visited France, Switzerland and Italy with him in 1814, and saw through the press Part 1 of his *Italy*, 1822 (P. W. Clayden, *Rogers and his Contemporaries*, 1889, I, 314–35). George Ticknor described breakfast parties at her house in Hanover Terrace, Regent's Park, in 1838, itself "a sort of imitation . . . of her brother's at St. James's. . . . She has some good pictures . . . keeps autographs, curiosities, and objects of *virtù*, just like her brother" (*Life, Letters and Journals of George Ticknor*, ed. G. S. Hillard, 1876, II, 181). On her death, at the age of 82, Rogers is said to have only commented "What a great blessing! I wish I could die too" (Clayden, *op. cit.*, II, 444).

[2] Charles Edwards Lester (1815–90; *DAB*), of New York, journalist and writer of history and biography; for a short time a Presbyterian minister. An ardent abolitionist, he had come to England as a delegate to the World Anti-Slavery Convention held in Exeter Hall, June 40. American consul at Genoa 1842–7; on his return, *Times* correspondent in New York. His books included the story of a runaway slave, *Chains and Freedom*, 1839, translations from the Italian, several biographies, and some popular history. He visited CD July 40, with a letter of introduction from Thomas Campbell, and afterwards wrote a long and somewhat naïve description of the visit and CD's conversation as a letter addressed to Washington Irving. This—one of a series of letters addressed by him from England to prominent Americans, published as *The Glory and Shame of England*, 2 vols, 1841—was attacked at length in the *Examiner*, 11 Dec 41 (probably by Forster), for its absurdity. "There is some truth in this book", the *Examiner* review admitted grudgingly; "but its chief property is an exquisite badness of taste"; its "violation of the confidences of social life" had been "hardly surpassed by Mr. Willis himself". CD no doubt saw the English edition (Bentley,

day have an interest for my children) I am enabled to send you a scrap,[1] in compliance with your request; and have much pleasure in doing so.

Pray make my regards to your lady,[2] and give her from me the other little packet inclosed. It is the first specimen of the kind I have parted with—except to a hair-dresser—and will most likely be the last,[3] for if I were to be liberal in this respect, my next portrait would certainly be that of a perfectly bald gentleman.

Believe me Dear Sir | Faithfully Yours

To Charles Edwards[4] Lester.               CHARLES DICKENS

P.S. I should tell you perhaps as a kind of certificate of the Oliver scrap, that it is a portion of the original and only draught.—I never copy.[5]

## *To* THOMAS CAMPBELL,[6] 19 JULY 1840*

MS University of Texas. *Address:* Thomas Campbell Esquire | 61 Lincolns Inn Fields.

1 Devonshire Terrace. | York Gate Regents Park.<br>19th. July 1840.

My Dear Sir.

I cannot lay your letter[7] aside, without telling you how much pleasure it

---

1841) before he left for America, and—even if annoyed by the pages about himself, though they were full of praise—would have agreed that the book in general contained "some truth". To Lester, England's "glory" was her heritage of ancient buildings, historical associations, beautiful countryside; the gracious way of life of her gentry; her prosperity as shown in buildings, railways, trade and influence overseas—and CD himself. Her "shame" was the hopeless misery of the poor; the hungry, ragged children at work in mills and factories; the workhouses—"a dark cloud, that hangs on the vision of every poor man in England, when he looks into the future" (CD's descriptions in *Oliver* "will not do, we all know, for the majority of them; but . . . will do for many": i, 201–2); the poor rates and iniquitous Corn Laws. With these he contrasted the wealth and luxury of a haughty aristocracy; the philanthropist who would not give to starving children on "principle" (i, 128). "I would sooner", he wrote in his preface, "see the children of my love born to the heritage of Southern slavery, than to see them subjected to the blighting bondage of the poor English operative's life" (i, vii).

[3] The MS of 22 chapters, about two-fifths of the whole, is now in the Forster Collection, V & A—found at Bentley's office after CD's death, and bought by Forster at Sotheby's for £50 in July 70. The MS of the last ten chapters was in America—bought from Bentley for £60 by Carey, Lea & Blanchard in Oct 38 (see Vol. I, p. 322*n*).

[1] A leaf from Ch. 15, now in the Berg Collection (reproduced in *D*, VIII [1912], 295). See *Oliver Twist*, ed. Kathleen Tillotson, pp. xlvi–vii.

[2] Ellen, daughter of Capt. Haley Brown, of Sackett's Harbor, New York. They had married in 1837.

[3] Cf. *To* Mrs Hurnall, 27 Oct 41. He refused a request for a lock from the ladies of Plymouth, Massachusetts, on 21 Feb 42, but sent Mrs Colden a brooch containing a "very small specimen" of hair on 24 Feb 42.

[4] "Charles Edwards" inserted in an unknown hand in space left by CD between "To" and "Lester".

[5] But there is evidence of his making

gave me to hear from you, and how it came upon me—not as from a slight acquaintance, but from a very old and valued one; for if I have not known you intimately in the flesh, I have been upon most friendly terms with you in the spirit for a long, long, time.

I hope we shall improve this opportunity and become better known to each other. Believe me that you do not rank among the admirers of your genius one more sincere and earnest person than

Yours very faithfully

Thomas Campbell Esquire.         CHARLES DICKENS

## *To* DANIEL MACLISE, 22 JULY [1840]

MS Private (destroyed in Prestwick air-crash, Dec 1954). *Date:* 22 July was Wednesday in 1840; clearly refers to the "dreadful girl" mentioned in next.

Devonshire Terrace. | Wednesday July 22nd.

My Dear Maclise

Kate has a girl stopping here, for whom I have conceived a horrible aversion, and whom I *must* fly. Shall we dine together today in some sequestered pothouse, and go to some theatre afterwards? (My Examiner promise[1] in the latter respect, lies heavy on my mind.) If yea, will you be here at 4, *or as soon as you like.* If nay, whither can I turn from this fearful female! She is the Ancient Mariner of young ladies. She "holds me with her glittering eye", and I cannot turn away. The basilisk is now in the

fair copies of a few pages and various short passages of *Oliver* (see *Oliver Twist,* ed. K. Tillotson, pp. xlvi–vii).

[6] Thomas Campbell (1777–1844; *DNB*), poet. CD had met him once, at a dinner given by Bentley on 22 Nov 38 (see Vol. I, p. 460*n*) at which Moore described him as "broken and nervous" (*Memoirs, Journal, and Correspondence of Thomas Moore,* ed. Lord John Russell, 1853–6, VII, 245). On his death, Macready commented: "He outlived his acceptability, and was latterly intolerable in society; but what a charming poet" (*Diaries,* II, 272). A copy of the edition of his *Poetical Works* with engravings after Turner, 1837, inscribed by Campbell to Catherine, was in the Gad's Hill library at CD's death.

[7] No doubt the letter introducing C. E. Lester.

[1] Presumably Forster was away (cf. *To* Landor, 26 July) and CD had promised to write the general review of the London theatres which appeared in the *Examiner* on 26 July. The notice of the Haymarket, which CD visited on

Thurs 23rd (see next, *hn*) reads: "The *Lady of Lyons* was repeated on Thursday to a house crowded to the ceiling. . . . Power, as rattling and vivacious as ever, has sent merry audiences laughing to their beds". The Drury Lane summer concerts are described as "very agreeable"; "the theatre is not a temple of obscenity—which (its old-established character in that respect being remembered) is worthy of remark"; but the review refers sarcastically to "the wisdom of the patent which gives [the theatre] a monopoly in doing that which it never does" (i.e. confine itself to the legitimate drama: see *To* Horne, Feb 40, *fn*). Van Amburgh, at the Surrey, is mocked, and "Carter, the Lion King" at Astley's, preferred to him. The majority of the other theatres are described as offering "romantic dramas of intense interest and with terrific *denouements,* where the mischief-working character is a being so terrible that he cannot be named, but is expressed in the playbills by a thick black dash and a corpulent note of admiration."

dining room and I am in the study, but I *feel* her through the wall. She is of a prim and icy aspect, her breast tight and smooth like a sugar loaf,—she converseth with fluency, and hath deep mental lore—her name is Martha Ball[1]—she breakfasted in the dining room this morning, and I took my solitary food, tight locked-up in the study. I went out last night and in my desolation, had my hair cut—merely to avoid her. Evins, this is dreadful!

Your wretched friend<br>CHARLES DICKENS

P.S. Is Davis[2] of an excitable and ardent nature—I mean the enthusiastic sculptor? Do you think if I asked him here, he might be got to run away with this tremendous being? She is remarkable for a lack of development everywhere, and might be useful as a model of a griffin or other fabulous monster.

P.P.S Or would he make her bust, and "aggrawate" it. That would be some revenge.

### *To* THOMAS MITTON, [?23 JULY 1840]

MS Huntington Library. *Date:* Handwriting points to 1840, in which year the only Thursday performances for which both *The Lady of Lyons* and Power were billed were on 9, 16, 23 and 30 July. Among these four dates, CD was free to go only on the 23rd. Reference to the "dreadful girl" (see last) supports.

Your Office | Thursday

Will you come up and dine with us at 5?[3] We have a box at the Haymarket for Kate to take that dreadful girl, and perhaps you would like to go with us, though it's only the Lady of Lyons[4] and Power.[5]

Faithfully Yours

Thomas Mitton Esquire.                                    CD.

[1] Unidentified—unless a cousin of CD's, descended from the Balls of Claverley, Shropshire, one of whom was CD's paternal grandmother (housekeeper at Crewe Hall). Cf. mention of "a cousin from France" in *To* Macready, ?16 May.

[2] Presumably Edward Davis (1813–1878), sculptor, who exhibited 115 works at the RA 1834–77. He executed the portrait bust of Maclise commissioned by the RA 1870, now in Burlington House. His *Rebecca* (1862) was much admired.

[3] Underlined twice.

[4] By Bulwer. First performed Feb 38. Macready had been acting in it again at the Haymarket since 20 June

40. On 23 July Mrs Gore's *King O'Neil* was also performed, with Power as Capt. O'Neil.

[5] Tyrone Power (1797–1841; *DNB*), Irish comedian; immensely successful during the last 15 years in both England and America; "the very soul of whim, of fun, and Irish frolic" (Thomas Marshall, *Lives of the Most Celebrated Actors and Actresses*, [1847], p. 128). On 1 Aug 40 took his farewell benefit at the Haymarket before setting off on his fourth trip to America. Lost with the S.S. *President* on his return journey Mar 41. Letters in the Forster Collection (V & A) show him to have been a friend of Forster and Maclise.

### *To* W. C. MACREADY, [?23 JULY 1840]*

MS Morgan Library. *Date:* probably same day as last, mentioning the "dreadful girl"; handwriting supports.

Devonshire Terrace. | Thursday.

My Dear Macready.

We will come with the greatest pleasure and delight. We must bring the guest, and I'm sorry to say I can't recommend her. But as different people have different opinions, some preferring onions to apples, perhaps you'll like her.

That exquisite pun of yours about the fawning,[1] was almost lost through hieroglyphical penmanship. I had put your note away when suddenly it dawned upon my mind and a re-perusal convulsed me.

Faithfully Yours always
CD.

What time do you dine?—6?


### *To* THOMAS MITTON, 24 JULY 1840

MS Huntington Library.

Devonshire Terrace | 24th. July 1840.

My Dear Mitton.

Inclosed is a cheque (dated 6th. next month) for[2] the life Insurance.[3]

Don't fail to bear in mind [? you come ou]t[4] of town with us at the [beginning][5] of September, which I am sure would do you good. A Month at that time of year would not be too long a holiday, and you might come up to town for a day, mid way in that period, if necessary. I shall quite conclude that you go with us; and set it down as a solemn bargain.

I think Broadstairs will surely be the place.

Faithfully Yours ever
CHARLES DICKENS

---

[1] The pun was presumably on "faughning".

[2] The paper is rubbed and grubby down a vertical fold at the centre of the page; but "for" and several other words affected can be confidently read.

[3] £18.17.6, paid to the Britannia Life Assurance Co. (CD's Account-book, MS Messrs Coutts). Cf. *To* Chapman & Hall, 2 July.

[4] Two large stains at the transverse fold of the paper have obliterated several words. Infra-red photography has recovered a few; but here there is space for about 11 letters, of which the last two seem to be "ou", the rest illegible.

[5] About 9 letters are illegible here, but "beginning" seems certain. See references to the coming visit in *To* Mitton, ?10 and 27 Aug.

## *To* MISS BURDETT COUTTS, 25 JULY 1840*

MS Morgan Library. *Address:* Miss Coutts.

1 Devonshire Terrace | Saturday 25th. July 1840.

Mr. Charles Dickens presents his Compliments to Miss Coutts, and exceedingly regrets that having made an engagement to go into Devonshire[1] on Monday, whence he does not return for ten days, he is prevented from accepting her welcome invitation.

## *To* WALTER SAVAGE LANDOR, 26 JULY 1840†

MS Berg Collection.

1 Devonshire Terrace | 26th. July 1840.

My Dear Landor.

Mr. Shandy's Clock[2] was nothing to mine—wind, wind, wind, always winding am I; and day and night the alarum is in my ears, warning me that it must not run down. When I received that Swing-like[3] letter of yours, such visions of Bath sprung up and floated about me that I rung the bell for my portmanteau and putting it on a chair, looked hard at it for three quarters of an hour. Suddenly a solemn sound from the Clock, jarred upon my ears; and sending it upstairs again, I sat down with a sigh, to write.

Gravely and seriously—for it *is* a serious matter—I have been looking forward to a glimpse of you were it only for one day, and am still looking forward, and shall be looking forward for Heaven knows how long. I am more bound down by this Humphrey than I have ever been yet—Nickleby was nothing to it, nor Pickwick, nor Oliver—it demands my constant attention and obliges me to exert all the self-denial I possess. But I hope before long to be so far ahead as to have actually turned the corner and left the Printer at the bottom of the next sheet[4]—and then—!

In the meanwhile, when you have the grace to write a long letter *I* will have the grace to answer it with one of corresponding dimensions, so take care what you do, and what inflictions you call down upon that poetical sconce,[5] on which be all peace and happiness and sunny light for evermore!

Boz.

I was going to put in this place such an effusion (impromptu of course) about *her*,[6] but as I've only got the first line and the last, and it wants a

---

[1] To visit his parents at Alphington.

[2] *Tristram Shandy*, Chs 1 and 4.

[3] I.e. threatening (from a mythical "Capt. Swing", a name used in the 1830s by discontented labourers, in letters to farmers threatening to burn their crops).

[4] On 31 July he finished No. 21, pub-

lished 22 Aug. During the rest of 1840 he seems to have finished each number 18 or 19 days ahead of publication.

[5] Head.

[6] Rose Caroline Paynter (*b.* 1818), youngest daughter of David R. Paynter; lived in Bath 1818–34, and again 1843 until her marriage to Charles Brune

dozen or so to express the vast idea, I shall defer it until my next, when I shall certainly dispatch it to you. Until then, give her my love, or if you won't—and upon my word I mistrust you—add it to that little private store of your own, and say nothing about it.

Regards to Mrs. Painter[1] and the rest of the family of course. Also to that blighted reed[2] who whispers softly according to the custom of his family and was grown in the softest soil conceivable.

Forster is out of town, but comes home next Wednesday.[3]

Graves Sawle (later Liberal MP for Bodmin) in 1846. First met Landor in Florence 1834–5, and later wrote of the meeting: "On hearing that my mother was the half-sister of Rose Aylmer, his first love, and that I was named after her, he came to see us; and from that time onward there was the closest friendship between him and my family" (*Sketches from the Diaries of Rose Lady Graves Sawle*, 1908, p. 19). CD had met the Paynters on his visit to Bath Feb–Mar 40. On 8 Mar Landor wrote to Theodosia Garrow (later Mrs T. A. Trollope):

"Both of my friends [*CD and Forster*] were smitten by Miss Paynter—See my reproof.

Now Dickens! by the Saints! if you *Pretend* to . . what I truly *do*, I cannot choose but run you thro, And then myself.—Quick. Swords for two!

He said 'It will be a lucky fellow who gathers that Rose'.

Rondeau

Under the Rose, my hearty Dickens, What gamecock but would rear his chickens And glance at them with brighter eye To see them bask or scamper by Under the Rose? Under the Rose lay thou thy bays, Where mine are laid for all my days. Thou praisest them . . for this alone Praise them henceforth . . that they have grown Under the Rose"

(Sotheby's catalogue, March 1960). On this visit to Bath Rose and her sister "introduced [CD] to the original of Quilp; a frightful little dwarf named Prior, who let donkeys on hire" and used a heavy stick impartially on his wife and the donkeys (*Sketches from the*

*Diaries*, p. 55). The following month she dined with CD and Catherine in London in the company of Landor, Forster, Quin, Kenyon and Maclise, the evening ending with charades; and with her sister went down in the diving-bell at the Polytechnic with CD and Landor. She apparently received several letters from CD (*op. cit.*, p. 53); but these have not been traced.

[1] Mis-spelt by CD. Sophia Paynter, *née* Price (1790–1863), half-sister of Rose Aylmer, whose death in 1800 inspired Landor's famous lines. Mrs Paynter and her daughters, Rose and Sophia, were the chief delight of Landor's life in Bath: see R. H. Super, *W. S. Landor*, 1957, *passim*.

[2] John Edmund Reade (1800–70; *DNB*), poetaster and novelist, much of whose work was plagiarism. Lived most of his life in Bath and the West of England. Frequently mocked by Landor; described by Bulwer as "an elongated, moth-eaten-looking individual" (Super, *op. cit.*, p. 299); referred to by Macready, to whom he wanted to dedicate a play 1839, as "that ludicrously wretched fellow" (*Diaries*, 1, 498). CD's Gad's Hill library contained Reade's *Catiline*, privately printed, 1839, inscribed: "June 25, '39. To Charles Dickens, Esq., this Drama is presented with sentiments of highest estimation from the Author. St. James's Square: 45. Bath"; also Reade's *The Drama of a Life*, 1840 (*Catalogue of the Library of CD*, ed. J. H. Stonehouse, 1935, pp. 92 and 93).

[3] On 9 Aug Landor, clearly having heard in the meantime from Forster of CD's visit to Devonshire (see last), replied: "It is enough to drive any man mad, who wants but little driving that way, to be told that he was within hail of

## *To* W. C. MACREADY, [26 JULY 1840]\*

MS Morgan Library. *Date:* clearly 1840 on signature. Basingstoke was on the way to Devonshire, where CD stayed 27 July to 4 Aug. Mrs Macready took her children to Broadstairs on 7 Aug (*Diaries*, II, 72).

Devonshire Terrace | Sunday

My Dear Macready.

I send you Bryant[1]—not with any idea, however, of your finding time to read the same. Indeed this would have prevented my sending it to you at all, but that the man who forwarded it to me from America, has marked the best pieces in the Index, which saves trouble. I think they are all famous, but perhaps these *are* the best.

I forgot to tell Mrs. Macready to bear especially in mind at Broadstairs in connection with bottled stout, ale, punch, wines and spirituous liquors, Mr. Ballard[2] of the Albion Hotel—one of the best and most respectable tradesmen in England. He has a kind of reverence for me (you will admire his simplicity) and on the mention of my name will send his very best.

If it clears up, we think of going by the Railroad as far as Basingstoke tonight.

Faithfully Yours always

CHARLES DICKENS

## *To* JOHN FORSTER, 31 JULY [1840]

MS Victoria & Albert Museum (FC). *Date:* 31 July was Friday in 1840; paper is watermarked 1840; signature supports that year.

Alphington | Friday Night July 31st.

My Dear Forster.

Bradburys told me you were going to write, but as I have not heard from you, I scrawl a very *short* note (having just finished my number)[3] to say that we shall be home, please God, on Tuesday Evening. I have taken our places by the Telegraph, albeit it is a monstrously dangerous coach. Coming down, we were *twice* as nearly over as you can conceive. The hills are very steep, and the pace tremendous.[4]

a person he would have walked thirty miles to see. But neither that person nor another he could mention has he seen since he left Bath, now a fortnight. Forster also told me, in his last note, that he had gone as far as Clifton on his road to me—Why could he not have told me of his intention. | Now as to what I am to write on the blank page of the two Dramas [*copies of* Andrea of Hungary *and* Giovanna of Naples], stick on it what you may tear off the other side—I do not mean the top or the center, for I shall write it so as neither to be creased or blotted." The inscrip-

tion follows on p. 3 of the letter: "To Charles Dickens, | the only man living to whom I owe tribute, these two small coins are paid willingly. | W. S. Landor" (MS Berg).

[1] Possibly *Selections from the American Poets*, compiled by W. C. Bryant, 1840; called "Mr. Bryant's volume" in the *Knickerbocker*, Dec 40, XVI, 545.

[2] James Ballard (?1806–74): see Vol. I, p. 303n.

[3] No. 21 (see *To* Cattermole, ?7 Aug), published 22 Aug.

[4] Only seven months before, his father had been involved in an accident

I don't believe there is anywhere such a perfect little doll's house as this.[1] It is in the best possible order—beautifully kept—the garden flourishing, the road lively, the rooms free from creeping things or any such annoyance, and the prospect beautiful. I wish you could see it, and but that you have been so roving of late should have asked you to come down and return with us. It is quite a queer thing, and if it were not for recent demonstrations (I speak of those you know of)[2] would give me unmingled satisfaction. I wonder more than ever how he had the heart to write as he did. I hope that's all over.

They *seem* perfectly contented and happy. That's the only intelligence I shall convey to you except by word of mouth.

Kate joins in kindest remembrances.

Always believe me Dear Forster

Your faithful friend

CHARLES DICKENS[3]

## *To* MESSRS CHAPMAN & HALL, [31 JULY 1840]

Mention in *To* Cattermole, ?7 Aug 40. *Date:* CD had finished the No. on 31 July (see last). *From* Alphington.

*Sending the MS of No. 21 and mentioning "an old Gateway"[4] as a subject for illustration.*

## *To* DR JOHN ELLIOTSON,[5] [5 AUGUST 1840]

MS Wisbech Museum & Literary Institute. *Date:* Signature points to Summer 1840; CD had clearly returned to London on Tues 4 Aug as planned (*To* Forster, 31 July).

Devonshire Terrace | Wednesday Morning

My Dear Doctor Elliotson.

I only returned to town from Devonshire, late last night. I shall be truly

to the Exeter coach "Defiance" (see Vol. I, p. 620*n*).

[1] Mile End Cottage, Alphington, which CD had taken for his parents on 5 Mar 39 (see Vol. I, pp. 517–20).

[2] Doubtless the letter from John Dickens which CD had forwarded to Mitton on 14 June, with a draft of his reply, giving permission for both to be shown to Forster.

[3] During this visit, says Forster, CD and Catherine had one day's real holiday, "when Dawlish, Teignmouth, Babbacombe, and Torquay were explored" (F, II, viii, 160). On 3 Aug CD was entertained at an evening party by the Mayor of Exeter (*Western Times*,

8 Aug); earlier, the *Western Times* (1 Aug), in an article eulogizing him, had criticized Exeter for not granting him the Freedom of the City.

[4] Put in expressly for Cattermole: see ?7 Aug.

[5] John Elliotson, MD (1791–1868; *DNB*): see Vol. I, p. 461*n*. After his resignation from University College Hospital in Dec 38—following attacks by the *Lancet* on his practice of mesmerism—he gave up medical teaching and concentrated on his private practice, within which he continued to use mesmerism. In 1840 he published *Human Physiology*; and in 1841 *A Memoir of Courvoisier* (the murderer),

glad to dine with you on Saturday, and also to meet Mr. Townshend[1]
from whom I have found two kind notes on my table.

Mr. Forster's address is No. 58 Lincolns Inn Fields.

Faithfully Yours always

Doctor Elliotson.                                            CHARLES DICKENS


*To* GEORGE CATTERMOLE, [?7 AUGUST 1840]

MS Benoliel Collection. *Date:* The "old Gateway" was a subject for Ch. 27
(No. 21, published 22 Aug); reference to his visit to Devonshire strongly
suggests first Friday after CD's return to London.

Devonshire Terrace | Friday Morning.

My Dear Cattermole.

I sent the MS of the inclosed proof marked Z up to Chapman and Hall
from Devonshire, mentioning a subject of an old Gateway which I had
put in expressly with a view to your illustrious pencil.[2] By a mistake,
however, it went to Browne instead.[3] Chapman is out of town, and such
things have gone wrong in consequence.

The subject to which I wish to call your attention is in an *un*written No.
to follow this one, but is a mere echo of what you will find at the conclusion

as No. 1 of G. R. Lewis's *Illustrations of Phrenology: Comprising Accounts of Persons Remarkable in Some Mental Respect . . . and . . . Delineations of their Heads.* For further attacks on him, and CD's indignation at them, see *To Macready*, 24 Aug 41. Became godfather to CD's second son, Walter, 4 Dec 41.

[1] The Rev. Chauncy Hare Townshend (1798–1868; *DNB*), poet, antiquarian, dilettante, and collector of pictures and precious stones (bequeathed to the V & A). Bulwer, who had known him as a young man, noted: "His beauty of countenance was remarkable at that time.—Those who knew Byron said it was Byron with bloom and health. He grew plain in later life—an accomplished man—but effeminate and mildly selfish" (MS Lytton Papers). Published a volume of *Poems*, 1821; was one of the colleagues of Macaulay, Praed and Moultrie when they founded *Knight's Quarterly Magazine* 1823–4; and contributed five articles to *Blackwood's* (Sep 1829–Feb 1830, and Aug 37). Published *A Descriptive Tour in Scotland*, Brussels, 1840.

Lived much of his life abroad. Greatly interested in mesmerism: dedicated *Facts in Mesmerism*, 1840, to Elliotson (and gave Bulwer a copy, 29 Feb 40, urging him to draw on mesmerism in a future novel; for he saw in him "a *German* depth . . . peculiarly calculated to invest the mysteries of Mesmerism with solemnity and grandeur": MS Lytton Papers). Gave a number of demonstrations with his Belgian "magnetic boy", Alexis, both on the Continent and in England (see *To Lady Blessington*, 2 June 41 and *fns*). In a letter dated "Tuesday" (?11 May 41) he wrote to CD: "I must remind you of your *pledge* to cultivate my friendship. I only lack *opportunity* to do the same by one, who has lightened many a weary hour of my life, and whom I *love* in his works" (MS Huntington). For CD's dedicating *Great Expectations* to him and giving him the MS, and Townshend's appointing CD his literary executor, see later vols.

[2] The subject being architectural.

[3] It was therefore Browne who did the illustration, "Quilp at the Gateway", for Ch. 27.

of this proof marked Z.[1] I want the cart—gaily decorated—going through the street of the old town with the Wax Brigand displayed to fierce advantage, and the child seated in it also, dispensing bills—as many flags and inscriptions about Jarley's wax-work fluttering from the cart, as you please. You know the Wax Brigands, and how they contemplate small oval miniatures? That's the figure I want. I send you the scrap of MS which contains the subject.[2]

Will you, when you have done this, send it with all speed to Chapman and Hall as we are mortally pressed for time, and I must go hard to work to make up what I have lost by being dutiful and going to see my father.

I want to see you about a frontispiece to our first Clock Volume[3] which will come out (I think) at the end of September[4]—and about other matters. When shall we meet, and where?

I say nothing about our cousin[5] or the baby, for Kate bears this, and will make me a full report and convey all loves and congratulations.

Could you dine with us on Sunday at 6 o'Clock sharp? I'd come and fetch you in the morning and we could take a ride and walk. We shall be quite alone unless Macready comes. What say you?

Don't forget dispatch, there's a dear fellow and ever believe me.

Heartily Yours

George Cattermole Esquire CHARLES DICKENS

## *To* THOMAS HILL, 8 AUGUST 1840

Composite text from facsimile in Maggs Bros catalogue No. 486 (*aa*) and N, I, 267 (*bb*).

aDevonshire Terrace | 8th. August 1840.

My Dear Mr. Hill. I call you "Mr." because you are such a veteran,[6] though my inclination is to drop any word that *seems* to imply any formality between us, and assume the most irreverential familiarity of address.

I cannot tell you how much pleasure I have derived from your kind note,

[1] The last paragraph but one of Ch. 28 (No. 21) brings in the Brigand, in the cart advertising Jarley's waxworks, contemplating the miniature of his lady. The next No. opens with a fuller description.

[2] Perhaps the subject did not appeal to Cattermole or he had not time; for it was Browne who did the illustration of Nell and the waxworks for Ch. 29.

[3] See *To* Cattermole, 13 Aug.

[4] It was advertised in *Master Humphrey* No. 27 (3 Oct) as to be published on 15 Oct, and was included in the *Athenæum's* weekly "List of New Books" on 17 Oct.

[5] Mrs Cattermole (1812–92): see Vol. I, p. 576*n*.

[6] There were numerous jokes among Hill's acquaintances about his age, which nobody knew. Theodore Hook "circulated the apology that his baptismal register could not be found, because it was burnt in the Tower of London" (*Diary, Reminiscences, and Correspondence of H. Crabb Robinson*, ed. T. Sadler, II, 403); others questioned him on the Norman Conquest or the Spanish Armada, which they "insisted he must have been contemporary with" (J. R. Planché, *Recollections and Reflections*, revised edn, 1901, pp. 91–2).

and how cheering it is to me to be assured of the friendly interest of one whom I so warmly and truly esteem. I receive your congratulations with true gratification, for I know they are sincere and am proud of a place in your kind recollection and warm heart.

Carry with you to Paris and bring back again, my earnest and hearty friendship. Be a reader as long as I am a writer, and let us hope that we may regard each other with the*a* *b*same feelings as those which animate us now, in some other world where if there will be very few books, there will be (if my faith be at all near the right one) marvellously few Booksellers. Mrs. Dickens's "love".

Faithfully Yours*b*<br>[CHARLES DICKENS]

## *To* THOMAS MITTON, [?10 AUGUST 1840]

MS Huntington Library. *Date:* paper watermarked 1840. Clearly refers to the Broadstairs visit beginning 31 Aug 40; cannot have been written the day before *To* Mitton, 18 Aug; presumably, therefore, a week earlier.

Devonshire Terrace. | Monday Morning

My Dear Mitton

Will you dine with us on *Wednesday* at 5 instead of to-day? I owe a visit to a gentleman who leaves England tomorrow for a long time; and as the said gentleman addressed a Sonnet to me, have been obliged to engage myself.[1]

As Macready's house will not be vacant soon enough for our purpose[2] we have written to Broadstairs today about our old one. We purpose going *on Monday the 31st*. Prepare accordingly.

Faithfully Ever<br>CD.

[1] Probably refers to Chauncey Hare Townshend, whom CD had met the previous week (*To* Elliotson, 5 Aug). Townshend generally spent his winters abroad, and his *Sermons in Sonnets and Other Poems*, 1851, included a sonnet addressed "To the Author of Oliver Twist, Nicholas Nickleby &c" (undated, but—on evidence of the dedication—possibly written between *Nickleby* and *Master Humphrey's* appearance as a book: the volume includes even earlier poems). The sonnet reads:

Man of the genial mind! to thee a debt
No usurer records I largely owe!
Thy portraitures of life so warmly glow,
They clear the spirit of its old regret,
And, from the very heart that's smarting yet,

At human baseness, bid kind feelings flow.
'Tis thine our nature's lights and shades to show,
Redeeming these by those, till we forget
The evil in the good. Thy vigorous hand
Smites but to heal, and turns with master-ease
The mighty engine of the popular mind
To indignation, which shall purge the land
Of sanction'd sins. For such high services
I thank thee in the name of human kind!

[2] See next, *hn*.

## *To* W. C. MACREADY, [10 AUGUST 1840]*

MS Morgan Library. *Date:* Handwriting points to 1840. Mrs Macready took her children to Broadstairs on Fri 7 Aug: hence the invitation to Macready who was alone until Sat 29th. Since CD was at Alphington on the Monday before Mrs Macready's departure, this letter was presumably written the Monday after. Macready dined with him on 16 and 23 Aug (*Diaries*, II, 74–5).

Monday.

My Dear Macready

We hope that until we go to Broadstairs you will dine with us every Sunday when you are not better engaged. Is it a bargain?

As you were asking after that little boy who wrote the copies,[1] I send you the last accounts of him. They have just reached me.

I've got a word.—It's a mineral, and isn't to be found in England.[2] You have guessed it already, I have no doubt!

Always My Dear Macready | Faithfully Yours

CD.

## *To* ALFRED DICKENS,[3] 12 AUGUST 1840

Text from N, I, 267.

Devonshire Terrace | 12th August 1840

My dear Alfred,

I am very glad to learn that you have so good a prospect of continued employment in your old quarters.[4]

By a kind of fatality the servants, among them, lost that unfortunate dog on the day your letter arrived. He had grown very much, looked handsome, and was in high favor. He has not returned, nor can we get any news of him. I have determined never to keep another, be he who or what he may.

We are going to Broadstairs again, on the 31st and have been to Alphington where we found them very well, and looking exceedingly comfortable. The children are "charming" and desire their loves. On our return from

---

[1] The poor schoolmaster's favourite scholar, first spoken of in *Old Curiosity Shop*, Ch. 24 (No. 19, published 8 Aug). CD must have been sending proofs of the No. published 15 Aug, in which (Ch. 25) the boy dies.

[2] I.e., presumably, gold—to be found in America. This no doubt answered a letter from Macready mentioning his worries about money. On 9 Aug he had recorded them in his diary: "The house last night was humiliating—the charm of my name, as an attraction, seems broken up; my Haymarket income is

trembling" (*Diaries*, II, 73). But he did not think "seriously" of paying another visit to America until Jan 43 (*Diaries*, II, 192).

[3] Alfred Lamert Dickens (1822–60): see Vol. I, p. 44n.

[4] According to a MS note in a copy of *Sketches of Young Couples* (Widener Collection, Harvard) given by Alfred to a fellow engineering student, he was working for George and Robert Stephenson at Tamworth, on the Midland Railway, throughout 1840 and 1841.

Devonshire, we found the baby[1] extremely unwell, and Pickthorn considered it advisable to call in Doctor Davis.[2] We were very much distressed at first, but on consultation they thought there was nothing to be alarmed at, and since then she has improved greatly. She is still very thin, however, and paler than she should be.

I send you on the other side three signatures which I suppose will serve your purpose. There is no news in London—everybody is hurrying out of town—the two great theatres are shut up—and all the watering places are crammed with hot people.

Kate sends her best love. And I am always
                              You affectionate brother
                                        [CHARLES DICKENS]


## *To* SAMUEL ROGERS,[3] 13 AUGUST 1840

MS Comtesse de Suzannet.

                        Devonshire Terrace | Thursday 13th. August 1840.
My Dear Sir.
I have decided to publish Master Humphrey's Clock in half yearly volumes—*a*each volume, containing, of course, the collected Numbers for that period. As the first of these will be out at the end of September,[4] and I want to settle a point I have in my mind, let me ask a favor of you at once.*a*

Have you any objection to my dedicating the book to you, and so having one page in it which will afford me earnest and lasting gratification? *b*I will not tell you how many strong and cordial feelings move me to this enquiry; for I am unwilling to parade, even before you, the sincere and affectionate regard which I seek to gratify.[5]

If I wrote a quire of notes I could say no more than this. I must leave a great deal *understood*, and only say with a most hearty adaptation of what has passed into a very heartless form, that I am always
                              My Dear Sir | Faithfully Yours
Samuel Rogers Esquire                       CHARLES DICKENS*b*

---

[1] Katey, *b.* 29 Oct 39.
[2] Probably Dr Henry Davis, of 66 Stanhope Street, MRCS 1841, LSA 1842. A Dr Henry Davis was called in to see Catherine on Sydney Dickens's birth in Apr 47.
[3] Samuel Rogers (1763–1855; *DNB*): see Vol. I, p. 602*n*.

[4] In fact 15 Oct (see *To* Cattermole, ?7 Aug, *fn*).
[5] Rogers consented. For the two dedications CD wrote, one discarded, the other used, see *To* Forster, 6 Sep, *fn*, and *To* Rogers, ?8 or 9 Sep 40.

## *To* GEORGE CATTERMOLE, 13 AUGUST [1840]†

MS University of Texas. *Date:* 13 Aug was Thursday in 1840.

Devonshire Terrace | Thursday August 13th.
My Dear Cattermole.

Will you turn your attention to a frontispiece for our first Volume, to come upon the left hand side of the book as you open it, and to face a plain, printed title? My idea is, some scene from the Curiosity Shop, in a pretty border or scroll work or architectural device; it matters not what, so that it be pretty. The scene even might be a fanciful thing partaking of the character of the story but not representing any particular passage in it, if you thought that better for the effect.[1]

I ask you to think of this, because, although the volume is not published until the end of September, there is no time to lose. We wish to have it engraved with great care, and worked very skilfully; and this cannot be done unless we get it on the stocks soon.

They will give you every opportunity of correction, alteration, revision, and all other ations and isions connected with the Fine Arts.

Always believe me | Faithfully Yours
CHARLES DICKENS

*a*Loves to Cousin and—by the bye what relationship is there between us and the last of the Cattermoles—We[2] must look into this—I have no doubt the nurse can tell—baby meanwhile.*a*

## *To* W. C. MACREADY, 17 AUGUST [1840]†

MS Morgan Library. *Date:* 17 Aug was Monday in 1840.

Devonshire Terrace | Monday August 17th.
My Dear Macready.

*b*Many thanks for the book. I think so well of it *as to have it bound,* and when that's done, you must put your name in it for me.[3]

[1] In a distinguished, but not at all "pretty", border composed of halberds, armour and grotesque men in armour, the only recognizable scene from *Old Curiosity Shop* is Dick and Fred Trent sitting over "the rosy". Quilp appears, looking up at a couple of armed angels; Nell appears, in a halo, giving her grandfather a drink; then, older, kneeling before him by a church doorway. The centre is divided into two: above, Master Humphrey sits with his friends (who are asleep); below, the two Wellers, the housekeeper, and barber sit asleep. It was not an enlivening frontispiece. When *Old Curiosity Shop* was published without the Master Humphrey sections (1841), Cattermole's illustration "The shop" (previously the headpiece to No. 4) took its place.
*aa* Not previously published.
[2] Initial letter not clearly written; but the alternative "he" seems unlikely.
*bb* Not previously published.
[3] No such book has been traced.

Tuesday the Twenty Fifth shall (God willing) be the day.[1] We have arranged accordingly. Time and so forth we will settle next Sunday.[b2]

What can I say to you, about last night?[3] Frankly, nothing. Nothing can enhance the estimation in which I hold you, or the affectionate and sincere attachment I bear towards you, my dear friend,—and not even your manly and generous interposition can make me eloquent upon a subject on which I feel so deeply and singly.

I am very much grieved, and yet I am not penitent and cannot be, reason with myself as I will. With all the regard I have for Forster, and with all the close friendship between us, I cannot close my eyes to the fact that we do not quarrel with other men; and the more I think of it, the more I feel confident in the belief that there is no man, alive or dead, who tries his friends as he does. I declare to you solemnly, that when I think of his manner (far worse than his matter) I turn burning hot, and am ashamed and in a manner degraded to have been the subject of it.

[1] For the christening of Katey—Catherine Elizabeth Macready Dickens —at St Marylebone parish church. As godfather, Macready presented a watch and chain which he "was pleased to see very much admired" (*Diaries*, II, 75). His diary entry describes the happenings of the day. At the service the parson, the Rev. Brian Burgess, aroused his wrath (always latent against the Established Church), first by beginning before the arrival of a baby who was brought late, and not troubling to repeat the part already said ("The hypocrites! The villains! The liars to God, the cheats to human nature!"); then by expressing compliments on the "*distinction*" of CD's party. Afterwards Macready lunched at CD's house with Angus Fletcher and the two godmothers; in the afternoon, with CD and Fletcher, was taken over Coldbath Fields prison by Chesterton; then dined with CD and "some relations of his, uncles; Miss Ayrton, Mrs Burnett, Maclise, Jerdan, Forster, Mr Charlton, etc". "Rather a noisy and uproarious day", he ends; "—not so much *comme il faut* as I could have wished" (*op. cit.*, II, 76).

[2] Macready dined with CD on Sun 23 Aug, in the company of Fanny Burnett, Maclise, Fletcher, Collinson, also Forster—"who was there just the same as ever" (*Diaries*, II, 75): see next note.

[3] On Sun 16 Aug Macready, Forster and Maclise dined with CD. Macready recorded in his diary the "painful scene" he witnessed after dinner: "Forster got on to one of his headlong streams of talk (which he thinks argument) and waxed warm, and at last some sharp observations led to personal retorts between him and Dickens. He displayed his usual want of tact, and Dickens flew into so violent a passion as quite to forget himself and give Forster to understand that he was in his house, which he should be glad if he would leave. Forster behaved very foolishly. I stopped him; spoke to both of them and observed that for an angry instant they were about to destroy a friendship valuable to both. I drew from Dickens the admission that he had spoken in passion and would not have said what he said, could he have reflected; but he added he could not answer for his temper under Forster's provocations, and that he should do just the same again. Forster behaved very *weakly*; would not accept the repeated acknowledgment communicated to him that Dickens regretted the passion, etc., but stayed, skimbling-skambling a parcel of unmeaning words, and at last finding he could obtain no more, made a sort of speech, accepting what he had before declined. He was silent and not recovered—no wonder!—during the whole evening. Mrs. Dickens had gone out in tears" (*Diaries*, II, 74).

I have found the soul of goodness in this evil[1] thing at all events, and when I think of all you said and did, I would not recal[2] (if I had the power) one atom of my passion and intemperance, which carried with it a breath of yours.

Ever believe me | My Dear Macready
Yours affectionately and heartily
CHARLES DICKENS

## *To* J. P. HARLEY, 17 AUGUST 1840

MS Bryn Mawr College, Pennsylvania.

1 Devonshire Terrace | Monday August 17th./40

Deserter of your friends.

A babby is to be christened and a fatted calf killed on these premises on Tuesday the 25th. Instant. It (the calf; not the babby) is to be taken off the spit at 6. *Can* you come, and gladden the heart of the indignant

J. P. Harley Esquire                                               BOZ

## *To* SAMUEL ROGERS, 17 AUGUST [1840]*

MS The Earl of Harrowby. *Date:* 17 Aug was Monday in 1840.

Devonshire Terrace | Monday 17th. August.

My Dear Sir.

A Hundred thanks for your kind note which I found, on returning from a walk, within two or three minutes after you had called.

We go to Broadstairs at the end of this month, and remain there for five weeks. We are in great hopes of having you for a neighbour again.[3]

Believe me My Dear Sir
Your faithful friend
CHARLES DICKENS

Samuel Rogers Esquire

## *To* THOMAS MITTON, [?17 AUGUST 1840]

Extract in John Waller catalogue No. 133 (1882); *MS* (signed initials) 2 pp.; from Devonshire Terrace. *Date:* probably the day before *To* Mitton, 18 Aug —which seems to have been written the day CD had intended to go to Broadstairs (since he had not gone, he could ask Mitton to dinner).

I find that if I would have a House at Broadstairs, I must go there and get one. With this view I shall start tomorrow morning, will you run down with me? Say "yes", and come and sleep here tonight.

---

[1] Cf. *Henry V*, IV, i, 4.
[2] Thus in MS.
[3] They did: see *To* Rogers, 4 Oct. CD's "we" was not a mere formality; for through meeting Catherine at Broadstairs Rogers formed a friendship with her shown in later letters.

## *To* UNKNOWN CORRESPONDENT, [?17 AUGUST 1840]

Mention in next. *Date:* probably same day as last.


## *To* THOMAS MITTON, 18 AUGUST [1840]

MS John Rylands Library. *Date:* Letter is endorsed, in an unknown hand: "Given me by Mr. Mitton, at Broadstairs Sepr. 1840".

Devonshire Terrace | Tuesday 18th. August.

My Dear Mitton

This comes to say that I didn't go to Broadstairs (thinking better of it) but wrote. Wherefore if you will dine with us *to day* at half past 5, we shall be glad to see you.

Faithfully Always
CHARLES DICKENS

Thomas Mitton Esquire


## *To* JOHN FORSTER, [?19 AUGUST 1840]

Extract in F, II, vii, 147. *Date:* probably the day before he began Ch. 33 (the first chapter in No. 24, published 12 Sep), which opens with a description of Sampson Brass's house. Since CD finished No. 25 on 2 Sep (*To* Forster, that day), and was writing on an average one No. a week, the likely date for his beginning No. 24 seems about 20 Aug.

I intended calling on you this morning on my way back from Bevis-marks,[1] whither I went to look at a house for Sampson Brass. But I got mingled up in a kind of social paste with the jews of Houndsditch,[2] and roamed about among them till I came out in Moorfields, quite unexpectedly. So I got into a cab, and came home again, very tired, by way of the city-road.


## *To* HENRY COLBURN,[3] 19 AUGUST [1840]

MS Comtesse de Suzannet. *Date:* 19 Aug was Wednesday in 1840.

Devonshire Terrace | Wednesday August 19th.

My Dear Sir.

Mrs. Dickens and I, very much regret that we have an old engagement for tomorrow evening, and cannot have the pleasure of accepting your kind Invitation; which we should otherwise have done with exceeding pleasure.

---

[1] An area in Aldgate once owned by the Abbots of Bury.

[2] Less than 100 yards east of Bevis Marks Synagogue.

[3] Henry Colburn (*d.* 1855; *DNB*): see Vol. 1, p. 170n. Still pre-eminent as a publisher of society novels: his 1840–1 list included Bulwer, Lady Morgan, Lady Blessington, Mrs Gore and Theodore Hook.

I send this *in*formal reply to your card, in order that I may take the opportunity of dashing[1] even this small piece of friendly intercourse, with business. I had this morning a most urgent note from poor Mrs. Macrone enquiring after her book and imploring me not to delay getting the money for her fatherless children. I assure you that I have been greatly pained and grieved by the contents of her letter, and am deeply and earnestly anxious to bring the matter to an issue.

When do you propose to publish it and in what state is it? For God's sake do not delay it beyond November.[2] And let us have a final meeting upon the subject one day between this and the 31st. when I leave town for six weeks.

Don't forget this, but be a worthy and considerate bookseller,[3] and I'll preserve your image in spirits in my mental Museum as a good agreeable phaenomonon.[4]

My Dear Sir Very truly Yours

Henry Colburn Esquire                          CHARLES DICKENS

## *To* THOMAS MITTON, [?20] AUGUST [1840]

Text from Eleanor E. Christian, "Recollections of CD", *Temple Bar*, LXXXII (1888), 482–3.[5] *Date:* clearly misdated. 19 Aug was Thursday in 1841; but Mrs Christian's references to the rumour that CD was mad ("Reminiscences", p. 338: cf. *To* Forster, 6 and 13 Sep 40) and to Angus Fletcher's eccentricities (*ibid*: cf. *To* Maclise, 2 Sep, *To* Forster, 20 Sep) show that the holiday she shared with the Smithsons at Broadstairs took place in 1840.[6]

Devonshire Terrace, | Thursday, 19th August.

My dear Mitton.

The only intelligence we can get about the houses on the Terrace at Broadstairs is, that there are two to let, or nearly to let, one (certainly empty at this moment) a little to the left of our old house, supposing you were looking out of the window upon the blue, the fresh, and ever free;[7] the other a little more to the left still, and commonly called or known by the name of Barfield's Cottage.

[1] I.e. mingling (*OED*).

[2] *The Pic Nic Papers* (for which see Vol. I, p. 371 and *n*) was at last published 9 Aug 41. Mrs Macrone received £50 in Aug 38, and a further £400 on 23 July 41 (Receipt, MS Mr C. C. Dickens).

[3] I.e. publisher.

[4] Thus in MS.

[5] First published in Mrs Christian's "Reminiscences of CD", *English-woman's Domestic Magazine*, X (1871), 337, but with dashes for Mitton and Smithson instead of their names.

[6] According to her "Reminiscences" and "Recollections", she had first met CD and Catherine shortly before the visit to Broadstairs, at dinner at the house of a relative of hers (clearly Mrs Smithson, a connection by marriage of her future husband).

[7] Cf. "The sea! the sea! the open sea!

The blue, the fresh, the ever free!" (from "The Sea" in B. W. Procter's *English Songs*, 1832—from which CD also quoted in *To* Forster, 2 July 37; I, 280).

This Barfield's Cottage will be vacant (we are told) upon the twenty-first. But the **devil** of it is that at this season of the year they won't keep the houses even a week for you, and consequently Barfield's Cottage is meat for our masters.[1] The other house must be either the one which Smithson looked at, or one close to and exactly like it.

If he wants to get up a picture of this last-named tenement in his mind, ask him if he don't remember going with Kate and me and the man from the library to look at a house, and stealing in at the kitchen-door past the water-butt and coal-cellar.[2] That house was next the library on the side nearest London—the library being between it and ours. I am not sure that this particular house is the same, but it must be either the next door to it, or the next door but one. The terms I don't know, but they are certainly *not more than* five guineas per week, I should say. . . .

In short, nothing can be done without going down in person, for the place is very full indeed, and the people wildly rapacious and rearing up on their hind legs for money. The day to go down upon is *a Monday*, for there is a chance of some family having gone out upon that morning, it being a great departure day. If you put all this into your partner's pipe, tell him that I wish, for his sake and my own too, I could fill it with more substantial matter.[3]

---

[1] Elizabethan proverbial saying. Cf. *2 Henry IV*, II, iv, 118. Listed in article on Barham in *A New Spirit of the Age*, 1844, as common slang "in vogue in the time of our fathers and grandfathers".

[2] Clearly refers to Smithson's one-day visit to Broadstairs on 14 June 40 (*To* Mitton, that day). CD then had a house next door to the library (*To* Mitton, ?31 May).

[3] Mrs Christian describes the Broadstairs holiday which followed. The Smithson and Dickens parties met, it seems, daily, and "got up ridiculous relations to each other"; CD pretended to be engaged "in a semi-sentimental, semi-jocular, and wholly nonsensical flirtation" with "Milly T——" (i.e. Amelia Thompson, "Billa"), aged 29, and Emma Picken (as Mrs Christian then was), aged 19 or 20; they "generally addressed each other in the old English style of euphuism" ("Wilt tread a measure with me, sweet lady?" &c); they all played guessing games, charades, vingt-et-un; they danced a quadrille at the end of a jetty at dusk, and CD, "possessed with the demon of mischief", seized Emma, proclaiming that he would hold her in the rising tide till it submerged them both ("the lovely E. P. drowned by Dickens in a fit of dementia"), and did so, long enough to spoil her silk dress ("Reminiscences", pp. 337 and 339). Mrs Christian remarks on his sudden changes of mood, "which we could tell at one glance at his face". His eyes could be like "danger lamps", and then she and Milly would "run round corners to get out of his way" (*op. cit.*, p. 341). Of Mrs Christian's two accounts of the Broadstairs holiday and her acquaintance with CD before and after it, the "Reminiscences" of 1871 are to be preferred to the "Recollections" of 1888— a rearrangement of the 1871 material, but with some omissions and additions. "Recollections" omits Fletcher's emergence from the sea, in the buff; CD's "disporting in the waves" less than six yards away, "but with only his head and shoulders visible" (i.e. nude too, presumably); two instances of CD's running Emma down a jetty under breaking waves and again spoiling her clothes (she was poor and this mattered); and the carving of her name on a rock by either CD or Fred. "Recollections" mentions that CD's mother, the two Burnetts and Letitia were staying with CD and Catherine, and describes

## *To* MISS BURDETT COUTTS, [?24 AUGUST 1840]*

MS Morgan Library. *Date:* CD probably went down to Broadstairs on Wed 26 Aug and stayed the night; for he had in person "engaged a house" there by the morning of Thurs 27th (*To* Mitton from Broadstairs, that day). No other visit to Broadstairs on a Wednesday is known during the period in which he was writing to Miss Coutts in the third person. If written on 24 Aug, the note is disingenuous; but CD (engaged all Tuesday with Katey's christening celebrations) did not dare postpone his house-hunting in Broadstairs beyond Wednesday, and the beginning of the family holiday seemed the best excuse. *Address:* Miss Burdett Coutts.

Devonshire Terrace. | Monday Evening

Mr. Charles Dickens presents his Compliments to Miss Coutts and greatly regrets that he cannot have the pleasure of dining with her on Wednesday, as he leaves town on that morning for a few weeks on the Coast.

Mr. Dickens deferred answering Miss Coutts's kind note until tonight in the hope that he might have been enabled to postpone his departure for one day. He finds, however, that he could not do so without great inconvenience to others, and is reluctantly obliged to abide by his previous arrangements.

## *To* THOMAS MITTON, [27 AUGUST 1840]

MS Huntington Library. *Date:* PM 27 Aug 40. *Address:* Thomas Mitton Esquire | 23 Southampton Buildings | Chancery Lane | London.

Broadstairs. Thursday Morning.

My Dear Mitton

In case I should not see you in Devonshire Terrace when I arrive at home this evening (which, however, I have my doubts about) I write you the glad tidings that I have engaged a house—a *very good one*[1]—and purpose taking possession of it, next Sunday. Let me see you to know if we take steam together, and so forth.

In haste | Always Faithfully Yours

Thomas Mitton Esquire　　　　CHARLES DICKENS

them. But its statement that Emma first met Fred during this Broadstairs visit is incompatible with the statement that she had seen him on the night before the Courvoisier execution.

[1] Lawn House, Broadstairs, on the road to Kingsgate; then separated from the sea by a cornfield (F, II, vii, 147).

## *To* WILLIAM HALL, [?28 AUGUST 1840]

Text from N, I, 285. *Date:* probably 1840 or 41 since not fully dated by CD; an envelope in Eastgate House, Rochester, addressed "William Hall Esquire | 186 Strand" with PM 28 Aug 40 (Friday), may possibly belong with it.

Devonshire Terrace | Friday Evening
My dear Sir,

My feelings will not admit of my doing more than acknowledging the receipt of your note and enclosures, and begging you to transmit to Mrs. Hall (*without delay*) the enclosed outpouring of a grateful heart.[1]

Faithfully yours,
[CHARLES DICKENS]

## *To* JOHN FORSTER, [2 SEPTEMBER 1840]

Extract in F. II, vii, 147–8. *Date:* 2 Sep according to Forster. *From* Broadstairs.

I have been at work of course and have just finished a number. I have effected a reform by virtue of which we breakfast at a quarter before eight, so that I get to work at half-past, and am commonly free by one o'clock or so, which is a great happiness. Dick is now Sampson's clerk, and I have touched Miss Brass in Number 25, lightly, but effectively I hope.[2]

## *To* DANIEL MACLISE, 2 SEPTEMBER 1840†

MS Berg Collection.

The Lawn House Broadstairs. | September 2nd. 1840.
My Dear Maclise.

*a*Since that melancholy night when we parted in Covent Garden I have been hard at work; you must therefore consider this in the light of "a trifle from Broadstairs" which is of no intrinsic worth and is only valuable for the *sender*'s sake.*a*

You know that *we* know Fletcher didn't go into the Sea that day at Ramsgate?[3] Well—I had good corroborative evidence yesterday. Seeing me going into one of the Machines he plucked up and said he'd have another. He had the next one. I undressed, went in, waited, still no Fletcher. Determined that he should not escape, I waded under the hood

---

[1] Possibly thanks—from either CD or Catherine—for a christening present for Katey.

[2] Dick becomes Sampson's clerk in Ch. 33 (No. 24, published 12 Sep). Sally Brass is described in the same chapter; she appears in No. 25, but mainly as a foil to her brother.

*aa* Not previously published.

[3] During CD's June visit to Broadstairs, Smithson came over from Ramsgate for the day (*To* Mitton, 14 June), and presumably CD and Maclise paid him a return visit at Ramsgate.

of his bath and seeing him standing with only his coat off, urged him to make haste. In about five minutes more he fell heavily into the water, and feeling the cold, set up a scream which pierced the air! You never heard anything so horrible! And then he splashed like a fleet of Porpoises, roaring most horribly all the time, and dancing a maniac dance which defies description. Such a devil—such a bald, howling, fearful devil in buff, I never beheld.[1]

He distinctly said afterwards that being the *first* time &c &c.

He sketches here, gets beggars and idiots to sit to him on the sands and pier, dresses them in fragments of his own attire (all this, in public) and rewards them with shillings for their pains. He makes acquaintance with old Prout[2] as he sketches the Pier, endeavours to reconcile Miss Collins[3] to [Strivens][4] (the rival bather) goes up into lofts where sails are made, and asks if they can find him half a dozen old apostles to come and sit in the same—and, in short, commits all manner of absurdities. He is decidedly calmer though, than he was in town, but he is as greedy as ever, and he is *here,* and don't say when he'll be anywhere else—there's the Rub.

Come down for a week, come down for a fortnight, come down for three weeks, come down for a month. Arrange to come—arrange to come. It's charming, and the house a most brilliant success—far more comfortable than any we have had.

[a]Alas! There is no intelligence of The Modest Quencher.[5] I have

---

[1] Mrs E. E. Christian has a bathing story about Angus Fletcher too. Mitton, it seems, came running to the house to tell CD that "F——" had "walked out of the sea, without a rag on him, right among the people on the beach". CD rushed off to do what he could, but "found F—— had returned into the water as fast as he got out" ("Reminiscences of CD", *Englishwoman's Domestic Magazine*, x, 338). According to Forster, Fletcher was staying with CD during most of this visit, and CD's letters contained numerous descriptions, "too private for reproduction", of his eccentricities (F, II, viii, 161). But one of these letters Forster could not resist giving—in a footnote to CD's tour of the Highlands: see 20 Sep 40.

[2] Samuel Prout (1783–1852; *DNB*), one of the outstanding water-colour painters of his time and a major contributor to exhibitions of the Society of Painters in Water Colours. A pencil drawing by him of Broadstairs was in a Loan Collection of Drawings by Prout and William Hunt, exhibited at the Fine Art Society's Galleries 1879–80 (see *Notes by Mr. Ruskin on Prout and*

*Hunt*, 1880). At the time of his death CD owned Prout's drawing of Beauvais Cathedral (*Catalogue of the . . . Pictures . . . of CD*, ed. J. H. Stonehouse, 1935, p. 125).

[3] Unidentified. Cf., in *To* Rogers, 22 Mar 42, "Miss Collins the Bather". Possibly the Miss "Collin" who appears, also at Broadstairs, in *To* Leech, 9 Oct 49 (N, II, 179–80), as a drinker.

[4] Name not written clearly; but presumably "Strivens" (not "Strevens"), since three people of this name appear in local directories of 1845. Of these, Miss H. Strivens of 13 Queen Street Ramsgate, seems the most likely.

[a][a] Not previously published.

[5] Normally, something to quench thirst: cf. "Mr. Swiveller replied . . . that he was still open to a modest quencher" (*Old Curiosity Shop*, Ch. 35, No. 25—which CD had been writing that day: see next, *To* Forster). But here the "Alas!" and "shrinking purity" suggest that the phrase is used jokingly of some woman about whom Maclise had inquired—a quencher of ardour. Such jokes at this time were usually about Marion Ely, Talfourd's niece.

explored Ramsgate, lingered in Margate, flitted like a ghost through Saint Peters, and refused to be comforted in Broadstairs—Still no Quencher. The Moozler[1] *I have seen* in that quarter of Margate where Moozlers most do congregate—but the Modest Quenchers—ah! where do *they* preserve their shrinking purity!

The theme grows painful. Kate (forgive me for mentioning her) is quite well and desires her best regards. So are the children, and so do they. So am I, and so do I. And I am always

My Dear Maclise | Heartily Yours

Daniel Maclise Esquire[a]                              CHARLES DICKENS

## *To* JOHN FORSTER, 6 SEPTEMBER 1840

MS Victoria & Albert Museum (FC).

Broadstairs | Sunday 6th. Septr. | 1840.

My Dear Forster.

Just look at this dedication[2] and preface, and let me have a line from you by return.

First of the Preface—Would you say anything more? Would you allude to the mad report?[3] Would you touch on anything else or treat anything differently? If so, say so, and I'll consider it.[4]

Secondly, the Dedication. The reason of it, is there. Would you state it? I think I should.[5]

Your note I got this morning with great pleasure. I have been blundering over the Preface so long that I'm deadly stupid and can't answer it.

Faithfully Always

CD.

---

[1] Perhaps a corruption of "muzzler", one who drinks to excess (cf. "muzzle", *v*. 2, *OED*). Just conceivably Talfourd. Cf. Macready's diary-entry for 11 Sep 40: "Maclise, Forster and Talfourd came to dine . . . Talfourd grew so tipsy that he quite impeded conversation" (*Diaries*, II, 79).

[2] Of *Master Humphrey*, to Rogers: see below.

[3] A rumour had been circulated, apparently quite extensively, that CD was mentally deranged and under treatment in an asylum (see F, II, viii, 160). No newspaper source for it has been found.

[4] The original Preface (MS V & A) to Vol. I of *Master Humphrey* ended "and the clock will be about to stop for ever". For CD's additions to it, see *To* Forster, Sep 40, *fn*, p. 126.

[5] CD's uncertainty shows that the dedication he was enclosing was the one he afterwards discarded. It read: "To | Samuel Rogers | One of the Few Men | (qy.) | Whom Riches and Honors | Have Not Spoiled, | And who Have Preserved | In High Places | Active Sympathy With | The Poorest | And Humblest | Of Their Kind, | These Unworthy Pages | Are Dedicated | By | His Faithful Friend" (MS Forster Collection, V & A). The "(qy.)", written between lines 3 and 4, clearly referred to line 4. Forster probably advised against this dedication on the grounds that Rogers deeply disliked any mention of his wealth (see, e.g., Harriet Martineau, *Biographical Sketches, 1852–1875*, 1885, p. 369). For the dedication published instead, see next.

## To SAMUEL ROGERS, [?8 or 9 SEPTEMBER 1840]

MS Victoria & Albert Museum (FC). *Date:* probably two days or three after last, Forster having no doubt replied by return as CD requested.

### TO SAMUEL ROGERS ESQUIRE

My Dear Sir.

Let me have *my* Pleasures of Memory[1] in connection with this book by dedicating it to a Poet whose writings (as all the World knows) are replete with generous and earnest feeling; and to a man whose daily life (as all the world does not know) is one of active sympathy with the poorest and humblest of his kind.

Your faithful friend

CHARLES DICKENS[2]

## To JOHN FORSTER, [?9 SEPTEMBER 1840]

Extract in F, II, vii, 148. *Date:* This and next letter are both dated 9 Sep by Forster, but surely mistakenly; for the two mornings referred to are obviously different. Impossible to be sure which was the earlier of the two; but 9 Sep seems a probable date for his beginning No. 27 (Chs 38 and 39) with which Vol. II opened (on Sun 13 Sep he had a corrected proof of No. 26 to send Forster). *From* Broadstairs.

I have opened the second volume with Kit;[3] and I saw this morning looking out at the sea, as if a veil had been lifted up, an affecting thing that I can do with him bye and bye.[4] Nous verrons.

[1] The title of Rogers's best known poem, published 1792.

[2] This dedication was published in No. 26 on 26 Sep. It appeared at the beginning of *Master Humphrey* when the 26 weekly Nos were collected and published as Vol. I (on 15 Oct). When *Old Curiosity Shop* and *Barnaby* were detached from *Master Humphrey* and published separately (1841), the dedication was given to *Old Curiosity Shop*—while in his Preface to *Barnaby* (originally the Preface to *Master Humphrey*, Vol. III) CD acknowledged his indebtedness to Rogers for a "beautiful thought" in *Old Curiosity Shop*, Ch. 72, taken from "Ginevra" (in Rogers's *Italy, a Poem*): "And long might'st thou have seen | An old man wandering *as in quest of something,* | Something he could not find—he knew not what" (CD's italics). Cf. CD's: "wandered here and there as seeking something".

[3] Clearly the decision that Nell should die had been made before CD opened Vol. II. Forster, stressing his own responsibility for the tragic ending (a claim supported by *To* Forster, ?17 Jan 41), says: "He had not thought of killing her, when, about half way through, I asked him to consider whether it did not necessarily belong even to his own conception" (F, II, vii, 151). But C. E. Lester's account of his visit to CD in July implies that Forster's suggestion had been made rather earlier than "half way through". To Lester's hope that Nell would "find a quiet and happy home" CD (who had probably just finished No. 19, containing Chs 23 and 24) replied: "I hardly know what to do. But if you ever hear of her death in a future number of the Clock, you shall say that she died as she lived" (*The Glory and Shame of England*, II, 15).

[4] Almost certainly Kit's arriving at Nell's house, her birdcage in his hand, not knowing that "the strong heart of [the bird's] child mistress was mute and motionless for ever" (Chs 70 and 71). That CD attached importance to this is shown in his later plan for No. 43 (see *To* Forster, 16 Dec, *fn*).

## *To* JOHN FORSTER, [SEPTEMBER 1840]

Extract in F, II, viii, 160. *Date:* not the same day as last, as given by Forster, but in the same week. CD had corrected the proof of the Preface by 13 Sep (see *To* Forster, that day, *fn*). *From* Broadstairs.

I was just going to work when I got this letter, and the story of the man who went to Chapman and Hall's knocked me down flat.[1] I wrote until now (a quarter to one) against the grain, and have at last given it up for one day. Upon my word it is intolerable. I have been grinding my teeth all the morning. I think I could say in two lines something about the general report with propriety. I'll add them to the proof, giving you full power to cut them out if you should think differently from me, and from C and H, who in such a matter must be admitted judges.[2]

## *To* JOHN FORSTER, 13 SEPTEMBER 1840

MS Victoria & Albert Museum (FC).

Broadstairs | Sunday Morning 13th. Septr./40.

My Dear Forster.

I send you the proofs of 26[3]—cut here and there, but not otherwise corrected.[4] *I* am decidedly for the mention in the Preface, leaving out the

[1] The new rumour perhaps concerned his "place of confinement" (see *fn* below).

[2] On returning the proof CD also sent a page in MS, headed "To form the *last* paragraph of the Preface", which dealt with the "mad report". A second proof was then run off, incorporating the new last paragraph. In this, perhaps on Forster's or Chapman & Hall's advice, CD cancelled (after mention of the "report that he had gone raving mad") "has been made a subject of grave discussion in England, Ireland, Scotland, America, Germany, France, and the East and West Indies". He then drafted the following addition (on the back of the proof): "and was made the subject of much great discussion occasioning some strong disputation relative to his exact place of confinement; one party inclining to St. Luke's, another insisting peremptorily on Bedlam, and a third happening to know on circumstantial evidence quite as indisputable as Sir Benjamin Backbite's" [the MS ends in mid-sentence]. This also he cancelled, and finally wrote on the back of the same proof the passage "was made

the subject of considerable dispute . . . Northamptonshire" which (with three minor alterations made to the lines on Backbite's "evidence" in Forster's hand) appeared in the printed Preface.

Apart from the new last paragraph, the only significant addition to the first proof had been the sentence (perhaps suggested by Forster: see 6 Sep): "It was never the intention of the Author to make the Members of Master Humphrey's clock, active agents in the stories they are supposed to relate." (The first and second proofs, with the various MS additions, are all in the Forster Collection, V & A.)

[3] I.e. of *Old Curiosity Shop*, Ch. 37 and the Preface, published 26 Sep—the last weekly number in Vol. I.

[4] I.e. leaving their final correction to Forster. This division of labour on the proofs probably dates from the beginning of CD's present visit to Broadstairs, with which the first *Old Curiosity Shop* proofs preserved in the Forster Collection (V & A) coincide. Of Chs 44 and 45 there are two sets of proofs, one marked by CD, the other by Forster; and comparison of the two shows how

word "raving" which you will see I have struck out.[1] Kate is for it too—Mitton against.[2]

What do you think of the quotation in the title page?[3] To be, or not to be? I'm not particular.

Mitton sublimely absurd[4]—Fletcher horribly mad[5]—further particulars in future bills.

Always Faithfully
CD.

the work was divided on this occasion—and probably on many others also. CD marked the cuts to be made, and a few alterations and insertions. These Forster copied into his own set, making a few stylistic alterations himself, and adding heavily to CD's very sketchy punctuation. Sometimes the cutting of the number was left to Forster too: see, e.g., 16 Dec 40 (and, for *Barnaby*, 26 Mar and 29 Apr 41). While CD was out of London the proofs clearly went first to Forster, who forwarded them, sometimes with suggestions (see, e.g., 4 Oct 40); CD, after working on them, returned them to Forster, who made the final corrections on his own set which he then sent to the printer. Even after CD's return to London it was usually Forster's set which went to press: 19 out of the 28 chapters (or part-chapters) of *Old Curiosity Shop* surviving in proof in the V & A are marked in his hand. Several bear marginal instructions such as: "*I hope I have taken out enough*—but if I have not, you must cancel this par. Let it stand if possible. J.F.*"—of the penultimate paragraph in Ch. 47; and "Let this stand unless it is *necessary* that it should come out. J.F.*"—of the two paragraphs before the last in Ch. 48. (Both stood.) Ch. 48 he endorsed: "Send me revises in the morning"—clearly because the No. contained two long deletions.

[1] "Raving" is retained before "mad" in the Preface, having first been deleted in proof, then restored. Reviewing the book in the *Athenæum*, 7 Nov, Thomas Hood wrote: "We are rejoiced to learn, from so good an authority as his own preface, that in spite of certain crazy rumours to the contrary, he has never been 'raving mad' and we sincerely and seriously trust that he never will be 'off his head', except when, like Quilp's

urchin, he chooses to be on his feet."

[2] On 13 Sep Macready was consulted about the Preface by Forster, and "made objections" (*Diaries*, II, 80).

[3] Under the title and his name, CD had written into the proof a quotation from Addison's "The Uses of the Spectator" (*Spectator*, 12 Mar 1710), beginning: "I know several of my friends and well-wishers are in great pain for me, lest I should not be able to keep up the spirit of a paper which I oblige myself to furnish weekly; but to make them easy in this particular, I will promise them faithfully to give it over, as soon as I grow dull." Presumably Forster advised against it; for it was omitted on publication.

[4] Cf. Mrs Christian: "Mr. Mitton's laughter began with an abrupt *bray* and terminated in such an extraordinary sound that it was invariably provocative of mirth in every one else. No one caused so much merriment to Dickens as this friend ... I have known him to be sitting apart in apparently deaf-and-dumb abstraction, when Mitton would give out some fresh absurdity which caused Dickens to break into a chuckle of intense enjoyment; this success would act on the other as a further incentive, and he then became utterly ungovernable" ("Recollections of CD", *Temple Bar*, LXXXII [1888], p. 487).

[5] Written with some feeling, no doubt. See Mrs Christian's anecdote linking Fletcher's eccentricities with the "rumour flying about that Dickens had gone insane". During a walk on the beach, with Fletcher "behaving in a very flighty manner", some strangers passing stopped to look after him. " 'Ah', said one, with a lugubrious look ..., 'you see it's quite true! Poor Boz! What a pity to see such a wreck!' Dickens scowled at them, and then

Will you let Henry in his spare time look out the Clock MS, that I may "arrange" it when I come home?[1]
Anxiously expecting yours.

## To JOHN FORSTER, [15 SEPTEMBER 1840]

Extract in F, II, viii, 160–1. *Date:* 15 Sep according to Forster. *From* Broadstairs.

I have been rather surprised of late to have applications from roman-catholic clergymen, demanding (rather pastorally, and with a kind of grave authority) assistance, literary employment, and so forth. At length it struck me, that, through some channel or other, I must have been represented as belonging to that religion. Would you believe, that in a letter from Lamert[2] at Cork, to my mother, which I saw last night, he says "What do the papers mean by saying that Charles is demented, and further, *that he has turned roman-catholic?*"—![3]

called out, 'Hollo, F——, I wish you'd moderate your insane gambollings! There are fools among the British public who might mistake you for me' " ("Reminiscences of CD", *Englishwoman's Domestic Magazine*, x, 338).

[1] *Old Curiosity Shop* is the first novel of which the MS survives complete. By "arrange" CD presumably meant detach the novel from *Master Humphrey*, with a view to separate publication at some future date (cf. *To* Miss Coutts, 20 Apr 41 and *fn*). Possibly at the same time he separated the Weller episodes (now preserved in the Forster Collection, V & A, although the other "Master Humphrey" sections are lost).

[2] Matthew Lamert (1774–1848), born in Germany; had had a distinguished and adventurous career as an Army surgeon; wounded at Alexandria 1801 and thanked in General Orders for care of the sick at Gibraltar 1813. Stationed at Chatham on half-pay as a widower with five children, he married in Dec 1821 Mrs Mary Allen (*née* Barrow), widowed elder sister of CD's mother. James Lamert, who first took the young CD to the Theatre Royal, Rochester, *c.* 1821 (R. Langton, *The*

*Childhood and Youth of CD*, 1883, p. 53) and was managing Warren's blacking warehouse when CD worked in it 1824, was his son according to Forster and Langton—but not one of the five children above, so presumably illegitimate. Soon after his marriage Matthew moved to Cork where his wife died Sep 1822. In 1824 married Susanna Travers; in 1830 became Deputy Inspector-General of Military Hospitals. Died in Cork. He left a graphic MS record of his experiences in many campaigns 1795–1810. Forster had no doubt that he was the original of Dr Slammer in *Pickwick* (F, I, i, 7).

[3] Cf. letter from W. B. Hodgson to a Mr Wotherspoon, 28 Sep 41: " 'Humphrey's Clock', every Saturday, is a great relief to me. When I read there No Popery Riot stories, however, I ask myself, 'are we one jot better now?' Dickens, I am told, is a Roman Catholic; Catholic, in the best sense, he is, whether Roman, or Greek, or aught else" (*Life and Letters of W. B. Hodgson*, ed. J. M. D. Meiklejohn, Edinburgh, 1883, pp. 36–7). No newspaper report of his becoming a Roman Catholic has been found.

## *To* JOHN FORSTER, [20 SEPTEMBER 1840]

Extract in F, ii, xi, 182*n*. *Date:* 20 Sep according to Forster. *From* Broadstairs.

Mrs. M.[1] being in the next machine the other day heard him[2] howl like a wolf (as he does) when he first touched the cold water. I am glad to have my former story in that respect confirmed. There is no sound on earth like it. In the infernal regions there may be, but elsewhere there is no compound addition of wild beasts that could produce its like for their total. The description of the wolves in *Robinson Crusoe* is the nearest thing; but it's feeble—very feeble—in comparison.

An alarming report being brought to me the other day that he was preaching, I betook myself to the spot and found he was reading Wordsworth[3] to a family on the terrace, outside the house, in the open air and public way. The whole town were out. When he had given them a taste of Wordsworth, he sent home for Mrs. Norton's book,[4] and entertained them with selections from that. He concluded with an imitation of Mrs. Hemans[5] reading her own poetry, which he performed with a pocket-handkerchief over his head to imitate her veil[6]—all this in public, before everybody.

## *To* JOHN FORSTER, [21 SEPTEMBER 1840]

Extract in F, ii, vii, 148. *Date:* "twelve days later" than letter of 9 Sep according to Forster: i.e. twelve days had passed between CD's beginning No. 27 and receiving a letter written by Forster after reading it in proof. This interval seems likely. *From* Broadstairs.

I am glad you like that Kit number[.][7] I thought you would. I have altered that about the opera-going. Of course I had no intention to delude the many-headed into a false belief concerning opera nights, but merely to specify a class of senators.[8] I needn't have done it, however, for God knows they're pretty well all alike.

[1] Clearly Mrs Macready: see ?13 Nov 40. Misprinted as "Mrs N." in J. W. T. Ley's edition of F.

[2] Angus Fletcher.

[3] Whom he knew personally. Fletcher's mother now lived at Grasmere; he had spent the earlier part of the summer with her, and they had together seen the Wordsworths frequently (*Autobiography of Mrs Fletcher, of Edinburgh*, privately printed, Carlisle, 1874, pp. 214–15).

[4] Probably *The Dream, and Other Poems*, 1840.

[5] Felicia Dorothea Hemans (1793–1835; *DNB*), poetess; immensely popular, in her day, in both England and America. Her complete works had recently been published in 7 vols (Edinburgh, 1839). Perhaps best remembered now as author of "The boy stood on the burning deck". Fletcher had exhibited busts of her at the Liverpool Academy in 1830 and 1832.

[6] The veil, shown in portraits, was an idiosyncrasy of hers in a period when women wore caps by day, and had a choice of hats, berets, turbans, toques, ribbons, combs &c, for the evening.

[7] No. 27 (Chs 38 and 39; published 3 Oct), recounting Kit's meeting with the single gentleman at the notary's and the visit to Astley's.

[8] The sentence in paragraph four of

## To [JOHN] EDMONDS,[1] [?27 SEPTEMBER] 1840

Extract in Goodspeed's Book Shop catalogue, Nov 1914; *MS* 3rd person;
dated Lawn House, Broadstairs, 1840. *Date:* N, I, 274 mentions a letter
to Mr Edmonds dated 27 Sep 40—very probably the same letter.

*Saying that* when he wants anything more in either way [*jewellery or plate*]
he will have pleasure in ordering it of Mr. Edmonds.

## To HENRY COLBURN, 28 SEPTEMBER 1840

MS Mrs A. M. Stern.

Broadstairs | September 28th. 1840.

Dear Sir.

Having occasion to send some other papers to our friend Mr. Forster, I
have forwarded him the introduction[2] and title to Mrs. Macrone's book,
which he will give you on your application.

Faithfully Yours

Henry Colburn Esquire                    CHARLES DICKENS

## To MESSRS CHAPMAN & HALL, 2 OCTOBER 1840

MS Comtesse de Suzannet.

Broadstairs. | Friday October 2nd. 1840.

Dear Sirs.

I send you eleven slips of MS herewith.[3] I am suffering,—and have
suffered all night, and during the greater part of yesterday—insupportable
torture from some complaint in the face—whether rheumatism, tic
doloreux,[4] or what not, Heaven knows. I have had fomentations of various

Ch. 38 in the published No., which ends "whistled down on Wednesday nights", originally ended with "whistled down". This CD changed in MS to "whistled down by opera-going Senators on Wednesday nights". Challenged by Forster, he made some alteration to the proof—cancelling (if the printed text is to be trusted: the proof itself has disappeared) "by opera-going Senators", but allowing "on Wednesday nights" to stand. But since his letter shows that his aim was to prevent false beliefs about "opera nights", not about opera-goers, the wrong phrase seems to have been cancelled—perhaps by printer's error.

[1] No doubt John Edmonds, jeweller and silversmith, 14 Strand. CD's Account-book (MS Messrs Coutts) shows a payment to "Mr. Edmonds" of £16.5 on 1 Oct 40; the cheque was probably enclosed in this letter.

[2] Dated July 41, it appeared at the beginning of Vol. II of *The Pic Nic Papers*, published 9 Aug 41. It spoke of Macrone as "a young publisher in the prime and vigour of his years" who had died "at the moment when his prospects were brightest and the difficulties of his enterprise were nearly overcome"; said that the book was for the benefit of Mrs Macrone and her children; and (in spite of the numerous delays) ended, on behalf of the contributors: "They are happy to acknowledge the liberality and promptitude of Mr Colburn in seconding their object."

[3] Probably of No. 30 (Chs 44 and 45), published 30 Oct.

[4] Thus in MS.

kinds, but with little or no relief, and am desperately beaten in consequence. I am as bad as Miss Squeers—screaming out loud all the time I
write.[1]

Yours inflammatorily and despondingly<br>
CHARLES DICKENS

I haven't the heart to flourish.[2]

## *To* JOHN FORSTER, [4 OCTOBER 1840]

Extract in F, II, vii, 148. *Date:* 4 Oct according to Forster. *From* Broadstairs.

You will receive the proof herewith. I have altered it. You must let it
stand now.[3] I really think the dead mankind a million fathoms deep, the
best thing in the sentence.[4] I have a notion of the dreadful silence down
there, and of the stars shining down upon their drowned eyes—the fruit,
let me tell you, of a solitary walk by starlight on the cliffs. As to the child-
image I have made a note of it for alteration.[5] In number thirty there will
be some cutting needed, I think. I have, however, something in my eye
near the beginning which I can easily take out.[6] You will recognize a

---

[1] See *Nickleby*, Ch. 15.

[2] I.e. to make the flourish under his signature.

[3] The alterations Forster had urged were probably all to the first few paragraphs of Ch. 42 (No. 29), in the third of which comes the phrase quoted by CD in his next sentence. In that paragraph CD deleted in the proof "with Heaven and Earth" after "and she was alone", and substituted "stars" for "planets". At the end of the next paragraph he deleted "avoided speaking with her if he could, and while he loved her no less than before" after "he evaded all inquiry." Further cuts later in the chapter are scarcely of the sort to have been inspired by Forster.

[4] The description is of Nell's seeing the reflection of the stars in the river, "shining in the same majestic order as when the dove beheld them gleaming through the swollen waters, upon the mountain tops down far below, and dead mankind, a million fathoms deep". The last phrase is underlined and marked with a query in the proof—by CD, presumably while considering Forster's comment on it.

[5] Probably refers to the image used of Nell at the end of the third paragraph of Ch. 43, deleted (not altered) in proof: "and the child of that night was no more the child of yesterday, than the bleak bare heath on which she stopped to rest with the cold night-sky above, were fitting couch and canopy for one so young and tender".

[6] After paragraph five of Ch. 44, a passage of 29 lines is deleted in the proof—clearly by CD (copied in Forster's proof: see 13 Sep, *fn*). It compared the poor cottages of the open countryside Nell and her grandfather had left with the "stys, in which the working townsmen . . . huddled"—in filthy courts, "big with fever, loathsome humours, madness, and a long ghastly train of ills". " 'Misery! Pooh, pooh! I don't believe a word of it' ", said a portly well-fed gentleman that very night. After paragraph ten there is another deletion, of 14 lines in which Nell cheerfully encouraged the distraught old man although "there was something in the action with which she pressed her hand upon her drooping heart, sorely at variance with her speech" (Forster Collection, V & A).

description of the road we travelled between Birmingham and Wolver-hampton:[1] but I had conceived it so well in my mind that the execution doesn't please me quite as well as I expected.[2] I shall be curious to know whether you think there's anything in the notion of the man and his furnace-fire.[3] It would have been a good thing to have opened a new story with, I have been thinking since.


## *To* SAMUEL ROGERS, 4 OCTOBER 1840*

MS University of Kentucky.

Broadstairs | Sunday Night Octr. 4th./40.

My Dear Sir

I send you my paper,[4] in case you should not have seen one. I should have sent you at the same time yesterday's Clock, but not knowing where you may have left off, forbear to bore you with it on the chance.

Further of these 'shoulds'. I should have come to see you to day, but I have been troubled with a raging face, and being out for a few minutes was visited by certain admonitory symptoms which sent me home again, faster than I came out.

I am always My Dear Sir

Heartily Yours

Samuel Rogers Esquire.                          CHARLES DICKENS

Compts. to Mr. Maltby.[5]

---

[1] On their visit to Birmingham six months before. In Ch. 45 Nell and her grandfather cover the same ground.

[2] Presumably CD is referring here to his description of the industrial scene—smoke-blackened suburbs, interminable factory chimneys, shrieking machinery, derelict houses, &c—not to the melo-dramatic description he imposed on this of a violent mob made up of people who were, as Humphry House has said, "not Chartists, but ... typical of what a great part of the industrial workers were thought to be in the Chartist period, a barbarous and awful horde" (*The Dickens World*, 1941, pp. 179–80). The terror of the mob was fully developed a year later in *Barnaby*.

[3] Which had been "nurse" to him when his mother died and his father reared him, secretly at first, in its ashes) and was now his friend and book: "We talk and think together, all night long" (Ch. 44).

[4] Presumably No. 26 of *Master Humphrey*, which contained the dedica-tion to Rogers. (For similar uses of the word see *To* Williams, 31 Mar 40, and Macready, *Diaries*, II, 70.) No. 26 was now a week old; but CD may have kept it until he could deliver it by hand on Rogers's arrival at Broadstairs.

[5] William Maltby (1763–1854; *DNB*), lifelong friend of Samuel Rogers: see Vol. I, p. 643*n*. It was probably only as an appendage of Rogers that CD met him—e.g., on 31 Jan 41, when dining with Rogers (Macready, *Diaries*, II, 118).

## *To* THOMAS MITTON, 6 OCTOBER [1840]*

MS University of Texas. *Date:* presumably 6 Oct 40, since on 7 Oct Mitton paid £20 into CD's bank (Account-book, MS Messrs Coutts); handwriting supports. *Address:* Private | Thomas Mitton Esquire | 23 Southampton Buildings | Chancery Lane | London.

Broadstairs | 6th. October

My Dear Mitton

If you succeeded in drawing the needful, I wish you would pay that £20 into Coutts's for me, *directly*,[1] if possible. I had overlooked a payment of £60,[2] which, with the expences of leaving here, will run me for a few weeks very near indeed.[3]

Should you want it again in a month or so, of course you can have it.

Faithfully Always

CD.

All well.

## *To* SAMUEL ROGERS, 7 OCTOBER [1840]

Mention in Goodspeeds Book Shop catalogue, Jan 1910; dated Broadstairs, Wed 7 Oct—presumably 1840, the only year in which CD was at Broadstairs on that date.

## *To* JOHN FORSTER, 12 OCTOBER [1840]

MS Victoria & Albert Museum (FC). *Date:* 12 Oct was Monday in 1840; handwriting supports that year. *Address:* John Forster Esquire.

Devonshire Terrace. | Monday 12th. October.

My Dear Forster.

I have a few letters to write, which will take me an hour or so to finish. I will be with you between One and Two.

Faithfully Always

CD.

I didn't hear your ring last night. *Did* you pull the bell?

[1] Underlined twice.

[2] On 14 Oct CD's account-book (MS Messrs Coutts) shows a payment of £59.18.6 to "Miles & Co"—possibly Edmund Miles & Co., West Indian Merchants, of Throgmorton Street; or Miles & Edwards, furniture-printers, upholsterers and cabinet manufacturers, of 134 Oxford Street.

[3] After Chapman & Hall's payment to him of £200 on 14 Oct, he had about £80 in his account; their next payment (£200) was on 6 Nov. On 17 Oct CD told Macready of the "heavy expenses of *Humphrey's Clock* eating up so very much of the profits" (*Diaries*, II, 90). The illustrations were doubtless the main expense. The provision of two woodcuts to each weekly number meant that each monthly part had a minimum of eight—against the usual two steel engravings a month of *Pickwick*, *Oliver* and *Nickleby*. Although "woodcuts dropped into the text" were cheaper than steel engravings, such an increase in the number provided monthly must have more than offset the saving on them.

*To* THOMAS SIBSON, [12 OCTOBER 1840]

Mention in next.


*To* WILLIAM SMITH WILLIAMS,[1] 12 OCTOBER 1840

Text from N, I, 275.

Devonshire Terrace | 12th Octr. 1840

My dear Sir,

I have just returned to town after six weeks' absence, and hasten to thank you for your friendly congratulations and good wishes, which I do, most cordially.

I have written to Mr. Sibson[2] by this Post.

Believe me | Faithfully yours
[CHARLES DICKENS]


*To* GEORGE CATTERMOLE, 13 OCTOBER 1840

Photograph, Dickens House.

Devonshire Terrace. | 13th. October 1840

My Dear Cattermole

All the Clock Corps dine here on Tuesday next, at Six for half past exactly, to celebrate the completion of the first Volume. You have shewn

---

[1] William Smith Williams (1800–75), book-keeper since 1827 to Hullmandel & Walter, lithograph printers. Originally apprenticed to Taylor & Hessey, publishers of the *London Magazine*; had come to know Leigh Hunt, Keats and Hazlitt, and had contributed to the *Spectator* and *Athenæum*. Employed by George Smith 1845–75 as Smith, Elder's reader and general publication manager; soon on cordial terms with Thackeray, Ruskin, Charlotte Brontë and G. H. Lewes (whose radical opinions he and his family evidently shared: see *The George Eliot Letters*, ed. G. S. Haight, 1954–6, I, lxviii).

[2] Thomas Sibson (1817–44; *DNB*), artist; self-taught through assiduous sketching (over 1400 of his sketches are now in the Print Room, BM). Published, in weekly issues without text, *Sibson's Racy Sketches of Expeditions, from the Pickwick Club*, 1838 (10 etchings illustrating *Pickwick*), *Sibson's*

*Sketches of Life and Humour*, 1838, and *Illustrations of Master Humphrey's Clock*, 72 etchings, in 18 monthly parts, published Tyas, 1840–1, and in 2 vols, 1842. Illustrated part of the Abbotsford edn of the Waverley novels. A close friend of W. J. Linton, and of William Bell Scott who considered that his Dickens illustrations were on a higher level than those of "the astonishingly facile Phiz", who "owned that he never carried a sketch-book, and never made a memorandum from nature in his life!" (*Autobiographical Notes of the Life of William Bell Scott*, ed. W. Minto, 1892, I, 206). For reproductions of his *Pickwick* illustrations see Joseph Grego, *Pictorial Pickwickiana*, 1899. Grego points out their most striking quality—"a dashing *abandon* ... an exuberance of life, action, and movement in harmony with the sprightly narrative by which they were inspired" (I, 453).

your interest in the matter too well to leave me in any doubt of your joining us, and joining us heartily. Therefore I count upon you.

*My* missis's love to your'n,—and mine.

Faithfully Yours always

George Cattermole Esquire                     CHARLES DICKENS

## *To* CHARLES GRAY,[1] 13 OCTOBER 1840

MS Berg Collection.

1 Devonshire Terrace | York Gate, Regents Park
13th. October 1840.

Mr. Charles Dickens sends his compliments to Mr. Gray, and if he has no better engagement for next Tuesday, begs the favor of his company to dinner (at Six o'Clock for half past punctually) to meet their fellow-labourers in the Clock, and celebrate the completion of the first Volume.

## *To* [R. S. HORRELL],[2] 14 OCTOBER 1840

MS Public Library of Victoria, Melbourne.

1 Devonshire Terrace, York Gate | Regents Park London
14th. October 1840.

Sir.

I should have answered your letter immediately after you sent it to me, had it reached my hands. But as I have been out of town for nearly two months, and as letters addressed to my publishers' are not forwarded to me at those times (being seldom important, and being usually of that kind from which I am anxious to escape) I did not receive your communication until this morning.

The great pressure and extent of my correspondence, added to my other occupations, oblige me to be a man of very few words in my epistolary conversation. First, let me say that I am sincerely and truly interested in the labours and aspirations of all young men. And secondly, that if you wish me to read your poems or any of them, I will cheerfully do so.

But, to this I must add that such a task is to me a very painful one, for I

---

[1] Charles Gray (*d.* 1845), engraver, born in Newcastle; apprenticed, with Landells, to Thomas Bewick's pupil Isaac Nicholson. George Dalziel was his pupil 1835–9. Engraved Browne's three illustrations to *Sunday under Three Heads*; and 74 of the illustrations to *Master Humphrey*.

[2] Robert Sydney Horrell, who wrote to CD under the assumed name of "S. Harford" (see subscription). CD only

addressed him by his real name in his seventh, and last, letter to him (2 Dec 42). N, I, 276*n* identifies him as a young solicitor's clerk at Exeter who later went to Australia for his health. The catalogue of the Pickwick Exhibition held in the Public Library of Victoria 1936 adds that he died in Australia of consumption shortly after CD's last letter to him, still in his twenties.

know, before I enter upon it, that I can do you no service. The influence I have with publishers is solely and entirely personal. While they care for me, they care nothing for my recommendation, as it does not carry profit with it; and I cannot call to mind any one instance in which it has been productive of any good result.

You will therefore place me in the distressing situation, either of telling you that I do not think your productions more likely to succeed than a thousand others which have been languishing in mothy manuscript and vainly trying to burst into butterfly type, for years; or that I consider them very good, and can do no more. But if either of these dicta would give you the smallest satisfaction, believe me that I shall be very happy to be the means towards such an end.

Faithfully Yours

S. Harford Esquire              CHARLES DICKENS

## *To* THOMAS HILL, 14 OCTOBER [1840]*

MS Berg Collection. *Date:* 14 Oct was Wednesday in 1840.

Devonshire Terrace. | Wednesday 14th. October

My Dear Sir.

Designers, printers, publishers, wood-cutters—in short, the whole of the works of Master Humphrey's Clock dine here next Tuesday at Six for half past exactly, to celebrate the completion of the first Volume. I look upon you as an essential part of the publication; and count surely on your joining us.

I regretted to hear from my brother Fred,[1] that you had not been very well—though I look upon your being anything but well and cheerful, as a sort of practical joke; not an agreeable thing, but still a thing too preposterous to be considered seriously.[2]

Always Heartily Yours

Thomas Hill Esquire              CHARLES DICKENS

## *To* W. G. TAUNTON,[3] 14 OCTOBER 1840*

MS New York Public Library.

Devonshire Terrace, York Gate. | Regents Park London<br>14th. October 1840.

My Dear Sir.

My father tells me you want an autograph of Mr. Macready's. I have looked among his notes, and have turned up the inclosed, which has

[1] Frederick William Dickens (1820–1868): see Vol. I, p. 47*n*.

[2] Hill was suffering from a severe chill caught at Rouen that autumn, but was at the Clock dinner on 20 Oct. He died on 20 Dec, after a fall in his chambers, aged 80.

[3] Unidentified. Perhaps a Devonshire acquaintance of John Dickens.

nothing in its contents to make its presentation to you, treasonable. I shall be extremely happy to see you if you ever come to town; and begging my compliments to your sister, am

W. G. Taunton Esquire

Faithfully Yours

CHARLES DICKENS

## *To* WALTER SAVAGE LANDOR, [?MID-OCTOBER 1840]*

MS Berg Collection. *Date:* 1840 on handwriting; Forster's letter on the back[1] seems likely to have been an invitation for a few days in London after a visit Landor paid to Cheltenham in mid-Oct.

My Dear Landor.

Here is a small sign-manual which includes a great deal—all manner of hearty recollections and cordial wishes, and all the friendly things you can think of. Come up to London forthwith, and go back when the Railroad's finished[2]—not an hour sooner.

Faithfully Yours always

BOZ.

(the short signature for convenience)

## *To* J. P. HARLEY, 16 OCTOBER [1840]*

MS Johns Hopkins University. *Date:* 16 Oct was Friday in 1840; handwriting supports that year.

Devonshire Terrace. | Friday October 16th.

My Dear Harley.

The *works* of the Clock-printers, publishers, designers, engravers, and wood-cutters, dine here on the completion of the accompanying Volume, next Tuesday at 6 for half past exactly. Don't tell me that they have put up anything at 'the Garden' which will prevent your joining us—don't, there's a worthy fellow.[3]

J. P. Harley Esquire

Faithfully Yours always

CHARLES DICKENS

[1] On the back is a fragment of a letter from Forster (out of which CD's note has been cut), which reads: "and that before you return to Bath you will come to London. *Do come for a few*".

[2] I.e. stay a long time: the Great Western Railway to Bath was not finished until June 1841.

[3] Harley jotted down his reply on p. 3 of CD's invitation: "Tuesday next is a good day as the bill stands. | Many thanks for Master Humphrey—my old Friends 'Pick' & Nick will be most happy to find Room for such an excellent Companion."

## *To* W. C. MACREADY, 20 OCTOBER 1840*

MS Morgan Library.

Tuesday Morning Octr. 20th. 1840

My Dear Macready.

Many thanks for the offer. If he[1] attends you here, and lends a hand in waiting at dinner, he will be of great service[2] I have no doubt.

I have thought of nothing but that Tragedy[3]—until last night; and since then, I have thought of nothing but Werner.[4]

Faithfully Yours ever

CD.

## *To* DANIEL MACLISE, 25 OCTOBER 1840*

MS Benoliel Collection. *Address:* Daniel Maclise Esquire | 14 Russell Place.

Sunday Morning | 25th. Octr. 1840.

My Dear Maclise

I promised to call on the modern Michael Angelo—Patric Park[5]—to arrange about Sittings, at *Two* to-day. If you are not painting, will you call

[1] Macready's "servant in livery" (*Diaries*, II, 75).

[2] At the Clock Dinner, no doubt. Macready had recorded the day before: "Forster gave me a mem. of the toasts to be drunk at Dickens's dinner to-morrow. What would I not do for dear Dickens?—but I had rather take so many doses of physic than drink my own toasts; 'the misérable!' " (*Diaries*, II, 90). An undated memorandum in the Forster Collection (Forster's hand) reads: "Toasts for The Clock Dinner | The Clock—Talfourd | Mrs Dickens Macready | Publishers Dickens | Printers Dickens | The Artists Forster | Wood Engravers Dickens | Macready Talfourd | Talfourd Macready | Forster Dickens | Harley Forster | And then Everybody proposes everything" (MS V & A). Forster relates this (F, II, ix, 167) to the second Clock Dinner, 10 Apr 41, but surely—in the light of Macready's diary entry—mistakenly. The month October is moreover supported by the following pencil endorsement, probably in Browne's hand: "Hablot Browne | Monday 31st. October | At 6 for ½ past 6 | 33 Howland Street | Fitzroy Sq.". (31 Oct 40 was a Saturday not Monday, but this would have been an easy slip on such a festive occasion.)

[3] Presumably this refers to Gerald Griffin's *Gisippus* which Macready had read to CD, Catherine, Forster and Maclise on 17 Oct. "All were delighted with it", he recorded (*Diaries*, II, 90). He produced it at Drury Lane 1842, and it ran for 20 nights. In *A New Spirit of the Age* R. H. Horne lists with sarcasm "the much-puffed *Gisippus*" as one of the "many great 'discoveries' " of Macready's which had vanished for ever.

[4] Macready had acted Werner (see ?6 May 41 and *fn*) at the Haymarket the night before.

[5] Patric Park (1811–55; *DNB*), sculptor, born in Glasgow. Began as a stone-cutter; studied under Thorwaldsen in Rome 1831–3, with the help of the Duke of Hamilton. Executed many large-scale heroic works, but made his living by portrait-busts, his sitters including Napoleon III, Macaulay and Thomas Campbell. Exhibited a bust of CD in the 16th Annual Exhibition of the Royal Scottish Academy 1843, another bust of him at the RA 1843, and a plaster head RA 1844. Elected an Associate of the Royal Scottish Academy 1849.

there with me? After that, the day being very fine, I should propose a walk 'till dinner.

Any way, I'll call upon you at a quarter before Two. If you're at work, reject me.

Forster being here last night, I sent to you, but you were otherwise and better engaged.

Faithfully Always

C.D.

## *To* EDWARD MOXON, 27 OCTOBER 1840

Extract in Parke-Bernet Galleries catalogue No. 262; *MS* 1 p.; dated Devonshire Terrace, 27 Oct 40.

Will you have the goodness to send me at your convenience, a copy of each of your famous reprints[1] (except the Shakespeare) and two copies of Beaumont and Fletcher,[2] as I want to make a present of one of them.[3]

*a*I include the Campbell in one volume, of course; Charles Lamb too by the bye, except the letters,[4] which I have.*a*

## *To* JOHN OVERS, 27 OCTOBER [1840]*

MS Berg Collection. *Date:* 27 Oct was Tuesday in 1840; handwriting supports that year.

Devonshire Terrace. | Tuesday 27th. October

Dear Mr. Overs.

First, with regard to the beautiful little model you have sent me, and which I return herewith. The Lion holds in his right paw, a maltese cross, which is made after this manner

✠

—that is to say, so that all the four parts are broad at the base, and go

---

[1] A very successful series of cheap single-volume edns of English authors, chiefly poets, brought out by Moxon in 1840, most of them priced at 2/6d. The series began in March with Rogers's *Pleasures of Memory and other Poems*, Campbell's *Poetical Works*, Lamb's *Essays of Elia* (2 vols) and *Rosamund Gray*, and Leigh Hunt's *Indicator* and *Companion*. They were followed in April by the vol. of Shelley's *Poetical Works* which led to Moxon's prosecution for blasphemy in 1841 (see *To* Moxon, 5 May 40, *fn*). The series

was praised in the *Examiner*, 15 Mar 40, as showing that the Copyright Bill need be no bar to cheap publications.

[2] *The Works of Beaumont and Fletcher.* With an Introduction by George Darby, 2 vols, 1840.

[3] To Overs (see next).

*aa* Catalogue describes this as a postscript.

[4] *Letters, with a Sketch of his Life by T. N. Talfourd,* 2 vols, 1837, also published by Moxon. It was in the Gad's Hill library at CD's death.

tapering up to the point whence they diverge.[1] Of the present itself, let me assure you that *in feeling* I have it—complete and perfect in all its parts—and that come when it will, it will be nothing new, or strange, or long in coming, to me.

Now, with reference to your letter. It was sent on to me at Broadstairs in Kent where I have been for nearly two months; and, as you may suppose, occasioned me a great deal of pain and surprise. I sat down to answer it a great many times, but I really could not bring myself to discuss the question in writing, and postponed it until I should see you. For I thought you would have that confidence in me, and that assurance within yourself that I could not be offended with what was honest and true in intention, that I never once dreamed of your imputing my silence to any feeling of coldness towards you, or any umbrage I had taken on the score of your communication.

But though I should have contemplated this possibility, I cannot, even now, answer your letter, as I would in speaking to you. I do not know and have never known a man on whom riches and honors have had less corrupting influence than the venerable old gentleman[2] who is the subject of our discussion. I do not know and have never known a more amiable, charitable, or just man in all he says and does. A kinder-hearted or more gentle creature I have never seen. And that he does, every day, a thousand worthy and generous acts, *I know.*

Now, what have I to put against these results of my own reason, observation, and experience, and the evidence of senses which I will not pretend are peculiarly acute, but which I have been accustomed to train to the pursuit of the Truth, and which I believe are as little to be dazzled by the false glitter of the world or its applause as those of most men? This story which is told you by somebody else, and which *must* have relation to some time long ago, or it is a monstrous farce. What do I find in it? That this old man, being then a younger one, had connection with some girl who prostituted herself for money, and had it. I have no reason to believe that he used force, stratagem, or any other arts to attain his object. She must have been a willing and consenting party. Supposing the story to be true,

[1] Overs had sent a model for the carving he afterwards did for CD of the crest used by John Dickens: "a lion couchant, bearing in his dexter paw a Maltese cross", as CD described it to J. O. Marples, 5 Apr 69. Originally granted in 1625 to William Dickens, citizen of London, the crest's true heraldic description is "a lion couchant, or in dexter, a cross patonce, sable". CD never recorded a pedigree in the College of Arms nor established his descent from William Dickens. But he used the crest with the Maltese cross for his book-plate (reproduced on title page of this edition), on his silver, and on many other possessions; and the crest with the true "cross patonce" on the china dinner service specially painted for him by Copeland. See T. P. Cooper in *D*, XVIII (1922), 194–5.

[2] Clearly Samuel Rogers—as evidenced by the almost identical wording of the opening of CD's alternative dedication of *Master Humphrey* (see *To* Forster, 6 Sep, *fn*). Overs had probably written a protest at CD's choice of dedicatee soon after the appearance of the dedication in No. 26 (published 26 Sep).

I find nothing in it but this. And good God if such sins were to be visited upon all of us[1] and to hunt us down through life, what man would escape! You speak of your own daughters. Do you know—*can* you know —that this girl had not gone through the same ordeal a hundred times, and sold her virginity—cheap or dear, according to the buyer's circumstances— over and over again? Consider whether you are not pressing very hard on vices which have been your own no less than his, and whether it would not be honest and right to let virtues which are not everybody's have their fair weight in the other scale.

I cannot write a hundredth part of what I should say, or of what I think, upon this matter. But doing full justice to your honest and upright impulses, I must add that *my faith is not shaken in the least,* and that I very strongly doubt the motives of your authority.

I received, and read, your notes on the Chartist book,[2] some of which I will shew to Mr. Carlyle[3] as I am sure he would be glad to see them. I wish you would bring me one of these Sundays two or three of your songs to choose from.[4] I shall have an opportunity, I hope, at the turn of the year to publish one with your name.[5]

[1] MS reads "us of us".

[2] Carlyle's *Chartism*, 1840. It had been planned as an article on the working classes for the *Quarterly Review*; but when Lockhart "dared not" print it (Carlyle's Journal, quoted by J. A. Froude, *Thomas Carlyle, a History of his Life in London, 1834–1881*, 1884, I, 173), it was published by Fraser as a 5/- booklet in late Dec 39. In it Carlyle put forward his remedies for "the-condition-of-England-question"— education and emigration. He had anticipated that it would be "equally astonishing to Girondins, Radicals, do-nothing Aristocrats, Conservatives, and unbelieving dilettante Whigs" (*op. cit.*, I, 172): and it found favour with no Party.

[3] Thomas Carlyle (1795–1881; *DNB*); settled in 5 Cheyne Row, Chelsea, since 1834; earlier in the year had delivered the lectures which became *Heroes, Hero-Worship, and the Heroic in History* (1841). The Barings, John Sterling and Milnes were already his friends. Of *Pickwick* he had written to Sterling, 28 July 37: "Thinner wash, with perceptible vestige of a flavour in it here and there, was never offered to the human palate. . . . Ought there not to be Books of that kind? It is not certain *Yes*; and yet not certain *No*" (*Letters of T. Carlyle to J. S. Mill, J. Sterling, and R. Browning*, ed. A. Carlyle, 1923, pp. 206–7). He first met CD at the Stanleys' house in Mar 40 (see Vol. I, p. 425n), and afterwards described him in a letter to John Carlyle as "a fine little fellow— . . . clear blue, intelligent eyes, eyebrows that he arches amazingly, large protrusive rather loose mouth, a face of most extreme *mobility*, which he shuttles about—eyebrows, eyes, mouth and all— in a very singular manner while speaking. Surmount this with a loose coil of common-coloured hair, and set it on a small compact figure, very small, and dressed à la D'Orsay rather than well— this is Pickwick. For the rest a quiet, shrewd-looking, little fellow, who seems to guess pretty well what he is and what others are" (J. A. Froude, *op. cit.* I, 177–8.) Carlyle was much preoccupied during 1840 with the founding of the London Library (Forster, Talfourd and Bulwer were on the Committee; and CD on the list of first subscribers, 1841).

[4] Among them were probably those published as "The Songs of the Months" in *Tait's Edinburgh Magazine*, Jan–Dec 42. See Vol. I, p. 590 and *n*.

[5] Presumably CD meant in *The Pic Nic Papers* (cf. *To* Shoberl, 27 Apr 41); but he did not do so.

I have a Beaumont and Fletcher for you too—a book in which you will find many great things that will please you highly.

Dear Mr. Overs | Faithfully Yours
CHARLES DICKENS

## *To* JOHN FORSTER, 28 OCTOBER [1840]

MS Victoria & Albert Museum (FC). *Date:* 28 Oct was Wednesday in 1840; watermark 1840 and handwriting support that year. *Address:* Wait | John Forster Esquire.

Devonshire Terrace | Wednesday Morning Oct 28

Dear Forster

How are you this morning? And what about the Pills?

Faithfully Always
CD.

## *To* T. W. WHITE,[1] 29 OCTOBER 1840*

MS Mrs R. H. Dabney.

Private              1 Devonshire Terrace | York Gate Regents Park London.
Thursday 29th. October 1840.

Dear Sir.

I hasten to acknowledge the receipt of your Southern Literary Messenger[2] which has been obligingly forwarded to me, by your friend Mr. Lyman[3] of New York.

In the short interval which has elapsed between the receipt of your kind favor and its acknowledgment, I have barely had time to do more than glance at the table of its contents. But I promise myself an early perusal of the work, and am sure (from the glance I have had already) that it will afford me great pleasure and interest.[4]

I know not how to thank you for your flattering remembrance of me. Such gifts,—and I have had many such from your great country—come upon me like the voices of friends, assuring me of awakened interest and cordiality in the land where most men would desire to be known and approved; and where, it is one of the chief pleasures of my life to learn that my writings have been received with favor.[5]

---

[1] Thomas Willis White (1788–1843; *DAB*), printer, of Richmond, Virginia; founder and owner of the *Southern Literary Messenger*.

[2] A monthly literary journal published in Richmond 1834–64. White's employment of Poe as editor 1835–6 helped to make it nationally known and, according to Poe, quadrupled its circulation. Poe wrote many of his early tales, poems, articles and reviews for it.

[3] Possibly Samuel P. Lyman (1804–

1869), lawyer in New York City; partner of Daniel Webster for a time, and associated with him in the Harrison Campaign 1840. Engaged in railway business enterprises, not always successfully. Erie Railway owed much to him in its early days, especially for aid obtained from the State.

[4] Nothing stands out in the journal's recent issues as of obvious interest to CD.

[5] CD was presumably unaware of the

Before many years are over, I shall hope, with God's leave, to shake hands with you and many other brothers in the New World. Meantime in heart and spirit believe me theirs and yours

CHARLES DICKENS

T. W. White Esquire

## *To* DANIEL MACLISE, 31 OCTOBER [1840]*

MS Colonel Richard Gimbel. *Date:* 31 Oct was Saturday in 1840; handwriting and "Maclise" in salutation support that year.

Devonshire Terrace. | Saturday Octr. 31st.

My Dear Maclise.

I *don't* sit to-day, but *do* tomorrow, from 12 till 2, between which hours I shall hope to see you in the studio of Patric Park.

Forster dines with us. And I told him that after we had done with sculpture, we would give him a call, in case he should be disposed to take a walk.

He (the Author of the Lives of the Statesmen of the Commonwealth) made divers enquiries of me yesterday touching the Feast of Lanthorns,[1] which, you may remember, we told him we were going to see. I described the same, but stopped at the street corner, and *said no more.*

*Another* visit must be paid to that world of enchantment; between which and all beside ourselves, there is a deep gulf fixed—shadowy, mysterious, and profound.

Yours my friend | In darkness

CHARLES DICKENS

Such a days[2] work as I have before me! And yet I can jest—but with a breaking heart.[3]

antagonistic reviews of his work which had appeared in earlier numbers of White's journal. *Sketches by Boz* had been highly praised by Poe in June 36, and *Pickwick* well reviewed the following Nov. But the Nos for May and Sep 37 contained slashing attacks on "The Public Life of Mr. Tulrumble", the first number of *Oliver*, and *Pickwick*, by Judge Beverly Tucker (see F. L. Mott, *A History of American Magazines, 1741–1850*, 1930, pp. 641–2). In May (III, 323–5) CD was accused of "an exhibition . . . degrading and disgusting"; the task of reading *Bentley's Miscellany*, Nos 1 and 2, was described as "loathsome"; and the name "Boz" was ridiculed. In Sep (III, 525–32) protests at the May review were answered, the Pickwickians derided, Pickwick himself charged with "pre-posterous incongruities", and CD attacked as a "kept writer" prostituting himself to a depraved public. Only the interpolated tales in *Pickwick* showed him to be "a writer of considerable power"; but the great body of the book was made up of "grimace and absurd caricature, and impossible incidents happening to beings that have no existence in nature".

[1] The *Examiner* of 17 Oct 46 advertised a "Feast of Lanterns", to be "exhibited, with increased splendour, every Evening this Week, from 7 till 10, at the Chinese Collection, Hyde Park Corner. A-shing and A-you will be in attendance. Blight's full Cornopean Band". But no similar advertisement has been found in 1840.

[2] Thus in MS.

[3] See *To* Forster, 3 Nov.

## *To* MISS MARION ELY, 1 NOVEMBER 1840

Mention in Hodgson & Co. catalogue, 20 July 1916; dated 1 Nov 40.

## *To* DANIEL MACLISE, 3 NOVEMBER 1840*

MS Benoliel Collection.

Devonshire Terrace | 3rd. November/40

My Dear Maclise.

I am dead (in spirit) with yesterday's work. I'll call on you—alone in the carriage—at 2. For Heaven's sake let us range the fields and get some freshness if its[1] only fresh rain. I want to read you what I did yesterday,[2] as it shadows out one or two ideas which, if you exert your pencil in my behalf at all, perhaps would suit you as well as any other.[3] For this purpose I have kept back the MS from the Printer, and will come with it in my pocket.

Faithfully Yours Ever

CD.

## *To* JOHN FORSTER, [3 NOVEMBER 1840]

Extract in F, II, vii, 149. *Date:* Subject and similar wording point to same day as last.

Maclise and myself (alone in the carriage) will be with you at two exactly. We propose driving out to Hampstead and walking there, if it don't rain in buckets'-full. I shan't send Bradburys' the MS. of next number till tomorrow, for it contains the shadow of the number after that, and I want to read it to Mac,[4] as, if he likes the subject, it will furnish him with one, I think. You can't imagine (gravely I write and speak) how exhausted I am to-day with yesterday's labours. I went to bed last night utterly dispirited and done up. All night I have been pursued by the child;[5] and this morning I am unrefreshed and miserable. I don't know what to do with myself. . . . I think the close of the story will be great.

[1] Thus in MS.

[2] Clearly the second chapter (Ch. 53) in the newly finished No. 34.

[3] Symbols of life and death run through the whole chapter: on a new child's grave an infant lies asleep; the sexton has gardening spades for "things that are to live and grow", not "moulder away and rot", besides his spade for grave-digging; he describes the well ("What is it but a grave!"); in the decaying church Nell feels "happy, and at rest"; she climbs the tower and at the top "the glory of the sudden burst of light" is "like passing from death to life". Three days later CD told Mac-

lise which subject from this he would like him to illustrate: see 6 Nov.

[4] CD read them the No. at Jack Straw's Castle, says Forster (F, II, vii 149).

[5] Curiously, readers of the chapter did not realize that everything in it foreshadowed Nell's own death: Macready was "deeply touched and delighted" by the No. (*Diaries*, II, 94). It was only after publication of No. 35 on 21 Nov—with the return to the subject of the well (grave), and Maclise's unequivocal illustration—that CD's purpose became clear (see *To* Chapman & Hall, 24 Nov).

## *To* JOHN MAJOR,[1] 3 NOVEMBER 1840*

MS Mr L. T. Edwards.

Devonshire Terrace | Tuesday 3rd. November 1840.

Sir.

I assure you that I shall be exceedingly sorry if this reply to your note occasions you any feeling of disappointment; for then I shall have a solitary reason for regretting that we have corresponded.

I cannot give you a letter of recommendation to Messrs. Chapman and Hall—not because I deem your pieces unworthy of it; for, on the contrary, I think them very good—but because I have resolved never again to trouble those gentlemen with any such communications. I need not tell you that the influence I have with them is strictly personal, and that I have no right to dictate to or advise them in the conduct of their business. Now, if I had not prescribed this rule to myself, I should be its manager, and not they, for I believe there is not one man out of a dozen who has a proposal to make to them, who does not first write to me (as you have done) and urge me to back it.

Let me tell you frankly, for your consolation, that in submitting your proposals to them, you will stand on precisely as good a footing of your own, as if you had the strongest and most favorable introduction from me. In either case they would publish your book if they thought it would repay them, and reject it if they thought it would not. It will be a comfort to you to know that before I determined on my present system of non-interference, I *did* recommend several books to them, and (acting on this principle) they rejected them every one. And the last case, I perfectly remember, was one which I urged on behalf of one of our first authoresses, who would have appeared as "editing" the work.[2]

If you give me credit for a sincere desire to assist you if I had the power, you will only do justice to

Sir | Yours very truly

John Major Esquire                                       CHARLES DICKENS

## *To* DANIEL MACLISE, [6 NOVEMBER 1840]*

MS Colonel Richard Gimbel. *Date:* clearly the Friday between 3 Nov and the 12th, when Maclise saw the MS of the No. he was to illustrate (see *To Forster,* 12 Nov).

Devonshire Terrace. | Friday Morning

My Dear Maclise

Will you mind doing me a little design, embodying the bells above and

---

[1] Probably John Major (1782–1849; *DNB*), bookseller and publisher. Best known for his four editions of Walton and Cotton's *Compleat Angler*; also edited *Hogarth Moralised* and published several books of verse. Ruined through his entanglement in Thomas Dibdin's bibliographic ventures. Granted £25 by the Literary Fund in 1837, but was refused a second grant in Nov 40 on grounds of insufficient authorship (MS Royal Literary Fund). Lived in the Charterhouse from 1842 to his death.

[2] Apparently Caroline Norton (see *To* Lunn, 15 Nov 41).

the well below, and the old sexton and the child?[1] If you will do so, I'll tell them to send you a block forthwith.

I am obliged to ask you 'yes' or 'no' today, because time gets precious and if you don't, somebody else must. Topping (the gentle bearer) is going on to the Adelphi, and will call for an answer as he returns.

Ever Yours<br>CD.

## *To* DANIEL MACLISE, [?6 NOVEMBER 1840]*

MS Private. *Date:* probably same day as last—Maclise having sent an answer by hand immediately. CD was at the Adelphi all day on Sat 7 Nov (*To* Mitton, 9 Nov).

Dear Mac.

A *Million thanks.* I have sent directions to C and H. Remember that your illustration will come into the No. *after* the one of which you'll have the proof. Therefore if you like to put any more people in, young or old, do so at your own discretion, and I'll take care to account for 'em.[2] When you have done it, will you let *me* have it, that I may take care the text and it agree?[3]

Will you put on some shelf or nook, an old broken hour glass?[4]

Always Faithfully<br>CD

I am obliged to go down to the Adelphi tomorrow morning, and will call on you between 2 & 4.

## *To* [PATRIC PARK], 6 NOVEMBER 1840*

Photograph, Mr Leigh B. Block. *Address:* almost certainly to Patric Park, to whom CD was at this time sitting (see *To* Maclise, 25 and 31 Oct).

Devonshire Terrace | Friday 6th. November 1840

Dear Sir

Don't think me a false, inconstant, perjured sitter—pray. I was detained yesterday on my way to you by urgent business, and have now to tug at the

---

[1] Maclise agreed: see next.

[2] Apart from omitting the bells and showing only a bell-rope, Maclise kept to CD's earlier suggestion: Nell and the sexton are alone by the well.

[3] In two details they do not agree: in Ch. 55 the well is in a gloomy crypt reached by narrow steps, while in Ch. 53 (which Maclise's illustration follows) it is underneath the belfry; in Ch. 55 Nell is told to throw back the well-cover, while in the illustration the well is coverless. But no doubt CD was following Maclise's powerful illustration when he wrote: " 'Look in', said the old man, pointing downward with his finger. . . . 'It looks like a grave itself. . . . We shall see . . . on what gay heads other earth will have closed, when the light is shut out from here.' " This was Maclise's only illustration to the book.

[4] Not in the illustration.

oar and work my little galley, double tides. I am afraid I shall not be able to sit before next Tuesday; but I will write to you again.

Have faith in me,—and believe me always

Faithfully Yours
CHARLES DICKENS

## *To* DR JOHN ELLIOTSON, [6 NOVEMBER 1840]

Mention in next.

## *To* W. C. MACREADY, [6 NOVEMBER 1840]*

MS Morgan Library. *Date:* clearly the Friday before Mon 9 Nov, first night of *Old Curiosity Shop* at the Adelphi.

Devonshire Terrace. | Friday Evening

My Dear Macready.

I have been detained this week by some new arrangements with Chapman and Hall,[1] and shall have to[2] break tomorrow (which I had set aside for ten hours work) by going down to Yates and preventing his making a greater atrocity than can be helped of my poor Curiosity Shop, which is "done" there[3] on Monday Night.[4]

---

[1] Concerning the decision to serialize *Barnaby* in *Master Humphrey* immediately after the close of *Old Curiosity Shop*, instead of publishing it in the monthly parts specified in *To* Chapman & Hall, 2 July, and the *Barnaby* Agreement (Appx, p. 475). Ten days earlier, William Chapman had sent Smithson & Mitton a copy of *To* Chapman & Hall, 2 July, endorsed: "I send on the other side Copy Mr. Dickens' Letter as requested. I will not fail to be with you a little before 1 on Friday" (PM 28 Oct 40); and the new negotiations had presumably begun on Fri 30 Oct. On 10 Nov a meeting took place in Forster's chambers, at which the "understanding" was "minuted down" by Forster, and later given "bodily form" by Bacon (see W. Chapman *to* Smithson & Mitton, 12 June 41: Appx, p. 487). Mitton was present. According to Chapman, Forster's memorandum undertook that CD would agree to legal assignment of his copyrights as security, in consideration of Chapman & Hall's relinquishing the *Barnaby* Agreement; and the words "a lien in the nature of a Mortgage" showed (Chapman claimed in his letter of 12 June 41) that a Deed was "necessarily intended"—CD's letter of 2 July 40 having been "virtually superseded by the new arrangements". CD seems to have assumed, however, that that letter, taken together with Forster's memorandum, was all the security Chapman & Hall would need for the advance of £2250 that they had made on the original understanding that *Barnaby* was to be published in monthly parts independent of *Master Humphrey*; and no cloud in his relations with Chapman & Hall appeared until June 41, when Smithson told him of the Deed Bacon had based on Forster's memorandum, and how shocked he had been by it (see *To* Chapman & Hall, ?3 Aug 41 and *fns*).

[2] MS reads "shall to have to".

[3] At the Adelphi.

[4] For the first performance, see next, *fn*. The adaptation was by Edward Stirling; its full title *The Old Curiosity Shop; or, One Hour from Humphrey's Clock*; and the playbills described it as

At the last minute—I had not the resolution to breathe it to myself before—I am obliged to decide *not to go* tonight. You know how hard this is upon me as we were to have gone together—and I have a high regard for Elliotson[1]—but it is really no go in every sense of the word.

I send the carriage to take you there, and Topping is charged with a letter to convey instead of my portly person. I also send you herein a cheque[2] for the amount I am in your debt, with a thousand thanks.

The wine exhausts the language in its approving adjectives.

Ever Yours

I have *crossed* the cheque.                                          **CD.**

## *To* THOMAS MITTON, 9 NOVEMBER [1840]

MS Comtesse de Suzannet. *Date:* 9 Nov was Monday in 1840. *Address:* Thomas Mitton Esquire.

Devonshire Terrace. | Monday 9th. Novr.

My Dear Mitton

So far—all right.

I am *not* going to the Adelphi tonight[3]—I haven't the heart. Kate goes, and Fred takes her. I was at the Theatre all day on Saturday and made a great many improvements—especially in furnishing Bedford[4] with divers pieces of bye-play, in the invention of which, he seemed most woefully at sea. Yates will be *good*. The thing may be better than I expect, but I have no faith in it at all.[5]

Forster's appointment, if I remember right, stands for 11. I shall not see him, I think, today.

Faithfully Always

**CD.**

"a Burletta in Two Acts". It ended with an invented expulsion of Quilp by the Garlands, who had sheltered Nell and her grandfather, and with the strong implication that Nell would marry Dick Swiveller. The Codlin and Short scenes were made the excuse for acrobatic displays and for imitations of Macready, Kean, Harley and other actors.

[1] Elliotson's invitation was probably to one of his demonstrations of mesmerism. On another occasion he wrote to CD: "I am anxious that you should see human nature in a new state, and if you can come to my house to morrow at four precisely I will shew a very curious and perfectly genuine case of mesmerism" (Anderson Galleries catalogue, March 1916, dated "[May 41]").

[2] For £20.8.0 (CD's Account-book, MS Messrs Coutts).

[3] See last and *fns*.

[4] Paul Bedford (?1792–1871; *DNB*), who played Codlin. He made a great hit as Blueskin in the Adelphi *Jack Sheppard*.

[5] Despite scepticism about all such adaptations, the *Examiner* found in it "excellent snatches" of CD's genius and praised Yates's Quilp as "a performance of . . . amazing skill, and, all things considered, of . . . portentous relish and gusto" (15 Nov). The *Morning Chronicle* found Mrs Keeley "most natural and affecting" as Nell, and Yates beyond all praise: "his very rubbing of his hands had electric effect upon the house" (10 Nov). To Mrs Keeley herself Yates's Quilp was "so horribly real that [she] thought every moment he was going to pinch [her]!" (quoted in Walter Goodman, *The Keeleys*, p. 81).

## *To* JOHN FORSTER, [12 NOVEMBER 1840]

Extract in F, II, vii, 149. *Date:* 12 Nov according to Forster.

I will bring the MS and, for Mac's information if needful, the number before it.[1] I have only this moment put the finishing touch to it. The difficulty has been tremendous—the anguish unspeakable. I didn't say six. Therefore dine at half-past five like a Christian. I shall bring Mac at that hour.

## *To* MRS MACREADY,[2] [13 NOVEMBER 1840]*

MS Free Library of Philadelphia. *Date:* Handwriting suggests late 1840. It seems probable that Macready regularly received *Master Humphrey* on the day before publication: see four instances recorded in *Diaries* (II, 58, 89, 90, 94) and CD's words "regular course" in letter of 22 Jan 41. On Fri 13 Nov Macready read not only No. 33, published 14 Nov, but No. 34 as well (II, 94) —probably having received it through this letter to his wife. For CD's heavy cold, see next.

My Dear Mrs. Macready.

That madman—the Broadstairs bather whose grampus sounds you may remember[3]—turned up yesterday to the astonishment and horror of this peaceful household, and invited himself to dine here next Sunday. *Him* I would put off, to enjoy such pleasure as your note offers me, but my sister[4]

[1] I.e. the MS of No. 35 (Chs 54 and 55) and the proof of No. 34 (Chs 52 and 53).

[2] Catherine Macready (?1806–52), *née* Atkins, daughter of a scene-painter and actress. Macready first met her 1815 at Glasgow, when she was nine; next, on tour at Aberdeen, Summer 1820, when he found her playing Virginia to his Virginius—and the sole support of her parents. They became engaged 1823. But Macready's sister Letitia (aged 30) showed, on first meeting Catherine, such "disappointment, indeed repulsion", and wept so bitterly, that the marriage was postponed on her suggestion until June 1824—Catherine meanwhile going through a course of "education" by Macready and Letitia, and proving to Macready what he had "always maintained", "her wonderful aptness for improvement" (*Macready's Reminiscences*, ed. F. Pollock, 1875, I, 288–9). After accompanying Macready to America 1826, she settled down to child-bearing and domesticity—Macready still supervising her reading

(which included Locke and Bacon), and giving much practical instruction on how to manage her house and herself (A. S. Downer, *The Eminent Tragedian*, 1966, pp. 118–19). That Catherine Dickens felt at ease on visits to the Macreadys is understandable. Macready was a patient and devoted husband and father, and the marriage a success. He later told Letitia that the love of Dante for Beatrice reminded him of his for Catherine (Lady Pollock, *Macready as I Knew Him*, 1884, p. 69).

[3] Cf. *To* Forster, 20 Sep.

[4] Almost certainly Fanny who with her husband Henry Burnett was engaged on Sundays (until they moved to Manchester) to sing professionally at the Chapel of the Sardinian Ambassador and usually spent the Sunday evenings at CD's house (James Griffin, *Memories of the Past*, 1883, p. 171. The date of their move is not recorded. According to Griffin, Burnett, after his engagement at Bath (Jan–June 40: see *To* Mrs CD, 1 Mar), "hesitated a while" before resolving to leave the stage and move to

(being alone just now) usually dines with us on that day, and moreover my brother[1] whom I encourage so to do, as he is at an age when he might do worse. Now is there not *one* other day, early in next week, when we could meet for this delightful purpose? *Do* cast about in your mind for a snug, happy, undisposed-of evening, and say it shall be then. I am going out on no day but Thursday, and shall have no peace of mind until you write again. Therefore, pray relieve me soon from a despondency which is already stealing over my spirits, and unfitting me for Clock work.

Apropos of that—I send you next week's Number to look at, thinking that it may read none the worse for being exclusive. When the family have done with it, perhaps you'll let me have it back.

Our best loves at home. I don't know what word to use when I send remembrances to Macready, and have thoughts of coining one which shall be strong enough.

Always Faithfully Yours
CHARLES DICKENS

I have got *such* a cold! I have been crying all day, and upon my word I believe that my nose is an inch shorter than it was last Tuesday, from constant friction.


## *To* [PATRIC PARK], 14 NOVEMBER 1840*

MS Miss Elena Klasky. *Address:* see *To* [Patric Park], 6 Nov, *hn.*

Devonshire Terrace | Saturday Novr. 14th. 1840

My Dear Sir

I am afraid I cannot manage to sit to you before Tuesday at 12. But on that day, and on Wednesday, I will do so, with pleasure. It happens most unfortunately that I have been engaged in some extensive business arrangements[2] during the last fortnight, which have taken up so much of these short days that after a couple of hours writing in the morning, and then attending to them, it has been night again. In addition to these drawbacks I have had, and have still, a deplorable cold which almost prevents me from working.

I owe you an apology for this delay but I will make none, because I am sure *you* are sure that if I could have found the time to continue our pleasant sittings, I would most gladly have done so.

I am always My Dear Sir | Faithfully Yours
CHARLES DICKENS

Manchester; while a letter from Fanny to Griffin, dated 3 Oct (no year), mentions their settling in Manchester "a twelvemonth since" (*op. cit.*, p. 177). They probably left London *c.* Oct 41; for in Summer 1842 CD loaned them £100 to help with the expenses of their move (see Vol. III).

[1] Frederick, aged 20.

[2] Cf. *To* Macready, 6 Nov and *fn.*

## *To* GEORGE CRUIKSHANK, 17 NOVEMBER [1840]

MS Comtesse de Suzannet. *Date:* 17 Nov was Tuesday in 1840; reference
to *The Pic Nic Papers* supports that year.

1 Devonshire Terrace | Tuesday Seventeenth November
My Dear George.

As I know you are *sometimes* (!) engaged,[1] and fear your servant may
check me at your street door, unless previously admonished from Head
Quarters, I send this threatening letter to let you know that I mean to call
on you tomorrow at 3 o'Clock about Mrs. Macrone's book,[2] which is ripe
and ready. Poor thing, she needs its help, sadly.

Faithfully Always

George Cruikshank Esquire                         CHARLES DICKENS

## *To* T. J. SERLE,[3] 17 NOVEMBER 1840*

MS Colonel Richard Gimbel.

1 Devonshire Terrace, York Gate
Tuesday 17th. November 1840.

My Dear Sir.

I am so heartily favorable to all such Institutions as that to which your
note refers,[4] that I should have cheerfully complied with your request,
had it been urged by one with whom it afforded me no pleasure to communicate. As it is, if I had a dozen names you should be welcome to
them all.

Moreover, I shall hold myself in a manner bound to attend the dinner,[5]

[1] Naturally a joke, but Cruikshank's work did in fact fluctuate—only the *Comic Annual*, which he illustrated for Tilt 1835–53, providing him with a regular income. He was now illustrating Ainsworth's *The Tower of London* (in monthly parts, 1840) and *Guy Fawkes* (in *Bentley's Miscellany*, 1840–1841); but to his disgust Ainsworth did not employ him for *Old St. Paul's*, 1841; and although before CD's final break with Bentley it had been understood that Cruikshank would illustrate *Barnaby* (see Vol. I, p. 589), the new decision to serialize it in *Master Humphrey* inevitably resulted in the work's falling to Browne and Cattermole.

[2] Cruikshank contributed two illustrations to *The Pic Nic Papers*: "The Philosopher's Stone" (frontispiece to Vol. I) for CD's "The Lamplighter's Story", and "The Volunteer's Disaster" for "The Battle of Garscube". But CD's true purpose in proposing this

call was probably not to talk about the *Pic Nic* illustrations but to tell Cruikshank of the new arrangements for *Barnaby*. (For his suggestion—made perhaps to compensate Cruikshank for his loss of *Barnaby*—that they should collaborate over an Annual, see 17 Feb 41.)

[3] Thomas James Serle (1798–1889): see Vol. I, p. 355n. A play of his, *Master Clarke*, had been produced at the Haymarket Sep 40; in 1841 he published *Joan of Arc, the Maid of Orleans*, a historical romance. He was closely involved in the management of Drury Lane during Macready's lesseeship of 1841–3.

[4] The Southwark Literary and Scientific Institution.

[5] To celebrate the laying of the foundation-stone of the Institution's new building, 2 Dec 40 (see *To* Forster, 3 Dec 40).

and have made a memorandum of the day—when I hope nothing will occur to prevent me from joining the party.

The gentleman you mention, is *not* one of the Cheerybles I am happy to say—happy, because it is pleasant to think that there are more than two in the family, and that duplicates are wandering about the world in divers places.

Believe me | My Dear Sir | Faithfully Yours<br>CHARLES DICKENS

Thomas James Serle Esquire


## *To* THOMAS MITTON, 18 NOVEMBER 1840

MS Huntington Library.

Devonshire Terrace. | Eighteenth Novr. 1840.

My Dear Mitton

I shall be at home—tomorrow till six—Friday till 2 or 3, and in the evening; and Saturday all day.

Let me give you a hint. Make the *first* article of your Treaty, the period Smithson's name is to remain in the business. If you don't carry that point well, it would be madness to purchase it.[1] And upon that point—by far the most important of all—I see some reason to expect a little trimming on the other side.

Don't forget this. You will find sooner or later that it is important.

Faithfully Always<br>CD.


## *To* DANIEL MACLISE, 20 NOVEMBER 1840*

MS Private; seen before partial destruction in Prestwick air-crash, Dec 1954; fragment (*aa*) MS Colonel Richard Gimbel.

Friday November twentieth Eighteen forty

My Dear Mac

I have been writing all day, and mean to take a great, London, back-slums kind of walk tonight, seeking adventures in knight errant style. Will you come with me? And *a*as a preparation, will you dine with us at *a quarter before 5?*—Leg of mutton stuffed with oysters.

Reply 'Yes'.

Always & Ever<br>CD *a*

---

[1] Mitton's purchasing the practice had clearly been agreed by 29 Oct 41 (*To* Mitton, that day) and was a *fait accompli* by Apr 42 (*To* Mitton, 4 Apr 42). His name appeared alone in the 1843 *Law List*.

## *To* JOHN CLOSE,[1] 23 NOVEMBER 1840

MS Abbot Hall Art Gallery, Kendal.

1 Devonshire Terrace | York Gate Regents Park.
Twenty third November 1840.

Sir.

I hasten to say that the former communication to which you refer in your letter dated the twentieth and received today, has not reached me.—I have been out of town, and have little doubt that it is lying at my publisher's.

I cannot sufficiently thank you for the obliging and courteous terms in which you have addressed me, but I *can* assure you that it will give me great pleasure and satisfaction to receive a copy of your book,[2] and that I shall esteem it highly.

I am Sir | Faithfully Yours
CHARLES DICKENS

## *To* MESSRS CHAPMAN & HALL, 24 NOVEMBER 1840

MS Comtesse de Suzannet.

Devonshire Terrace | November twenty four | 1840.

Dear Sirs

I think the inclosed[3] is the sort of thing.—I have not shewn it to anybody.—If you have anything to suggest, let me know straightway.

I am inundated with imploring letters recommending poor little Nell to mercy.—Six yesterday, and four today (it's not 12 o'Clock yet) already!

Faithfully Always
Messrs. Chapman & Hall                        CHARLES DICKENS

## *To* JOHN FORSTER, [?NOVEMBER 1840]

MS Victoria & Albert Museum (FC). *Date:* Handwriting, supported by white paper, suggests Nov 40 to Feb 41; perhaps Nov 40 since later Catherine might have been too near child-birth for such an expedition. *Address:* John Forster Esquire.

Devonshire Terrace. | Tuesday Morning.

My Dear Forster.

Thompson, his two sisters,[4] Mrs. Burnett, and we, are away to Windsor

---

[1] John Close (1816–91; *DNB*), born at Gunnerside in Swaledale; poetaster, known as "Poet Close"; had been issuing verse tracts since a butcher's boy in his teens. Set up as a printer in Kirkby Stephen 1846. Bombarded potential patrons with copies of his verses. A Civil List pension unaccountably granted to him in 1860 was withdrawn the next year after public ridicule.

[2] Perhaps *The Satirist: or, Every Man in his Humour*, privately printed, Appleby, 1833, rather than one of his numerous verse pamphlets.

[3] Probably a draft of the announcement that *Barnaby* would be published

this morning, purposing to take a Dinner there, which we shall call a lunch, and to return by the Train at 5 o'Clock or thereabouts. Mac has suddenly taken it into his head to join the party, though I didn't ask either of you, lest you should think it a bore.

I wish to God you'd come down after us by the first train after you [have][1] this (they start every hour) and go straight to the White Hart, where, if we should not be at the moment, I'll leave full word of our whereabout.

Faithfully Yours<br>CD.

## *To* [R. S. HORRELL],[2] 25 NOVEMBER 1840

MS Public Library of Victoria, Melbourne.

Private                                    1 Devonshire Terrace | York Gate Regents Park.
                                                      Twenty fifth November 1840.

Sir.

I have read the little poems you sent me (and which I now return), and in compliance with your request, have to give you my opinion of them. I am by no means satisfied, nor do I wish you to be, that my conclusions are infallible; and I scarcely expect, and certainly do not desire, that you should attach any weight to them, whatever.

First, as the more grateful task, let me say what I have to say of praise. You are a very young man you tell me, with other occupations to employ your time; and you can only cultivate these thoughts and aspirations by stealth. A love of the good and beautiful, and a desire to illustrate it in one so circumstanced is always a thing to be commended—to be very highly commended. It should increase your own happiness whether it adds to the happiness and entertainment of mankind or no, and from pursuits so worthy and humanizing, I would not turn you aside by one discouraging word. The pursuit of excellence in any path which has the light of Truth upon it, is, in the abstract, a noble employment, and like the search for the Philosopher's Stone will reward you with a hundred incidental discoveries though you fall short of the one great object of your desire.

Beyond this, I think that you have many good thoughts—occasionally a power of expressing them, very simply and well—a love of nature and all creation—and, of course, (for these are its necessary companions) deep feeling and strong sympathy.

On the other hand, you have very much to learn. Your versification is often harsh and irregular, your conceits strained and unnatural, your images fraught with more sound than sense. The first fault is one which

---

in *Master Humphrey* (see *To* Forster, 16 Dec and *fn*).

[4] Mrs Smithson and Amelia Thompson.

[1] MS reads "leave"; presumably a slip.

[2] See *To* Horrell, 14 Oct, *fn*.

only time and reading can remove; a few instances of the other two, I have marked as they have struck me in the perusal. To spell a tiger from all thoughts of harm—to clasp blood springs with tendril fingers (which appears difficult, to say the least)—to make the sun unfurl his bannered robe—to engrave words *with* fire—to describe the birds as couching with gasping pants of bliss—to tear a man to pieces with links—to fold love's banner o'er a lady's brow—are so near being absurdities that I hardly know what else to call them. You may find, I know, startling and monstrous conceits in the writings of our greatest Poets; but you must remember that *they* were great, not because of these blots, but in despite of them, having for every one a crowd of beautiful and grand thoughts which bore down all before them. Never imitate the eccentricities of genius, but toil after it in its truer flights. They are not so easy to follow, but they lead to higher regions.

You have too much about faëry land, and faëry things—by far too much mention of nerves and heart strings—more agonies of despondency than suit my taste—mysterious promptings too in your own breast which are much better there, than anywhere else. It is not the province of a Poet to harp upon his own discontents, or to teach other people that they ought to be discontented. Leave Byron to his gloomy greatness, and do you

> Find tongues in trees, books in the running brooks,
> Sermons in stones, and good in everything.[1]

The young painter's last dream pleased me very much in its opening; the change of time and coming on of morning are very beautifully described, and the aspect of his room and the familiar things about it I really think *highly* of. But surely in the close of this piece you have quite perverted its proper object and intention. To make that face his comfort and trust—to fill him with the assurance of meeting it one day in Heaven—to make him dying, attended, as it were, by an angel of his own creation—to inspire him with gentle visions of the reality sitting by his bedside and shedding a light even on the dark path of Death—and so to let him gently pass away, whispering of it and seeking the hand to clasp in his—would be to complete a very affecting and moving picture. But, to have him struggling with Death in all its horrors, yelling about foul fiends and bats' wings, with starting eyes and rattles in his throat, is a ghastly, sickening, hideous end, with no beauty, no moral, nothing in it but a repulsive and most painful idea. If he had been the hero of an epic in seventy books, and had out-Lucifered Lucifer in every line of them, you could scarcely have punished him at last in a more revolting manner. I do hope that you will write this piece again with some such alteration. If you ever do so, I shall be glad to see it.

"Withered Leaves" opens, I think, very prettily. But it is not so well sustained, and treads rather closely at last (in the idea; not in the manner of

---

[1] Quoted again by CD in his speech at Hartford, 7 Feb 42 (*Speeches*, ed. K, J. Fielding, p. 24).

expressing it) upon a song of Mr. Lover's, founded on an Irish Superstition. It is called, if I remember right, the Four Leaved Shamrock.[1] The Ode to the Moon, very good. These are the only *data* I have, by which to form an opinion of your powers.

The advice I have to give you, is given in a very few words. I don't think you would ever find a publisher for a volume of such compositions unless at your own expence; and if you could, and have anything in you, the time would very soon come, when you would most heartily regret the having rushed into print. There are a great many people who write as well—many who write better. If you are to pass them, or are to take any place in the procession of Fame, you will do so none the later for keeping these effusions in your desk. At the same time, I see no objection to your sending some piece of moderate length—the painter for instance, but not in its present form—to such a Magazine as Blackwood's; and no improbability—no unusual improbability I mean—in the way of its acceptance and insertion. If you do this, give yourself the advantage of plain penmanship and a sheet of paper large enough to hold the lines, or it will never be read. And don't write to the Editor to tell him who you are or what you are, for he will care very little about that, and the public will care less.

It is impossible for me to say on such means as you have given me, whether I think you ever will be a great man, or whether you have God's gifts to become one. Some men would consider it their bounden duty to warn you off the dangerous ground of Poetry, but that I will not do,—firstly because I know you would still trespass there as boldly as ever, and secondly because for aught I know the land may be yours by right. Therefore, I make such remarks upon your writings as occur to me in reading them, and point out to you the course you would do best to take—the course I took myself when I was about one and twenty—and the course most writers have adopted when unknown and untried.

It is impossible that being unknown and untried, I could introduce you to a publisher with any beneficial result. I could not say that I thought your book would *pay* (that would be his first question); I could not even tell him that it was likely to attract public attention. I know but a dozen leaves of it, and if I said of those leaves to him, what I have said to you, he would be perfectly satisfied; and with the utmost deference and respect, and with the sincerest possible thanks, would decline the honor I proposed to confer upon him, and express the deepest gratitude for the preference.

You wish to know whether you do right in sacrificing so much time to what may fail at last. If you do so at the cost of any bitterness of heart, or any disgust with the employment in which you are engaged, you certainly do *wrong*. If you have strength of mind to do your duty cheerfully, and to make these toils a relaxation and solace of which nobody can deprive you, you do *right*. This is a question which none but yourself can determine. It is settled easily. When you have finished something care-

[1] One of Samuel Lover's "Songs of the Superstitions of Ireland" (*Songs and Ballads*, 1839, p. 17).

fully and to please yourself, make the trial I have suggested. If it fail in one quarter, try it again in another. If it fail in half a dozen, and each failure bring with it vexation and disappointment, lock up your papers, burn your pen, and thank Heaven you are not obliged to live by it.

Faithfully Yours

M[r. S.] Har[ford][1]                                CHARLES DICKENS

## *To* DANIEL MACLISE, 25 NOVEMBER 1840*

MS Private (destroyed in Prestwick air-crash, Dec 1954).

Devonshire Terrace.
Wednesday Night | November Twenty five 1840.

My Dear Maclise

It seems like an impertinence to put such a question to such a man as you, but have you thought in the various sleeping faces, of *dreaming expressions*—guards dreaming of fighting & roystering—ladies of love—and chamber women of flirting? It occurred to me last night, thinking of you, that there was a great field in this for such an imagination as yours, especially as the idea could be impressed upon the most leaden-headed of visitors by the catalogue description. Such a thing as a sleeping child among 'em, in the happiest repose, would point the notion—shewing how even sleep in after life becomes "grown up" and of the world.—Beautiful! Very beautiful![2]

So charming indeed, that I blush to sully such poetry with the prose announcement that we dine at half past four on Saturday, before the comedy,[3] but as we can't live on poetry alone (as the deaths of several spare authors have unhappily demonstrated) perhaps you'll forgive me.

Always Faithfully Yours

Daniel Maclise Esquire                          CHARLES DICKENS

## *To* JOHN OVERS, 26 NOVEMBER 1840

MS Free Library of Philadelphia.

Devonshire Terrace. | 26th. November 1840.

Dear Mr. Overs.

Any time on Sunday week the Sixth of December, between eleven and half past one, I shall be glad to see you.

[1] Name very faint and partly illegible: an attempt has sometime been made to erase it, presumably because a pseudonym.

[2] Obviously refers to Maclise's *The Sleeping Beauty*, exhibited at the RA 1841. The *Examiner* review, 9 May 41, suggests that Maclise kept to the traditional fairy-tale and did not follow CD's "Queen Mab" suggestions. The picture won the Art Union prize (cf. *To* Maclise, 18 Nov 41, *fn*); was in the possession of Sir John Pender 1887, sold at Christie's 1897, and has not been traced since.

[3] Bulwer's *Money*, which was to have been produced by Macready at the Haymarket on Sat 28 Nov, but had to be postponed to 8 Dec (see *To* Bulwer, 12 Dec, *fn*) owing to the death of Macready's small daughter.

I have gone through your two profiles, and marked them in pencil here and there. The Postilion[1] is much the better of the Two. I am sorry to say that I have not had time to go again through that weightier story, and fear I must reserve myself for the piece you will bring with you—which I am curious to see.

I am glad you are hearty with Beaumont and Fletcher—They are very good company. It will take you a long time to get through the two volumes, which are of a huge thickness and closely printed. Don't write about them, for I fancy it rather spoils the pleasure.

Always Faithfully Yours

Mr. J. A. Overs.                                        CHARLES DICKENS

## *To* W. C. MACREADY, [26 NOVEMBER 1840]

Mention in Macready, *Diaries*, II, 100. *Date:* On 26 Nov 40 Macready recorded: "Received a dear and affectionate note from Dickens, which comforted me as much as I can be comforted" (on the death of his daughter Joan).[2]

## *To* DANIEL MACLISE, 27 NOVEMBER [1840]*

MS Benoliel Collection. *Date:* two days after the death of Macready's daughter Joan.

Devonshire Terrace<br>Friday Morning Twenty Seventh Novr.

My Dear Mac

Perhaps you haven't heard that poor Macreadys have suddenly lost little Joan—the night before last, it was—and that little Henry is almost despaired of, also.

It is impossible, I am sure, that any people can more truly sympathize with the affliction of others, than we do for the sorrows of those to whom we are so strongly and ardently attached—and so I know you will say and feel. But I vow to God that if you had seen Forster last night, you would have supposed our Dear Friend was dead himself—in such an amazing

---

[1] Published in *George Cruikshank's Omnibus* No. 9, Jan 42, pp. 289–92. The other profile may have been one of the three collected by Overs in *Evenings of a Working Man*, 1844: "The Costar'monger", "Ring-a-tingle-dingle-ingle-ing-in-'n; Rap! 'Ba—ker!' ", and "The Carpenter".

[2] She had had jaundice (Forster *to* Bulwer, quoted in *Bulwer and Mac-*

ready, ed. C. H. Shattuck, p. 180), had seemed to be recovering, but—to Macready's intense grief—died very suddenly in the night of 25 Nov aged not quite three and a half. According to A. S. Downer, *The Eminent Tragedian*, p. 200, the true cause, which Macready would not admit, of this and later deaths in the family, was consumption.

display of grief did he indulge, and into such a very gloomy gulf was he sunk up to the chin.[1]

I wrote to Macready yesterday, but have not seen him of course. Poor fellow. He is a man of very strong affections, and I fear feels this misfortune keenly. If the second Child die, it will be a heavy blow indeed.[2]

We dine today at 5 or a quarter before, and I think Forster will take a little sustenance at that time. Will you come in, if you are not going anywhere? Burn this letter, for I generally see my autographs for six months past, lying about your room.

Faithfully Always

CD.

## *To* THOMAS MITTON, 28 NOVEMBER [1840]

Seen in Sotheby's, Oct 1967; dated 28 Nov—unmistakably 1840 on handwriting.

*Saying that he is bound to work that night,[3] and suggesting a meeting on the following Monday.*

## *To* CHARLES MOLLOY, 28 NOVEMBER [1840]

Extract in P. J. Dobell & Son catalogue No. 4 (1912); *MS* 1 p.; dated Devonshire Terrace, November Twenty-eighth—clearly 1840, the year of the failure of Wright's Bank (see *fn*).

I hope you have not been, or will not be, a great sufferer by Wright's failure.[4] Remembering you banked there, I feared you might be a loser, when I heard they had stopped payment.

---

[1] This is less than fair to Forster, the genuineness of whose feeling for Joan cannot be doubted. A man with strong untapped paternal instincts, he was Joan's god-father, and had become an established family friend (Macready many times recorded returning home to find Forster there: e.g. on 3 Oct, playing cards with the family). In the week after Joan's death he was the only friend Macready saw. Calling on Macready on 26 Nov, Forster "had supposed that it was Henry who was gone, and when he learned that dear Joan had been taken ... lost all self-control ... rushed out of the study, and remained away at least half an hour. When he returned he could say nothing; he left me greatly agitated", wrote Macready (*Diaries*, II, 100). But Macready clearly welcomed a friend who so fully shared his grief. Forster sat with him on the evenings of 27, 28, and 29 Nov; spent the whole of the day of the funeral (30th) with him (having the night before—when he saw the child's coffin—"promised not to give way to his emotions"); went into the country with him on 1 Dec; walked and dined with him on the 2nd. Their conversation on 28 Nov "composed" Macready (*op. cit.*, II, 104); from their day in the country he returned "very much renovated and cleared in mind" (*op cit.*, II, 106).

[2] Henry, aged nearly two, was dangerously ill with "thrush" (*Diaries*, II, 106), but recovered.

[3] Probably on No. 38 (Chs 60 and 61; published 19 Dec), in which Kit is arrested, and committed for trial.

[4] John Wright, principal managing partner of Wright & Co., 5 Henrietta Street, private bankers, had announced the bank's failure on 23 Nov. The

## *To* MESSRS CHAPMAN & HALL, 30 NOVEMBER 1840

MS John Rylands Library.

Devonshire Terrace | Monday Night Thirtieth Novr. | 1840.
Dear Sirs

I have spoken to two or three friends—judges in such matters—about the Barnaby Notice; and they are all of opinion that in the height and stir of the present story, Saturday week would be *too soon*.

Therefore, please let it stand over, until we have had time to discuss and consider it further.[1]

Faithfully Always
CHARLES DICKENS

## *To* JOHN FORSTER, [?LATE NOVEMBER 1840]

Extract in F, II, vii, 148. *Date:* given by Forster as written "just before" CD's return from Broadstairs in second week of Oct. But since on 12 Nov No. 35 was only in MS, Nos 36 and 37 could not both have been written before the last week in Nov; and proofs of No. 37 would have been received a few days later.

Tell me what you think of 36 and 37?[2] The way is clear for Kit now, and for a great effort at the last with the Marchioness.[3]

## *To* JOHN FORSTER, 3 DECEMBER [1840]*

MS Victoria & Albert Museum (FC). *Date:* the day after CD's speech of 2 Dec (see *fn*); handwriting supports 1840. *Address:* John Forster Esquire.

Thursday | Third Decr.
My Dear Forster.

*I believe you*[4]—as to my own brilliancy.[5] Serle, subdued.[6] Speeches,

deficiency amounted to *c.* £500,000. The majority of the depositors were members of rich Roman Catholic families. The legend once current that CD had invested "a large part of his slender means" in the bonds of the spurious Cairo City and Canal Co., which its organizer, Darius B. Holbrook, had sold through Wright & Co., was given publicity by John F. Snyder ("CD in Illinois", *Journal of the Illinois State Historical Society*, III [1910], 20–2). But Gerald G. Grubb (*Studies in Philology*, XLVIII [1951], 87–97) and H. G. Baetzhold (*D*, LV [1959], 169–75) have shown that no evidence for this exists.

[1] It was not published until 9 Jan 41: see *To* Forster, 16 Dec 40, *fn*.

[2] Chs 56–9, in which Sampson and Sally Brass carry out their plot against Kit, and Dick first names the small servant "the Marchioness".

[3] Clearly CD had in mind the revelation of the Marchioness's parentage in Ch. 66: see *To* Forster, 30 Dec, *fn*.

[4] Perhaps an echo of the actor Paul Bedford's "eternal 'I believe you, my boy!' " (see Clement Scott, *The Drama of Yesterday and To-day*, 1899, I, 19).

[5] On 2 Dec at Serle's invitation (see 17 Nov) CD had attended a banquet given at the Bridge House Hotel, Southwark, by the Southwark Literary and Scientific Institution and proposed the toast to its success: see *Speeches*, ed. K. J. Fielding, pp. 4–5. CD subscribed five guineas to the Institution in Dec 40,

excellent. I wish you had been there,[1] for you can form no idea of what these bodies are. I never saw such a good meeting, or a thing so well and handsomely done.

If you come up today, either come before half past 2 and go with me to Willesden and thereabouts—or at half past 4 to dinner. But not in the evening because I am only just up, and must be then, at work.

Faithfully Always

CD.

*a*A brilliant morning for a country walk.*a*

## *To* T. P. GRINSTED, 7 DECEMBER 1840*

MS Free Library of Philadelphia. *Address:* T. P. Grinsted Esquire | 3 Glo'ster Terrace | Brighton.

1 Devonshire Terrace, York Gate | Regents Park London

Seventh December 1840.

Sir.

I am cordially obliged to you for the interesting intelligence you have been kind enough to send me. A day or two after I received your letter, I had, from some other hand, a Port Nicholas Mens paper[2] containing an advertisement of the Club Meetings.[3] It was very curious to see the old familiar name in its unusual-looking columns.

I hope when you write to your friend, you will convey to him (and through him, to *his* friends) an assurance of the great gratification I have derived from the circumstance of their meeting together for social purposes, under this name. To be associated with their pleasant recollections of home in their hours of relaxation, is to me a most proud and happy distinction. I really cannot tell you how very much it has interested and pleased me.

and another five guineas on 31 May 41.

[6] Serle proposed the health of the chairman, Henry Kemble, MP.

[1] Forster was with Macready: see *To* Maclise, 27 Nov, *fn.*

*aa* Cf. F, II, i, 92: " 'What a brilliant morning for a country walk!' he would write, with not another word in his dispatch."

[2] Thus in MS. Presumably CD was misreading Grinsted's writing of "Port Nicholson Newspaper"—and not stopping to check the title from the actual paper sent by "some other hand". See below.

[3] Probably the issue of 16 May 40 of the *New Zealand Gazette*, Port Nicholson, the first newspaper in the colony. After announcing the formation of "The Pickwick Club of New Zealand" in Port Nicholson, Wellington (only four months after the arrival there of the New Zealand Company's settlers), and the holding of its meetings "at Mr W. Elsdon's Commercial Inn and Tavern", it commented: "It has already a considerable number of members. To our friends in England, this cannot fail to awaken the most pleasing sensations; as it tends to prove, that in this remote region of the globe—this land of savages—Englishmen relish the inimitable works of 'Boz'." A long report on the first quarter's activities of the Club followed on 22 Aug, mentioning, *inter alia*, that it now possessed a library of 100 books.

I hope the Brighton club still flourishes nobly. And again thanking you for your communication and good wishes, which I fully reciprocate, I am

Faithfully Yours

T. P. Grinsted Esquire                                        CHARLES DICKENS


## *To* GEORGE CRUIKSHANK, 7 DECEMBER 1840

MS Colonel Richard Gimbel.

Devonshire Terrace, York Gate
Seventh December 1840.

My Dear Cruikshank.
I'll call upon you next Wednesday about 2.[1]

Always Faithfully
CHARLES DICKENS

## *To* "JAMES FLEMING",[2] 8 DECEMBER 1840*

MS Clark Memorial Library, University of California.

1 Devonshire Terrace, York Gate | Eighth December 1840.

Mr. Charles Dickens cannot afford any assistance to the writer of the Letter signed "James Fleming", which reached him last night. The case stated is not one, in which he would feel justified in giving pecuniary assistance; to the exclusion of some living, and unhappy object.[3]

---

[1] This may well have been the call first proposed by CD for 18 Nov (see *To* Cruikshank, 17 Nov and *fn*), and perhaps postponed because Cruikshank was ill (the *Publishers' Circular*, 15 Dec, announced that the *Comic Almanack* had been "delayed by Mr. Cruikshank's indisposition" but would appear on 19 Dec).

[2] Unidentified.

[3] While recounting events of about this date (adding that he ought to have mentioned the subject earlier), Forster commends CD's essay, "The Begging-Letter Writer" (*Household Words*, 18 May 50, I, 169), as a description "without a particle of exaggeration" of "the extent to which he was made a victim by this class of swindler"; however, "for much of what he suffered he was himself responsible, by giving so largely, as at first he did, to almost every one who applied to him" (F, II, viii, 161). CD describes himself in the article as "a chosen receiver" of such letters for 14 years: i.e. from the time of his marriage. But this is the earliest answer to a begging-letter to come to light.

## *To* SIR EDWARD LYTTON BULWER, 12 DECEMBER 1840

MS Lytton Papers.

1 Devonshire Terrace, York Gate
Twelfth December 1840.

Dear Sir Edward.

Let me thank you for the copy of your comedy[1] received this morning.

I told Macready when he read it to me a few weeks since, that I could not call to mind any play since the Good Natured Man,[2] so full of real, distinct, genuine character; and now that I am better acquainted with it, I am only the more strongly confirmed in this honest opinion.[3]

You may suppose that "I was there to see",[4] last Tuesday;—I most heartily and cordially congratulate you on its brilliant reception and success, which I hope will encourage you to other efforts in the same Path.[5] I feel assured that you will tread it alone.

Faithfully Yours
CHARLES DICKENS

Sir Edward Lytton Bulwer.

## *To* GEORGE CATTERMOLE, 13 DECEMBER 1840

Extracts in Sotheby's catalogue, July 1914 (*aa*), and Parke-Bernet Galleries catalogue, Feb 1941 (*bb*); *MS* 2 pp.; dated *b*"Devonshire Terrace, Twelfth December, 1840 (I mean the Thirteenth)"*b*; salutation "My dear George".

*a*Here is that dinner of ours still to come off, and I gasping with anxiety to speak to you about divers closing subjects for poor Nell.*a*

[1] *Money*, dedicated to Forster, which had been produced by Macready at the Haymarket 8 Dec 40. A copy inscribed "From the Author" was in the Gad's Hill library at CD's death.

[2] Goldsmith's comedy. Both it and *Money* were among the plays rehearsed, though not performed, by CD's amateur company in Feb 48.

[3] On hearing it read, 17 Nov 40, CD had commented that he "had not supposed that Bulwer could do anything so good" (Macready, *Diaries*, II, 95); and in his speech at the General Theatrical Fund dinner, 17 Apr 48, he described it as the best comedy since Goldsmith. Bulwer himself felt that it was the first of his "attempts at Comedy . . . to have at all hit on the right vein" (Bulwer *to* Forster, [29 Aug 40], quoted in *Bulwer and Macready*, ed. C. H. Shattuck, p. 155). It was an immediate success, and ran continuously to the end of the Haymarket season 15 Mar 41. For the texts of letters between Bulwer, Macready and Forster, discussing the play and its production, see *op. cit.*, pp. 150–87.

[4] Cf. final lines of "The Diverting History of John Gilpin": "And when he next doth ride abroad, | May I be there to see!"

[5] During the next two years Bulwer struggled to find a subject for another play for Macready; searched classical and French authors; urged Macready himself to sketch a plot. "If I were writing a comedy for Farren, I should soon knock it off", he wrote [Aug 42]; "But strange to say, you are my stumbling-block—I cannot raise myself up to that grave high Humour which would alone suit your dignity" (*op. cit.*, p. 214). After *Money*, the only comedy of Bulwer's to be performed was *Not so Bad as We Seem* first played by CD's amateur company in 1851.

*<sup>b</sup>*I am going out Monday *Evening* but at no early hour—what do you say to dining with me at the Parthenon on that day at half 5?*<sup>b1</sup>* *<sup>a</sup>*I cannot make Mac or Forster of the party, because the laws of the Medes and *Parthenons*[2] forbid a member to indulge in more than one friend.*<sup>a</sup>*

## *To* LORD ASHLEY,[3] [13 or 14 DECEMBER 1840]

Mention in next.

## *To* DR SOUTHWOOD SMITH,[4] 15 DECEMBER 1840

MS Mrs Robert Nuttall.

1 Devonshire Terrace, York Gate | Fifteenth December 1840.
My Dear Sir.
I am greatly obliged to you for your kind note and inclosure of to day. I had never seen the Sanatorium pamphlet,[5] and have been greatly pleased

---

[1] Perhaps written "½ 5" by CD, and expanded in catalogue.

[2] For the Parthenon Club see Vol. I, p. 380*n*.

[3] Anthony Ashley Cooper, Lord Ashley (1801–85; *DNB*), later 7th Earl of Shaftesbury. Social reformer; Conservative (but virtually independent) MP 1826–51. During 1840 supported Bills for the emancipation of Jews, for Church extension, and for the prohibition of juvenile chimney-sweeps. Helped to found the Society for Extinction of the Slave Trade, which held its first meeting on 1 June 40. In Sep 40, after settlement of the Syrian Question, addressed a paper to Palmerston, proposing the return of the Jews to Palestine (E. Hodder, *Life and Work of the Seventh Earl of Shaftesbury*, 1886, I, 313). The Report of his Committee on child-labour in factories 1841, and Second Report 1843, led to the Factory Act of 1844. Given Hon. LL.D. by Oxford in June 41. See later vols.

[4] Thomas Southwood Smith, MD (1788–1861; *DNB*), sanitary reformer. MD 1816; Unitarian minister at Yeovil, simultaneously practising medicine, 1816–20. Published *Illustrations of the Divine Government*, Glasgow, 1816. From 1820 practised medicine in London. Consultant to the London Fever Hospital 1824. One of the projectors of the *Westminster Review*, for which he wrote his first articles on sanitary reform: "Contagion and Sanitary Laws" (Jan 1825, III, 134–167) and "Plague—Typhus Fever—Quarantine" (Apr 1825, III, 499–530). These were followed by *A Treatise on Fever*, 1830 (arguing that "penury and ignorance" could "at any time and in any place, create a mortal plague"); *The Philosophy of Health*, 1835–7; and by his Reports to the Poor Law Commissioners for East London 1835–9 and Reports on Sanitary Improvement 1838–57. An advocate of dissection, he had contributed "The Use of the Dead to the Living" to the *Westminster Review* (II [1824], 59–97), and dissected and lectured over Bentham's body (left him by Will) 1832 —later keeping the skeleton, dressed in Bentham's clothes, in his Finsbury Square consulting room (it is now in University College, London, encased in a wax replica). One of the original Committee of the Society for the Diffusion of Useful Knowledge 1825. He was main founder of the Health of Towns Association 1839. In 1841 Lord Normanby, the Home Secretary, used Smith's evidence to support his Drainage of Buildings Bill (shelved on the Govt's defeat).

[5] *The Sanatorium; a Self-Supporting Establishment for the Lodging, Nursing, and Cure of Sick Persons of Both Sexes* (reviewed with approval in the *Metropolitan*, Aug 40, XXVIII, 104).

with it. The reasons for such an Institution,[1] and the advantages likely to result from it, could not have been more forcibly or eloquently put. I have read it twice with extreme satisfaction.

You have given me hardly less pleasure by sending me the Instructions of the Childrens'[2] Employment Commission,[3] which seem to me to have been devised in a most worthy spirit, and to comprehend every point on which humanity and forethought could have desired to lay stress. The little book reaches me very opportunely; for Lord Ashley sent me his speech[4] on moving the Commission, only the day before yesterday, and I could not forbear, in writing to him in acknowledgement of its receipt, cursing the present system and its fatal effects in keeping down thousands upon thousands of God's images, with all my heart and soul.[5]

It must be a great comfort and happiness to you to be instrumental in bringing about so much good.[6] I am proud to be remembered by one who

---

[1] The sanatorium was intended "for the Lodging, Nursing and Cure of Sick Persons of the Middle Classes" (1842 prospectus). Southwood Smith was its prime mover. Meetings were held at the Marylebone Literary Institution, 11 Dec 39, and at the London Tavern, 6 Mar 40, to explain its aims. Expenses were to be met partly by members' subscriptions (a guinea *p.a.* or ten guineas for life), partly from patients' fees of up to two guineas a week. A provisional committee was formed on 16 May 40, for which additional members were canvassed later (see *To* Shee and *To* Macready, 3 June 41). The sanatorium was opened at Devonshire House, York Gate (nearly opposite CD's own house), in Apr 42. CD was a member of the new committee and interested himself in the appointment of a matron (*To* Mitton, 15 Nov 42; *To* Hood, Nov 42). Lord Ashley became its chairman. The sanatorium was always in financial difficulties. For CD's description of its principles and plea for financial support, see his speech when presiding at the Sanatorium dinner of 4 June 44 (*Speeches*, ed. K. J. Fielding, pp. 68–71).

[2] Thus in MS.

[3] The First Report of the "Commission for Inquiring into the Employment and Condition of Children in Mines and Manufactories", 1842, stated that the Commissioners' initial act was to draw up "Instructions for the guidance of the Sub-Commissioners in the collection and verification of evidence;

to construct Tabular Forms to be filled up by the Employers of Children and Young Persons and to draw up Queries to be answered by them".

[4] Delivered in the Commons on 4 Aug 40 (*Hansard*, 3rd. series, LV, 1260–1274). In demanding an inquiry, Ashley gave horrifying details of the conditions under which children, down to the age of five, worked in mines and in a large number of industries, and of the moral and physical effects on them. "My first grand object", he concluded, "is to bring these children within the reach of education. ... Only let us exhibit these evils—there is wit enough, experience enough, activity enough, and principle enough in the country, to devise some remedy." Ashley later thanked CD for his warm interest in the Commission and introduced to him Leonard Horner, one of the four Commissioners: "Your knowledge of the poorer Classes", he wrote (12 Feb 41), "might greatly assist the labours of the Commission; and I feel confident, therefore, that you will not only give them the benefit of your experience, but will also excuse the trouble this request may impose on you" (MS Huntington).

[5] For CD's letter to the *Morning Chronicle*, 25 July 42, in support of Ashley's Mines and Collieries Bill, and his review there of Lord Londonderry's attack on it, see Vol. III.

[6] Southwood Smith was one of the four Commissioners; and, according to his grand-daughter Mrs C. L. Lewes (*Dr Southwood Smith, A Retrospect,*

is pursuing such ends, and heartily hope that we shall know each other better.

My Dear Sir | Faithfully Yours

Dr. Southwood Smith.                                    CHARLES DICKENS

## *To* T. J. THOMPSON, 15 DECEMBER 1840

Text in MDGH, III, 16, checked from MS Sotheby's, 15 Dec 1964. *Address:* T. J. Thompson Esquire| Pall Mall.

Devonshire Terrace | Tuesday Fifteenth December | 1840.
My Dear Thompson.

I have received a most flattering message from the Head Turnkey of the Jail this morning, intimating that "there warn't a genelman in all London as he'd be gladder to shew his babies to, than Muster Dickens. And let him come wenever he would to that shop, he wos welcome". But as the Governor[1] (who is a very nice fellow, and a gentleman) is not at home this morning, and furthermore as the morning itself has rather gone out of town in respect of its poetical allurements, I think we had best postpone our visit for a day or two. I will write to you again on this head, as soon as I have finished my No.[2]

## *To* MISS BURDETT COUTTS, 15 DECEMBER 1840*

MS Morgan Library. *Address:* Free | Miss Coutts| Stratton Street.

Devonshire Terrace | Fifteenth December 1840.

Mr. Charles Dickens presents his compliments to Miss Coutts, and has great pleasure in accepting her kind Invitation for Thursday the Seventeenth.

## *To* JOHN FORSTER, [?16 or 18 DECEMBER 1840]

Extract in F, II, vii, 149–50. *Date:* 16 Dec according to Forster. But see *hn* to next.

"If you make believe very much it's quite nice; but if you don't, you know, it seems as if it would bear a little more seasoning, certainly."[3] I think that's better. Flavour is a common word in cookery, and among cooks, and so I used it. The part you cut out in the other number, which

1898, p. 73), it was at his instigation that its first report—on mines and collieries —was illustrated by drawings done on the spot (a main target of Londonderry's attack).

[1] Probably G. L. Chesterton, Governor of Coldbath Fields Prison (see Vol. I, p. 101*n*).

[2] Bottom of letter cut away, probably

removing no more than ending and signature.

[3] This sentence (in *Old Curiosity Shop*, Ch. 64, No. 40, published 2 Jan 41) originally ended: "but if you don't, you know, it hasn't much flavour" (MS Forster Collection, V & A). Clearly Forster had objected to the word "flavour" in the Marchioness's mouth.

was sent me this morning, I had put in with a view to Quilp's last appearance on any stage, which is casting its shadow upon my mind;[1] but it will come well enough without such a preparation, so I made no change. I mean to shirk Sir Robert Inglis,[2] and work to-night. I have been solemnly revolving the general story all this morning.[3] The forty-fifth number will certainly [be the] close.[4] Perhaps this forty-first[5] which I am now at work on, had better contain the announcement of *Barnaby* ?[6] I am glad you like Dick and the Marchioness in that sixty-fourth chapter—I thought you would.

[1] Forster had cut two passages in the proof of No. 39 (Forster Collection, V & A), one from the beginning of Ch. 62 and the other from the end, each of them ironically foreshadowing Quilp's drowning at the end of the story. The first (of 11 lines) describes Brass's fears as he halts on his way to Quilp's wharf, and wonders who would come, in a place "so cursed lonely—so dreary and so dark", if it "was necessary to scream for help". In the second (of 13 lines)—probably the passage CD refers to here—Quilp stands on "the very brink of the wharf", soliloquizing with great satisfaction on how easily he could become a widower: "I need only invite Mrs. Quilp to take tea here one foggy night—the water's very near the door to be sure. If she took the wrong turning and her foot slipped—ah!" He finds it "a tempting spot". How deaf he would be if anybody he hated had fallen over and was screaming to him!—but he would hear the splash.

[2] Sir Robert Harry Inglis, Bart (1786–1855; *DNB*), anti-Catholic Tory politician, opponent of parliamentary reform, and strong churchman (Macready called him "that fat monk": *Diaries*, II, 333). Supporter, however, of Ashley's campaigns for factory reform and condemner of the slave trade. MP, Oxford University, 1829–54. Presided at the Anniversary Festival of the Literary Fund Society, 13 May 40, where CD probably met him.

[3] The MS of CD's plans for Nos 41–44 is preserved in the Forster Collection, V & A. These are the first number-plans of his known. They show some uncertainties about No. 41: "hint of Nell—qy."; "hints of Nell | no"; "small servant—parentage. qy." (cf. *To* Forster, 30 Dec, *fn*). No. 42 is

outlined only briefly. But the plan for No. 43 (published 23 Jan 41) shows that CD already had Chs 69–70 visually in mind ("snow—hard weather—travelling by night . . . cottages—people abed —lights in windows"), and these were to lead up to "The bird" (the "affecting thing" he had probably had in mind three months earlier: see *To* Forster, ?9 Sep and *fn*). For No. 44 (Ch. 71) the plan has only the monosyllable "Dead".

[4] F, 1872–4, I, 186, reads "will certainly close".

[5] Published 9 Jan 41.

[6] It did. The announcement was printed at the top of the reverse side of the cover and read: "BARNABY RUDGE IN MASTER HUMPHREY'S CLOCK. | MESSRS CHAPMAN AND HALL have the pleasure of announcing that | BARNABY RUDGE | WILL FORM THE NEXT TALE IN 'MASTER HUMPHREY'S CLOCK.' | It will commence immediately upon the completion of 'The Old Curiosity Shop', which will extend to about the Forty-fifth Number of the Work. | BARNABY RUDGE, though originally projected with a view to its separate publication in another and much more expensive form, will be, like its predecessor, written by MR DICKENS expressly for these pages. | 186, STRAND, *January*, 1841." This was repeated in No. 42 (16 Jan). In Nos 44 and 45 a shorter announcement appeared: "MESSRS CHAPMAN & HALL beg to announce that No. 45 of MASTER HUMPHREY'S CLOCK will contain the last Chapter of 'THE OLD CURIOSITY SHOP;' and that the commencement of 'BARNABY RUDGE' (which will be published continuously, from week to week) will appear in No. 46. | 186, STRAND, *January* 1841."

*To* SIR ROBERT INGLIS, [?16 or 18] DECEMBER 1840

Mention in N, I, 283. *Date:* given in N as 18 Dec, but possibly incorrectly: if a note of excuse for shirking the engagement with Inglis mentioned in last, presumably written the same day. Either Forster's or N's dating is to be doubted.

*To* MISS BURDETT COUTTS, [?17 DECEMBER 1840]*

MS Morgan Library. *Date:* Handwriting suggests 1840; possibly refers to the invitation for 17 Dec which CD had accepted on the 15th.

Devonshire Terrace. | Thursday 5 O'Clock.

Mr. Charles Dickens presents his compliments to Miss Coutts, and exceedingly regrets that a sudden necessity for his going a few miles from town on business, prevents his having the honor of dining with her to-day. But Mr. Dickens hopes to have the pleasure of paying his respects to Miss Coutts in the course of the Evening, if he can by any means return to town in time.

*To* MISS BURDETT COUTTS, 18 DECEMBER [1840]*

MS Morgan Library. *Date:* 18 Dec was Friday in 1840; handwriting supports that year. *Address:* Miss Coutts.

Devonshire Terrace | Friday Eighteenth December
Dear Miss Coutts.
I cannot thank you sufficiently for your great kindness, and am most happy to avail myself of it.
I have kept the order for this Evening,[1] and beg to return you the other.
I beg my compliments to Miss Meredith,[2] and assure you that I am always *with great sincerity*

Faithfully Yours
Miss Coutts.                                              CHARLES DICKENS

[1] Perhaps for Miss Coutts's box at Covent Garden (see *To* Miss Coutts, 24 Nov 41), where *The Merry Wives of Windsor* was played that night, with *The Critic*.
[2] Hannah Meredith (*d.* 1878), later Mrs William Brown, Miss Coutts's former governess (since 1821) and lifelong companion and friend. *A Summary Account of Prizes for Common Things . . . Awarded by Miss Burdett Coutts . . .* , [1856], contains (p. 10) a letter from Miss Coutts, acknowledging indebtedness to her "not only for whatever information I may possess, but for my first interest in [philanthropic] subjects". She was the "one of [CD's] lady friends, very familiar to him indeed" on whom he based Rosa Dartle's "peculiarity of never saying anything outright, but hinting it merely, and making more of it that way" (F, VI, vii, 556); also her argumentativeness. See Margaret Cardwell, "Rosa Dartle and Mrs. Brown", *D*, LVI (1960), 29–33.

### *To* J. P. HARLEY, 18 DECEMBER [1840]*

MS Berg Collection. *Date:* 18 Dec was Friday in 1840; handwriting supports that year. *Address:* J. P. Harley Esquire | Upper Gower Street.

1 Devonshire Terrace | Friday Evening Decr. 18th.

My Dear Harley.

Come and dine here on the last day of this good old year, at *6 sharp*. Make them put up something you don't play in, or if they won't mind you, come when you *have* played.¹ We have no serious party—only George Cruikshank, Quin, and one or two more who are friends of all of us—and want to see the year out with some charades and other frolics. I won't tell you simply that you could come in dirty boots, but that stockings alone would be considered court dress.

Faithfully Always

J. P. Harley Esquire                                                               Boz.

### *To* GEORGE CATTERMOLE, [?18 DECEMBER 1840]

Extract in Goodspeeds Book Shop catalogue No. 8 (1902); *MS* 1 p. *Date:* probably, like letters to Ainsworth and Harley, an invitation for 31 Dec 40.

Will you dine with us on the last day of the old year—just to see it jollily out.

### *To* W. HARRISON AINSWORTH, 18 DECEMBER 1840

Extract in Sotheby's catalogue, 2 June 1932; *MS* 1 p.; dated Devonshire Terrace, 18 Dec 40. *Address* (envelope, MS Private)*:* William Harrison Ainsworth Esquire | Kensal Lodge | Harrow Road. PM 19 Dec 40.

Behold your Sketch.² I want to make you promise to dine here on the last day of the old year at *6 exactly*—quite at home and unceremoniously to see it out with forfeits and such like exercises. So make the promise— kiss the children, and remember me to the ladies (heartily).³

---

¹ On 31 Dec Harley played Bottom in *A Midsummer-Night's Dream* at Covent Garden.

² Presumably "The Old London Merchant, a Fragment", Ainsworth's sole contribution to *The Pic Nic Papers* which initially he and CD were to have edited jointly (see Vol. I, pp. 371–2).

With Cruikshank's illustration to it, it reappeared in *Ainsworth's Magazine* (Jan 46, IX, 1–5) under the title "Sir Lionel Flamstead. A Sketch".

³ This was CD's first invitation to Ainsworth after a lapse in their friendship of over 20 months: see *To* Forster, ?21 Dec, *hn* and *fn*.

## *To* UNKNOWN CORRESPONDENT, 19 DECEMBER 1840

Text from John Waller catalogue No. 135 (1883); dated Devonshire Terrace, 19 Dec 40.

Dear Sir,

I shall certainly do myself the pleasure of seeing you next Wednesday, and am always, faithfully yours,

CHARLES DICKENS

## *To* GEORGE CATTERMOLE, 21 DECEMBER [1840]

Text from MDGH, I, 33. *Date:* 1840, since CD's instructions for *Old Curiosity Shop*, Ch. 70 (No. 43).

Devonshire Terrace, December 21st.

My dear George,

Kit, the single gentleman, and Mr. Garland go down to the place where the child is, and arrive there at night. There has been a fall of snow. Kit, leaving them behind, runs to the old house,[1] and, with a lanthorn in one hand and the bird in its cage in the other, stops for a moment at a little distance with a natural hesitation before he goes up to make his presence known. In a window—supposed to be that of the child's little room—a light is burning, and in that room the child (unknown, of course, to her visitors, who are full of hope) lies dead.[2]

If you have any difficulty about Kit, never mind about putting him in. *The two others to-morrow.*

Faithfully always

[CHARLES DICKENS]

## *To* JOHN FORSTER, [?21 DECEMBER 1840]

Extracts in F, II, viii, 162. *Date:* According to Forster, CD was here describing the "motive, as well as the principle that guided him" in his "last successful labour of the year ... the reconciliation of two friends". The friends were no doubt Forster himself and Ainsworth;[3] and this letter probably told Forster of Ainsworth's acceptance of the invitation of 18 Dec. The letter's opening words must refer to CD's thoughts about Nell's coming death, while writing instructions to Cattermole: see last.

In the midst of this child's death, I, over whom something of the bitterness of death has passed, not lightly perhaps, was reminded of many

[1] Cf. *To* Forster, ?16 or 18 Dec, *fn.*
[2] Through having been drawn from the description in this letter, Cattermole's illustration, "The ruin in snow", does not agree with the text in one important detail. It has no "curtain drawn across the lower portion of the window" (see Ch. 70): so Kit could have seen into the room where Nell lies dead without difficulty.
*aa* Omitted in MDGH, 1882, MDGH, 1893, and N.
[3] Estranged since Spring 1839, when CD accused Ainsworth of acquiescing

old kindnesses, and was sorry in my heart that men who really liked each other should waste life at arm's length.

I have laid it down as a rule in my judgment of men, to observe narrowly whether some (of whom one is disposed to think badly) don't carry all their faults upon the surface, and others (of whom one is disposed to think well) don't carry many more beneath it. I have long ago made sure that our friend is in the first class; and when I know all the foibles a man has, with little trouble in the discovery, I begin to think he is worth liking.

## *To* JOHN FORSTER, [?22 DECEMBER 1840]

Extract in F, II, viii, 162. *Date:* the day following last according to Forster, who also calls it CD's "latest letter of the year"—which it was almost certainly not.[1] CD was probably writing about plans for Christmas Day.[2]

*The letter closed with the hope that he and Forster might enjoy together* fifty more Christmases, at least, in this world, and eternal summers in another.

## *To* GEORGE CATTERMOLE, [?22 DECEMBER 1840]

MS Mr Roger W. Barrett. *Date:* not dated by CD; but he probably sent Cattermole the two subjects on 22 Dec (the date supplied by MDGH and copied in N), as promised on 21 Dec.

Dr. George

The child lying dead in the little sleeping room which is behind the

in attacks on Forster by Bentley which he knew to be false (see *To* Ainsworth, 26 Mar 39; I, 530–2). S. M. Ellis (*W. H. Ainsworth and his Friends*, 1911, I, 389) asserts that no breach in CD's and Ainsworth's "intimate friendship" followed the letter (which he quotes, though omitting some of the most damaging passages); but the lack of letters from CD to Ainsworth between 1 Apr 39 and 18 Dec 40 disproves this. Ellis hints at a breach with Forster, but shifts the blame on to Forster's antagonistic review of *Jack Sheppard* in the *Examiner* (3 Nov 39), which he attributes to jealousy of its sales exceeding *Oliver's*: of this Ainsworth spoke "sorrowfully many years after" (*op. cit.*, I, 358–9). It was in fact Ainsworth who made the first reconciliatory move, in inviting CD and Forster to be among about 60 guests at a dinner on 12 Dec 40 to celebrate his completion of *The Tower of London*. But clearly a full reconciliation could only take place on a more intimate occasion. Hence CD's

invitation of 18 Dec for New Year's Eve—when friendly relations were apparently restored (see *To* Ainsworth, 25 Jan 41). Ainsworth, however, had been finally replaced by Maclise in the "trio" with CD and Forster.

[1] Forster had presumably decided that the letters of 28 and 30 Dec did not belong in 1840. The letter of 28 Dec has four date endorsements in his hand: "1839", "9 if the Chuzzlewit | doubtful", "1840" and "1841". That of 30 Dec (not endorsed) could, were it not for the handwriting, belong in any one of several years (N places it in 1842). Letter above, with its reference to Christmas, could scarcely be 31 Dec; nor is the reconciliation-letter likely to have been a second written on 30 Dec.

[2] Forster dined with Macready on Christmas Day 1840; but Macready records that, earlier, CD and Forster called on him and the three of them "walked round the Park at a posting rate together—a delightful afternoon" (*Diaries*, II, 112).

oaken screen. It is winter time, so there are no flowers; but upon her breast, and pillow, and about her bed, there may be slips of holly, and berries, and such free green things.—Window overgrown with ivy—. The little boy who had that talk with her about angels, *may* be by the bedside, if you like it so, but I think it will be quieter and more peaceful if she is quite alone. I want it to express the most beautiful repose and tranquillity, and to have something of a happy look, if death can.[1]

2nd.

The child has been buried *inside* the church, and the old man who cannot be made to understand that she is dead, repairs to the grave every day, and sits there all day long, waiting for her arrival, to begin another journey. His staff and knapsack, her little bonnet and basket, &c lie beside him.[2] "She'll come tomorrow" he says when it gets dark, and goes sorrowfully home. I think an hour-glass running out, would help the notion.[3]—Perhaps *her* little things upon his knee, or in his hands—

————

I am breaking my heart over this story, and cannot bear to finish it.

Love to Missis

Ever & always heartily

CD

## *To* MRS CHARLES SMITHSON, 23 DECEMBER 1840

Mention in *American Book Prices Current*, 1901.

## *To* THOMAS MITTON, 24 DECEMBER 1840*

MS University of Texas.

Christmas Eve 1840.

My Dear Mitton

Father[4] tells me he saw you today—I thought you told me you were going out of town.—The Smithsons are coming to play at charades

---

[1] Cattermole drew Nell alone in the "little sleeping room". For the effect of the illustration on Macready, see *To* Macready, 22 Jan 41, *fn.*

[2] Most of these details are in the illustration; but Cattermole devoted as much—if not more—care to the architecture of the church and its tombs.

[3] Cattermole drew the hour-glass, though not in the church but in the background of his previous illustration —"Nell dead". CD had made the same suggestion to Maclise for his illustration "Nell and the Sexton" (see ?6 Nov 40).

[4] CD's parents had presumably come up to London to spend Christmas with him.

tonight.[1] If you are really not gone, for God's sake come. I can't tell you how surprised and vexed I am to think I mistook you—as I suppose I must have done.

I have sent a copy of this to New Inn.[2]

Always faithfully
CD.

## *To* HENRY AUSTIN, 26 DECEMBER 1840*

MS Morgan Library. *Address:* Henry Austin Esquire.

Devonshire Terrace. | December Twenty Sixth 1840.

Dear Henry.

John Forster Esqre. 58 Lincolns Inn Fields.

Daniel Maclise Esqre. 14 Russell Place Fitzroy Square.

[          ]

Henry Austin Esquire                       [CHARLES DICKENS][3]

## *To* BASIL HALL,[4] 28 DECEMBER 1840

Extracts in Retz & Storm catalogue No. 8 (*aa*) and N, I, 284 (*bb*); dated
1 Devonshire Terrace, Twenty-Eighth December 1840.

*[a]Thanking Hall for a copy of* Patchwork.[5] I have been pursuing the

[1] Probably this was the "small charade party at the Dickens's" for which Emma Picken, on calling at the Smithsons one evening after the Broadstairs holiday, found Mrs Smithson and Amelia Thompson dressing. "Milly immediately proposed to take me with them, but Mrs. S—— said, looking puzzled and uncertain, that she feared Mr. Dickens might think it a liberty!" ("Reminiscences of CD", *Englishwoman's Domestic Magazine*, x, 342). Whether Mrs Smithson was nevertheless persuaded to take her the "Reminiscences" do not say, though their silence implies that she was not. But Emma's (in general less reliable) "Recollections" state that after the return from Broadstairs "we continued to have our charade parties", and describes one at which Maclise arranged a striking "tableau-non-*vivant*" representing—with hat-stand, cake-basket, Catherine's bonnet-feathers &c &c—"Alonzo the brave and the fair Imogene". This may have been the party of 24 Dec, or else one of the many Broadstairs parties moved into the

Devonshire Terrace setting. Before the end of the year CD had clearly decided that his high-spirited flirtation with Emma must end. She lunched with him and Catherine soon after their return from Broadstairs and found him preoccupied and "changed in manner" ("Reminiscences", p. 342). The payment to "Miss Picken" of £3.3.0, recorded in CD's account-book (MS Messrs Coutts) on 26 Oct 40, may well have been for the drawing she had made of Catherine, which CD refused to look at (see *ibid*).

[2] The copy, reading "Southampton Buildings" for "New Inn", is in the Huntington Library.

[3] A piece has been cut out of the paper here, probably only removing the ending and signature.

[4] Basil Hall, FRS (1788–1844; *DNB*), Capt, RN: see Vol. I, p. 604*n*. Now living at Portsmouth with his wife and family. A great admirer of CD's work, he saw any pathetic incidents that came his way as potential material for CD's pen, and wrote him long descriptions of

fortunes of the child in whom you take so much interest, ever since its receipt, and have only had time to cut it, to read the preface, and to devour (very gluttonously) the paper called the Gallows and the Guillotine,[1] which struck me very much indeed. It is a great piece of description.[2] *He then gives his views on public executions.*[a]

[b]What can I say to you in acknowledgement of your high commendation of the tale I am drawing to a close—with no common regret and pain I do assure you—for I am loath to finish it—and of the cheering encouragement you give me. It would be idle to tell you that such expressions[3] of interest from thinking and gifted men are a source of the purest happiness and delight. You know that, I am sure, and I cannot thank you enough for your generous applause.[b]

[a]*CD closes with the hope that Hall will accept, with his compliments, copies of* Master Humphrey *as the parts are issued.*[a]

them. As he told CD in a letter of 28 June 41, he had himself published "19 Volumes already", and had by him "no fewer than 81 Volumes of old Journals . . . pretty well milked dry"; yet there remained "an infinity of trash" which he still might publish "to the augmentation of [his] miserable half pay, . . . 10/6 a day" (MS Huntington). But his mind broke down in 1842 and *Patchwork* was his last book.

[5] *Patchwork*, 3 vols, 1841 (in fact published Dec 40), a collection of travel stories.

[1] Vol. II, pp. 61–96: a comparison between the English and French methods of execution. The executions of Thistlewood and his associates in the Cato Street Conspiracy of 1820 and of a French murderer—both witnessed by Hall—are described; and hanging is favoured as being more solemn, more likely to deter and no more painful.

[2] Replying to this letter on 10 Jan 41, Hall wrote: "In my gallows chapter— (which I inserted *solely* from the encouragement which some parts of your writings gave me to be bold—) I added the letter about the boy expressly in the hope that it would touch you—& I rejoice greatly to find that it did." The "letter about the boy" was written from Newgate on 30 Apr 1820 by one of Thistlewood's associates, on the eve of his execution for high treason, to his

son. It began: "My little dear boy William, I hope you will live to read these few lines, when the remains of your poor father is mouldered to dust" (*Patchwork*, II, 74–5). Hall's letter to CD went on: "In one of my Chapters called the End of Life [*Patchwork*, *I*, *182–96*] . . . also, I ventured, here & there, on a touch in your vein—but as I have a great horror at the crime of imitation I hope I have not betrayed my secret to any eye but yours. Human nature, it is true is so wide that there is room for all of us—but *you* must know right well what a pack of harriers your success has set yelping at your tail" (MS Huntington). "The End of Life" is a somewhat morbid account of the last days and death of a widowed Swiss woman whom Hall had gone out to help at the request of her former English employers. The *Edinburgh* reviewer, Sir John Barrow, thought the chapter "would much better have been omitted", being "of too dismal a colour" to match with the rest—which included brilliant descriptions of the Alps, Paris, Etna and Vesuvius. "The Gallows and the Guillotine" (which CD devoured "very gluttonously") "might as well have been left out" too (*Edinburgh Review*, Apr 41, LXXIII, 41–54).

[3] Thus in catalogue. N reads "expression".

## *To* JOHN FORSTER, 28 DECEMBER [1840]

MS Victoria & Albert Museum. *Date:* clearly 1840. CD's Account-book (MS Messrs Coutts) shows £200 credited on 29 Dec 40, £300 on 11 Jan 41, and the monthly £200 reduced to £150 from Jan onwards. *Address:* John Forster Esquire | 58 Lincolns Inn Fields.

Parthenon. | Tuesday twenty eighth December

My Dear Forster.

Knowing that you are out by this time, I write to you instead of calling again.

After I saw you to day and had been into the city, I called at Chapman and Hall's. I saw the latter, who told me that he had paid into Coutts's *£200*. Now, the two should be a five—that is, £200 for the month,[1] and £300 which was (you recollect?) to be advanced at this time, and deducted in monthly fifties.

As you were kind enough to negociate this matter with them,[2] and as I have never interchanged a syllable with them about it, I wish you would be so good as to send for Mr. Hall tomorrow morning, and get this mistake corrected. I need not say that it is rather a serious one at this time of year,[3] and that the sooner it is set right, the better.

I would have spared you this trouble, but as I am not in a condition to remind them of what passed, (not having heard it) I think it but right and necessary to leave the matter with you.

Faithfully Always

John Forster Esquire                CHARLES DICKENS


## *To* JOHN FORSTER, 30 DECEMBER [1840]

MS Victoria & Albert Museum (FC). *Date:* undoubtedly 1840, on handwriting.

Devonshire Terrace | December Thirtieth

My Dear Forster.

I think there is plenty inserted to fill the inclosed. I question, however, whether it will be necessary now to strike anything out. I hope you may think it the better for the alterations.[4]

It will be necessary to have a revise.[5]

What about dining today?

Faithfully Ever

CD

---

[1] I.e. £50 for each weekly number under the terms of the Agreement for *Master Humphrey* of 31 Mar (see Appx, p. 465).

[2] Exactly when Forster negotiated this advance is not known; but clearly it was not at the meeting of 10 Nov when CD must have been present. The firm made CD other advances between July 40 and June 41: see CD's reference, in *To* Chapman & Hall, 31 July 41, to a total advance of £769.9.5 (called by William Chapman "about £1000" in his letter to Smithson & Mitton, 12 June 41: see Appx, p. 488).

[3] CD's bank balance at the end of

## *To* JOHN OVERS, 30 DECEMBER 1840

MS Free Library of Philadelphia.

Devonshire Terrace. | Wednesday 30th. December | 1840.
Dear Mr. Overs.

I could not find time to read your paper before to-day. Having done so, I think it is a good magazine piece—I am speaking, mind, as if I knew nothing of the author, or the circumstances under which it was written—and *quite equal* to the general run of such things. If you will make the little corrections I have marked, and keep it by you until you have finished the other, I will think in the mean time where you will do best to try it.

I object on principle to making Wat such a thorough-paced villain, because a rebel on such grounds has a certain claim to one's sympathy, and I feel that if I had lived in his time, I should have been very likely to have knocked out the Collector's brains myself,—or at all events to have looked upon the man who did so, as a demi-God. Fathers may naturally object to having gross indecencies practised upon their daughters even by government servants; and bystanders can scarcely shew their manhood better than by resenting such things when they are done before their eyes.[1]

Therefore, if Wat Tyler and his followers when their passions were once let loose, had burnt down the City and got drunk with blood, I should still entertain some respect for their memory.

Apart from this, I have been greatly pleased with the performance, and I

1840 was £232.8.0 (Account-book, MS Messrs Coutts).

[4] Presumably "the inclosed" was the corrected galley-proof of No. 41 (Ch. 66), published 9 Jan 41, which shows numerous small additions made to counterbalance a cancelled passage of 43 lines in the course of which Sally Brass reveals that she is the Marchioness's mother. (The passage is quoted in full by Gerald Grubb in *Modern Language Notes*, LXVIII [1953], 162–3.) In Ch. 51, where Quilp first meets the Marchioness, questions her, observes her narrowly, and is suddenly convulsed with mirth, CD was presumably preparing for this later revelation. But even while writing Ch. 66 he had been uncertain whether to make it (see *To* Forster, 16 Dec, *fn*), and now he had clearly decided that it was best to confine himself to hints. One hint was already there—Sally's "curious kind of spasm about her mouth" and "cunning" expression, reminiscent of the Marchioness's "look of infinite cunning" as she "screwed up her mouth very tight and round" in Ch. 51; and

CD added a further hint, when Sally, in the presence of the notary, flushes on mention of the Marchioness and is immediately on the defensive, but relaxes on hearing that the charge against herself mainly concerns Kit. CD never gave the information about the Marchioness's parentage explicitly; but it appears in the form of speculations by Dick in a single sentence in the final chapter of the book.

[5] The revise (Forster Collection, V & A) shows that CD when altering the galley had not inserted enough to fill the No. On the last page some padding is therefore introduced into Mr Witherden's surprising communication to Dick, and the final sentence of the chapter ("And she shall walk in silk attire . . .") added.

[1] The story of Wat Tyler's killing the tax-collector, after the insult to his daughter, derives from John Stow's *The Chronicles of England* [1580]. It was retold by Thomas Keightley, whose *History of England*, 3 vols, 1839, was one of the sources for CD's *A Child's History of England*.

speak most seriously when I say that in the way of improvement, you have done *wonders*.[1]

Beware of writing things for the eyes of everybody, which you would feel the smallest delicacy in *saying* anywhere. Mrs. Scutfidge[2] may have stripped in public—I have no doubt she did—but I should be sorry to have to tell young ladies so in the nineteenth Century, for all that.

Faithfully Yours<br>CHARLES DICKENS

## *To* MRS F[?ILLONNEAU], [WINTER 1840–1]

Mention in next.

## *To* JOHN FORSTER, [WINTER 1840–1]

MS Victoria & Albert Museum (FC). *Date:* Signature (on outside) and handwriting suggest Winter 1840-1. *Address:* John Forster Esquire.

My Dear Forster

Yes—I wrote to that effect to the beautiful Mrs. F,[3] whose eyelashes are in my memory.

Would you know this hand? Oh Evins how misty I am!

Always Faithfully<br>CD

Come tonight[4]

## *To* UNKNOWN CORRESPONDENT, [1840]

Mention in *Autograph Prices Current*, VI (1921–2); *MS* 1 p.; from Devonshire Terrace, 1840.

*Referring to the purchase of some port.*

---

[1] The paper was not, however, included in Overs's *Evenings of a Working Man*, 1844.

[2] Not a known historical character.

[3] Possibly Amelia Fillonneau, Henry Austin's sister, who had married André Fillonneau in 1837 (see Vol. I, pp. 18 and 283*n*). CD implied more than once that he found her beautiful: in 1847, for instance, he sent her a recipe for punch, hoping that it would make her "a beautiful Punchmaker in more senses than one" (*D*, I [1905], 205). The Fillonneaus lived at this time in London and later in Paris. See W. J. Carlton in *D*, LI (1955), 150–4.

[4] Written large, with a flourish beneath.

*To* UNKNOWN CORRESPONDENT, [1840]*

Text from typescript, Huntington Library.

*Private.*                    1 Devonshire Terrace, | Sunday Morning, 1840.
Dear Sir,
        I had retained your tale with the view of reading it next week, when I
should have had sufficient leisure for the purpose—inferring from the tone
of the letter which did *not* miscarry, that you still wished me to peruse it.
        In the propriety and truth of all that you state in that letter with equal
manliness and modesty, I entirely concur. I wish you saw your way to
the attainment of your moderate wishes, and assure you sincerely that if I
can at any time help you towards that end, you may command such aid as I
can render you.

                                                Very truly yours,
                                                CHARLES DICKENS

        I did not quite understand whether you wished to see me this morning,
and have therefore left your parcel out, deeming it very probable that you
might not have any such desire. If you have, I shall be very happy to
afford you an interview at half past one o'clock on any Sunday you may
name.

*To* THOMAS MITTON, [?1840]

Mention in American Art Association and Anderson Galleries catalogue,
Jan 1935; *MS* (signed initials) 1 p.; dated Devonshire Terrace, Monday
morning [1840].

*Requesting Mitton to change the hour of their appointment and mentioning
Miss Coutts.*

*To* THE REV. WILLIAM HARNESS,[1] 2 JANUARY 1841

Text from MDGH, I, 37.

                            Devonshire Terrace | Saturday Morning, Jan. 2nd, 1841
My dear Harness,
        I should have been very glad to join your pleasant party, but all next
week I shall be laid up with a broken heart, for I must occupy myself in
finishing the "Curiosity Shop", and it is such a painful task to me that I
must concentrate myself upon it tooth and nail, and go out nowhere until
it is done.
        I have delayed answering your kind note in a vague hope of being

---

[1] William    Harness    (1790–1869;
*DNB*). For CD's dining with him 5
Feb 39 see Vol. I, p. 639. They had
possibly first met at the Athenæum on
26 Oct 38: Harness noted in his diary
(MS Mrs E. Duncan-Jones) the names
of those dining there that evening; CD's
he underlined.

heart-whole again by the seventh. The present state of my work, however (Christmas not being a very favourable season for making progress in such doings), assures me that this cannot be, and that I must heroically deny myself the pleasure you offer.[1]

Always believe me, | Faithfully yours
[CHARLES DICKENS]

## *To* T.N. TALFOURD, 2 JANUARY 1841

Mention in *To* Harness, 10 Jan.

## *To* JOHN FORSTER, 5 JANUARY [1841]

MS Victoria & Albert Museum (FC). *Date:* 5 Jan was Tuesday in 1841; handwriting supports that year.

Devonshire Terrace. | Tuesday Morning | Fifth January.
My Dear Forster.

On the whole we were tremendous last night,[2] though rather slack at first. We had two very long Sir Roger de Coverleys, and after supper about eight very good Charades. Among them was conspicuous "Morning Herald" invented by your humble.

I shall certainly not stir out today, for we were not home until half-past five, and not up until half-past twelve. Unless I look very sharp, I shall not have done the No. by tomorrow night[3]—for I drank punch last evening in considerable quantities.

Always Faithfully
CD.

As you don't say how the face is, I suppose it was a false alarm.

## *To* DANIEL MACLISE, 6 JANUARY [1841]

Text in N, I, 292 checked from MS Sotheby's, 15 Dec 64. *Date:* Charley was four in 1841.

Devonshire Terrace. | Wednesday Morning Sixth January
My Dear Maclise.

To day is Charley's birth-day. He attains the tremendous age of four. If

[1] CD did, however, accept a later invitation from Harness for 29 Jan (see Diary entry, Appx, p. 463).

[2] Perhaps at Mrs Fillonneau's: see *To* Forster, Winter 1840–1.

[3] No. 43 (Chs 69 and 70), in which Mr Garland, the single gentleman and Kit travel to the village where they have discovered Nell lives and are directed to her house by the sexton. On the journey the single gentleman tells Mr Garland the Trent family history and reveals that he is the old man's younger brother, returned from his self-imposed exile "with wealth for both". It was probably shortly before this that CD wrote the page of notes on the Trent family, beginning "Single gentleman and old man brothers—loved the same girl", of which the MS is in the Forster Collection (V & A).

you have nothing better to do, perhaps you'll look in this evening. Forster
will be here, but nobody else.

Faithfully Yours always

Daniel Maclise Esquire.                    CHARLES DICKENS

## To W. C. MACREADY, [?6 JANUARY 1841]*

MS Morgan Library. *Date:* almost certainly 6 Jan, referring to Ch. 70
(finished that day), which ends with Kit's arrival at the house in which—
although no one yet knew it[1]—Nell lies dead. By Wed 13 Jan the final
"murdering" had already been done; CD spent that day and the next on
Ch. 72, and read Chs 71 and 72 to Forster on the night of Thurs 14th (F,
II, vii, 150).

Devonshire Terrace. | Wednesday Morning.

My Dear Macready.

Why do you always leave the name which is most pleasant and welcome
to me,—when I am not at home?

Are you going to Elliotson's on Friday? If so, I'll take you there, and
call for you.

I am slowly murdering that poor child, and grow wretched over it. It
wrings my heart. Yet it must be.

Faithfully Always<br>CD.

## To DANIEL MACLISE, [?7 JANUARY 1841]*

MS Benoliel Collection. *Date:* from Nov 40 onwards on "Mac" in salutation; before July 41 on handwriting. If referring to Talfourd's dinner of 7
Jan (see *To* Harness, 10 Jan), CD's promise would have been made while
inflamed by punch and Sir Roger de Coverley on the 4th (*To* Forster,
5 Jan). *Address:* Wait | Daniel Maclise Esquire.

My Dear Mac

Kate and Fanny have Raised the Standard of Rebellion this morning,
and placed me in what the Americans would call "a slantindicular[2] fix"
—swearing that I promised to bring them to see your picture[3] to day;
being at the moment inflamed with wine and "the Mazy".[4]

What's to be done? May they come about 3 or so? After that, as I want
to call at Brompton,[5] let you and I go and ride in the Parks until Talfourd's

---

[1] "Will Nelly die?", wrote Lady
Stanley to her daughter-in-law after
Quilp's death in No. 42; "I think she
ought" (*The Ladies of Alderley*, ed.
N. Mitford, 1938, p. 2).

[2] Portmanteau word from "slanting"
and "perpendicular"; fig., "indirect"
(slang, 1840).

[3] Perhaps *The Sleeping Beauty*, for
which CD had made suggestions on
25 Nov.

[4] "The mazy dance": cf. Dick
Swiveller's "thread the windings of the
mazy" (*Old Curiosity Shop*, Ch. 56).

[5] Perhaps on Edward Chapman, then
living at Clare Villa, Old Brompton.

dinner is ready, and Elyian[1] blandishments convert our present sweet seeming into bitter gall.[2]

Faithfully Always
CD

## *To* MISS HANNAH MEREDITH, 7 JANUARY [1841]*

MS Morgan Library. *Date:* 7 Jan was Thursday in 1841; handwriting supports that year.

Devonshire Terrace | Thursday Jany. 7th.

My Dear Miss Meredith.

On *Wednesday* next,[3] I shall most gladly enjoy the pleasure your note offers.

Begging my compliments to Miss Coutts, I am always

Faithfully Yours

Miss Meredith. CHARLES DICKENS

## *To* JOHN FORSTER, [?8 JANUARY 1841]

Extract in F, II, vii, 150. *Date:* Fri 7 Jan according to Forster; but 7 Jan was Thursday. CD had probably finished No. 43 on 6 Jan (see *To* Forster, 5 Jan), begun No. 44 on 7 Jan, and was now, on 8 Jan, still writing Ch. 71— at the end of which Kit, Mr Garland, the single gentleman, the schoolmaster and the bachelor follow the old man into Nell's room and find her dead.

Done! Done!!! Why bless you, I shall not be done till Wednesday night. I only began yesterday, and this part of the story is not to be galloped over, I can tell you. I think it will come famously—but I am the wretchedest of the wretched. It casts the most horrible shadow upon me, and it is as much as I can do to keep moving at all. I tremble to approach the place a great deal more than Kit; a great deal more than Mr. Garland; a great deal more than the Single Gentleman. I shan't recover it for a long time. Nobody will miss her like I shall. It is such a very painful thing to me, that I really cannot express my sorrow. Old wounds[4] bleed afresh when I only think of the way of doing it: what the actual doing it will be, God knows. I can't preach to myself the schoolmaster's consolation,[5]

[1] Cf. *To* Maclise, 2 June 40.
[2] Cf. *Romeo and Juliet*, I, v, 89–90: "but this intrusion shall, | Now seeming sweet, convert to bitterest gall".
[3] By which time he hoped to have finished No. 44 (Chs 71 and 72).
[4] Inflicted by Mary Hogarth's death, 7 May 37.
[5] See Ch. 54: "Nell, Nell, there may be people busy in the world at this instant, in whose good actions and good thoughts these very graves ... are the chief instruments. ... Forgotten! oh, if the good deeds of human creatures could be traced to their source, how beautifully would even death appear; for how much charity, mercy, and purified affection, would be seen to have their growth in dusty graves!" (a passage particularly admired by Washington Irving: see 21 Apr 41, *fn*).

though I try. Dear Mary died yesterday, when I think of this sad story. I don't know what to say about dining to-morrow—perhaps you'll send up to-morrow morning for news? That'll be the best way.[1] I have refused several invitations for this week and next, determining to go nowhere till I had done. I am afraid of disturbing the state I have been trying to get into, and having to fetch it all back again.[2]

## *To* THE REV. WILLIAM HARNESS,
## 10 JANUARY [1841]*

MS Mr Richard C. Hatchwell. *Date:* 10 Jan was Sunday in 1841; handwriting supports that year.

> Devonshire Terrace.
> ⎧Tenth January—Sunday, and
> ⎨therefore the better day to
> ⎩unburden a guilty conscience.

My Dear Harness.

See what a false, and yet what a true fellow I am!

On the day I answered your kind Invitation,[3] I had one from Talfourd (for that same Thursday) to which I returned exactly the same reply. But on the night following this answer, I had another letter from Russell Square, urging me for various weighty reasons therein set forth to break my resolution rather than the Serjeant's party. The man waited—I am not as firm as I ought to be—I yielded—and went. Now, curse, or forgive me.

Apart from duty, I would have better liked to dine with you, because of those few words we said together at Miss Coutts's.[4] I really feel as though I had committed some grave offence against you, and am impelled to this full and free confession. If it be any consolation to you to know that going out in the midst of the work I had resolved nothing should interfere with, has, up to this time, broken it off and protracted the heartbreaking, you have it in full force I do assure you.

Believe me | Faithfully Yours

Reverend William Harness.                          CHARLES DICKENS

---

[1] Probably when asking CD to dine with him on the 9th Forster invited Maclise too, and it is to this occasion that the following undated note to CD from Maclise refers: "Forster wrote to me last evening—He expects us to dinner with him to-day at half past five—Will you call for me as you pass—? | I can fancy it grieves you to kill poor Nell. I am heartily sorry for the suppositious necessity" (MS Huntington).

[2] A sentence which shows the sort of effort it was to write Ch. 71. Probably, when the time came to write of the death he had had in mind since July 40 (see *To* Forster, ?9 Sep 40, *fn*), CD found he had deliberately to bring thoughts of Mary Hogarth's death into his mind, in order to produce the "state" he needed to be in.

[3] See 2 Jan.

[4] Probably on 17 Dec 40, when CD, cancelling his dinner engagement with Miss Coutts that day, said he hoped to call on her in the course of the evening.

## *To* JOHN FORSTER, 11 JANUARY [1841]

MS Victoria & Albert Museum (FC). *Date:* 11 Jan was Monday in 1841;
handwriting supports that year; paper watermarked 1840.

Devonshire Terrace | Monday Morning | January Eleven

Dear Forster
Behold George's note.[1] I shall meet you there at 5 sharp. 23 Amwell
Street Pentonville—name on door—brass plate.

Faithfully<br>CD.

## *To* DANIEL MACLISE, 11 JANUARY [1841]*

MS Colonel Richard Gimbel. *Date:* same day as last; handwriting supports.

Monday | January Eleven

My Dear Mac
Cruikshank tells me we are fully expected today, to discuss the promised
edgebone.[2] The time 5 *sharp*. The place 23 Amwell Street Pentonville.
Name on door.

Faithfully Always<br>CD.

## *To* GEORGE CATTERMOLE, 14 JANUARY [1841]

MS Free Library of Philadelphia. *Date:* 14 Jan was Thursday in 1841.

Devonshire Terrace | Thursday January Fourteen

My Dear Cattermole.
I cannot tell you how much obliged I am to you for altering the child,[3]
or how much I hope that my wish in that respect didn't go *greatly*[4] against
the grain.
I saw the old Inn[5] this morning. Words cannot say how good it is. I
can't bear the thought of its being cut, and should like to frame and glaze
it in statu quo for ever and ever.
Will you do a little tail piece for the Curiosity story—only one figure if

---

[1] See next.
[2] Corruption of "aitchbone" (*OED*), the cut of beef lying above the rumpbone. CD is no doubt recalling Lamb's "Old Benchers of the Inner Temple" in *Essays of Elia*, where "the omniscient Jackson" favoured this spelling.
[3] Nell on her deathbed, in Ch. 71.
What alteration Cattermole made is not known.
[4] Underlined twice.
[5] Cattermole's drawing of the Maypole Inn, mullion-windowed and elaborately gabled, which formed the headpiece to *Barnaby Rudge*.

you like—giving some notion of the etherealised spirit of the child—something like those little figures in the Frontispiece. *If* you will, and can dispatch it at once, you will make me happy.[1]

I am, for the time being, nearly dead with work—and grief for the loss of my child.

Always | My Dear George | Heartily Yours
                                          CHARLES DICKENS


## *To* MISS BURDETT COUTTS, 14 JANUARY [1841]*

MS Morgan Library. *Date:* 14 Jan was Thursday in 1841; handwriting supports that year. *Address:* Miss Coutts.

Devonshire Terrace. | Thursday January Fourteen.
Dear Miss Coutts.

On *Monday* I am disengaged, and shall be but too happy to enjoy a Library Dinner.[2]

Many thanks to you for the book. I am quite ashamed to have given you the trouble of sending it,—and was about to send for it when your messenger arrived.

Always believe me

Faithfully Yours
Miss Coutts.                              CHARLES DICKENS


## *To* DANIEL MACLISE, 14 JANUARY 1841

Mention in Sotheby's catalogue, June 1950; *MS* 1 p. (signed initials); dated 14 Jan 41; salutation "My Dear Mac".


## *To* BASIL HALL, 15 JANUARY 1841

Extracts from *Autograph Prices Current*, VI, 50 (*aa*), and Anderson Galleries catalogue, 1924 (*bb*); *MS* 2½ pp.; dated Devonshire Terrace, January Fifteenth, 1841.

*a*I have been breaking my heart with such constancy over the Curiosity Shop, that I have not been able to write one note since I received your welcome letter, . . .*a*3

[1] In the tailpiece to the final chapter of *Old Curiosity Shop* Cattermole showed Nell being carried heavenwards, on a cloud, by four angels, very similar to the four holding swords and shields in the border of the frontispiece.

[2] I.e., presumably, an informal dinner in Miss Coutts's library.

[3] On 10 Jan Hall sent CD a copy (offering to send others if he was willing to distribute them) of a letter he had written to the *Hampshire Telegraph* (published 11 Jan), appealing for contributions for the widow and eight children of Capt. Hewett, lost on the HMS *Fairy* while surveying in the North Sea, Nov 40. His letter, Hall said, was meant "to appeal rather to the reason than to the heart", but he had introduced "sundry affecting points".

*b*The clock does not stop, and was never intended to.[1] It goes on—but with a new story.*b*

## *To* [R. S. HORRELL], 15 JANUARY 1841

MS Public Library of Victoria, Melbourne.

Private.

1 Devonshire Terrace. | Fifteenth January 1841.

Sir.

I cannot forbear saying a very few words in reply to your letter of the Ninth. As my time is short, I must say them briefly.

I did not expect you to defer to my opinion *now*. I should say that in three years time you will be more disposed to entertain it, and that in five —at the longest—we shall have come to think alike.

He went on: "Old stager as I am (three & twenty years I have been at it!) I have learned many things from your exquisite taste & discretion in writing. Among others . . . the vast effect of very slightly touching on the pathetic—& then going off to something else. How well, by the way, that old fellow Shakespeare understood this!" CD's "little touch in the Fleet, in Pickwick—where the poor ruined father lays his only child in his little coffin" had cost him "many a tear". He attempted to describe his family's interest in CD's delicious "Hummy", as the children called it, but broke off with: "I am afraid to say more—as an idea has got abroad that you do not like to be spoken to about your works." However, he went on to speak of Nell. His eldest daughter seemed to him "just such a reflecting— considerate—kind—high principled child" as CD made his; and when he asked his second daughter which was her favourite character she replied: "Oh —Nell's being so much above her situation—is what interests me most.— Next to her, I like the small servant." "By the way", wrote Hall, "what an enchanting hit the title of *Marchioness* is! It has flashed through all ranks of society." He liked Swiveller too. But CD's "expressly good characters" failed to move him: they were " 'less in natur' as the elder Weller would say— than those in which a mixture occurs. So of the rogues—whose villainy would be vastly more villainous if the characters were relieved by some shade of— of—what shall I call it?—goodness— no!—but of that frailty of feeling—a certain weakness—a 'whoreson tingling' as Falstaffe says which belongs, I fully believe, to the veriest ruffian on earth." Thus he applauded the passage in which Ralph Nickleby's thoughts flew back "to the days of his innocence & youth", and welcomed Quilp's "sense of ridicule—his excessive delight at a joke—bloodthirsty jokes though his be", which relieved the "jet black of his character" (MS Huntington).

On 15 Jan, not having had an answer to his letter of the 10th, Hall wrote again from Portsmouth—this letter clearly crossing CD's. He reported that the subscription for Mrs Hewett was going well, described a "singularly poetical & touching" dream his elder daughter had had about a midshipman lost on the *Fairy*, and suggested that CD "might immortalise it by giving it as a dream of poor Nell's" (MS Huntington). On 17 Jan, after receiving CD's letter, he sent a few more copies of his printed letter, and reported the "non-arrival of Hummy" on the previous day: "I verily believe if the news of the Pss. Royals death had come upon us it would not have produced as much sensation! I was half afraid to go home" (MS Huntington).

[1] Hall had ended his letter of 10 Jan: "hoping that you are not serious in proposing to stop the Clock in a few numbers—pray wind it up & let us have 100 more such" (MS Huntington).

Are you quite sure that you do not confound my means of estimating your genius, with your own? Pray consider that I am ignorant of the feelings which you admit, yourself, you express inadequately—that I have not been the companion of your thoughts—that I have seen but a very few lines of your writing—and that you would be a very extraordinary man, indeed, if on so short an acquaintance I could pronounce you in my own mind—a Poet.

You seem to desire that I should expressly say whether you would do best to pursue this bent, or to abandon it for ever. I am not in a condition to do so. I have not sufficient knowledge of your abilities. It is impossible for me to acquire it from the data you have given me. And I am confident that if you laid those same pieces before any man who considered the responsibility you imposed upon him, he would say in so many words what I now tell you.

In answer to some of the objections I ventured to suggest to you, you plead the absence of needful revision and correction. Now, I must say you are foolish and wrong in this. The question you wish me to decide, has reference, not only to what you think, but to your power of expressing what you think. How can I judge of that, upon you[r] mere assurance that you have the power of writing regular verse, but have not taken the trouble to exert it? For aught I know, a great many men may *think* poetry—I dare say they do—but the matter between us, is, whether you can write it or no.

Do not suppose that the entertaining a distaste for such extremely light labour as reading and revising your own writings, is a part of the true poetical temperament. Whatever Genius does, it does well; and the man who is constantly beginning things and never finishing them is no true Genius, take my word for it.

I do not remember to have ever had, within the last four or five years, any composition sent me by a young man (and I have had a great number) who did not give me to understand that it was the worst he had ever written, and that he had much better ones at home.

I tell you candidly that I am interested in you—that I should be glad if you would do justice both to yourself and me, and give me the means of knowing what you really can do—and that I should be delighted to cheer and encourage you if I found I could. I should like to see the Young Painter's Dream with its altered (that is, with its original) conclusion; and if I should not receive them from you by any other mode, I shall certainly if I visit Exeter next summer—as I think I shall—hope to take the two poetical tales from your own hand.

I hope you will not misunderstand me in anything I have said to you, either in this, or in my former letter. If I seem cruel, it is only to be kind,[1] believe me. You do not know, and can form no conception of the misery (often untold to any other ears) which I see every day of my life in young men who mistook their vocation when they were younger, and have become the very beggars of Literature. It is because I know the bitterness

[1] Cf. *Hamlet*, III, iv, 178.

and anguish of such mistakes, and looking along the path you wish to tread, see these dismal scarecrows in it, that I must know well what your qualification is, before I encourage you in your perilous desire.

If my last letter to you were unsatisfactory, it was so because the specimens you sent me were unsatisfactory too, and insufficient. What I have seen of yours, I should have read with pleasure if it had caught my eye by chance. I cannot say more, unless I repeat that I see every day, writing which is to my mind quite as good. You say you can write better. I wish to be enabled to say so too.

I regret very much to hear that you have been unwell, and sincerely hope your health is now improving. Assuring you that your confidence needs no apology or excuse, I am

Faithfully Yours

S. Harford[1] Esquire            CHARLES DICKENS

## *To* JOHN FORSTER, [?17] JANUARY 1841†

MS Victoria & Albert Museum (FC).[2] *Date:* 17 Jan was Sunday in 1841; curiously, CD seems to have been mistaken in the day of the week, not the date in the month.[3]

Devonshire Terrace | Monday Seventeenth January | 1841.

My Dear Forster.

I can't help letting you know how much your yesterday's letter pleased me.[4] I felt sure you liked the Chapters when we read them on Thursday

[1] The assumed name of R. S. Horrell: see 14 Oct 40, *fn.*

[2] In Forster's copy of *Old Curiosity Shop.*

[3] The letter from Forster (see below) referred to in paragraph 1 was clearly written on two consecutive days: begun on Fri 15 Jan (the day after CD had read him Chs 71 and 72) and finished on the Saturday morning, 16th. CD's "after you left last night" in paragraph 4 must surely have referred to the call Forster's postscript had promised for Saturday evening. During it Forster presumably gave CD his letter of the 15th/16th, perhaps asking him not to read it until he had gone. CD then worked until 4 a.m. on the Sunday, and wrote this letter to Forster during the day—clearly sending it by hand, since Forster was to give Macready a message the same day. (On Sundays Macready habitually had people to dinner or himself dined out.)

[4] Forster had written: "I could not say to you last night my dear Dickens how much this last Chapter has moved me. But I cannot resist the impulse of sending this hasty line to say it now. | It is little to tell you that I think it is your literary masterpiece. The deeper feeling it has left with me goes beyond considerations of that kind. | And so far *I* had gone yesterday when the Examiner & the Face Ache stopped me. I was about to say that I had felt this death of dear little Nell as a kind of discipline of feeling and emotion which would do me lasting good, and which I would not thank you for as an ordinary enjoyment of literature. But the stoppage disables me from saying it as intelligibly as I might have said it yesterday, and you must take the will for the deed. | Believe me at least, that if anything could have increased my affection for you, this would have done it. You and I have sometimes had hasty differences—such only as such intimate friends are apt to fall into—but certain am I, that if, at any time hereafter, a word or tone that might possibly give

night, but it was a great delight to have my impression so strongly and heartily confirmed.

You know how little value I should set on what I had done, if all the world cried out that it was good, and those whose good opinion and approval[1] I value most, were silent. The assurance that this little closing of the scene, touches and is felt by you so strongly, is better to me than a thousand most sweet voices[2] out of doors.[3]

When I first began *(on your valued suggestion)* to keep my thoughts upon this ending of the tale,[4] I resolved to try and do something which might be read by people about whom Death had been,—with a softened feeling, and with consolation. *I was moved, therefore, to have poor Bradbury's note yesterday,[5] and was glad to think he felt as I would have had him.*

After you left last night I took my desk up stairs, and writing until four o'Clock this morning, finished the old story. It makes me very melancholy to think that all these people are lost to me for ever,[6] and I feel as if I never could become attached to any new set of characters.

*I wish you would give my love to Macready (I suppose you dine there today) and tell him that on Friday night, I will send him the next week's number, in order that he may read the two together, which I should like him very much to do. Tomorrow morning, please God, I shall be with you—about twelve.

                    Always My Dear Forster | Your affectionate friend
John Forster Esquire.                              CHARLES DICKENS*

## *To* MISS BURDETT COUTTS, [18 JANUARY 1841]*

MS Morgan Library. *Date:* clearly 18 Jan, the day fixed for the "Library Dinner" (*To* Miss Coutts, 14 Jan); signature supports. *Address:* Miss Coutts.

                              Devonshire Terrace | Monday Afternoon.
Dear Miss Coutts.

It is with no slight disappointment, I assure you, that I have been

you pain should threaten to rise to my throat, I'd gulp it down in the memory of Nell. | God bless you my dear Dickens and give you life to write many more such books and me the power to subscribe myself ever | Your grateful & affectionate friend | . . . PS. I shall be with you today—but as I shall have to call at one or two places, don't wait an instant for me. I hope to be with you at 5—& shall certainly be with you very shortly after. | Saturday Morning" (MS Private).

[1] Changed to "approbation" in F, II, vii, 150.

[2] Cf. *Coriolanus*, II, iii, 169.

[3] I.e. than the greatest praise from other people.

*aa* Given in italics in F, II, vii, 150.

[4] A decision made *c.* Aug 40 (see *To* Forster, ?9 Sep 40, *fn*).

*bb, cc* Not previously published.

[5] Bradbury, as printer, had no doubt read the chapters in MS. Having lost a young daughter in 1839 (see Vol. I, p. 515), he would have been particularly moved.

[6] Cf. "Master Humphrey from his Clock Side in the Chimney-Corner", following the last chapter of *Old*

obliged to make up my mind—on the doctor's orders—to stay at home this evening. I should not mind a bad cold, but I have the additional pleasure of a swelled face, which is too large even to be amusing—to look at— otherwise I should certainly have presented it in its deformity, despite all injunctions to the reverse.

I hope this is not the *last* "Library Dinner"; and with that hope, console myself.[1]

Believe me always | Faithfully Yours
Miss Coutts.                                          CHARLES DICKENS

## To W. C. MACREADY, 19 JANUARY 1841

Text from N, I, 295.

Devonshire Terrace | Nineteenth January 1841
My Dear Macready,

I don't know whether you have seen the inclosed. I only send it to you because I promised Basil Hall that I would distribute a few copies for him.[2]

There is a separate subscription for the widows of the other officers, and the men.[3] I mean to divide what I did intend to give to the Lord Holland testimonial[4] between the two lists.[5]

Always, my Dear Macready, | Faithfully yours
[CHARLES DICKENS]

## To JOHN OVERS, 21 JANUARY 1841

Text from Walter T. Spencer catalogue ;n.d., in Eastgate House, Rochester.

Devonshire Terrace | Twenty-first January, 1841.
Dear Mr. Overs,

They have sent me from Chatham a copy of that immortal work, which I beg you to accept, as it contains a very good song of yours.[6] It is in company which will by no means discourage you.

I also send a little hand-bill, by which you will see that due honour has been done to your name.

Faithfully yours,
CHARLES DICKENS

*Curiosity Shop* (No. 45), in which Master Humphrey reproaches himself for looking forward to the ending of his tale, "as if it were a kind of cruelty to those companions of my solitude whom I had now dismissed, and could never again recall".

[1] The invitation was renewed for 30 Jan: see *To Miss Coutts, 22 Jan, fn.*

[2] See *To Hall, 15 Jan, fn.*

[3] A separate subscription for the widows and children of the seamen and marines of the *Fairy* had been opened by Capt. Hornby, Superintendent of Woolwich Dockyard (*Examiner,* 17 Jan 41).

[4] Lord Holland had died on 22 Oct 40. Lord Lansdowne organized a subscription for a monument to him, erected in Westminster Abbey 1844.

[5] CD sent Hall three guineas (Account-book, MS Messrs Coutts).

[6] The *Kentish Coronal,* containing Overs's song "The Trysting Tree" (see *To Adams, 18 Jan 40*).

## *To* THOMAS BEARD, 21 JANUARY 1841

MS Dickens House. *Address:* Wait. | Thomas Beard Esquire | or | Miss
Beard | 42 Portman Place | Edgeware Road.

Devonshire Terrace. | Twenty First January 1841.
My Dear Beard
Will's[1] haunch is scientifically carved by your humble, next Sabbath
Day at 5. Come and try it. And Kate desires me to say (with all manner
of loves and remembrances, wherein I join) that if your sister will join
you, we shall be delighted to see her.

Always My Dear Beard | Heartily Yours
CHARLES DICKENS

## *To* MESSRS CHAPMAN & HALL, 21 JANUARY 1841*

MS Benoliel Collection.

Devonshire Terrace.
Thursday Evening January 21st. | 1841.
Dear Sirs.
Instead of the usual two of No. 44,[2] let me have half a dozen tomorrow
night, if you please, as I wish to send them *confidentially* to one or two
friends who would consider it a mighty recollection of them, and a great
anticipation of the many-headed.

Faithfully Yours
CHARLES DICKENS

## *To* JOHN FORSTER, [22 JANUARY 1841]

Extract in F, II, ix, 164. *Date:* 22 Jan 41 according to Forster.

I am at present in what Leigh Hunt would call a kind of impossible state
—thinking what on earth Master Humphrey can think of through four
mortal pages.[3] I added, here and there, to the last chapter of the *Curiosity*

---

[1] Probably William Beard (1812–
1905): see Vol. 1, p. 51*n.*
[2] Containing Chs 71 and 72 (published 30 Jan).
[3] CD had originally ended *Old
Curiosity Shop*, Chapter the Last (the
first part of No. 45), with Master Humphrey's extraordinary statement that he
was himself the "single gentleman",
Trent's younger brother, Nell's great-

uncle (a revelation quite incompatible
with the opening of the book and with
the Preface to *Master Humphrey*, Vol. 1,
of Sep 40). He now moved the passage
from "Chapter the Last" and made it
part of the "four mortal pages" he had
to fill for "Master Humphrey from his
Clock Side in the Chimney-Corner"
(the last part of No. 45; published 6
Feb).

*Shop* yesterday,[1] and it leaves me only four pages to write. I also made up, and wrote the needful insertions for, the second number of *Barnaby*[2]—so that I came back to the mill a little.

## *To* CLARKSON STANFIELD, 22 JANUARY 1841*

MS Berg Collection.

Devonshire Terrace.
Friday Twenty Second January 1841.

My Dear Stanfield

On Wednesday the 27th. at the hour you *don't* name, I shall be delighted to join you, and to know Marryat.[3] Until then, and then, and always afterwards,

believe me | Heartily Yours
CHARLES DICKENS

[1] The MS list of *Old Curiosity Shop* characters now in the Forster Collection (V & A) may well have been made by CD while planning who was to be rounded off in this final chapter. Against "Miss Monflathers" he has written "no"; against "Young Trent" and "Sexton", "qy"; the rest on the list are ticked. Quilp is not on it, no doubt because dead; but bringing his corpse into the chapter was perhaps one of CD's additions of 21 Jan; others may have been the fates of List, Jowl, Groves, and Fred Trent—who comes to an unexceptionably bad end.

[2] Through the addition to his original MS of three passages (mostly of conversation in the Maypole), amounting to 1⅓ closely written pages, CD was able to convert the two chapters he had written in 1839, now redivided, into the three which made up the first two weekly numbers of *Barnaby*, and thus start with two numbers in hand.

[3] Frederick Marryat (1792–1848; *DNB*): see Vol. 1, p. 339n. Lived 1840–1841 in his mother's large house at Wimbledon and later in London (separated from his wife, with whom he did not live again). In 1840 published *Poor Jack* (see *To* Longmans, 11 Jan 40 and *fn*) and *Olla Podrida* in 3 vols—articles reprinted chiefly from the *Metropolitan*; in 1841 *Joseph Rushbrook, or the Poacher* and Vol. 1 of *Masterman Ready, or the Wreck of the Pacific* (Vols. II and III followed 1842). His *Diary in America* (6 vols, 1839) was attacked not only in the American Press as anti-American, Tory, and anti-democratic, but also in the *Edinburgh Review* (Oct 39, LXX, 123–49)—in an article thought by Marryat to be by Harriet Martineau, but in fact by William Empson, its future editor. Marryat was a favourite member of Lady Blessington's circle: as a novelist she found him "full of talent, originality, and humour" (*The Idler in France*, 1841, II, 85); he helped her with her Annuals; and in Sep 41, following a complaint that Peel had given him no employment despite his past work for the Conservatives, she wrote to Peel on his behalf—though without success (R. R. Madden, *Literary Life and Correspondence of the Countess of Blessington*, 1855, III, 225, 228). Stanfield had written to CD on 22 Jan: "I have before told you that my friend Captain Marryat is very anxious to have 'what all covet' the pleasure of your acquaintance and if therefore you have no objection to meet him will you come and take a beef steak with me on Wednesday 27; or if that day will not suit you, on the Saturday following. I will ask Maclise and Jerdan to meet you. . . . I thank you for sending the circular of the loss of the Fairy. I will do all in my power" (MS Huntington).

## *To* MISS BURDETT COUTTS, 22 JANUARY [1841]

MS Morgan Library. *Date:* CD was clearly sending Miss Coutts one of the six copies of *Master Humphrey* No. 44 requested from Chapman & Hall on 21 Jan 41.

Devonshire Terrace.
Friday Evening | January Twenty Second.

Dear Miss Coutts.

It has occurred to me—this is a kind of vanity to which the meekest of authors are occasionally liable—that when you came to read this week's number of the Clock, you might possibly desire to know what the next one contained, without waiting seven days. I therefore make bold to send you, inclosed, the two numbers together, begging you not to be at the trouble of returning them, as I have always plenty by me.[1]

Beseeching you to with-hold this mighty revelation from all the world—except Miss Meredith, who is free to share it to the utmost, I am always

Dear Miss Coutts | Faithfully Yours

Miss Coutts.                                             CHARLES DICKENS

## *To* W. C. MACREADY, 22 [JANUARY 1841]*

MS Morgan Library. *Date:* Must refer to *Master Humphrey*, the only work of CD's originally published in weekly Nos (Apr 40 to Nov 41). But 22 Dec 40 was Tuesday not Friday. Clearly CD meant Fri 22 Jan [41], the day on which Macready received the "next week's" No. (one of the six advance copies of No. 44): see *fn.*

Friday Evening | Twenty Second Decr.

My Dear Macready.

I believe Forster mentioned to you that I wished you to read this week's Number, and next week's together.[2] As you will no doubt have received the first in regular course tonight, I send you the second herewith.[3] Do not be at the trouble of returning it, for I have plenty more.

---

[1] Miss Coutts replied on 23 Jan 41: "My dear Sir, | On my return home I found your most welcome parcel, for which pray accept my best thanks & rest assured that I shall successfully preserve the secret & that we are so *very* glad not to be kept in suspense a week. Still it is with no small regret that we look forward to parting with the friends with whom we have passed so many pleasant moments and that we shall see no more 'the child'.—I hope by this time you are recovered, if so would either Wednesday or Saturday next suit you to join a 'Library Dinner' at ½ past Six o'c. ... As you said I might keep the numbers I have availed myself of your kindness and done so" (MS Huntington).

[2] See *To* Forster, ?17 Jan.

[3] Macready wrote under date 22 Jan 41: "Found at home notes from Ransom, and one from Dickens with an onward number of *Master Humphrey's Clock.* I saw one print in it of the dear dead child that gave a dead chill through my blood. I dread to read it, but I must get it over." Later, "I have read the two numbers; I never have read printed words that gave me so much pain. I could not weep for some time. Sensation, sufferings have returned to me, that are terrible to awaken [*his much-loved daughter Joan had died Nov 40*]; it

I have read the Tragedy,[1] and will report thereupon in a separate note.[2]
Always My Dear Macready | Faithfully Yours

CHARLES DICKENS

## *To* THOMAS BEARD, 23 JANUARY 1841

MS Dickens House. *Address:* Thomas Beard Esquire | 42 Portman Place | Edgeware Road.

Devonshire Terrace.
Saturday Night | January Twenty Third | 1841.

My Dear Beard.

I am sorry to say that the Haunch must be presented before a solitary carver tomorrow, and not to a jovial half dozen as I had hoped.

Kate was taken very unwell at Four o'Clock this morning,[3] and has remained so ever since. Nothing has come of it so far, and all appearances indicate another night of watching and suspence.[4] I expected some such state of things about this time, and am resignedly putting the best face possible (a very sleepy one though) upon it.

My regards to your sister—and always believe me

Dear Beard | Faithfully Yours

CHARLES DICKENS

is real to me; I cannot criticize it" (*Diaries*, II, 116). On 25 Jan he wrote to CD: "I do not know how to write to you about the papers I read last night:—I would almost wish to defer any further thought upon them—I have suffered so much in reading them, and even now in returning to them I have a recurrence of painful sensations and depressing thought. This beautiful fiction comes too close upon what is miserably real to me to enable me to taste that portion of pleasure, which we can often extract (and you so beautifully do) from reasoning on the effect of pain, when we feel it through the sufferings of others.—You have crowned all that you have ever done in the power, the truth, the beauty and the deep moral of this exquisite picture—but my God—how cruel after all!—It is true that we must be taught in all things through endurance—and the best charity is clear and bright through every lesson you teach.—I have had thoughts and visions of angelic forms and pictures of the last sad truth of our being here, in constant succession through the night.—I cannot banish the images you have placed before us.— . . . Go on, my dear, my excellent friend —make our hearts less selfish and teach us the duty of love to one another by disclosing to us in your own language so full of eloquence, simplicity and poetry, how much there may be in the depths of our common nature to pity, to revere & love. I cannot express my own opinion of what you have done in terms too enthusiastic—to be sincere. God bless you—All well I hope?—Ever & ever yours" (MS Huntington).

[1] On 21 Jan Macready noted in his diary: "Called on Dickens and gave him Darley's first copy of 'Ethelstan'"; he recorded also that they walked out together and called on Rogers, went to leave a card and note on Darley, called in at the Athenæum, "where Dickens took some refreshment", and went on to CD's printers in Fleet Street. While they were with Rogers Macready asked CD "to spare the life of Nell . . . and observed that he was cruel. He blushed" (*Macready's Reminiscences*, ed. Sir Frederick Pollock, 1875, II, 169).

[2] This, if ever written, has apparently not survived. *Ethelstan; or, the Battle of Brunanburh,* 1841, a "Dramatic Chronicle" by George Darley (1795–1846; *DNB*), was never performed.

[3] Her baby was nearly due.

[4] Thus in MS.

## *To* MISS BURDETT COUTTS, 25 JANUARY 1841*

MS Morgan Library.

Devonshire Terrace. | Twenty fifth January 1841.
Dear Miss Coutts.

I have contrived to get rid of my cold, and shall be happy to reconcile myself to my late disappointment, by dining with you on Saturday.[1]

Believe me | Faithfully Yours

Miss Coutts.                                             CHARLES DICKENS

## *To* W. HARRISON AINSWORTH, 25 JANUARY 1841

MS Brotherton Library, Leeds.

Devonshire Terrace | Twenty fifth January 1841.
My Dear Ainsworth.

I shall be truly happy to dine with you on the Fourth, and remember the day well.[2] Forster and I dining together on the last Fourth of February, drank your health most heartily, and wished that would come about which has since been accomplished.[3]

I have not had an opportunity of telling you how generous and manly I felt your conduct to be on that first occasion of your dining here.[4] It gave me throughout the most unfeigned and cordial pleasure, and if I stop here and say no more, it is only because I cannot express to you my approval and admiration.[5]

My wife has been (and is) exceedingly unwell, and I have not been to bed for eight and forty hours. I hoped the event we are expecting would have

[1] Miss Coutts replied on 27 Jan, asking if he could dine with her on the following Monday, Tuesday or Wednesday, instead of Saturday; and inviting him to a party on "Friday Evg. next the 27th . . . any time from 10 to 12 o'C." She added as a postscript: "Since I wrote last we have read the Numbers . . . but I must not say anything more not having sufficiently recovered from the loss of our little favourite" (MS Huntington).

[2] On 23 Jan Ainsworth had written from Kensal Lodge: "Pray dine with me on the fourth of February at six o'clock?—It is my birthday, as you may, perhaps, recollect, so I shall calculate upon seeing you" (MS Huntington).

[3] Ainsworth's and Forster's recon-

ciliation (cf. *To* Forster, ?21 Dec 40, *hn* and *fn*).

[4] On 31 Dec 40, presumably.

[5] N (I, 296n) connects with this an undated letter from Laman Blanchard to Ainsworth who had written to apologize for his part in a "fray" at some dinner the night before, which began with "that good natured ass", Moran, lauding Lady Bulwer and Kean at the expense of Bulwer and Macready, whereupon Ainsworth called Macready a humbug and Blanchard flared up. But clearly that letter to Ainsworth and this of CD's are quite unconnected; they have been mistakenly associated through having once been together in the Suzannet collection (now both in the Brotherton Library).

taken place before now—but patience, in this matter and in all others, is the sovereign virtue.

> With best regards to the Ladies
> Believe me My Dear Ainsworth
> Heartily Yours
> CHARLES DICKENS

Forster and I, called upon you yesterday, but you were out.

## *To* JOHN FORSTER, [26 JANUARY 1841]

Extract in F, II, ix, 164. *Date:* according to Forster, four days after letter to him of 22 Jan (during which CD had "done nothing").

I have been looking (three o'clock) with an appearance of extraordinary interest and study at *one leaf* of the *Curiosities of Literature*[1] ever since half-past ten this morning—I haven't the heart to turn over.[2]

## *To* BASIL HALL, [27 JANUARY 1841][3]

Extract in Parke-Bernet Galleries catalogue, Jan 1941; *MS* 1 p. *Date:* clearly written between Hall's two letters to CD of 27 Jan; see *fns* to this and *To* Hall, 28 Jan. *Address* (from Sotheby's catalogue, June 1913): Captain Basil Hall, R.N.

I am sorry to say that I dare not go out in the morning (being very busy) until next Tuesday, sorely tempted as I am to be undutiful for the sake of Miss Edgeworth[4] . . . As you never read Oliver,[5] I promise myself the pleasure of sending you a copy this morning . . . C.D.

[1] By Isaac D'Israeli. Both series, 6 vols, 1823–4, were in CD's library at his death.

[2] He entered in his Diary on 26 Jan: "Forster at half past five"; and on 27 Jan: "Stanfield at 6" (see Appx, p. 462).

[3] Hall had written to CD that morning saying that Maria Edgeworth would much like to meet him, and suggesting that they should call on her together between 11 and 12 (MS Huntington).

[4] Maria Edgeworth (1767–1849; *DNB*), novelist. Had given much literary advice to Basil Hall since 1827; e.g. on 14 Aug 31: "In your new volumes do not weaken the effect by giving too much of a good thing; do not be lengthy; cut well before you go to press" (*Life and Letters of Maria Edgeworth*, ed. Augustus Hare, 1894, II, 191). Of CD she wrote to a friend in 1843: "Dickens's *America* is a failure; never

trouble yourself to read it; nevertheless, though the book is good for little, it gives me the conviction that the man is good for much more than I gave him credit for; a real desire for the improvement of the lower classes, and this reality of *feeling* is, I take it, the secret, joined to his great power of humour, of his ascendant popularity" (*op. cit.*, II, 299).

[5] Hall's letter ended: "I take it quite for granted, you see, that you will be pleased to make the acquaintance of so distinguished a person who, I assure you, appreciates your talents fully. I was much struck with an expression she made use of. She was describing to me a scene (which, by the way, I had not read, but I suspect it is in Oliver Twist) in which a man unjustly jealous of a woman murders her, under that erroneous impression, just after she had been

## *To* MISS BURDETT COUTTS, [28 JANUARY 1841]\*

MS Morgan Library. *Date:* Clearly CD was replying to Miss Coutts's letter
of 27 Jan (see *To* Miss Coutts, 25 Jan, *fn*). *Address:* Miss Coutts.

Devonshire Terrace. | Thursday Morning

Dear Miss Coutts.

Next Monday—I have written the word, but I mean *Tuesday*—will suit
me exceedingly well. I shall therefore hold myself engaged for that day
instead of Saturday. And if I can do myself the pleasure of joining your
party on Friday the 27th.[1] I shall be most happy to do so.

Believe me | Faithfully Yours

Miss Coutts.                                    CHARLES DICKENS

## *To* BASIL HALL, 28 JANUARY 1841

MS Comtesse de Suzannet.

Devonshire Terrace. | Twenty Eighth January 1841.

My Dear Sir.

I am not, I confess, a good hand at roaring,[2] and do indeed shrink from
it with most invincible repugnance. But you really do me injustice in the
matter of Miss Edgeworth, whom I should have been *glad* to see.[3] The
plain Truth is that in the beginning of a new story—with all my thoughts
and interest hanging about the old one—and the difficulty of settling
down into the track I must pursue, when I have sickness and anxiety
at home[4]—to say nothing of engagements which I cannot avoid, and
which seldom leave me a quiet evening—I cannot break in upon my
mornings[5] work. Just at this time I have but one holiday in the week, and
that is Tuesday.—Tuesday therefore, I named to you.

risking her own life to save his. Miss
Edgeworth's version of it was sufficiently fearful—but she said 'I certainly
never read anything so effective—out
of Shakespeare!' You must be an awful
glutton if you quarrel with this limita-
tion" (MS Huntington).

[1] Thus in Miss Coutts's letter of 27
Jan (see 25 Jan, *fn*); but Friday was the
29th.

[2] Hall, obviously annoyed by CD's
declining his invitation to call with him
on Maria Edgeworth on 27 Jan, had
replied the same day: "I shrewdly suspect, my friend, that you have a great
fancy for wagging your tail, & that this
is the explanation of your inability to go
out a roaring in the woods! No matter
—that is your affair—not mine—& I
only hope you will forgive me for having
proposed the thing. A mere accident
prevented me from seeing Lord Byron

& possibly you may regret some day that
you have cut old Maria Edgeworth.
Perhaps, however, I am wrong after all
—if so—pardon my suspicions" (MS
Huntington).

[3] The invitation was certainly an
honour. Maria Edgeworth had chosen
to visit London at this quiet time of
year (she wrote to George Ticknor, 19
Nov 40) particularly to avoid "the
bustle and dissipation and lionising";
for though she was "such a minnikin
lion now, and so old, literally without
teeth or claws", there were people who
might "rattle at the grate" to make her
"stand up to play tricks for them", and
this she was "not able or inclined to do"
(*Life and Letters of Maria Edgeworth*,
ed. A. Hare, II, 281).

[4] Cf. *To* Ainsworth, 25 Jan.

[5] Thus in MS.

If I were not resolute in shutting myself up now and then, either to write or think as the case may be, there would soon be no Clock. If the Queen were to send for me at such times, I wouldn't go to her.

I should be sorry if you left town under a wrong impression, and therefore dispatch this missive.

Always Faithfully Yours

Captain Basil Hall
CHARLES DICKENS

## *To* THOMAS MITTON, [?28 JANUARY 1841]

MS Huntington Library. *Date:* CD's difficulty in concentrating on *Barnaby* points to the Thursday between letters to Forster of 26 and 29 Jan.

Devonshire Terrace. | Thursday Morning.

My Dear Mitton.

I have been so terribly delayed by Kate's illness, goings out to dinner, and the extreme difficulty of fixing my thoughts on Barnaby after so recently shutting up the "Shop", that I am afraid I must shut up myself now, and go to work tonight.

If you will let our pleasanter engagement for tonight stand over, I will come down to you as soon as I have finished my Number—which will be (if no new obstacles interpose) either on Monday, or Tuesday.

Kate continues much the same. She will be no better until this little business is finally disposed of.

Now and always | Faithfully Yours

Thomas Mitton Esquire
CHARLES DICKENS

## *To* GEORGE CATTERMOLE, 28 JANUARY 1841†

MS Comtesse de Suzannet.

Devonshire Terrace. | Thursday Night January 28. | 1841.

My dear George.

I sent to Chapman and Hall yesterday morning, about the second subject for No. 2 of Barnaby[1]—but found they had sent it to Browne.

The first subject of No. 3,[2] I will either send to you on Saturday, or at latest on Sunday morning. I have also directed C and H to send you proofs of what has gone before, for reference if you need it.

I want to know whether you *feel* Ravens in general, and would fancy Barnaby's raven in particular. Barnaby being an idiot my notion is to have him always in company with a pet raven who is immeasureably more knowing than himself. To this end, I have been studying my bird, and

---

[1] No. 47 of *Master Humphrey*, published 13 Feb. See *To* Cattermole, 30 Jan, *fn.*

[2] See *To* Cattermole, 30 Jan.

think I could make a very queer character of him. Should you like the subject where this raven makes his first appearance?[1]

Faithfully Always<br>CHARLES DICKENS

[a]Loves to Cousin—We are in statu quo at home.[2]—Did you ever write on greasy paper? This is like butter. The pen *won't* mark.[a]

### To JOHN FORSTER, [29 JANUARY 1841]

Extract in F, II, ix, 164. *Date:* 29 Jan according to Forster.

I didn't stir out yesterday, but sat and *thought* all day; not writing a line; not so much as the cross of a t or dot of an i. I imaged forth a good deal of *Barnaby* by keeping my mind steadily upon him; and am happy to say I have gone to work this morning in good twig,[3] strong hope, and cheerful spirits.[4] Last night I was unutterably and impossible-to-form-an-idea-of-ably miserable.... By the bye don't engage yourself otherwise than to me, for Sunday week, because it's my birthday. I have no doubt we shall have got over our troubles here by that time, and I purpose having a snug dinner in the study.

### To GEORGE CATTERMOLE, 30 JANUARY 1841†

MS Huntington Library.

Devonshire Terrace<br>Saturday Evening | January Thirtieth | 1841.

My Dear George.

I send you the first four Slips of No. 48,[5] containing the description of the Locksmith's house, which I think will make a good subject, and one you will like. If you put the 'Prentice in it, shew nothing more than his paper cap, because he will be an important character in the story, and you will need to know more about him as he is minutely described.[6] [b]I may as well say that he is *very short.*[b] Should you wish to put the locksmith in,[7]

---

[1] Cattermole clearly declined; for Browne did all the illustrations containing Grip the raven. Grip's first appearance was in the headpiece to Ch. 6.
[aa] Not previously published.
[2] I.e. the baby had not yet arrived.
[3] Style, fettle (slang). Cf. *Barnaby*, Ch. 11: "You're in twig to-night, I see."
[4] He was working on Ch. 4, the first entirely new chapter that he wrote this year (cf. *To* Forster, 22 Jan, *fn*).
[5] Of *Master Humphrey*. It was No. 3 (Chs 4 and 5) of *Barnaby*; published 27 Feb.
[6] CD prepared for this illustration on p. 5 of his MS, where Varden, entering his workshop, catches sight of "his 'prentice's brown paper cap ducking down to avoid observation"; but Cattermole must have received the whole of Ch. 4, with its minute description of Simon Tappertit, in time for his illustration. He drew Simon, alone in the workshop, with folded arms and curling lip uttering "with supreme contempt the monosyllable 'Joe!' ".
[bb] Added over a caret.
[7] "let Chapman know directly, as Browne has done him" cancelled here.

you will find him described in No. 2 of Barnaby (which I told C and H to send you)—Browne has done him in one little thing,[1] but so very slightly that you will not require to see his sketch, I think.

Now, I must know what you think about the Raven,[2] my buck, otherwise I am in this fix.—I have given Browne *no* subject for this No., and time is flying. If you would like to have the Raven's first appearance, and don't object to having both subjects, so be it. I shall be delighted. If otherwise, I must feed that hero forthwith.[3]

I cannot close this hasty note, my dear fellow, without saying that I have deeply felt your hearty and most invaluable co-operation in the beautiful illustrations you have made for the last story—that I look at them with a pleasure I cannot describe to you in words—and that it is impossible for me to say how sensible I am of your earnest and friendly aid. Believe me that this is *the very first time* any designs for what I have written have touched and moved me, and caused me to feel that they expressed the idea I had in my mind. I am most sincerely and affectionately grateful to you, and am full of pleasure and delight.

> Believe me,
> My Dear Cattermole | Always Heartily Yours
> C.D
> Over

*a*We are just the same at home. But next week, I should say, *must* put us all to rights.*a*

## *To* W. C. MACREADY, [31 JANUARY 1841]*

MS Morgan Library. *Date:* CD's Diary entry for 31 Jan 41 reads "Rogers at" but names no time; and Macready's for the same day: "Dickens called for me and I accompanied him to Rogers's, where we dined" (*Diaries*, II, 118). Since CD expected to see Macready that same night and then reclaim from him the end of *Old Curiosity Shop*, he was clearly writing on the day of Rogers's dinner.

My Dear Macready

What time does Rogers dine? I forget. I'll call for you, if you'll let me know. We will not be too soon, for there is usually what you call "a long wait" there.

I inclose you the end of the Curiosity Shop, which I must ask you for again tonight. Don't be afraid of it. It's very cheerful, or intended to be so.[4]

---

[1] "The wounded man", tailpiece to Ch. 3 (No. 2).
[2] See *To* Cattermole, 28 Jan and *fn*.
[3] The raven did not appear until the next number. Browne illustrated a different subject—Varden, Dolly and Simon at breakfast (Ch. 4).

*aa* Not previously published.
[4] Macready replied at once: "Many thanks for your healing application of Mast. Humphrey, and for your promised lift.—Quarter before seven was Rogers's hour. . . . I will give you the No.—when you call" (MS Huntington).

You are not disposed for a walk this delicious morning, are you? I am going to ride out at 2, and get down on Hampstead Heath or some high and dry road to walk.

Best regards at home. We are here in statu quo.

Faithfully Ever

W. C. Macready Esquire                         CHARLES DICKENS


*To* MRS GORE,[1] 31 JANUARY 1841

MS Berg Collection.

1 Devonshire Terrace
Sunday Thirty First January | 1841.

Dear Mrs. Gore.

Let me thank you cordially for the two Magazines,[2] and for that delicate and most touching attention which I recognize in the maiming of the cover. If the name be never whispered in Heaven (as I should think it never was) it is no doubt muttered very often in the other place,[3] and it is a great relief to be free of it.[4]

I have been greatly pleased with both papers, but especially with the

---

[1] Catherine Grace Frances Gore (1799–1861; *DNB*), *née* Moody, novelist and dramatist. Married Capt. Charles Arthur Gore 1823, and had ten children of whom only two survived her. Had already by Jan 41 published 28 of her 59 works of fiction listed by Sir Michael Sadleir; 1841 saw three more—one of them *Cecil: or the Adventures of a Coxcomb*, described in *A New Spirit of the Age*, 1844, as "that clever, but surpassingly impudent book, . . . a perfect representation of the worst, but certainly the most dazzling aspect of Mrs. Gore's genius". "No one," says Sadleir, "seeking to recreate the affectations, arrogance and pasteboard splendours of smart Society during the eighteen-thirties and forties, can afford to ignore [Mrs Gore's novels]. Nor would one wish to do so, for her tongue is as witty as it is cruel" (*XIX Century Fiction*, 1951, I, 144). CD himself, thanking her for dedicating *The Dean's Daughter* to him in 1853, wrote of her power, humour, knowledge of humanity and wit. They met rarely, but one of the most outspoken letters he wrote about

his separation from Catherine was to Mrs Gore.

[2] *Bentley's Miscellany* for Feb 41 (see below) and presumably the Jan issue—to which Mrs Gore had contributed "Abdications. A Prize Essay, by Albany Poyntz". They came with the following note: "I send you the Magazines, and cannot tell you how glad I am to have made your acquaintance. As I am certain you feel as strongly as I do the worthlessness of dinnertable conversation towards accomplishing such an object, I hope some day when you are at leisure, you will come and see me. —I always remain at home on Sunday. I have a pretty clever little daughter who travelled to Mecklenburgh Square last night in hopes of being presented to you, and was greatly disappointed. My affectionate croak to the Raven!" (MS Huntington).

[3] Cf. Catherine Fanshawe, "Enigma, the letter H"—"'Twas whispered in heaven, 'twas muttered in hell".

[4] The name was no doubt "Bentley". Mrs Gore had presumably "maimed" the cover by cutting his name out of it.

children of the Mobility.[1] Those books[2] are the gall and bitterness of my life. I vow to God they make me wretched, and taint the freshness of every new year. Your satire is most admirable, and to pluck the peacock's feathers from such daws is worthy of you.

What do you think of a book in serious earnest—a true, strong, sledge-hammer book—about the children of the people; as much beaten out of Nature by iron necessity as the children of the nobility are, by luxury and pride? It would be a good thing to have the two extremes—Fairlie[3] and Fielding—Hogarth and Chalon[4]—the Princess Royal[5] whom the nurse daren't kiss—and the baby on the step of a door whose mother tried to strangle it.

I have seen in different towns in England, and do see in London whenever I walk alone into its byeways at night, as I often do, such miseries and horrors among these little creatures—such an impossibility of their ever growing up to be good or happy—that these aristocratic dolls do turn me sick. I only know one good those books are likely to achieve. If I were a poor labouring man and saw them in the shop windows as I went slouching home, I should think of my own children and the no-regard they had from anybody, and be a greater Radical than ever. I hope they may be productive of some advantage that way.

You see what *I* am. I can't help it. It's more genteel to be on the other side, but Truth doesn't always keep its carriage, and is sometimes content to go in hob-nailed shoes and wheelbarrows.

I heartily reciprocate the pleasure you so kindly express at our having met the other night; and hope we shall be better acquainted. As a means to this end, I shall not fail to call upon you—if not next Tuesday, at all events on the Tuesday following. I was very sorry to leave Harness's so soon t'other night,[6] but I was anxious to get away as early as I could, and refrained from going up stairs again, lest I should be tempted to stay.

Believe me | Dear Mrs. Gore | Faithfully Yours
CHARLES DICKENS

[1] "The Children of the Mobility, versus the Children of the Nobility, by Albany Poyntz", *Miscellany*, Feb 41, IX, 164. In it the discomforts endured by fashionable children, especially as portrayed in the series *Portraits of the Nobility*, are contrasted with the freedom of ordinary children. ("Mobility": the mob; the lower classes.) Cf. Leech's *Portraits of Children of the Mobility Drawn from Nature*, 1841.

[2] *Portraits of the Nobility*, 1838–41, a series of engravings by Chalon and other artists, with accompanying verses, edited by Mrs Fairlie. Among the contributors of verse were Marryat, Lady Blessington, L.E.L., Bulwer, Disraeli, Procter and Landor.

[3] Mrs Louisa Fairlie (1810–43), *née* Purves. Favourite niece of Lady Blessington, whose Annuals she contributed to and helped to edit.

[4] Alfred Edward Chalon (1780–1860; *DNB*), painter of French extraction. RA 1816. The first to paint Queen Victoria after her accession; and appointed painter in water colours to her. For CD's reference later this year to "the maudlin taint | Of the sweet Chalon school of silk and ermine", see his "subjects for pictures after the manner of Peter Pindar", F, II, xii, 191.

[5] *b.* 21 Nov 40.

[6] 29 Jan; he was going on to an evening party at Miss Coutts's (entry in CD's Diary).

The Raven sends his duty. He has just [w]aylaid[1] and attacked a butcher, whose pantaloons [ha]ve suffered considerably. He (the butcher) [th]reatens to throw poison over the garden wall, [bu]t my groom is of opinion that I needn't be [u]neasy, for the Raven wouldn't have it at no [pr]ice. *He* knows better than that, he says, bless you.

Mrs. Gore.

## *To* NATHANIEL ELLISON,[2] 3 FEBRUARY 1841*

MS Messrs Clark & Smith, Solicitors.

Devonshire Terrace. | Third February 1841.

Sir.

Mr. Harness in a note to me this morning, mentioned the object with which you called upon me on Sunday last.[3] If I could have anticipated it, I should have been happy to have seen you, but, as you may suppose, I am obliged to deny myself to those visitors (for their name is Legion) whom I have not the pleasure of knowing.

I have a distinct recollection of having at pretty long intervals received three or four letters from the young gentleman in whom you are interested. Taking it for granted that they had their origin in some unfortunate delusion, I have not noticed them in any way. If I should have any further communication on the same topic, I will forward it to you immediately.[4]

Yours very obedtly.

Nathaniel Ellison Esquire                                    CHARLES DICKENS

## *To* W. HARRISON AINSWORTH, [4 FEBRUARY 1841]

Mention in next.

*Apologizing for not being able to dine with him that day as arranged.*

---

[1] Beginnings of several words of postscript are obscured by frame in the album in which letter is laid.

[2] Nathaniel Ellison (*b.* ?1786), barrister of Lincoln's Inn since 1811. Fellow of Merton College, Oxford, 1806–23. Commissioner of Bankruptcy 1842.

[3] On 2 Feb Harness had written to tell CD that Ellison's nephew, Nathaniel Bates, who was "evidently mad", had taken it into his head that he had been attacked by CD in *Oliver Twist* and by Samuel Warren in *Ten Thousand a Year*, and was talking, "if his second [thought] fit, of calling [them] both to account". Ellison had called on CD, Harness said, to ask if he would forward to him any letters he received from Bates (MS Huntington).

[4] For two letters from Bates sent on to Ellison by CD, see *To* Ellison, 15 Feb, *fn.*

## *To* JOHN FORSTER, [4 FEBRUARY 1841]

MS Victoria & Albert Museum (FC). *Date:* clearly 4 Feb 41 (Ainsworth's birthday), when Forster and CD were to have dined with him; CD's Diary entry for 3 Feb reads "Dr. Smith at 6 o'Clock". Handwriting supports.

Devonshire Terrace. | Thursday Morning

My Dear Forster.

[          ]¹

There will not be time to write Ainsworth by post. Please, therefore, to hand him the inclosed—which is an excuse on the score of Kate.²

I didn't go to Southwood Smith's yesterday, and last night went out roaming. I tapped at your Window with my stick soon after Ten (to carry you to the Parthenon, and broiled bones) but you were not at home. At the club I stumbled upon Thompson when I had had my supper, and with him sat drinking Gin and Water until 3 this morning.

Faithfully Always

CD.

Mac is laid up with a cold, he says, in a note just this moment received, and don't go either.³

## *To* JOHN FORSTER, [4 FEBRUARY 1841]*

Forster's summary of letter and his copy of extract from it, MS Victoria & Albert Museum (FC).⁴ *Date:* headed "Devonshire Terrace Thursday" by Forster; clearly later in the same day as last, referring again to the visit to Ainsworth cancelled on the score of Kate, and to CD's spree of the night before.⁵

*About going to Ainsworth's.⁶ Remorseful about his bachelor's doings.* I

¹ A paragraph of 4½ lines has been heavily cancelled here, presumably by Forster. It begins "It's lucky that fit of Christian"; and ends "to myself) came upon you, for I don't mean to go to-day." The rest is illegible. Probably the paragraph stated that CD was crying off the dinner that night at Ainsworth's and it was therefore lucky that Forster had decided to go.

² I.e. an excuse for himself on the score that Kate was still awaiting the birth of her baby.

³ Maclise had written: "I am wretched in not being able to join you for Ainsworths—I have got exactly the cold that destroys all one's self esteem—my nose is actually crooked from a neighbouring swelling— | To live in the hope of being able to get out on

LCD—H

Sunday [*CD's birthday*] I must stay at home now" (MS Free Library of Philadelphia). Forster had been invited for Sunday 7th also (see 29 Jan). Possibly the invitation, at least to Maclise, was cancelled, or he was still unwell; for on 7 Feb he wrote: "How is the good lady—I drink to you—many happy returns of this your birthday. Is it to be the birthday of another. If so—health to that other" (MS Mr P. J. Radford).

⁴ Clearly one of the many letters from CD to himself that Forster destroyed.

⁵ Forster had presumably answered CD's previous note at once, protesting that if he could spare a night away from Catherine, drinking, he had no excuse for not coming to Ainsworth's.

⁶ Forster's destruction of this letter and failure to copy the passage about

finished the number yesterday and then broke loose.[1] Upon my word and honour I have serious thoughts of retiring, as soon as K is confined, to the seaside, & getting out of harm's way.

## *To* GEORGE CATTERMOLE, [4 FEBRUARY 1841]

MS Dickens House. *Date:* presumably the Thursday before Walter's birth; for CD's engagement to dine with Cattermole on 13 Feb ("Saturday *week*"), see *To* Cattermole, that day.

Devonshire Terrace. | Thursday Afternoon

My Dear George.

As this business of Kate's is not yet over, and don't seem to advance at all (my mind begins to run very much on Joanna Southcote)[2] I should like, if it will not inconvenience you, to postpone our Athenæum dinner until Saturday *week*. Will this suit you?

Always Faithfully Yours

George Cattermole Esquire                    CHARLES DICKENS

## *To* W. HARRISON AINSWORTH, 5 FEBRUARY 1841

MS Free Library of Philadelphia.

Devonshire Terrace. | Fifth February 1841.

My Dear Ainsworth.

Will you tell me where that Punch is to be bought, what one is to ask for, and what the cost is. It has made me very uneasy in my mind.

Mind—I deny the beer. It is very excellent; but that it surpasses that meeker, and gentler, and brighter ale of mine (oh how bright it is!) I never will admit.[3]

My gauntlet lies upon the cask. Yours in defiance.

CHARLES DICKENS

"going to Ainsworth's", following the cancellation in CD's earlier letter of 4 Feb, strongly suggests that his aim, both in cancelling and in destroying, was suppression of any hint that relations with Ainsworth had been strained and a reconciliation only recently effected (see *To* Forster, ?21 Dec 40 and *fn*).

[1] Finishing No. 3, begun with a great effort on 29 Jan (see *To* Forster, that day), fully explained his sudden need to break loose.

[2] Joanna Southcott (1750–1814; *DNB*), fanatic, whose symptoms of approaching maternity, after her announcement (1813) that she was to become "the mother of Shiloh", proved to have been entirely stimulated by her imagination. When Sally Brass, in a passage cancelled in proof (*Old Curiosity Shop*, Ch. 66: see *To* Forster, 30 Dec 40, *fn*), announces that she is the Marchioness's mother, Sampson ejaculates "I'd sooner believe in Mrs. Southcote and *her* child. Non-sense!"

[3] Presumably Forster had brought CD samples of the punch and beer he had missed the night before.

## *To* JOHN FORSTER, [?6 FEBRUARY 1841]

MS Victoria & Albert Museum (FC). *Date:* on white paper watermarked 1840 and used by CD up to Mar 41; depressed tone suggests shortly after his return to *Barnaby* (cf. *To* Forster, 26 Jan). However, not Sat 23 Jan, since Catherine was taken ill that morning, and probably not Sat 30 Jan when he wrote cheerfully to Cattermole; perhaps 6 Feb, CD having relapsed into his mood of 28 Jan (see *To* Forster, 29 Jan). *Address: Wait* | John Forster Esquire | 58 Lincolns Inn Fields.

Saturday Morning.

My Dear Forster.

I am deadly stupid this morning—perfectly swinish and brutal in an intellectual point of view, and of no use whatsomdever excepting out of doors.

Can you come to Hampstead—while the day is bright, not when it has dwindled away to nothing—or to Greenwich—or to Windsor— or anywhere  ?  ?  ?  ?  ?  ?[1]

Faithfully
CD.

## *To* EDWARD MARJORIBANKS, ?7 FEBRUARY 1841

Mention in *To* Marjoribanks, 9 Feb 41.

## *To* THOMAS MITTON, [8 FEBRUARY 1841]

MS Huntington Library. *Date:* Handwriting shows that the birth this refers to was Walter's (8 Feb 41). *Address:* Thomas Mitton Esquire | 23 Southampton Buildings.

Devonshire Terrace. | Monday 1 O'Clock

My Dear Mitton.

You will be glad to hear that Kate was safely confined at 12 oClock to-day—a jolly boy.[2] She had a very hard trial indeed, but thank God is thriving now, amazingly.

Ever Yours

Thomas Mitton Esquire                                      CD.

---

[1] Cf. Forster's rendering of this letter (F, II, I, 93): "Where shall it be—*oh where*—Hampstead, Greenwich, Windsor? WHERE? ? ? ? ? ? while the day is bright, not when it has dwindled away to nothing! For who can be of any use whatsomdever such a day as this, excepting out of doors?"

[2] Walter Landor Dickens (1841–63), CD's fourth child; the first of the five sons born at Devonshire Terrace.

## *To* GEORGE CATTERMOLE, 9 FEBRUARY [1841]

MS Colonel Richard Gimbel. *Date:* 9 Feb was Tuesday in 1841; signature supports that year.

Devonshire Terrace. | Tuesday Ninth February.

My Dear George.

My notes tread upon each others' heels. In my last,[1] I quite forgot business.

Will you for No. 49 do the locksmith's house, which was described in No. 48[2]—I mean the outside. If you can, without hurting the effect, shut up the shop as though it were night, so much the better. Should you want a figure, an ancient watchman in or out of his box, very sleepy, will be just the thing for me.[3]

I have written to Chapman, and requested him to send you a block of a long shape, so that the house may come *upright* as it were.[4]

Faithfully ever

George Cattermole Esquire                    CHARLES DICKENS[5]


## *To* MESSRS CHAPMAN & HALL, 9 FEBRUARY 1841

Extract in *Autograph Prices Current*, v (1919–21); *MS* 2½ pp.; dated 9 Feb 41.

I have written to Mr. Cattermole and told him that I want for the end of No. 49 the outside of the locksmiths[6] House (at night) as described in the beginning of No. 48. I have also told him that Mr. Chapman will let him have a block of an upright shape—the size is not material; it needn't be very large—the house may come as it were thus [*here CD outlines the shape*]—in the shape of a house. Do you understand? . . . Mrs. Dickens and the child are not merely as well as can be expected, but a great deal better.


## *To* HABLOT K. BROWNE, [9 FEBRUARY 1841]

Mention in next.


[1] Possibly written the day before to announce the birth of Walter.

[2] At the beginning of *Barnaby*, Ch. 4.

[3] Cattermole did not do this illustration for Ch. 7 (No. 49), presumably because he was ill (see 13 Feb and *fn*), but did it later for Ch. 16 (see 26 Feb and *fn*).

[4] Wording suggests that this was not the first time that CD arranged for Cattermole to do his own drawing on wood. For how long Browne copied his designs (see ?21 Jan 40) is not known; but it seems unlikely that he had a hand in the architectural subjects of the later part of *Old Curiosity Shop*.

[5] Cattermole replied on 10 Feb: "I believe I have now *three* notes of yours to answer!" He promised an early call to "wipe off all together"; sent congratulations on the birth of Walter; and agreed to "undertake the *exterior* at once", directly he received the block. He had sent away "the Slips" (CD's pages of MS), but imagined that he could now have a proof (MS Huntington).

[6] Thus in catalogue.

## *To* JOHN FORSTER, [9 FEBRUARY 1841]

Extracts in F, II, ix, 164 (*aa*), and F, II, x, 173 (*bb*). *Date:* 9 Feb according to Forster, the day after Walter's birth.

*a*Thank God, quite well. I am thinking hard, and have just written to Browne enquiring when he will come and confer about the raven.*a1*
*b*I mean to call the boy Edgar, a good honest Saxon name, I think.*b2*

## *To* EDWARD MARJORIBANKS, 9 FEBRUARY 1841*

MS Morgan Library. *Address:* Private | Free | Edward Marjoribanks Esquire | Messrs. Coutts and Compy. | Strand.

Devonshire Terrace. | Ninth February 1841
My Dear Sir.

Many thanks for your kind note.

I see now how it was that you came to talk of "finance", and I could not for my life understand you. You were obscure, like some streams and rivers, by reason of your excessive depth. Miss Meredith interposes and asks what you say. "Nothing" you reply; "only a little matter of finance." And then I—this is a humiliating confession—instead of thinking "Good God how ready he is!", exclaim within myself "Finance! What *can* he mean!"

Seriously, I had been vexed not many days before by the practices of my unknown representative who lords it fearfully in my name at watering places and country inns, and sometimes doesn't pay his bills.[3] Not understanding you, and being on the alert for some new discovery, I tortured myself with the possibilty of some monstrous or impertinent application having been made to you in my name.[4] The chances were ninety nine to one that there was nothing in it, but while that one remained I was not quite at ease, and so occasioned you the trouble of writing one note and reading two—for which I know you will forgive me.

My Dear Sir Faithfully Yours
CHARLES DICKENS

P.S. I am delighted to find that rascal Dunn,[5] so well trounced. But if

[1] See *To* Cattermole, 28 Jan, *fn.*
[2] "He changed his mind in a few days, however, on resolving to ask Landor to be godfather", says Forster (F, II, x, 173).
[3] CD had suffered from an unknown forger of his name the previous winter (see *To* Molloy, Jan 40).
[4] The wording here suggests that CD's real fear may have been that John Dickens had used his name to obtain a loan from Coutts's: see *To* Latimer, 18 Feb, and *To* Mitton, 6 Mar. On 24

Mar 42 John Dickens unsuccessfully applied to "Miss Coutts & Co." for a loan of £25 on his own security (MS Morgan).
[5] Richard Dunn (*d.* 1890), an Irish barrister who had been pestering Miss Coutts with love-letters and calls since 1838. Prosecuted 1840 and confined to the Fleet for the costs since May of that year, on 6 Feb 41 he had failed in a claim for damages for alleged assault and false imprisonment against a Mr Alexander, at whose house he had tried

Miss Coutts had electrified her knocker in the first instance, or had procured "the Pet of the Fancy", or "the Slashing Sailor Boy", or "Young Sawdust"[1] or some such gentleman to accomodate[2] him with a customer[3] as the sporting phrase is, I should have been still better pleased.

### *To* C. L. EASTLAKE,[4] 10 FEBRUARY 1841*

MS Free Library of Philadelphia.

Devonshire Terrace | Tenth February 1841.

My Dear Sir.

I deferred answering your note, in the hope that I should be enabled to tell you that I had attended the ballot at the Athenæum and voted for your friend.[5] I regret to say, however, that some family circumstances obliged me to dine at Hampstead on Monday[6] and that I did not return to town in time.

Let me assure you of the pleasure it would have given me to comply with this, or any request of yours, and believe me My Dear Sir

Faithfully Yours

C. L. Eastlake Esquire CHARLES DICKENS

### *To* E. HENDERSON,[7] [EARLY FEBRUARY 1841]

Mention in Henderson *to* CD, 11 Feb 41.[8]

### *To* DANIEL MACLISE, 10 FEBRUARY [1841]*

MS Colonel Richard Gimbel. *Date:* See *To* Forster, 9 Feb; 10 Feb was Wednesday in 1841.

Devonshire Terrace. | Wednesday Tenth February

My Dear Maclise.

Browne (who is coming to sketch the Raven) dines with me in the study

to see Miss Coutts, 18 May 40. He continued his letters and demands for money until his release in 1845, and after it.

[1] Typical nicknames of boxers, taken from the boxing slang of the day: "the Fancy" was the boxing profession; "Sawdust", the ring.

[2] Thus in MS.

[3] To provide him with an opponent.

[4] Charles Lock Eastlake (1793–1865; *DNB*), historical painter and writer on art. RA 1830; PRA 1850, when knighted. Keeper of the National Gallery 1843–7; first Director 1855. Commissioner for the 1851 Exhibition. Did much to promote art in England.

[5] Eastlake supported three candidates —none of them apparently known to CD.

[6] I.e. on the day of Walter's birth—when he was best out of the house.

[7] Unidentified.

[8] Henderson replied from the Home Office on 11 Feb: "No reliable man needs any apology for writing to me on behalf of any one in whom he has confidence. I may be permitted to say I think you are a reliable man: therefore if you please I will note the wish of your friend for employment and if I can hereafter serve him I shall be very glad" (MS Huntington).

to-day *en garçon* at five. The gay and festive Thompson also joins us. Will you make a fourth? Say yes.

Ever Yours<br>CD.[1]

All going on famously.


## To DANIEL MACLISE, 11 FEBRUARY 1841*

MS Mrs Percy W. Valentine.

Devonshire Terrace. | Eleventh February 1841.

My Dear Maclise.

We were speaking of Ethelstan.[2] Le voici.

I am sorry the water bottle[3] held you so long last night. We adjourned from the Private Box to the Parthenon, and were rather jolly.

Hot joints here on Sunday at Five o'Clock.[4]

Faithfully Always<br>BOZ.


## To WALTER SAVAGE LANDOR, [?11 FEBRUARY 1841]

Summary from F, II, x, 173.[5] *Date:* a few days after letter of 9 Feb according to Forster; probably 11 Feb—the day Elliotson answered a similar request.

*Asking Landor to be godfather to his newly-born son and telling him that it would give the child something to boast of, to be called Walter Landor, and that to call him so would do his own heart good. For, as to himself, whatever realities had gone out of the ceremony of christening,[6] the meaning still re-*

---

[1] Maclise replied: "The 10th of Feb —to-day I go to the Academy to vote for—I suppose—C Landseer—but as this will not take place before 8 oClock I don't see why I should not dine with you beforehand" (MS Huntington).

[2] See *To Macready, 22 Jan, fn.*

[3] Frequently used in CD's letters to Maclise as symbol for business at the RA.

[4] Maclise replied on Sat 13th: "I shall want to work to the last moment to-morrow by day light—and I fear by Lamplight too—So expect not me to your hospitable board, and believe me wretched in making such a sacrifice— Ethelstan I return you having read it through—very, *very* beautiful!!" (MS Huntington). The last words are perhaps an echo of CD's "Beautiful! Very beautiful!" in *To Maclise, 25 Nov 40.*

Cf. his quoting CD's "I can no more" (*To Maclise, 2 June 40, fn*).

[5] Presumably Forster came on this letter when going through Landor's papers for his *W. S. Landor* (1869).

[6] For Landor's own, anti-Tractarian, view of baptism, see his pamphlet *Popery: British and Foreign*, 1851, p. 35, where he identifies himself with the "many sound and earnest Christians, who believe that sprinkling a few drops of water on an infant's face is no more baptism than a sandwich is a dinner". But Catherine took one aspect of christening very seriously: "The consequences of a child's dying without being baptized are very dreadful as they cannot be buried on consecrated ground", she wrote to her cousin Mary on 30 May 37 (MS Free Library of Philadelphia; see *D*, LXIII [1967], p. 80).

*mained in it of enabling him to form a relationship with friends he most loved: and as to the boy, he held that to give him a name to be proud of was to give him also another reason for doing nothing unworthy or untrue when he came to be a man.*[1]

## *To* GEORGE CATTERMOLE, 13 FEBRUARY 1841*

MS Mr Edward S. Moore III.

Devonshire Terrace. | Thirteenth February 1841.

My Dear George.

I am very sorry to hear you are an Invalid.[2] I, too, am under the doctor's hands for a violent fit of indigestion; and as I may only eat with

[1] Landor replied (in a letter postmarked 14 Feb 41): "All the men in Europe, uniting their forces, could not confer on me so great and acceptable an honour as you have done. First, let me wish the boy health—then, everything else which such parents can contribute. It creates in me a somewhat new sentiment, it makes me religious, to think of him. Now do not turn round and say to Mrs. Dickens | When the devil was ill &c | and least of all the close | When the devil was well the devil a Saint was he." He went on: "I am well enough again—only that my throat is a little relaxt. Tripped-up indeed I was, and gagged, but soon upon my feet again. Three nights of fever, without the power of swallowing —two days afterwards I was in Gt. Bedford St, well again, talking, listening, too happy for laughing, bathing and buoyed up in a tepid relaxing gladness. But do not imagine that I am the prince, or either of the three (altho by this time they must be about my age) 'who purchased the certain rose which, coming near the pillow of any patient, tho in articulo mortis, immediately restored him'. No indeed, I have not 'the rose [*i.e. Rose Paynter*] always *at hand*'. I wish to God I had. | Alas! mine grows in Faery-land | And never is to be *at hand*. | I shall certainly lay your letter before the Judge—If you are permitted to defend yourself in person, instead of counsel, happy you. | God bless you! | Ever Affectionately Yours | and my godchild's" (MS Huntington).

Elliotson, invited to be Walter's other godfather, replied: "I shall be delighted to become father in God to your little bopeep: you still retaining your title of his father in the flesh, with all the rights, privileges, perquisites & duties thereto annexed, from the moment you determined to construct him to the end of life. | I should, however, have been compelled to forego this delight had you not absolved me from religious duties & every thing vulgar—For nothing could I consent to teach him in the vulgar tongue—nor would I have spoiled him for arithmetic by teaching him that three are one & one is three, or defaced his views of the majesty of God by assuring him that the maker of the Universe once came down & got a little jewess in the family way, & so gave himself up to fun as to manage that he himself should be the little master she produced when in the way she was because she loved her Lord & was favoured beyond all other damsels." He continued: "Oh, how as a human being I thank you for your delightful Clock. I look forward to every friday night with impatience; for after dinner one of us reads the new number aloud. But last friday week we were beaten to the earth —Symes, who reads most beautifully, at last threw down the book & sobbed, & Wood [*see* To *Macready, 24 Aug 41*, fn] & myself cried a deluge: & we all agreed that you must be a good man to be able to write thus—Not that I ever heard your goodness doubted" (MS Huntington).

[2] Earlier the same day, Cattermole had written: "I have been so unwell for

great discretion, and may not drink at all, am truly rejoiced that our dinner does not come off.

Thank God, we are brilliant up stairs. Fish yesterday—boiled fowl to day—up to dinner tomorrow—drawing room by the middle of next week. Kate is asleep at[1] this moment, and I defer giving her your inclosure (which will afford her great pleasure I know) until she wakes.

                    With best regards | Always Heartily Yours
George Cattermole Esquire                    CHARLES DICKENS


## *To* THOMAS MITTON, 15 FEBRUARY 1841

MS Huntington Library.

                    Devonshire Terrace | Monday Fifteenth February | 1841.
My Dear Mitton
    If you have nothing else to do, will you come and play a game at cribbage with me this evening? I shall be alone and at home any way.
                                        Faithfully Ever
Thomas Mitton Esquire                    CHARLES DICKENS


## *To* NATHANIEL ELLISON, 15 FEBRUARY 1841*

MS Messrs Clark & Smith, Solicitors.

                    1 Devonshire Terrace | Fifteenth February 1841.

    Mr. Charles Dickens sends his compliments to Mr. Ellison, and begs, in compliance with his request, to forward him the inclosed,—received this morning.[2]

some days past with what (for want of a more definite name) I must call a *disorder of the nerves* that I have not been out of my room or I would have performed my anxious desire to call upon you: I know that our engagement to dine together stands for to-day [*see To Cattermole, 4 Feb*], and I am quite unable to go out: let it therefore stand over a little and send word by my messenger a good account of Mrs Dickens and your little son" (MS Huntington).
    [1] Squeezed in to replace " 'till" cancelled.
    [2] A letter dated 11 Feb, from Nath-

aniel Bates (see *To* Ellison, 3 Feb, *fn*,) repeating the earlier charge: "Since the publication of Oliver Twist many are *inclined to cast in my Teeth* if I may so express myself that *you wished to insult both me and my mother* that you intended to represent me both as a Pickpocket & a Bastard", and adding to it: "If the Character Miss Sally Brass is meant in any way as an insult to my Sister *you are not a Gentleman*." CD also, at some time, sent on to Ellison a letter from Bates (endorsed "Received 26 Jany 1841") dissociating himself from his uncle, Nathaniel Ellison (MSS Messrs Clark & Smith).

## *To* W. HARRISON AINSWORTH, [?15 FEBRUARY 1841]

Mention in Ainsworth *to* CD, 15 Feb 41.[1]


## *To* T. N. TALFOURD, 16 FEBRUARY 1841

MS Historical Society of Pennsylvania.

1 Devonshire Terrace | Tuesday February Sixteen | 1841.
My Dear Talfourd.

A friend of mine—a man you will say of most extraordinary tastes—wants to go into the Gallery of the House of Commons next Friday. Can you give me an Order for that day, and will you send it me by post?

Tell Mrs. Talfourd your Nickleby and Clock are in course of binding—by the slowest man in England.[2]

Faithfully Yours
CHARLES DICKENS


## *To* MR LLOYD,[3] [16] FEBRUARY [1841]*

MS Berg Collection. *Date:* Someone (apparently not CD) has written "1840" beneath CD's "February"—perhaps because 18 Feb 40 was Tuesday. A third hand, in different ink, has changed the "o" to "1". Handwriting and reference to *Master Humphrey* confirm 1841; but in that year 18 Feb was Thursday. Probably CD was wrong in the date of the month, not the day of the week, and was writing on Tues 16 Feb.

1 Devonshire Terrace, York Gate | Tuesday 18th. February

Mr. Charles Dickens presents his compliments to Mr. Lloyd, and begs to assure him that Master Humphrey's Clock is really, decidedly, and unquestionably of his manufacture.

Mr. Dickens owes an apology to Mr. Lloyd for not returning an earlier reply to his note.


[1] On 15 Feb 41 Ainsworth wrote from Kensal Lodge: "The accompanying Paper has been sent to me by the writer of a critical notice of Master Humphrey's Clock (a Mr. Price), begging I would forward it to you. I do so. Your note has just arrived. We will foregather one of these days at the Parthenon. Just now, I am much bothered. I rejoice to hear that Mrs. D's troubles are over, and that all is doing well. The opening of Barnaby Rudge is capital" (MS Huntington).

[2] See *To* Miss Coutts, 20 Apr and *fn.*

[3] Unidentified; perhaps a relation of Miss Lloyd (see next). They were possibly both autograph-hunters.

## *To* MISS LLOYD,[1] 17 FEBRUARY 1841*

MS Berg Collection.

Faithfully Yours
CHARLES DICKENS

1 Devonshire Terrace, York Gate | Regents Park London.
Wednesday Seventeenth Feby. 1841.

Mr. Charles Dickens sends his compliments to Miss Lloyd, and complies with her request with pleasure.[2] And he begs to assure Miss Lloyd at the same time, in reference to one part of her note, that she is entirely and thoroughly mistaken in supposing him to be the author of Sketches of Young Ladies.[3]

## *To* GEORGE CRUIKSHANK, 17 FEBRUARY 1841

MS Colonel Richard Gimbel.

Devonshire Terrace. | Seventeenth February 1841.
My Dear Cruikshank.

Will you let me know whether you are willing or able to go into that matter of the Annual?[4] If you are, I will write you my views upon it and put you in possession of the means of determining whether you shall join it or no.[5]

Faithfully Yours
George Cruikshank Esquire.                    CHARLES DICKENS

[1] Unidentified.

[2] For an autograph: hence signature at head.

[3] *Sketches of Young Ladies: in which these Interesting Members of the Animal Kingdom are Classified, according to their Several Instincts, Habits, and General Characteristics*, by "Quiz" [E. Caswall], with six illustrations by "Phiz", Chapman & Hall, 1837. The confusion persisted, and *Sketches of Young Ladies* and CD's *Sketches of Young Gentlemen* and *Sketches of Young Couples* (see *To* Forster, 3 Jan 40, *fn*) were later reprinted together in one volume—all three as by "Quiz".

[4] Just possibly the "book . . . about the children of the people" envisaged by CD as a counterblast to annuals such as Mrs Fairlie's: see *To* Mrs Gore, 31 Jan and *fns*.

[5] Cruikshank called on CD the same day (visit referred to, as having taken place on "Wednesday", in Cruikshank

*to* CD, 22 Feb, asking him to "send pr. bearer, one small four & sixpenny umbrella, also two sketches for the 'Pic Nic' ", which he had left at CD's house). Presumably at that meeting Cruikshank told CD that his own projected *Omnibus* (see 2 May 41, *fn*) might rule out his co-operation in an Annual; for on 27 Feb he wrote: "I find that I have proceeded [so] far in that said speculation with Mr. Tilt [*publisher, with Bogue, of his* Omnibus] that I cannot in honor recede—indeed I am bound under peculiar circumstances to others as well—so that I *must* now go on— | It is of no use expressing my regret that we are not working together (as we ought to have done from the first)—and should this said speculation of mine *unfortunately* fail—I shall be ready to join you in any way, & work on if agreeable, to the last" (MSS Huntington).

## *To* JOHN FORSTER, 18 FEBRUARY [1841]

MS Victoria & Albert Museum (FC). *Date:* 18 Feb was Thursday in 1841;
handwriting supports that year. *Address:* John Forster Esquire.

Devonshire Terrace. | Thursday Eighteenth Feby.
My Dear Forster.

I think it probable I *shall* be out to day, and in your neighbourhood at
about 2 or 3 o'Clock. If so, I will call, of course.

I am walking round and round the garden this exquisite morning, trying
to think of the subjects for next No.,[1] and indulging in visions of the
country. What a day for a Greenwich Steamer!

Faithfully Ever
CD.

## *To* THOMAS LATIMER,[2] 18 FEBRUARY 1841*

MS Rosenbach Foundation.

*Most Private*                    1 Devonshire Terrace | York Gate Regents Park.
                                      Thursday Eighteenth Feby. | 1841.
My Dear Sir.

Your letter has occasioned me great grief and distress. It opens a very
painful subject—one that has been a source of constant anxiety, uneasiness, and expence to me for some years; and which I fondly hoped, when
I settled my father in Exeter, would haunt me no more.

I need scarcely tell you (for I am sure you will have anticipated it
already) that he *should have* had no need to borrow money of you, or of
any man; and that his making your note of hand payable at my publishers'
was a moral outrage which words can scarcely censure enough. They felt
it so, as they knew I should, and refrained from informing me of the
circumstance, knowing how much it would hurt me.

Will you let me know how I shall remit you the amount—whether I shall
send you a cheque on my own Bankers in town—whether I shall desire
them to pay it to Saunders's in Exeter[3]—or whether I can pay it, to your

---

[1] No. 51 (*Barnaby*, Chs 10 and 11),
finished by 26 Feb (see *To* Cattermole,
that day); published 20 Mar.

[2] Thomas Latimer (1803–88), radical journalist. Managing editor of the
Liberal *Western Times* 1835–73, and a
great local personality. Strongly anti-
clerical, he consistently attacked the
Tory and High Church Bishop of
Exeter, Henry Phillpotts; and in 1848
was acquitted, amid public rejoicing, on
a charge of criminally libelling him.
He had met CD in May 35 as a fellow-
reporter of the Exeter election, and

again in Mar 39, on CD's house-
hunting expedition to Alphington (R. S.
Lambert, *The Cobbett of the West:
a Study of Thomas Latimer*, 1939,
pp. 71–2, 99); and in Aug 40 he
criticized Exeter Town Council for not
giving CD a civic welcome. He had
also known George Hogarth when
Hogarth was editing the Tory *Western
Luminary* 1831–2.

[aa] Added over a caret.

[3] Sanders & Co., bankers, Cathedral
Yard, Exeter.

credit, with anyone in London?[1] I shall desire to write you more at length, and to beg a favor of you, when I have heard from you on this head. Meantime believe me

Faithfully Yours

T. Latimer Esquire                          CHARLES DICKENS

### *To* BASIL HALL, 19 FEBRUARY 1841

MS Brotherton Library, Leeds.

Devonshire Terrace. | Friday Nineteenth February 1841.

My Dear Sir.

Many thanks to you for the MS.[2] I have not had time to read it yet, and intend to reserve it until after dinner on Sunday.[3] Your wishes in relation to it, I shall religiously observe, of course.[4]

I quite understand how you all laughed when the friend came in, and am glad you did so, because I know how truthful and hearty the crying must have been that went before. My love to the whole audience.[5]

---

[1] On 16 Mar CD's account-book (MS Messrs Coutts) shows a payment of £14 to Latimer.

[2] On 13 Feb Hall had sent CD an account in MS by his sister, Lady De Lancey, of her experiences at Waterloo (see *To* Hall, 16 Mar and *fn*).

[3] CD did not in fact read it until 15 Mar.

[4] In his letter enclosing the MS, Hall had requested that the account should be shown only to CD's "fireside circle".

[5] In the same letter Hall described the reception of *Master Humphrey* No. 44 (*Old Curiosity Shop*, Chs 71 and 72): "It was . . . brought in triumph to the drawing room, where in two minutes, all the family were assembled—all work left off—& every mind & heart bent on the fate of poor Nell & the old man. The effect was such as you might expect—I mean the first effect—but you will hardly anticipate the result— though, indeed, you have too much of old Shakespeare's kidney about you to be surprised at the apparent incongruities of human feelings.—All the party were in deep affliction—weeping & sobbing as if their hearts were breaking, when first one ludicrous incident, & then another, gave a fresh direction to their emotions. A Lady, a neighbour & a great friend of ours, hearing the shout which announced the arrival of the Clock, had come in & joined the 'Niobe' group. But it chanced that she had left her pocket handkerchief at home—& after swabbing away with her sleeves for some time, she was obliged to borrow the end of my eldest girl's handkerchief—& there they were, tugging at the opposite ends of it, when the door opened—& in walked Sir Edward Codrington's flag captain!—No order had been given (as usual when a number of the clock arrived) to deny company:—the door bell had not been heard—& so in came Capn. Montague. The contrast between his merry face, & astonished look—& the speechless grief of the weeping circle, was so great, that— after a pause of three seconds—they all burst out a laughing! | For the rest—*I* shall only say, that I would rather be the author of the eight lines from the 12th. to the 20th. inclusive, of page 214 of the aforesaid number, than of all I have ever penned—not nearly so much for the matchless beauty of the diction —as for the useful, virtuous, reflections it is calculated to excite in so many breasts" (MS Huntington). The passage on p. 214 runs from "Oh! it is hard to take to heart the lesson that such deaths will teach, but let no man reject it" to "In the Destroyer's steps there spring up bright creations that defy his power, and his dark path becomes a way of light to Heaven."

I am happy to say that Kate (that's my wife) is in a brilliant state, and is rather sitting in the drawing room up stairs as a matter of form, than for anything that prevents her coming down here. The three *old* children (they seem quite grown up, now there's another baby) are well and hearty, and the young one appears to be in the same condition. I can vouch for his lungs, which are dreadfully good.

As to his outward boy—about which you want to know something—all I know is that he has large dark eyes, and no nose at all as yet—that he seems to live in a state of perpetual sleepiness and intoxication (except when he cries)—is very fat—and looks when he is being washed, like a plucked turkey. His name, after one of his godfathers, is Walter Landor. And now you know as much of him as I do.

Have you ever had two babies in the house at once?—of your own I mean. Our third child can't walk yet, and here is a fourth upon her heels. I am expecting every day to be gray, and have very nearly persuaded myself that I am gouty.

Always My Dear Sir | Faithfully Yours

Captain Basil Hall CHARLES DICKENS

## *To* GEORGE CRUIKSHANK, 19 FEBRUARY 1841

MS Colonel Richard Gimbel.

Devonshire Terrace. | Nineteenth February 1841

My Dear Cruikshank.

The Bearer Lord Lindsey[1] has just come to town from Lincolnshire and wants to see the live Lions, among whom he justly puts you foremost. Therefore show yourself if you will, shake your mane, and roar at me for giving you the trouble.

My Dear Cruikshank | Faithfully Yours always
CHARLES DICKENS

## *To* JOHN FOWLER,[2] [?19 FEBRUARY 1841]

Envelope only, MS Private. *Date:* PM Sheffield 20 Feb 41 (clearly day of receipt). *Address:* John Fowler Esquire | Mechanics Institution | Sheffield.

[1] George Augustus Frederick Albemarle Bertie, 10th Earl of Lindsey (1814–77), of Uffington, near Stamford. Of weak intellect, he was a family problem: see *Lady Charlotte Guest, Extracts from her Journal 1833–1852*, ed. the Earl of Bessborough, 1950, pp. 1–3. Cruikshank commented in his reply of 22 Feb: "Your 'Lion' hunter call'd. The same I suppose who hath been slightly of the character of the wild animals himself"; and then again on 27 Feb: "It is well you took the precaution of ommiting [*thus*] to mention any of *his Lordships* peculiarities in your note for I found his Lordship had carried it off with him, what a rum 'un eh?—My wife saw him first & came & told me that there was a man either drunk or mad—I said, 'Show him up'! —and when he got into my room hang me [if] I do not think that he thought he was making hay—he pitched the papers about so!" (MSS Huntington).

[2] Secretary of the Sheffield Mechanics' Institute (see later vols).

## *To* THOMAS MITTON, [?20 FEBRUARY 1841][1]

MS Chas J. Sawyer Ltd. *Date:* Signature points to Feb 41; possibly not long after *To* Latimer, 18 Feb.

Devonshire Terrace | Saturday Morning

My Dear Mitton.

The inclosed, I had from my mother yesterday. If you have heard this morning, please let me know by Bearer. I shall be at home all day.

I have told John[2] to wait, *in case* you have any news.

Always Faithfully

Thomas Mitton Esquire. CHARLES DICKENS

## *To* T. N. TALFOURD, [?22 FEBRUARY 1841]

Envelope listed in John Anderson Jr. catalogue No. 343; postmarked 22 Feb 41; addressed "Mr. Serjeant Talfourd, M.P. | &c &c."

## *To* GEORGE CATTERMOLE, 22 FEBRUARY 1841

MS Dickens House.

Devonshire Terrace | Twenty Second February/41.

My Dear Cattermole.

I find I shall have so many little things to do tomorrow, that I must forego the *morning* part of our Engagement. Therefore I shall expect you to a snug dinner in the study at 6.

Punctival.

Best Regards. Always Faithfully

George Cattermole Esquire CHARLES DICKENS

## *To* JOHN TOMLIN,[3] 23 FEBRUARY 1841

Text from MDGH, I, 40.

1, Devonshire Terrace, York Gate, Regent's Park,
London, Tuesday, Feb. 23rd, 1841.

Dear Sir,

You are quite right in feeling assured that I should answer the letter you have addressed to me. If you had entertained a presentiment that it would

---

[1] Printed twice in N: in 1840 (N, I, 285) and in Dec 42 (N, I, 493).

[2] Possibly John Thompson, CD's man-servant from some date in the 40s until 1867.

[3] John Tomlin (1806–50), postmaster of Jackson, Tennessee, minor writer and autograph-collector. Author of *Shelley's Grave and Other Poems*, privately printed, [?1845], and of *Tales of the Caddo*, Cincinnati, 1849. He published CD's letter, together with a highly eulogistic note on him, in *Graham's Magazine*, Feb 42, XX, 83–4; and reprinted it, with a further letter from him (13 Jan 43), in "The Autobiography of a Monomaniac", by "Joe Bottom", *Holden's Dollar Magazine*

afford me sincere pleasure and delight to hear from a warm-hearted and admiring reader of my books in the backwoods of America, you would not have been far wrong.

I thank you cordially and heartily both for your letter and its kind and courteous terms. To think that I have awakened a fellow-feeling and sympathy with the creatures of many thoughtful hours among the vast solitudes in which you dwell, is a source of the purest delight and pride to me; and believe me that your expressions of affectionate remembrance and approval, sounding from the green forests on the banks of the Mississippi, sink deeper into my heart and gratify it more than all the honorary distinctions that all the courts in Europe could confer.

It is such things as these that make one hope one does not live in vain, and that are the highest reward of an author's life. To be numbered among the household gods of one's distant countrymen, and associated with their homes and quiet pleasures; to be told that in each nook and corner of the world's great mass there lives one well-wisher who holds communion with one in the spirit, is a worthy fame indeed, and one which I would not barter for a mine of wealth.

That I may be happy enough to cheer some of your leisure hours for a very long time to come, and to hold a place in your pleasant thoughts, is the earnest wish of "Boz".

And, with all good wishes for yourself, and with a sincere reciprocation of all your kindly feeling,

I am, dear Sir, | Faithfully yours
[CHARLES DICKENS]

## *To* JOHN FORSTER, [25 FEBRUARY 1841]

Extract in F, II, ix, 165. *Date:* 25 Feb 41, from Brighton,[1] according to Forster.

I have (it's four o'clock) done a very fair morning's work,[2] at which I have sat very close, and been blessed besides with a clear view of the end of the volume.[3] As the contents of one number usually require a day's

(New York), Jan 49, III, 29–30. This serial story (Nov 48–Nov 49) also contains texts of letters to Tomlin from Landor, Macaulay, Tennyson, Talfourd, Fenimore Cooper, Longfellow, Poe, and other English and American writers: see T. O. Mabbott in *Notes & Queries*, 6 Jan 1934.

[1] He had gone there to get "out of harm's way" (*To* Forster, 4 Feb, 2nd letter), "for a week's quiet labour" (F, II, ix, 165).

[2] On *Barnaby*, Ch. 10 (No. 51, published 20 Mar), the MS of which he sent to Cattermole next day.

[3] Vol. II of *Master Humphrey* ended with the next No. (No. 52), which contained Ch. 12 (six pages only), in which Haredale and Chester meet at the Maypole, and decide to thwart the intended marriage of Emma and Edward. The rest of the 12 pages of the No. was made up by the frontispiece, title-page and a two-page Preface to the Volume. The frontispiece was to have been done by Cattermole, but illness prevented this. In a letter dated "Sunday Morning" [?7 Mar] Browne wrote to CD: "Will you give me some notion of the sort of design you wish for the frontispiece to

thought at the very least, and often more, this puts me in great spirits. I think—that is, I hope—the story takes a great stride at this point, and takes it WELL. Nous verrons. Grip will be strong, and I build greatly on the Varden household.

## *To* GEORGE CATTERMOLE, 26 FEBRUARY 1841

MS Mrs A. M. Stern.

Old Ship Hotel Brighton.
Twenty Sixth[1] February 1841.

My Dear Kittenmoles.

I passed your house[2] on Wednesday—being then atop of the Brighton Æra[3]—but there was nobody at the door, saving a solitary poulterer, and all my warm-hearted aspirations lodged in the goods he was delivering.—No doubt you observed a peculiar relish in your dinner. That was the cause.

I send you the MS. I fear you will have to read all 5 slips, but the subject I think of, is at the top of the last, where the guest, with his back towards the spectator, is looking out of window.[4] I think, in your hands, it will be a very pretty one.

Then, my boy, when you have done it, turn your thoughts (as soon as other engagements and prostrations will allow) first to the outside of the Warren—see No. 1[5]—secondly, to the outside of the locksmith's house by

second vol. of *Clock*? Cattermole being put *hors de combat*—Chapman with a careworn face (if you can picture that) brings me the block at the eleventh hour, and requires it finished by Wednesday. Now as I have two others to complete in the meantime—something nice and *light* would be best adapted to my *palette*, and prevent an excess of perspiration in the relays of wood-cutters. You shall have the others to criticise on Tuesday. | . . . How are Mrs. Dickens and the 'Infant'?" (F. G. Kitton, *"Phiz", a Memoir*, 1882, p. 23). Prominent in Browne's frontispiece is an hour-glass, with figures tumbling through, some of them suggestive of the coming riots. Above and to the left are scenes from both *Old Curiosity Shop* and *Barnaby*—old Trent weeping on Nell's death-bed (which follows Cattermole's death-bed illustration fairly closely, but shows a prettier Nell); Swiveller on one knee proposing to the Marchioness; Edward Chester lying wounded as the "stranger" gallops off. Most of the design is "lightly" engraved and flowing.

[1] MS reads "Sixthe".

[2] On Clapham Rise. Cattermole's son, Leonardo, describes (in F. G. Kitton, *CD by Pen and Pencil*, 1890–2, II, 177–80) CD's rather later visits to the house, by coach; its "very 'George Cattermolean'" drawing-room, with "draperies reminding one of those of the 'Maypole' bed" and heavy carved furniture which had been Byron's; and its tapestry and armour-hung studio, with carvings of "hideous, gaping 'Old Curiosity Shop' faces" on an escritoire, and lamplight glinting on antique swords and firelocks.

[3] Apparently diphthong in MS.

[4] Cattermole's illustration to *Barnaby*, Ch. 10, in fact shows John Chester warming his hands in front of a massive fireplace.

[5] Described there vaguely as "the great house . . . the old red brick house . . . that stands in its own grounds" (*Barnaby* No. 1, *Master Humphrey* No. 46). Cattermole emphasized the grounds both in this illustration (the headpiece to Ch. 13, first chapter in Vol. III, published 3 Apr) and in another in Ch. 29.

night—see No. 3.[1] Put a penny pistol to Chapman's head, and demand the blocks of him.[2]

I have addled my head with writing all day, and have barely wit enough left to send my love to my cousin, and—here's a genealogical poser—what relation of mine may the dear little child be[3]—at present, I desire to be commended to her clear blue eyes.

Always My Dear George | Faithfully Yours

George Cattermole Esquire                                        Boz.

## *To* THOMAS HOOD,[4] [?LATE FEBRUARY 1841]

Mention in Hood *to* CD, ?Feb or Mar 41 (i.e. after the move to 2 Union Row which Hood reported to his doctor on 1 Feb, and probably before the improvement in his health that spring). *Date:* not on first reading in Nov 40 Hood's review of *Master Humphrey*, but shortly before Hood's reply, below.[5]

*Saying how much he had been pleased by Hood's review of* Master Humphrey *in the* Athenæum *of 7 Nov 40,[6] and by his earlier praise of other books.[7]*

[1] An illustration CD had asked Cattermole for before (see 9 Feb and *fn*) and clearly much wished him to do, knowing the result would be something architecturally remarkable: as indeed it was. The "shy, blinking house" had the features described in No. 3 (Ch. 4)—the conical roof, garret windows &c—but with an elegant neo-classical structure running up two floors above the porch (see Ch. 16; *Master Humphrey* No. 54, published 10 Apr).

[2] CD had asked Chapman & Hall for the blocks for the locksmith's house on 9 Feb, without result. On 1 Mar Cattermole wrote to Edward Chapman himself (MS Comtesse de Suzannet).

[3] Cf. *To* Cattermole, 13 Aug 40.

[4] Thomas Hood (1799–1845; *DNB*), poet and humorist. As assistant sub-editor of the *London Magazine* 1821–3 had become friendly with De Quincey, Lamb, Hazlitt and J. H. Reynolds, whose sister he married 1824. After producing a few volumes of prose and verse 1825–9, launched in 1830 his *Comic Annual* (well received, though CD found the issue for 1839 "rather poor": see Vol. I, p. 505); published a 3-vol. novel, *Tylney Hall*, 1834, *Hood's Own*, 1839 (lent by CD to Cattermole, to read on his honeymoon: see Vol. I, p. 576), and in 1840 his unsuccessful *Up the Rhine*. Dogged by ill-health and

financial troubles, he lived abroad 1835–40. His appointment, on Hook's death in Aug 41, as editor of the *New Monthly Magazine* at £300 *p.a.* was a great relief from anxiety.

[5] None of CD's and Hood's biographers have made clear the beginning of their relationship. When CD read the *Athenæum* review he did not know the identity of its author; but he had already met Hood (see Hood's letter below, mentioning the "last time" he saw CD—clearly in June 40)—though this he apparently later forgot (see *To* Miss Coutts, 18 Mar 45). According to the 1848 Preface to the Cheap Edn of *Old Curiosity Shop*, CD did not discover Hood's authorship of the *Athenæum* review until "long after" its publication (which may be interpreted as four or five months after). He then presumably wrote to Hood at once.

[6] The review began with criticism of the sections in which Master Humphrey and his friends appear. (What, he asked, appealing to Mr Weller Senior, could make "a more hock'erder start"?) Then turning to the new story, he said he did not know where he had met in fiction with "a more striking and picturesque combination of images" than the simple childish figure of Nell amidst the chaos which formed the stock-in-trade of the Curiosity Shop (and he

## *To* HENRY AUSTIN, ?28 FEBRUARY 1841\*

MS Morgan Library. *Date:* 1 Mar 41 was Monday; probably CD was writing on Sun 28 Feb.

Old Ship Hotel Brighton | Sunday First March 1841.

My Dear Henry.

I shall be at home next Wednesday Evening. May I hope to find a note

pointed the reader not to CD's own description but to Williams's picture of the child asleep): "it is like an Allegory". As for Nell herself, he went on, we would say that "she thinks, speaks, and acts, in a style beyond her years, if we did not know how poverty and misfortune are apt to make advances of worldly knowledge to the young at a most ruinous discount". He commented on the truth to nature of old Trent and Swiveller; disliked in Quilp the too common "association of moral with physical deformity"; and applauded CD's good characters—painted with a relish which proved that he believed in their goodness. He then, in "a few words of Boz himself", rejoiced to learn from CD's Preface that he had "never been 'raving mad'". So struck was CD, it seems, by Hood's review that when, later in 1841, he detached the "Master Humphrey" sections from *Old Curiosity Shop* and wrote new passages to fill the gaps, he inserted four paragraphs (before the last in Ch. 1) which dwelt on Nell's surroundings as she lay asleep, and even added: "she seemed to exist in a kind of allegory".

[7] Heading his letter simply "2 Union Row | High Street | Camberwell", Hood replied: "Your kind letter arrived very opportunely, when I was laid up in bed, for it served to give me great pleasure in the midst of great pain. I am confined, as you know, to slops . . . | As to the review . . . the beauty of the country that was passed over was a sufficient reward. That it was written with a kindly feeling towards you, is true, for books which put us in a better humour with the world in general must naturally incline us towards the Author in particular. (So we love Goldsmith for his Vicar of Wakefield)—Add . . . that I felt you had been unfairly used in

a certain Critique [*possibly Richard Ford's review of* Oliver *in the* Quarterly, *June 39*]—& you will have the whole Animus. Yet I was critical too, & found all the faults I could pick. | My opinion of your books is a deliberate one:—and in spite of an early prejudice that Boz was all Buzz. Some ill-chosen extracts which reached me abroad, with the rumour that one of the Prominences was a stage coachman & the other a Boots (what grammar!) led me to think that the Book was only a new strain of Tom-&-Jerryism [*see Vol. 1, p. 463 and* n]—which is my aversion. So strong was this notion, that I did not properly enjoy the work itself on a first perusal, or detect that 'soul of goodness in things evil' the goodness of Pickwickedness. I afterwards read it several times with increased delight & finally packed off the whole set to a friend, a Prussian Officer, but English by birth & feeling [*Lieut. Philip de Franck*], that he might enjoy its Englishness—to my taste a first rate merit. | Go on, and prosper!— and I wish it most sincerely. Though no man in England has so legitimate a right to envy you, for *my* circulation is so bad that I can hardly keep my hands warm . . . | . . . Some happy day, Lord knows when, I will certainly come, Lord knows how, & see you in Devonshire. I drop the Terrace, because to *me* you are a county or two distant . . . In the mean time I heartily grasp & shake the hand you autographically hold out to me, & embrace your friendship with my whole heart. A friendship that promises to endure, if from nothing better, thro the mere difficulty of falling in, & consequently out, with each other. . . . | By the bye, the last time I saw you, I was on a very happy errand, & you of course on a pleasurable one. Mine to Ostend to fetch home my dear children—yours to Ramsgate or

from you, telling me when you can come and have a little talk with me?[1]
I have my reasons for not coming to you, which you may perhaps guess;
and which our conversation will explain, if you do not.[2]

My love to Letitia

                          In haste | Always Heartily Yours
Henry Austin Esquire                    CHARLES DICKENS

## *To* THE DIRECTORS OF THE NEW ZEALAND COMPANY,[3] 4 MARCH 1841*

MS Public Record Office, London. *Address:* To | The Board of Directors |
of | The New Zealand Company.

                          1 Devonshire Terrace, York Gate, Regents Park.
                                          Thursday Fourth March 1841

My Lords and Gentlemen.

A younger brother of mine, Mr. Alfred Dickens, being desirous to try
his fortune in your new Colony, and to procure an appointment as Assistant Surveyor and Civil Engineer, of the First Class, I take the liberty of
recommending him to you as a young man who is in every respect qualified to serve you in that capacity.

He has been educated for his profession under the very best auspices,
and has been practically employed for the last four years, without cessation, on Great Public Works.[4] He is extremely intelligent, active, and
enterprising; and I trust I need hardly say that unless I were well assured

Margate [*clearly in June* 40], the two steamers paddling for some time, side by side. . . . | Pray present my Respects to Mrs. Dickens, and believe me Bozitively | Yours ever very truly" (MS Huntington). The development of Hood's and CD's friendship no doubt dates from this period. On 13 Apr 41 Hood wrote to de Franck: "Boz is a very good fellow, and he and I are very good friends" (*Memorials of Thomas Hood*, ed. [Mrs Broderip and Thomas Hood], 1860, II, 96–7).

[1] Presumably on what was to be done about John Dickens's debts and attempts to raise money on the security of CD's name: see *To* Latimer, 18 Feb. See also *To* Macready, 6 Mar, *fn.*

[2] No doubt CD felt the discussion would worry Letitia.

[3] Founded as the New Zealand Land Company in 1839, through the amalga-mation of the New Zealand Association,

formed 1837 by Col. Edward Gibbon Wakefield (1796–1862; *DNB*), the New Zealand Colonization Company (1838), and William Huskisson's Colonizing Company (1825). Despite the Govt's hostility, the Company's first settlers sailed in the *Tory* on 5 May 39 and landed at Port Nicholson in the North island on 24 Sep, with Wakefield's brother William in charge. They quickly founded Wellington (originally named Britannia, but re-named after the Duke), and purchased from the Maoris some 20 million acres of land, eventually cut down by the Govt to 283,000 acres. Largely through Wake-field's efforts in London, Lord John Russell, as Colonial Secretary, granted the Company a charter of incorporation in Feb 41.

[4] See *To* Alfred Dickens, 12 Aug 40, *fn.*

of his fitness for the office, I would, on no consideration whatever, countenance his application.

> I have the honor to be
> My Lords and Gentlemen | Your faithful Servant
> CHARLES DICKENS[1]

The Directors | of | The New Zealand Company.

## *To* [?ALEXANDER] BLACKWOOD,[2] [EARLY MARCH 1841]

Mention in *To* Overs, 5 Mar 41.

## *To* JOHN FORSTER, [?4 or 5 MARCH 1841]

MS Victoria & Albert Museum (FC). *Date:* on the pale blue watermarked paper that CD began using Mar 41, but before July 41 when he changed his initial "y" (see *To* Forster, 23 July, *fn*). "That monstrosity" may well have been the news of John Dickens which infuriated CD to the point of publicly repudiating his debts (see *To* Mitton, 6 Mar and *fn*).

My Dear Forster

I have already sent to Mac, who is to be here at a quarter before 5. Therefore I have told Henry *not* to take the note.

---

[1] Alfred's own letter (no doubt drafted by CD) read as follows: "33 Argylle [*thus*] Street New Road. | Thursday March 4th. 1840 [*thus*]. | My Lords and Gentlemen | I beg respectfully to offer myself to you as a Candidate for the Office of an Assistant Engineer and Surveyor of the first class to the New Zealand Company. | I am Twenty years of age, have been educated as a Civil Engineer, possess a thorough knowledge of Land Surveying and Civil Engineering; and having been constantly employed for the last four years, on different Railways and public Buildings, am perfectly and practically acquainted with the most important duties of my Profession. | I am at present engaged by the Birmingham and Derby Railway Company, in whose employment should I prove unsuccessful in this application, I shall still remain. But as I am anxious to try my fortune in a wider sphere, I have come up to London for the purpose of submitting this application to you; and with it such testimonials, as I presumed you would require. | I beg to submit those certificates herewith. I also take the liberty of laying before you a letter from my brother Mr. Charles Dickens, which I trust will serve as a guarantee for my respectability and trustworthiness. | I have the honor to be | My lords and Gentlemen | Your most obedient humble Servant | Alfred L. Dickens | To the | Board of Directors of the | New Zealand Company" (MS Public Record Office). Office endorsements of this letter read: "4 Mar 41" and "too young 1st. class | postponed for interview. 2nd." Informed of this, Alfred applied on 10 Mar as a Second Asst. On the 18th he sent another letter (dictated by CD: see *To* Mitton, 19 Mar) to the Chief Clerk, F. Dillon Bell, saying that he was anxious to know whether the Directors had come to any decision, as he had waited in town solely to hear the result and was therefore absent from his Derby Railway duties. No reply to this appears in the file; but Alfred's original letter is endorsed "rejected insufficient | 10 March" (MSS Public Record Office).

[2] The head of the publishing firm of Blackwood's (see *To* Forster, 30 June 41, *fn*).

That monstrosity of yesterday has played the very devil with me. To complete my cheerfulness, I was seized last evening with a fearful tooth ache which is pulling my jaw to pieces this morning. I have sent to the Dentist, but am afraid he's out.

I have sent Topping to order dinner—Six, I said, that we might ride gently there, by the pleasantest road.

Faithfully Always

CD.

## *To* JOHN OVERS, 5 MARCH 1841

MS Free Library of Philadelphia. *Address:* Paid | Mr. J. A. Overs | Messrs. Springweiler & Compy. | 2 Duke Street | West Smithfield.

Devonshire Terrace. | Friday Evening Fifth March | 1841.

Dear Mr. Overs.

I have only time to write you half a dozen words.

Since you sent me your paper, I have had sickness at home[1]—family affairs of a trying nature to arrange[2]—and have been out of town. I have gone through it at last (the improvement is *immense*)[3] and have sent it to Blackwood with an earnest private letter. What the upshot will be, I cannot tell of course,—for I fear they will not set much store by my recommendation of a paper when I don't write for them—but directly I hear anything, I shall not fail to communicate with you.

I have given it a second name. It stands now, Norris and Anne Boleyn. An English Chronicle.[4]

The new introduction[5] is—except the latter part[6]—the best of the whole. When you do anything fresh, throttle your jesters, remorselessly.[7]

Faithfully Yours

Mr. J. A. Overs.                                          CHARLES DICKENS

## *To* THOMAS MITTON, 6 MARCH 1841*

MS Hr Jacob Christensen.

Devonshire Terrace. | Saturday Sixth March 1841.

My Dear Mitton.

I return you the form of advertisement,[8] corrected; and have marked

---

[1] Whooping-cough (*To* Macready, 11 Mar).

[2] See next, *To* Mitton.

[3] Underlined twice.

[4] The story was apparently not accepted by *Blackwood's*, but was published in Overs's *Evenings of a Working Man*, 1844 (pp. 115–75), called simply "Norris and Anne Boleyn".

[5] CD presumably meant the introductory chapter, describing Christmas at Hever Castle in 1525.

[6] No doubt the final chapter, describing the tournament won by Henry Norris, wearing—unknown to himself—Anne Boleyn's glove; the King's rage; the imprisonment and execution of them both—movingly told. (Overs's one quoted source was Lingard's *History of England*.)

[7] Both the King and Wolsey have jesters—their "wit" modelled on that of Shakespeare's clowns.

[8] On 6 Mar Macready noted in his

upon the back the papers in which it must be inserted, which, indeed, are all the morning and evening ones.[1] The Sundays we may leave alone.

Let there be no misunderstanding, for this is a very serious matter, relative to what I said to you this morning. Mind. If he communicate with you, the following are the only conditions to which I will assent.

First. That he goes abroad—to Calais, Boulogne, or Antwerp. The last, I think, is the best place, but let him please himself.

Secondly. That he takes Augustus[2] with him, whom, immediately on their arrival, I will send as a weekly boarder to the best school I can find in the place, and clothe, and find in pocket money.[3] I say weekly boarder, because I should wish the boy, for more reasons than one, to be at home from Saturday night to Monday Morning.

Thirdly. That if my mother should object to go—I think it very likely she may, but I have had no communication whatever with her upon the subject—he allows her out of his pension,[4] for her support, forty pounds a year.

On these conditions, I will allow him £20 a year, which will make his income a hundred[5]—a very good one mind, abroad—put the amount of the last quarter's allowance to whatever the furniture at Alphington will fetch, and apply the amount to paying or compounding for the Devonshire debts—and I will give him besides £10 to leave England with.

If these concessions are accepted, you have full power from me to carry them out immediately. *But I will consent to nothing short of, or beyond them*; and I know after the solemn injunctions I have laid upon you to the

---

diary: "Forster told me to-day that Dickens would put an advertisement in the paper on Monday in reference to his father—which I told him he *ought not* to do" (*Diaries*, II, 126).

[1] It appeared in all the main London newspapers on 8 Mar as follows: "CAUTION.—We, the undersigned Solicitors for Charles Dickens, of No. 1, Devonshire-terrace, York-gate, Regent's Park, in the county of Middlesex, Esquire, do hereby give notice, that certain persons bearing, or purporting to bear, the surname of our said client, have put into circulation, with the view of the more readily obtaining credit thereon, certain acceptances made payable at his private residence, or at the offices of his business agents; that no person whatever has any right, title, or authority to make promissory notes, acceptances, or other pecuniary securities, payable either at the private residence of the said Charles Dickens, or at his publisher's or banker's; and that

such bills made payable as aforesaid will not be paid. And we do further give notice, that from and after the date hereof, the said Charles Dickens will not discharge or liquidate any debt or debts, save those of his own or of his wife's contracting, and that any application made to him on account of the debts of any other person whomsoever will be made in vain. | SMITHSON and MITTON, |23, Southampton-buildings, Chancery-lane. | Dated this 8th day of March, 1841" (*Morning Herald*).

[2] Augustus Newnham Dickens (1827–1866): see Vol. I, p. 485n.

[3] *To* Mitton, 3 Jan 42, suggests that CD was already paying his school fees at Exeter.

[4] £145.16.8 (5/12ths of his former salary of £350: W. Huskisson *to* J. W. Croker, 9 Mar 1824, MS Public Record Office).

[5] In fact, including £20 from CD, it would have been £125.

contrary, that you will not hold yourself justified in entertaining any other proposition for a moment.[1]

Always | Dear Mitton | Faithfully Yours

Thomas Mitton Esquire                                    CHARLES DICKENS[2]


## *To* DANIEL MACLISE, 7 MARCH 1841

Mention in Sotheby's catalogue, June 1950; *MS* 1 p.; dated 7 Mar 41; salutation "My Dear Mac", signed initials.


## *To* JOHN FORSTER, 8 MARCH [1841]

MS Victoria & Albert Museum (FC). *Date:* 8 Mar was Monday in 1841; handwriting and blue watermarked paper support that year.

Monday 8th. March.

My Dear Forster.

I am writing the Oliver preface,[3] and will give you a call—I hope—at about 4. Will you dine here at 5 any way?

I want to have some talk with you. Please Sir, did you ring the bell at half past Eleven last night?

Faithfully Always

CD


[1] John Dickens, however, did not accept this plan, but continued to live at Alphington. That CD had been making him an allowance of £20 a quarter is suggested by payments to Mitton of £20 in Sep 40, £40 in Apr 41, £20 in June 41 (Account-book, MS Messrs Coutts). No similar round sums to Mitton appear in CD's later 1841 accounts; but his Diary entry for 15 June (Appx, p. 463) implies that an allowance was continued.

[2] An envelope addressed "Thomas Mitton Esquire" (MS Morgan) might conceivably belong with this letter. On the back CD has written: "Be very sharp upon the fraudulent second part." Date is clearly 1841, on handwriting; probably Mar-May, on final "e"s of "the" and "Esquire".

[3] Probably first thought of in Feb 40, as a means of defending *Oliver* against the charge that it glamourized vice (see *To* Horne, Feb 40 and *fn*); explicitly mentioned in June 40, as a possible means of helping off the stock of *Oliver* when CD recaptured the copyright (see *To* Forster, 17 June 40 and *fn*). The preface, dated Apr 41, appeared in the edition of *Oliver* published by Chapman & Hall on 15 May 41.

## *To* DANIEL MACLISE, 8 MARCH 1841\*

MS Benoliel Collection. *Address:* Daniel Maclise Esquire.

Monday Eighth March 1841

My Dear Mac

I'll write you tomorrow, and fix either that, or Wednesday night, for our foregathering.[1]

In the last haste | Faithfully
CD.

## *To* RICHARD MONCKTON MILNES, [?8 MARCH 1841]\*

MS Trinity College, Cambridge. *Date:* Signature points to Mar 41; light blue watermarked paper supports; perhaps connected with first paragraph of *To* Milnes, 10 Mar.

Devonshire Terrace | Monday Morning

My Dear Milnes.

Look at the inclosed, which came in an envelope directed to me. Have you anything for *me* in return?

Faithfully Yours always

Richard M. Milnes Esquire CHARLES DICKENS

## *To* THOMAS MITTON, 9 MARCH 1841†

MS Huntington Library.

Devonshire Terrace
Tuesday Evening Ninth March 1841.

My Dear Mitton.

I have been thinking over what we spoke of this morning, and write to ask you to put to him[2]—even more distantly and unpromisingly than you have already settled in your own mind—the matter of the debts. Independently of the worth of the money, *[a]*I am more fearful than I can tell you, of encouraging his expectations.*[a]*

Faithfully Ever

CHARLES DICKENS

---

[1] Possibly CD's answer to an undated note from Maclise reading: "There is not a bit of the Man left in me—I have sworn to myself to ornament the top of an Arch to-night—an employment over which I grudge to spend day-light— I want very much to see you.—I am forced every week day to go to the RA, at five. This drives me mad— | Will you call for me to-morrow evening at 8, *there* or meet me at The Athenaeum at that hour— | Ever yours | D. Maclise | P.S. My hair is all falling off. I am now quite bald a-top" (MS Huntington). By July he was wearing a wig (see *To* Maclise, ?16 Aug 41, *fn*).

[2] John Dickens (see *To* Mitton, 6 Mar and *fn*).

*[aa]* Extract given in N. Letter otherwise unpublished.

## *To* RICHARD MONCKTON MILNES, 10 MARCH 1841

MS Trinity College, Cambridge.

Devonshire Terrace. | Wednesday March Tenth | 1841.

My Dear Milnes.

I thank you very much for the Nickleby correspondence, which I will keep for a day or two, and return when I see you. Poor fellow! The long letter is quite admirable, and most affecting.[1]

I am not quite sure, either of Friday or Saturday; for independently of the Clock (which for ever wants winding) I am getting a young brother off to New Zealand[2] just now, and have my mornings sadly cut up in consequence. But knowing your ways, I know, I may say that I will come if I can—and that if I can't, I won't.

That Nellicide was the Act of Heaven, as you may see any of these fine mornings when you look about you. If you knew the pain it gave me—but what am I talking of—if you don't know, nobody does.[3]

I am glad to shake you by the hand again autographically, and am always

Faithfully Yours

Richard M. Milnes Esquire                          CHARLES DICKENS

## *To* [?EDWARD CHAPMAN], 10 MARCH 1841*

MS Dickens House. *Address:* His correspondent's access to the proofs of *Barnaby* (see *fn*) and the words "kind care" suggest Chapman or Hall; probably Chapman, the more literary of the two.

Devonshire Terrace. | Wednesday Tenth March 1841.

My Dear Sir

I have looked back to the Annual Register, and find you are quite right about the one pound notes.[4] Very many thanks to you for your kind care.

Faithfully Yours

CHARLES DICKENS

[1] No explanation of this paragraph has been found.

[2] See *To* the Directors of the New Zealand Co., 4 Mar and *fn*.

[3] Perhaps Milnes's *Poetry for the People, and Other Poems*, 1840, had come to CD's mind, and "The Violet-Girl" in particular—plying her "small commerce in the chill March weather". He would also obviously have been in sympathy with themes such as "the sacred Patience of the Poor", "the charities of Poor to Poor", in the sequence "Specimens of Poetry for the

People"—though scarcely with Milnes's acceptance of the "line between the Rich and Poor" as God-ordained. For a full discussion of Victorian "Benevolence" in the period, see Humphry House, *The Dickens World*, 1941.

[4] See *Barnaby*, Ch. 11 (No. 51, published 20 Mar): "that chap, whose mother was hung . . . for passing bad Notes". The MS reads: "for passing bad one pound notes" (Forster Collection, V & A). Notes under £5 were not issued until 1797.

## *To* JOHN FORSTER, [?10 MARCH 1841]

MS Victoria & Albert Museum (FC). *Date:* Almost certainly refers to the first day of the sale of Thomas Hill's library 10–17 Mar by Messrs Evans of 93 Pall Mall: see *fn*; handwriting supports. *Address:* John Forster Esquire.

My Dear Forster

*Of course* I am going to the Sale; and was just dressing to repair to the Parthenon,[1] when your note arrived.

It's a farce proposing to be later than *a quarter past 2*, for if I am to be in Southampton Buildings at 4, what in God's name would be the use of going to Evans's at 3? I shall wait at the Parthenon from 2 to a quarter past, and if you don't come, repair to the Auction.[2]

Will you dine with me afterwards—at home at 5?

Faithfully Always
CD.

## *To* W. C. MACREADY, 11 MARCH 1841*

MS Morgan Library.

Devonshire Terrace.
Thursday March the Eleventh. | 1841.

My Dear Macready.

When your note arrived yesterday,[3] I had left home and gone to Evans's where I bought some of poor Tom's books, and whither I have dispatched an agent today, to purchase more.[4] There's a cup, made from the Bard's

---

[1] CD was now a member of the Committee: see *To* Beadnell 26 July 40 (*Addenda*, p. 496).

[2] On the first day CD bought Cowper's Translation of Homer, 4 vols, 1802 (12/-); *Don Quixote*, with Notes by Lockhart, 4 vols, 1820 (13/-); and Cobbett and Howell's *Complete Collection of State Trials* (to 1784), 21 vols, 1809 (£5.10). The whole library, containing 1684 lots, fetched £1424.3.6 (*Catalogue of the Valuable Library, Prints, Autographs and Manuscripts, of the late Thomas Hill Esq.*, with MS record of buyers and prices, BM).

[3] Macready had written the day before: "Do you intend to look in on poor Tom Hill's effects?—and to lounge through any other auction rooms?—Because if you do, you will tempt us to go too?—You will hold yourself double booked for Monday 22nd. ¼ before 7—on pain of extermination for default—no bail will be taken.— | Today is the first day of T. Hill's books &c." (MS Huntington).

[4] On the second day of the sale the marked copy of the Hill catalogue (BM) shows that CD acquired Chatterton's *Works*, with his Life by Gregory, ed. Southey, 3 vols, 1803 (£1.5); Canova's *Works*, 2 vols, 1824 (£1.13); *The Dance of Death*, ed. Douce, Pickering, 1833 (17/-); J. C. Dunlop's *History of Fiction*, 3 vols, 1814 (£1.3); Defoe's Novels, ed. Sir Walter Scott, 12 vols (1–3 missing), 1831 (£1.13); *English Poets from Chaucer to Cowper*, with their Lives by Johnson and Chalmers, 21 vols, 1810 (£9.9); and Dekker's *Gull's Hornbook*, 1812 (8/-). During the remaining days he acquired Joseph Glanvill on *Witches and Apparitions*, 1726 (6/-); J. P. Malcolm's *Anecdotes of the Manners and Customs of London*, 2 vols, 1808, 1811 (16/-); Spenser's *Works*, with Life and Notes by Todd, 8 vols, 1805 (£3.13.6); Shakespeare's *Plays and Poems*, with Notes and Glossary by Malone, 21 vols, 1821 (£7.7); and P. F. Tytler's *England under the Reigns of Edward VI and Mary*, 2 vols, 1839

Mulberry tree, and presented by somebody or other, to Garrick.[1] It is quite clear to me that this relic *must* be yours; the more especially as you have very good stuff to put into it—no man better.

I have booked Monday the 22nd. at a quarter before seven, for a full inside.[2] A sort of madness is upon me (occasioned by seeing the buds come out) which prevents me from doing anything but walk round and round the garden,[3] haunted by a ghostly clock which I don't seem to care for.

                                      Always My Dear Macready | Faithfully Yours
W. C. Macready Esquire                                      CHARLES DICKENS

Fine weather for the hooping-cough. Since such things must be, it is a most fortunate time.


## *To* MRS BENNETT,[4] 11 MARCH 1841

Mention in N, I, 303.[5]


## *To* DANIEL MACLISE, 12 MARCH 1841

MS Victoria & Albert Museum (FC). Endorsed by Forster: "Enormous Black Seal on Envelope".

                                                      Devonshire Terrace.
                                      Friday Evening | March The Twelfth 1841.
My Dear Maclise.

You will be greatly shocked and grieved to hear that the Raven[6] is no more.

He expired to-day at a few minutes after Twelve o'Clock at noon. He had been ailing (as I told you t'other night) for a few days, but we anticipated no serious result, conjecturing that a portion of the white paint he swallowed last summer might be lingering about his vitals without having

---

(15/-). By the end he had acquired 15 lots for £36.0.6—adding 105 volumes to his library. Two presentation copies from himself to Hill were also sold: *Oliver*, 3 vols, 1838, with a CD letter in it (£1.5), and *Nickleby* (£1.8). A copy of *Sketches by Boz*, Second Series, fetched 2/6, and 38 weekly numbers of *Master Humphrey* 3/6.

[1] "Garrick's Celebrated Cup formed from the Mulberry Tree planted by Shakspeare ... with an Inscription on the Stem from Garrick's Ode". It was bought on the last day of the sale for £44.2 by a Mr Jolley (Sale catalogue, BM), and is now in the Garrick Club.

[2] I.e., presumably, to help ensure a full meeting of the Siddons Committee: see *To* Macready, 22 Mar, *fn.*

[3] Cf. *To* Forster, 18 Feb.

[4] Unidentified.

[5] Perhaps merely an autograph: on the same day CD gave autographs to a Miss Theobald and a Miss Tryon.

[6] One of the two ravens who were the originals of Grip (see Preface to the First Cheap Edition of *Barnaby*, 1849). Stuffed, in a glass case, he fetched £126 in Christie's sale of 9 July 70. He is now owned by Colonel Richard Gimbel.

any serious effect upon his constitution. Yesterday afternoon he was taken so much worse that I sent an express for the medical gentleman (Mr. Herring)[1] who promptly attended, and administered a powerful dose of castor oil. Under the influence of this medicine, he recovered so far as to be able at 8 o'Clock p.m. to bite Topping. His night was peaceful. This morning at daybreak he appeared better; received (agreeably to the doctor's directions) another dose of castor oil; and partook plentifully of some warm gruel, the flavor of which he appeared to relish. Towards eleven o'Clock he was so much worse that it was found necessary to muffle the stable knocker. At half past, or thereabouts, he was heard talking to himself about the horse and Topping's family, and to add some incoherent expressions which are supposed to have been either a foreboding of his approaching dissolution, or some wishes relative to the disposal of his little property—consisting chiefly of halfpence which he had buried in different parts of the garden. On the clock striking twelve he appeared slightly agitated, but he soon recovered, walked twice or thrice along the coach-house, stopped to bark, staggered, exclaimed "Halloa old girl!" (his favorite expression) and died.

He behaved throughout with a decent fortitude, equanimity, and self-possession, which cannot be too much admired. I deeply regret that being in ignorance of his danger I did not attend to receive his last instructions. Something remarkable about his eyes occasioned Topping to run for the doctor at Twelve. When they returned together our friend was gone. It was the medical gentleman who informed me of his decease. He did it with great caution and delicacy, preparing me by the remark that "a jolly queer start had taken place", but the shock was very great notwithstanding.

I am not wholly free from suspicions of poison—a malicious butcher has been heard to say that he would "do" for him—his plea was, that he would not be molested in taking orders down the Mews, by any bird that wore a tail—other persons have also been heard to threaten—among others, Charles Knight[2] who has just started a weekly publication, price fourpence;[3] Barnaby being, as you know, Threepence. I have directed a

---

[1] William Herring, dealer in birds and live animals, 21 Quickset Row, New Road, London.

[2] Charles Knight (1791–1873; *DNB*); author and publisher, son of a Windsor bookseller. His main ambitions from youth onwards were to edit Shakespeare and become a popular instructor. Publisher for the Society for the Diffusion of Useful Knowledge (see *To* Nugent, 26 Aug 41, *fn*) 1829–46; for the Poor Law Commission 1835; and in 1836 began publication of a number of major illustrated works in monthly parts. His *Pictorial History of England*, 8 vols, 1837–44, was in CD's library at his death. In later years Knight could not remember exactly when he and CD first met; but they were "on tolerably familiar terms" by 7 Dec 39, the date of the final dinner of the Shakespeare Club (see Vol. I, p. 611*n*), to which Knight had been elected in recognition of his *Pictorial Shakespeare* 1838–41 (Knight, *Passages of a Working Life*, 1864–5, III, 38). A warm friendship between them developed later.

[3] *London*, ed. Knight, issued in weekly parts 6 Mar 41 to 2 Mar 44, at 4d.

post mortem examination, and the body has been removed to Mr. Herring's school of Anatomy for that purpose.

I could wish, if you can take the trouble, that you would inclose this to Forster when you have read it. I cannot discharge the painful task of communication more than once.[1] Were they Ravens who took Manna to somebody in the wilderness? At times I hope they were, and at others I fear they were not, or they would certainly have stolen it by the way. In profound sorrow, I am ever Your bereaved friend. CD.

Kate is as well as can be expected, but terribly low as you may suppose. The children seem rather glad of it. He bit their ancles. But that was play——[2]

## *To* THOMAS LATIMER, 13 MARCH 1841†

MS Berg Collection.

Devonshire Terrace | Saturday Thirteenth March | 1841.

My Dear Sir.

I thank you heartily for your kind letter, and shall hope to hear from you again at your convenience.

[1] Maclise sent the letter on to Forster with the following note: "Dickens desires me to transmit to you the enclosed announcement of the Ravens decease—which took place in Devonshire Terrace March ... 1841" (MS Forster Collection, V & A). He illustrated it with a sketch. At the foot of the note is the raven (very black) lying dead on a rectangular slab; from it rises a white raven with eyes upturned. At the head of the note three white ravens, with legs folded across their breasts, look down through clouds (a background to the note itself). Beneath the dead raven is written "HIC"; at bottom right the initials "DM" sign both note and drawing. In the left margin Forster has written "apotheosis"—the word he uses to describe the note in F, 1872, I, 213, where it is reproduced. The sketch could be a caricature of the tailpiece to *Old Curiosity Shop* (see *To* Cattermole, 14 Jan, *fn*).

[2] Replying, Maclise continued the joke—in parts a trifle heavily: "I received the mournful intelligence of our friends decease last night at eleven, and the shock was great indeed— ... | I know not what to think as the probable cause of his death. I reject the idea of the Butcher Boy ... | I rather cling to the notion of felo de se—but this will no doubt come out upon the post mortem—How blest we are to have such an intelligent Coroner in Mr. Wakley [*cf. CD's joke in* To *Maclise, 13 Feb 40*] —I think he was just of those grave melancholic habits, which are the noticeable signs of your intended suicide—his solitary life—those gloomy tones, . . . his solemn suit of Raven black which never grew rusty—Altogether his character was the very prototype of a Byron Hero—and even of a Scott a Master of Ravenswood.—We ought to be glad he had no family I suppose—he seems to have *intended* it however for his solicitude to deposit in those Banks in the Garden his Savings were always very touching— | I suppose his obsequies will take place immediately. It is beautiful—the idea of his return even after death to the scene of his early youth ... having clearly booked his place in that immortality Coach driven by Dickens— | Yes, he committed suicide . . ." (MS Huntington). In his Preface to the First Cheap Edition of *Barnaby*, CD cleared the mystery up: the raven ate "a pound or two of white lead", left in the stable by workmen who were repainting it.

I don't think any object would be gained by concealing the fact of my having paid the bill.[1] So long as he is left to suppose that I traced it from Chapman and Hall's and took it up, all the end we need have in view is gained.

I received a paper from you[2] after I had written the first paragraph of this note. *It is curious that I have always fancied the Old Curiosity Shop to be my XXX,[3] and that I never had the design and purpose of a story so distinctly marked in my mind, from its commencement. All its quietness arose out of a deliberate purpose; the notion being to stamp upon it from the first, the shadow of that early death.[4] I think I shall always like it better than anything I have done or may do. So much for authorship.*

Bulwer who read it through t'other day holds exactly my opinion,[5] and Lord Jeffrey[6] was—and is I believe but I have not seen him since its conclusion[7]—of the same mind. I know a great many people are of yours,[8] or I shouldn't say so much.

My raven died suddenly yesterday at noon. He is a great loss to me. He buried in his lifetime immense quantities of treasure (in halfpence) in

---

[1] See *To* Latimer, 18 Feb, *fn.*

[2] The *Western Times* for 6 Mar, containing a brief *résumé* of *Master Humphrey* Nos 40–45 (the last nine chapters of *Old Curiosity Shop*) and a general opinion of the whole.

*a a* Extract given in N; letter otherwise unpublished.

[3] I.e. my best (metaphor from brewing).

[4] The review praised *Old Curiosity Shop* for its "breadth of humour, depth of pathos, force and elegance of narrative, vividness of description, and interest of incident", but pronounced it "without much elaborateness of plot, or apparently fixedness of purpose in the mind of the author"—in this implying, presumably, that CD had not originally intended that Nell should die. Nor had he, on the evidence of *To* Forster, ?17 Jan 41.

[5] In an undated letter to Forster (MS Lytton Papers), Bulwer had written of *Old Curiosity Shop*: "It perfectly fascinated me. I think it contains patches of the most exquisite truth & poetry"; he thought Nell "wonderful" and "the comic of 'the rosy' ... admirable"; he would not discuss "the merits of the construction", for here CD seemed "to entertain a wilful contempt for the art"; but he "found in the beauty of the writing from the first page to the last— (despite the early numbers which are inferior to the rest)—a most vivid & delicious interest." "All this", he ended, "is honest praise which I repeat everywhere." Perhaps it was in the glow of hearing of this letter that CD, on 5 Mar, when writing his 1841 Preface to *Oliver* (see *To* Forster, that day), dissociated Bulwer's "admirable and most powerful novel of Paul Clifford" from the novels of crime he was deploring. Bulwer thought less well of *Barnaby*. On 9 July he wrote to Forster (MS Lytton Papers): "Dickens is greatly improved in the art of story— but does not seem to be so good in character—Barnaby is too Scott like. Ditto the smith & his daughter—Old Chester is a failure—his son a non entity—the finest thing is the flitting about of the starved Villain" (singled out for praise by Forster too: see F, IX, i, 723).

[6] Francis Jeffrey, Lord Jeffrey (1773–1850; *DNB*): see Vol. I, p. 479*n*.

[7] Nor indeed ever. They first met on 6 Apr 41.

[8] Daniel O'Connell, for instance, who thought it obvious that CD "had not sufficient talent to maintain Nell's adventures with interest to the end and bring them to a happy issue, so ... killed her to get rid of the difficulty" (W. F. Fitzpatrick, *Correspondence of Daniel O'Connell*, 1888, II, 113).

various parts of the garden—so much, indeed, that if it were not spring time I should certainly have it dug up. His death was characteristic. He had had some castor oil, and a little warm gruel to assist its operation; and having swallowed the last-named medicine with infinite relish, walked the Stable twice or thrice—very slowly—from end to end. Suddenly he stopped, staggered, called my man by his name, walked on again, stopped, cried "Halloa old girl!"—which I take to be an apostrophe to death, which is feminine in Latin—and expired. The medical gentleman (one Herring, a bird fancier) arrived immediately afterwards and broke the intelligence to me. He did it with great delicacy, preparing me with the remark that "a jolly queer start as ever he know'd had took place back'ards there" (the stable is in the rear of the premises) but the shock was very great of course.

I am not without suspicions of Poison—a butcher having been heard to threaten—and have directed a Post Mortem examination.

Excuse this rambling note, for *my* commission is always opening and never shutting up again.[1]

Faithfully Yours always

Thomas Latimer Esquire                                  CHARLES DICKENS


## *To* BASIL HALL, 16 MARCH 1841

MS Berg Collection.

Devonshire Terrace
Tuesday Evening Sixteenth March | 1841.

My Dear Hall—for I see it must be juniores priores,[2] and that I must demolish the ice at a blow.

I have not had courage until last night to read Lady De Lancey's narrative,[3] and but for your letter[4] I should not have mustered it even then. One glance at it when (through your kindness) it first arrived here, impressed me with a foreboding of its terrible truth; and I really have shrunk from it, in pure lack of heart.

After working at Barnaby all day, and wandering about the most wretched and distressful streets for a couple of hours in the evening—searching for some pictures I wanted to build upon[5]—I went at it, at about

---

[1] I.e. his duty to produce *Master Humphrey* weekly. What Latimer's "commission" was has not been discovered. Possibly he was a candidate for the Exeter Improvement Commission, to which he was elected 1849. He became a JP in 1851.

[2] I.e. he must take the initiative, although 24 years younger than Hall, in dropping the "My Dear Sir".

[3] Which Hall had sent him in MS on 13 Feb (see *To* Hall, 19 Feb).

[4] Of 12 Mar, asking for its return for a friend who wished to see it (MS Huntington).

[5] In *Barnaby*, Ch. 16 (No. 54), presumably, which begins with an attempt to re-create the dark streets of London at the time of the story (1780).

ten oClock.[1] To say that the reading that most astonishing and tremendous account has constituted an epoch in my life—that I never shall forget the lightest word of it—that I cannot throw the impression aside and never saw anything so real, so touching, and so actually present before my eyes, is nothing. I am husband and wife, dead man and living woman, Emma[2] and General Dundas,[3] doctor and bedstead,—everything and everybody (but the Prussian officer[4]—damn him) all in one. What I have always looked upon as masterpieces of powerful and affecting description, seem as nothing in my eyes. If I live for fifty years, I shall dream of it every now and then from this hour to the day of my death with the most frightful reality. The slightest mention of a battle will bring the whole thing before me. I shall never think of the Duke any more, but as he stood in his shirt with the officer in full dress uniform,[5] or as he dismounted from his horse when the gallant man was struck down.

It is a striking proof of the power of that most extraordinary man Defoe, that I seem to recognize in every line of the narrative, something of him. Has this occurred to you? The going to Waterloo with that unconsciousness of everything in the road, but the obstacles to getting on—the shutting herself up in her room and determining not to hear—the not going to the door when the knocking came—the finding out by her wild spirits when she heard he was safe, how much she had feared when in doubt and anxiety—the desperate desire to move towards him—the whole description of the cottage; and his condition; and their daily shifts and contrivances; and the lying down beside him in the bed and both *falling asleep*; and his resolving

---

[1] It was a detailed day-by-day account by Lady De Lancey of her experiences between 8 June 1815, when she accompanied her husband, Colonel Sir William Howe De Lancey (?1781–1815; *DNB*), to Brussels, and 26 June when he died from a wound received while speaking to Wellington (whose Quartermaster-General and friend he was) at the Battle of Waterloo. She nursed him for a week in a cottage in the village of Waterloo, in primitive conditions. Eight ribs were detached from his spine, and one driven into his lung; in spite of frequent bleedings there was little hope. They had been married for six weeks when he died; and she had known him for only six weeks before their marriage. She wrote her Waterloo narrative at Hall's request. The family were opposed to publication but made copies at various times (one came into the possession of Samuel Rogers). In 1888, however, a condensed account was published in the *Illustrated Naval and Military Magazine* (VIII, 414); the

full narrative appeared in the *Century Magazine*, New York, in Apr 1906, and that same year in book-form—*A Week at Waterloo in 1815*, with informative introduction and notes by Major B. R. Ward. Lady De Lancey married again 1819, but died 1822.

[2] Lady De Lancey's maid.

[3] General Francis Dundas (d. 1824; *DNB*), for whom the dying De Lancey asked and who spent the night before his death in the cottage where he lay.

[4] Who had tried to prevent Lady De Lancey's carriage passing the military waggons on the road between Antwerp and Brussels, as she made her way towards her dying husband (*A Week at Waterloo*, pp. 65–6).

[5] The night before the battle De Lancey found Wellington "standing looking over a map with a Prussian general, who was in full-dress uniform —with orders and crosses, etc.—the Duke was in his chemise and slippers, preparing to dress for the Duchess of Richmond's ball" (*op. cit.*, p. 45).

not to serve any more but to live quietly thenceforth; and her sorrow when she saw him eating with an appetite, so soon before his death; and his death itself—all these are matters of truth which only that astonishing creature, as I think, could have told in fiction.

Of all the beautiful and tender passages—the thinking every day how happy and blest she was—the decorating him for the dinner—the standing in the balcony at night, and seeing the troops melt away through the gate—and the rejoining him on his sick bed—I say not a word. They are God's own and should be sacred. But let me say again with an earnestness which pen and ink can no more convey than toast and water, in thanking you heartily for the perusal of this paper, that its impression on me never can be told; that the ground she travelled (which I know well)[1] is holy ground to me from this day; and that please Heaven I will tread it every foot, this very next Summer,[2] to have the softened recollection of this sad story on the very earth where it was acted. You won't smile at this, I know. When my enthusiasms are awakened by such things, they don't wear out.[3]

Have you ever thought within yourself of that part where having suffered so much by the news of his death, she *will not* believe he is alive? I should have supposed that unnatural if I had seen it in fiction.

I shall never dismiss the subject from my mind, but with these hasty and very imperfect words I shall dismiss it from my paper with two additional remarks—firstly that Kate has been grievously putting me out by sobbing over it while I have been writing this, and has just retired in an agony of grief—and secondly that *if* a time *should* ever come when you would not object to letting a friend copy it for himself, I hope you will bear me in your thoughts.[4]

---

It seems the poorest nonsense in the world to turn to anything else—that

[1] From his visit to Belgium with Catherine and Browne in July 37 (see Vol. I, p. 281).

[2] He did not visit Belgium again until 1845, on his way back from Italy.

[3] Others to whom Hall had shown the MS had been deeply moved by it too. Moore recorded in his diary for 29 Aug 1824 that he read it in bed that night "till near two o'clock, and finished it; made myself quite miserable, and went to sleep, I believe, crying" (*Memoirs, Journal, and Correspondence of Thomas Moore*, ed. Lord John Russell, 1853–6, IV, 240). Scott wrote to Hall on 13 Oct 1825: "I never read any thing which affected my own feelings more strongly or which, I am sure, would have a deeper interest on those of the public"; he asked Hall's view on whether it could now be published, saying that Constable thought "with great truth that it would add very great interest as an addition to the letters which I wrote from Paris soon after Waterloo, and certainly I would consider it as one of the most valuable and important documents which could be published as illustrative of the woes of war" (*Letters of Sir Walter Scott*, ed. H. J. C. Grierson, 1932–7, IX, 247–8).

[4] There is no evidence that CD saw the MS again. On 19 Mar Hall wrote to him: "Of all opinions I have heard on my sister's narrative none has ever appeared to me so just or forcible as yours" (MS Huntington). In the same

is, seems to me being fresher in respect of Lady De Lancey than you—but my Raven's dead. He had been ailing for a few days but not seriously, as we thought, and was apparently recovering, when symptoms of relapse occasioned me to send for an eminent medical gentleman (one Herring; a bird fancier in the New Road) who promptly attended, and administered a powerful dose of castor oil. This was on Tuesday last. On Wednesday Morning he had another dose of castor oil; and a teacup-full of warm gruel, which he took with great relish, and under the influence of which he so far recovered his spirits as to be enabled to bite the groom severely. At 12 o'Clock at noon he took several turns up and down the stable with a grave, sedate air—and suddenly reeled. This made him thoughtful. He stopped directly, shook his head, moved on again, stopped once more, cried in a tone of remonstrance and considerable surprise "Halloa old girl!"—and immediately died.

He has left a rather large property (in cheese and halfpence) buried, for security's sake, in various parts of the garden. I am not without suspicions of poison.—A butcher was heard to threaten him some weeks since—and he stole a clasp knife belonging to a vindictive carpenter, which was never found. For these reasons I directed a post mortem examination, preparatory to the body being stuffed; the result of it has not yet reached me. The medical gentleman broke out the fact of his decease to me with great delicacy, observing that "the jolliest queer start had taken place with that 'ere knowing card of a bird, as ever he see'd—" but the shock was naturally very great. With reference to the jollity of the start, it appears that a raven dying at two hundred and fifty or thereabouts, is looked upon as an infant. This one would hardly, as I may say, have been born for a century or so to come, being only two or three years old.

I want to know more about the promised "tickler"[1]—when it's to come —what it's to be—and in short all about it, that I may give it the better welcome. I don't know how it is, but I am celebrated, either for writing no letters at all, or for the briefest specimens of epistolary correspondence in existence. And here I am—in writing to you—on the Sixth side! I

---

letter he told CD how in 1809 his frigate had picked up De Lancey who was adrift in a boat after the battle of Corunna, but that they never met again.

[1] In his letter of 12 Mar Hall had told CD that he was "engaged in a new work, some parts of which will tickle you". On the 19th he wrote that its subject was Portsmouth and its title might be "The Naval Arsenal"; he had "already sketched out more than a dozen chapters of the Dock yard alone—it is full to overflowing of subjects capable of the most graphic painting—& I am 'Wain' enough to fancy that I am just the man to paint em. *You* could do it

50 thousand times better—no doubt— if you had one fifty thousandth part of my professional knowledge—but as I have been living half my life in a dock yard, ... I should have some small advantage—". He went on to list the other subjects: "I have seen things in Haslar [*Hospital*] which, handled *im*-properly, would make people's hair stand on end—but which, properly handled, may kindle their gentlest sympathies". Hall never wrote this book; his mind gave way the following year, and he was himself put into Haslar Hospital where he died 1844.

won't make it a seventh any way: so with love *to* all your home circle, and *from* all mine, I am now and always

Faithfully Yours

CHARLES DICKENS

I am very glad you like Barnaby.[1] I have great designs in store, but am sadly cramped at first for room.

## *To* JOHN FORSTER, [18 MARCH 1841]

Extract in F, II, x, 174. *Date:* given by Forster as 18 Mar—the day after the Hill sale had ended.

I have done nothing today but cut the *Swift*,[2] looking into it with a delicious laziness in all manner of delightful places, and put poor Tom's books away. I had a letter from Edinburgh this morning,[3] announcing that Jeffrey's visit to London will be the week after next; telling me that he drives about Edinburgh declaring there has been "nothing so good as Nell since Cordelia,"[4] which he writes also to all manner of people; and informing me of a desire in that romantic town to give me greeting and welcome.[5] For this and other reasons I am disposed to make Scotland my destination in June rather than Ireland.[6] Think, *do* think, meantime (here are ten good weeks), whether you couldn't, by some effort worthy of the owner of

[1] Hall had written on 12 Mar: "Barnaby is admirable—quite equal & in some respects superior to anything you have done before. The touch about the young man having exchanged shadows with a lady [*Barnaby*, *Ch. 6*, *published 6 Mar*], is charming—& to me quite new—Shakesperean in the conception & Walter Scottish in its expression. . . . Master Basy has found out, to his great joy that the Clock is obtainable on Thursday—& we have our snug reading by regular appointment on that day. We all say—with the Prophet 'Oh King (of writers) live for ever!'—for, faith, I dont know what we should do without this, our weekly bread!" (MS Huntington).

[2] A set of Swift's *Works*, with Notes and a Life by Sir Walter Scott, 19 vols, 1814, is listed in the Hill sale catalogue; bought Bohn, £7.17.6—possibly for Forster, who acquired books at the sale (F, II, x, 174), though not under his own name. But this edn of Swift is neither in the Forster Collection (V & A), nor listed by Stonehouse in his *Catalogue* of CD's library.

[3] Probably from Angus Fletcher (see 8 Apr).

[4] For Mrs Henry Siddons's story that she found Jeffrey weeping in his library, and that he told her "little Nelly, Boz's little Nelly, is dead", see J. C. Young, *A Memoir of Charles Mayne Young*, 1871, II, III. Jeffrey had himself lost a son of a few weeks old in 1832.

[5] CD's Scottish reviews had been excellent. "It is surely no common pen", said the *Scotsman* (13 Feb 41), "that can enlist the sympathies of so many thousands in behalf of two such unobtrusive and harmless wanderers as Nell and her grandfather".

[6] Where he had thought of going for the purposes of *Master Humphrey* when envisaging it as a miscellany (see 14 July 39; I, 564). No doubt his aim now —as in Nov 43 when planning his visit to Italy—was to "enlarge [his] stock of description and observation" by seeing a new country (F, IV, ii, 304).

the gigantic helmet,[1] go with us. Think of such a fortnight—York, Carlisle, Berwick, your own Borders,[2] Edinburgh, Rob Roy's country, railroads, cathedrals, country inns, Arthur's-seat, lochs, glens, and home by sea. DO think of this, seriously, at leisure.

### *To* THOMAS MITTON, 19 MARCH 1841*

MS Dr De Coursey Fales.

Devonshire Terrace. | Nineteenth March 1841.

Dear Tom.

I'll come down to you at a quarter to four. I am hard at work (having been fearfully lazy since Monday) but will take a couple of hours before dinner, and resume at night.

I am, as you are, much surprised that Alfred has not heard from the New Zealand folks. I dictated a letter to him yesterday, which he wrote and sent to the chief clerk.[3] It cannot fail, I think, to bring something decisive soon.

Faithfully Always

Thomas Mitton Esquire.                                                    CD

I thought this a good opportunity of sending you the C & H accounts.

### *To* T. N. TALFOURD, 22 MARCH 1841

MS Historical Society of Pennsylvania.

Devonshire Terrace.
Monday March Twenty Second | 1841.

My Dear Talfourd

That immortally sluggish binder has at length completed your Nickleby, which I pray you accept herewith. The two Clock Volumes are in progress.

The mention of them brings me to asking a favor of you. I must have *the works* to dinner again. Will Saturday April the Tenth at a quarter past six, suit you?—And if so, will you on that day again kindly do for me what no man can do so well, or with so much pleasure to all his hearers?[4]

---

[1] Alfonso the Good in Walpole's *The Castle of Otranto*. The Christmas pantomime at Covent Garden 1840 had been J. R. Planché's *Harlequin and the Giant Helmet; or, The Castle of Otranto.*
[2] I.e. Northumberland.

[3] See *To* the Directors of the New Zealand Co., 4 Mar, *fn.*
[4] I.e. preside, as he had done at the first *Clock* dinner (see *To* Macready, 20 Oct 40).

The celebration of the Second Volume[1] entails these pains and penalties upon you.[2]

With best regards to Mrs. Talfourd and to Miss Ely.

Believe me ever

My Dear Talfourd | Faithfully Yours

Mr. Serjeant Talfourd                              CHARLES DICKENS[3]


## *To* W. C. MACREADY, [22 MARCH 1841]*

MS Morgan Library. *Date:* clearly Mon 22 Mar 41, the day the Siddons Committee met at Exeter Hall and Macready recorded in his diary: "Then Bulwer came; an excuse from Dickens and Tom Moore" (*Diaries*, II, 129).

Devonshire Terrace. | Monday Morning.

My Dear Macready.

I have had this morning a grievous letter from the Printer which *obliges* me—either to dine at home this evening, or stay at home this morning. I choose the lesser evil of the two, and send you this, to beg that in the Siddons matter you will at this first Meeting do all for me that you do for yourself.[4]

In haste | Always My Dear Macready

Faithfully Yours

W. C. Macready Esquire                           CHARLES DICKENS[5]

---

[1] *Master Humphrey*, Vol. II, ended with No. 52 (*Barnaby*, Ch. 12), published 27 Mar.

[2] Talfourd replied from Hereford on 25 Mar: "Mrs. Talfourd has sent me your Note, and informed me of the arrival of the beautiful and everlasting book which accompanied it very much to her delight. Hoping to be at home by *your* Saturday—though I shall not be there much before—I shall look forward to solemnizing the Birth Day of ea[ch] Volume on the 10th. April" (MS Huntington).

[3] Apparently John Dickens waylaid Talfourd, who was at Monmouth 29–31 Mar (on the Oxford circuit), and obtained this letter from him; for it has been refolded and addressed on the outside "Dr. R. S. Mackenzie | Salopian Journal | *Shrewsbury*", postmarked 1 Apr 41; and a note beneath the address reads: "Monmouth Mar 31/41 | D Sir, | As you are an Autograph-er this may be of use to you. | Talfourd gave it me today. | I am etc | Jn D. | Will Mister be hanged? J.D." (Josiah Mister was tried and found guilty of attempted murder, 23 Mar 41.) CD's letter is printed by Mackenzie in his *Life of CD*, Philadelphia, [1870], p. 217.

[4] The committee, with Lord Lansdowne in the chair, resolved that a monument should be erected to Mrs Siddons in Westminster Abbey and that the expenses should be met by public subscription. Chantrey, whom Macready—the prime mover in the matter—had approached as early as 1834 (*Diaries*, I, 99), was to be invited to be the sculptor. But public response was poor; and although Macready worked hard to obtain subscribers and arranged two benefit performances at Drury Lane (1843 and 1848), he finally had to make good the deficit himself by nearly £200 (*Diaries*, II, 442). Chantrey died 1842, and the bust was executed instead by Thomas Campbell (1790–1858; *DNB*).

[5] In a letter, also dated 22 Mar, which clearly crossed CD's, Macready told him the time he himself would be going to Exeter Hall, and wrote: "A note has been lying for you on my table since Saturday night, which I have not

## *To* JOHN SCOTT,[1] 22 MARCH 1841

MS Comtesse de Suzannet.

1 Devonshire Terrace. | York Gate Regents Park.
March The Twenty Second 1841.

My Dear Sir.

I really cannot tell you how much pleasure I have derived from the receipt of your warm-hearted and welcome note; nor can I thank you for it sufficiently.

Although I know in my heart and conscience that every action of my life and every impulse by which I am guided give the lie to the assertion, I am still greatly pained to learn that you have ever heard me charged with forgetting old friends or associates. Those who know me best, best know how such a charge would wound me, and how very undeserved it is. There is no character I so detest and abhor as a man who presumes on his prosperity. I feel its baseness so strongly that if I supposed my children could at any future time believe me to have been a creature of that kind, I should be wretched.

Happily, although I have made many friends, I have never since my schooltime lost *one*. The pleasantest and proudest part of my correspondence is that in which I have stored the congratulations of some from whom I had been separated by distance or accident for several years; and believe me that from a little pale schoolmaster[2] who taught me my letters (and who turned up miraculously the other day in a high state of preservation) to those who have more recent and more fleeting claims on my regard, I have never in my life—and especially in my later life—no, not once, treated any single human being with coldness or hauteur. I have a capacity, and a strong inclination, for feeling warmly towards all those whom I have

had an opportunity of sending.—It only says very imperfectly what I am sure you know well, that any remembrance from you has a value to me which words are not calculated to explain or sum up —You know that I have a pleasure at my very heart in thanking you, as I do for this elegant little volume;—part of it has amused me very much already— I look for something more serious in its object, and of deep interest in the pictures it draws, from the concluding descriptive essay.—You know how entirely I sympathise with you in your desire to better the condition of the poor and lowly, and can only say to you in all your efforts to this end, 'Ever right, Menenius' [*Cf. Coriolanus, II, i, 183*]" (MS Huntington). The "elegant little volume" was *Sketches of Young Couples,* 1840, inscribed: "W. C. Mac-

ready from his faithful friend Charles Dickens, 20th. of March, 1841". It is now in the Free Library of Philadelphia.

[1] Probably a friend of CD's in his reporting days; according to Thomas Beard (quoted by Charles Kent in "CD as a Journalist", *Journalist,* 1 [1879], 23), "old Scott" was one of the two colleagues who protected CD's notebook from the rain at Exeter, 1835 (see Vol. I, p. 58*n*). Identified in N, 1,308*n* as editor of the *Morning Advertiser*: cf. reference in *To* Wills, 27 Sep 51 (N, II, 346) to "Scott of the Advertiser"; but no evidence of his being editor has been found. He was apparently a friend of W. F. Lemaitre of the *Morning Chronicle* (see *To* Scott, 13 Sep 41, *fn*).

[2] Probably William Giles: see Vol. I, p. 429*n*.

known in less successful times; and any man who reports me unjustly in this respect, either does me wilfully an envious and grudging wrong, or acquiesces too easily in a falsehood, of which he may convince himself at the smallest possible expence of trouble and justice.

Let me thank you again, very faintly and imperfectly, for your honest letter. I shall put it among the grateful records to which I have referred; and I do not despair of increasing their bulk before I die, by communications not very dissimilar, even from those who now mistake me most.

Pray, if you should have reason to think when you read the Clock that I have written anything about this time in extremely good spirits, believe that you have had a large share in awakening them—and believe besides that I am with sincerity

My Dear Sir | Faithfully Yours

John Scott Esquire                                    CHARLES DICKENS


To JOHN FORSTER, [?23 MARCH 1841]*

MS Victoria & Albert Museum (FC). *Date:* Macready recorded in his diary for 22 Mar 41: "Mrs. Jameson, Mrs. Pierce Butler, Kenney, Dickens, Travers, Harness and Rogers dined with us" (*Diaries*, II, 129). Presumably CD's note was in answer to a letter from Forster asking who had been present at the dinner, and was written next day or soon after.

My Dear Forster
I shall be out between 2 and 4, and will call on you.

Faithfully Always<br>CD.

An anonymous man with grey whiskers[1]
Rogers
Kenney[2]
Mrs. Butler[3]
Mr.[4] Jameson[5]
Harness

[1] Clearly Travers, the only one of Macready's guests not named by CD. Benjamin Travers (1783-1858; *DNB*), distinguished surgeon. FRCS 1806; Fellow of the Royal Society 1813. The first hospital surgeon in England to devote himself to surgery of the eye.

[2] James Kenney (1780-1849; *DNB*), popular dramatist; a frequent guest of Rogers, at whose house CD had met him at dinner on 31 Jan (Macready, *Diaries*, II, 118). Through Kenney's exertions Macready, though blackballed 1835, was elected to the Athenæum 1838; in the same year he produced Kenney's *Love Extempore*. For CD's special interest in Kenney's *Love, Law and Physic*, see *To* Forster, 12 May 42.

[3] Fanny Kemble (1809-93; *DNB*), actress and writer, daughter of Charles Kemble and niece of Mrs Siddons; "a girl of genius" (John Wilson, *Noctes Ambrosianæ*, No. LI). After a great success on the London stage 1829-33, toured in America with her father, and married (1834) Pierce Butler, discovering afterwards with dismay that he was a Southern planter employing slaves, in Georgia—her future home. Her marriage, already precarious when she, Butler and their two children came to England Oct 40, finally broke up 1845.

## *To* JOHN FORSTER, [25 MARCH 1841]

Extract in F, II, ix, 166. *Date:* 25 Mar according to Forster.

I see there is yet room for a few lines, and you are quite right in wishing what I cut out to be restored. I did not want Joe to be so short about Dolly, and really wrote his references to that young lady carefully[1]—as natural things with a meaning in them. Chigwell, my dear fellow, is the greatest place in the world.[2] Name your day for going. Such a delicious old inn[3] opposite the churchyard—such a lovely ride—such beautiful forest scenery—such an out of the way, rural, place—such a sexton! I say again, name your day.

## *To* JOHN FORSTER, [26 MARCH 1841]

Extract in F, II, ix, 167. *Date:* 26 Mar according to Forster.

I have shut myself up by myself to-day, and mean to try and "go it" at the *Clock*;[4] Kate being out, and the house peacefully dismal. I don't remember altering the exact part you object to, but if there be anything here you object to, knock it out ruthlessly.[5]

She returned to the stage 1847; a divorce followed 1848, her husband gaining custody of the children. She had published her *Journal* describing her first American visit in 1835; later she published several other autobiographical works, including *Journal of a Residence on a Georgian Plantation*, 1863.

[4] Thus in MS; but clearly a slip of CD's. Mrs Jameson appears frequently in Macready's *Diaries*, and was a friend of Fanny Kemble's.

[5] Anna Brownell Jameson, *née* Murphy (1794–1860; *DNB*), writer. Married Robert Jameson, later Attorney-General of Ontario, but soon separated from him. Her best known works were *Characteristics of Women* (essays on Shakespeare's female characters, dedicated to Fanny Kemble), 1832, *Companion to the Public Picture Galleries of London*, 1842, a similar guide to the private collections, 1844, and *Sacred and Legendary Art*, 1848, 1850 and 1852, and a fourth volume completed after her death by Lady Eastlake. Among her numerous friends were the Brownings, Lady Byron and Ottilie von Goethe.

[1] Clearly refers to *Barnaby*, Ch. 14 (No. 53, published 3 Apr), in which Joe speaks to Edward Chester of Dolly. CD did not restore the further references to her which he had deleted in proof; and they add little.

[2] Chigwell, and Epping Forest generally, were favourite resorts for Londoners. CD describes an excursion to Chigwell in "The Young Ladies' Young Gentleman", *Sketches of Young Gentlemen*, 1838.

[3] Probably the old King's Head Inn at Chigwell. What is now known as the King's Head, Chigwell, was in 1841 a private house—a large gabled building (adjoining the old inn) which CD probably had in mind when describing the Maypole in *Barnaby*. He is thought to have placed his Maypole on the site of an inn of that name not in Chigwell but in Chigwell Row (see *D*, XXIII [1927], 122–6). He and Forster made the proposed expedition; and Forster records CD's delight in "the double recognition, of himself and of *Barnaby*, by the landlord of the nice old inn" (F, II, ix, 167).

[4] No. 55, presumably, which was in proof 5 Apr (see *To* Forster, that day, and *fn*).

[5] Nothing appears to have been cut in No. 53 except the Dolly passages, cut **by** CD not Forster (see last); and nothing at all in No. 54.

## *To* GEORGE CATTERMOLE, 27 MARCH 1841

MS Free Library of Philadelphia.

Devonshire Terrace | Twenty Seventh March 1841.
My Dear Cattermole.

Will you book Saturday the Tenth of April at a quarter past 6 (that's this day fortnight) to dine here with our Clock Works, in honor of the new Wolume?[1] And will you furthermore get the steam up to an extent which will enable you to toast the Ali Babas or wood cutters,[2] to the concern?

Always Faithfully | And at present hastily
George Cattermole Esquire CHARLES DICKENS

## *To* CHARLES GRAY, 27 MARCH 1841*

MS Goodspeed's Book Shop.

1 Devonshire Terrace | Saturday Twenty Seventh March 1841.
My Dear Sir.

Will you do me the favor to dine with me on Saturday the Tenth of April, at a quarter past six, to welcome our new volume?

Faithfully Yours
—Gray Esquire CHARLES DICKENS[3]

## *To* WILLIAM SHOBERL,[4] 29 MARCH 1841

Extract in John Waller catalogue No. 98 (1873); *MS* 2 pp.; dated 29 Mar 41.

I want to know when I shall revise the proofs of the end of the second volume,[5] comprising the latter portion of Mr. Landor's paper, which I wish that Gentleman to correct.[6]

---

[1] For Cattermole's acceptance, see 1 Apr, *fn*. Browne was naturally invited too and replied: "I shall be most happy to remember not to forget the 10th. April. And, let me express a *dis*interested wish, that having completed and established one 'shop' in an 'extensive line of business', you will go on increasing and multiplying such like establishments in number and prosperity, till you become a Dick Whittington of a Merchant with pockets distended to most Brobdignag dimensions ... I return you the Riots [*probably Holcroft's*

Narrative of the Riots in London (*see* To *Forster, 3 June,* fn)] with many thanks" (MS Huntington).
[2] Ali Baba was a woodcutter.
[3] Only the signature is in CD's hand.
[4] William Shoberl (*d.* 1853), elder son of Frederic Shoberl (1775–1853; *DNB*); assistant to Colburn, and later a publisher at 20 Great Marlborough Street. Author of *A Summer's Day at Greenwich, Being a Guide to the Royal Hospital and Park*, 1840.
[5] Of *The Pic Nic Papers*.
[6] See *To* Colburn, 1 Apr.

## *To* BASIL HALL, [?31 MARCH 1841]

Mention in Hall *to* CD, 1 Apr (see *fn*). *Date:* written between Hall's letters of 29 Mar and 1 Apr.

*Acquiescing in Hall's wish to possess a bust of him and have it done by Mr Joseph*[1] *and to give him a bust of himself by Joseph; approving of his notion of writing "Seaport sketches";*[2] *and saying that Hall's humility about his own writing made him uneasy.*[3]

## *To* J. C. PRINCE,[4] 31 MARCH 1841*

MS Winifred A. Myers Ltd.

1 Devonshire Terrace | York Gate Regents Park
Thirty First March 1841.

Mr. Charles Dickens sends his compliments to Mr. Prince, and begs to assure him that he will have great pleasure in subscribing to his book.[5]

---

[1] Samuel Joseph (*d.* 1850; *DNB*). Hall had written to CD on 29 Mar: "I have a favor to ask of you . . . I wish you to allow your Bust to be done for me, by my friend Mr. Joseph the Sculptor"; and had explained that Joseph was in financial difficulties (MS Rutgers University Library). Replying on 1 Apr to CD's answer to this request, Hall wrote: "Thanks, noble Sir, for your prompt acquiescence with my wish. 'Bis dat &c' " (MS Huntington). On the back of Hall's letter is a list in an unknown hand of 33 people whose busts were at this time "in Mr. Joseph's collection" (presumably executed by him)—among them William IV, George IV, Flaxman, Brougham, Sir Thomas Lawrence, William Allan, Wilkie (the bust now in the Tate Gallery), Wilberforce (bust now in Westminster Abbey), and Hall himself. Joseph exhibited in the RA 1811–46. For CD's sitting to him, see 15 Dec 41.

[2] See *To* Hall, 16 Mar, *fn*.

[3] In his letter of 29 Mar Hall had written: "You might perhaps fancy it mock humility, were I to say that I feel my literary inferiority so much, that I dare scarcely term myself a brother author—& that I shrink from offering you a bust of my own Phisog. by the same skilful hand. But if you would accept it, & put it anywhere, in a corner, I should be singularly gratified".

Clearly, on receiving CD's answer to this, Hall felt that he had over-stated his "humility". He replied on 1 Apr, rather defensively, that occasional feelings of insignificance were common to all writers who aimed higher than they could reach. But he admitted to one "twinge of genuine jealousy". On a recent visit to Bradbury & Evans's office, he had asked: "What was that enormous pile of sheets. 'Oh, Sir', said the fellow—'there lie sixty thousand copies of the next No. of Humphrey's Clock!'—I turned me about & said 'What's that small bundle?' 'Oh Sir' said the dog, grinning from ear to ear—'*that* is *one* [*underlined 5 times with exclamation mark written above*] thousand of *your* new book!'—I could have cuffed the Imp." "Seriously!", he went on, "I know enough of letters, & of their mysteries . . . to respect most unaffectedly, the genius, as well as the talents which can give birth to such beings as Nell—(a sort of blood relation to Ariel)". He admitted that to have said anything of his and CD's "relative positions in the monarchy of Letters" might have been lacking in taste; but he neither felt nor pretended to feel humility, knowing he had worked successfully in his own "humble walk". He ended: "I hope you will forgive all this: for, really,—after what you said of my humility having made you uneasy—

## *To* GEORGE CATTERMOLE, 1 APRIL 1841

Extract in J. F. Drake catalogue No. 191; *MS* 1 p.; dated Devonshire Terrace, 1 Apr 41.

With all my heart—at half past six next Saturday, in the Athenaeum dining room.[1] I shall want to walk into Lord Northampton's and out again in the course of the Evening as it is the last "swarry" and I have not been yet; but that will not interfere.[2]


## *To* FRANCIS SMEDLEY,[3] 1 APRIL 1841*

Text from typescript, Huntington Library.

Devonshire Terrace, | April The First, 1841.

Dear Sir,

I am exceedingly obliged to you for your kind note. I am not "free" of Tothill Fields Bridewell (I am of most other jails), and do entertain a curiosity to see the Palace Victim;[4] strongly doubting the popular belief in his sharpness of intellect.[5]

Therefore, I will call on you next Tuesday, as you are good enough to leave the day to me, at a quarter after twelve.[6]

Faithfully yours

Francis Smedley Esquire.                           CHARLES DICKENS

I could not say less . . .—I am really rejoiced that you approve of my 'Seaport' notion" (MS Huntington).

[4] John Critchley Prince (1808–66; *DNB*), poet, son of a Wigan reed-maker; published his first poems, *Hours with the Muses*, Manchester, [1841], while working as a reed-maker in an Ashton-under-Lyne cotton factory. Later lived in Manchester, mainly on his writing, but in constant financial difficulties.

[5] CD subscribed to *Hours with the Muses*, which ran to 3 edns by May 42.

[1] Cattermole had written earlier that day: "I am yours for Saturday week, with all my heart. Meanwhile a phantom dinner haunts me: will you help me to lay the Ghost in such sober . . . simple realities as the Athenaeum Cuisine may afford" (extract in John Heise catalogue No. 2454). "Phantom" dinner became due it had been twice postponed (see *To* Cattermole, 4 and 13 Feb).

[2] At the Athenæum Macready ran into them, and went with CD to Lord Northampton's. Elliotson, Stanfield, Pickersgill, Rogers, and Crabb Robinson were there among others (*Diaries*, II, 131).

[3] Francis Smedley (1791–1858), High Bailiff of Westminster; father of Francis Edward Smedley, the novelist.

[4] William Jones (Edmund Jones in some reports), known as "the Boy Jones", a 17-year-old apothecary's errand-boy, now serving a three-months' sentence in Tothill Fields Prison after being discovered in Buckingham Palace for the third time. Arrested at 1 a.m. on 16 Mar 41 while eating cold meat from the Palace larder, he claimed that his only object in entering the Palace "was to hear the conversation of her Majesty and Prince Albert, in order to 'write a book' " (*Examiner*, 21 Mar 41). Soon after his release he was placed on an emigration ship bound for Brazil, as an apprentice seaman.

[5] On his first apprehension, Jones had been discharged as of unsound mind; the same plea was put forward by his father, a tailor, on his two subsequent arrests, but was not accepted. In his curiosity to see him, CD no doubt had Barnaby in mind.

[6] The visit was postponed until the 26th: see *To* Smedley, 5 and 19 Apr.

## *To* R. S. HORRELL, 1 APRIL 1841

MS Public Library of Victoria, Melbourne.

Private

1 Devonshire Terrace. | April The First 1841.

My Dear Sir.

I think the improvement you have made in the inclosed MS, *very great.* My objection is entirely removed, and I have read it with the greatest pleasure.

You will not consider me hypercritical if I suggest to you that in lieu of the "shriek" at page 5, a groan or sigh or murmur would be more in consonance with the spirit of the piece. At page 7 marréd is awkward I think. Sullied would be better. And going back to page 5 again, I would rather see "good creature" or something to that effect than "Ha! woman" when he is apostrophising the nurse. This, however, is altogether a matter of taste.

I don't think it needs any other alteration whatever; and I shall be very happy to receive the copy from you, whenever it suits your leisure and convenience.

If I were you, I would send it to Blackwood's—you are not to be discouraged, mind, if it be rejected[1]—with some such note as this: "S.H presents his compliments to the Editor of Blackwood's Magazine, and earnestly begs that he will do him the favor to *read* the accompanying paper which is very short, and which he forwards with much diffidence and self-distrust." The shorter such a communication is, the better; and I always found when I edited a Magazine, that a modest note arrested me when I had been wading through seas of nonsense and was growing almost too dull to see the words upon the paper.

With best wishes for your success, believe me

Faithfully Yours

[S]. H[arford][2] Esquire                    CHARLES DICKENS

## *To* HENRY COLBURN, 1 APRIL 1841

Facsimile[3] in *CD's Original Autograph Copy of his Letter to Henry Colburn ... Together with a Note to Forster*, privately printed for Cumberland Clark, 1918.

(Copy)

1 Devonshire Terrace | York Gate Regents Park.

April The First 1841.

Sir

As I address you upon a matter of business, and not a mere question of

---

[1] It apparently was.

[2] Presumably CD addressed this to Horrell by his pseudonym "S. Harford" (see *To* Horrell, 14 Oct 40). Only the "H" is now clear, the rest having been erased.

[3] Apparently a facsimile of a skilful tracing of CD's original draft: the handwriting at times lacks CD's flow, parts of several words are slightly miswritten, and the words beneath various cancellations are either mismanaged or non-existent.

gentlemanly and courteous treatment, I count upon receiving an answer.

Last June, you objected to the quality of some essays by Mr. Walter Savage Landor[1] which I had forwarded to you for insertion in the Pic Nic Papers, in my capacity as Editor of that work. Mr. Forster, himself an intimate friend of Mr. Landor's, saw you upon the subject (I being then out of town) and pointed out to you your mistake—You withdrew—to reconsider it.

Since then, I have several times requested to see a complete proof of these articles, in which you had—without any communication with me—stopped the Printer some weeks previously. Of these applications you have taken no notice whatever. In the mean time I have with-held my paper, in the hope of bringing you by that means to do your duty.

It is apart from my object to characterize this proceeding of yours in reference to myself, or to discuss your competency to sit in judgment on the productions of Mr. Landor. I content myself with asserting my right as Editor of the book to choose the matter for its pages, and denying any authority on your part to interfere with my selection.

If the book were publishing as my own property or for my own profit, I would not forego this right though I retarded its publication a dozen years and wanted bread the while. But as the case is one of "charity", and as I cannot resist, and do not hold myself justified in resisting, the urgent appeals of the lady for whose benefit our price is to be paid, I will no longer delay it by with-holding my contribution. I have therefore to request that you will, in reply to this, send me back that Manuscript of Mr. Landor's which you refuse to print, and in reference to which, you have taken my office on yourself;—in order that I may return it to that gentleman with a statement of the circumstances leading to his receiving it.[2] This done, the Printer will receive my tale, and the book will be completed.

CHARLES DICKENS

## *To* JOHN FORSTER, 1 APRIL 1841

Facsimile in *CD's Original Autograph Copy of his Letter to Henry Colburn ... Together with a Note to Forster,* privately printed for Cumberland Clark, 1918.

April The First 1841

My Dear Forster[3]

Here is a copy of the letter to Colburn—sent along with an imaginary

[1] Colburn's objection had been that "his literary friend" had told him Landor's paper " 'wasn't Protestant'!!!!!!!!!!" (*To* Hunt, 19 July 42). For Landor's earlier relations with Colburn, see R. H. Super, *The Publication of Landor's Works* (Supplement to the Bibliographical Society's Transactions, No. 18), 1954, pp. 40–3.

[2] CD's and Landor's relations were unaffected by what had happened. A few weeks later Crabb Robinson records Landor declaring, with characteristic superlatives, that CD was "with Shakespeare the greatest of English writers, though indeed his women are superior to Shakespeare's. No one of our poets comes near him" (*Henry Crabb Robinson*

gauntlet, to day. Preserve it,[1] for I have no other. The letter to Landor I will write when I have received an answer from this sneaking vagabond.

Faithfully Yours always<br>CD.

## *To* EDWARD DUBOIS,[2] 2 APRIL 1841

MS Harvard College Library.

Devonshire Terrace. | April The Second 1841.

My Dear Sir.

Thank you for your note of yesterday.

I was a *leetle* startled when I first went to Evans's, by the autographic department of the Catalogue,[3] but a moment's reflection assured me that the Executors had no choice in the matter; for those who have a gratification in preserving such things during their lives, usually contemplate their sale at some distant time, and have a pleasure in anticipating the little bustle it will make.

You are quite right in your philosophy. The pooh-poohers[4] and Lord Burleighs[5] have it hollow, all the world through—but we won't allow Hill to have been one of that kind.

He used to tell me often that he had kept a Diary for—I am afraid to say how many years, but I know it was a great number. I am looking forward with great expectation to your publishing it.[6] I have in my mind's eye at this minute the expression of face, with which he told me he intended it to see the light—an unfathomable face—with something of John Murray, hinted, and perhaps a dim suggestion of three Volumes—but all the rest a deep, inscrutable mystery. It was behind a door he whispered it—He gave me to understand that between ourselves it would throw a light on certain

---

*on Books and their Writers,* ed. E. J. Morley, 1938, II, 593).

[3] This note is written on the fourth side of *To* Colburn, 1 Apr, following the word "Over", cancelled. The note is itself crossed through. As with *To* Colburn, above, the facsimile seems to be of a tracing of the original.

[1] How the letter and note escaped preservation by Forster is not known.

[2] Edward Dubois (1774–1850; *DNB*), wit and writer. One of Thomas Hill's two executors and residuary legatees. At one time a contributor to periodicals; edited the *Monthly Mirror* when owned by Hill, and for a few years the *Lady's Magazine* and *European Magazine*. His works included translations, and *Old Nick; a Satirical Story in Three Volumes,* 1801, dedicated to Hill. Was

the original of Duberly in Hook's *Gilbert Gurney*—in which Hill appeared as Hull.

[3] In the sale of Hill's Library 10–17 Mar, 104 lots were MSS, most of them autograph letters. Besides letters from people who were dead (Shenstone, Burns, Sheridan, Byron, Hazlitt, Scott, Coleridge, Mozart, Gluck and others), there were letters from the living—Wordsworth, Southey, Campbell, Moore, Rogers, Talfourd, Brougham, Hook, and CD himself.

[4] One of Hill's own catch-phrases was "Pooh! pooh! I happen to know".

[5] I.e. people like the Lord Burleigh in Sheridan's *The Critic* who has no time to speak because of the weightiness of his thoughts.

[6] It was not published.

autobiographies—that somebody hadn't represented something quite correctly somewhere—that he knew all about that, bless you (God knows what) before *she* (God knows who) was trusted with it. And so, with one nudge of his elbow and three nods, he dismissed the subject and fell upon another no less weighty and secret.[1]

I really did love him. He seems to have carried away with him half the pleasant, good-humoured little eccentricities of the world—of *my* world at least, as Charles Lamb says.[2]

Faithfully Yours

Edward Du Bois Esquire                          CHARLES DICKENS


## *To* J. P. HARLEY, 3 APRIL 1841

MS Comtesse de Suzannet.

Devonshire Terrace. | April The Third 1841.

My Dear Harley.

The "works" of the Clock dine with me next Saturday at a quarter past 6, in honor of our new volume. It is Passion week, and I devoutly hope you have no engagement to prevent you from joining the little party[3] which you have gladdened so often on the like occasions.[4]

Always believe me | Faithfully Yours

J. P. Harley Esquire.                           CHARLES DICKENS

---

[1] Crabb Robinson saw Hill as "the real original Paul Pry, ... the man whom everybody laughed at, and whom, on account of his good-nature, many tolerated, and some made use of as a circulating medium" (*Diary, Reminiscences, and Correspondence*, ed. T. Sadler, II, 403). J. R. Planché, who disliked him, could only explain his being tolerated by "many of the most brilliant men of the time" by the fact that, though not witty himself, he was "the cause of wit in others"; "scandal was, of course, the great staple of his conversation" (*Recollections and Reflections*, revised edn, 1901, pp. 91–2). The most common view of him was Serjeant Ballantine's: "He acted the *rôle* of a busybody for the amusement of his friends, but was too much liked ever to have been a mischievous one" (*Some Experiences of a Barrister's Life*, 1882, I, 112).

[2] At the end of "The Praise of Chimney Sweepers" (*Essays of Elia*) Lamb says of James White that he "carried away with him half the fun of the world when he died—of my world at least".

[3] The two patent theatres, Covent Garden and Drury Lane, were closed by law on the Wednesday and Friday in Passion Week, although the other London theatres were open for performances of a non-dramatic character, and "Passion Week itself was unknown in the theatres two or three miles from St. James's Palace" (J. R. Planché, *Recollections and Reflections*, revised edn, p. 290).

[4] Harley replied on 5 Apr: "We have only this morning set the wheels in motion for our *Easter* works, and should no winding up, and regulating be requisite on Saturday Evening, next—I shall be *too* happy to make *one* among you" (MS Berg). In fact, this year Covent Garden was closed throughout the week, opening on Easter Monday with the extravaganza *Beauty and the Beast*, in which Harley played John Quill.

## *To* WALTER SAVAGE LANDOR, [4] APRIL 1841*

MS Mrs A. M. Stern. *Date:* 5 Apr 41 was a Monday; presumably CD
was writing on the 4th.

Devonshire Terrace | Sunday Night | April The Fifth 1841.
My Dear Landor.

I shall look for the end of the month right earnestly, and shall be heartily
glad and pleased to see you.

I am in fearfully low spirits tonight—bilious, behind-hand in my work
in consequence, blue devil haunted and miserable. Thank God there are
no real causes for this (saving, I suppose, some slight disorder in the
system) and it's no great matter to me and less to you, except as an explanation of this poor note—for which reason I mention it.

Four months! I don't believe a word of it. If you're away from Bath
four whole months consecutively, I'll write four novels for fourpence.
Four months![1] In the very high time and season of roses![2] Your note
bears date on the First of April, or it would have no such wild and monstrous statement in it, I'll be sworn.

Don't talk of such rash acts. Don't think of them. Come to London.
Go to Paris. But return to Bath at short intervals wherever you go. How
can a man live without sun, light, heat—How are you to be inspired—How
are you to go on writing (as I know you do)—how are you to go on at all?
It *cannot*[3] be done. Or if it can, it must be by some frozen-hearted, slow-
blooded, torpid wretch; and you are not the man to do it.

If you do, I renounce you. I hold the Landor faith no more, and
publicly recant.

Always Faithfully—but at present | conditionally | Yours
CHARLES DICKENS

All well and blooming—your dutiful Godson included.

## *To* H. P. SMITH,[4] 5 APRIL 1841*

MS Miss Mabel Hodge.

Devonshire Terrace. | Monday Morning April Fifth | 1841.
My Dear Sir.

I am so very much indisposed by a bilious attack, that we are reluctantly
compelled to deny ourselves the pleasure of being with you to day. I

---

[1] Landor's son Walter was on his way
from Italy to England, and Landor had
planned to meet him in Paris. He
stayed in London with Lady Blessington
on the way there (5–9 May), returned
from Paris with Walter in the second
week of June, stayed about three days
with Forster, and was back in Bath by
about 28 June—after less than two

months' absence (see R. H. Super,
*W. S. Landor*, pp. 326–9).

[2] For earlier rose-jokes, see *To*
Landor, 26 July 40, *fn.*

[3] Heavily underlined three times.

[4] Henry Porter Smith (1797–1880),
actuary. Had started life as an Ensign
in the 52nd (Oxfordshire) Foot Regt
1814; Lieut. 1819–21; then retired on

assure you it grieves me very much to lose so good an opportunity of improving your acquaintance though I hope to have very many more— but indisposition is a serious matter to me who am so constantly engaged, and I am obliged[1] to drive it away by vigorous and rigid measures, whereof the first is keeping at home and living abstemiously.

Mrs. Dickens begs me to present her compliments to Mrs. Smith. I doubt whether my bilious and most uncomfortable regards are worth acceptance, but I venture to add them notwithstanding.

My Dear Sir | Faithfully Yours

H. P. Smith Esquire                                     CHARLES DICKENS

## *To* FRANCIS SMEDLEY, 5 APRIL 1841

Extract in N, I, 312, from catalogue source; dated Devonshire Terrace, 5 Apr 41.

I am extremely unwell with a vile bilious disorder which must be

half pay. Married Penelope Lloyd (daughter of John Lloyd, wine merchant of 163 Fleet Street) 1823; a daughter was born 1824; through Lloyd became secretary and actuary to the Eagle Life Assurance Co. 1828–48. An old friend of Macready's, and often consulted by him on business and personal matters (see, e.g., *Diaries*, I, 339; II, 132, 137; and *Macready's Reminiscences*, ed. F. Pollock, 1875, II, 74). According to Macready he had had a tragedy published in 1834 (*Diaries*, I, 102). On 16 Dec 38 he was one of a group invited to Macready's to hear him read Bulwer's *Richelieu* and give their opinions. Browning, Fox and Blanchard were enthusiastic; only Smith was critical: "He rarely approves without discovering something to alter", wrote Macready to Bulwer, 21 Dec; "he has written plays, and . . . the dramatist peeps out in his criticisms" (*Bulwer and Macready*, ed. C. H. Shattuck, p. 111). Smith was the actuary who investigated for the Eagle the affairs of Thomas Griffiths Wainewright (1794–1852; *DNB*) after the suspicious death Dec 1830 of Wainewright's young sister-in-law Helen Abercromby, whose life had been insured between Mar and Oct 1830 for £18,000—£3000 of it with the Eagle. He testified at the insurance trial of Dec 35, and after Wainewright's arrest

1837 and imprisonment in Newgate (where CD saw him: see Vol. I, p. 277n) was sent to France to collect the papers Wainewright—who had earlier fled there—had left behind (see Jonathan Curling, *Janus Weathercock*, 1938, *passim*). These he kept possession of, and in 1846 lent to Bulwer, who drew on them for *Lucretia* (see Lytton, *The Life of Edward Bulwer*, 1913, II, 87n). It seems likely that the rumour current in 1848 that one of the Eagle actuaries had fallen in love with Helen Abercromby, and himself pursued Wainewright to Boulogne, concerned Smith; and the following note in CD's Book of Memoranda, which may have been based on a confidence from Smith (and was later drawn on for *Hunted Down*, 1859), lends support: "Devoted to the Destruction of a man. . . . The secretary in the Wainewright case, who had fallen in love (or supposed he had) with the murdered girl" (F, IX, vii, 749). The phrase "or supposed he had" could well fit Smith, who is only known to have met Helen Abercromby twice, but is inapplicable to the feelings of the actuary in *Hunted Down*. For the development of his friendship with CD, who asked him to be godfather to two of his children (Dora, who died when a baby, and Sydney), see later vols.

[1] Written "obiged".

promptly subdued and has been taken in hand by the doctor[1] with a most unpleasant alacrity[2].

## *To* JOHN FORSTER, [5 APRIL 1841]

Extract in F, II, ix, 167. *Date:* 5 Apr according to Forster.

Don't fail to erase anything that seems to you too strong. It is difficult for me to judge what tells too much, and what does not.[3] I am trying a very quiet number[4] to set against this necessary one. I hope it will be good, but I am in very sad condition for work. Glad you think this powerful. What I have put in is more relief, from the raven.[5]

## *To* JOHN FORSTER, [7 APRIL 1841]

Extract in F, II, ix, 167. *Date:* two days after 5 Apr according to Forster.

I have done that number[6] and am now going to work on another. I am bent (please Heaven) on finishing the first chapter[7] by Friday night.

[1] Francis Pickthorn (see Vol. I, p. 390n) was still the family doctor. Payments to him of £10 on 8 Apr 41 and £3 on 15 May are shown in CD's account book (MS Messrs Coutts). But after that date he seems to have been called in only once, when Charley had convulsions on his parents' return from America.

[2] Presumably the rest of the note asked for a postponement of the visit to Tothill Fields Prison arranged on 1 Apr for the 6th.

[3] Clearly refers to the proofs of Chs 17 and 18 (No. 55, published 17 Apr)—the one set of *Barnaby* proofs to survive in the Forster Collection, V & A. In Ch. 17 Forster cut five passages. One (continuing Rudge's threat to Mrs Rudge, after "if you betray me"): " 'By this right hand, whose history you know, and by this devil's seal stamped on me, you remember when, I will!' | He pulled his slouched hat from his brow, ... pointing, as he spoke, to the gash upon his cheek . . ."; another (between "As she said this wildly," and "there came a heavy knocking"): "and towered above him as though she could have crushed him in her passion". CD's growing awareness that while writing he was often a poor judge of what was "too strong" is illustrated in Kathleen

Tillotson's analysis of the "consistent and progressive curbing of overemphatic expression" in his revisions of *Oliver* (see *Oliver Twist*, ed. K. Tillotson, pp. xxxi, xxxii, xxxvi, and footnotes to text). This awareness he undoubtedly owed to Forster, who—in his *Examiner* review (4 Dec 41) of the completed *Master Humphrey*—rewarded him with: "The tendency to exaggerate is less."

[4] He would have been writing the comparatively quiet No. 56 (Chs 19 and 20), describing the Varden household, their expedition to the Maypole, and Dolly's visit to Emma Haredale.

[5] As with *Old Curiosity Shop* (see *To* Forster, 13 Sep 40, *fn*), they clearly each had sets of the proofs of this No.: Forster marked on his set (now in the V & A) what he felt should be cut; CD, on his set (lost), wrote the additions. He put in, as further "relief" to Ch. 17, Barnaby's insistence that that day must be his birthday and Grip's reception of the news (eight paragraphs, six of them dialogue).

[6] Presumably No. 56: see last, *fn*.

[7] Ch. 21, in which Dolly, on her way back to the Maypole in the dusk, is waylaid by Hugh, rescued by Joe, but has meanwhile lost the letter entrusted to her by Emma Haredale.

I hope to look in upon you to-night, when we'll dispose of the toasts for Saturday.[1] Still bilious—but a good number, I hope, notwithstanding. Jeffrey has come to town and was here yesterday.

## *To* ANDREW BELL,[2] 7 APRIL [1841]*

MS Huntington Library. *Date:* 7 Apr was Wednesday in 1841; handwriting supports that year.

1 Devonshire Terrace | York Gate Regents Park.
Wednesday April The Seventh.

Dear Sir.

It gave me very great pleasure, I assure you, to receive your letter last night. I read the paper[3] you did me the favor to send with it, before I went to bed, and was much amused and *interested* with it. Charles Lamb would have been charmed with it, I am sure.

I beg you to use my name among your other credentials, as freely and fully as you please.

And in thanking you for the many services I have received at your hands in the exercise of your painful calling[4] (which I have often observed, and often commended) let me couple with my very sincere acknowledgments, my cordial wishes for your prosperity and success. It will afford me real gratification to hear that you are doing well; and if any commendation[5] of mine can serve you at any time, it will be heartily at your service.

Faithfully Yours

Mr. Andrew Bell.                                          CHARLES DICKENS

---

[1] The day of the second *Clock* dinner.

[2] Andrew Bell, author (under the pseudonym A. Thomason) of *Men and Things in America; Being the Experience of a Year's Residence in the United States, in a Series of Letters to a Friend*, 1838 (2nd edn, privately printed at Southampton, 1862, under his own name). He also published an *Imperial Dictionary* and *Historical Sketches of Feudalism*, 1852.

[3] Unidentified.

[4] *Men and Things in America* contains some autobiographical matter, but is never explicit concerning the business Bell had been "apprenticed" to (p. 118), his "one trade" (p. 276), the work on the strength of which he called himself "brother artisan" to the artisans of the United States (p. 288). Presumably his trade was one of those he lists pp. 279–80 when discussing American wages. Among these, one is given a sentence to itself: "Book printers are lower paid than in England, and still less sure of getting work" (he had himself failed to find work in New York: p. 137). It is conceivable that his "painful calling" was that of compositor, employed by Bradbury & Evans (to whose works *To* Bell, 12 Oct 41, is addressed), and recently active on CD's MSS.

[5] CD first wrote "recommendation", then apparently cancelled the "re".

### *To* ANGUS FLETCHER, 8 APRIL 1841

MS John Rylands Library.

Devonshire Terrace.
Thursday April The Eighth | 1841.

My Dear Fletcher.

On the Twenty First of June, God willing, and no accident or misfortune interposing, I shall leave this for Edinburgh; staying one night, or possibly two, upon the road.

The choice of the Hotel I will leave to you; and some week or ten days beforehand, I will write to entreat you to take the trouble to bespeak the needful accommodation for us—a trouble I know you will take.

In the matter of the dinner or rumours of dinner, I feel bound to say—stop nothing. You know my "quiet ways", but coming Northward really as an acknowledgment of the kind opinion of the Northern people,[1] and with a cordial desire to shake hands with them one and all, I would not for the world reject any compliment they, or any of them, sought to offer me. Therefore I say, stop *nothing*; and be assured that I should accept any testimonial of that, or any other kind, in the full height of the spirit in which it would be bestowed—and very gladly and proudly.

Jeffrey called on me two or three days ago, and I went to him this morning.[2] He was in great force and charmed me exceedingly. His enthusiasm relative to the Old Curiosity Shop, exceeded even what you had prepared me for,[3] and upon my word I c[a]me[4] out of the house more delighted than if I had been ten thousand pounds the richer than when I went in—as I was in the true wealth undoubtedly.

The Bust[5] arrived safe, and is considered by everybody (by Maclise at the head of them) *much more like* in the Marble than in the Cast. Kate wrote to thank you for it, but was guilty of the small omission (a very slight one) of forgetting to put it in the post. She is[6] going to write again, and I have no doubt you will get her note, either with this, or immediately afterwards.

Somebody has been talking to me all the time I have been writing this. I am afraid it's illegible. But you would rather have it than wait, I know, and I would rather you had—so here (it) goes.

Always Dear Fletcher | Faithfully Yours
CHARLES DICKENS

---

[1] Cf. *To* Forster, 18 Mar.

[2] Jeffrey's friendship with CD developed quickly; and before he left London, says Forster, "the visit to Scotland in June was all duly arranged, to be initiated by the splendid welcome of a public dinner in Edinburgh, with Lord Jeffrey himself in the chair" (F, II, x, 174).

[3] For Jeffrey's weeping over the death of Nell, see *To* Forster, 18 Mar, *fn*.

[4] MS reads "come".

[5] Fletcher's bust of CD, exhibited in the RA 1839.

[6] MS reads "was is".

You shall be our "Dougal"[1] to the Highlands, and I your bailie. It *was* Forster who noticed Susan Hopley.[2] He has *sent* me the book to read.

*Note*

There was, as you will see by the erasures, a redundancy of L's in the above paragraph.[3] The talking man was the occasion of it.

## *To* EDWARD MARJORIBANKS, 8 APRIL 1841†

MS Morgan Library. *Address:* Edward Marjoribanks Esquire | &c &c.

Devonshire Terrace. | Thursday April the Eighth 1841.

My Dear Sir

*a*Twice a year—that is, at the end of each volume—I hold, not a solemn supper,[4] but a solemn dinner, whereat all the Clock "Works", publishers, printers, artists, engravers, &c &c assemble together in high festival.*a* And we make wonderful speeches I assure you, and strange things happen— such as men in black who were never seen to smile before, cutting jokes— and songs breaking out in unexpected places—and many other moral Vesuviuses of that nature.

Unhappily next Saturday is the great day. Three white waistcoats have been seen on lines in suburban districts under suspicious circumstances, and I have reason to suppose are preparing for the occasion; a studious-looking man has been observed in Saint John's Wood muttering such scraps as "Gentlemen I rise"—"—on the present occasion"—"more than I can express" and so forth—and the description tallies exactly with a renowned engraver.[5] Under *any*[6] other circumstances (I am serious now) I would have a cold immediately, but in this predicament I have nothing for it but to regret most heartily you didn't say Monday or any other day, indeed, but this.

Dear Sir Faithfully Yours always

Edward Marjoribanks Esquire                                    CHARLES DICKENS

[1] The turnkey of the Glasgow prison in *Rob Roy*, who joins Francis Osbaldistone and Bailie Nicol Jarvie in their search for Rob Roy in the Highlands. Perhaps linked with Fletcher in CD's mind not only as a guide to the Highlands but for his wild appearance and antics: e.g. on touching the gold Frank gives him, he springs "twice or thrice from the earth . . ., flinging out first one heel and then another in a manner which would have astonished a French dancing master" (Ch. 36): cf. Fletcher's "insane gambollings" (*To* Forster, 13 Sep 40, *fn*).

[2] Catherine Crowe's *Adventures of Susan Hopley; or Circumstantial Evidence*, published anonymously, was reviewed in the *Examiner*, 28 Feb 41.

In a long notice Forster summed it up as "powerful, beyond all question; but unsatisfactory". In *To* De la Rue, 9 Mar 54, CD called it "rather a clever story". He apparently met Mrs Crowe (?1800–76; *DNB*) when staying with Jeffrey (see 3 July, *fn*).

[3] CD first wrote "Dougall" and "baillie", then cancelled an "l" in each.

*aa* Quoted in N. I, 314, from catalogue source; letter otherwise unpublished.

[4] *Macbeth*, III, i, 14: "To-night we hold a solemn supper, Sir".

[5] Probably Thomas Landseer (1795– 1880; *DNB*), who lived in Cunningham Place, St John's Wood. See Vol. I, p. 601*n*.

[6] Underlined twice.

### *To* HENRY AUSTIN, 8 APRIL 1841*

MS Morgan Library.

Devonshire Terrace | Thursday April the Eighth | 1841.

My Dear Henry

Remember that the time for the Clock Works is a quarter past 6 on Saturday next.

Love to Letitia.

Affectionately Always

Henry Austin Esquire          [CHARLES DICKENS][1]

### *To* THE REV. THOMAS ROBINSON,[2] 8 APRIL 1841

Tracing of MS by Mr R. L. McCulloch.

Private        1 Devonshire Terrace | York Gate Regents Park
Thursday April The Eighth/41.

Dear Sir

I am much obliged to you for your interesting letter. Nor am I the less pleased to receive it, by reason that I cannot find it in my conscience to agree in many important respects with the body to which you belong.

In the love of virtue and hatred of vice, in the detestation of cruelty and encouragement of gentleness and mercy—all Men who endeavour to be acceptable to their Creator in any way, may freely agree. There are more roads to Heaven, I am inclined to think, than any Sect believes; but there can be none which have not these Flowers garnishing the way.

I feel it a great tribute, therefore, to receive your letter. It is most welcome and acceptable to me. I thank you for it heartily, and am proud of the approval of one who suffered in his youth, even more than my poor child.[3]

While you teach in your walk of life the lessons of tenderness you have learnt in sorrow, trust me that in mine, I will pursue cruelty and oppression, the Enemies of all God's creatures of all codes and creeds, so long as I have the energy of thought and the power of giving it utterance.

Faithfully Yours

The Reverend | Thomas Robinson     CHARLES DICKENS

[1] Signature has been cut away.
[2] According to MDGH, 1882, 41, a dissenting Minister who had been a workhouse boy.

[3] Clearly refers to Oliver.

## *To* W. C. MACREADY, 8 APRIL 1841*

MS Miss Christina Macready.

Devonshire Terrace.
Thursday April The Eighth. | 1841.

My Dear Macready.

If Mrs. Macready isn't going to have an evening party next Saturday, may I ask you to bring Meyrick[1] with you, as you were kind enough to do on the last Clock work occasion?[2]

Faithfully always
CHARLES DICKENS

## *To* W. C. MACREADY, 9 APRIL 1841*

MS Morgan Library.

Friday April The Ninth 1841.

My Dear Macready.

I think No. 1[3] will suffice. Thank you no less for the offer of No. 2.

I am afraid I shall not be able to go out today. Perhaps if you are not anxious to call at Lord Northampton's now, you will let it stand over until one day next week. Then, I shall be happy to go with you.[4]

My courage rises higher and higher now that you have settled for Drur[y] Lane.[5] I feel more strongly than [ever][6] that it is the position you alone should occupy—the position you alone can maintain—[an]d the venture tha[t] is as sure as a[ny] man's can be [to][7] be crowned in the end, with a m[           ][8] and success.

Always Faithfully Yours | My Dear Macready
CHARLES DICKENS

[1] I.e. Macready's manservant Merrick (see *Diaries*, II, 208). On reading the note through, CD added an exclamation-mark in the margin—no doubt amused by his own spelling of the name and perhaps by the thought of Macready's bringing Sir Samuel Rush Meyrick (1783–1848; *DNB*) to wait at the *Clock* dinner. Meyrick would have been known to Macready through the assistance he gave Planché in the reform of theatrical costume.

[2] See *To* Macready, 20 Oct 40.

[3] Merrick: see last.

[4] Presumably to leave cards, following Lord Northampton's "swarry" (see *To* Cattermole, 1 Apr and *fn*).

[5] For the last three months Macready, who had been far from happy at the Haymarket under Webster's management (see *To* Macready, 2 Dec 41 and *fn*), had been considering applying for the lesseeship of Drury Lane and re-opening the theatre *"as a theatre"* (*Diaries*, II, 129). Since Alfred Bunn's bankruptcy 1840, James Hammond, manager of the Strand, had had the theatre at a reduced rental, but he also had to close Mar 41—the remainder of the season being filled out with concerts and some opera. On 6 Apr the General Committee of Drury Lane agreed to give Macready the management from Oct 41. He opened with *The Merchant of Venice* on 27 Dec.

[6] The paper is torn at the fold and tattered at the right edge. Several words are slightly affected, but only three are wholly gone. Here a short word is missing, presumably "ever".

[7] Short word missing at end of line.

[8] Bottom corner of page torn away.

## *To* JOHN FORSTER, [12 APRIL 1841]

Extract in F, II, ix, 167. *Date:* given by Forster as "five days later" than *To* Forster, 7 Apr (itself "two days later" than letter dated by him 5 Apr).

I finished the number[1] yesterday, and, although I dined with Jeffrey, and was obliged to go to Lord Denman's[2] afterwards (which made me late), have done eight slips of the *Lamplighter*[3] for Mrs. Macrone, this morning. When I have got that off my mind, I shall try to go on steadily, fetching up[4] the *Clock* lee-way.

## *To* MESSRS COX & SONS,[5] 13 APRIL 1841*

MS Clark Memorial Library, University of California.

Devonshire Terrace | April The Thirteenth 1841.

Mr. Charles Dickens presents his compliments to Messrs. Cox and Sons, and begs to say that he will leave out his contribution to the Pic Nic Papers, under cover to them, if they will have the goodness to send a boy for it on Monday Morning.

## *To* MISS CATHERINE HUTTON,[6] 13 APRIL 1841

Text from N, I, 314.

1 Devonshire Terrace, York Gate, Regents Park, London
April the Thirteenth, 1841

Dear Madam,

Mr. Charles Knight punctually executed your commission and sent me

[1] Probably No. 57 (Chs 21 and 22), begun 7 Apr (*To* Forster, that day); published 1 May.

[2] Thomas Denman, first Baron Denman (1779–1854; *DNB*), Lord Chief Justice 1832–50. Had been Queen Caroline's Solicitor-General 1820, and at her trial summed up her case in a speech bitterly resented by George IV. As Lord Chief Justice was responsible for a number of legal reforms, including abolition of the death penalty for forgery 1837. Championed extinction of the slave trade in pamphlets and speches 1843–52, when his rapidly deteriorating health led him to a violent attack on *Bleak House*, and Mrs Jellyby in particular, in a series of letters to the *Standard*. CD always thought highly of him.

[3] "The Lamplighter's Story" for *The Pic Nic Papers*—an adaptation of the farce CD had written for Macready who rejected it (see *To* Forster, 4 Dec 38 and *n*; I, 465).

[4] Making up (*OED*).

[5] J. L. Cox & Sons, 75 Great Queen St., Lincoln's Inn Fields, printers of *The Pic Nic Papers*, Vol. I.

[6] Catherine Hutton (1756–1846; *DNB*), writer, needlewoman, collector of fashion-plates and autographs. Bulwer, Ainsworth and Augusta Leigh were among her many correspondents. For her varied accomplishments and remarkable industry to the age of 90, see *Reminiscences of a Gentlewoman of the Last Century*, ed. Mrs C. H. Beale, Birmingham, 1891. Besides completing her father's Life (see below) and his history of Birmingham, she published three novels, some minor works, and articles.

your father's biography.[1] I should have acknowledged its receipt immediately, but I had forgotten your address, and hoped to have my memory refreshed by hearing from you again.

I have not yet had time to do more than dip into the volume just before going to bed, but what I have read has interested me greatly. The part on which I chanced to light on cutting the leaves was that which described Mr. Hutton's "running away", and first entry into Birmingham.[2] I was much struck with the whole description of his journey—very much—and felt as if I were reading some new story by DeFoe.

Let me thank you very cordially for your kind recollection of me in sending me the book which I am sure I shall read with strong interest throughout, and with hearty good wishes for your health and happiness, believe me, Dear Madam,

Faithfully yours<br>[CHARLES DICKENS]

## *To* LORD JEFFREY, [?14 or 15 APRIL 1841]

Mention in Jeffrey *to* CD, "Thursday 15th" [Apr 41]: see *fn.*

*Confirming an invitation for 26 Apr.*[3]

[1] *The Life of William Hutton, Stationer, of Birmingham; and the History of his Family. Written by Himself. With Some Extracts from his Other Works* (one of Knight's "English Classics"), 1841. Catherine Hutton had originally published it in 1816, edited by herself, without the extracts from his other writings. William Hutton (1723–1815; *DNB*), author of *The History of Birmingham*, 1781, began work in a Derby silk-mill at the age of seven and rose to be a leading Birmingham citizen. A friend of Joseph Priestley, he was mobbed and his house sacked in the riots of 1791 (his "Narrative of the Riots" was published posthumously in his daughter's edition of the *Life*, 1816).

[2] The section entitled "The History of a Week", pp. 10–16. It is an unadorned, vivid description of the 17-year-old William Hutton's running away, after a severe beating, from his uncle at Nottingham, to whom he was apprenticed as a stocking-weaver. It recounts how he walked to Derby with 2/- in his pocket, had his bags containing all his possessions stolen at Lichfield, walked on to Birmingham, where he slept for three-half-pence but failed to find work, and finally walked back to

his father's lodgings at Derby, where he was reconciled with his uncle.

[3] Jeffrey replied: "I am sorry you have had the trouble of writing—I shall come to you on Monday 26th.—with very great pleasure" (MS Huntington). Clearly the invitation was first given by word of mouth, probably on 14 Apr during a call by CD in response to a note from Jeffrey, dated "Tuesday", ?13 Apr (MS Huntington). Three weeks later, on 4 May, Jeffrey wrote to Lord Cockburn: "I have seen a good deal . . . of Charles Dickens, with whom I have struck up what I mean to be an eternal and intimate friendship. He lives very near us here, and I often run over and sit an hour *tête à tête*, or take a long walk in the park with him— the only way really to know or be known by either man or woman. Taken in this way I think him very amiable and agreeable. In mixed company, where he is now much sought after as a lion, he is rather reserved, &c. He has dined here . . . and we with him, at rather too sumptuous a dinner for a man with a family, and only beginning to be rich, though selling 44,000 copies of his weekly issues" (Cockburn, *Life of Lord Jeffrey*, 1852, II, 338).

## *To* DANIEL MACLISE, [?15 APRIL 1841]*

MS Private. *Date:* Initials (not wholly reliable) suggest Mar–Apr 41, in which period 15 Apr seems the only possible Thursday. *Address:* Daniel Maclise Esquire.

Devonshire T. | Thursday

Dear Mac.

Forster dines here today at ½ past 5. Will you dine with us? I mean to leave off, and go out for a ride—*now.* Will you come with us? Kate waits, and will bring you to me.

In haste | Always
CD

## *To* [?SIR FRANCIS AND LADY BURDETT], [?15] APRIL [1841]*

MS Bodleian Library. *Date:* endorsed 1841 in contemporary hand; style of date ("April The Sixteenth") supports. But since 16 Apr 41 was a Friday, CD was probably writing on Thurs 15th. *Address:* see *fn.*

Devonshire Terrace. | Thursday, April The Sixteenth.

Mr. Charles Dickens has very great pleasure in accepting [?Sir Francis and Lady Burdett's][1] kind Invitation for tomorrow.

## *To* ALBANY FONBLANQUE,[2] 16 APRIL 1841*

Text from typescript, Huntington Library.

1 Devonshire Terrace, | April The Sixteenth, 1841.

My Dear Sir,

Have you anything better to do on Monday Week the Twenty Sixth, than to dine here at 7 o'clock—only to meet Jeffrey, and one or two others whom you know?[3]

If you have not, I shall be truly glad to see you.[4]

Faithfully yours,

Albany Fonblanque Esquire.                    CHARLES DICKENS

[1] Name or names have been cut out of the MS, leaving space for up to 28 letters (including spaces between words). Since the MS is in a Burdett collection, "Sir Francis and Lady Burdett's" seems possible. A curve not cut away, 7 letters from the end, could be the top of "B". For Sir Francis Burdett, Bart (1770–1844; *DNB*), see Vol. I, p. 472*n.* He had married Sophia Coutts (1775–1844) in 1793.

[2] Albany Fonblanque (1793–1872; *DNB*): see Vol. I, p. 205*n.*

[3] Samuel Rogers accepted a similar invitation on 17 Apr (MS Huntington). Sydney Smith (see Vol. I, p. 431*n*) declined on 17 Apr because he would be dining with Lady Holland, and added: "We are constant readers here of all you write—You have many attributes —but I love your humor most—Miggs Swiveller Miss Brass are all admirable. | We have routes [*thus*] for 4 Weeks every Thursday beginning the 22nd. most happy to see you at them all" (MS Huntington).

[4] Fonblanque accepted (MS Huntington).

## To HENRY AUSTIN, 17 APRIL 1841*

MS Morgan Library.

Devonshire Terrace.
Saturday April The Seventeenth | 1841.

My Dear Henry.

The pamphlet[1] is extremely well got up, and looks capital. The following names occur to me—should I think of any others, I will send them to you.

Affy. always

CD.

Sir Martin Archer Shee,[2] P.R.A.  32 Cavendish Sqe.
The Right Hon The Marquis of Lansdowne[3]
    54 Berkeley Square
The Right Hon The Marquis of Northampton
    145 Piccadilly.
The Right Hon The Lord Monteagle[4]
    8 Mansfield Street.

[1] *Thoughts on the Abuses of the Present System of Competition in Architecture; with an Outline of a Plan for the Remedy*, 1841, written as a letter to Earl de Grey (1781–1859; *DNB*), first President of the Royal Institution of British Architects (founded 1834). "I fearlessly assert", wrote Austin, "that the root from which all the evils of the present system have sprung, is the total ignorance of those whom architects allow to sit in judgment"—i.e. the amateur Building Committees in charge of architectural competitions since these became fashionable (following the competition for the Houses of Parliament 1835–6). The Committees advertised for designs, giving wholly inadequate instructions, said Austin; some competitors attempted to win through influence; others submitted designs "on a scale of great magnificence" (which would have cost "twenty times the stipulated amount"), having employed "skilful artists to prepare coloured, showy elevations and false perspective views . . . to catch the Committee's unpractised eye". The results were a laughing-stock and outrage, degrading to the profession. To remedy these ills, Austin urged that the Institute of British Architects should announce its willingness to work with any Building Committee if consulted before a competition was opened; that it should ensure that competitors were given every necessary detail; that the designs submitted should be exhibited in the Institute; and that the five designs most favoured by the competing architects themselves should be finally judged by a joint committee of members of the Institute and of the Building Committee concerned. CD's choosing to make the main character in his next novel a self-styled architect (who entered his pupils' work for competitions) must have owed something to Austin.

[2] Sir Martin Archer Shee (1769–1850; *DNB*), portrait painter; RA 1800, PRA 1830–50. Also won a literary reputation, by his *Rhymes on Art*, 1805, *Elements of Art*, 1809, poems, two novels and a tragedy. His presidency fell in a difficult time; but he successfully resisted all attempts to bring the RA under Parliamentary instead of the Sovereign's control 1834–9 (see Sir W. R. M. Lamb, *The Royal Academy*, revised edn, 1951, pp. 36–40). He and CD had met at the Artists' Benevolent Fund dinner, 12 May 38 (see *Speeches*, ed. K. J. Fielding, p. 2).

[3] Henry Petty-Fitzmaurice, 3rd Marquess of Lansdowne (1780–1863; *DNB*), Whig statesman and patron of the arts. A trustee of the British Museum from 1823; of the National Gallery from 1834; President of the Literary Fund from 1838.

[4] Thomas Spring-Rice, 1st Baron Monteagle of Brandon (1790–1866;

Sir Francis Chantrey[1] R.A.   30 Lower Belgrave Place
Pimlico
His Majesty The King
of the
Cannibal Islands[2]
Cannibal Islands.
World.

And all the R.As and architects you can think of. I should say Ewart M.P[3] certainly. I don't know his address, but you'll find it in any list of Members.[4]

I sent one copy to Forster, and begged him to notice it.[5]


## *To* MRS [?HURNALL],[6] 17 APRIL 1841*

MS University of Texas. *Address:* see *fn.*

Devonshire Terrace.
Saturday April The Seventeenth | 1841.

Dear Madam.

I should have written to you the first thing this morning, had I not been anticipated by your messenger (whom I fear I have detained some time,

---

*DNB*), Whig politician, Chancellor of the Exchequer 1835–9; raised to the peerage 1839. Trustee of the National Gallery.

[1] Sir Francis Legatt Chantrey (1781–1841; *DNB*), sculptor, primarily of portrait busts, who had risen from humble origins to great distinction and wealth, to which marriage to a rich wife 1807 contributed. RA 1818, knighted 1835. Death prevented his executing the Siddons monument (see *To* Macready, 22 May, *fn*). Left a fortune of £159,000, which on his wife's death was to go to the Council of the RA, instructed in his Will to buy "Works of Art of the highest merit in Painting and Sculpture" by artists living or dead of any nation, so long as their work was executed in England—to form a "public National Collection". (£3000 *p.a.* from the Chantrey Bequest became available to the RA Council from 1877; but its choice of works was soon under heavy attack.)

[2] "The King of the Cannibal Islands" was a popular comic song, written and sung by A. W. Humphreys; first published *c.* 1830 and still current in the '60s.

[3] William Ewart (1798–1869; *DNB*), advanced liberal politician, at this time MP for Wigan; advocated easier admission to museums and galleries, drew up the report of a committee "on the connection between arts and manufactures", 1836, from which stemmed the Schools of Design at Somerset House, 1837. Campaigned for abolition of capital punishment; urged entry to civil and diplomatic services and army by examination; and carried a bill for establishing free public libraries 1850.

[4] On the back of CD's letter is the following list (presumably in Austin's hand), no doubt of the people to whom the pamphlet was to be sent: "Lawrence | Archt. Socy. | Lord Monteagle | Sir M. Wood | Gally Knight | Aldn Humphery | Visct. Duncannon | A. Milne Esquire | Hon. C. A. Gore | J. Philipps Esquire. R.A. | Earl de Grey | Lewis Cubitt | Ewart M.P. | Sir H. Ellis | Sir F. Chantrey | Sir Martin Shee".

[5] The pamphlet was very favourably reviewed in the *Examiner* on 25 Apr.

[6] Unidentified. CD's subscription reads "Mrs. Harnace". But what seems almost certainly the same letter is advertised in Sotheby's catalogue,

for I was not up when he arrived) to appoint tomorrow for calling on you, and to tell you that I was unexpectedly summoned out of town yesterday morning, and did not return 'till Evening.

I regret to say that this is always with me the busiest day in the week, and that this morning I could not on any account leave home. I must therefore defer the pleasure of seeing you—very unwillingly—until your next visit to town. Wishing you health and happiness in the mean time, and trusting that I may have the good fortune to increase your stock of cheerfulness in time to come, as you make me happy by telling me I have, in time past, I am Dear Madam

Faithfully Yours

Mrs. Harnace                                              CHARLES DICKENS

## *To* MRS SMITHSON, 18 APRIL 1841

Mention in *American Book Prices Current*, 1901; dated 18 Apr 41.

## *To* SIR EDWARD LYTTON BULWER, 19 APRIL 1841

MS Lytton Papers.

1 Devonshire Terrace. York Gate<br>Monday April The Nineteenth 1841.

My Dear Sir Edward.

If you have no better engagement—as you easily may have—for next Monday the Twenty Sixth, will you dine with me at Seven o'Clock?[1] I shall be heartily glad to see you, if you will.

Always Believe me | Faithfully Yours

Sir Edward Lytton Bulwer.                          CHARLES DICKENS

March 1903, as *To* Mrs Hurnall (2 pp., dated Devonshire Terrace, 17 Apr 41; "a reply to an invitation to pay a visit"); and CD's letter to Mrs Hurnall, 21 July 41, referring to his "promise" to see her in London, connects with paragraph 2 of letter above. CD's "Harnace" is probably, therefore, a misreading of Mrs Hurnall's signature; and Sotheby's attribution correct through their knowledge of the letter's provenance.

[1] Jeffrey, Rogers and Fonblanque had accepted for that evening. Bulwer replied, on Wed [21 Apr]: "I should have been most happy to dine with you, on Monday—but unluckily it is the day of our great debate on the Irish Registration—& as the tactics seem uncertain—there may be an early Division either after going into Committee or on the first clause—I must therefore tho' very reluctantly forego the pleasure you propose to me" (MS Huntington). The following from Maclise to CD, dated "Monday Night" [?26 Apr], may well have been in answer to a last minute invitation to the same dinner party: "I did not get your note till it was too late, quarter to five— and I undressed—unshaved— | I was obliged to substitute—for the entertainment of your society, and the good things of The Castle said and done— the delices of the green cloth and water bottle—to which I am subjected again to-morrow and every night this week" (MS Berg). Maclise had been appointed on 20 Apr 41 to the RA Arranging Committee: hence, probably, his being

## *To* FRANCIS SMEDLEY, 19 APRIL 1841

Text from *D*, x (1914), 214.

Devonshire Terrace, | April the Nineteenth, 1841.
My dear Sir,
Unless you forbid me, I mean to call upon you next Monday between 12 and 1, and avail myself of your good offices in the matter of "The Boy Jones",[1] as the Sunday newspapers denominate him in very fat capitals.
Faithfully yours
Francis Smedley Esquire.                                    [CHARLES DICKENS]

## *To* OCTAVIAN BLEWITT, 19 APRIL 1841*

MS Royal Literary Fund.

Devonshire Terrace | April The Nineteenth 1841
My Dear Sir.
I shall be happy to act as one of the Stewards at the next Anniversary Dinner, and beg you to assure the Committee of my ready and cordial co-operation on the occasion.[2]
Faithfully Yours
Octavian Blewitt Esquire                                    CHARLES DICKENS

## *To* MISS BURDETT COUTTS, 20 APRIL 1841

MS Morgan Library.

Devonshire Terrace.
Tuesday April The Twentieth 1841.
Dear Miss Coutts.
I thank you very much for the order (which I intended calling for to-day, to save you trouble); and as you are so good as to offer your box at the German Opera, I will avail myself of your kindness, if you please, on Thursday Night.[3]

engaged "every night this week". (As subscription to his note, Maclise made a couple of attempts at CD's signature, including flourish—presumably from memory, since not as CD ever wrote it.)
[1] See *To* Smedley, 1 Apr, *fn.*
[2] CD chaired a meeting of the stewards and the sub-committee of the Literary Fund on 11 May, and attended the Anniversary Festival dinner the next day, when one of the toasts was "Mr. Charles Dickens and The Novelists"; his speech was the last he made in support of the Fund (see *Speeches*, ed. K. J. Fielding, pp. 6–7).

[3] When sending the order on 19 Apr (probably for Covent Garden on 20 or 21 Apr, to see *London Assurance* and *Beauty and the Beast*—an extravaganza, with Mme Vestris), Miss Coutts had offered her Box at Drury Lane for the following Thursday and Friday: "I really advise you not to wait for Schumann as the German Opera is beautiful without her" (MS Huntington). CD would have heard *Fidelio* on Thurs 22 Apr.

I have at length been enabled to discover the benevolent Porkman. His name is Edward Hurcomb; his address, 19 William Street Lisson Grove. The poor distracted creature who stole the pork (I think it *was* pork) lives, or did live then, at No. 1 Carlisle Mews Paddington. Her name is Maria Robinson. The circumstance occurred on Monday December the Twenty Eighth, and was reported in the Newspaper Police Accounts of the following day.[1]

I have given my binder instructions to put up an Old Curiosity Shop in one Volume, and when it is becomingly dressed, to send it to you.[2] I hope I may venture to beg your acceptance of it, in this more pleasant shape, as a slight but very sincere tribute of my respect and esteem, and as conveying the author's most cordial and hearty regard.

I should add two more sentences in reference to this Copy of the Tale which I am proud to believe has added something to your stock of pleasant associations. The first is, that the binder to whom I have sent it, is the slowest man in England.[3] The second, that as I have told him to weed out all the foreign matter that was mixed up with its earlier pages, in the Clock,[4] it will have some blank sides here and there, and will be regularly irregular in the numbers at the top of the leaves.[5] But it will be all together, and free from interruptions, and will serve you, I hope, until it comes to be printed in a more convenient form, some years hence.

The Raven's body was removed with every regard for my feelings, in a covered basket. It was taken off to be stuffed, but has not come home yet.

[1] The facts were as CD gives them. Hurcomb, the pork butcher, visited Maria Robinson's lodgings, found that her husband had been unemployed for many weeks, and stated: "I found six young children there with scarcely any thing to cover them, and, taking it altogether, the condition of the whole family was piteous in the extreme; it was indeed a most heart-rending sight" (*Times*, 29 Dec 40). He refused to prosecute and she was discharged.

[2] CD also gave instructions for a special copy of *Old Curiosity Shop* in one volume to be prepared for Jeffrey (see *To* Jeffrey, 11 May and *fn*). For Miss Coutts's letter of thanks on receiving the book, 16 May, see 23 May, *fn*. Inscribed "Miss Burdett Coutts with the sincere regard and esteem of Charles Dickens", it is now in the possession of Colonel Richard Gimbel.

[3] Possibly James Hayday (see Vol. I, p. 340 and *n*), who, according to *D*, xl (1944), 78, was the binder of the one-volume *Old Curiosity Shop* published at the end of the year; alternatively, Francis Bedford (1799–1883), "the best binder in England or perhaps Europe" according to F. Boase, who is given in Parke-Bernet Galleries catalogue, 4 Jan 1940, as binder of the copies given to Frederick Salmon of *Master Humphrey*, Vols I and II, and of the first independent edition of *Barnaby*.

[4] I.e. the "Master Humphrey" interpolations. But the sections "Master Humphrey from his Clock-Side in the Chimney-Corner" at the beginning and end of *Old Curiosity Shop* were retained in the copies specially prepared. Perhaps at this date CD still planned to keep the "Master Humphrey" framework and considered only the stories and Pickwick incidents "foreign". In the Preface to the First Cheap Edn, 1848, he described himself as "especially unwilling"—when detaching *Old Curiosity Shop* from *Master Humphrey* (as he did completely for the first separate edn)—to cancel "the opening paper" (see *To* Macready, 29 Jan 40, *fn*).

[5] For the paging of the first edn of *Old Curiosity Shop*, see *To* Macready, 27 Dec 41, *fn*.

He has left a considerable property (chiefly in cheese and halfpence) buried in different parts of the garden; and the new Raven—for I have a successor[1]—administers to the effects. He had buried in one place, a brush[2] (which I have made two efforts to write plainly) a very large hammer, and several raw potatoes, which were discovered yesterday. He was very uneasy just before death, and wandering in his mind, talked amazing non-sense.—My servant thinks the hammer troubled him. It is supposed to have been stolen from a carpenter of vindictive disposition.—He was heard to threaten,—and I am not without suspicions of Poison.

Believe me at all times | Faithfully Yours<br>CHARLES DICKENS

I beg my compliments to Miss Meredith whose cold, I hope, is better.

## *To* WASHINGTON IRVING, 21 APRIL 1841

MS Huntington Library.

1 Devonshire Terrace York Gate | Regents Park London<br>April The Twenty First 1841.

My Dear Sir.

There is no man in the World who could have given me the heartfelt pleasure you have, by your kind note of the Thirteenth of last Month.[3] There is no living writer, and there are very few among the dead, whose approbation I should feel so proud to earn. And with everything you have written, upon my shelves, and in my thoughts, and in my heart of hearts, I may honestly and truly say so. If you could know how earnestly I write this, you would be glad to read it—as I hope you will be, faintly guessing at the warmth of the hand I autographically hold out to you, over the broad Atlantic.

I wish I could find in your welcome letter, some hint of an intention to visit England. I can't. I have held it at arm's length, and taken a bird's-eye view of it after reading it a great many times, but there is no greater encouragement in it this way than on a microscopic inspection. I should love to go with you—as I have gone, God knows how often—into Little Britain, and Eastcheap, and Green Arbour Court, and Westminster Abbey.[4] I should like to travel with you, outside the last of the coaches, down to Bracebridge Hall.[5] It would make my heart glad to compare notes with you about that shabby gentleman in the oilcloth hat and

---

[1] Not up to his predecessor: see *To* Mrs S. C. Hall, 2 Dec.

[2] Crossed out twice and written a third time.

[3] Described in F, III, 1, 196, as "a very hearty letter . . . about little Nell and the *Curiosity Shop*" (cf. Irving *to* Mrs Storrow, below), which "very

strongly revived" CD's earlier idea of going to America (see Vol. 1, p. 564).

[4] All these are described in *The Sketch-Book of Geoffrey Crayon, Gent.*, 1820.

[5] For the coach-journey, followed by Christmas at Bracebridge Hall, see *The Sketch-Book.*

red-nose who sat in the nine-cornered back parlor at the Masons' Arms[1]—
and about Robert Preston[2]—and the tallow chandler's widow[3] whose sitting
room is second nature to me—and about all those delightful places and
people that I used to walk about and dream of in the daytime when a very
small and not over-particularly-taken-care-of boy. I have a good deal to
say too about that dashing Alonzo De Ojeda[4] that you can't help being
fonder of than you ought to be—and much to hear concerning Moorish
Legend, and poor unhappy Boabdil.[5] Diedrich Knickerbocker[6] I have
worn to death in my pocket—and yet I should shew you his mutilated[7]
carcass—with a joy past all expression.[8]

I have been so accustomed to associate you with my pleasantest and
happiest thoughts, and with my leisure hours, that I rush at once into full
confidence with you, and fall—as it were naturally, and by the very laws of
gravity—into your open arms. Questions come thronging to my pen as to
the lips of people who meet after long hoping to do so. I don't know
what to say first, or what to leave unsaid, and am constantly disposed to
break off and tell you again how glad I am this moment has arrived.

My Dear Washington Irving I cannot thank you enough for your cordial
and generous praise, or tell you what deep and lasting gratification it has
[given me].[9] I hope to have many letters from you, and to exchange a
frequent correspondence. I send this to say so. After the first two or three,
I shall settle down into a connected style, and become gradually rational.

[1] See "The Boar's Head Tavern, Eastcheap" in *The Sketch-Book*. In his speech at the New York Dinner, Feb 42, CD referred again to the man with a red nose and oilskin hat, whom Irving had "left sitting" in the small back parlour of the "Mason's Arms"—and was still "sitting there" when CD came away: "Yes, gentlemen, it was the same man . . ." (*Speeches*, ed. K. J. Fielding, p. 30).

[2] "Whilom drawer" at the Boar's Head, whose ghost, while "airing itself in the churchyard" one night, heard "the well-known call of 'Waiter!' from the Boar's Head, and made its sudden appearance in the midst of a roaring club" (*The Sketch-Book*).

[3] "The venerable chronicler of East-cheap" in the same sketch.

[4] A Spanish adventurer, described by Irving in *Voyages and Discoveries of the Companions of Columbus*, 1831, as a "hot-headed and bold-hearted cavalier". He led a rival expedition to the West Indies 1499, but was finally outwitted by Columbus's lieutenant.

[5] Boabdil el Chico, Moorish King of Granada; known as El Zogoybi, "the unfortunate", because the astrologers predicted at his birth that the kingdom of Granada would fall to the Spaniards during his reign. This and the many other misfortunes which befell him are described in Irving's *A Chronicle of the Conquest of Granada*, 1829.

[6] *A History of New York*, ... By Diedrich Knickerbocker, 1809. Leading up from the creation of the world to the present time, it burlesqued the pride and pedantry of many American histories. In this "masterpiece of learned spoofing", says Van Wyck Brooks (*The World of Washington Irving*, 1945, p. 137), "Irving's talent declared itself, the first high literary talent the country had known."

[7] Written "mutilitated".

[8] Well as CD knew Irving's work (see also his speech in New York, 18 Feb 42: *Speeches*, ed. K. J. Fielding, pp. 29–31), its influence on his writing was of little account, though some contemporary English (but not American) reviewers claimed to have found evidence of it in *Sketches* and *Pickwick*.

[9] Cancelled by CD, but nothing else written in its place.

You know what the feeling is after having written a letter, sealed it, and sent it off. I shall picture you reading this and answering it, before it has lain one night in the Post Office. Ten to one that before the fastest packet could reach New York, I shall be writing again.

Do you suppose the Post office clerks care to receive letters? I have my doubts. They get into a dreadful habit of indifference. A Postman, I imagine, is quite callous. Conceive his delivering one to himself, without being startled by a preliminary double knock—!

Always your faithful friend

CHARLES DICKENS[1]

[1] On 25 May 41 Irving told his niece Mrs Storrow of the arrival of this letter "from that glorious fellow, Dickens (Boz), in reply to the one I wrote, expressing my heartfelt delight with his writings, and my yearnings towards himself. See how completely we sympathize in feeling" (*The Life and Letters of Washington Irving*, ed. Pierre Irving, 1862–4, III, 128). He replied on 26 May: "My dear Sir, | I cannot tell you how happy the receipt of your letter has made me, for it has convinced me that I was not mistaken in you; that you are just what your writings made me imagine you, and that it only wanted a word to bring us together in heart and soul. Do not suppose me, however, a man prompt at these spontaneous overtures of friendship. You are the only man I have ever made such an advance to. In general I seek no acquaintances and keep up no correspondences out of my family connexion; but towards you there was a strong impulse, which for some time I resisted, but which at length overpowered me; and I now am glad it did so. | You flatter my languid and declining pride of authorship by quoting many of my sketchings of London life, written long since, and too slight as I supposed, to make any lasting impression; but what are my slight and isolated sketches to your ample and complete pictures which lay all the recesses of London life before us? And then the practical utility, the operative benevolence which pervade all your portraitures of the lowest life, and give a value and dignity to your broadest humor; that exquisite tact which enables you to carry your readers through the veriest dens of vice and villainy, without a breath to shock the ear or a stain to sully the robe of the most shrinking delicacy.... I have a peculiar relish for your pictures of low English life, and especially those about the metropolis, and connected with public fairs &c., from having studied them much during my residence in England. I had a perfect passion for exploring London, and visiting every place celebrated in story or song ... I wanted to write about all these scenes ... but some how or other my pen seemed spell bound; ... I felt too much like a stranger in the land ... All this makes me the more sensible to the fullness as well as the fidelity of your picturings.... | I have just been reading again your Pickwick papers ... Old Pickwick is the Quixote of commonplace life, and as with the Don, we begin by laughing at him and end by loving him. Sam Weller and his father I could swear I had seen fifty times in my loiterings about Coach offices and Inn yards—all the world knows the truth and force of their portraits. I have a great fancy, however, for the less obtrusive merits of those worthies Bob Sawyer and Ben Allen; ... Dick Swiveller too, the exquisite Dick Swiveller who is so continually within a hair's breadth of becoming a scamp but is carried safely through every temptation by the native goodness of his heart.... Let me ask you one question. Mantalini, the inimitable Mantalini! is he a mere creation of the brain or did any mortal sit for the portrait. For judging as an artist, I should think you had the "living subject" for a model, but that you clothed and heightened it by the copious additions of your fancy. | I have been dwelling on your comic picturings but

## *To* AUGUSTUS TRACEY,[1] 26 APRIL [1841]*

MS University of Texas. *Date:* 26 Apr was Monday in 1841.

1 Devonshire Terrace | York Gate Regents Park.
Monday Evg. April The Twenty Sixth.

My Dear Sir.

Since I left you to-day, I have been greatly distressed in my mind, concerning our wretched friend the (supposed) tailor.[2] May I ask you to apply the inclosed trifle in any way that you think will do him the most good, and to exercise your own discretion—for none can have so good a one as you in such a case—either to pay his fine and give him the rest, or keep him his five days,[3] and then let him have the whole to start with. In either case, I would like to send him, besides, a suit of cast-off clothes, which (if you give me your permission to forward them to the jail; I don't like to venture on sending them without it) my man shall bring directly.

I cannot express to you how much moved I have been by witnessing the results of your humanity and goodness.[4] Men who have so much in their

you have proved yourself equally the master in the dark and terrible of real life: not the robbers, and tyrants and villains of high strained romance and feudal times and castellated scenes; but the dangerous and desperate villainy that lurks in the midst of the busy world and besets the every day haunts of society . . . And then the exquisite and sustained pathos, so deep, but so pure and healthy, as carried throughout the wanderings of little Barbara [*thus*!] and her poor old Grandfather. I declare to you there is a moral sublimity and beauty wrought out with a matchless simplicity of pencil in the whole of this story, that leaves me at a loss how sufficiently to express my admiration— and then there are passages (like that of the schoolmasters remarks on neglected graves) which come upon us suddenly and gleam forth apparently unde-signedly, but which are perfect gems of language. . . ." (MS Huntington).

[1] Lieut. Augustus Frederick Tracey, RN (1798–1878), Governor of the Westminster House of Correction, Tot-hill Fields, 1834–?55. In the Navy from 1811; saw service as midshipman on the *Royal Oak* in the battle for New Orleans Dec 1814, in which G. L. Chesterton (see Vol. 1, p. 101*n*), though then unknown to him, also took part; obtained his commission 1828; served in the Mediterranean 1830–1 and

1833–4; placed on retired list 1834. CD first met him on the visit to Tothill Fields 26 Apr arranged for him by Francis Smedley (see *To* Smedley, 1 Apr and *fn*), to see "the Boy Jones". Like Chesterton, Governor of Coldbath Fields, became a personal friend of CD's, taking a keen interest in Urania Cottage, Miss Coutts's home for fallen women in Shepherd's Bush, many of whose inmates came from his prison.

[2] Unidentified. This and *To* Tracey, 28 Apr and 11 May, seem all to refer to the same man, admitted while CD was present (see 11 May).

[3] The normal term at Tothill Fields was anything from one week to three years—though the prison also housed a few debtors and political prisoners (e.g. the Chartist Ernest Jones) for longer periods.

[4] Tracey was a conscientious Gov-ernor, and his prison well run—on the "silent system". It was nevertheless one of London's harshest: no trades were taught, and oakum-picking and the treadwheel were the only labour provided (see Philip Collins, *Dickens and Crime*, 1962, pp. 65–6). For CD's un-favourable comparison of prisons he saw in America with Tothill Fields (and Coldbath Fields—which dealt with similar offenders, but was equipped for weaving, shoemaking and tailoring as well as oakum-picking and the tread-

power and acquit themselves so well, deserve the gratitude of mankind. Accept the thanks and assurances of esteem of one among them who loves, and truly loves the rest. It is the only qualification I have for offering them to you.

Very faithfully Yours

Lieut. Tracey | &c &c &c                     CHARLES DICKENS

## *To* BASIL HALL, 27 APRIL 1841

MS Brotherton Library, Leeds.

Devonshire Terrace | April The Twenty Seventh 1841.

My Dear Hall.

Post just going—compression of sentiments required—Bust received[1]—likeness *amazing*—recognizable instantly if encountered on the summit of the Great Pyramid—Scotch anecdote most striking and most distressing[2]—dreamed of it—babbies well—wife ditto—yours the same, I hope?—Seaport sketches,[3] one of those ideas that improves in promise as they are pondered on—*Good*, I am certain—Ever faithfully, and at present hastily —[4]

BOZ.

wheel), see Vol. III. The interest to him of the "(supposed) tailor" (not a real criminal) seems partly to have been that his wits were "ricketty" (*To* Tracey, 28 Apr)—like Barnaby's.

[1] Hall had written on 14 Apr: "My brother writes to me that the cast of my Bust [*see* To *Hall, ?31 Mar and* fn] is ready for you, & I shall tell him, by this post, to have it sent to your house." He then spoke of the varying responses that requests of his had met, now that he was "on half pay & in plain clothes"—sometimes "painful snubs", at other times "ready kindnesses": "I have seldom, accordingly, felt more anxious than I did for *your* answer to my request about the bust. I could not but know that you would at once see through the case, & detect that my proximate object was a job for Joseph & I felt uncertain how far your good will for me, personally, or your favourable consideration of my lucubrations, printiwise [*thus*], might induce you to spare me the great mortification of a rebuff" (MS Huntington).

[2] On 19 Apr Hall had written to CD: "There is a touch in your way in one part of the following extract which I think will strike you. It is from a friend in Scotland, who being in some distress at home wished to have the assistance of a friend. | 'But' says the writer 'I cannot get her to help me for she is in attendance on the death bed of her young cousin Mrs. [*a blank in MS*]. You know who I mean?—poor thing—she was married just two months ago, & went with her husband to visit his family before setting off with him to India. She took cold, & inflamation [*thus*] there, & has been brought home in a rapid consumption. She was just a fortnight gone when she was brought back to die. The flowers I sent to deck out her wedding breakfast, were still unwithered when I called to enquire about her, & heard the Doctor say there was not a shadow of hope! She is quite calm & happy, poor thing' " (MS Rutgers University Library).

[3] Hall's proposed book about Portsmouth, never published (see 16 Mar, *fn*).

[4] A letter as Alfred Jingle would have written it.

## *To* T. N. TALFOURD, 27 APRIL [1841]

Text from R. S. Mackenzie, *Life of CD*, Philadelphia, 1870, p. 214. *Date:* misdated 1840 by Mackenzie and N; 27 Apr was Tuesday in 1841; references to the sonnet and Ewart (see *To* Forster, 3 May) support that year.

Devonshire Terrace,
Tuesday, April the Twenty-seventh.

My Dear Talfourd,

Many thanks for the Sonnet.[1] Do you know Ewart? I want, on behalf of an oppressed lady,[2] to remind him of a promise he made her relative to the presentation of a petition to the House. I don't like to approach a man of his kidney, without an introduction. Can you give me one in a couple of lines?[3]

Faithfully Always,
CHARLES DICKENS

## *To* LEITCH RITCHIE,[4] 27 APRIL [1841]

MS John Rylands Library. *Date:* clearly 1841 on handwriting.

1 Devonshire Terrace | York Gate Regents Park
April The Twenty Seventh.

My Dear Sir.

Believe me that *pecuniary* considerations would have no influence with me, if I could possibly comply with your request, in the matter of the Friendship's Offering.[5] But I cannot. While the Clock is going, my hands are tied. I have not turned aside from it to write one line for anything else, although I have been very strongly and earnestly solicited; nor can I. If I could, I would most cheerfully assist you.

You will be glad to hear that the book for Mrs. Macrone's benefit to which you kindly sent a very interesting contribution,[6] is coming out *at last*.

Dear Sir | Faithfully Yours

Leitch Ritchie Esquire.                                  CHARLES DICKENS

[1] Clearly the sonnet "Composed in view of Eton College, after leaving a Son there for the first time", Talfourd's contribution to *The Pic Nic Papers* (1, 54): see next letter.

[2] Possibly Mrs Booth: see letter to her of 4 May—the day after CD's visit to Ewart "about 'the Cry from the Oppressed' " (*To* Forster, 3 May).

[3] Talfourd replied: "I send you a note to [Ewart]. It is too much honor for the like of him to be introduced to you . . . you will gain no redress for the fair Petitioner from the House of Commons" (Anderson Galleries catalogue, March 1916, omitting Ewart's name).

[4] Leitch Ritchie (?1800–65; *DNB*), novelist and writer of books of travel (letterpress for *Heath's Picturesque Annual* and *Turner's Annual Tour*); for some time editor of the *Era*, and first editor of the *Indian News and Chronicle of Eastern Affairs*, 1840; in later life edited *Chambers's Journal*.

[5] *Friendship's Offering: a Literary Album*, an Annual, with steel engravings after Chalon and others. Ruskin contributed some of his earliest poems to it 1840–1, while at Oxford. The 1842 vol. was the first Ritchie edited.

[6] "Some Account of Marcus Bell, the Convict" (*The Pic Nic Papers*, 1, 85).

## *To* WILLIAM SHOBERL, 27 APRIL 1841*

MS Morgan Library.

Devonshire Terrace | April The Twenty Seventh 1841.

My Dear Sir

I couldn't write to you yesterday, for I had not heard from Mr. Browne. He says that *certainly* he will finish his plates by the middle of next week—and I have no doubt he will.[1] Please to send him two steel plates directly, and to tell the Printer to be quick in sending me a set of the proof sheets,—with a view to the subjects of the designs.[2]

Mr. Serjeant Talfourd's Sonnet I inclose. I have a little song I should wish to find room for.[3] It will not occupy more than a page. You shall have it tomorrow.

Mr. Forster, it seems, is writing a short paper.[4] If you will instruct the printer to send a boy to 58 Lincolns Inn Fields for it on Friday Morning, it will be ready.

Have you sent to Mr. Cruikshank?[5]

Faithfully Yours

W. Shoberl Esquire. CHARLES DICKENS

## *To* AUGUSTUS TRACEY, 28 APRIL 1841*

MS University of Texas.

Devonshire Terrace
Wednesday The Twenty Eighth April | 1841.

Dear Sir.

I was in the very act of acknowledging the receipt of your first note, and assuring you that I heartily reciprocated all its friendly contents, when your second arrived.

It is impossible to doubt the wisdom and propriety of your intention, in reference to our love-lorn friend,—respecting whose ricketty intellects by the way, I would rather take his face's evidence than his sister's. If you

[1] Browne, presumably in reply to an urgent note from CD, had written: "I have just got one boot on, intending to come round to you, but you have done me out of a capital excuse to myself for idling away this fine morning. ... I think by the beginning of next or the middle (*certain*) I shall have done the plates—but, in the scraps of copy that I have I can see but *one good* subject, so, if you know of another pray send it me" (MS Huntington).

[2] Browne did six illustrations for *The Pic Nic Papers*.

[3] Probably one by Overs (see *To*

Overs, 27 Oct 40), but not included in the book.

[4] Clearly "John Dryden and Jacob Tonson" (*The Pic Nic Papers*, I, 55), signed "I.F.". A list of the proposed contents of *The Pic Nic Papers* in CD's hand (MS Berg; drafted Summer 1838 on evidence of the handwriting) includes "Booksellers of the last Queen's reign—John Forster"; and Tonson, Dryden's publisher, would have been one of them.

[5] To inquire about his two plates for *The Pic Nic Papers* (cf. *To* Cruikshank, 13 May).

will bestow the fifteen shillings[1] in any portions you please on any objects who may seem deserving of such poor aid when they travel into the world again, from your seclusion, you will gratify me very much.

As you say nothing about the clothes, and as I take it for granted that his master will not like him the worse for a slight improvement in his appearance, I send them herewith. They will do the poor creature no harm at any rate, and may do him service.

I am truly indebted to you on every score for the kind interest you have shewn in this matter, and the very great pains you have taken. But the being regardless of trouble when good is to be done, must be so common with you, that it would be impertinence to thank you for it.

Believe me with sincerity | My Dear Sir

Lieutenant Tracey                               [CHARLES DICKENS][2]
&c   &c   &c

## *To* W. HARRISON AINSWORTH, 29 APRIL 1841

MS Morgan Library.

Devonshire Terrace | April The Twenty Ninth /41,
My Dear Ainsworth.

With all imaginable pleasure. I quite look forward to the day.[3] It is an age since we met, and it ought not to be.

The artist has just sent home your Nickleby. He suggested variety, pleading his fancy and genius. As a wilful binder must have his way, I put the best face on the matter and gave him, his. I will bring it, together with the Pickwick, to your house-warming with me.

The old Royal George went down in consequence of having too much weight on one side.[4] I trust the New First Rate of that name,[5] won't be

---

[1] The "trifle" sent on 26 Apr was presumably a sovereign (see 11 May). Five shillings of it had probably been used by Tracey to pay the "(supposed) tailor's" fine (see 26 Apr).

[2] Signature has been cut away.

[3] On 28 Apr Ainsworth had written from Kensal Manor House, to which he had moved in Mar 41 from Kensal Lodge (where CD had in earlier days so often visited him): "I begin to think it long since we met; and I also long to show you my new house. Will you therefore dine with me on Saturday the 8th. of May at six o'clock, and set both my longings at rest?—I have been often intending to call upon you—but perhaps you know from experience that the best intentions are seldom fulfilled. The meeting of Saturday will be a sort of inaugural dinner, being the first I

shall give in my new abode. Do not disappoint me" (MS Huntington). Forster had also been invited, and wrote to CD on 29 Apr "Do you go to THE MANOR HOUSE?" (MS Private). The Manor House, so called because built, early in the century, on the manorial lands of Willesden, was a large one-storied house to which Ainsworth, needing a large house for his three daughters and his own entertaining, added another storey. Mrs Touchet (see Vol. 1, p. 277*n*) continued to live in a part of Kensal Lodge near by.

[4] The flag-ship HMS *Royal George* (subject of Campbell's famous poem) had sunk at anchor in Spithead 29 Aug 1782. Attempts to raise her continued until 1840.

[5] No. 1 of *George Cruikshank's Omnibus* (see *To* Cruikshank, 2 May,

heavy anywhere.  There seems to me to be too much whisker for a shilling,[1]
but that's a matter of taste—

Faithfully Yours always
CHARLES DICKENS[2]

William Harrison Ainsworth Esquire

## *To* JOHN FORSTER, [29 APRIL 1841]

Extract in F, II, ix, 167 (*aa*), dated 29 Apr by Forster; extract in F, II, x,
173 (*bb*), dated simply "April" by Forster, but clearly also 29th since both
extracts answer a letter from Forster dated "Thursday" [29 Apr].[3]

[a]I am getting on very slowly.  I want to stick to the story; and the fear of
committing myself, because of the impossibility of trying back or altering a
syllable, makes it much harder than it looks.[4]  It was too bad of me to give
you the trouble of cutting the number,[5] but I knew so well you would do it
in the right places.  For what Harley would call the "onward work" I
really think I have some famous thoughts.[a]

[b]How often used Black[6] and I to quarrel about the effect of the poor-law
bill![7]  Walter comes in upon the cry.[8]  See whether the whigs go out upon
it.[b9]

*fn*).  In a postscript to his letter Ainsworth had said: "Our friend G. C.
brings out his Omnibus this month.  I
hope it will not turn out to be the Loss
of the Royal George—or what would be
still worse the George and blue *bore*."

[1] I.e. too much Cruikshank—whose
whiskers, covering his chin, were
notable in a mainly beardless period.
The *Omnibus* cost 1/-.

[2] CD received two further invitations
to dinner with Ainsworth during 1841
(MSS Huntington): one for 28 June
when he was in Scotland, the other undated.

[3] Forster's letter (MS Private) asked:
"How do you get on?"  A few lines
lower it announced: "Walter is returned
for Nottingham"—a reference to the
Nottingham by-election of 26 Apr 41
(see below).

[4] Almost certainly refers to No. 60
(Chs 27 and 28; published 22 May), in
which Mr Chester embarks on his plot
to alienate Edward and Emma.

[5] Presumably No. 59.  The proofs are
not extant; but comparison of the MS
and printed text reveals the cutting—in
a rhetorical passage in Ch. 25 (paragraph
5, after "eternal frown")—of "ye lim-
ners of God's attributes who can devise

no fitter crown for Mercy's head than
wreaths of ever-burning fire; ye
fashioners of a false cross from twisted
thunderbolts and scourges", where
CD's pen had clearly run away with
him.

[6] John Black (1783–1855; *DNB*),
editor of the *Morning Chronicle*: see
Vol. I, p. 83*n*.

[7] The Poor Law Amendment Act,
1834, which CD had attacked in the
early chapters of *Oliver* (see Vol. I,
p. 231*n*).  In 1840 the powers of the
three Poor Law Commissioners had
been renewed for a year only.  A bill to
continue the Act's working for ten years
had been moved by Lord John Russell
29 Jan 41; but over 500 petitions against
it had followed, and it was withdrawn
May 41.  It finally became law July 42
under the Conservative Govt, for a
period of five years.

[8] John Walter (1776–1847; *DNB*),
chief proprietor of *The Times* and
moving spirit behind its rise to emin-
ence, fought his by-election campaign
as Conservative candidate for Nottingham, a Liberal stronghold for 30 years,
exclusively on opposition to the New
Poor Law.  The alliance between Tory
and Radical opponents of the Poor Law

## *To* GEORGE CRUIKSHANK, 2 MAY 1841

MS Colonel Richard Gimbel.

Devonshire Terrace | Sunday May The Second 1841.

My Dear George.

Many thanks for, and all good wishes to, the "Buss".[1] It is wery light, wery easy on the springs, well horsed, driv in a slap up style, and altogether an uncommon spicy con-sarn. "Mind Coachman" as the old ladies say "you take me as fur as ever you go, and don't you put me down till you come to the very end of the journey."

I object, Sir, to one thing—and that is, your treatment of that 'ere wind-galled, wall-eyed, spavined, knock-knee'd, gallows-bred leader, Grant[2]—known down our yard as the Blunderer. You an't half nor a quarter sharp enough with him Sir;[3] you should have established a raw on him as 'ud ha' made him wince till sich time as he wos made into dog's meat for halfbred mongrels—the only animals as 'ud condescend to eat him—and them only on account of his amazing sarce. I should ha' liked to have had the punishing of him Sir. *I* wouldn't ha' let him off so easy.[4]

Seriously. A man has no right to live upon lies, and to trade in reputations as that scoundrel does. With an air of truth, he deliberately sits down, to tell at so much a line, what he knows to be lies about you (because he invented them) and which are calculated to give people a most unfavourable impression of your habits and character.[5] Vermin, when caught, are

became known as "the Treaty of Nottingham". Walter was returned on 26 Apr by 238 votes, but was defeated by the Liberal candidate in the General Election that summer.

[9] It was in fact on the Corn Law issue that Melbourne's Govt was defeated at the end of May, but the anti-Poor Law alliance was a strong factor in the Conservative victory at the General Election which followed.

[1] *George Cruikshank's Omnibus*, No. 1, edited by Laman Blanchard and lavishly illustrated by Cruikshank. Nine monthly Nos appeared, May 41–Jan 42.

[2] James Grant (1802–79; *DNB*): see Vol. I, p. 131*n*.

[3] The first No. of the *Omnibus* opens with "My Portrait", in which Cruikshank quotes 11 statements made about him in Grant's *Portraits of Public Characters*, 1841, II, 236–51, qualifies some and mockingly refutes others.

[4] Apparently CD had not read Grant's *Portraits* (in a letter of 3 Jan

54 he told him he had read none of his books); so his comments in this letter must have been based on excerpts Cruikshank had quoted in his *Omnibus* (and perhaps a general report from Forster). Grant lavished praise on Cruikshank as "one of the most original geniuses . . . which the world ever witnessed", and described his humorous drawings as "unequalled, nay, unapproached, by any other artist which the present or any previous age has produced"; but all this Cruikshank acknowledged with no more than the statement that "the writer . . . was evidently animated by a spirit of kindness"—and went on to show that Grant had misrepresented him as a person.

[5] The impression of Cruikshank as a frequenter of low public-houses ("the gallery in which George first studied his art"); as an old and close friend of Hone, then an "infidel"; as a "decided liberal"; and, in social life, eccentric and rude.

never tickled, but killed outright; and having got my foot upon that louse of literature, I'd have squashed him ruthlessly.[1]

Faithfully Yours always

George Cruikshank Esquire      CHARLES DICKENS

## *To* J. BLACKBURN, 3 MAY 1841

MS Free Library of Philadelphia.

Devonshire Terrace | Monday May The Third 1841

My Dear Sir.

Many thanks to you for the Magazine, which is a great curiosity. As you may suppose that I haven't read my second self "right through", you will not give me any credit for returning them within the specified time.[2]

Good God how hot these Oriental Magazines look! You're so used to them, that I dare say you don't see it, but the pages are parched—burnt up—suggestive of drought and scorching heat. Some Indian birds we have, began to sing directly the parcel was brought in. *I* began to drink claret out of a tumbler before I had turned over the leaves of the Second Number. And all last night, I dreamed about Vishnu, and Hindoo Temples, and Indian Jugglers sitting upon nothing, and Tigers coming unexpectedly to dinner parties and bounding away into remote Jungles with English Butlers—Elephants too were so common as to be quite ridiculous; and I ate rice by hundred weights.

Faithfully Yours

J. Blackburn Esquire      CHARLES DICKENS

## *To* JOHN FORSTER, 3 MAY [1841]

MS Victoria & Albert Museum (FC). *Date:* 3 May was Monday in 1841; handwriting and pale blue watermarked paper support that year.

Monday Morning the Third of May.

My Dear Forster.

I should have been very glad to go to that hallowed spot on which the eyes of Europe and the beating hearts of the civilized world are unalter-

---

[1] Grant's portraits were gossipy and over-personal, and no doubt often inaccurate; but what would have infuriated CD most were probably the passages about his subjects' monetary affairs. The portrait of Macready, for instance, contained references to financial help he had given to relations, and the statement (II, 235): "[Mr. Macready] lately was, and I believe still is, the proprietor of the Granby Hotel, at Harrowgate [*thus*], which, if my information be correct, brings him in £400 per annum." (Macready had in fact invested in this hotel 1833, but disposed of it 1835: *Diaries*, I, 58 and 259.) Writing on Cruikshank, Grant gave the sums he had recently been receiving for each plate as 12–15 guineas. (For *Oliver* he received 12 gns a plate: see *Oliver Twist*, ed. K. Tillotson, p. 392.)

[2] Blackburn had probably sent him the numbers of the *Lighthouse*, Madras, containing "Pickwick in India", in seven chapters, by the Editor. See later vols.

ably fixed[1]—but I had previously made an engagement to be with Ewart at 4 o'Clock, about "the Cry from the Oppressed" &c.[2]

From the eloquent and illustrious Member for Wigan, I shall come straight to you. Wherefore, between half past four and five, expect the writer hereof.—Perhaps at half price[3]—there *is*[4] one Bullock[5] to be seen— I say no more—

Dinner at the Grays Inn, I suppose?

Faithfully

CD.

This rain will do good.


## *To* MRS BOOTH, 4 MAY 1841†

MS Colonel Richard Gimbel.

Private

Devonshire Terrace. | Tuesday May The Fourth 1841.

Dear Mrs. Booth.

*a*I was not home until very late last night, and did not see your letter until this morning. I have an appointment, I am sorry to say, which will take me out at the hour you name; but I shall be visible on Sunday at one, or[6] tomorrow afternoon at half past four.*a*

I could not bring Mr. Booth[7] to Lord Jeffrey's recollection, neither was

---

[1] Presumably the RA Summer Exhibition: this was the first day of public admission.

[2] Possibly Mrs Booth: see next.

[3] A suggestion that they should go to the theatre, for the later part of the performance.

[4] Underlined twice.

[5] Possibly a joke-name for the actor Henry Wallack, to whose "ominous jowls" a letter from Bulwer to Forster, 5 Nov 40, refers (see *Bulwer and Macready*, ed. C. H. Shattuck, p. 171). He was appearing at the Haymarket on 3 May 41 in the second piece (W. B. Bernard's *St. Mary's Eve*), so CD and Forster would have seen him "at half price". An otherwise unexplained letter from Forster to CD of 13 May looks like a continuation of the joke: "My Dear Dickens | You will be delighted to hear that our friend Bullock was presented to Her Majesty last night— yesterday, that is, at Levee. | 'Mr Henry Bullock by Viscount Maynard'— is the significant announcement of the fact. | It is reported that Her Majesty means to make B. the medium of com-

munication with her new premier, | God bless her! | Ever Yours | John Forster" (MS Mr L. C. Staples).

*aa* Previously unpublished.

[6] "tomorrow evening between seven" cancelled here.

[7] David Booth (1766–1846; *DNB*), author of *An Analytical Dictionary of the English Language*, 1835 (only Vol. 1 published). Born in Scotland; self-taught; settled in London *c.* 1820. Superintended for several years publications of the Society for the Diffusion of Useful Knowledge, for which he wrote *The Art of Brewing*, 1829, and *The Art of Wine-making in All its Branches*, 1834. Published *A Letter to the Rev. T. R. Malthus*, 1823, and other works. Dr Robert Blakey (*Memoirs*, ed. H. Miller, 1879, p. 75) described him as "one of the most extraordinary personages [he had] met with for some time": he was scarcely five feet high, "of very dark visage, eyes very red and watery, and presenting altogether an impish and fiendish look. He was, however, most kind"—and there the likeness to Quilp ends.

he acquainted with his writings. I would advise you not to urge the matter in that quarter, as I think he does not wish to interfere. I know something of Macauley,[1] and if you like will inclose him Mr. Booth's memorial, myself; but it *must* have added to it the facts of his apoplexy and illness, strongly stated. As it stands, I am quite certain the case is not strong enough to attract attention among a hundred others.[2]

Faithfully Yours

Mrs. Booth                                              CHARLES DICKENS

## *To* JOHN HUDSON,[3] 5 MAY 1841

MS University of Texas.

Private

1 Devonshire Terrace, | York Gate, Regents Park, London.<br>Wednesday May The Fifth./41.

Mr. Charles Dickens sends his Compliments to Mr. Hudson, and begs to inclose him a cheque for the amount of his account.[4] Mr. Dickens does so, by reason of its easy transmission; but if it should be inconvenient, he begs Mr. Hudson to return it, and mention any other mode of payment that may suit him better.

Mr. Dickens has to thank Mr. Hudson for the ingenious legend concerning the Punch, which he has read with breathless interest. With regard to the Punch itself, it is impossible to praise it too highly, as all who taste it at Mr. Dickens' table agree in saying.

## *To* W. C. MACREADY, [?6 MAY 1841]*

MS Private. *Date:* Handwriting points to Mar–May 41. Clearly after Macready's decision of 6 Apr to take over Drury Lane, but not in Apr when the Haymarket was closed; almost certainly refers to the only tragedy Macready performed in during May—Byron's *Werner*, on the 5th.

My Dear Macready.

Kate will be delighted.[5]—Maclise knows all about it.

---

[1] Thus in MS. Thomas Babington Macaulay (1800–59; *DNB*). At this time Whig MP for Edinburgh, contributor to the *Edinburgh Review*, and had begun his *History of England*. CD had possibly met him at Holland House or through Rogers.

[2] Booth had been granted £50 by the Literary Fund in Dec 40, after suffering a third attack of paralysis; he was given further grants of £30 in June 42 and £40 in Dec 45 (MS Royal Literary Fund). Peel sent him £50 from the Royal Bounty Fund in 1844.

[3] John Hudson, partner in J. & F. Hudson, wine merchants, 26 Lambeth Hill, Upper Thames Street.

[4] CD's account-book (MS Messrs Coutts) shows a payment of £7.1.0 to J. Hudson on 14 May 41.

[5] Possibly CD was accepting an invitation to meet Rachel (see *To* Miss Coutts, 23 May and *fn*), whom Macready had called on the day before and invited to dinner on the 9th. But he and Catherine are not among the guests Macready listed as present that evening.

I meant to have written you a long letter this morning about last night. But if I followed the dictates of my own heart, I should write to you every time I see you play. There is nothing I know, or can imagine, so exquisitely beautiful, so manly, noble, dignified, true, and brave, as that most exquisite and touching performance.[1] It's Nature refined to the very highest pitch of refinement—its[2] everything it ought to be, or can be: and to talk about it, is presumption and arrogance.

I yearn for the Drury days.—I want King Lear—I want everything— I want 'em all at once.

Always Your faithful friend<br>
and admirer from the heart<br>
CHARLES DICKENS

## *To* LORD JEFFREY, 11 MAY 1841

MS Widener Collection, Harvard.

Devonshire Terrace | Eleventh May 1841.

My Dear Lord Jeffrey.

I told you I was going to beg the favor of your acceptance of a Copy of the Old Curiosity Shop. Here it is.[3] The binder, agreeably to my directions has cut out and pasted out all foreign matter, and it has the unique advantage, consequently, of being regularly irregular in the paging.[4]

It is in a more durable form than its ordinary dress,[5] and as it is not likely to appear in any other fashion for some years to come,[6] I hope you will receive it and keep it for my sake. If you knew how much I *mean* in sending it to you,[7] you would not wonder at my only *saying* that the praise you have bestowed upon the tale[8] has afforded me more real and enduring pleasure than any other man living could give me.

Believe me with sincere regard | Faithfully Yours

Lord Jeffrey

CHARLES DICKENS

[1] Werner was generally considered his finest performance of all. Macready's greatness, says G. H. Lewes, was not in representing high, heroic, ideal characters, but in depicting a wide range of the unheroic, among them Werner (see "Was Macready a Great Actor?", *Leader*, 8 Feb 51; reprinted in *Dramatic Essays, John Forster, G. H. Lewes*, ed. William Archer and R. W. Lowe, 1896, pp. 126–34). What he could do with an "unheroic" character CD's epithets show.

[2] Thus in MS.

[3] It is now in the Widener Collection, Harvard, inscribed: "Lord Jeffrey With the regard and esteem of Charles Dickens. Eleventh May 1841".

[4] For a similar copy prepared for Miss Coutts see 20 Apr and *fns*.

[5] Weekly Nos or Monthly Parts.

[6] It did not appear with the correct pagination until the Cheap Edition, 1848.

[7] Cf. Jeffrey's letter of 13 May to Macvey Napier asking him to send the latest *Barnaby* on Saturday, as he "could not possibly live over till Monday without seeing it", and continuing: "You know, I hope, that Dickens and I have sworn eternal friendship" (*Selection from the Correspondence of the late Macvey Napier, Esq.*, ed. by his son, Macvey Napier, 1879, pp. 347–8).

[8] See *To* Forster, 18 Mar.

## *To* AUGUSTUS TRACEY, 11 MAY 1841

Text from N, I, 319.

Devonshire Terrace | Tuesday, Eleventh May 1841

My Dear Sir,

I was afraid our poor friend was damaged in his intellects. Any man who goes to a Police Office without absolute necessity, must be raving mad.

I shall look out for the suit of clothes with some curiosity. I saw a hat going down Oxford Street yesterday, which looked remarkably like mine, and I am pretty sure was the tile of this ill-fated House.

Good God! When I think of him standing in the sun after he got out of the van, with his face to the wall like a scriptural mourner—and call up his desolate figure—with things upon his legs which were a kind of compromise between jack-boots and gaiters—and remember how he burst into tears when you questioned him kindly, and rubbing his dim eyes with his sooty hands wept tears of milk—when I picture him after his real fashion, and think of a clean and very flesh-coloured cupid with blue wings and scarf and bow and arrow complete, looking over his shoulder, I don't know whether to laugh or cry, or to be sad or merry. Heaven knows he is no less an object of pity for his imbecility of mind; and if he could have walked off in as many suits of clothes as there are of cards, he should have been welcome to them.

How right you were about the Sovereign! If he had had it, he would not have been a bit the better for the money, and would have come back the sooner, I dare say.[1]

I suppose you couldn't, in your ingenuity and knowledge of dealing with these unfortunate creatures, bring about a match between him and the fair unknown, formerly in man's attire? If he could be brought to love her instead of the deceitful charmer, and she could be brought to love him instead of the aspiring Footman, and they could go off arm in arm to a Westminster Chapel with a Turnkey to give the girl away, and some light offender who was good company—say Jones—to act as Bridegroom's man, what a happy thing it would be. But I am afraid neither of them can ever forget. There are no waters of oblivion in the silent Gruel.[2]

I am going to ask you one day next week, to let me introduce you to my friend Doctor Elliotson (who is a good, as well as clever man) whose utmost interest I have awakened by a very imperfect description of your humane and wise government. I will write you a line the day before, that I may be sure of not putting you to inconvenience.

My dear Sir | Faithfully yours

[CHARLES DICKENS]

[1] Chesterton at Coldbath Fields seems to have been more lenient over the giving of "small gratuities" to prisoners on their discharge, and found that it worked (see Hepworth Dixon, *The London Prisons*, 1850, pp. 242–3).

[2] "silent" because Tothill Fields was a "silent system" prison; "Gruel", as part of prison diet.

## *To* THOMAS MITTON, 12 MAY 1841

MS Huntington Library.

Twelfth May 1841.

My Dear Mitton

Can't you manage—for once—to be here by 5 tomorrow? I tell you why I ask you. I have been out every day this week, and have scarcely seen the children. If we dine so late as 6, it is their bedtime when the cloth is removed[1]—and I don't like to deprive them of the opportunity of coming down—

Faithfully Always

CD.

## *To* GEORGE CRUIKSHANK, 13 MAY 1841*

MS Dr De Coursey Fales.

Devonshire Terrace. | May The Thirteenth 1841.

My Dear George

I am sorry to trouble you—but obliged—for the Press is stopping. *When* can you let us have the plates for Mrs. Macrone?[2]

One word in answer.

Faithfully Yours always

George Cruikshank Esquire                    CHARLES DICKENS

## *To* T. J. THOMPSON, 13 MAY 1841

Facsimile in George R. Sims, *Among my Autographs*, 1904, p. 31.

Devonshire Terrace | May The Thirteenth 1841.

My Dear Thompson.

Your sisters[3] are going to dine with us—and no strangers, or indeed anybody else that I know of—on Sunday at five. Will you give me the pleasure of seeing you? Take your blister off,[4] and come.

Faithfully Yours

T. J. Thompson Esquire                       CHARLES DICKENS

---

[1] Punctuation confused: possibly comma changed to a dash.

[2] Cruikshank replied the same day: "I think I may safely say in one week from this time—they are nearly finished —but the 'Omnibus' has pushed them aside for a few days" (MS Berg).

[3] Mrs Smithson and Amelia Thompson.

[4] I.e., literally, "your plaster off"; but possibly a joke about Thompson's life of ease (see ?9 Feb 40), and meaning "Pull yourself together".

## *To* AUGUSTUS TRACEY, 18 MAY 1841*

MS University of Texas.

Devonshire Terrace. | Tuesday May The Eighteenth 1841.
My Dear Sir.
If I don't hear from you that it will be any inconvenience, I shall trespass on your kindness so far as to bring the friend I spoke of[1] and two others[2] to view your charge at a quarter past one Tomorrow.[3]

## *To* JOHN OVERS, [?22] MAY [1841]*

MS Mr Robert K. Black. *Date:* The only Sat 21 May during CD's acquaintance with Overs was in 1842—when CD was in America. Handwriting points clearly to 1841. CD was probably writing on Sat 22 May, that year.

Devonshire Terrace | Saturday May The Twenty First.
Dear Mr. Overs.
I have been so very much engaged since I saw you, that I have not had time to read your papers; neither have I seen Mr. Cruikshank[4] who has been very busy too. Therefore, instead of coming tomorrow, wait a few days, and I will write to you.

In haste | Faithfully Yours
CHARLES DICKENS

## *To* MISS BURDETT COUTTS, 23 MAY 1841

MS Morgan Library.

Devonshire Terrace | Sunday Evening
May The Twenty Third 1841.
Dear Miss Coutts.
I return you the Curiosity Shop with the *something* inserted. I meant so much in asking you to accept the book, that I forgot to say anything. Pray forgive me.[5]

[1] Elliotson (see *To* Tracey, 11 May).

[2] One of them was presumably Chauncey Hare Townshend, who in a letter dated "Tuesday" asked CD to tell him "at what hour we are to go to the prisons tomorrow". He ended his letter: "When shall I really enjoy your society? Not in London I fear—heartless London—where idle business chokes the affections, or at least closes over them for a time, even with those whose hearts are warmest" (MS Huntington).

[3] Ending of letter cut away.

[4] About the possible acceptance of Overs's "The Postilion" for *George*

*Cruikshank's Omnibus* (see *To* Cruikshank and *To* Overs, 21 July 41).

[5] Miss Coutts had written on 16 May: "I have just received 'The Old Curiosity Shop' [*see* To *Miss Coutts*, 20 *Apr, and* fn] 'the slowest man in the world' has done his part. But there is *something* sadly wanting in the title page which would greatly enhance its value, I take the liberty of sending it to you in the hope that you will kindly supply what is wanting. At the same time I must beg you to excuse me for I feel I am very troublesome . . . Have you seen Madlle. Rachel if not *pray do*" (MS Huntington).

I have not seen Rachel[1] yet, being unwilling to be forced to believe that anybody or anything could impart an interest to Racine.[2] I mean to wait for Mary Stuart;[3]—I am told she is a wonder, and am prepared to think so.

If anybody should entreat you to go to the Polytechnic Institution[4] and have a Photographic likeness done[5]—don't be prevailed upon, on any terms. The Sun is a great fellow in his way, but portrait painting is not his line. I speak from experience, having suffered dreadfully.

Always believe me, with sincerity,

Faithfully Yours

CHARLES DICKENS

## *To* MRS E. J. STANLEY,[6] 23 MAY [1841]*

MS (copy) Mr George Howard. *Date:* 23 May was Sunday in 1841; the copied signature supports that year. *Address:* clearly Mrs E. J. Stanley since copy is among the Carlisle papers (see *fn*).

Devonshire Terrace. | Sunday Twenty Third May.

Dear Mrs. Stanley.

I am exceedingly sorry to say that I have an engagement for Tuesday which binds me to dine elsewhere, far less pleasantly; but if I should be

---

[1] Elisa Rachel Felix (1821–58), great tragic actress; born in Switzerland of poor Jewish parents; excelled in Corneille and Racine. Made her first of six visits to London in 1841, appearing first in Racine's *Andromaque*, 10 May, at Her Majesty's Theatre. She was greeted with immense enthusiasm.

[2] A view attacked in G. H. Lewes's notice of *Phèdre* in the *Leader*, 6 July 50, as characteristic of too many in Rachel's audience: "They form their views of Art exclusively upon the Shakespeare model, and aiding their prejudices with an adequate ignorance of the language . . . pronounce Racine no poet" (reprinted in *Dramatic Essays*, ed. W. Archer and R. W. Lowe, 1896, p. 82). But Greville, who was present at Rachel's English *début* on 10 May 41, in spite of his "little habitude of French tragedy, and difficulty of hearing and following, . . . thought her very good" and wished "we had anything as good" (*The Greville Memoirs*, Second Part, 1885, II, 6).

[3] By Pierre-Antoine Lebrun (1785–1873), performed 14 June—"an atrocious piece" according to Thackeray (*The Letters and Private Papers of W. M. Thackeray*, ed. G. N. Ray, II,

23); only a well worked out third act gave scope to Rachel's "genius for sarcasm and fury", wrote G. H. Lewes (*Leader*, 27 July 50; reprinted in *Dramatic Essays*, p. 100).

[4] The Royal Polytechnic Institution for the Advancement of the Arts and Practical Science, Cavendish Square, founded 1838.

[5] In Mar 41 a photographic studio was opened at the Polytechnic Institution, where Daguerreotype portraits were taken by a Mr Richard Beard, who had bought Daguerre and Niépce's patent for £1000. The studio was in an attic "with an extensive skylight to secure every available ray of the sun, and tinted . . . with a pale-blue colour, by which the eyes are secured from being dazzled. The sitter takes his or her place on an elevated seat, looking towards the sun". The exposure lasted five seconds. (*Morning Herald*, 19 Mar 41.) Beard's was one of two photographic studios in London; takings were often as much as £50 a day (W. J. Harrison, *History of Photography*, 1888, pp. 42–3).

[6] Henrietta Maria (1807–95), daughter of Viscount Dillon. A consistent Radical, advocate of women's education

so fortunate as to be able to release myself early in the evening, I shall make bold to look in, and pay my compliments to you.

Believe me | Faithfully Yours<br>CHARLES DICKENS

## *To* PATRIC PARK, 26 MAY [1841]\*

MS Miss Madge Pemberton. *Date:* 26 May was Wednesday in 1841.

Devonshire Terrace | Wednesday Twenty Sixth May.

My Dear Park.

I find that I am obliged—sorely against my will, and by a confounded engagement which I can't avoid—to postpone my sitting until six tomorrow; when I shall hope to see you.[1]

Always believe me | Faithfully Yours

Patric Park Esquire.                                         CHARLES DICKENS

## *To* BASIL HALL, 26 MAY [1841]

MS Brotherton Library, Leeds. *Date:* The death of Hall's youngest son, Frederick Richard, aged 4, was announced in *The Times* of 25 May.

Devonshire Terrace. | Wednesday May The Twenty Sixth.

My Dear Hall.

I saw the paper yesterday, and had sorrowful thoughts of you.

The traveller from this World to the next, found the Infant Child he had lost many years before, wreathing him a bower in Heaven.[2] It must be something to you, even in your grief, to know, that one of the Angels called you father upon Earth.[3]

God bless you, and send you in the comforting presence of your other children and the impression of this calamity upon their minds, a lasting source of consolation.[4]

Your faithful friend<br>CHARLES DICKENS

and one of the founders of Queen's College, London, and Girton College, Cambridge. One of her daughters married the ninth Earl of Carlisle; another, Lord Amberley, son of Lord John Russell and father of Bertrand Russell. For her husband, afterwards second Baron Stanley of Alderley, see Vol. I, p. 424*n*. She had taken a keen interest in *Old Curiosity Shop*: see *To* Macready, ?6 Jan, *fn*.

[1] For Park's busts of CD, see *To* Maclise, 25 Oct 40, *fn*.

[2] See Fielding, *A Journey from this World to the Next*, Ch. 8.

[3] "Your idea of little Freddy playing among the angels & calling me his pups [*thus*] ...!", Hall commented on 28 May; and on 28 June he wrote: "Your charming idea my friend of the angels playing about & talking of their earthly Papas, has often helped assuage my grief" (MS Huntington)—which was not quite what CD had said.

[4] Hall did not open CD's letter until the 28th, but he wrote on the 27th to tell him this and explain it: "The truth is—that during the whole of the last fortnight—by far the most anxious & interesting—albeit the most melancholy

## *To* SIR G[EORGE] CAYLEY,[1] 26 MAY [1841]

Extract in Sotheby's catalogue, July 1923; *MS* 1 p.; dated Devonshire
Terrace, 26 May. *Date:* 31 May was Monday in 1841 and 1847. Since in
May 47 CD was in Brighton or at 1 Chester Place, 1841 seems certain.

If the Fates will keep themselves to themselves, until and on Monday
the thirty-First, I'll dine with you on that day.

of my life—*you* have been mixed up
with the whole proceedings in the most
singular manner—& my wish is—or
rather has been—to give you some
notion of this. ... At every turn of
these harassing incidents I caught myself saying 'Oh here is a point for
Dickens'—'how will he value this!'
'here is nature laid actually bare' & so
on,—till, at length, even moments of
the deepest distress took a personal sort
of character in connexion with you. ...
There was fever, no doubt, in all this—
but I dont suppose it was less true to
nature, or less fit for your great pur-
poses, on that account. | I fear much,
however, that I shall not be able to
accomplish my purpose—for three
reasons,—first—& chiefly, I am in such
real distress in consequence of this loss,
that I feel weakened in powers of expression & description—2ndly. I cannot
write at all to the purpose unless I have
rest at night—& my remaining children
are all still so ill with the hooping
cough—& as two of them sleep in the
same room with me—or rather cough
in the same room in which I lie awake—
& one in the same bed—I am exhausted
for want of sleep—& 3rdly. as I before
hinted, I feel even the most remarkable
passages gliding away from my memory
in such a way that I question if I shall
now be able to catch hold even of their
traces. | But as I very much wish to give
them a chance—& as I have a sort of
a notion that your unopened letter may
contain something to disturb the remarkable trains of thought & sentiment
alluded to, I refrain from opening it at
present" (MS Huntington). The following day, having opened CD's letter, he
wrote: "I find it totally out of the
question my giving you ... a picture of
the last fortnight. But . . . as the
tendency of all you do is good—I should
feel very happy if I could contribute any
pencil sketches from nature which you

might turn to account for the improvement of dispositions disposed to good
but not very well knowing how to set
about it" (MS Huntington). CD
apparently did not answer either of these
letters. But in a letter to D. M. Moir,
17 June 48 (N, II, 102–3), apropos of the
response of bereft parents to the death
of Nell, he wrote: "Poor Basil Hall lost
a little boy for whom he had a great
love.—I think his insanity began about
that time—, and he wrote out all the
secret grief and trial of his heart to me,
wherever he went afterwards, always
referring to the same work" (not in fact
quite true). On 28 June Hall wrote
again, at enormous length, first telling
CD he would be in London from 5 to
12 July and would like to discuss with
him whether he should accept an offer
to write for *Chambers's Edinburgh
Journal*, to augment his "miserable
half-pay"; next describing in great
detail his child's funeral and grave, and
where he took his wife and children (still
ill) for change of air; finally mentioning
his thoughts of wintering in Malta (MS
Huntington). CD was in Scotland when
Hall was to be in London, so they did
not meet. One more letter from Hall
has survived in the Huntington Library,
written on "H.M.S. Indus Off Algiers"
on 3 Sep 41, to ask if CD would return
"a devil of a long letter" he had written
him from Trafalgar, because he wanted
it for his Journal which he had decided
in future to write for publication. He
described his family as "half dead with
anxiety to know how Mr. Haredale is to
deal with the murderer whom he succeeded in getting down", and enclosed
a small sketch he had made of Mount
Etna for Catherine's Album. This was
the end of the correspondence. No
answers from CD to Hall's last four
letters are known.

[1] Presumably Sir George Cayley,
Bart (1773–1857), "the father of aerial

## *To* GEORGE CRUIKSHANK, [26 MAY 1841]

Mention in next.


## *To* [HENRY COLBURN], 27 MAY 1841

MS Berg Collection.

Devonshire Terrace. | May The Twenty Seventh 1841.
My Dear Sir.

Not seeing Mr. Cruikshank yesterday, I wrote to him last night. His answer is "My dear Dickens—the plates will be at Mr. Colburn's, either tomorrow (to day, that is) or Friday."

I will look over the Lamplighter and send him back to you tonight. I hope we may be out next week[1]—I suppose we can, if Mr. C redeems his pledge?

Faithfully Yours always
CHARLES DICKENS


## *To* DANIEL MACLISE, 27 MAY 1841*

MS Benoliel Collection.

Twenty Seventh May 1841.
My Dear Maclise

Are you going out tonight? If not, and you should be disposed for a stroll through some of the queer places and bye ways, come here at half past 7. My other half is going (oh!) to Samivel Carter Hall's—the Rosary[2] —Old Brompton.

A word in answer.

Always Faithfully
CD


navigation". Built and flew the first man-carrying glider, 1852–3; invented the tension-wheel, hot-air engine and caterpillar tractor; and carried out a system of arterial drainage in Yorkshire on a principle previously unknown in England. He was the first to promote and adopt the cottage allotment system; was founder and chairman of the Polytechnic Institution, London, 1838; and chairman of the Whig Club at York. He and CD probably met through

Jeffrey, who, in a note dated "Friday 30th." [Apr], wrote to CD: "If you can come here—(it is all on your way) rather before two o'clock on Sunday—I shall be most happy to marshall you the way to Sir Geo Cayley's" (MS Huntington).

[1] *The Pic Nic Papers* was in fact published 9 Aug 41.

[2] Apparently thus in MS. "The Rosary" in Hall's *A Book of Memories of Great Men and Women of the Age*, 1871.

## *To* GEORGE LOVEJOY,[1] 31 MAY 1841

Text from MDGH, I, 44.[2]

> 1, Devonshire Terrace, York Gate, Regent's Park,
> Monday Evening, May 31st, 1841.

Sir,

I am much obliged and flattered by the receipt of your letter,[3] which I should have answered immediately on its arrival but for my absence from home at the moment.[4]

My principles and inclinations would lead me to aspire to the distinction you invite me to seek, if there were any reasonable chance of success,[5] and I hope I should do no discredit to such an honour if I won[6] and wore it.[7] But I am bound to add, and I have no hesitation in saying plainly, that I cannot afford the expense of a contested election. If I could, I would act on your suggestion instantly. I am not the less indebted to you and the friends to whom the thought occurred, for your good opinion and approval. I beg you to understand that I am restrained solely (and much against my will) by the consideration I have mentioned, and thank both you and them most warmly.[8]

> Yours faithfully
> [CHARLES DICKENS][9]

[1] George Lovejoy, bookseller, stationer and librarian, of 117 London Street, Reading; the local Liberal agent. He left a collection of scrapbooks concerning Reading to the Reading Reference Library.

[2] The letter is also quoted in a pamphlet by E. M. Tull, *CD and Reading*, Reading, n.d., p. 4, from the original then in the possession of Lovejoy's daughter. But the MDGH text is fuller and seems, except in instances noted below, more accurate.

[3] Lovejoy had written on 29 May: "Allow me in confidence to submit a query to you—The election of a new Parliament is near at hand.—We have one learned and talented literary Member—your friend Mr. Sergeant Talfourd—Would a seat be worth your trying for?—Reading is at present in want of a candidate to succeed the liberal member Mr. Fyshe Palmer who retires from public life.—The expenses of a contest are not great, but still the Candidate must be prepared to bear them.—The thought has occurred to a few friends to hint it to you—hence this application." He asked CD for an early answer, and referred him to Talfourd

for more information (MS Huntington).

[4] On the back of Lovejoy's letter CD wrote in shorthand a draft of his reply. It has been deciphered by Mr W. J. Carlton, who reads this paragraph as beginning: "I am much touched and flattered by the receipt of your note".

[5] A Conservative victory in the coming General Election seemed almost certain, and CD's chances of success at Reading would have been minimal. Talfourd did not stand either. He explained this in a letter to Leigh Hunt on 14 Sep 41: "I could not have retained my own seat (if at all) without a great expence which I cannot afford, and without also submitting to the dictation of the Radicals at Reading" (MS BM). (He was re-elected in 1847.) Two able Conservatives were returned for Reading in 1841—Charles Russell and Lord Chelsea. For an account of the election, see *Reminiscences of Reading, by an Octogenarian* [W. S. Darter], Reading, 1888.

[6] Tull reads "won it and wore it".

[7] Cf. *2 Henry IV*, IV, v, 222.

[8] Shorthand reads "heartily".

[9] According to Tull, "an interview

## *To* JOHN FORSTER, [MAY 1841]

Extract in F, VI, vii, 551. *Date:* May 41 according to Forster.

I have a letter from my father lamenting the fine weather, invoking congenial tempests, and informing me that it will not be possible for him to stay more than another year in Devonshire, as he must then proceed to Paris to consolidate Augustus's French.[1]

## *To* H. G. ADAMS, [?MAY 1841]

MS (fragment) Francis Edwards Ltd. *Date:* Signature suggests *c.* May 41.

I hasten to answer your note, and am obliged to do so thus briefly or I should lose another Post.

Faithfully Yours

H.G. Adams Esquire                         CHARLES DICKENS

## *To* THOMAS BEARD, 2 JUNE 1841

MS Dickens House. *Address:* Thomas Beard Esquire | 42 Portman Place | Edgeware Road.

Devonshire Terrace. | June The Second 1841.

My Dear Beard.

If you have not yet stirred in the matter of the Newspaper Dinner[2]— don't. I feel that I ought to be at work on Saturday Evening, for I have much to do before going to Edinburgh and but a little time to do it in.

Kate tells me to say that we shall expect your sister Marion[3] to dinner also on Sunday. So none of your nonsense, but bring her.

5[4]                         Faithfully Yours always
                         CHARLES DICKENS

If *you* go to the Whacking[5] dinner, or have pledged yrself in any way— I will.

took place between several of the leading adherents of the Liberal party" and CD, at Lovejoy's office, before CD's final refusal (10 June 41). No corroboration of this has been found; but according to Forster CD's strong desire to make himself heard on the subject of the Poor Law caused him to hesitate before finally refusing (F, II, x, 173).

[1] On 24 Mar 42, taking advantage of CD's absence in America, John Dickens wrote to "Miss Coutts & Co." announcing that—as was "settled" between him and CD before he left, "but rather more hastily, in consequence of his then numerous engagements, than was consistent with a systematic arrangement"

—he was "to rid himself of all obligations" binding him to Alphington, so that he could return to London when Augustus left school the following July; he asked for £25, which was refused (MS Morgan).

[2] The fourth anniversary dinner of the Newspaper Press Benevolent Association, held at the London Tavern, 5 June 41 (see *Spectator*, 12 June 41).

[3] Marion Beard (*d.* 1902), the youngest of Beard's five sisters. She married Alexander Pearson Fletcher.

[4] Written huge.

[5] From journalists' slang for a portion of a speech to be taken down in shorthand.

## *To* DR SOUTHWOOD SMITH, 2 JUNE 1841

MS Mr W. A. Foyle. *Address:* Dr. Southwood Smith | New Broad Street |
City.

Devonshire Terrace.
Wednesday June The Second 1841.

My Dear Dr. Smith.

I find it can't be done.[1] The artists, engravers, printers, and every one
engaged, have so depended on my promises and so fashioned their Engagements by them, that I cannot, with any regard to their comfort or convenience, leave town before the Nineteenth.  At any other time, I would
have gone with you to John o' Groats for such a purpose; and I don't
thank you the less heartily, for not being able to go now.

If you should see one place which you would like me to behold of all
others, and should find that I could get easy access to it, tell me when you
come back, and I'll see it on my way to Scotland, please God.

I will send your papers[2] home by hand tomorrow.

In haste | Believe me with true regard
Faithfully Yours

Dr. Southwood Smith.                                         CHARLES DICKENS

## *To* THOMAS MITTON, 2 JUNE 1841

Mention in N, I, 322; *MS* I p.; dated Devonshire Terrace, 2 June 41.

## *To* THE COUNTESS OF BLESSINGTON, 2 JUNE 1841

MS Benoliel Collection.

Devonshire Terrace. | Wednesday June The Second /41.

Dear Lady Blessington.

The year goes round so fast, that when anything occurs to remind me
of its whirling, I lose my breath and am bewildered.  So your handwriting
last night had as startling an effect upon me as though you had sealed
your note with one of your own eyes.[3]

---

[1] Apparently a "proposed expedition,
in the course of which Dickens was to
see on the spot some place where children were at work in a coal-mine" (Mrs
C. L. Lewes, *Dr Southwood Smith*, p.
86).

[2] Presumably either evidence for the
Report of the Children's Employment
Commission or papers connected with
the Sanatorium (see *To* Southwood
Smith, 15 Dec 40, *fn*). CD was now a
member of the Sanatorium committee.

[3] On 31 May Lady Blessington had
written: "Though you promised me

last year, that you would kindly let me
have something from your pen, for the
Book of Beauty, or Keepsake for 1842,
I really feel reluctant to intrude on you
for the fulfilment of this promise because I know the value of a page from
you too well not to be aware of the
sacrifice you make in granting me one.
If however, I did not remind you of the
promise, I might appear insensible of
its importance, so with great hesitation
I venture to recall it to your mind and to
add that even the slightest contribution
from a pen that delights every class of

I remember my promise,[1] as in cheerful duty bound, and with Heaven's grace will redeem it. At this moment I have not the faintest idea how, but I am going into Scotland on the nineteenth to see Jeffrey, and while I am away (I shall return, please God, in about three weeks) will look out for some accident, incident, or subject for small description, to send you when I come home. You will take the will for the deed, I know; and remembering that I have a Clock which always wants winding up, will not quarrel with me for being brief.[2]

Have you seen the Magnetic boy?[3] You heard of him no doubt from Count D'Orsay.[4] If you get him to Gore House,[5] don't, I entreat you, have more than eight people—four is a better number—to see him. He fails in a crowd, and is *marvellous* before a few.[6]

I am told that down in Devonshire there are young ladies innumerable,

readers, will confer on me a great obligation, and save you the repetition of an importunate request" (MS Huntington).

[1] Of 16 Apr 40.

[2] In Nov 41 CD was still hoping to redeem his promise (*To* Lady Blessington, 23 Nov), and finally did so in July 43.

[3] Alexis Didier, clearly the young medium referred to throughout Townshend's *Facts in Mesmerism* as "E.A.", and the subject of several demonstrations described there. Townshend claimed to be able to mesmerize him in a few seconds. Born at Boom, in Belgium, he was 15 in Feb 39, when Townshend began experimenting with him, and a musician (*Facts in Mesmerism,* 1840, p. 563).

[4] Alfred, Count D'Orsay (1801–52; *DNB*), son of a French general and the illegitimate daughter of the Duke of Würtemberg; an officer in the Garde du Corps until he met the Blessingtons 1821 when he resigned his commission and toured with them on the Continent. Fascinated Lord Blessington who in 1823 added a codicil to his will leaving D'Orsay his Dublin estates on his marrying one of his daughters. Married Harriet, aged 15, 1827. After Lord Blessington's death, moved to London (1831) with Lady Blessington and his wife, who later in the year left him, causing scandalous rumours that he was Lady Blessington's lover and had only married Harriet as a cover. A formal separation followed 1838. Strikingly handsome, the "Prince of Dandies", charming, generous, and a

talented artist, he lived a brilliant social life 1832–41, dining, gambling, race-going, &c, but also had friends outside the fashionable world such as Forster, CD, Bulwer and Macready (whom he advised on clothes and the scene in Crockford's for Bulwer's *Money*). Recklessly overspent the income from his marriage settlement; and, on its becoming known (1840–1) how much less his expectations from the Blessington estate were than he had supposed, his creditors closed in on him. He had now left his small house in Kensington Gore and was living in Gore House with Lady Blessington—self-imprisoned to avoid arrest, but emerging on Saturdays after midnight and then "to be seen at Crockford's, always gay and smiling, as if he had no anxiety or fears", and again there on Sunday nights until 11.30 "when he left, so as to reach Gore House before the Cinderella hour of twelve . . . safe until the last stroke" (Lord Lamington, *In the Days of the Dandies*, 1906, pp. 28 and 35). During the summer of 1841 he tried unsuccessfully to obtain through Henry Bulwer a diplomatic post at the French Embassy in London, and at this time settled more seriously to making portrait-drawings and portrait-busts. For CD's sitting to him, see *To* Lady Blessington, 23 Nov 41, *fn*.

[5] No evidence has been found of a mesmeric demonstration by Alexis at Gore House.

[6] CD had apparently both heard him play and seen him mesmerized at Townshend's on 12 May (Townshend

who read crabbed Manuscript with the palms of their hands—newspapers with their ankles[1]—and so forth, and who are, so to speak, literary all over. I begin to understand what a blue-stocking means, and have not the smallest doubt that Lady Stepney[2] (for instance) could write quite as entertaining[3] a book with the sole of her foot, as ever she did with her head.

I am a believer, in earnest, and I am sure you would be, if you saw this boy under moderately favorable circumstances—as I hope you will, before he leaves England.

Believe me Dear Lady Blessington<br>Faithfully Yours<br>CHARLES DICKENS

## *To* W. C. MACREADY, [?3] JUNE 1841*

MS New York Public Library. *Date:* 3 June 41 was Thursday; but since Macready—and Talfourd, to a similar request (see next, *fn*)—replied on the 4th, CD was probably mistaken in the day of the week, not date of the month.

Devonshire Terrace. | Wednesday June The Third 1841.
My Dear Macready.

Will you (like a good man) empower me to add your name to the Sanatorium committee? It is a most excellent Institution, and they are exceedingly desirous to have you.

Such weather as it is here, for warmth and sunshine, was never seen. You are so languid, I suppose, with playing in [h]ot Theatres every night, that if I were to write you a long letter you would swoon at the sight of it.—Don't be alarmed at my going over leaf, [?I'll just write][4] four lines and no more.

*to* CD, ?11 May 41, in which he is referred to as "the celebrated clairvoyant Somnambulist, mentioned in my book": MS Huntington), and on 12 May had told Macready of "the wonder of this boy, under the effect of magnetism, producing such wonderful effects" (Macready, *Diaries*, II, 135–6). In Townshend's experiments Alexis "saw" through his forehead or even the back of his head (*Facts in Mesmerism*, pp. 564–6); and Townshend claimed that mesmerism improved his character and sensibility (p. 169) and gave him visionary insight into the soul (p. 168). Fanny Kemble describes a *séance* of his at her house on 21 May 41 (*Records of Later Life*, 1882, II, 77–8).

[1] Apparently "ancles" written first (as in *To* Maclise, 12 Mar 41); then "k" written over the "c". A reference to the absurd claims of early mesmerists, who, as Townshend said, talked of their patients' "seeing *with* the epigastrium—the fingers, &c." (*Facts in Mesmerism*, p. 385).

[2] Name omitted in MDGH and subsequent editions. Catherine Lady Stepney (d. 1845; *DNB*), *née* Pollok, fashionable novelist and contributor to Annuals; patroness of authors and artists. Miss Mitford claimed that all her work was rewritten by L. E. L. "or the grammar and spelling would have disgraced a lady's maid" (*Life of Mary Russell Mitford*, ed. A. G. L'Estrange, 1870, III, 94). Macready found her "a very dull and empty person—a mindless beauty" (*Diaries*, I, 394).

[3] Written "entertaining".

[4] The paper is tattered, torn, stained, and the ink faded. Here "I" is clear, " 'll" probable; then 10–11 letters missing.

Mrs. Macready is *amazing* at the charades. The way she *wouldn't* go into a Station House the other night, was masterly in the extreme. You couldn't have done it better in a Domestic Tragedy. Comparisons are odious, but I shall have my eye on you at Drury Lane—My faith is shaken.

Always believe me | My Dear Macready | Heartily Yours

CHARLES DICKENS[1]

I am [?verging] on the [      ].[2]

## *To* SIR MARTIN ARCHER SHEE, 3 JUNE 1841

MS Harvard College Library.

1 Devonshire Terrace. | York Gate Regents Park.<br>June The Third 1841.

Dear Sir Martin Shee.

I don't know whether you happen to have seen anything of the inclosed project—a most excellent and worthy one—which is now about to be carried into immediate operation. The Committee (among whom are Drs. Southwood Smith and Arnott,[3] Macready, Talfourd,[4] the leading merchants and bankers in the City, and many whom you know) are extremely desirous to have your name, as representing a class which includes a great number of young Students whose friends are resident at a distance, and to some of whom, at one time or other, the Sanatorium might prove of inestimable service. As I look upon your sanction and influence as being of very great importance and value, I volunteered at the last Meeting to write to you upon the subject. Therefore I trouble you with this Note.

[1] On 4 June Macready replied, from the Adelphi Hotel, Liverpool: "I could not put my name into better trust, and beg you will use it as you think may in any way serve the interests of the Institution you advocate, and which I really wish so much to see flourish. My only concern is that I must be such an inefficient member, for I can scarcely promise a single attendance—You will perhaps explain so much for me. | I look at the sunshine like a prisoner through his iron bars, for I am confined to the Theatre by business and to the room I occupy by indisposition, from which I have not been free since I left London. —The terrible necessity involved in the fact 'il faut manger' drives me on, and makes me crawl up to the best whirlwinds of passion that I can lose myself in—to tumble back into my usual grunting decrepitude.—This is no joke—but I shall get well on my legs again, as soon as I can get a little rest. | If all else fails, the Station House may be a good hit for Drury Lane—I have written to my wife about it" (MS Huntington).

[2] The postscript is extremely faint: "verging" might be "urging"; and about six words at the end are wholly illegible.

[3] Neil Arnott, MD, FRS (1788–1874; *DNB*), physician, natural philosopher and inventor. Physician extraordinary to the Queen 1837; prominent member of the Royal Institution. He had many philanthropic interests.

[4] Macready and Talfourd had not yet consented to be on the committee. Talfourd replied on 4 June: "You may make any use of my name that you please;—therefore, although the Institution rejoices in an appellation more sickly than classical, you may place it on the Committee" (MS Huntington).

I will not take up your time by urging the point. It is enough that I convey to you the respectful and earnest desire of the Committee, and beg you to forgive me this intrusion, for the object's sake.

If you should desire any further information on the subject, they will be most happy to give it you.

I beg to remain | Faithfully Yours

Sir Martin Archer Shee                              CHARLES DICKENS[1]
&c   &c   &c


## To DR SOUTHWOOD SMITH, 3 JUNE 1841

Mention in C. F. Libbie catalogue, Sep 1909; dated Devonshire Terrace, "June the Third, 1841"; salutation "My Dear Dr. Smith".

*Apologizing for his absence from a Sanatorium Committee meeting and mentioning Talfourd and Macready.*[2]


## To JOHN FORSTER, [3 JUNE 1841]

Extract in F, II, ix, 168. *Date:* 3 June according to Forster.

Solomon's expression I meant to be one of those strong ones to which strong circumstances give birth in the commonest minds. Deal with it as you like.[3] ... Say what you please of Gordon,[4] he must have been at heart

[1] In a letter dated 6 May 41 (clearly a mistake for 6 June), Shee replied: "Altho' I candidly confess that I am so much *overdone* in the way of subscriptions, the very sound of the word gives me a pain in my *pocket*, yet I cannot resist your application. If therefore you will accept the very humble mite of two guineas, with the expression of my regret that the vulgar quality called prudence forbids a more liberal contribution, my name if it be considered of any use, is very much at the service of the Institution which you have so eloquently advocated" (MS Huntington). CD's own subscription, shown in his account-book (MS Messrs Coutts) on 11 May 41, was three guineas.

[2] No doubt saying that he had written to ask if their names might be added to the Sanatorium committee.

[3] Clearly refers to Solomon Daisy's revelation in Ch. 33 (No. 63, published 12 June; presumably the final proofs). Forster may have objected that on Solomon's realizing it was the 19th of March, anniversary of the murder, his "It came

upon me with a kind of shock, as if a hand had struck the thought upon my forehead" was out of character. He did not, however, cut this or any other part of Solomon's narrative; but either he or CD deleted two paragraphs (immediately before Solomon begins his story) in which Mr Willet imagines the "mischief" he will do the little man if he delays telling it a quarter of a minute more.

[4] Lord George Gordon (1751–93; *DNB*), son of the 3rd Duke of Gordon; fanatical anti-Papist. MP 1774–80. First President 1779 of the Protestant Association, formed to secure repeal of the Act removing Catholic disabilities. After the anti-Catholic riots of 6–8 June 1780, was sent to the Tower for eight months, but acquitted of high treason Feb 81. Died in Newgate after serving a sentence of five years' imprisonment on two charges of libel. He had become a Jew, calling himself Israel bar Abraham George Gordon (cf. his prophetic dream in *Barnaby*, No. 65, Ch. 37).

a kind man,[1] and a lover of the despised and rejected, after his own fashion. He lived upon a small income, and always within it; was known to relieve the necessities of many people; exposed in his place the corrupt attempt of a minister to buy him out of Parliament;[2] and did great charities in Newgate.[3] He always spoke on the people's side, and tried against his muddled brains to expose the profligacy of both parties.[4] He never got anything by his madness, and never sought it. The wildest and most raging attacks of the time, allow him these merits: and not to let him have 'em in their full extent, remembering in what a (politically) wicked time he lived, would lie upon my conscience heavily. The libel he was imprisoned for when he died, was on the queen of France;[5] and the French government interested themselves warmly to procure his release[6]—which I think they might have done, but for Lord Grenville.[7]

[1] "I had objected to some points in his view of this madman, stated much too favourably as I thought", says Forster (F, II, ix, 168)—commenting, no doubt, on No. 64 (Chs 35 and 36), in which Gordon makes his first appearance. Cf. Hood's review of the finished book: "We protest against calling the great Leader the misled—the designating of his wickedness as weakness, and the sheltering the misdeeds of this 'poor crazy lord' under the plea of insanity" (*Athenæum*, 22 Jan 42). CD's picture of Gordon seems based on the more sympathetic accounts he had read—e.g. on Robert Watson's *Life of Lord George Gordon: with a Philosophical Review of his Political Conduct*, 1795, and the "Anecdotes of the Life of Lord George Gordon" which are printed at the end of *A Plain and Succinct Narrative of the Late Riots ...* By William Vincent [Thomas Holcroft], 1780, but are not themselves by Holcroft. (According to a MS note on the title-page of the BM copy of the 2nd edn, 1780, they are by "J Perry"—presumably James Perry [1756–1821; *DNB*].) CD owned Holcroft's pamphlet with the appended "Anecdotes". For probable echoes, in this letter to Forster, of Watson's *Life* and the "Anecdotes", see below.
[2] "Anecdotes" (pp. 60–1) gives Gordon's income as between £700 and £800 a year, and tells the story of his publishing in the House Lord North's "infamous attempt to bribe him with a place of 1000*l*. a year, to give up his seat in Parliament".
[3] Cf. Watson (p. 109): "No man was more beloved by his fellow prisoners than Lord George; he divided his substance with those who had no money, and did every thing in his power to alleviate their distress."
[4] Cf. "Anecdotes" (p. 62): "He has said some of the severest, and at the same time the wittiest things against both sides of the House".
[5] In a notice published in the *Public Advertiser*, Aug 1786, Gordon had accused Marie-Antoinette and the French Ambassador in London of a conspiracy against Count de Cagliostro (then living in Gordon's house), following the scandalous "case of the Diamond Necklace".
[6] Watson prints Gordon's unsuccessful petition to the French National Assembly (23 July 1789), asking that they should apply to "the Court of London" for his release; also the sympathetic reply of the Secretary, Henri Grégoire (24 Feb 1790).
[7] William Wyndham, Baron Grenville (1759–1834; *DNB*), cousin and supporter of Pitt. Secretary of State for the Home Department 1789; and for Foreign Affairs 1791. A consistent supporter of Catholic Emancipation, he was naturally hostile to Gordon.

## *To* CHARLES OLLIER,[1] 3 JUNE 1841

MS Comtesse de Suzannet.

Devonshire Terrace. | Thursday June The Third 1841.
My Dear Sir.
Many thanks to you for your kind offer, but I don't need the trials.[2]
What I wanted from Upcott was a *portrait* of Lord George, which I got
from him.[3] As to the Riot, I am going to try if I can't make a better one
than he did.[4]

Believe me | Faithfully Yours
Charles Ollier Esquire.                                        CHARLES DICKENS


## *To* HENRY COOK,[5] 4 JUNE 1841

Extract (in part from facsimile) from Charles Hamilton catalogue, 16 May
1963; *MS* 1½ pp.; dated Devonshire Terrace, 4 June 41.

. . . cordial thanks for the present of your Poem,[6] and for the very kind and
welcome expressions with which you have accompanied it. As the earliest
opportunity I shall have of reading it, will be, most likely, in a fortnight's
time in Scotland, I cannot refrain from acknowledging its receipt before
perusal . . .
My warm assurance of the gratification I have derived from your letter.
Believe me | Dear Sir | Faithfully Yours
Henry Cook Esquire                                          CHARLES DICKENS

[1] Charles Ollier (1788–1859; *DNB*),
publisher and author. A friend of
Leigh Hunt's, through whom he met
Keats. In partnership with his brother
James as a publisher 1816–*c.* 1821; published Keats's first poems, and works by
Shelley and Lamb. Began the short-
lived *Ollier's Literary Miscellany*, 1820.
On having to wind up his business,
became assistant to Colburn; and after
the dissolution of the Colburn-Bentley
partnership, 1832, remained with Bentley as a member of his staff until 1839.
Later contributed to *Ainsworth's Magazine*. His own literary output was three
volumes of tales and a romance.

[2] CD already owned Cobbett and
Howell's *Complete Collection of State
Trials*, 21 vols, 1809 (see *To* Forster,
?10 Mar 41, *fn*), which included Lord
George Gordon's trial for high treason,
5 Feb 1781.

[3] This was no doubt one of the 3000
portraits owned by Upcott and sold

with his library in June 46. Among his
other possessions listed in the sale
catalogue were Daniel Lysons's "Historical Collections", in 5 vols, consisting of broadsides, newspaper cut-
tings &c, covering, among other events,
the Gordon riots. It would be surprising if he had not shown these to CD.

[4] I.e. than Gordon did. Cf. *To* Cay,
21 July.

[5] Henry Cook (1819–?90), painter
and poet; studied painting at the RA
and in Rome. Published *Adrian, a Tale
of Italy . . . and Other Poems* in 1839.
Settled in Italy 1859 and was commissioned by Napoleon III to paint a
series of pictures commemorating the
Italian campaign. A presentation copy
of his *Scenery of Central Italy*, 1846 (26
coloured lithographs), was in the Gad's
Hill library at CD's death.

[6] Probably *Pride, or the Heir of
Craven. A Tale of the Fifteenth Century
in Six Cantos*, 1841.

## *To* MESSRS CHAPMAN & HALL, 7 JUNE 1841

MS New York Public Library.

Devonshire Terrace. | Monday Seventh June 1841.

Dear Sirs

Mr. Browne has the MS of another Number.[1] If you will send up to him, No. 33 Howland Street Fitzroy Square, any time this evening, he will leave it out for your Messenger.

Faithfully Yours always
CHARLES DICKENS

## *To* DAVID BARNES, 7 JUNE 1841*

MS Free Library of Philadelphia.

1 Devonshire Terrace | York Gate Regents Park.
Monday Seventh June 1841.

Dear Mr. Barnes.

We purpose coming to Broadstairs this year, please God, on Saturday the Thirty First of July, and remaining until Saturday the Ninth of October; and as we are going into Scotland on the nineteenth of this month, we wish, if we can, to arrange about a house before leaving town.

Mrs. Dickens and I, think (though we don't quite remember its accomodations)[2] that your small Library House[3] would suit us very well. If you are disposed to let it for this term, we shall be glad to hear from you on the subject. If you are otherwise engaged, perhaps you will look about for us and give us the benefit of your advice. We wish to be on the Terrace if possible.

Faithfully Yours
Mr. Barnes                                       CHARLES DICKENS

## *To* THE REV. CHAUNCY HARE TOWNSHEND, [?EARLY JUNE 1841]

Mention in Townshend *to* CD, "Wednesday" [?9 June 41].[4]

[1] Probably No. 65, published 26 June, in which Browne illustrated "Hugh in Gashford's room" (Ch. 37) and "The No-Popery Dance" (Ch. 38). CD seems to have been finishing his instalments of *Barnaby* about three weeks ahead of publication, but was probably now trying to get further ahead in preparation for the visit to Scotland. Browne may well have received No. 65 some days before the 7th.

[2] Thus in MS.

[3] See *To* Mitton, ?31 May 40, *fn.*

[4] In a letter to CD written earlier in the same week Townshend had enclosed three of his "brain's children", i.e. poems, and said: "I have no patience with the heartless engagements of London, which have kept me from seeing you, & above all, from mesmerising you—which I am sure I could do, and which I long to do"; he would be leaving London on Saturday, so begged CD to breakfast with him on the Thursday and give him a "mesmeric

## *To* SIR MARTIN ARCHER SHEE, [9 JUNE 1841]

Extract in 11th Cooperative Catalogue of Members of the Middle Atlantic
Chapter of the Antiquarian Booksellers' Association of America; *MS* 1 p.;
dated London, 9 June 41.

I thank you very much for your kind . . . acquiescence in the matter of
the Sanatorium. I should have mentioned when I sent you Dr. Smith's
pamphlet . . . that the design—honestly—was not upon your pocket, but
upon the sanction of your name and station.

## *To* ANGUS FLETCHER, [9 JUNE 1841]

Mention in next.

*A formal acceptance of the invitation to the Edinburgh dinner in his honour.*

## *To* ANGUS FLETCHER, 9 JUNE 1841*

MS Free Library of Philadelphia.

Devonshire Terrace. | June The Ninth 1841.

My Dear Fletcher.

You are the *other* Dromio,[1] an't you? You convene, I think?[2] I am lost
between you and the unknown Angus.[3]—The formal reply comes along
with this, and will be right in any case.

I needn't tell you what I think of this testimony. It knocked me over
this morning just as I was going to work, and threw me into such a flurry
of pleasure that I *think* I spoiled a Number.[4] I never was so gratified in
my life, nor ever had such reason to be.

Now, about our operations. We leave here, please God, next Saturday

---

trial" (MS Huntington). Clearly CD
declined (being doubtless busy and
probably also unwilling to be mesmerized) and invited Townshend to dinner
on the Friday instead. Townshend
had to decline, but added (on ?9 June):
"Perhaps I shall run up to town before
the 20th, & I then should hope to see
you. When you see Wilson, remind him
of his old contributor to Blackwood's"
(MS Huntington). Reference to the
20th (a mistake for 19th, the day CD
left London) and to John Wilson
("Christopher North") makes a date not
long before CD's visit to Edinburgh
certain.
[1] Twin servant in *The Comedy
of Errors*. There were two Angus

Fletchers, cousins, both assisting at the
Edinburgh dinner on 25 June.
[2] The Dromio of Ephesus gave the
summons to dinner in *The Comedy of
Errors*, I, ii.
[3] Angus Fletcher of Dunans (1805–
1875), advocate; solicitor to Inland
Revenue 1842. Belonged to numerous
literary societies, and was sought after
as a speaker. Proposed the health of
Mrs CD and the Ladies at the Edinburgh dinner. CD called him "a capital
fellow to know" (*To* Macready, ?13
Mar 45).
[4] Either the end of No. 66 or the beginning of No. 67. When he left London on the 19th, CD had finished No.
68.

Morning,—*a*I mean the 19th. which is Saturday week*a*—Per Rail. Sunday
we spend with some friends within 20 miles of York.[1] Monday Morning
we shall start forward again in a posting carriage which I have ordered at
that City—taking the Railway as far as Darlington, and sleeping that night
upon the road—Tuesday we shall push on again—early enough, I hope, to
be in Edinburgh by 6 o'Clock.

Now, will you order dinner for Kate and you and me, at that hour?—A
good, Scotch, comfortable, perfectly cosy dinner? And will you order us
comfortable rooms at whatever hotel you please (if they could include a
little antichamber of any kind, in which I could write o'mornings,[2] it
would be a great relief)—and will you, furthermore, write again when you
have done all this, tell me where we are to come to, and any news you have,
besides? I have a horror of Kate's boxes. If I should find she contemplates
a very big one, I shall despatch it Pr. Steam beforehand.

I have been thinking that the best plan will be, to make an indomitable,
savage, unalterable resolve to leave Edinburgh on the Saturday week, in the
morning,—and to stick to it. Our route in the Highlands we will plan
together. I suppose a week would be a liberal allowance?—I should like
to have a three days halt at some intensely romantic tavern, to refresh from
the excitements and hospitalities of Auld Reekie.[3]—All this, and much
more, we will talk about, over that unparalleled repast I have just spoken of.

As Kate will be mad to see the house she was born in,[4] and all the rest
of it, let us be *alone* that evening, we three—and with the sun next morning,
let you and I cut up to the top of Arthur's Seat,[5] and stand upon its
highest crag. I am on the highest crag of expectation now, and shan't come
down again 'till I have been there.

It has just been told to me that Wilkie[6] is dead. I can hardly believe it.[7]
'Tis in the papers, they say. You will know the truth or falsehood of the
tale, as soon as I.

Always Dear Fletcher | Faithfully Yours<br>CHARLES DICKENS

*aa* Added over a caret.

[1] The Smithsons, at Easthorpe Hall, near Malton.

[2] In the event, CD failed to write anything in Edinburgh. But he wrote Nos 69 and 70 while in the Highlands (see *To* Forster, 9 July and *fns*).

[3] Edinburgh.

[4] 8 Hart Street, Edinburgh.

[5] The highest of Edinburgh's seven hills (822 ft).

[6] Sir David Wilkie (1785–1841; *DNB*): see Vol. 1, p. 569*n*.

[7] Rather delicate, but still in his prime, Wilkie had left England Aug 40, and after six weeks in Holland, Germany and Austria had gone on to Constantinople where, held up by the war in Syria, he spent three months and painted the Sultan; thence he went to Smyrna and Beirut, and on to the Holy Land in late Feb, with a Bible in hand as guide-book. After five weeks sketching in and near Jerusalem, he left for home in mid-April; began a portrait of the Pacha of Egypt on the way; was taken ill at Malta, following a stomach attack some weeks earlier; and died on 1 June, while at sea off Gibraltar. Kate Perugini refers to him as the first artist her father knew "intimately" ("CD as a Lover of Art and Artists", *Magazine of Art*, 1903, p. 164).

## *To* JOHN FORSTER, [?9 JUNE 1841]

Extract in F, II, x, 174. *Date:* presumably same day as last; written, says
Forster, on hearing of Wilkie's sudden death, in which CD "refused to
believe" at first.

My heart assures me Wilkie liveth. He is the sort of man who will be
VERY old when he dies.

## *To* CHARLES SMITHSON, [?9 JUNE] 1841

Composite text from Sotheby's catalogue, Nov 1903, and George D. Smith
catalogues, 1901 and 1907; *MS* 2 pp.; dated Devonshire Terrace, 1841—
possibly 9 June, the date of a letter of 2 pp. to Smithson mentioned (without
text) in N, I, 325.

My dear Smithson,
      I have but a minute before post time, and must therefore be as short as
the twenty-first of December. The carriage, I think, is decidedly cheap.
I hope it is a good 'un to look at, as well as a good 'un to go. . . . *ª*but I am a
galley slave, as you know. Why wasn't I born with a golden ladle in my
mouth as well as a pen*ª*
      *ᵇMentions the visit to Edinburgh and gives details of the journey.ᵇ* Kate
will write to Mrs. Smithson the day before. As we shall be desolate at the
station, I shall look out for one of Wallace's[1] whiskers.
                                                        *ᶜ*Love to the Ladies*ᶜ*[2]

## *To* GEORGE LOVEJOY, 10 JUNE 1841

Text from MDGH, I, 44.[3]

                                        Devonshire Terrace, June 10th, 1841.
Dear Sir,
      I am favoured with your note of yesterday's date,[4] and lose no time in
replying to it.[5]

*ªª, ᵇᵇ, ᶜᶜ* From Smith catalogue.

[1] Joseph Wallace, manservant, aged
30, was shown as at Easthorpe Hall in
the census of 12 June 41.

[2] Both Mrs Smithson and Thompson's other sister, Amelia, were shown
as at Easthorpe Hall in the same census
(also T. J. Thompson's two children,
Thomas aged 7 and Matilda aged 6).

[3] The text in E. M. Tull, *CD and
Reading*, p. 5 (see 31 May, *fn*), is in-
complete and seems less accurate than
MDGH's.

[4] Lovejoy had written on 9 June to
assure CD that the expenses would be
trifling compared with those in some

other places: "Something less than
£1000 would do well I think, and if
this be more than you would think it
prudent to spend I have no doubt the
Reform Club would put you in the way
of overcoming the difficulty. The
difference of *four* [*underlined twice*]
votes is of too much importance to
Ministers at the present crisis to be
thought lightly of. | No doubt you are
acquainted with a friend who would
manage the matter for you . . . | P.S.
The registration is favorable and the
chances of return good" (MS Huntington).

The sum you mention, though small I am aware in the abstract, is greater than I could afford for such a purpose; as the mere sitting in the House and attending to my duties, if I were a member, would oblige me to make many pecuniary sacrifices, consequent upon the very nature of my pursuits.

The course you suggest did occur to me when I received your first letter, and I have very little doubt indeed that the Government would support me—perhaps to the whole extent. But I cannot satisfy myself that to enter Parliament under such circumstances would enable me to pursue that honourable independence without which I could neither preserve my own respect nor that of my constituents. I confess therefore (it may be from not having considered the points sufficiently, or in the right light) that I cannot bring myself to propound the subject to any member of the administration whom I know. I am truly obliged to you nevertheless, and am

Dear Sir, | Faithfully yours

[CHARLES DICKENS]

## *To* LADY HOLLAND, 10 JUNE 1841*

MS The Earl of Ilchester.

Devonshire Terrace. | June The Tenth 1841.

Dear Lady Holland.

I am truly obliged to you for your kindness in the matter of Lord Lauderdale,[1] and thank you sincerely.[2] I hope I shall be able to call upon him while in Scotland, and shall make a point of doing so if I possibly can.[3]—I fear I shall be very much at other peoples'[4] disposal, however, all the time.

I should have had great pleasure in dining with you on Saturday the Nineteenth, had I not arranged to leave town that very morning. Nor can I postpone my departure for a day (as I would gladly have done), for I am obliged to turn out of my road in Yorkshire to visit some friends, and am obliged to be in Edinburgh punctual to my appointed time,—as I yesterday received formal announcement of a public Dinner in my honor.

I should be much delighted if I could execute any commission for you in the North; and am always Dear Lady Holland,

Yours faithfully and obliged

CHARLES DICKENS

[5] On the back of Lovejoy's letter—as of his previous letter (31 May)—CD wrote in shorthand a copy or draft of his reply.

[1] James Maitland, 9th Earl of Lauderdale (1784–1860), Tory MP for Appleby 1826–32; Lord Lieutenant of Berwickshire 1841–60. His father, the 8th Earl (a Whig until the trial of Queen Caroline when he became a Tory), had been an intimate friend of the Hollands.

[2] On Wednesday [9 June] Lady Holland had written: "Dear Sir, | Pray return me the enclosed [*a letter of introduction to Lord Lauderdale*] when you have read it—I hope you will be able to arrange your time so as to see Ld. Lauderdale. | Will you do me the favor of dining here on Saturday 19th. | Yrs. truly | E H" (MS Huntington).

[3] He was apparently not able to.

[4] Thus in MS.

## *To* CHARLES SMITHSON, 13 JUNE 1841*

MS University of California, Los Angeles.

Devonshire Terrace. | Sunday Thirteenth June 1841.
My Dear Smithson.

It has occurred to me that if Malton is not horribly out of the way to
Edinburgh, it will be best not to take the Darlington Rail Road at all, but
to go straight on from your door. If you consider this a wise and Dickens-
like idea, perhaps you will kindly arrange for me accordingly. In that case
it would be best for us to take the carriage from the station to Easthorpe
(the hired one from York I mean) and order Post horses again at 7[1] on
Monday Morning. Considering the ghastly absurdity one becomes when
one is hoisted bodily, carriage and all, on a Railway Truck, I think this will
be what Mitton would call "a tidy move".

I don't know how you may be in the North just now, but here we have
come to the conclusion that there's a mistake in the almanacks. The
blankets are put on again, the fires lighted, great coats and mackintoshes
taken out of lavender; and a Policeman, it is reported, was frozen to death
on Ludgate Hill last Friday Night.

Love to the ladies—from theirs and your  [          ]

Charles Sm[ithson Esquire][2]


## *To* MISS ROGERS, 14 JUNE 1841*

MS Mr John Greaves.

Devonshire Terrace. | Fourteenth June 1841.
Dear Miss Rogers.

I should have been extremely happy to dine with you next Monday, but
that I leave town for Scotland on Saturday Morning.

I wish I could execute any commission for you across the border. On
*that* side and on this, I am always

Faithfully Yours
Miss Rogers.                                                    CHARLES DICKENS


## *To* DANIEL MACLISE, 15 JUNE 1841*

MS Benoliel Collection.

Tuesday Fifteenth June 1841.
My Dear Mac

Forster and Stanfield are on the vagabond tack tonight, being now at the

---

[1] Underlined four times.                     removing part of ending and subscrip-
[2] The signature has been cut away,   tion.

Grays Inn,[1] where they want us to meet them and then repair to some place of amusement. Shall we go? If so, I will call on you between 7 and ½ past.

> Faithfully
> CD.


## *To* CHARLES SMITHSON, 15 JUNE 1841*

MS University of Oregon.

> Devonshire Terrace | Fifteenth June 1841.

My Dear Smithson.

Our letters crossed upon the road.

I quite understood the terms.—To take a carriage from London would be a great expense,[2] as you say; and I should not like to incur it. Therefore, please to do the best for me you can, and be sure that what you do, will please me.

> Love to the Ladies | Always Faithfully
> CD.

*a*In great haste—having been working all day, and the Post just going.*a*


## *To* ANGUS FLETCHER, 15 JUNE 1841†

MS Berg Collection.

> Devonshire Terrace. | Fifteenth June 1841.

My Dear Fletcher.

Many thanks for your welcome letter.

Ten days let us say—good ten days in the Highlands. But to secure this liberty we must be immoveable[3] in the matter of leaving Edinburgh—stone—steel—adamant. Therefore on the morning of the Saturday week after the dinner, we bolt summarily.[4]

Grip *is* no more. He was only ill a day. I sent for the medical gentleman (a bird-fancier in the New Road) on the first appearance of his indisposition. He promptly attended, and administered castor oil and warm gruel. Next day, the patient walked in a thoughtful manner up and down the stable till the clock struck Twelve at Noon; then staggered twice; exclaimed "Hal-loa old girl"—either as a remonstrance with his weakness, or an apostrophe to Death: I am not sure which—and expired.

Suspectful of a butcher who had been heard to threaten, I had the body opened. There were no traces of poison, and it appeared he had died of influenza. He has left a considerable property, chiefly in cheese and

---

[1] No doubt the Gray's Inn coffee house, High Holborn.

[2] Spelt thus—uncharacteristically. CD was perhaps following Smithson's spelling.

*aa* Written across top of the page, above address.

[3] Thus in MS.

[4] They did not in fact get away from Edinburgh until Sun 4 July.

halfpence, buried in different parts of the Garden. The new raven (I *have* a new one, but he is comparatively of weak intellects) administers to his effects, and turns up something every day. The last piece of bijoutrie[1] was a *hammer* of considerable size—supposed to have been stolen from a vindictive carpenter who had been heard to speak darkly of vengeance, "down the Mews".

The medical gentleman, himself—habituated to Ravens—assured me that he "never see sich a thorough going, long-headed, deep, outdacious file" in the whole course of his practice. And he wound up by saying, in reference to Topping "Why, wot was *he* agin that bird? That 'ere little man could no more stand agin him in pint of sense and reason, than I could agin the ghost of Cobbett".[2]

Good Christians say in such cases "it was all for the best perhaps!" I try to think so,—he had ripped the lining off the carriage and eat the paint off the wheels. In the course of the summer while we were at Broadstairs, I think he would have eat it all, bodily.

I have been fearfully hard at work, morning, noon, and night. I have done now, for the present, and am all impatience to start.—I shall not be quite myself (now that having done I can venture to think of it) until we have taken our first glass of wine at the Royal.[3]

Until when—and always—

Believe me Dear Fletcher
Faithfully Yours

Angus Fletcher Esquire                                    CHARLES DICKENS

[a]I have been greatly importuned by the people of Reading, to stand for the next Parliament, but I can't afford it myself, and don't choose to be bound hand and foot to the Reform Club. Therefore I don't. Your friend Hall, the Jotter, stands for Taunton.[4]—There is a Heaven above us![a]
[b]I think it much better that Jeffrey shod. *not* be in the Chair at the dinner.[5] I dare say he has a delicacy in connection with that.—Wilson[6] is on every ground a better man for the purpose.[b]

---

[1] Thus in MS.

[2] Renowned for his "slaughtering invective" (*The Times*, 20 June 35).

[3] The Royal Hotel, Edinburgh, where CD and Catherine stayed 22 June–4 July.

[aa] Not previously published. In tiny writing, squeezed in to the left of the signature with a line drawn round it.

[4] James Hall (see Vol. I, p. 603n), Basil Hall's brother, stood unsuccessfully as a Conservative candidate for Taunton in the General Election June 41. In 1839 he had published *The Jotting Book; a Political and Literary Experiment; by an Amateur*, an attempt to work out a comprehensive political philosophy, both conservative and progressive.

[bb] Not previously published. Written crosswise at the top of p. 1 above the address.

[5] A sentence of roughly 15 words has been heavily cancelled here. In it CD no doubt explained why he was glad that the original plan had been changed. He was probably anxious not to appear too much as Jeffrey's *protégé*.

[6] John Wilson (1785–1854; *DNB*), "Christopher North" of *Blackwood's* (who with Lockhart had flung himself into the creation 1817 of this Tory rival to Jeffrey's *Edinburgh Review*); Professor of Moral Philosophy at Edin-

## *To* JOHN FORSTER, [15 JUNE 1841]

Extract in F, II, x, 174. *Date:* 15 June according to Forster.

I heard from Edinburgh this morning.[1] Jeffrey is not well enough to take the chair,[2] so Wilson does. I think under all circumstances of politics, acquaintance, and *Edinburgh Review*, that it's much better as it is—Don't you?

---

burgh 1820–51; chief author of *Noctes Ambrosianæ* 1822–35. Something of a legend in Edinburgh: a "Norse Demigod" to Mrs Oliphant (*Annals of a Publishing House, William Blackwood and his Sons*, 1897, I, 315); reminded people of "the first man, Adam" (Harriet Martineau, *Biographical Sketches*, 1869, p. 339); was wayward, reckless, guileless, crusty and magnanimous. Scott placed him "among the list of originals" (Scott *to* Joanna Baillie, 17 Jan 1812: *Letters of Sir W. Scott*, ed. H. J. C. Grierson, 1932–7, III, 61). For CD's first impression of him, see *To* Forster, 23 June. He presided at the Edinburgh dinner (for his speech see *To* Forster, 26 June, *fn*). Apparently he and CD did not meet again; but CD subscribed to his memorial statue. For a contemporary caricature, "Boz's Introduction to Christopher North", see frontispiece.

[1] From Fletcher (see last).

[2] Jeffrey had fainted in Court on 5 June and was too weak to perform his duties for most of the session. On 17 June he wrote to CD: "Tho' I cannot keep myself fresh in your memory, by issuing a delightful weekly circular, to some 40,000 particular friends—I hope you do not entirely forget me?—And I do not believe you do—But I begin to be nervous and impatient about your coming—and anxious to have the assurance, and the particulars—if it be not too much trouble—under your own hand—If you come with Mrs Dickens only, I hope you will gratify me by taking up your abode with me—If you bring children and nurses, I am not sure that I can well accommodate you—especially as I live a migratory sort of life at this season—being four days in the week at Craigcrook (about 3 miles out) and three, here in town—which marching and counter marching might not be quite convenient for such small infantry—tho' I daresay even that might be managed —if you were all as *agreeable* to the reunion, as I am sure I shall be—We shall see— | But the immediate business is this—They will have you at a Public Dinner, you see, on Friday the 25th.— Now I am not strong enough to go to such things—and I think they are generally tantalising—and suspect indeed that you would have been better pleased to have been let alone—at least till you knew a little who was who— and what was what, in these latitudes— But what I want now is, that you must promise to dine with me at Craigcrook on Saturday the 26th.—and also—at all events—on Tuesday after—29th.— which days I wish to fix, that I may contrive to have a few friends to meet you. If you are kind enough to become my inmate, we shall arrange better afterwards ... My brother Judge, Lord Murray (late Lord Advocate) is very anxious that you should name some day when you can dine with him—and I have promised to intimate his humble petition to you— | I thank you every Saturday Evg.—and every Sunday morning, for a Barnaby—But I want somebody to love heartily—and you have not yet given me one—I am very saucy you will say—and so I am—but it is your pampering that makes us all so difficult—I shall not be difficult however when I see you—and so, with kindest remembrances to Mrs Dickens —Grip, and the rest of the family— Believe me always | Faithfully and affectly. Yours" (MS Huntington).

## *To* HENRY AUSTIN, 15 JUNE 1841*

MS Morgan Library.

Tuesday Evening June Fifteenth 1841.

My Dear Henry.

Let us dine on Thursday, at the Parthenon, and take a stroll afterwards. I shall be at your end of the Town,[1] in the afternoon, and will call for you between 4 and 5.

Always Affectionately Yours

C. D.

Love to Lætitia


## *To* HENRY JACKSON,[2] 16 JUNE 1841†

MS Free Library of Philadelphia. *Address:* Free | Henry Jackson Esquire | Birkendike's Hotel | York.[3]

Devonshire Terrace | Sixteenth June 1841.

*a*Dear Sir.

I don't know whether this letter will find you; but I write to acknowledge the receipt of yours, and to thank you for the trouble you have taken in the matter of the carriage.*a*

I have been endeavouring to picture to myself what a Mail Phaeton may be[4]—whether it has one, two, three, four, or six wheels—whether it has a head, a front, a back, a pole, a drag, a box, a boot—and can't settle the question at all. *b*It runs very fast in my mind, but has no bodily existence that I know of.

I have no doubt it will suit us well. And am always

Faithfully Yours

Henry Jackson Esquire.                    CHARLES DICKENS*b*

---

[1] In Jan 42 Austin was living at 87 Hatton Garden.

[2] Unidentified.

[3] Presumably this was the Red Lion Inn, near Monk Bar—a coaching house owned and occupied by James Bickerdike 1831–46.

*aa, bb* Not previously published.

[4] It was a large, open, four-wheeled carriage, much in fashion for long journeys, especially abroad; so named because underneath it resembled a mail coach.

## *To* CHARLES BABBAGE,[1] 17 JUNE 1841

MS British Museum.

Devonshire Terrace. | June The Seventeenth 1841.

My Dear Sir.

Many thanks to you for the pamphlets on the Corn Laws,[2] which I have read with great interest.

I am very sorry I was not able to have the pleasure of seeing you on either of the two last Saturdays. I am going to Scotland the day after tomorrow, and have had to work so hard before going away, that for the last three weeks I have been nowhere.

Believe me | Faithfully Yours

Charles Babbage Esquire.                    CHARLES DICKENS
&c &c &c

## *To* JOHN FORSTER, [23 JUNE 1841]

Extracts in F, II, x, 175–6. *Date:* 23 June, the day after their arrival in Edinburgh, according to Forster.

I have been this morning to the Parliament-house, and am now introduced (I hope) to everybody in Edinburgh. The hotel is perfectly besieged, and I have been forced to take refuge in a sequestered apartment at the end of a long passage, wherein I write this letter. They talk of 300 at the dinner. We are very well off in point of rooms, having a handsome sitting-room, another next to it for *Clock* purposes, a spacious bed-room, and large dressing-room adjoining. The castle is in front of the windows, and the view noble. There was a supper ready last night which would have been a dinner anywhere.

*He describes some of the eminent people he had met.*

[1] Charles Babbage (1792–1871; *DNB*), mathematician and inventor; FRS 1816; helped to found the Astronomical Society 1820, and the Statistical Society 1834. Began work on his celebrated calculating machine (which anticipated the modern digital computer) 1823, but abandoned it 1842 after spending £17,000 of public money and *c.* £20,000 of his own. Professor of Mathematics, Cambridge, 1828–39. Gave regular Saturday *soirées*; was a friend of Samuel Rogers, Miss Coutts and Macready—through whom CD probably first met him. For his turbulent character, close relationship with Byron's daughter, Lady Lovelace (herself a gifted mathematician), quarrels with other scientists, and increasing bitterness at lack of belief in his machine, see M. Moseley, *Irascible Genius*, 1964. CD owned his *Ninth Bridgewater Treatise*, 1837, a work on the use of mathematics to religion, and alluded to it in a speech in 1869 (see *Speeches*, ed. K. J. Fielding, p. 399).

[2] N misreads as "comedians". No pamphlets on this subject by Babbage himself have been discovered; but during 1840 alone over a million anti-Corn-Law pamphlets and leaflets were distributed (A. Prentice, *History of the Anti-Corn-Law League*, 1853, I, 173). For CD's own reference to the Corn Laws in his *Examiner* verse-satires, see *To* Forster, 13 Aug 41, *fn.*

The renowned Peter Robertson[1] is a large, portly, full-faced man with a merry eye, and a queer way of looking under his spectacles[2] which is characteristic and pleasant. He seems a very warm-hearted earnest man too, and I felt quite at home with him forthwith. Walking up and down the hall of the courts of law (which was full of advocates, writers to the signet, clerks, and idlers) was a tall, burly, handsome man of eight and fifty, with a gait like O'Connell's, the bluest eye you can imagine, and long hair—longer than mine—falling down in a wild way under the broad brim of his hat. He had on a surtout coat, a blue checked shirt; the collar standing up, and kept in its place with a wisp of black neckerchief; no waistcoat; and a large pocket-handkerchief thrust into his breast, which was all broad and open. At his heels followed a wiry, sharp-eyed, shaggy devil of a terrier, dogging his steps as he went slashing up and down, now with one man beside him, now with another, and now quite alone, but always at a fast, rolling pace, with his head in the air, and his eyes as wide open as he could get them. I guessed it was Wilson, and it was. A bright, clear-complexioned, mountain-looking fellow, he looks as though he had just come down from the Highlands, and had never in his life taken pen in hand. But he has had an attack of paralysis in his right arm, within this month. He winced when I shook hands with him; and once or twice when we were walking up and down, slipped as if he had stumbled on a piece of orange-peel. He is a great fellow to look at, and to talk to; and, if you could divest your mind of the actual Scott, is just the figure you would put in his place.[3] . . .

Allan[4] has been squiring me about, all the morning. He and Fletcher have gone to a meeting of the dinner-stewards, and I take the opportunity of writing to you. They dine with us to-day, and we are going to-night to

[1] Patrick Robertson (1794–1855; DNB), advocate; often known by the diminutive "Peter". A friend of John Wilson's. Became a Lord of Session 1843, and took his seat on the bench as Lord Robertson. Known for his warm-heartedness and wit. At the Edinburgh dinner proposed the health of Scott. "With what enthusiasm", he said, "—with what delight and cordiality would the author of Waverley have hailed the advent of the author of the Pickwick Papers." He envisaged various meetings between characters in Scott's and CD's novels: how, e.g., Davie Gellatley (the half-witted servant in Waverley) would "jump with delight to hail his brother Barnaby Rudge" (a parallel Bulwer clearly recognized too, though with disapproval: see To Latimer, 13 Mar, fn); and how at Dotheboys Hall "Dominie Sampson would have ex-

claimed at the arrangements of Squeers —Pro-digious!'" (Caledonian Mercury, 26 June 41). Robertson and CD met again in 1844.

[2] In two sketches of Robertson reproduced in Mrs Gordon's 'Christopher North', A Memoir of John Wilson, new edn, Edinburgh, 1879, pp. 163 and 165, his spectacles are halfway down his nose and he looks over them; in the caricature "Boz's Introduction to Christopher North", he seems to look under them: i.e. what was characteristic was his not looking through them.

[3] For CD's description of Wilson when proposing his health at the Edinburgh dinner, see Speeches, ed. K. J. Fielding, pp. 11–12.

[4] Whom CD already knew. For the sketch he made of CD at the Edinburgh dinner, see To Landseer, 11 May 40, fn.

the theatre. M'Ian[1] is playing there. I mean to leave a card for him before evening. We are engaged for every day of our stay, already; but the people I have seen are so very hearty and warm in their manner that much of the horrors of lionization gives way before it. I am glad to find that they propose giving me for a toast on Friday the Memory of Wilkie.[2] I should have liked it better than anything, if I could have made my choice. Communicate all particulars to Mac. I would to God you were both here. Do dine together at the Gray's-inn on Friday, and think of me. If I don't drink my first glass of wine to you, may my pistols miss fire, and my mare slip her shoulder.[3] All sorts of regard from Kate. She has gone with Miss Allan[4] to see the house she was born in, &c.[5] Write me soon, and long, &c.

## *To* SIR CHARLES BELL,[6] 24 JUNE 1841*

Text from typescript, Huntington Library.

Royal Hotel, Princes Street
Thursday Morning. | June 24. 1841

Mr. Charles Dickens presents his compliments to Sir Charles Bell, and begs to hand him the inclosed letter and accompanying little parcel, with which he was entrusted, previous to leaving town, by Mr. Thomas Landseer.[7]

---

[1] Robert Ronald M'Ian (1803–56; *DNB*), actor and painter; "a Highlander and fierce Jacobite" (W. P. Frith, *John Leech*, 1891, II, 4). As an actor, specialized in playing Highland characters. Performed (1835–9) at the English Opera House, Covent Garden, and Drury Lane, meanwhile training himself in art. His portrait of Mrs S. C. Hall 1838 was praised by Camilla Toulmin (*Landmarks of a Literary Life*, 1893, p. 125). Figured as the jester, mounted on a donkey, in the Eglinton Tournament, 28 Aug 39, and "was generally voted an intolerable bore" (Henry Vizetelly, *Glances back through Seventy Years*, 1893, I, 183). Advised Macready on the part of McIan in *Glencoe*, 1840 (Macready, *Diaries*, II, 60). Before long gave up the stage to devote himself entirely to art—mainly painting scenes of Highland history or life. For his

wife, Fanny M'Ian, a painter too, see Vol. III.

[2] The third speech CD made at the dinner: see *To* Forster, 26 June, *fn*.

[3] *The Beggar's Opera*, I, 13; Macheath to Polly.

[4] William Allan's niece.

[5] See *To* Fletcher, 9 June, *fn*.

[6] Sir Charles Bell (1774–1842; *DNB*), discoverer of the functions of the nerves. Practised medicine and lectured in London 1804–36, when he returned to his birthplace, Edinburgh, as Professor of Surgery. Published *The Nervous System of the Human Body*, 1830. Lifelong friend of Lord Jeffrey. He was on the platform at the dinner of 25 June.

[7] Landseer may have attended the lectures on anatomy which Bell gave to artists in London. Bell was a skilled draughtsman and illustrated many of his own anatomical works.

## *To* JOHN FORSTER, [26 JUNE 1841]

Extracts in F, II, x, 176–7. *Date*: Sat 26 June according to Forster.

The great event[1] is over; and being gone, I am a man again.[2] It was the most brilliant affair you can conceive; the completest success possible, from first to last. The room was crammed, and more than seventy applicants for tickets were of necessity refused yesterday. Wilson was ill, but plucked up like a lion, and spoke famously.[3] I send you a paper herewith,[4] but the report is dismal in the extreme.[5] They say there will be a better one —I don't know where or when. Should there be, I will send it to you. I *think* (ahem!) that I spoke rather well.[6] It was an excellent room, and both

---

[1] The dinner in CD's honour held at the Waterloo Rooms, Edinburgh, on 25 June. The elaborately decorated dinner ticket is reproduced in *D*, XXII (1926), 219.

[2] *Macbeth*, III, iv, 108.

[3] For a long extract from Wilson's speech from the Chair, see F, II, x, 176*n*. He described CD as "perhaps the most popular writer now alive". CD had formidable competitors, not only among the living, but in the minds of people familiar with Defoe, Richardson, Fielding, Smollett and Scott; and Wilson understood that he had "no external aids to trust to". His popularity then must be attributed to his "almost divine insight into the workings of human nature", his originality, his power to transmute "what was base into what was precious", and "the benign spirit" which pervaded all his creations. He was a satirist, but only of selfishness and hard-heartedness. Wilson then came to his one criticism: "I shall not say that our distinguished guest has done full and entire justice—that he has entirely succeeded wherein he and every man must be most anxious to succeed—in a full and complete delineation of the female character [*Laughter, and cries of Hear*]—Who has succeeded with the exception of Shakspeare? ... But this he has done— ... he has represented his female characters as inspired with the love of domestic duty, of purity, innocence, charity, faith, and hope, which makes them discharge, under the most difficult and trying circumstances, their duties, and always brings over their path on earth some glimpses of the light of heaven [*Loud cheers*]" (*Caledonian*

*Mercury*, 26 June 41). Here Wilson seems to have been paying lip-service to Nell, of whom he doubtless knew Lord Jeffrey's view and how differently Jeffrey, if chairing the dinner, would have treated the subject. On reading an account of this speech Landor wrote to Lady Blessington: "I am delighted to find how gloriously my friend Dickens has been received at Edinburgh. But the Scotchmen could not avoid ill-placed criticisms, and oblique comparisons. One blockhead talked of his deficiency in the female character—the very thing in which he and Shakespeare most excel" (R. R. Madden, *The Literary Life and Correspondence of the Countess of Blessington*, 1855, II, 386).

[4] Probably either the *Edinburgh Evening Courant* or the *Caledonian Mercury* of 26 June.

[5] The *Caledonian Mercury* gave CD's speech only a little over a quarter of the space it gave Wilson's; but the *Evening Courant*'s report was fuller. The *Scotsman* of 30 June remarked that "the report of the proceedings in Saturday morning's papers was necessarily very imperfect, and conveyed but a feeble idea of the style and effect of [CD's] eloquence". Its own report was extremely brief, and contained no direct quotation from his speeches.

[6] A considerable part of CD's reply to Wilson's speech centred on Nell's death (which Wilson had not mentioned): "I feel", he said, "as if the deaths of the fictitious characters, in which you have been kind enough to express an interest, had endeared us to each other as real afflictions deepen friendships in real life". Later in the

the subjects (Wilson and Scottish Literature, and the Memory of Wilkie)[1] were good to go upon. There were nearly two hundred ladies present.[2] The place is so contrived that the cross table is raised enormously: much above the heads of people sitting below: and the effect on first coming in (on me, I mean) was rather tremendous. I was quite self-possessed however, and, notwithstanding the enthoosemoosy, which was very startling, as cool as a cucumber. I wish to God you had been there, as it is impossible for the "distinguished guest" to describe the scene. It beat all natur'. . . .

I have been expecting every day to hear from you, and not hearing mean to make this the briefest epistle possible. We start next Sunday (that's to-morrow week). We are going out to Jeffrey's to-day (he is very unwell), and return here to-morrow evening. If I don't find a letter from you when I come back, expect no Lights and Shadows of Scottish Life[3] from your indignant correspondent. Murray the manager[4] made very excellent, tasteful, and gentlemanly mention of Macready,[5] about whom Wilson had been asking me divers questions during dinner.

speech he defended his adherence to the end he had had in view—Nell's death, in which he knew they were disappointed; but, "not untried in the school of affliction" himself, he hoped his "little work of pleasant amusement" might "substitute a garland of fresh flowers for the sculptured horrors which disgrace the tomb" (*Edinburgh Evening Courant*, 26 June). This seems an instance of CD's overestimating the impact of Nell's death on the general public.

[1] The two toasts that CD proposed later in the evening. For texts of his three speeches, taken from the *Evening Courant*, 26 June, see *Speeches*, ed. K. J. Fielding, pp. 9–14. Both the *Evening Courant* and the *Scotsman* praised his spontaneity; R. S. Mackenzie (*Life of CD*, p. 131) quotes a letter from one of his audience: "He is as happy in public speaking as in writing—nothing studied, nothing artistical; his were no written speeches, conned, and got by heart, but every sentence seemed to be suggested on the impulse of the moment" ("seemed": but he had probably prepared in advance the passages on Nell, and was not to be put off by Wilson's virtually ignoring her). The *Evening Courant* reported that he was "much affected" in the delivery of his speech on Wilkie.

[2] Catherine, accompanied by 150 other ladies, came into the gallery when the dinner was over, to hear the speeches. Angus Fletcher proposed their health, declaring that CD "owed much of his distinction to his having selected as a partner for life a Scottish lady". Replying, CD said that it was true that his wife was a Scotchwoman, born in Edinburgh; "and he had always looked with pleasure upon his children as half bred English and Scotch" (*Caledonian Mercury*, 26 June).

[3] An allusion to Wilson's *Lights and Shadows of Scottish Life*, 1822; also referred to in CD's speech, as "that beautiful book to which I have turned again and again" (*Speeches*, p. 12). He had read it in the British Museum in 1830 (see Vol. I, p. 9n), but apparently did not own it until he acquired Wilson's complete *Works*, 1855–8.

[4] William Henry Murray (1790–1852; *DNB*), actor and manager. For 33 years manager of the Edinburgh Theatres—first succeeding his brother-in-law Henry Siddons (Mrs Siddons's son) 1815 to 1829 (when the patent granted to Henry Siddons expired); then in direct management of the Adelphi and Theatre Royal 1830–48. Acted in numerous adaptations of Scott's novels 1817–26—more than half of them adapted by himself. His adaptation of *Oliver* was produced in Mar 40. Managed CD's amateur dramatics in Edinburgh July 48.

[5] Presumably in his speech (the last

## *To* MESSRS CHAPMAN & HALL, 26 JUNE 1841

MS Mrs A. M. Stern.

Royal Hotel Edinburgh. | Saturday Twenty Sixth June 1841.
Dear Sirs.

The great event is over. It was the most brilliant affair you can possibly imagine. The room was crammed to the throat, and more than seventy people were turned away yesterday who had come from different parts of Scotland,—in consequence of the room being full. Besides the diners there were nearly two hundred ladies, and the whole place rings to-day with the noise of the affair.

I send you a couple of newspapers, but the report is very dismal indeed. Blackwoods have been here this morning and intend to publish a corrected account in a pamphlet,[1] which of course you shall have.

I shall be glad if you will send me, so that I may receive it in the course of the week, a fifty pound note, and deduct it with the other extras from the monthly payment into Coutts's. The Highland arrangements seem to be more extensive than I had supposed, and I have no cheque book here, nor did I make any arrangement for a credit at the bank in this place before I came away; not thinking I should require it.[2]

I shall be very glad to hear from you. We are going to Lord Jeffrey's tonight, and shall stop there a day or two, but I shall be sure to be in Edinburgh again by the time the Post returns.

Mrs. Dickens sends her best regards.

Always Believe me | Faithfully Yours
Messrs. Chapman and Hall.                              CHARLES DICKENS


## *To* GEORGE CATTERMOLE, 26 JUNE 1841

MS Dickens House.

Royal Hotel Edinburgh | Saturday 26th. June 1841.
My Dear George.

I have barely time to write six words, having some sixty letters to dispatch. The dinner was the most brilliant success ever known here. They turned away more than 70 people yesterday for whom there was no room, and besides the 250 or 270 who dined, there were nearly 200 ladies. It was a most magnificent show, and the shouting perfectly awful.

I send you a newspaper, but the report is intensely dismal. Blackwoods have been here this morning to tell me that they mean to publish a cor-

---

but one of the evening) replying to the toast proposed by Robertson to "Mr Murray and the Theatre". According to the *Caledonian Mercury*, 26 June, the applause during it was so deafening that no report was possible.

[1] They did not in fact do so. For CD's dining with them on 30 June, see *To* Forster, that day, and *fn.*

[2] The letter is endorsed: "Sent a £50 pound Note. | No. 32439. 6th. March 1841. | June 28th. 1841. WE".

rected account in a pamphlet, of which I promise myself the pleasure of sending you a copy.

With best regards from Kate in which I heartily join,

Believe me | Always Faithfully Yours

George Cattermole Esquire                    CHARLES DICKENS


## *To* WILLIAM JERDAN, 28 JUNE 1841

Extracts in N, I, 329 and Anderson Galleries catalogue, Feb 1922 (*aa*); *MS* 2 pp.; dated Royal Hotel, Edinburgh, 28 June 41.

The dinner was a very brilliant affair indeed—they say here the best on record. *It included all parties and persuasions.* They were obliged for lack of room to turn away nearly a hundred applicants for tickets, and besides the diners we had more than a hundred and fifty ladies. Blackwoods are going to publish a good account of the speechifying. When they do so, I'll send you one. Meanwhile I forward you two papers wherein the reporting is dismal.

It's November here. I hope it may be June in London.


## *To* THE LORD PROVOST OF EDINBURGH,[1]
### [30 JUNE 1841]

Mention in next.


## *To* JOHN FORSTER, [30 JUNE 1841]

Extracts in F, II, x, 177–80, dated by Forster four days after letter of 26 June; and extract in F, II, ix, 168, dated 30 June.

A hundred thanks for your letter. I read it this morning with the greatest pleasure and delight, and answer it with ditto, ditto. Where shall I begin—about my darlings? I am delighted with Charley's precocity. He takes arter his father, he does. God bless them, you can't imagine (*you!* how can you!) how much I long to see them. It makes me quite sorrowful to think of them. . . . Yesterday, sir, the lord provost, council, and magistrates voted me by acclamation the freedom of the city, in testimony (I quote the letter just received from "James Forrest, lord provost") "of the sense entertained by them of your distinguished abilities as an author." I acknowledged this morning in appropriate terms the honour they had

---

[1] Sir James Forrest, Bart (1780–1860), advocate; Lord Provost of Edinburgh since 1838. A ruling elder of the established Church of Scotland until 1843, when he joined the Free Church. Grand Master of the Freemasons in Scotland.

done me, and through me the pursuit to which I was devoted. It *is* handsome, is it not?[1]

The men who spoke at the dinner were all the most rising men here, and chiefly at the Bar. They were all, alternately, whigs and tories; with some few radicals, such as Gordon,[2] who gave the memory of Burns. He is Wilson's son-in-law and the lord advocate's nephew—a very masterly speaker indeed, who ought to become a distinguished man. Neaves,[3] who gave the other poets, a *little* too lawyer-like for my taste, is a great gun in the courts. Mr. Primrose[4] is Lord Rosebery's[5] son. Adam Black,[6] the publisher as you know. Dr. Alison, a very popular friend of the poor.[7] Robertson you know. Allan you know. Colquhoun[8] is an advocate. All these men were selected for the toasts as being crack speakers, known men,

[1] A Minute of the Town Council records, 29 June 41, the unanimous voting to CD of the Freedom of the City on the Lord Provost's motion; and Forrest's letter to CD of the same date is copied into the Letter Book. CD's Burgess Ticket was sent him on 12 Aug with a covering note from Forrest (also copied in the Letter Book). The "Ticket" (a parchment scroll) hung framed in CD's study until his death (F, II, x, 177). It was given to the Huntly House Museum, Edinburgh, in 1940, by Mr H. C. Dickens.

[2] John Thomson Gordon (1813–65), advocate; married John Wilson's daughter Mary 1837; sheriff of Aberdeen 1847–8; of Midlothian 1849–65. With his wife lived in Wilson's house 1837–48, and introduced him to new friends from "the camp of the enemy" such as Cockburn, Jeffrey, and his uncle, Rutherfurd; under his influence, Wilson's "old prejudices disappeared" (Mrs Gordon, 'Christopher North', *A Memoir of John Wilson*, new edn, 1879, p. 415). Proposed the Memory of Burns at the Edinburgh dinner. Later became a friend of CD's—"not less intimate", says Forster (F, VI, vi, 530), than Jeffrey.

[3] Charles Neaves (1800–76; *DNB*), Tory advocate-depute 1841–5; Solicitor-General for Scotland 1852–3; regarded as one of the best case-lawyers of the day. Judge in the Court of Session 1853, with the title Lord Neaves. A frequent contributor to *Blackwood's*. Proposed the health of Wordsworth, Campbell and Moore at the Edinburgh dinner.

[4] The Hon. Bouverie Francis Primrose (1813–98), who had proposed Robertson's health at the dinner.

[5] Archibald John Primrose, 4th Earl of Rosebery (1783–1868; *DNB*).

[6] Adam Black (1784–1874; *DNB*), liberal politician and publisher; established the publishing house with his nephew Charles, in 1827 acquiring the copyright of the *Encyclopaedia Britannica*. Proposed "the Universities of Great Britain and Ireland" at the dinner.

[7] William Pulteney Alison, MD (1790–1859; *DNB*), Professor of the Institutes of Medicine, Edinburgh University, since 1822. First gained knowledge of working-class sufferings as physician to the New Town dispensary, Edinburgh, 1815. He was convinced that poverty must be attacked before disease, and that private benevolence was utterly inadequate (though devoting more than half his own income to relieving the poor of Edinburgh). Expressed these ideas in a highly influential pamphlet, *Observations on the Management of the Poor in Scotland, and its Effects on the Health of Great Towns*, 1840, demanding compulsory Poor Relief, and insisting that the proper way to control population was through "general felicity". In Jan 43 the Govt appointed a Royal Commission to inquire into the Scottish Poor Laws, and the Scottish Poor Law Amendment Act was passed 1845.

[8] Ludovick Colquhoun (1807–54), advocate 1832, who had proposed Jeffrey's health.

and opposed to each other very strongly in politics. For this reason, the professors and so forth who sat upon the platform about me[1] made no speeches and had none assigned them. I felt it was very remarkable to see such a number of grey-headed men gathered about my brown flowing locks; and it struck most of those who were present very forcibly.[2] The judges, solicitor-general,[3] lord-advocate,[4] and so forth, were all here to call, the day after our arrival. The judges never go to public dinners in Scotland. Lord Meadowbank[5] alone broke through the custom, and none of his successors have imitated him. It will give you a good notion of *party* to hear that the solicitor-general and lord-advocate refused to go, though they had previously engaged, *unless* the croupier[6] or the chairman were a whig. Both (Wilson and Robertson) were tories, simply because, Jeffrey excepted, no whig could be found who was adapted to the office. The solicitor laid strict injunctions on Napier[7] not to go if a whig were not in office. No whig was, and he stayed away. I think this is good?—bearing in mind that all the old whigs of Edinburgh were cracking their throats in the room. They give out that they were ill, and the lord-advocate did actually lie in bed all the afternoon; but this is the real truth, and one of the judges told it me with great glee. It seems they couldn't quite trust Wilson or Robertson, as they thought; and feared some tory demonstration. Nothing of the kind took place; and ever since, these men have been the loudest in their praises of the whole affair.[8]

[1] Professors Christison, Traill, and Syme were on the platform; also Sir George Warrenden, Sir William Hamilton, the Lord Provost, Sir Charles Bell, D. M. Moir, and others.

[2] CD rose to reply to Wilson amidst cordial applause, "subdued by the astonishment with which the crowded assembly obviously regarded the Shakspeare of his day, the juvenility of whose appearance was found to have been faithfully depicted in the published portraits" (*Caledonian Mercury*, 26 June).

[3] Thomas Maitland (1792–1851; *DNB*), Solicitor-General under Whig Ministries 1840–1 and 1846–50; brother-in-law of Cockburn and a close friend of Jeffrey's; edited a volume of Jeffrey's contributions to the *Edinburgh*, 1843. A Lord of the Court of Session 1850, taking the title Lord Dundrennan.

[4] Andrew Rutherfurd (1791–1854; *DNB*), Lord Advocate under Whig Ministries 1839–41 and from 1846. Member of the Privy Council 1851, with the title of Lord Rutherfurd.

[5] Alexander Maconochie, later Maconochie-Welwood, Lord Meadowbank (1777–1861; *DNB*), judge. A Tory.

[6] I.e. the Assistant Chairman who sat at the lower end of the table (*OED*)—Patrick Robertson.

[7] Macvey Napier, FRS (1776–1847; *DNB*), editor of the *Edinburgh Review* since Jeffrey's resignation 1829, distinguishing himself by the tact and firmness with which he handled difficult contributors (notably Brougham); under him the *Edinburgh* became not so much the voice of liberal ideas but of the Whig party. First Professor of Conveyancing, Edinburgh University, 1824. Edited the *Encyclopaedia Britannica*, 7th edn, completed 1842.

[8] Party antagonism had become violent at the time of the Whigs' advocacy of Napoleon, and even after his death supporters of the two parties only met as friends occasionally. See, for instance, Scott's tentative explanation (8 Dec 1826) of the pleasantness and "capital good cheer" on such an occasion as a dinner at Murray's, continuing (9 Dec): "I believe both parties met with the feeling of something like novelty" (*The Journal of Sir Walter Scott 1825–26*, ed. J. G. Tait, Edinburgh, 1939, pp. 288–9). Both Wilson and Robertson referred in

A threat reached me last night (they have been hammering at it in their papers, it seems, for some time) of a dinner at Glasgow.[1] But I hope, having circulated false rumours of my movements, to get away before they send to me; and only to stop there on my way home, to change horses and send to the post-office. . . . You will like to know how we have been living. Here's a list of engagements, past and present. Wednesday, we dined at home, and went incog. to the theatre at night, to Murray's box:[2] the pieces admirably done, and M'Ian in the *Two Drovers* quite wonderful, and most affecting. Thursday, to Lord Murray's;[3] dinner and evening party. Friday, *the* dinner. Saturday, to Jeffrey's, a beautiful place about three miles off,[4] stop there all night, dine on Sunday, and home at eleven. Monday, dine at Dr. Alison's, four miles off. Tuesday dinner and evening party

their speeches to the coming General Election, Wilson calling the dinner to CD "a sort of truce".

[1] A letter in the *Glasgow Courier* on 15 June, expressing the hope that the citizens of Glasgow would not lag behind those of Edinburgh in inviting CD to a public dinner, seems to have been the only reference in Glasgow papers.

[2] At the Adelphi. The programme consisted of *Lo Zingari* (founded on a novel by Tyrone Power); *The Twa Drovers* (with M'Ian as Robin Oig the Highland Drover); and *The Inchcape Bell* (with M'Ian as the Pirate, and the Dumb Boy played by Taglioni). During the week, Murray also put on CD's *The Strange Gentleman*—"nightly received in a manner which testifies to the author's popularity more unequivocally, perhaps, than the distinguished compliment paid to his genius by the more select few among his admirers in the city last night" (*Scotsman*, 27 June 41).

[3] John Archibald Murray (1779–1859; *DNB*), created Lord Murray on leaving politics to become a judge of the Court of Session 1839. Contributed to the *Edinburgh Review* (only five certain articles listed in *The Wellesley Index to Victorian Periodicals*, 1966, Vol. I). An ardent liberal; succeeded Jeffrey as Lord Advocate 1835; a charming and most hospitable man. Provided CD with a map of the Highlands and letters of introduction for his tour (*To* Lord Murray, 21 July 41). With his wife visited CD later at Devonshire Terrace (F, VI, vi, 531).

[4] Before leaving for Jeffrey on the 26th, CD apparently dined with the Lord Advocate (Lord Rutherfurd), and wrote the following appeal: "MONUMENT TO MRS. SIDDONS BY CHANTREY, IN WESTMINSTER ABBEY. A Committee has been formed in London, of which the Marquess of Lansdowne is President, for the purpose of erecting a Monument to Mrs. Siddons, by Guinea subscription, in Westminster Abbey. The Committee is composed of a few gentlemen the most distinguished in Art, Literature and rank; and the Sculptor himself is one of their number. It was suggested to me as a member of the body, before I left town, that in Edinburgh where Mrs. Siddons was so much admired, the object could not fail to be supported. I have therefore opened this list. The amount of subscription is limited to one guinea for each person subscribing. | CHARLES DICKENS | Saturday June The Twenty Sixth 1841" (MS Mr A. G. Schaw Miller). This is now accompanied by the following MS note: "The above was written by Mr Dickens at a Dinner Party given by the Lord Advocate. The company consisted of the Honle. Lord Murray, Lady Murray, The Right Honle. The Lord Advocate, the Solicitor Gen. for Scotland and Mrs Maitland, The Honle. Lord Cockburn, Wm. Murray Esqre. of Henderland and Angus Fletcher Esqre. Sculptor, each of whom subscribed a guinea towards the erection of the monument." Interest in the appeal (see *To* Macready, 22 Mar, *fn*) could be expected in Edinburgh, with its existing link with Mrs Siddons (see *To* Forster, 26 June, *fn*).

at Allan's. Wednesday, breakfast with Napier, dine with Blackwoods[1] seven miles off, evening party at the treasurer's of the town-council,[2] supper with all the artists (!!).[3] Thursday, lunch at the solicitor-general's, dine at Lord Gillies's,[4] evening party at Joseph Gordon's,[5] one of Brougham's earliest supporters. Friday, dinner and evening party at Robertson's. Saturday, dine again at Jeffrey's; back to the theatre,[6] at half-past nine to the moment, for public appearance; places all let, &c. &c. &c. Sunday, off at seven o'clock in the morning to Stirling, and then to Callender, a stage further. Next day, to Loch-earn, and pull up there for three days, to rest and work. The moral of all this is, that there is no place like home; and that I thank God most heartily for having given me a quiet spirit, and a heart that won't hold many people. I sigh for Devonshire-terrace and Broadstairs, for battledore and shuttlecock; I want to dine in a blouse with you and Mac; and I feel Topping's merits more acutely than I have ever done in my life. On Sunday evening the 17th of July I shall revisit my household gods, please heaven. I wish the day were here. For God's sake be in waiting. I wish you and Mac would dine in Devonshire-terrace that day with Fred. He has the key of the cellar. *Do.* We shall be at Inverary in the Highlands on Tuesday week, getting to it through the pass of Glencoe, of which you may have heard! On Thursday following we shall be at Glasgow, where I shall hope to receive your last letter before we meet. At Inverary, too, I shall make sure of finding at least one, at the post-office. . . . Little Allan is trying hard for the post of queen's limner[7] for Scotland, vacant by poor Wilkie's death. Every one is in his favor but ——[8] who is jobbing for some one else. Appoint him, will you, and I'll give up the premier-ship.—How I breakfasted to-day in the house where Scott lived seven and twenty years;[9] how I have made solemn pledges to write about [mining][10] children in the *Edinburgh Review*, and will do my best to keep them; how I have declined to be brought in, free gratis for nothing and qualified to boot, for a Scotch county that's going a-begging, lest I should

---

[1] Alexander (1805–43) and Robert (1807–52), the two eldest sons of William Blackwood, founder of *Blackwood's Magazine*, whose publishing house they ran jointly from his death in 1834. John, the sixth son (1818–79; *DNB*), who later took over the firm, was at this time working at the London branch.

[2] William Drysdale, Writer to the Signet; entered the Town Council as councillor Nov 38; Treasurer from Nov 40.

[3] Among them, presumably, Allan, Fletcher and the M'Ians.

[4] Adam Gillies, Lord Gillies (1760–1842; *DNB*), judge. Took little part in politics; his views were Whig in early life, but changed to Tory. Sir Archibald Alison thought highly of him: he "possessed no family influence, and his rise at the Bar was the result of his own force and originality of mind" (*My Life and Writings*, 1883, 1, 276).

[5] Probably Joseph Gordon (1777–1855), Writer to the Signet, of Gordon, Stuart & Cheyne, 5 Royal Terrace.

[6] See *To* W. H. Murray, 3 July, *fn.*

[7] He was successful.

[8] Name omitted by Forster.

[9] 25 St George's Square. Scott lived there 1778–97. Napier was living there now.

[10] Forster reads "missing", clearly mistakenly: see *To* Napier, 8 Aug, *fn.*

be thought to have dined on Friday under false pretences; these, with other marvels, shall be yours anon.

*a*You may suppose, I have not done much work—but by Friday night's post from here I hope to send the first long chapter of a number and both the illustrations;[1] from Loch-earn on Tuesday night, the closing chapter of that number; from the same place on Thursday night, the first long chapter of another, with both the illustrations; and, from some place which no man ever spelt but which sounds like Ballyhoolish,[2] on Saturday, the closing chapter of that number,[3] which will leave us all safe till I return to town.*a*

I must leave off sharp, to get dressed and off upon the seven miles dinner trip. Kate's affectionate regards. My hearty loves to Mac and Grim.[4]

## *To* A. S. LOGAN,[5] 1 JULY 1841*

MS National Library of Scotland.

Royal Hotel Edinburgh | First July 1841.

Dear Sir.

I find to-day that I must receive some gentlemen here, on Saturday morning, and that after I have done with them I must fulfil so many engagements (all of which I have postponed to that last day of my stay) that I shall not have time to see Mr. Harvey's[6] pictures, to which you so kindly offered to introduce me. Having two engagements for the evening besides, I shall really not have a moment to spare between morning and night.

With reference to Stirling too, I am obliged, having regard to my letters from London this morning, to *get on*; and I grieve to say that I must not stop there except to change horses. So the castle and the battle fields must be visited when I come again;—I hope it will not be very long before I do.

*b*I beg my compliments to Mrs. Logan, and am Dear Sir,

Faithfully Yours,

A. S. Logan Esquire                          CHARLES DICKENS*b*

*aa* This passage (from F, II, ix, 168), quoted by Forster in his chapter on *Barnaby*, seems clearly to belong at this point in CD's letter.

[1] I.e. instructions for the illustrations.

[2] Ballachulish.

[3] He had in fact finished the two numbers of *Barnaby* (Nos 69 and 70, Chs 45–8, published 24 and 31 July) by Fri 9 July: see *To* Forster, that day. They contained the following illustrations: "Widow Rudge's cottage" and "Stagg at the Widow's" (Ch. 45), "Barnaby refuses to sell the raven" (Ch. 47), and "Lord George ordering Barnaby to join the mob" (Ch. 48)—all by Browne, although in Hatton's

"Bibliographical List" (*Retrospectus and Prospectus*, The Nonesuch Dickens, 1937) "Widow Rudge's cottage" is given as by Cattermole.

[4] No doubt Macready: in *To* Maclise, 12 July, CD says he has had letters from "Grims and Elliotsons", and in *To* Forster, 9 July, from Macready and Elliotson.

[5] Alexander Stewart Logan (1810–1862), advocate, sheriff of Forfarshire.

[6] Probably George Harvey 1806–76; *DNB*), painter, chiefly of figure-pictures and landscapes. President Royal Scottish Academy 1864, when knighted.

*bb* Not in CD's hand. The ending has

## *To* LORD JEFFREY, 1 JULY 1841

MS Mr A. G. Schaw Miller.

Royal Hotel. | Thursday First July 1841.

My Dear Lord Jeffrey.

Do not fear that either my spouse or I had forgotten, or were in danger of forgetting, our engagement for next Saturday. It is much too pleasant and happy.

I wish most earnestly that it were in my power to remain with you over Sunday and enjoy a quiet day, but I am sorry to say that our arrangements are made for leaving Edinburgh at Seven on Sunday morning, and that I am bound to be virtuous, and constant to my plans. I am a poor Slave of the Lamp, and tomorrow it will have been rubbed thrice, with no response from me.[1] It is impossible to work or think here, and I must fly for my life—or for my living, which is the same thing.

I shall be obliged, moreover, to leave Craigcrook at a quarter before nine. I have been terribly beset by Murray to go to his theatre, and having made a vague promise that I would, am anxious to redeem it, lest I should seem to set too high a store by my gracious presence. Therefore I have settled to be there at half past nine.—It's martyrdom to me, but there is no help for it.

You see how defenceless I am, and knowing how much rather I would be with you, will be sorry for me, I am sure.

I beg my compliments to Miss Browne.[2] She told me she would like to see the inclosed pamphlet, which I happened to have in my desk, and which I send for her perusal.

Kate desires her best regards. And I am always

Dear Lord Jeffrey
With truth and heartiness
Faithfully Yours
CHARLES DICKENS

I hope, and have no doubt, that your coming holidays will set you up completely.

## *To* LORD JEFFREY, 3 JULY 1841*

MS Mills College, Oakland, California.

Royal Hotel. | Saturday July The Third 1841.

My Dear Lord Jeffrey.

I need not say that we are truly sorry for the cause of our disappointment to day, and that we are extremely anxious to hear how you are, when

---

been cut away (and "given to a friend" according to endorsement); but the portion removed was copied first.

[1] He had not written a word since he finished No. 68 (published 17 July) on 15 June (*To* Fletcher, that day).

[2] Thus in MS. Harriet Brown, Jeffrey's niece, daughter of his sister Marion and Dr Thomas Brown, a leading Glasgow physician.

we reach town tomorrow fortnight.  If you could find time to write me one line, you would gratify me very much.  If not, I hope Miss Brown will do us that favor.

We took solemn council together just now, whether we should come round and see you, and shake hands before parting.  We have come to the conclusion that we had better not; firstly, because you have been enjoined repose, and secondly—to tell the truth—because parting even for a few months from one whom I hold in such esteem and regard, is a thing I cannot bear.—I have been contriving all the morning, a hundred ways of getting off from your dinner table without saying good bye.  Writing it, is nearly as bad, but not quite.

God bless you.  We shall always remember with delight the few most pleasant hours we have spent at Craigcrook,[1] and shall look forward to your next visit to London with as much real pleasure as any of your thousand friends.[2]

Believe me Dear Lord Jeffrey | Faithfully Yours

CHARLES DICKENS

Our united best regards to Miss Browne[3]—with whom I am very much in love.[4]

[1] Over the previous week-end. It was probably then that CD gave Jeffrey a horn snuff-box, inscribed round the silver rim: "To Lord Jeffrey from Charles Dickens Edinburgh 1841" (now in the possession of Colonel Richard Gimbel).  Since the silver emblem on the face of the box is engraved "C.D. Gad's Hill", it was clearly returned to CD sometime after Jeffrey's death.

[2] On 20 July Jeffrey wrote: "I can scarcely believe that it is little more than a fortnight since you left Edinburgh—and *ought* to have dined with me at Craigcrook!  The time since has passed but heavily with me—not merely because *you* have been at a distance, but, I am sorry to say, because I have been in a very shabby, shaky, good for nothing state of health—You saw the beginning of it, that nice day we strolled on my little terrace and wooed the sylvan muse (in the shape of Mrs Crowe! [*who lived at 2 Darnaway Street, Edinburgh*]) in the shades of Dalmeny . . . —I have always a good day I observe *on Saturday* [*publication day of* Master Humphrey]—and have a strong belief therefore, that a *private prescription* from the great Doctor who mends the hearts of all the world, on that day,

would be of infinite service to me— . . . | Well, God bless you and all that belongs to you!—I regret direly that I saw so little of you while you were here—But I have seen enough to do me a great deal of good—and to feel assured (is that very presumptuous ?) that you will rely on my sincere friendship for life—It is a pity that I am so old, that my constancy will not be put to a great trial—But that melancholy seniority gives me a right to counsel you—to which I am aware I have no other pretension—and therefore I venture to say—do not spend your money as you get it—but secure as near as you can, a full *independence*—and pray give us something to love and weep over—better than Dolly—and more touching than even Mrs Rudge. Have you gathered any traits of *Scotch* character and feeling on your visit ? I do not wish you to take *ludicrous* subjects from among us—for those would be merely provincial and less generally intelligible than those which you know better—But there are peculiarities of thoughtful tendency and homely devotedness which would tell anywhere and are strictly *national*—You must have been struck with many of them I think in Scott— | Remember me very

## *To* MISS ALLAN, 3 JULY 1841*

MS Albion Hotel, Broadstairs.

Royal Hotel. | July The Third 1841.

My Dear Miss Allan.

When you come up to London, to assist at Miss Liston's sacrifice,[1] don't forget to remind your iron uncle of our Broadstairs engagement, to which I hold you bound. A good sea—fresh breezes—fine sands—and pleasant walks—with all manner of fishing boats, light houses, piers, bathing machines and so forth are its only attractions, but it's one of the freshest and free-est little places in the world. Consequently the proper place for you.

Always believe me with sincere regard
Faithfully Yours
CHARLES DICKENS

## *To* W. H. MURRAY, 3 JULY 1841*

MS Morgan Library.

Royal Hotel. | Third July 1841.

My Dear Sir.

Will you take some supper with us tonight after the play?[2] I have ordered it at 11, and sincerely hope to see you. And will you let me know in one word, by bearer (if one word will hold it) what time your half price goes in?

Believe me always | Faithfully Yours

W. H. Murray Esquire.                    CHARLES DICKENS

kindly to Mrs Dickens—whose nationality I hope has lost nothing of its ardor, by this little peep of her native land—or the proofs it has given of its sympathy of choice with her—as to the being it most delights to honor . . . Do let me have a line to cheer my dull convalescence" (MS Huntington).

[3] Thus in MS. "Brown" in paragraph 1.

[4] Ever since CD's visit, wrote Jeffrey in his letter of 20 July, Miss Brown "has talked, and dreamed . . . of your airy tete a tete (over poor Mrs Dickens' head and mine) during our drive to Dalmeny—She obliged me to give her a certain tender *postscript* to the farewell letter you afterwards sent me— . . . However she declines putting any postscript to this—far gone as she is otherwise!"

[1] Anne, eldest daughter of Robert Liston (1794–1847; *DNB*), distinguished surgeon, was married to A. Dalrymple, of Norwich, at St James's, Piccadilly, on 24 Aug 41.

[2] The Adelphi programme consisted of four plays: J. R. Planché's *Charles XII; or, the Siege of Stralsund; L'Atelier de Canova;* J. Poole's *Simpson & Company;* and *L'Amour et la Folie.* The *Scotsman* and the *Edinburgh Evening Courant* reported that CD would probably be present; the *Caledonian Mercury* announced: "Tonight will be a bumper, for Dickens is expected". On his entrance the orchestra improvised "Charley is my Darling"—"amid tumultuous shouts of delight" (F, II, x, 179n).

## *To* JOHN FORSTER, [5 JULY 1841]

Extracts in F, II, xi, 182–3. *Date:* Mon 5 July according to Forster. *From* Loch-earn-head.[1]

Having had a great deal to do in a crowded house on Saturday night at the theatre, we left Edinburgh yesterday morning at half past seven, and travelled, with Fletcher for our guide, to a place called Stewart's-hotel, nine miles further than Callender. We had neglected to order rooms, and were obliged to make a sitting-room of our own bed-chamber; in which my genius for stowing furniture away was of the very greatest service. Fletcher slept in a kennel with three panes of glass in it, which formed part and parcel of a window; the other three panes whereof belonged to a man who slept on the other side of the partition. He told me this morning that he had had a nightmare all night, and had screamed horribly,[2] he knew. The stranger, as you may suppose, hired a gig and went off at full gallop with the first glimpse of daylight. Being very tired (for we had not had more than three hours' sleep on the previous night) we lay till ten this morning; and at half past eleven went through the Trossachs to Loch-katrine, where I walked from the hotel after tea last night. It is impossible to say what a glorious scene it was. It rained as it never does rain anywhere but here. We conveyed Kate up a rocky pass to go and see the island of the Lady of the Lake, but she gave in after the first five minutes, and we left her, very picturesque and uncomfortable, with Tom[3] holding an umbrella over her head, while we climbed on. When we came back, she had gone into the carriage. We were wet through to the skin, and came on in that state four and twenty miles. Fletcher is very good natured, and of extraordinary use in these outlandish parts. His habit of going into kitchens and bars, disconcerting at Broadstairs, is here of great service. Not expecting us till six, they hadn't lighted our fires when we arrived here; and if you had seen him (with whom the responsibility of the omission rested) running in and out of the sitting-room and the two bed-rooms with a great pair of bellows, with which he distractedly blew each of the fires out in turn, you would have died of laughing. He had on his head a great highland cap, on his back a white coat, and cut such a figure as even the inimitable can't depicter . . .

The Inns, inside and out, are the queerest places imaginable. From the road, this one looks like a white wall, with windows in it by mistake. We have a good sitting-room though, on the first floor: as large (but not as lofty) as my study. The bedrooms are of that size which renders it impossible for you to move, after you have taken your boots off, without chipping pieces out of your legs. There isn't a basin in the Highlands which will hold my face; not a drawer which will open after you have put your

---

[1] Which they had reached " 'wet through' at four that afternoon" (F, II, xi, 182). For CD's route in the Highlands, see Map.

[2] One of Fletcher's peculiarities,

notes Forster (F, *ibid*), and quotes in support CD's letter of 20 Sep 40.

[3] "The servant they had brought with them from Devonshire-terrace" (F, II, xi, 183).

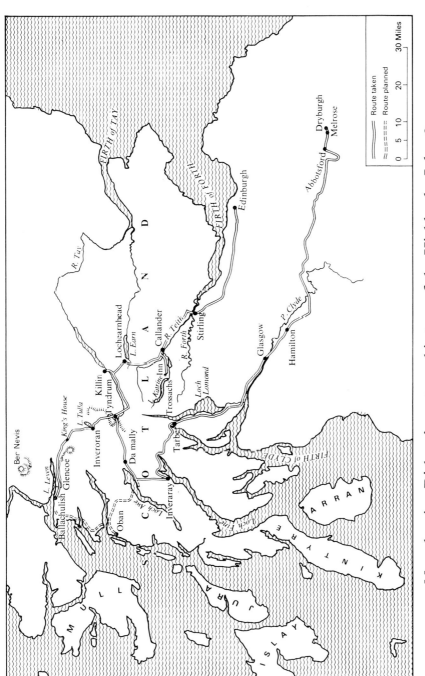

Map showing Dickens's route on his tour of the Highlands, July 1841

Ben Nevis

L. Leven

Ballachulish Glencoe
King's House
L. Tulla
L. Etive
Inveroran
Da mally
Oban
Loch Awe
Inveraray
Loch Fyne

MULL
JURA
ISLAY
KINTYRE
ARRAN
FIRTH OF CLYDE

FIRTH OF TAY
R. Tay
Lochearnhead
L. Earn
Killin
Tyndrum
Callander
R. Teith
Katrine Inn
Trossachs
Loch Lomond
Tarbet
Stirling
R. Forth
FIRTH of FORTH
Edinburgh

SCOTLAND

Glasgow
Hamilton
R. Clyde
Abbotsford
Dryburgh
Melrose

Route taken
Route planned

0   5  10      20      30 Miles

clothes in it; not a water-bottle capacious enough to wet your toothbrush. The huts are wretched and miserable beyond all description. The food (for those who can pay for it) "not bad", as M[1] would say: oatcake, mutton, hotch potch, trout from the loch, small beer bottled, marmalade, and whiskey. Of the last named article I have taken about a pint to-day. The weather is what they call "soft"—which means that the sky is a vast water-spout that never leaves off emptying itself; and the liquor has no more effect than water. . . . I am going to work to-morrow, and hope before leaving here to write you again. The elections have been sad work indeed. That they should return Sibthorp[2] and reject Bulwer,[3] is, by Heaven, a national disgrace. . . . I don't wonder the devil flew over Lincoln.[4] The people were far too addle-headed, even for him. . . . I don't bore you with accounts of Ben this and that, and Lochs of all sorts of names, but this is a wonderful region. The way the mists were stalking about to-day, and the clouds lying down upon the hills; the deep glens, the high rocks, the rushing waterfalls, and the roaring rivers down in deep gulfs below; were all stupendous. This house is wedged round by great heights that are lost in the clouds; and the loch, twelve miles long, stretches out its dreary length before the windows. In my next, I shall soar to the sublime, perhaps; in this here present writing I confine myself to the ridiculous. But I am always,

## *To* JOHN FORSTER, 9 JULY 1841

Extracts in F, II, xi, 183–6 and F, II, ix, 168–9. *Date:* "Ballechelish,[5] Friday evening, ninth July, 1841, half past nine, P.M." (F, II, xi, 183–4).

I can't go to bed without writing to you from here, though the post will not leave this place until we have left it, and arrived at another. On looking over the route which Lord Murray made out for me, I found he had put down Thursday next for Abbotsford and Dryburgh-abbey, and a journey of seventy miles besides! Therefore, and as I was happily able to steal a march upon myself at Loch-earn-head, and to finish in two days what I thought would take me three, we shall leave here to-morrow morning; and,

---

[1] Probably Mitton.

[2] Colonel Charles de Laet Waldo Sibthorp (1783–1855; *DNB*), MP for Lincoln 1826–55, with only one short break. An ultra-Tory; anti-Catholic, anti-Reform Bill, anti-railways, anti-Great Exhibition xenophobic. CD devoted three stanzas to him in his *Examiner* squib, 2 Aug (see *To* Forster, 13 Aug, *fn*). Became *Punch's* most frequent butt. His chief political success up to date had been the reduction of Prince Albert's settlement from £50,000 to £30,000 *p.a.* in Jan 40.

[3] Bulwer lost his seat to Collett, a Tory. He had been Radical member for Lincoln 1832–41, last speaking in the House May 38 in support of abolition of Negro Apprenticeship. In the 11 years before his re-election to Parliament he devoted himself to writing.

[4] Proverbial saying: "He looks as the devil over Lincoln".

[5] As spelt locally—properly Ballachulish; well-known for its slate quarries, described by Basil Hall in *Patchwork*, 1841, II, 261–76.

by being a day earlier than we intended at all the places between this and
Melrose (which we propose to reach by Wednesday night), we shall have
a whole day for Scott's house and tomb, and still be at York on Saturday
evening, and home, God willing, on Sunday. . . . We left Loch-earn-head
last night, and went to a place called Killin, eight miles from it, where we
slept. I walked some six miles with Fletcher after we got there, to see a
waterfall: and truly it was a magnificent sight, foaming and crashing down
three great steeps of riven rock; leaping over the first as far off as you could
carry your eye, and rumbling and foaming down into a dizzy pool below
you, with a deafening roar. To-day we have had a journey of between 50
and 60 miles, through the bleakest and most desolate part of Scotland,
where the hill-tops are still covered with great patches of snow, and the
road winds over steep mountain passes, and on the brink of deep brooks
and precipices. The cold all day has been *intense*, and the rain sometimes
most violent. It has been impossible to keep warm, by any means; even
whiskey failed; the wind was too piercing even for that. One stage of ten
miles, over a place called the Black-mount, took us two hours and a half to
do; and when we came to a lone public called the King's-house, at the
entrance to Glencoe—this was about three o'clock—we were well nigh
frozen. We got a fire directly, and in twenty minutes they served us up
some famous kippered salmon, broiled; a broiled fowl; hot mutton ham
and poached eggs; pancakes; oatcake; wheaten bread; butter; bottled
porter; hot water, lump sugar, and whiskey; of which we made a very
hearty meal. All the way, the road had been among moors and mountains
with huge masses of rock, which fell down God knows where, sprinkling
the ground in every direction, and giving it the aspect of the burial place
of a race of giants. Now and then we passed a hut or two, with neither
window nor chimney, and the smoke of the peat fire rolling out at the door.
But there were not six of these dwellings in a dozen miles; and anything
so bleak and wild, and mighty in its loneliness, as the whole country, it is
impossible to conceive. Glencoe itself is perfectly *terrible*. The pass is an
awful place. It is shut in on each side by enormous rocks from which great
torrents come rushing down in all directions. In amongst these rocks on
one side of the pass (the left as we came) there are scores of glens, high up,
which form such haunts as you might imagine yourself wandering in, in
the very height and madness of a fever. They will live in my dreams for
years—I was going to say as long as I live, and I seriously think so. The
very recollection of them makes me shudder. . . . Well, I will not bore you
with my impressions of these tremendous wilds, but they really are fearful
in their grandeur and amazing solitude. Wales[1] is a mere toy compared
with them.

  We are now in a bare white house on the banks of Loch-leven, but in a
comfortably furnished room on the top of the house—that is, on the first
floor—with the rain pattering against the window as though it were Decem-

---

[1] Where he had spent three nights in Nov 38 (see Diary entries, Vol. 1, pp.
635–6).

ber, the wind howling dismally, a cold damp mist on everything without, a blazing fire within halfway up the chimney, and a most infernal Piper practising under the window for a competition of pipers which is to come off shortly.

*a*"I have done all I can or need do in the way of *Barnaby* until I come home, and the story is progressing (I hope you will think) to good strong interest. I have left it, I think, at an exciting point, with a good dawning of the riots.[1] In the first of the two numbers I have written since I have been away, I forget whether the blind man, in speaking to Barnaby about riches, tells him they are to be found in *crowds*. If I have not actually used that word, will you introduce it?[2] A perusal of the proof of the following number (70) will show you how, and why.*a* [3]

The store of anecdotes of Fletcher with which we shall return, will last a long time. It seems that the F's are an extensive clan, and that his father[4] was a highlander. Accordingly, wherever he goes, he finds out some cotter or small farmer who is his cousin. I wish you could see him walking into his cousins' curds and cream, and into their dairies generally! Yesterday morning between eight and nine, I was sitting writing at the open window, when the postman came to the inn (which at Loch-earn-head is the post office) for the letters. He is going away, when Fletcher, who has been writing somewhere below stairs, rushes out, and cries "Halloa there! Is that the Post?" "Yes!" somebody answers. "Call him back!" says Fletcher: "Just sit down till I've done, *and don't go away till I tell you.*"— Fancy! The General Post, with the letters of forty villages in a leathern bag!... To-morrow at Oban. Sunday at Inverary. Monday at Tarbet. Tuesday at Glasgow (and that night at Hamilton). Wednesday at Melrose. Thursday at Ditto. Friday I don't know where. Saturday at York. Sunday —how glad I shall be to shake hands with you. My love to Mac. I thought he'd have written once. Ditto to Macready. I had a very nice and welcome letter from him, and a most hearty one from Elliotson.... P.S. Half asleep. So, excuse drowsiness of matter and composition. I shall be full of joy to meet another letter from you!... P.P.S. They speak Gaelic here, of course, and many of the common people understand very little English.

*aa* This passage (from F, II, ix, 168–9), quoted by Forster in his chapter on *Barnaby*, seems likely to belong at this point in CD's letter.

[1] Ch. 48 (No. 70) closes with Mrs Rudge "thrown to the ground" and Barnaby "whirled away into the heart of a dense mass of men, and she saw him no more."

[2] The MS of this passage in Ch. 46 reads: "... not in solitary places like those you pass your time in, but where there's noise and rattle." Forster changed it to: "... but in crowds, and where there's noise and rattle."

[3] In Ch. 48 Barnaby urges his mother to join the London rioters: "You remember what the blind man said, about the gold. Here's a brave crowd! Come!"

[4] Archibald Fletcher (?1744–1830), advocate; a Whig; brought up in Rannoch, Perthshire, his mother claiming descent from a Highland chieftain, McNaughton, known as the "Black Knight of Loch-Awe", hereditary Keeper of the King's Castles before the Campbells established themselves there (*Autobiography of Mrs. Fletcher, of Edinburgh*, Carlisle, 1874, pp. 60–1).

Since I wrote this letter, I rang the girl upstairs, and gave elaborate directions (you know my way) for a pint of sherry to be made into boiling negus; mentioning all the ingredients one by one, and particularly nutmeg. When I had quite finished, seeing her obviously bewildered, I said, with great gravity, "Now you know what you're going to order?" "Oh yes. Sure." "What?"—a pause—"Just"—another pause—"Just plenty of *nutbergs*!"

## *To* THE POSTMASTER, OBAN, [10 JULY 1841]

Mention in next (penultimate sentence).

## *To* JOHN FORSTER, 11 JULY 1841

Extracts in F, ii, xi, 186–9. *Date:* "Dalmally, Sunday, July the eleventh, 1841" (F, ii, xi, 186).

As there was no place of this name in our route, you will be surprised to see it at the head of this present writing. But our being here is a part of such moving accidents by flood and field[1] as will astonish you. If you should happen to have your hat on, take it off, that your hair may stand on end without any interruption. To get from Ballyhoolish (as I am obliged to spell it when Fletcher is not in the way; and he is out at this moment) to Oban, it is necessary to cross two ferries, one of which is an arm of the sea, eight or ten miles broad. Into this ferry-boat, passengers, carriages, horses, and all, get bodily, and are got across by hook or by crook if the weather be reasonably fine. Yesterday morning, however, it blew such a strong gale that the landlord of the inn, where we had paid for horses all the way to Oban (thirty miles), honestly came upstairs just as we were starting, with the money in his hand, and told us it would be impossible to cross. There was nothing to be done but to come back five and thirty miles, through Glencoe and Inverouran, to a place called Tyndrum, whence a road twelve miles long crosses to Dalmally, which is sixteen miles from Inverary. Accordingly we turned back, and in a great storm of wind and rain began to retrace the dreary road we had come the day before. . . . I was not at all ill pleased to have to come again through that awful Glencoe. If it had been tremendous on the previous day, yesterday it was perfectly horrific. It had rained all night, and was raining then, as it only does in these parts. Through the whole glen, which is ten miles long, torrents were boiling and foaming, and sending up in every direction spray like the smoke of great fires. They were rushing down every hill and mountain side, and tearing like devils across the path, and down into the depths of the rocks. Some of the hills looked as if they were full of silver, and had cracked in a hundred places. Others as if they were frightened, and had broken out into a deadly sweat. In others there was no compromise or division of streams, but one great torrent came roaring down with a deafening noise, and a rushing of water that was quite appalling. Such a *spaet*, in

[1] *Othello*, i, iii, 135 (cf. Vol. i, p. 610).

short (that's the country word), has not been known for many years, and the sights and sounds were beyond description. The post-boy was not at all at his ease, and the horses were very much frightened (as well they might be) by the perpetual raging and roaring; one of them started as we came down a steep place, and we were within that much (——) of tumbling over a precipice; just then, too, the drag broke, and we were obliged to go on as we best could, without it: getting out every now and then, and hanging on at the back of the carriage to prevent its rolling down too fast, and going Heaven knows where. Well, in this pleasant state of things we came to King's-house again, having been four hours doing the sixteen miles. The rumble[1] where Tom sat was by this time so full of water, that he was obliged to borrow a gimlet, and bore holes in the bottom to let it run out. The horses that were to take us on, were out upon the hills, somewhere within ten miles round; and three or four bare-legged fellows went out to look for 'em, while we sat by the fire and tried to dry ourselves. At last we got off again (without the drag and with a broken spring, no smith living within ten miles), and went limping on to Inverouran. In the first three miles we were in a ditch and out again, and lost a horse's shoe. All this time it never once left off raining; and was very windy, very cold, very misty, and most intensely dismal. So we crossed the Black-mount, and came to a place we had passed the day before, where a rapid river runs over a bed of broken rock. Now, this river, sir, had a bridge last winter, but the bridge broke down when the thaw came, and has never since been mended; so travellers cross upon a little platform, made of rough deal planks stretching from rock to rock; and carriages and horses ford the water, at a certain point. As the platform is the reverse of steady (we had proved this the day before), is very slippery, and affords anything but a pleasant footing, having only a trembling little rail on one side, and on the other nothing between it and the foaming stream, Kate decided to remain in the carriage, and trust herself to the wheels rather than to her feet. Fletcher and I had got out, and it was going away, when I advised her, as I had done several times before, to come with us; for I saw that the water was very high, the current being greatly swollen by the rain, and that the post-boy had been eyeing it in a very disconcerted manner for the last half hour. This decided her to come out; and Fletcher, she, Tom, and I, began to cross, while the carriage went about a quarter of a mile down the bank, in search of a shallow place. The platform shook so much that we could only come across two at a time, and then it felt as if it were hung on springs. As to the wind and rain!... well, put into one gust all the wind and rain you ever saw and heard, and you'll have some faint notion of it! When we got safely to the opposite bank, there came riding up a wild highlander, in a great plaid, whom we recognized as the landlord of the inn, and who without taking the least notice of us, went dashing on, —with the plaid he was wrapped in, streaming in the wind,—screeching in Gaelic to the post-boy on the opposite bank, and making the most frantic gestures you ever

[1] Back portion of a carriage adapted for servants' seats or luggage.

saw, in which he was joined by some other wild man on foot, who had come across by a short cut, knee-deep in mire and water. As we began to see what this meant, we (that is, Fletcher and I) scrambled on after them, while the boy, horses, and carriage were plunging in the water, which left only the horses' heads and the boy's body visible. By the time we got up to them, the man on horseback and the [man][1] on foot were perfectly mad with pantomime; for as to any of their shouts being heard by the boy, the water made such a great noise that they might as well have been dumb. It made me quite sick to think how I should have felt if Kate had been inside. The carriage went round and round like a great stone, the boy was as pale as death, the horses were struggling and plashing and snorting like sea-animals, and we were all roaring to the driver to throw himself off and let them and the coach go to the devil, when suddenly it came all right (having got into shallow water), and, all tumbling and dripping and jogging from side to side, climbed up to the dry land. I assure you we looked rather queer, as we wiped our faces and stared at each other in a little cluster round about it. It seemed that the man on horseback had been looking at us through a telescope as we came to the track, and knowing that the place was very dangerous, and seeing that we meant to bring the carriage, had come on at a great gallop to show the driver the only place where he could cross. By the time he came up, the man had taken the water at a wrong place, and in a word was as nearly drowned (with carriage, horses, luggage, and all) as ever man was. Was *this* a good adventure?

We all went on to the inn—the wild man galloping on first, to get a fire lighted—and there we dined on eggs and bacon, oat-cake, and whiskey; and changed and dried ourselves. The place was a mere knot of little out-houses, and in one of these there were fifty highlanders *all drunk*. . . . Some were drovers, some pipers, and some workmen engaged to build a hunting-lodge for Lord Breadalbane[2] hard by, who had been driven in by stress of weather. One was a paper-hanger. He had come out three days before to paper the inn's best room, a chamber almost large enough to keep a New-foundland dog in; and, from the first half hour after his arrival to that moment, had been hopelessly and irreclaimably drunk. They were lying about in all directions: on forms, on the ground, about a loft overhead, round the turf-fire wrapped in plaids, on the tables, and under them. We paid our bill, thanked our host very heartily, gave some money to his children, and after an hour's rest came on again. At ten o'clock at night, we reached this place, and were overjoyed to find quite an English inn, with good beds (those we have slept on, yet, have always been of straw), and every possible comfort. We breakfasted this morning at half past ten, and at three go on to Inverary to dinner. I believe the very rough part of the journey is over, and I am really glad of it. Kate sends all kind of regards.

[1] Printed text reads "men"—plainly a mistake: see "wild man" both above and below.

[2] John Campbell, 2nd Marquis of Breadalbane (1796–1862; *DNB*). Lord Rector of the University of Glasgow 1840–2. One of the largest landowners in Scotland.

I shall hope to find a letter from you at Inverary when the post reaches there, to-morrow. I wrote to Oban yesterday, desiring the post-office keeper to send any he might have for us, over to that place. Love to Mac.

## To [JAMES BOGLE[1] AND OTHERS, 12 JULY 1841]

Mention in next.

## To JOHN FORSTER, [12 JULY 1841]

Extracts in F, II, xi, 189. *Date:* "from Inverary the day following his exciting adventure [of 10 July]", says Forster (F, *ibid*). But reference to the invitation from Glasgow (see *fn*), which CD received on 12 July (*To* Maclise, that day), shows that he must have been writing not the day after the adventure but the day after his letter about it: i.e. on the 12th.

*Promising another letter from Melrose (lost, or possibly never written) and enclosing the invitation to a public dinner at Glasgow.*[2]

I have returned for answer that I am on my way home, on pressing business connected with my weekly publication, and can't stop. But I have offered to come down any day in September or October, and accept the honour then. Now, I shall come and return per mail; and if this suits them, enter into a solemn league and covenant to come with me. *Do.* You must. I am sure you will[3] ... Till my next, and always afterwards, God bless you. I got your welcome letter this morning, and have read it a hundred times. What a pleasure it is. Kate's best regards. I am dying for Sunday, and wouldn't stop now for twenty dinners of twenty thousand each.

Always your affectionate friend

Boz.

Will Lord John meet the parliament, or resign first?[4]

[1] Writer to the Signet; member of Glasgow Town Council 1838–44; and Bailie of the River.

[2] The *Scotsman*, 10 July 41, printed the following from the *Glasgow Herald*: "PROPOSED DINNER TO MR DICKENS AT GLASGOW | At three o'clock on Thursday afternoon a highly respectable meeting of gentlemen, admirers of the genius of Mr Dickens, was held in the Committee Room of the Royal Exchange, to consider the propriety of inviting that gifted individual to Glasgow. Mr James Bogle was called to the chair, and the meeting was unanimous in the resolution to offer their humble testimony of their high appreciation of the genius of the author of Pickwick. A Committee was appointed to transmit the invitation, and make the necessary arrangements, should Mr Dickens return a favourable response as is most earnestly wished."

[3] "I agreed to accompany him to Glasgow", says Forster (F, *ibid*); "but illness [*see* To *Forster, 19 Sep*, fn] intercepted that celebration".

[4] Lord John Russell's last-minute attempt to stave off the fall of Melbourne's Govt, by proposing to modify the duty on corn, had made him the virtual Whig leader, though Melbourne was still Prime Minister. The General Election had begun on 28 June; by 11 July a Conservative victory for Peel was certain; his final majority was 76. The new Parliament met on 24 Aug, with the Whigs still in office; but after defeats on the Royal Address in both Houses, the Govt resigned (30 Aug).

## *To* DANIEL MACLISE, 12 JULY 1841*

MS Rosenbach Foundation.

Inverary. | July The Twelfth 1841.

My Dear Mac.

You're a nice man. Why in the name of Heaven, have you never written to me—why didn't you say a word in acknowledgment of the receipt of those newspapers—why do you fix your thoughts exclusively on green cloths and water bottles,[1] and leave your bosom friends uncongratulated, when Grims and Elliotsons[2] write him long letters brim full of friendly enthusiasm—does R. A. stand for coldness, forgetfulness, insensibility, or what?[3]

And who has scraped out the beautiful eyes of those sweet summer-evening girls?[4] Who has reduced the Modest Quencher to a state of darkness,[5] and quenched the lustre of the gentle Sophy?[6] If you had no interest in my affairs, do you think it was mutual, and I had none in yours? But Shee shall answer for this, if he lives 'till my return. It's his doing, I know.

The mountain passes we have traversed, the rushing streams in which we have been nearly drowned, the torrents that have roared and raged in our ears, the heather we have plucked, the rocks we have climbed, the lochs whereon we have glided, shall all be yours anon. *Do* ask Forster for my

---

[1] Cf. *To* Maclise, 11 Feb 41 and *fn*.

[2] CD had had letters from Macready and Elliotson: see *To* Forster, 9 July.

[3] Maclise replied on 16 July: "I fling back upon you the term villain [*used by CD later in his letter*]—You are the villain—I *recollect distinctly* thro the fog of forgetfullness [*thus*] that I conjured around me on that last fatal, farewell, Friday night, when we stopped so long —you with Cattermole and others, at one end of the table, and I blessed and happy beyond mortal man, endeavouring to be coherent to The Aimable [*thus*] and Lovely [?*Marion Ely*] at the other, when I thought, at that late hour, that I never could leave you, and began already to dream of the possibility of making a hasty packing up, to accompany you, 'to swell your triumph, and partake your gale' [*cf. Pope*, Essay on Man, *1, 385*]—I say I distinctly recollect your saying to me you would write to me—These remarkable words, have shone out in the gloom of my thoughts, and glowing of my jealousies, as if they were written in a Belshazzan style of

penmanship, or expressed in the exploding lights of 500 Dozen of Lucifer Match boxes" (MS Huntington).

[4] The *Examiner*, 3 July 41, reported "a wanton outrage" at the RA on 25 June. Four paintings had been mutilated—including Maclise's *Hunt the Slipper at Neighbour Flamborough's* (a scene from *The Vicar of Wakefield*, Ch. 11)—"by some person having completely scratched out the eyes of every figure portrayed upon the canvas". Maclise commented (16 July): "great exaggeration about that picture—no eyes at all torn out—the canvass scraped at the lower part near the frame—some child we suppose—other pictures indeed damaged."

[5] Clearly Maclise had painted "the Modest Quencher" (?Marion Ely) as one of the girls. He frequently introduced portraits of his friends into his pictures: e.g. Crofton Croker, P. W. Banks, and Maclise's sisters appear in *All Hallow E'en in Ireland* (see O'Driscoll, *Daniel Maclise*, 1871, p. 48*n*).

[6] Sophia Primrose.

last letter, and see what perils we encountered. I wrote it for your edification no less than his.[1] Unkindly villain!

—Or stay—was it love for Fortescue[2] that kept your thoughts from me? If so, I am satisfied. We always agree on those points, you know.—When I last saw her, I *think* her nose turned up at the end. Is it so? Let me know the worst, and I will bear it.[3]

Tomorrow night, we sleep at Hamilton—on Wednesday at Melrose—on Thursday at Melrose too—on Friday, somewhere on the road, but I don't know where—on Saturday at York. Let me hear from you though it be only to the amount of six words. To see your handwriting will be summ'at.

And *do* be in Devonshire Terrace on Sunday evening. And *do*[4] bear

---

[1] To this Maclise replied (16 July): "Forster, I must say kindly, kept from me the perusal of your letters, except the first one and I did not see them all 'till last evening, he would now and then say, Dickens desires to be remembered to you, and mysteriously move a large packet of your letters from one pocket to another. At home, from the side recesses of his frowsy dressing gown—and abroad from the coat tail of his blue frock coat—but he would not do more—Once he even inflamed me to the last pitch, by shewing me a letter from Mrs. Dickens, who after addressing him in the most glowing style, coldly enquires after the state of my health. If any thing were wanting to exaggerate this case, it was furnished when Cattermole told me, you had written to him and I've no doubt in my own mind that Grim Visage, and Blue Beard [*Macready and ?Elliotson. See CD's letter*] have also been so distinguished—I leave this subject for the present. | You gave us I assure you a most fearful interest in the description of the Arm of the Sea Ferry and I bless God Mrs. Dickens was not submitted to the surpassing terrors of that damn'd situation."

[2] Julia Sarah Hayfield Fortescue (1817–99), actress. Played Rose Maylie in Yates's *Oliver Twist* at the Adelphi Nov 38; was now appearing as Barnaby at the English Opera House (see *To Selby, 20 July, fn*); later played Mary Graham in *Martin Chuzzlewit*, Meg Veck in *The Chimes*, and Dot in *The Cricket on the Hearth*; also acted with CD's amateur company in 1845 and 1848. Macready, who saw her play

Barnaby on 7 July, "with great vivacity and grace and power" (*Macready's Reminiscences*, ed. Sir F. Pollock, II, 180), thought she showed excellent promise, but was disappointed when she acted with him in *The Two Gentlemen of Verona*, Drury Lane, Dec 41. In 1842 she gave birth to a son by Alan Legge Gardner (1810–83); other sons by him followed in 1843 and 1846, but she continued to act. After his wife's death 1847, she was generally supposed to have married Gardner (Burke's *Peerage* dates the marriage 1848). In fact she had two more children by him first, daughters born 1853 and 1856, and the marriage took place later in 1856 (CD sent Macready news of it on 13 Dec 56).

[3] "Yes. Fortescue is transcendent", Maclise replied in his letter of 16 July, "—you have heard what Mac the first says—'she is really and truly charming'. —Is her nose turned up—? Allow me —I think you are not quite clear as to that point—but if so—you are altogether absorbed in the wild attractions of her legs, and her general suave movement—her voice is regulated to the most perfect scale of modulation. You must expect to see as to the personation —an Operatic Barnaby of course in a degree—the small waist, the neatly turned leg—and the woman bust—the tunic exactly reaching where we wish it, the straws, and Peacock Feather placed Plume like and the half bend—point toe—close knee—wrist bend movement, but still you will like her—love her—doat upon her."

[4] Underlined three times.

this in mind—that I have had to-day an invitation to a great dinner, from the Glasgow people—that I have declined it for the present, being on my way home for Clock purposes—that I have offered to come back in September or October[1]—and that if this suits them, I shall come down by Mail and go back by ditto. You'll join me in that? Now say you will, once and for all. The only thing I felt at the Edinburgh Dinner (and I felt it very strongly) was, that except Kate there was nobody I cared for, there to see.

She sends her best regards. She thinks with me that you are a villain, but like me is meek and forbearing. Fletcher desires to be remembered. I *think* I have some good stories of him.—You shall judge.

Let us dine together every day next week. I look forward to Sunday, with a delight past all expression.[2]

Always Dear Mac<br>Your affectionate friend

Daniel Maclise Esquire                                 CHARLES DICKENS

## *To* CHARLES SELBY,[3] 20 JULY 1841

Text from N, I, 339.

*Private.*

1 Devonshire Terrace | July the Twentieth 1841

My Dear Sir,

Your letter of I don't know what date, but not a very recent one, has been following me over Scotland. It was forwarded with others from town, and did not reach me until I was coming home within these few days.

It would be ridiculous for me to deny that I am always most intensely mortified and very much aggravated by having my stories anticipated in their course;[4] and that I think the state of the law which permits such

---

[1] For a further reference to the proposed visit to Glasgow see *To* Paul, 9 Sep.

[2] "Hurrah for Sunday Evening", wrote Maclise in a postscript.

[3] Charles Selby (?1802–63; *DNB*), character-actor and writer and adapter of numerous plays, mostly burlettas and farces. In 1841 published *Maximums and Speciments of William Muggins*, illustrated by Onwhyn, written throughout in cockney in the spirit of his earlier farce, *The Unfinished Gentleman* (1834).

[4] Selby and Charles Melville had dramatized *Barnaby* when only half the story had appeared. Sub-titled "A Domestic Drama", the play contained neither Riots nor any kind of historical action, but concentrated on the "mystery" plot (which it rather spoilt, as a

mystery, by making it clear to the audience that the "Stranger" was Rudge and the murderer). It had run at the English Opera House since 28 June, Selby playing Mr Chester and his wife Mrs Rudge. The *Examiner* (3 July) regretted that Selby had "flown in the face of Mr Dickens' own earnest and well warranted protest against all piratical doings of that kind", but, "with this reservation", praised it as "the best imagined, best executed, and, in some few characters, the best acted adaptation, we can remember to have seen." Other versions before completion of the novel were C. Z. Barnett's at Sadler's Wells (9 Aug) and Stirling's at the Strand (14 Aug). On 20 Dec Frederick Yates put on a new version (perhaps also by Stirling) at the Adelphi,

things, is disgraceful to England.[1] At the same time, I am so far from blaming you in the matter, that if I could give you a patent for dramatizing my productions I would gladly do so; inasmuch as if they *must* be done at all, I would rather have them done by gentlemanly hands, and by those who really desire to act fairly and honorably as I am sure you do.

Mrs. Dickens will be glad if you can let her have a private box tonight; and I hear so much of Miss Fortescue,[2] that I shall endeavor to accompany her. If this should not find you at the Theatre, will you do me the favor to leave such instructions with the doorkeeper as will insure us a quiet and quick reception?

Believe me always | Faithfully yours<br>[CHARLES DICKENS]

## *To* WILLIAM SHOBERL, 20 JULY 1841*

MS Mr J. W. Nyberg.

Devonshire Terrace. | July The Twentieth 1841.

My Dear Sir.

I have been in Scotland for more than a month, and on my return home yesterday,[3] found your note of Saturday's date.

I shall be happy to see you tomorrow at Ten, and am

Faithfully Yours

W. Shoberl Esquire                                   CHARLES DICKENS

## *To* WILLIAM SHOBERL, 21 JULY 1841

Text from N, i, 341.

Devonshire Terrace | Twenty-First July 1841

Dear Sir,

I beg to acknowledge the receipt of your letter in answer to mine of this morning,[4] which is quite satisfactory. I need not, I am sure, point out the

which included the Riots: the *Spectator* (25 Dec) found its "mob scenes not well managed", but liked the "No-Popery hornpipe" by Tappertit and his "Brother Bulldogs".

[1] The right of dramatization was not included under English copyright law until the Copyright Act of 1911.

[2] E.g. from Maclise and Macready: see *To* Maclise, 12 July and *fns*. According to Forster, CD had been only "more or less satisfied" with such performances as Yates's Quilp and Mantalini, and Mrs Keeley's Smike, but on Julia Fortescue's Barnaby he always dwelt "with a thorough liking" (F, IV, iii, 321). In his letter to CD of 16 July, Maclise

commented on the other characters in Selby's production: "Miggs excellent— Hugh like a big headed *Smith*, as he is in a Pantomime, but devilish wild hoarse, and grotesque to perfection—Willet the worst of all, no attempt at his [*here a sketch of a rotund, open-mouthed Willet*] —and Joe a rotten snob. Varden Tappertit and Dolly so so" (MS Huntington).

[3] He had in fact returned on Sun 18 July, as planned: see *To* Murray, 21 July.

[4] Ambiguous; but must mean "your letter received this morning". In it Shoberl suggested calling at 8 p.m. instead of 10 a.m. (see next).

necessity of being very particular in respect of the form of advertisement in the Weekly papers [.A]s[1] there has been ample time for correction, I am sure you will have attended to it.[2]

Faithfully yours
[CHARLES DICKENS]

## *To* DANIEL MACLISE, 21 JULY 1841*

MS Benoliel Collection.

Devonshire Terrace | Twenty First July 1841.

Dear Mac

I can't go tonight—at all events until late; for a man[3] is coming here at 8, to settle (mirabile dictu) the matter of Mrs. Macrone's book, for ever.

All you have to do, is, to go to the Strand Theatre,[4] and ask for Forster's box.

I shall see you I hope, at least a dozen times, between this and Sunday. But don't forget that you dine with us on that day at 6.—Will you lounge first?

Faithfully
CD.

I think it very likely I may come in tonight about 9.

## *To* JOIIN FORSTER, 21 JULY 1841

Forster's summary of letter, made before destruction, MS Victoria & Albert Museum (FC); dated Devonshire Terrace, 21 July 41.

*As to the Pic Nic book. He and Shoberl.*

## *To* LORD MURRAY, 21 JULY 1841*

MS Public Archives of Canada.

1 Devonshire Terrace
York Gate Regents Park London
Twenty First July 1841.

Dear Lord Murray.

I know that when you see the inclosed letters,[5] you will think me a

---

[1] N reads ",as".

[2] Clearly an earlier advertisement (untraced) of *The Pic Nic Papers* had failed to state that it was to be published in book form. Shoberl does not seem to have "attended to" the correction at once; for in the announcement of 31 July that the work was "unavoidably delayed on account of the Plates by Cruikshank, Phiz, &c." it was still omitted. The weekly papers of 7 Aug were the first to announce it as "complete in 3 vols. . . . and not in Parts, as some Persons have erroneously supposed".

[3] Shoberl.

[4] The programme consisted of Leman Rede's *The Frolics of the Fairies*, with Mrs Keeley, followed by *The Devil and Dr. Faustus*, and *Aldgate Pump*.

[5] Of introduction given him by Murray.

villain—dead to a sense of Highland grandeur and Highland hospitality—
unworthy of that memorable chart[1] which I have worn into a perfect fringe
by frequent reference—and in short a worthless character, utterly un-
deserving your interest and kindness.

But believe me that notwithstanding your judicial habits, all this is a
mistake. I have—if I may say so, who shouldn't—a particular capacity for
feeling and remembering such genial treatment as yours; a vivid recollection of anything that is true and earnest; and, by consequence, a most
distinct remembrance of everything you said and did, advised and recommended—and a strong desire to stand well with you.

I plead guilty to never having intended to deliver these fatal missives,
simply for this one reason—that I was bound by a great many considerations, to be in London last Sunday night—that I mistrusted my power of
resisting the Lady of the Lake[2] (for which you will please attack the Laird
of Dunans,[3] who gave me a heart rending account of her and filled my soul
with a vague idea that Mr. Callandar[4] had done something personal in
marrying so fair a creature)—and that I wanted to see as many places as
I could, in so short a space of time. These are several reasons in one, but
they all go to the same point, and therefore I use the singular number. For
this reason then, I put the letters away, when you gave them to me, in the
very bottom of my Portmanteau, and said within myself that they would
give me an excuse for writing to you when I got home. You see that I am
not slow to avail myself of it; this is their real use, and a very good one
too—as *I* think.

That I was delighted and astonished beyond all measure by what I saw;
and that I never could have seen what I did, without your aid; I need not
say. As I have you associated in my mind with Glencoe, Loch Katrine,
and everything that was wild wonderful or beautiful in the expedition, I
hope my friends on this side of the Tweed will not charge upon you a new
failing of which I am sensible. I am strongly apprehensive that I have
come back, a bore. Strange desires to talk about Scotland come upon me
at improper seasons. I prose fearfully after supper. The mind of my most
intimate friend wandered last night as I related some moving adventures
at Inverouran, and described the dreariness of Tyndrum. I see that
visitors begin to avoid the subject; and when I put my hand into my desk,
and drawing out a greasy paper, say—"this was the little route which Lord
Murray—" they recollect engagements, and think they left their hats
outside.

[1] The itinerary Murray had prepared for him: see *To* Forster, 9 July.

[2] Perhaps Jane, daughter of the 2nd Baron Erskine, who had married James Callander (see below) in Aug 1837. Scott's poem, *The Lady of the Lake*, 1810, is set in the region of Loch Katrine.

[3] Angus Fletcher, cousin of Angus Fletcher the sculptor. Dunans, the family seat, was in Argyllshire.

[4] Middle of the word confused; CD was clearly uncertain of the spelling. Probably James Henry Callander (1804–1851), of Craigforth House, Stirling-shire, and Ardkinlas Lodge, Argyllshire. The two seats are about 40 miles apart, Loch Katrine lying between them.

I am on the subject now, and will be warned in time. Not another word shall pass my pen's lips, except that I beg my compliments to Lady Murray;[1] that Mrs. Dickens desires to be remembered cordially, both to you and her; and that I am, with a most unaffected sense of your great kindness,

Dear Lord Murray

Yours faithfully and obliged

The Honorable | Lord Murray                          CHARLES DICKENS


## *To* MRS MARY HURNALL, 21 JULY 1841

MS Free Library of Philadelphia. *Address:* Free | Mrs. Mary Hurnall | Clipston | Market Harborough.

1 Devonshire Terrace | York Gate Regents Park.

July The Twenty First 1841.

Dear Madam.

I have been in Scotland for some weeks past, and find so many letters to answer on my return, that I am obliged to send a more brief reply to yours than I desire.

Accept my sincere thanks, both for your note, and the Invitation it contains. I fear it is not likely that it will ever be in my power to accept it in deed, but in spirit I do, and so do Mrs. Dickens and my children—you are right; I have four.

Be assured that I am not unmindful of my promise, and that if you should come back to London at any time, I shall, please God, make a point of seeing you.[2]

Your remark—a very natural and proper one—on the blind man in Barnaby, is only another proof to me, among many others which present themselves in various forms every day, of the great disadvantages which attend a detached and desultory form of publication. My intention in the management of this inferior and subordinate character, was to remind the World who have eyes, that they have no *right* to expect in sightless men a degree of virtue and goodness to which they, in full possession of all their senses, can lay no claim—that it is a very easy thing for those who misuse every gift of Heaven to consider resignation and cheerfulness the duty of those whom it has deprived of some great blessing—that whereas we look upon a blind man who does wrong, as a kind of monster, we ought in Truth and Justice to remember that a man who has eyes and is a vicious wretch, is by his very abuse of the glorious faculty of sight, an immeasurably greater offender than his afflicted fellow. In a word, I wished to show that the hand of God is at least as manifest in making eyes as in unmaking them, and that we do not sufficiently consider the sorrows of those who

---

[1] Mary, daughter of William Rigby of Oldfield Hall, Cheshire; she had married Lord Murray in 1826.

[2] Cf. *To* ?Mrs Hurnall, 17 Apr 41 and *fn.*

walk in darkness on this earth, when we set it up as a rule that they *ought* to be better than ourselves, and that they are required to be by their calamity. Calamity with us, is made an excuse for doing wrong. With them, it is erected into a reason for their doing right. This is really the justice of rich to poor, and I protest against it because it is so.[1]

All this you would have seen if you could have had the whole book before your mental vision.[2] As it is, I can only hope to bring my meaning before you by very slow and gradual degrees, and after you have formed a first impression on the subject.

That it is a real pleasure and delight to me to know that I afford you any consolation or amusement, you may believe with your whole heart. And believe also that I am, Dear Madam with an unaffected interest in your happiness

Faithfully Yours

Mrs. Hurnall. CHARLES DICKENS

## *To* JOHN CAY,[3] 21 JULY 1841*

MS Free Library of Philadelphia.

1 Devonshire Terrace | York Gate Regents Park.<br>July The Twenty First 1841.

My Dear Sir.

Many thanks for your letter, and for the Index to the same.[4] They both reached me, safely.

My Barnaby plans are so laid, that I am not sure (especially as I think I can make a better riot than Lord George Gordon did) whether I could

---

[1] The coincidence, in time, of Mrs Hurnall's protest at CD's treatment of Stagg and the change in his treatment of him, suggests that CD received her letter, with others, in Scotland, between writing Chs 45 and 46, and that his addition to Ch. 45 (in very small writing above the line) of "for we are accustomed to see in those who have lost a human sense, something in its place almost divine" was an afterthought inspired by her. He then proceeded in Ch. 46 to develop the theme as summarized in this letter.

[2] If CD had written the addition to Ch. 45 and Stagg's defence in Ch. 46 as a result of Mrs Hurnall's letter, this is clearly disingenuous. Certainly nothing in Stagg's earlier appearances prepares for it. Nor was it usual for CD to complicate a minor character. In *Old Curiosity Shop*, Ch. 44, for instance, he had decided against associating virtue with deformity in the "good" furnace keeper, and carefully cancelled in proof all references to his being a cripple. (It was a theme he avoided until he could do it justice in Tiny Tim, 1843.) However, he had read Hood's stricture about Quilp (see *To* Hood, ?Feb/Mar 41, *fn*), and the possibility that he had already planned Stagg's defence of his right to be both blind and bad cannot be completely ruled out.

[3] John Cay (1790–1865), of Edinburgh, advocate; sheriff of Linlithgowshire 1822 to his death. Eldest son of R. H. Cay, Judge Admiral of Scotland. Member of the Royal Society of Arts. Author of *An Analysis of the Scottish Reform Act*, two parts, 1837 and 1840. He had been on the platform at the Edinburgh dinner of 25 June.

[4] Presumably Cay had annotated his own letter.

make any use of any new discoveries. But being interested in the subject I should very much like to see the two books of which you so kindly proffer me the loan. And if you will have the kindness to address them to me to the care of the Clock agent—Mr. Menzies, Bookseller of Prince's Street—I have no doubt he will have the means of forwarding them.

I am delighted to hear that the Orsons are at peace, and that you, Valentine, got home again undamaged.[1] I was half afraid to look into the print shop windows at Glasgow as I rode through the town, lest I should see a lithographic representation (on the model of the picture of Captain Cook's death)[2] of certain Irish excavators beating you to death with clubs. I bless my stars—and the Military—for your preservation.[3]

Mrs. Dickens desires to be kindly remembered to you, and I am, with many thanks,

My Dear Sir | Faithfully Yours
CHARLES DICKENS

P.S. I should state that I have the remarkable property of taking care of borrowed books, and of returning them.

## *To* R. S. HORRELL, 21 JULY 1841

MS Public Library of Victoria, Melbourne.

Devonshire Terrace. | July The Twenty First 1841.
Dear Sir.
You must not be down-hearted about Blackwood. You may write a civil

[1] The story of the wild Orson, tamed by his brother the knightly Valentine, was well known to CD from an early age. It appeared in chapbooks; and there were numerous 18th and 19th century editions (with titles such as "The Famous History of Valentine and Orson"), besides plays on the subject (e.g. an O'Keefe, 1795, and a Dibdin, 1804). In "The Child's Story" (*Household Words*, Christmas No., 1852), CD refers to "the most astonishing picture-books: all about ... caverns and forests and Valentines and Orsons"; and in "A Christmas Tree" (*op. cit.*, 21 Dec 50, II, 291), Valentine is named with Robin Hood. In *Barnaby*, CD saw Hugh ("more brute than man") as Orson. Mr Chester calls him "Bruin" (Ch. 40); and among the descriptive headlines added by CD for the Charles Dickens edn of 1867, those for Ch. 23 (in which Chester first interviews Hugh) read "Valentine and Orson" and "Orson Tamed".

[2] CD had probably seen Zoffany's painting of the clubbing to death of Capt. James Cook by the Sandwich Islands natives in 1797. It was given to Greenwich Hospital in 1835 by Mrs Cook's executor, and exhibited in the Painted Hall from then on. (It is reproduced in Alan Moorehead, *The Fatal Impact*, 1966, facing p. 78.) He may also have known the picture by George Carter (1737–94; *DNB*), frequently engraved, and reproduced in many early biographies of Cook.

[3] A violent quarrel had broken out between the Highlanders and Irish labourers working on the Edinburgh and Glasgow Railway. On 27 June several Highlanders were severely injured by bludgeons; and the next day the Linlithgow authorities called in military aid from Edinburgh to prevent a battle between 1500 Irish and a larger number of Scots (report in the *Scotsman*, 30 June). As sheriff, Cay would have been closely involved.

note, I think—enquire after the Young Painter's fate—and beg to have the MS returned, if rejected. I should like to know what they say to you.

I see no objection to your trying Mr. Heraud[1] certainly, though I believe (but this is between ourselves) that he and some other gentlemen inclose themselves in a magic circle formed of their own Manuscripts, and perform wondrous incantations which seldom reach beyond it. However, a fellow feeling makes us wondrous kind,[2] and perhaps the Young Painter may see the light, even amidst their brightness. Try the Monthly by all means.[2]

I [hope][3] you have received some benefit from your Voyage. I should have written to you sooner, but I have been in Scotland for some weeks, and only returned home last Monday.

Faithfully Yours<br>CHARLES DICKENS

I fear I shall not be able to get to Exeter this year.


## *To* GEORGE CATTERMOLE, 21 JULY 1841*

MS Free Library of Philadelphia.

Devonshire Terrace. | July The Twenty First 1841.

My Dear George.

Come and dine with me on Sunday at 6 exactly[4]—nobody here but the two Macs and Forster. I am at home again, you see. Traitor! Why didn't you write to me after I sent you that paper ? ? ?[5]

Loves at home nevertheless<br>Yours indignantly

George Cattermole Esquire                                     CHARLES DICKENS


[1] John Abraham Heraud (1799–1887; *DNB*), editor of the *Monthly Magazine* 1839–42. Poet and dramatist; had attempted two grand epics, *The Descent into Hell*, 1830, and *The Judgment of the Flood*, 1834. A close friend of the Carlyles. Contributed to the *Athenæum* from 1843, later becoming its dramatic critic. Horrell's paper was not published in either *Blackwood's* or the *Monthly Magazine*.

[2] Cf. Garrick, "An Occasional Prologue on Quitting the Theatre", 1776.

[3] MS reads "I have you have".

[4] Cattermole had last dined with CD on the evening before he left for Scotland (letter of acceptance, MS Huntington; and see *To* Maclise, 12 July, *fn*).

[5] The newspaper describing the Edinburgh dinner (see 26 June). Cattermole replied: "It was not for me to put in any claim upon your time and attention whilst both must have been so fully occupied in responding to the homage of the Nations! It was enough to know that my memory would *keep* till your return: Still pleasanter was it to *feel* in the thrill which responded to the echoes of *their* gladness, how deep is the interest I take in all that makes your greatness and your happiness! ... I need not say I am *sure* for Sunday" (MS Rutgers University Library).

## *To* UNKNOWN CORRESPONDENT, 21 JULY 1841*

MS Dunedin Public Library, New Zealand.

Devonshire Terrace. | Twenty First July 1841.
Dear Sir.

I have been in Scotland for some weeks, and have only just returned to get your note. Nothing less should have prevented my answering it immediately.

Faithfully Yours
CHARLES DICKENS

## *To* MRS PERRY,[1] 21 JULY 1841

Mention in *American Book Prices Current*, IV, 1918–9; *MS* 2 pp.; dated 21 July 41.

*Answering an inquiry about a gentleman.*

## *To* GEORGE CRUIKSHANK, 21 JULY 1841

MS Colonel Richard Gimbel.

Devonshire Terrace. | Twenty First July 1841.
My Dear George

I am just home from Scotland.

What about the Postilion. Is he "all right", or "all wrong"—Vich?[2]

Faithfully Yours always
George Cruikshank Esquire                        CHARLES DICKENS

## *To* JOHN OVERS, 21 JULY 1841*

Transcript by Dr J. B. Solley, owner of MS in 1939.

Devonshire Terrace | Twenty First July 1841
Dear Mr. Overs.

I write hastily to you, because I have been in Scotland for some weeks, and have only just returned to find your letter lying upon my table.

I have not seen Mr. Cruikshank, of course. But as I think it cannot prejudice you now, to spur his memory, I have done so by letter. The result you shall hear, directly *I* hear it.

I am concerned to hear that you are ill, and trust you have sound advice.

---

[1] Unidentified.

[2] On 3 Apr, acknowledging Overs's "The Postilion", Cruikshank had written to CD: "I have introduced the 'Postboy'—to the 'Conductor' of the 'Omnibus' & hope he may get a *Sitiva-* *tion* for I think you know that I am, like yourself, always ready to lend a helping hand to those who want it" (MS Berg). For his acceptance of the sketch, see *To* Overs, 8 Aug, *fn.*

If you have any doubt upon that subject, let me know, and I will take care that the best authority shall set your mind at ease on that score. You need have no hesitation in doing this, for most of our skilful doctors are my friends, and any one of them would be glad, I know, to wait upon you without charge.

This brings me to something else.—I hope you don't want money; but if you do, I hope you know whom to ask for it. Lest you should have any doubt upon the subject, here is the man's name at full length.

Mr. J. A. Overs CHARLES DICKENS

## *To* JOHN OVERS, 23 JULY 1841*

MS Carl and Lily Pforzheimer Foundation.

*a*In haste to save the Post.*a*

---

Devonshire Terrace. | Twenty Third July 1841.

My Dear Mr. Overs.

I am truly pleased to hear you are so much better. You must have suffered very much. *One* of your complaints I am, and have been from a child, subject to myself. I can feel for you.

Will you—if you can comfortably—acknowledge the safe receipt of the inclosed, in one line? I hope it is enough for your present purpose.[1]

I shall be in town until Saturday week; and after that, at Broadstairs in Kent, where all letters will find me. Whenever I hear from Mr. Cruik-shank, depend upon my writing. In case I should be addressing you at a wrong place, you had better let me know when you return to town.

Faithfully Yours always

Mr. J. A. Overs. CHARLES DICKENS

## *To* JOHN FORSTER, 23 JULY 1841

Forster's summary of letter, made before destruction, MS Victoria & Albert Museum (FC); dated Devonshire Terrace, 23 July 41.

*As to Shoberl matters.[2] And some misprinted words in proof.[3]*

*aa* Appears to have been written by CD before starting letter.

[1] Overs had accepted CD's offer of money (see last). CD's account-book (MS Messrs Coutts) shows payments to him of £5 on 27 July, 30 Aug and 27 Sep.

[2] Cf. *To* Shoberl, 21 July and *fn.*

[3] Presumably proof of *Barnaby* No. 70 (Chs 47 and 48, published 31 July), written in Scotland. The misprints were almost certainly a result of the printer's misreading CD's initial *Y* or *y* (see Plate 2). In letters of 21 July, and in the MS of *Barnaby* No. 71 (written this week), a new bold *Y* appears occasionally. In letters later in July, and in the MS of *Barnaby* Nos 72 and 73, *y* (as well as *Y*) appears in the new bold form, side by side with the earlier form of each. By Ch. 55 (the first in No. 74), begun 2 Aug, and in letters from the beginning of Aug, the new *Y* and *y* have virtually ousted the old (see Plate 3).

### *To* THE REV. CHAUNCY HARE TOWNSHEND, 23 JULY [1841]

MS Wisbech Museum & Literary Institute. *Date:* clearly the year of CD's visit to Scotland; signature supports.

Devonshire Terrace. | Twenty Third July.

My Dear Townshend.

On Wednesday I will dine with you please God. At what hour?

I am horribly hard at work,[1] after my Scotch honors, and dare not be mesmerized, lest it should damage me at all. Even a day's head ache would be a serious thing just now.[2]

—But a time *will* come—as they say in melo dramas[3]—no more—

Except that I am always | Faithfully Yours

CHARLES DICKENS

The Reverend | Chauncey Hare Townshend.

### *To* THOMAS BEARD, 25 JULY 1841

MS Dickens House. *Address:* Free | Thomas Beard Esquire | 42 Portman Place | Edgeware Road.

Devonshire Terrace | Sunday July Twenty Fifth 1841.

My Dear Beard.

This is to give you notice that I am safe at home—that the children and other valuables repair to Broadstairs next Saturday—and that self and Partner follow them, this day week.

You have not changed your mind, I hope, in respect of your weekly visits, dips, and airings? If not, come and dine with me (alone) at 5 on Thursday, and we'll enjoy everything in anticipation. It'll freshen you up and make a man of you till next Autumn, so break it out to Easthope forthwith.

Always Faithfully

Loves and regards

BOZ.

[1] Probably on No. 71 (Chs 49 and 50, published 7 Aug), which he must have begun immediately after his return from Scotland on 18 July. But he may have been already beginning No. 72, which was presumably finished when, on 28 July, he gave Cattermole a subject for No. 73. He was now writing rapidly—partly to make up for time lost in Scotland, but also because the chapters describing the riots came easily to him.

[2] Townshend replied the next day: "½ past 6 is our dinner-hour on Wednesday. I will promise to keep my hands off you, however much they may be itching to perform mesmeric evo-lutions about your head—& I will try to get up a case for you to *see*. It would be a shame there should be 2 operators present (for Elliotson makes one of my party) and no *stigmatising*, as a little boy of one of my friends calls it" (MS Hunt-ington). Probably the patient he or Elliotson provided was a Miss Critchley; for in his letter to CD of ?4 Aug (see *To* Hudson, 29 July, *fn*) Elliotson wrote of having that morning produced in a patient "*all* the phenomena, that you witnessed in Miss Critchley . . . in *one* minute at the utmost, she was senseless & rigid, & so remained" (MS Hunt-ington).

[3] Thus in MS.

### *To* JOHN FORSTER, 26 JULY 1841

MS Brotherton Library, Leeds.

Devonshire Terrace
Monday Morning | July Twenty Sixth 1841.

My Dear Forster.

The broad light of day, shews me that I ought not to go to Greenwich tomorrow; for unless I keep my mind upon my work, I shan't do it; and if I don't do it, I'm done. Wherefore I declare off virtuously.

Faithfully Always
CHARLES DICKENS
Over

I had written this when your note came. I must stick to it, like wax, pitch, glue, cement. Pity and protect
The Slave.

I have told the boy to bring Stanfield's note back to you for reconsideration.
What about Friday?[1] I shall see you between this and then. We might—I say we *might*—breakfast at the Parthenon perhaps.
! ! ! ! ! ! ! !

### *To* DANIEL MACLISE, 28 JULY [1841]*

MS Colonel Richard Gimbel. *Date:* 28 July was Wednesday in 1841; handwriting, and references to the "fete" (see last, *fn*) and to Broadstairs support.

Devonshire Terrace | Wednesday July The Twenty Eighth.

My Dear Mac.

Will you let me know when I see you on Friday at that dazzling fete, whether you purpose going to Broadstairs with us on Sunday.

Recollect that all the time we are there, there is a bedroom most heartily at your service. I only ask in order that the servants (who go on Saturday morning) may know for whom they are to prepare.

Faithfully Always
CD.

---

[1] On Fri 30 July Macready described in his diary that day's "long-promised expedition" (cf. Macready *to* CD, 4 June 41: "Shall we ever reach that most remote geographical position—Belvedere?": MS Huntington). The Macreadys, Stanfields and Catherine set off in one carriage; CD, Forster, Maclise and Cattermole in another. After visiting the house and grounds of Belvedere, they returned to Greenwich, saw the Hospital, and met Elliotson, Quin and David Roberts. They dined at the Trafalgar (*Diaries*, II, 139).

## *To* GEORGE CATTERMOLE, 28 JULY 1841

MS University of Texas.

Devonshire Terrace.<br>
Wednesday Evening | July The Twenty Eighth 1841.

My Dear George.

Can you do for me by *Saturday Evening*—I know the time is short, but I think the subject will suit you, and I am greatly pressed[1]—a party of rioters (with Hugh and Simon Tappertit conspicuous among them) in old John Willet's bar—turning the liquor taps to their own advantage—smashing bottles—cutting down the grove of lemons—sitting astride on casks—drinking out of the best punchbowls—eating the great cheese—smoking sacred pipes &c &c—John Willet, fallen backward in his chair, regarding them with a stupid horror, and quite alone among them, with none of the Maypole customers at his back.

It's in your way, and you'll do it a hundred times better than I can suggest it to you, I know.[2]

Faithfully Always

George Cattermole Esquire                 CHARLES DICKENS


## *To* EDWARD CHAPMAN, 28 JULY [1841]*

MS Dr William A. Whittaker. *Date:* clearly same day as last; handwriting supports.

Devonshire Terrace. | Wednesday Twenty Eighth July.

My Dear Sir.

I forgot to tell you—I have given Mr. Cattermole a subject for No. 73[3]—a full one—and asked him to get it done by *Saturday Evening*. Look him up ac-cor-din-ly.

Faithfully Yours always

Edward Chapman Esquire.               CHARLES DICKENS


## *To* JOHN FORSTER, [29 JULY 1841]

Extract in F, II, ix, 169. *Date:* 29 July according to Forster.

Have you seen no. 71? I thought there was a good glimpse of a crowd, from a window—eh?[4]

---

[1] He was going away to Broadstairs the following Sunday and no doubt wanted to finish his number and see Cattermole's illustration to it first.

[2] Cattermole's illustration, "The mob at the Maypole", appeared in *Barnaby*, Ch. 54 (No. 73, published 21 Aug). Simon Tappertit surveys the scene from a raised chair and Hugh is in the centre, brandishing a cudgel and holding aloft a punchbowl.

[3] "The mob at the Maypole": see last.

[4] Clearly refers to the last paragraph but two in Ch. 50 (No. 71, published 7 Aug), in which Gashford looks down from a window on the torch-lit mob returning from the wrecking of Catholic churches.

### *To* JOHN HUDSON, 29 JULY 1841*

MS Berg Collection.

Devonshire Terrace | July Twenty Ninth 1841.

Dr. Sir.

The bottle has been a great success, and has provoked a great many enquiries—as I hope you will find.

I want to make a present of some of the Illustrious Punch, to my friend Doctor Elliotson. Will you be good enough to have two dozen nicely packed, and to send it to that gentleman (Carriage Paid) 37 Conduit Street, Bond Street, London?[1]—The account, of course, to me. We are going to the seaside for a couple of months, but when we return I shall want some more for myself.

                                        Yours

Mr. John Hudson.                        CHARLES DICKENS

### *To* MESSRS CHAPMAN & HALL, 31 JULY 1841

MS[2] Widener Collection, Harvard.

                                    1 Devonshire Terrace | 31st. July 1841

My Dear Sirs

The terms upon which you advanced to me on the 2nd. July 1840 the sum of £2250 for the purchase of the Copyright and Stock of Oliver [on][3] my behalf and also upon which you have since advanced to me the su[m][3] of £769..9..5 making together the sum of £3019.9.5 are underst[ood][3] between us to be these.

That this sum is not to be called in by you before the 2nd. day of July 1845 and to be without interest in the mean time—That you are to have a lien to this amount on the property belonging to me that is now and will be then in your hands namely my shares in the Stock and Copyright of "Sketches by Boz" "The Pickwick Papers" "Nicholas Nickleby" "Oliver Twist" and "Master Humphrey's Clock" in which we do not include my share of the current profits of the last named Work which I still remain at

---

[1] Elliotson wrote on Wed [4] Aug (letter dated "Wednesday, 3–"): "You are resolved to punch out all my wits— *Two dozen* punches! I had made up my mind to half a dozen: but two dozen who shall stand! | Joking apart, you make me ashamed with your overflowing of the *milk* of kindness. I would send you two dozen Judies in return— but what would Mrs. Dickens say! | Accept my best thanks" (MS Huntington).

[2] Only the signature is in CD's hand, the rest presumably in a clerk's. Based

on *To* Chapman & Hall, 2 July 40, the letter incorporates alterations and additions made by William Chapman to bring it into line with "the existing state of things" (see Chapman *to* Smithson & Mitton, 10 July 41: Appx, p. 488). CD's insurance policy and a Bond which he had agreed to sign, having rejected the Deed Chapman had drawn up (see ?3 Aug 41), were to be held by Chapman & Hall as securities.

[3] Paper is tattered at the edge; in four places words or parts of words are missing. For the fourth see next page.

liberty to draw at the times stated in our Agreement except as to one half
of the profits arising to me over and above the Weekly sum of £50 which
one half is to be applied towards the reduction of the said sum of £3019.9.5
—That you are also to appropriate [to] gradual liquidation of the said sum
of £3019.9.5 whatever sum you may receive from the Sale of the Stock
of Oliver Twist deducting the sum of £5 pr. cent for Commission on the
Sale thereof and all charges of Advertizing and of foreign Commission.

I have also caused my Life to be insured with the Britannia Life Asse.
Company for £2000 the policy for which (Numbered 2251)[1] I am willing
that you should hold as a further Security and the same will this day be
handed over to you by my solicitors.

Dear Sirs | faithfully Yours

Messrs. Chapman & Hall                          CHARLES DICKENS[2]

## *To* MESSRS CHAPMAN & HALL, [31 JULY 1841]

Mention in *To* Chapman & Hall, ?3 Aug 41. *Date:* written immediately
after signing the Bond of 31 July, and sent with Mitton's letter to Chapman
& Hall closing the business.

*Peremptorily demanding the return of the private letter to Edward Chapman, 2 July 40, in which he had thanked him for the firm's loan of £2250.*[3]

## *To* JOHN FORSTER, [31 JULY 1841]

Extract in F, II, xii, 193. *Date:* 31 July according to Forster.

I subscribed for a couple of copies of this little book.[4] I knew nothing
of the man, but he wrote me a very modest letter of two lines, some weeks
ago. I have been much affected by the little biography at the beginning,[5]
and I thought you would like to share the emotion it had raised in me. I
wish we were all in Eden again—for the sake of these toiling creatures.

---

[1] Before leaving for America in Jan 42, CD also handed over to Chapman & Hall, as security, his original Britannia policy, No. 794, endorsed for America (MS Mr C. C. Dickens).

[2] For the Bond, signed 31 July, see Appx, p. 489.

[3] On receiving this, Chapman & Hall were much pained, and wrote CD a letter which completely changed his feelings (see ?3 Aug).

[4] Possibly *A Narrative of the Experience and Sufferings of William Dodd, a Factory Cripple, written by Himself,* 1841 (in CD's library at his death: *Catalogue of the Library of CD,* ed. J. H. Stonehouse, p. 88); published by L. &

G. Seeley, 41 pp., price 1/-. It is dated 18 June 41 from 23 Little Gray's Inn Lane, and dedicated to Lord Ashley, who had seen an earlier brief outline.

[5] CD was perhaps referring to the following summary on the title-page: "Giving an account of the hardships and sufferings [Dodd] endured in early life, under what difficulties he acquired his education, the effects of factory labour on his mind and person, the unsuccessful efforts made by him to obtain a livelihood in some other line of life, the comparison he draws between agricultural and manufacturing labourers, and other matters relating to the working classes." Born in 1804,

## *To* DANIEL MACLISE, [?31 JULY 1841]*

MS Private. *Date:* later than CD's Broadstairs visit of Sep–Oct 40 on reference to "the Maniac" (i.e. Fletcher: see *To* Forster, 13 Sep); clearly some Saturday when CD had "packed up" before leaving home; probably 31 July 41 (he left for Broadstairs on 1 Aug). *Address:* Daniel Maclise Esquire.

Devonshire Terrace | Saturday

My Dear Maclise

Let me make you lazy today, for I have packed up all my tools and can't do anything. The Maniac joins us at "Mister Ryan's"[1] at half past 6. Meanwhile let us lunch and walk. I'll be with you in a quarter of an hour after the receipt of this.

Faithfully Yours Always
CD.

## *To* UNKNOWN CORRESPONDENT, [?JULY] 1841

Extract in Charles De F. Burns catalogue, Feb 1896; *MS* (signed initials) 1 p.; dated 1841—possibly July when he was hard at work making up for time spent in Scotland.

I am hard at work, but will take a couple of hours before dinner and resume at night.

## *To* THOMAS BEARD, 2 AUGUST 1841

MS Dickens House. *Address:* Thomas Beard Esquire | 42 Portman Place | Edgeware Road | London.

Broadstairs | Monday. August The Second | 1841.

My Dear Beard.

You cannot (as you know) come too soon, or too often, or stay too long. I am alone, and anxiously expecting you.

The *Ramsgate* boat starts from the Wharf at London Bridge, every morning at 9 to the moment. All you have to do, is to go aboard of her, and when you come off Margate or thereabouts, tell the captain you want to go ashore at Broadstairs.

When you know, write and tell me the day, that I may be on the look out for you. And may I ask you to stop your cab at No. 1 Devonshire

---

Dodd worked at card-making at the age of five and began as a piecer in a textile factory a year later. When 15 he was crippled from the work. The whole book is autobiographical; but in the latter part there are reflections on the factory system, and finally an impassioned indictment of its evils.

[1] Possibly the Theatre Royal, Richmond, of which John Ryan (*d.* 1850), one-time member of the resident company, had been manager 1839–40. CD had subscribed to his benefit on 5 Nov 39 (Malcolm Morley, "Dickens Goes to the Theatre", *D*, LIX [1963], 169).

Terrace, and bring down a small basket Topping shall have ready packed and waiting for you—together with any letters he may have on hand? The Sea, with long creation,[1] seems to me to get fresher every year.

Always My Dear Beard | Faithfully Yours

CHARLES DICKENS

Best regards from Kate, and from Fred, who is here—in tight boots[2] of course. Love from children.

## *To* JOHN FOWLER, 2 AUGUST 1841

Mention in N, 1, 343. *Address* (envelope, MS Private): John Fowler Esquire | Occupation Road | Sheffield; PM Sheffield 3 Aug 41.

## *To* MESSRS CHAPMAN & HALL, [?3 AUGUST 1841]†

MS[3] Huntington Library. *Date:* Handwriting points unmistakably to Aug 41 at earliest. Presumably *To* Chapman & Hall, 31 July (like CD's insurance policy), was delivered by hand that same day; Chapman & Hall would probably have replied on Mon 2 Aug, and CD written the answer below on the 3rd. An apparently post-reconciliation letter from William Chapman to Mitton, about CD's insurance premium, is dated 4 Aug (MS Mr C. C. Dickens). *From* Broadstairs (see below).

Dear Sirs.

I desire, no less earnestly than yourselves, that the spirit of confidence which has always—until lately—prevailed between us, and which of late has doubtless undergone a[4] suspension, should be restored. But I owe it to myself, and to the[5] reliance I have always felt[6] in you, [a]and always endeavoured earnestly to [      ],[a] to say that its suspension is in no wise attributable to me, or to any act or expression on the part of any person who has mediated, on my behalf, between us.

When [b]I applied to you to advance[b] me the money for the purchase of Oliver Twist and for my extrication from the hands of the nefarious[7] Mr. Bentley, I did so because you knew me well—because you had profited largely by such abilities and powers of perseverance and application as are

---

[1] Possibly a distant echo of Byron's invocation to the ocean in *Childe Harold's Pilgrimage*, Canto IV, verse 182: "Time writes no wrinkle on thy azure brow— | Such as creation's dawn beheld, thou rollest now."

[2] Which were highly fashionable: see, e.g., "A Chapter on Boots" in *Punch*, 24 July 41. Fred's boots are mentioned again in *To* Fletcher, 24 Mar 44.

[3] A draft, showing frequent changes of mind as CD wrote it; afterwards revised, with alterations and additions

by him in pencil (all, with one exception, ignored in N, 1, 285–7). The last two paragraphs are written entirely in pencil.

[4] "total" cancelled here in pencil.

[5] "generous" cancelled here in pencil.

[6] Added in pencil above "reposed" cancelled.

[a][a] Added in pencil over caret; last word smudged and illegible.

[b][b] Written above "you advanced" cancelled.

[7] "dog whose name is" cancelled; "Mr." added over caret.

my only Bank—because *you had my copyrights—because* you knew me to be a man of truth and honor in my dealings—because we were closely and intimately connected in business transactions of present and prospective profit, both to you and to me. For all these reasons I considered that I had a claim upon you; and having it, that it was better to get the money from you than from any of the dozen strangers who would have thrust it into my pockets, and hampered me with hard conditions.

You advanced it. I wrote you an acknowledgement[1] which I considered, and do consider, was between truthful men a sufficient security. I also wrote you a private letter in which I expressed, as I always do, what I felt, *and always endeavoured [        ].* I had a strong sense of the ready and kind way in which you had come forward with the money, and of the personal interest you had shewn in the matter—this made it in my eyes something of a more pleasant nature than a mere matter of business, and[2] I was glad to be affected by it, and to think it a gratifying circumstance.

The *acknowledgement I wrote you* was "to be put into law".[3] Well, I thought, perhaps, on reflection, you would not consider this necessary. But as I had had the money, and had parted with it, I made no objection.

The next I heard of the business was this:—I was taken aside one day by Mr. Smithson (no very great private friend of mine—not in my confidence, and not having much reason that I know of to be partially interested in my proceedings)[4] who told me that a few nights previous, he had opened a parcel addressed to the firm, containing a draught of a deed from Mr. Chapman of Richmond[5]—that he had read it, and during the perusal could not refrain from expressing to those who were about him, at the moment, his unbounded surprise at the conditions it recited—that he held them to be most degrading in reference to myself, quite unwarrantable in reference to you; *of a most hard,* stringent, and overbearing kind—and that it was a deed such as no client of his, apart from any delicate[6] consideration arising out of previous dealings between the parties, should ever sign with his consent.[7] He expressed himself with the greatest warmth, and said that if you had instructed Mr. Chapman to prepare such

*cc* Added over caret.

[1] His letter of 2 July 40.

*dd* Added in pencil over caret; 3 or 4 words at end illegible.

[2] "connected it in my mind" cancelled here.

*ee* Written above "letter" cancelled.

[3] See William Chapman *to* Smithson & Mitton, 25 July 40, quoted in *To* Chapman & Hall, 2 July 40, *fn.*

[4] This seems somewhat disingenuous.

[5] William Chapman (1802–74), solicitor, Edward Chapman's elder brother. Admitted 1823; practised in Richmond all his life. Clerk to the Richmond Union, joint clerk to magistrates. Senior churchwarden 1852.

*ff* Written above "and under any circumstances" cancelled.

[6] Added over caret.

[7] See Appx, pp. 482–6 for the draft Deed, dated 26 May 41; also for three letters from William Chapman to Smithson & Mitton. In the first, 4 June, he defended the Deed as "the necessary result of both Mr Dickens' Letter & the arrangements entered into at our meeting at Mr Forsters"; on 12 June he elaborated the point and put forward the view (which would have particularly infuriated CD) that as "the £2250 was the purchase money (partly) of 'Barnaby Rudge' ", the book by being published in *Master Humphrey* was "in

an Instrument, it was his duty to have remonstrated with you, and to have endeavoured to dissuade you from attempting to carry such an intention into effect. He said that he felt great hesitation in interfering with the business, as this was the first he had heard of it, and it was managed by Mr. Mitton. But that he had told Mr. Mitton what he thought, and found that that gentleman entirely concurred with him, and was as much surprised as himself.[1] He wound up by telling me in so many words that he thought it would be much better if I empowered Mr. Mitton to negociate an advance of two thousand pounds in some other quarter & repay the money to you—and rid me of a burden *"you sought to render"* so insupportable and oppressive.

On this I communicated with Mr. Mitton directly—*"After reading the deed I"* told him flatly that I *would not* sign any such document, that I believed Mr. Chapman of Richmond was more to blame than you—and that it might go back to him as so much waste paper, as soon as he pleased.

The upshot of all the subsequent legal conferences and discussions *"(from which I was quite unable to separate your [              ])"* is simply this. The letter I wrote you was a security in equity, but not in law. Mr. Chapman of Richmond—acting with no very strong family likeness to Mr. Chapman of the Strand, and not always expressing himself, as I am told, in the most courteous or becoming terms—demanded to have *both*. As the least offensive way of putting me into double irons, Mr. Mitton recommended the bond; and wearied to death with opposition and delay, disgusted with the whole course of proceeding and thoroughly sick at heart, I signed the bond.

But when I did so, I told Mr. Mitton that as you had trusted nothing to me, and had treated me like a stranger, I would not leave on record between us a private letter (he had never seen or heard of it) which I had sent to Mr.

fact being paid for twice over, unless the £2250 & about £1000 subsequently advanced [were] in some manner secured"; on 20 July he enclosed a draft showing how CD's letter of 2 July 40 should be altered to fit the new arrangements—and generally climbed down. It is hard to see how CD's letter of 31 July 41 and the Bond, taken together, mortgaged his copyrights and insurance policy any less fully than the detested Deed would have done. But what seems to have mattered to CD was that the business should be done as informally as possible, should be something of a "gentlemen's agreement". He rebelled against the rigid legalism of the Deed—too reminiscent of his embittering Agreements with Bentley. But why Smithson, a lawyer himself, should have thought the conditions of the Deed "degrading"—unless vicariously —is not clear.

[1] William Chapman wrote to them on 4 June that he could by no means share their "surprize as to how Mr Bacon 'came to hit upon the present mode'" (the Deed incorporating CD's letter of 2 July 40 and Forster's memorandum of 10 Nov). They wrote, he said in his next letter (12 July), as if the objections were purely theirs, "as matters of business"; but he assumed that they were CD's too; and his clients had "that respect for and confidence in [CD] that they would desire to consult his wishes in every respect".

*aa* Added over caret.

*bb* Added in pencil above the line.

*cc* Added in pencil over a caret; 6 words illegible.

Chapman immediately after the money was put down; and[1] which, left unrecalled, would be a lie. I therefore took up the pen with which I had signed the bond, and with my own hand wrote those words which you say occasioned you so much pain; and peremptorily required that he should add them to the letter in which he closed the business.

This done, I left town, as you know, and coming down here, tried to dismiss the subject from my thoughts. Your letter of yesterday (received this morning) has re-opened it, and rendered it necessary that I should tell you exactly what I have thought, and felt, and known about it. *aI have done so without the least reserve.a*

[2]That my sentiments have undergone a complete change since the receipt of that letter; and that it has done more to awaken the feelings which have so long subsisted and should always subsist between us, than whole years of uninterrupted good understanding without any allusion to this theme, could have effected, it would be ungenerous in me to conceal for a moment. I make the avowal with great delight and pleasure; and rest assured that in the negociation of our new undertaking,[3] you will find me[4] as ready to respond to you in a frank and cordial spirit, and as earnestly desirous to meet you on all points with a liberal construction, and a confidence, founded on mutual [knowledge][5] and esteem as I ever have been at any period of our intercourse.

As you think you can trust me without the bond, I would rather you threw it into the fire with your own hands—for I can trust you to do it.

## To JOHN FORSTER, [5 AUGUST 1841]

Extract in F, II, ix, 169. *Date:* 5 Aug according to Forster. *From* Broadstairs.

I am warming up very much about *Barnaby*.[6] Oh! If I only had him, from this time to the end, in monthly numbers. *N'importe!* I hope the interest will be pretty strong—and, in every number, stronger.

## To MESSRS CHAPMAN & HALL, [?6 AUGUST 1841]

Mention in next.

---

[1] "that if I left it in existence between us" cancelled here.

[aa] This sentence omitted in N, I, 287, although written in ink.

[2] From this point to end letter is written entirely in pencil.

[3] The novel which was to follow *Master Humphrey*.

[4] "what I always have been" cancelled here.

[5] Reading apparently "knodge"—a contraction.

[6] He was at work on *Barnaby* No. 74, containing Chs 55 and 56—the burning and plundering of the Warren, and Haredale's capture of Rudge: see *To* Cattermole, 6 Aug.

## *To* GEORGE CATTERMOLE, 6 AUGUST 1841

Text from MDGH, I, 46–7.

Broadstairs, Friday, August 6th, 1841.

My dear George,

Here is a subject for the next number;[1] the next to that I hope to send you the MS. of very early in the week,[2] as the best opportunities of illustration are all coming off now, and we are in the thick of the story.[3]

The rioters went, sir, from John Willet's bar (where you saw them to such good purpose)[4] straight to The Warren, which house they plundered, sacked, burned, pulled down as much of as they could, and greatly damaged and destroyed. They are supposed to have left it about half an hour. It is night, and the ruins are here and there flaming and smoking. I want—if you understand—to show one of the turrets laid open—the turret where the alarm-bell is, mentioned in No. 1; and among the ruins (at some height if possible) Mr. Haredale just clutching our friend, the mysterious file, who is passing over them like a spirit; Solomon Daisy, if you can introduce him, looking on from the ground below.[5]

Please to observe that the M. F. wears a large cloak and a slouched hat. This is important, because Browne will have him in the same number,[6] and he has not changed his dress meanwhile. Mr. Haredale is supposed to have come down here on horseback, pell-mell; to be excited to the last degree. I think it will make a queer picturesque thing in your hands.[7] I have told Chapman and Hall that you may like to have a block of a peculiar shape for it.[8] One of them will be with you almost as soon as you receive this.

*a*We are very anxious to know that our cousin is out of her trouble, and

---

[1] *Barnaby* No. 74 (published 28 Aug), which CD had probably just finished.

[2] No. 75 was finished, "all but two slips", on Wed 11 Aug (see *To* Forster, that day).

[3] Both illustrations to No. 75, "The arrest of Barnaby" (Ch. 57) and "Barnaby in gaol" (Ch. 58), were in fact done by Browne—possibly because CD did not receive Cattermole's illustration to No. 74 until 13 Aug (see below) and wished to press ahead.

[4] In his illustration to No. 73, "The mob at the Maypole" (Ch. 54).

[5] On 12 Aug Cattermole wrote: "I cannot hope you will make much out of this accompanying scratch: I suppose the spectator to be placed upon the roof of one of the wings of the Warren house and towards him are rushing —— and Mr Haredale as they issue from a small

door in the tower whereunto is attached (as part & parcel of the same) the bell-turret: a small closet through which they pass to the roof has been dismantled or rather thrown down and ruined by the fire and the other spoilers: on the grass below is rooted Solomon Daisy in an ecstacy of wonder &c. &c. beyond are clouds of smoke apassing over and amongst many tall trees and all about over-head their tenants the frightened rooks are flying and cawing like mad" (MS Huntington).

[6] Browne's illustration (to Ch. 55) shows Rudge entering the dismantled Maypole bar where John Willet sits tied hand and foot to his chair.

[7] The illustration, "The Turret", appeared at the end of Ch. 56.

[8] The shape of the illustration is not unusual.

you free from your anxiety.[1] Mind you write when it comes off. And when she is quite comfortable come down here for a day or two, like a bachelor, as you will be. It will do you a world of good. Think of that.[a]

Always, dear Cattermole, | Heartily yours

[CHARLES DICKENS]

[b]P.S.—When you have done the subject, I wish you'd write me one line and tell me how, that I may be sure we agree. Loves from Kate.[b]

## *To* DR SOUTHWOOD SMITH, [?EARLY AUGUST 1841]

Mention in next.

## *To* MACVEY NAPIER, 8 AUGUST 1841

MS British Museum.

Broadstairs, Kent | Sunday August The Eighth 1841

My Dear Sir.

I write to you in great haste,—to save at once the Post, and my character.

I wrote to Southwood Smith, the chief commissioner in the Infant Labour Commission,[2] as we agreed; and have an answer from him[3] in which he says:

"I hope both report and evidence will be presented to Parliament during its next Sitting, that is, if it should not be prorogued earlier than 6 weeks or 2 months after its first meeting. As soon as these Documents are laid on the table of the House of Commons, they become public property, and may be treated accordingly; until that is the case, any communication of the matter contained in them must be strictly private and confidential. That you may be the better prepared to handle it, I will put you in possession of this matter as soon as I have put it in order, only it must be entirely for your own private study."

Therefore, I suppose the best plan will be, for me to write the paper[4] at my leisure, and for you to throw it over, until the Review after next— will it not? Southwood Smith, in other passages of this letter, lays extraordinary stress upon the facts they have got together—and from what I

---

[1] The Cattermoles' second child was born on 8 Aug. On the 9th Cattermole wrote: "In a snow-white, pink-lined little cot in the next room, fast asleep, with the settled and comfortable look of a veteran sleeper is—'My Son Sir!' ... all has gone capitally, and I almost contemplate the possibility of having a day with you as you propose. ... Tell this news the first moment you can to cousin Kate, ... and accompany it with my affectionate regards. God bless you all!" (MS Huntington).

[aa], [bb] Omitted in MDGH, 1882, 1893, and N.

[2] The "Commission for Inquiring into the Employment and Condition of Children in Mines and Manufactories", moved by Lord Ashley on 4 Aug 40 (see *To* Southwood Smith, 15 Dec 40).

[3] Not among the letters to CD of 1841 in the Huntington Library.

[4] Which he had promised Napier for the *Edinburgh Review* while he was in Edinburgh (*To* Forster, 30 June), but never in fact wrote. See 21 Oct.

know of them already, I am sure the subject is a most striking and remarkable one.[1]

Meanwhile, if any other should occur to me, I will communicate with you upon it.

I shall be glad to have one line from you.[2]  And am always

My Dear Sir | Faithfully Yours

CHARLES DICKENS

Mrs. Dickens desires her compliments—and joins me in remembrances to Miss Napier.

## *To* JOHN OVERS, 8 AUGUST 1841*

MS Dr Hugh Raven.

Broadstairs. | Sunday August The Eighth 1841.

Dear Mr. Overs.

You never found home so pleasant, as when you went back to it,—did you? I know the feeling well, and am glad sometimes (not often though) to go away by myself, for the purpose of enjoying it.

I was very glad to receive your note to day—not only because I am pleased to know you are so much better, but because I was very much fretted to have the inclosed good news from Mr. Cruikshank[3] lying idly here, and not being able to send it to you, until I should go to town; for want of your address—which I had forgotten.

I shall be glad to hear from you again soon, and to know how you are

---

[1] The findings of the Commission, published in their first Report of May 1842 (on mines), were sensational. "Perhaps even 'Civilisation' itself never exhibited such a mass of sin and cruelty. The disgust felt is very great, thank God", Ashley recorded in his diary (E. Hodder, *The Life and Work of the Seventh Earl of Shaftesbury*, 1886, I, 418). In his long speech of 7 June 42, asking leave to bring in a Bill (*Hansard*, LXIII [1842], 1319–51), he gave numerous examples, from evidence collected in the Report, of the appalling work in collieries and factories done by children from six years old, and by pregnant women; of their subsequent diseases; and of the brutality of individual employers.

[2] Napier replied on 12 Aug: "I was rejoiced to find, by your very obliging and welcome letter, that you had not forgotten me ... I am most anxious for your appearance in the Review as early as possible, and shall note you down for January. ... I have no doubt the subject will suit you, and that you will have no occasion to interfere with any of the doctrines maintained in the Review. The subject, if I rightly apprehend it, will be more *descriptive* than speculative, and will, under your graphic pen, make a far more interesting Paper than could be made of any thing of a theoretical nature. I think we talked of a couple of sheets, or thereabouts, as the probable length of it" (MS Huntington).

[3] Cruikshank had written to CD on 4 Aug accepting for his *Omnibus* Overs's sketch "The Postilion" (published Jan 42, I, 289–92) and saying: "I feel that he ought to have been taken into our service at once, considering the strong recommendation he had. But it's all the fault of my head man—who did not think he would do at first, but likes him very well now, upon taking a second look at him" (MS Morgan).

getting on. I don't think I shall be in town (unless for a day) until the eleventh or twelfth of October.

But here, or there, or anywhere, I am always

Faithfully Yours<br>CHARLES DICKENS

Your father, like many I know, takes after the birds, and forgets his children as soon as they can fly. But that's not the worst that can happen. I know some men who would be heartily glad, with reason, if their fathers would forget them altogether, instead of having dim glimpses of recollection as yours has.

## *To* MESSRS BRADBURY & EVANS, 10 AUGUST 1841*

MS Mr Cregoe D. P. Nicholson.

Broadstairs | August The Tenth 1841.

My Dear Sirs.

Since I have been here, I have not received a proof, of any kind or sort. Will you, by return of Post, send me proofs of the two Nos. 72 and 73[1]— and forward slips to me in future as soon as read.

Faithfully Yours always

Messrs. Bradbury and Evans. CHARLES DICKENS

## *To* THE EDITOR OF THE GATESHEAD OBSERVER,[2] 10 AUGUST 1841

MS Society of Antiquaries, Newcastle-upon-Tyne.

Broadstairs, Kent | August The Tenth, 1841

Sir.

Your paper of the Thirty First of last Month has been forwarded to me here, from London. It has made me desirous to depart from the rule I have found it necessary to establish in reference to any unfounded statements concerning myself that find their way into Print,—and to address these half dozen words to you with a twofold object.

Firstly, I beg to thank you with great cordiality for expressing your conviction that the charcoal sketch in Blackwood, of Cannie Newcastle,

[1] *Barnaby*, Chs 51–54, published 14 and 21 Aug. Both Nos were finished before he left London on 1 Aug.

[2] James Clephan (1805–88), journalist and antiquary. Trained as a printer and book-binder; worked in the offices of Messrs Ballantyne in Edinburgh while they were publishing Scott; later sub-editor of the *Leicester Chronicle*. Editor of the Whig *Gateshead Observer* 1838–1860. Afterwards a free-lance journalist on the staff of the *Newcastle Daily* and *Newcastle Weekly Chronicles*. Meanwhile wrote learned papers for the Newcastle Society of Antiquaries.

(which I have not seen) is not from my hand.[1] Secondly, to assure you that you are perfectly correct in your judgment, and that I know as much about it as I do of the heart of China.[2]

I am Sir | Very faithfully Yours
CHARLES DICKENS

To the Editor of | The Gateshead Observer.


## To JOHN FORSTER, [11 AUGUST 1841]

Extract in F, II, ix, 169. *Date:* six days after letter of 5 Aug, according to Forster. *From* Broadstairs.

I was always sure I could make a good thing of *Barnaby*, and I think you'll find that it comes out strong to the last word. I have another number ready, all but two slips.[3] Don't fear for young Chester. The time hasn't come[4]—there we go again, you see, with the weekly delays. I am in great heart and spirits with the story, and with the prospect of having time to think before I go on again.


## To THOMAS MITTON, 11 AUGUST 1841*

MS Huntington Library.

Broadstairs | August The Eleventh 1841.

My Dear Mitton

Take the will for the deed, and you will make a very long letter of this very short note. Until yesterday, I have been constantly at work. This is only my second holiday.

---

[1] The *Gateshead Observer* of 24 July had quoted a passage from "The June Gale", *Blackwood's*, July 41, L, 79, heading it "*Charcoal* Sketch (by *Blackwood*) of 'Cannie Newcastle' ", in which a traveller, who had passed through Newcastle on his way from London to Edinburgh, stigmatizes Newcastle as the worst of all the dingy, dirty, detestable towns in England or elsewhere, and describes its streets as "thronged with the most ill-favoured population we ever encountered—cripples, dwarfs, and drunkards". On 31 July the editor wrote that this paragraph had led to much gossip and had been "pretty generally ascribed to Mr. Dickens, who recently travelled as far north as Edinburgh. We allude to the circumstances . . . in order to contradict the conclusion to which our neighbours

have come. We see in the sketch no internal evidence of its production by the generous, good-natured mind of our friend *Boz*; nor will we believe him to be the author, unless authorized in the belief by himself. *Boz* is not a snarling, wholesale fault-finder; he is a man apt to find 'good in everything'."

[2] The *Gateshead Observer* of 14 Aug contained a denial of CD's authorship of the sketch and quoted his letter in full. The author was, in fact, the Rev. James White (later a friend of CD's).

[3] No. 75 (see *To* Cattermole, 6 Aug, *fn*), containing Barnaby's arrest and imprisonment (Chs 57 and 58), published 4 Sep.

[4] Edward Chester had been turned out of his father's house in No. 62 (Ch. 32). He reappeared at last in No. 82 (Ch. 71), to rescue Emma and Dolly.

I don't know what time the Saturday boats leave town, but that you can find out. On Sunday there is a boat from Margate at One; and on Monday at 8—that boat gets to town about one or half past.

Now write and tell me when you are coming, and how. I'll meet you whenever and wherever it is, please God. The weather here has been showery, but very fine and pleasant—crops decidedly good—today very squally.

Always Faithfully

CHARLES DICKENS

Forster writes me that he has had two letters from Father, which he don't mean to answer. This is not encouraging.

## *To* [WILLIAM] SHOBERL, 12 AUGUST 1841

Extract in T. F. Madigan catalogue No. 60 (1930); *MS* 1 p.; dated Broadstairs, 12 Aug 41. *Address:* mistakenly given in catalogue as *To* Frederic Shoberl; but clearly to William, Colburn's assistant. *From* Broadstairs.

I am greatly obliged to you for your note of the ninth (which has been forwarded to me here) and beg to assure you that I am quite convinced the omission was accidental, and that I entirely rely on your honorable and correct intentions.

## *To* JOHN FORSTER, [13 AUGUST 1841]

Extract in F, II, xii, 190. *Date:* 13 Aug according to Forster. *From* Broadstairs.

By Jove how radical I am getting![1] I wax stronger and stronger in the true principles every day. I don't know whether it's the sea, or no, but so it is.

---

[1] Since Peel's majority in the General Election of June–July. During Aug CD contributed three anti-Tory rhymed squibs to the *Examiner*, signed "W": " 'The Fine Old English Gentleman'. | New Version. | (To be said or sung at all Conservative Dinners.)", 7 Aug; "The Quack Doctor's Proclamation" (provoked by Peel's speech at Tamworth on 28 July), 14 Aug; and " 'Subjects for Painters' (After Peter Pindar)", 21 Aug —the last perhaps enclosed in this letter. Forster quotes from all three (F, II, xii, 190–2). For full texts see *The Poems and Verses of CD*, ed. F. G. Kitton, 1903, pp. 59–76. Peel's Tamworth speech was also satirized in *Punch* on 14 Aug, Peel appearing as "Rhubarb Pill (a travelling doctor)".

## *To* JOHN FORSTER, [?MID-AUGUST 1841]

Extract in F, II, xii, 191. *Date:* at a moment of sudden indignation at the
political outlook; placed by Forster after letter of 13 Aug. *From* Broadstairs.

*[a]CD thinks of carrying off himself and his household gods, like Coriolanus,
to a world elsewhere ![a1]* Thank God there is a Van Diemen's-land.[2] That's
my comfort. Now, I wonder if I should make a good settler! I wonder, if
I went to a new colony with my head, hands, legs, and health, I should
force myself to the top of the social milk-pot and live upon the cream!
What do you think? Upon my word I believe I should.

## *To* MISS BURDETT COUTTS, 16 AUGUST 1841

MS Morgan Library. *Address:* Miss Coutts | Stratton Street.

Broadstairs, Kent. | Monday August The Sixteenth | 1841.
Dear Miss Coutts.

A kind of daymare comes upon me sometimes, under the influence of
which I have dismal visions of your supposing me careless of your kind
Invitations—regardless of your notes—insensible to your friendship—and
a species of moral monster with the usual number of legs and arms, a head,
and so forth, but no heart at all.

This disorder, instead of diminishing within the cheerful influence of
the Sea, is so much aggravated by distance from Stratton Street and the
obstacles in the way of telling you about it by word of mouth, that I am
fairly driven to the desperate step of writing to you, to tell you how
notes and cards of Invitation from you have reached me in Scotland, in
Yorkshire, in Kent—in every place but London—and how I have reason
to suppose that some others are still taking sportive flights among the Post
offices, and getting very brown from change of air in various parts of the
United Kingdom.

I have too much pleasure and gratification in the sympathy you have
expressed, with my visionary friends, to let you forget me if I can help it.
In duty to myself therefore—this is a description of moral obligation which
most men discharge with the utmost punctuality—I raise my still small
voice from the ocean's brink, and humbly desire to live in your recollection
as an innocent, and not erring Individual, until next October.

If Miss Meredith should remember a fair young man with whom she had
a community of feeling in reference to the impossibility of getting up in the

---

[aa] Probably Forster's summary of the
earlier part of CD's letter.

[1] Cf. *Coriolanus*, III, iii, 137.

[2] Annexed by the British Govt 1803;
given colonial status and its name
changed to Tasmania 1856. The Van
Diemen's Land Co. had just been incorporated by charter.

morning during the Great Frost of eighteen hundred and forty one,—I beg to say that I am the person, and that I send my compliments.

Let me add that I am always with high regard and esteem,

Faithfully Yours

Miss Coutts.

CHARLES DICKENS[1]

## *To* JOHN FORSTER, [16 AUGUST 1841]

Extract in F, II, xii, 193. *Date:* Mon 16 Aug according to Forster. *From* Broadstairs.

I sit down to write to you without an atom of news to communicate. Yes I have—something that will surprise you, who are pent up in dark and dismal Lincoln's-inn-fields. It is the brightest day you ever saw. The sun is sparkling on the water so that I can hardly bear to look at it. The tide is in, and the fishing boats are dancing like mad. Upon the green-topped cliffs the corn is cut and piled in shocks; and thousands of butterflies are fluttering about, taking the bright little red flags at the mast-heads for flowers, and panting with delight accordingly. [Here the Inimitable, unable to resist the brilliancy out of doors, breaketh off, rusheth to the

---

[1] Miss Coutts replied on 19 Aug: "My Dear Sir | Notes and Cards were not the only means employed to find you, these failing, a body of Cavalry, headed by Mr. Marjoribanks and myself last Thursday week, made an attempt on your House, but with no other result, than the ascertaining that the House belonged to an Individual of your name, who was *just* gone out of Town, (the invariable answer to all enquiries) & whose identity it would have been as difficult to prove as that of Captn. Harvey Tuckett on a late celebrated trial [*whose identity—at the trial of the Earl of Cardigan (16 Feb 41) for wounding him in a duel—the prosecution was said to have failed to establish (see Cecil Woodham-Smith,* The Reason Why, *1953, pp. 64–5, 78–83)]—* Visionary reports of your having made excellent speeches in Scotland reached us, but like a Ghost, no one had themselves seen the Papers in which they were reported, at last on one occasion we traced a Newspaper into somebody's possession but on asking for it, were told it was just sent into the country that day, at last we gave ourselves up to the most gloomy reflections as to your probable or improbable fate, & as to the likelihood of your ever having existed & other useful speculations, & had not your Note arrived, containing not only an account of yourself but also the gratifying assurance that we were not forgotten, you would have seen advertised, as shortly ready, some new Historical Doubts [*cf. Richard Whately's* Historic Doubts Relative to Napoleon Bonaparte, *1829—a joke, proving he did not exist*] & even now I am not sure we should not have mentioned your Note as an instance of curious delusion on our part, owing to the strong deception we laboured under as to the fact of your existence had we not at the same time heard of you through the means of a *dumb* boy, the two reports together were too strong even for a theory & we are now quite willing to admit you are alive & that we shall have the pleasure of seeing you in October—Miss Meredith desires her best Compts., her forebodings *were* of the *most melancholy* kind, as she thought most likely you were smothered or expired suddenly trying to get up, if at least you have suffered as much as she has during the severe summer 1841 from the same 'community of feeling' as during the winter" (MS Huntington).

machines, and plungeth into the sea. Returning, he proceedeth:] Jeffrey is just as he was when he wrote the letter I sent you. No better, and no worse. I had a letter from Napier on Saturday, urging the children's-labour subject upon me. But, as I hear from Southwood Smith that the report cannot be printed until the new parliament has sat at the least six weeks, it will be impossible to produce it before the January number.[1] I shall be in town on Saturday morning and go straight to you. A letter has come from little Hall begging that when I *do* come to town I will dine there, as they wish to talk about the new story.[2] I have written to say that I will do so on Saturday, and we will go together; but I shall be by no means good company. . . . I have more than half a mind to start a book-seller of my own. I could; with good capital too, as you know; and ready to spend it. *G. Varden beware !*[3]

## *To* DANIEL MACLISE, [?16 AUGUST 1841]

Mention in Maclise *to* CD, [17] Aug (see *fn*). *Date:* Macready played in *William Tell* on 16 and 23 Aug; Maclise's letter almost certainly referred to the performance of the 16th and to CD's first visit to London (announced in *To* Forster, 16 Aug).

*Saying that he is coming up to London on the following Saturday, and suggesting a meeting at Forster's.*[4]

[1] See *To* Napier, 8 Aug.

[2] See *To* Mitton, 23 Aug.

[3] Cf. Simon Tappertit's "Beware, G. Varden!" and "Be warned in time, G. Varden" in *Barnaby*, Ch. 51 (No. 72, published two days before).

[4] Maclise replied: "I write 'thank you', for your very kind, and as usual hearty flavored letter, in the most common place manner, and I feel thank you in quite another sort of way—I am very glad you are coming up on Saturday. I hope to see you at Forster's at four—I dined with him yesterday the only time I have been outside the door since you left, or rather since we left you on that Saty. Evening—We sate like two Anchorites at the most frugal sure, of repasts—at least we were the mock hermits of the Raphael and Lamela caste [*Don Raphael and Ambrose Lamela, a pair of cunning rogues in* Gil Blas]. The Hermits of London. We had a long legged pullet as the point ['*d'appui*' *rubbed out*] de Resistance, with four bits of fried bacon. East West North South —french beans, I believe they call them —long green slips like green white bait [*sketch of them here*] rather slippery things to help—don't you know them? falling off the spoon?—opposite me— with potatoes cut like that staggering ball in one sort of Rouge et Noir table [*sketch of their shape here*] and very hardly done for me to help—removed by Artichokes, one a-piece—quite enough—I understand you don't know this creation. It is a soft sort of Fir tree fruit shaped production—made thus [*sketch of artichoke on plate*] served up with melted butter—and to be peppered. You detach with your fingers each layer, dip the rim in butter, and eat the tip and lining—dreadful nonsense. I class it with the much ado things of the Sparrow grass kind. Bulwer doats upon it—After this we had cheese and a Pat of Butter. Wine glasses—but we would not have or Port or Sherry—Cold water from the Pump in a Jug—for bringing it up in which— didn't Henry catch it? and I had Soda Water—Once we were very near breaking out and ordering up the finest Old Crusted but we knew we could not stop if once we went into the thing, that

### *To* HENRY AUSTIN, 16 AUGUST 1841*

MS Morgan Library.

Broadstairs | August The Sixteenth 1841.
My Dear Henry.

You would like this place, I think. Arrange to come down here with Letitia—say on the 1st. of September, and stop as long as you can.

The passage at the longest is 6 hours—the fare as many shillings—and you come ashore under the window—consequently, you can go backwards and forwards as often as you like.

My letters are of the briefest, because my relief is, *not* to write. But I mean a quirefull.

Kate joins me in love to Letitia and sends the same to yourself. Always believe her husband

[                    ]

Henry Austin Esquire                    [CHARLES DICKENS][1]

### *To* GEORGE CATTERMOLE, 19 AUGUST 1841

MS Benoliel Collection.

Broadstairs. | Nineteenth August 1841.
My Dear George.

When Hugh and a small body of the rioters cut off from the Warren unbeknown[2] to their pals, they forced into a ramshackle[2] post-chaise Dolly Varden and Emma Haredale, and bore them away with all possible rapidity; one of their company driving, and the rest running beside the chaise, climbing up behind, sitting on the top, lighting the way with their torches &c &c. If you can express the women inside without shewing them

we'd be carried away by our own Enthusiasm—so after mournfully smiling for an hour or so, we went off to see William Macready Tell embrace Mrs. W. Clifford his wife against his will—Of course we went behind and up stairs where we found *Him* unswathing, and taking the gummy mustachios off with hot water, and poor fellow with a real tooth ache—I cannot tell you how I always like him, and never more perhaps than when I see such a true fellow in that literally false position—doffing his dresses and tampering with that tin dressing box containing his smuts and rouges— | I feel when the time comes I shall not have firmness enough to resist going down with you for a day or two, but I am so damaged I do not like to impose myself—indeed I do not

enjoy myself—and the taking medicine and the wig, and the restriction and all that—But I should like to hear the sea swell again [*last few words written over a sketch of Broadstairs bay*]" (MS Huntington). Maclise had worn a wig for at least a month (for his going bald see 8 Mar 41, *fn*). In his letter to CD of 16 July he described himself as: "in a very bad state of health. Doctors!! here—my wig off and looking a good deal like that Maniac with his hand to his head in Hogarth's mad scene" (MS Huntington).

[1] Ending and signature have been cut away.

[2] N, following incorrect MDGH readings, gives "beckoned" for "unbeknown", "very remarkable" for "ramshackle".

—as by a fluttering veil, a delicate arm or so forth, appearing at the half closed window—so much the better. Mr. Tappertit stands on the steps, which are partly down, and hanging on to the window with one hand, and extending the other with great majesty, addresses a few words of encouragement to the driver and attendants. Hugh sits upon the bar in front—the driver sitting postilion wise—and turns round to look through the window behind him at the little doves within. The gentlemen behind are also curious to catch a glimpse of the ladies—one of those who are running at the side, may be gently rebuked for his curiosity by the cudgel of Hugh. So they cut away, Sir, as fast as they can.[1]

Always Faithfully
CD.

John Willet's bar is *noble*.[2]
We take it for granted that cousin and baby are hearty.—Our loves to them.

## *To* DR JOHN ELLIOTSON, 20 AUGUST 1841

Extract in Sotheby's catalogue, May 1949; *MS* 2 pp.; dated Devonshire Terrace, 20 Aug 41.

*Introducing John Overs, a cabinet maker who has literary aspirations and* really writes, in the intervals of his daily labour, *very well*.[3]

## *To* JOHN OVERS, 20 AUGUST 1841*

Text from typescript, Huntington Library.

Devonshire Terrace,
Friday, August Twentieth, 1841.

My Dear Mr Overs,
   Go to Doctor Elliotson (No 37 Conduit Street Bond Street) tomorrow morning between 10 and 12, and send in this card. I have written to him. I never knew him fail in any case where cure was possible, or care, humanity, and strong interest in his patient, coupled (I do believe) with greater skill than any other man possesses, could be of any avail. I am in town till Sunday morning. If you can come round here after you leave him, I shall be glad to hear your report of what he said to you.

Faithfully Yours always
CHARLES DICKENS

---

[1] Cattermole's illustration, "The chariot" (Ch. 59), which appeared in No. 76 (published 11 Sep), showed him unable to cope with so much detail and activity. All other such subjects were entrusted to Browne.
[2] CD had already praised this illus- tration (see 6 Aug), but had now pre- sumably seen it in proof or in an early issue of the published No. 73.
[3] Last two words underlined by CD. For Elliotson's kindness to Overs, see *To* Macready, 24 Aug.

### *To* W. C. MACREADY, 21 AUGUST 1841*

MS Morgan Library.

Devonshire Terrace.
Saturday Morning | August Twenty First 1841.

My Dear Macready.

Among the men I have an interest in, and help a little in their struggles through this workaday world, is one—Mr. Overs hight—a poor cabinet maker, who in the intervals of his work has taught himself for many years to think and feel like a man, and has written some[1] pretty ballads and good little prose sketches—of which latter commodity I am happy to say I have just got Cruikshank to take a sample for his Omnibus.

Now this cabinet maker (he is foreman to a manufacturer of medicine-chests, at some Thirty Shillings a week, wages) has a chronic affection of the pleura—but now discovered—which the doctors tell him will prevent his making cabinets any more, inasmuch as in doing that work he is obliged to *stand* for twelve hours a day at least—which they say won't do. I have sent him to Elliotson this morning, and no doubt he will confirm the opinion.

He is none of your maudlin gentry who think themselves neglected geniuses, but a straight forward, hard working, earnest man—above his station in nothing but having read and remembered a great many good books. It has occurred to me as just possible that you might at some time or other find you wanted such a person in some capacity about the Theatre —as a kind of upper messenger, or doorkeeper, or in any capacity where a diligent, respectable, sober fellow, of very creditable appearance and manners would be a desideratum. I can vouch for him most thoroughly in every respect. He has been in the habit of coming backwards and forwards to me for three years, and I know him to be a man of that kind that only this country and this time give birth to.

I think these few words will interest you in the poor fellow, and I am sure if you knew as much of him as I do, you would be greatly affected with his little history. Will you bear him in mind?

I meant to have spoken to you last night,[2] and in the coach had the words, once, upon my lips. But something arose to put it out of my head, and I forgot it.

My Dear Macready | Always Your faithful friend
CHARLES DICKENS

[1] Apparently "poetry" cancelled here.
[2] Macready was not acting on 20 Aug; but he and CD may have been at the Haymarket to see *The School for Scandal* that night.

L C D—N

## *To* JOHN OVERS, [22 AUGUST 1841]

MS Huntington Library. *Date:* clearly the day after Overs's visit to Elliotson and the call on CD suggested in *To* Overs, 20 Aug.

Devonshire Terrace | Sunday Morning | Half past 7.[1]

Dear Mr. Overs.

I was very much vexed to be obliged to go away without seeing you yesterday—but very glad to infer from the confused account of my servant (who for his good intentions and most imperfect execution might be the Devil's head pavior) that you had seen the doctor. I wish you would write and tell me what he said to you.

Thinking about you yesterday, and casting about for some light employment that would suit you, it occurred to me that Mr. Macready might be able to give you some employment, which would not tax your strength at all, at Drury Lane Theatre which—as you may have seen in the papers— he has taken. I wrote to him immediately telling him all about you, and I have very little doubt indeed—hardly any—from the answer he sent last night, that he will find a Post for you. In the hurry of starting for Broadstairs again, this morning, and the anguish of packing up, I cannot—for the life of me—lay my hand upon his note but you shall see it, for it will please you very much,—being of a scarce kind in these times.

I am obliged to come up to town next Saturday, to attend a meeting about a Monument to Sir David Wilkie.[2] Could you call upon me at the Parthenon Club, Regent Street, between 6 and 8 in the evening? Or would the morning suit you better? If so, I will make another appointment.

Write to Broadstairs.

In great haste | Always Faithfully Yours
CHARLES DICKENS

P.S. Keep up your spirits. There's more philosophy in "never *say*[3] die", than most people suppose.

## *To* THOMAS MITTON, 23 AUGUST 1841*

MS Berg Collection.

Broadstairs
Monday Morning August Twenty Third | 1841.

My Dear Mitton

After I left you on Saturday, I think an inspiration came upon me, which you will think highly of.

Being a little too early, I walked about Lincolns Inn, pondering all the Chapman and Hall matters in my mind, and reflecting on the proposed change from the weekly to monthly parts.[4] The impression it might have

---

[1] Address and date are written between the signature and postscript.

[2] See *To* Maclise, 28 Aug, *fn.*

[3] Underlined twice.

[4] For the novel he at first intended to begin on 31 Mar 42 (see p. 366, *fn*).

on the public mind,[1] the probable sale of the new work, the short pause, and so forth, I turned over again and again; and the more I thought of it, the more hazardous it seemed. I remembered that Scott failed in the sale of his very best works, and never recovered his old circulation (though he wrote fifty times better than at first) *because he never left off*.[2] I thought how I had spoilt the novel sale—in the cases of Bulwer, Marryatt,[3] and the best people—by my great success, and how my great success was, in a manner, spoiling itself, by being run to death and deluging the town with every description of trash and rot.[4] Then I thought if I could but have forseen[5] what would come to pass, and could but have made better bargains, now was the time—the very moment, with a view to my future fame and station— to *stop*—to write no more, not one word, for a whole year—and then to come out with a complete story in three volumes[6]—with no cuts or any expense but that of printing—and put the town in a blaze again.

When I had got into my head the enormous advantages of such a step, I came to this:—If my position is a strong one, and my reputation is as good as money, why not use it now, for this great object? I walked off to Forster, and said "Now will you in my presence say to Chapman and Hall for me after dinner to day (as I am not a very great demonstrator when my own affairs are at issue) what I am going to tell you"—"What is it?"

Then I told him. I see, I said, as in a clear bright glass that if I go to the monthly parts next March, I do so at a great hazard. Scott's life warns me that let me write never so well, if I keep on writing, without cessation, it is in the very nature of things that the sale will be unsteady, and the circulation will fall. The Clock shews us this, every week, for it started at 70,000, and is now 30,000—and this, notwithstanding that the Curiosity Shop made, without doubt, a greater impression than any of my other writings. I am doing what every other successful man has done. I am making myself too cheap. And although I still command a sale wholly unprecedented and unknown, even in Scott's case,[7] that sale is *shaky*, and trembles every day.

---

[1] In suggesting that CD's experiment with weekly parts had been a failure.

[2] An impression CD had presumably gained from Lockhart's *Life*, 1837–8. The truth seems rather that, after the steady rise from *Waverley*, 1814, to *Kenilworth*, 1821, Scott's sales fluctuated. *The Pirate*, 1822, sold less well, but after the success of *The Fortunes of Nigel*, 1822, the first printing of *Peveril of the Peak* (also 1822) was—like *Rob Roy's* in 1818—10,000. *Redgauntlet*, 1824, was received coldly, but *Tales of the Crusaders* (*The Talisman* and *The Betrothed*), 1825, was a great success. The novels published after the financial crash of 1825 did less well; but it was probably not those that CD classed as Scott's "best works". The fear of wearying his readers by overwriting had, in fact, been in Scott's own mind—but in relation to overwriting in a single vein (see his 1830 Introduction to *Ivanhoe*).

[3] Thus in MS.

[4] Another reference to the imitators of his monthly parts (see *To* Cattermole, 13 Jan 40, and *To* Longmans, 11 Jan 40, *fn*).

[5] Thus in MS.

[6] His original intention for *Barnaby* (see Agreements with Bentley, Vol. 1, pp. 654, 670, 674).

[7] Scott's highest first printing had been 12,000 for *The Monastery*, 1819. The whole first printing of 60,000 copies of *Master Humphrey* No. 1 was sold on the day of publication (see *To* Hall, ?7 Apr 40, *n*).

Propose this to Chapman and Hall. That the notice I have written[1] be cancelled directly[2]—that we contemplate no monthly parts at all—that we finish the Clock on the 27th. of November,[3] and advertize for that day twelve months a new book in three volumes.[4] And say to them this:—if Mr. Dickens is willing to let you have one half of the Copyright of that book, what can you afford, and what do you propose to give him for it, over and above Two Thousand Pounds which is to be paid to him in quarterly payments, for his subsistence through the year during which he retires from public notice?[5]

Little Hall with his pocketfull[6] of figures and estimates, gave, as soon as we were left alone after dinner, "Success to our new undertaking" where-upon Forster, who was a little piqued to do his best by something that had passed between us,[7] said that he was going to startle them by something I had mentioned to him half an hour before, but that he was sure it was *the*[8] thing, and certain all my friends would say so. He then stated (extremely well) what, in effect, I have just told you; throwing in a great many new considerations, and among others, the effect which a year's silence would have upon the sale of the back Nos. of the Clock, the sale of the Oliver—the Pickwick—and the Nickleby.

If you can imagine little Hall and big Chapman knocked down by a thunderbolt, you can form an imperfect idea of the minute's silence that ensued. Chapman was the first to break it; and he said in a very manly straight-forward way, that he *did* believe—looking forward for 20 years, and not for 2—that the effect of the year's silence would be tremendous. Then little Hall struck in, and said "Yes—he thought so too", but his doubt was, whether we should break it with three volumes or new monthly parts. To this, Forster and I rejoined,—the volumes certainly.[9] First, because it would be a great thing for me to try a new form. Secondly,

---

[1] His address "To the Readers of *Master Humphrey's Clock*", dated Aug 41. (Both the MS and a proof are in the Forster Collection, V & A.)

[2] On the return to him of the address, CD cancelled in proof the fifth para-graph, which announced that he would begin a new book in monthly parts, "under the old green cover", on 31 Mar 42; also, at the end of the para-graph, a series of metaphors illustrating the disadvantages of writing in weekly Nos ("I cannot help thinking that the effect of a flash of lightning would be materially impaired if it came in sparks", &c &c)—against which Forster had written "qy. | End this differently". Beyond this, he did nothing for the time being.

[3] It finished on 4 Dec.

[4] This plan was also altered, on CD's decision to go to America. For the

further stages by which the address to his readers reached its final form, see *To* Forster, 22 Sep, *fn*.

[5] About ten words cancelled here, apparently "and during which he is not to write one line". For the £150 a month which he was to receive for sub-sistence when not working, his pay per No. while working, and his share of the profits, see *To* Mitton, 30 Aug and *fns*.

[6] Thus in MS.

[7] Possibly Forster had been over-emphatic in decrying, on health-grounds, CD's previous intention to begin publication of the new novel as early as Mar 42 (the only hint of dis-agreement given in F, II, xii, 194).

[8] Underlined twice.

[9] But this decision was reversed at a meeting with Chapman & Hall on 28 Aug (see *To* Mitton, 30 Aug and *fns*).

because it was a cheap form. Thirdly because *after* we had done that, the question of any more publishing in numbers would be as open to us, as it was now. Then they both said that they had never desired to press Mr. Dickens—that they wished to consult Mr. Dickens's reputation[1] and[2]

## *To* JOHN FORSTER, [23 AUGUST 1841]

Extract in F, II, xii, 194. *Date:* Mon 23 Aug, the day after his return to Broadstairs, according to Forster.

*An enthusiastic letter about the share Forster had taken in* the development on Saturday afternoon; when I thought Chapman very manly and sensible, Hall morally and physically feeble though perfectly well intentioned, and both the statement and reception of the project quite triumphant. Didn't you think so too?

## *To* R. SHELTON MACKENZIE, 23 AUGUST 1841

Text from R. Shelton Mackenzie, *Life of CD*, Philadelphia, 1870, pp. 218-19.

Broadstairs, Kent, | Monday, Twenty-third August, 1841.
Dear Sir,

I am much obliged to you for your letter, and the scrap of paper enclosed in it. I was aware of the imposition soon after it was attempted, but had never seen the article.[3] I can bear, like a good Christian, the not having any more of it.

Let me thank you also for the newspaper I received from you. I found some lines in its columns which afforded me very great pleasure in the perusal.[4]

Faithfully yours,
Dr. Mackenzie.                    CHARLES DICKENS

[1] Clearly after CD's victory over the Deed (see ?3 Aug, *fn*), they would agree to virtually anything he proposed. Since he was their only major author until 1843 (when they started publishing Carlyle and Thackeray), his good will was of the utmost importance to them.

[2] Final page of letter missing.

[3] "What may have been written or printed on 'the scrap of paper' alluded to ... I do not recollect", says Mackenzie. It seems conceivable that it was some attempt by John Dickens to raise money: cf. his begging a CD letter off Talfourd and sending it to Mackenzie (*To* Talfourd, 22 Mar 41, *fn*), no doubt in the hope of being paid for it.

[4] Lines, according to Mackenzie, written in the Shrewsbury paper of which he was editor, on the recent death of his daughter; but no such lines have been found. Nor has anything of relevance to CD, except (in the *Salopian Journal* of 7 July 41) the following—of which the first few lines might have given him pleasure: "Master Humphrey's Clock | The interest of the story is much increased by the introduction of Lord George Gordon—who is drawn with great care. The sketch of his secretary is extremely good". But he would scarcely have liked the criticism that followed: "We suspect, from the manner in which 'Boz' takes the field against the 'No Popery' people of half a century since, that he intends giving a 'liberal' colouring to the circumstances of the times. If so, he may please a few—he must offend many. In a work of fiction we desire no *insinuation of politics.*"

## *To* W. C. MACREADY, 24 AUGUST 1841†

MS Morgan Library.

Broadstairs

Tuesday August The Twenty Fourth | 1841.

My Dear Macready

I *must* thank you—most heartily and cordially—for your kind note relative to poor Overs. I can't tell you how much it pleased me, or how glad I am to know that he thoroughly deserves such kindness.

What a good fellow Elliotson is! He kept him in his room a whole hour, and has gone into his case as if he were Prince Albert; laying down all manner of elaborate projects, and determining to leave his friend Wood[1] in town when he himself goes away, on purpose to attend to him. Then he writes me four sides of paper about the man, and says he can't go back to his old work for that requires muscular exertion, and muscular exertion he mustn't make—What are we to do with him? he says—Here's five pounds for the present—

I declare before God that I could almost bear the Tories[2] for five years, out of the pleasure I feel in knowing such things. And when I think that every dirty speck upon the fair face of the Almighty's creation, who writes in a filthy, bawdy[3] newspaper—every rotten-hearted pander who has been beaten, kicked, and rolled in the kennel, yet struts it in the Editorial We once a week—every vagabond that an honest man's gorge must rise at— every live emetic in that nauseous drug-shop, the Press—can have his fling at such men and call them knaves and fools and thieves,[4] I grow so vicious that with bearing hard upon my pen, I break the nib down, and with keeping my teeth set, make my jaws ache.[5]

[a]How Abraham must be smoothing his etherial robes, to make a warm place in his bosom for the Protestant champions of this time![6] What joy

---

[1] William Wood (?1816–92), Elliotson's clinical clerk and "chief mesmeriser" at University College Hospital; principal speaker in Elliotson's support at the students' meeting against his resignation on 5 Jan 39 (J. F. Clarke, *Autobiographical Recollections of the Medical Profession*, 1874, pp. 178–9). MD 1848; member of the Phrenological Society and Association; author of books on insanity.

[2] N, following MDGH, reads "Jones's".

[3] MDGH substitutes "beastly"; later editions and N follow.

[4] The *Lancet* over the past three years had taken every chance to attack and ridicule Elliotson's experiments in mesmerism. During 1841 most of the attacks were directed against French mesmerists; but on 7 Aug, after an editorial deriding the "fraud" of mesmerism in general, it reprinted its "exposure" of Elliotson's experiments on Elizabeth and Jane Okey of Aug 38 (see Vol. 1, p. 461*n*). Its attacks continued: on 11 Sep 41, for instance, it reprinted from *The Times* Elliotson's account of Elizabeth Okey's "power of foretelling death", with regret that *The Times*'s columns "should be polluted by such odious and disgusting trash".

[5] Punctuation and general style of this paragraph seem influenced by Macready's own.

[aa] Omitted in MDGH and later editions.

[6] CD no doubt had in mind the "Protestant champions" he had been depicting in *Barnaby*, and the lesson history taught—"that what we falsely call a religious cry, is easily raised by

in Holy Heaven when the angels look down on Sunday mornings, and read in bright blue letters that Mr. Westmacott[1] takes their part! Fancy the Standard, and the Morning Post—the Age—the Argus—and the Times—all on the side of Christ.[2] Celestial host![a]

I have put myself out of sorts for the day, and shall go and walk, unless the direction of this, sets me up again. On second thoughts, I think it will.

Always My Dear Macready | Your faithful friend
CHARLES DICKENS

## *To* JOHN OVERS, 24 AUGUST 1841*

MS Morgan Library.

Broadstairs
Tuesday August The Twenty Fourth | 1841.

My Dear Mr. Overs.

Doctor Elliotson has written me a full and particular account of your case. It arrived last night, and your letter reached my hands in due course this morning. He tells me, in effect, exactly what he told you—at greater length, perhaps, but without the least addition in the main point. He says emphatically, that he has cured several such cases. I *know* that, under God, there does not live a man in whose hands you would have so much reason to hope for a perfect restoration to health. If I were to tell you what I know of his skill, patience, and humanity, you would love and honor him as much as I do. If my own life, or my wife's, or that of either of my children were in peril tomorrow, I would trust it to him, implicitly.

He tells me in his letter that you cannot work; and he sends me, as a means towards keeping you from the present necessity of doing so, a five pound note. Tell me whether I shall send you the whole sum at once, or a part—and consider that I have put another five to it, and am your banker to the amount of Ten Pounds.

As I send you Mr. Macready's note, I should tell you what I said in

men who have no religion" (Preface to *Barnaby*, Nov 41). Now a Conference of over 600 dissenting ministers of all denominations, which had met at Manchester on 17 Aug to pray and preach for the repeal of the Corn Laws, had been scurrilously attacked in the pro-Corn Law Tory press, intent on mobilizing Established Church sentiment against them (see below).
[1] Proprietor and editor of the *Age* (see Vol. 1, p. 325n).
[2] On 15 and 22 Aug the *Age* had attacked the Dissenters as "Quakers" and "Jews" conspiring to enrich themselves; ridiculed their inability to agree on a common prayer, even the Lord's Prayer; and described them as enemies of the farmers, the poor and religion. The *Morning Post*, 20 Aug, called them "this conference of hypocrites and atheists"; and *The Times* (same date) added its ridicule. The *Argus*, which abused them under the heading "The Firebrands of Dissent" on 14 and 21 Aug, ended its editorial of 21 Aug: "And once more, thank God that we have the CHURCH OF ENGLAND." (On 7 Aug it had attacked CD himself for his sketch of "the country gentleman" in Ch. 47 of *Barnaby Rudge*—"which some irreverently call *Barnaby Rubbish*".)

writing to him. I told him, in a few simple words, what you had been by trade—what your weekly earnings were—and how I had come to know you—and I said that you were not one of the maudlin persons (of whom he and I know many) who consider themselves great geniuses neglected, but that you had always worked hard until you were taken ill, and had worked none the worse for having improved yourself by reading and writing in your few leisure hours. He is a most generous and high-minded man, having as great a sympathy with all struggling persons as anyone I know—and instantly sent back the note I inclose. His word is his oath, and you may rest assured he will not forget you.

You see that it is unnecessary to write to him. When I am in town, I see him almost every day; and when I am away, we are in very frequent correspondence. Leave the matter where it stands. He will not require any hint from either of us.

Always Faithfully Yours

Mr. J. A. Overs. CHARLES DICKENS

P.S. I ought to tell you (I don't think he desires this to be known) that Drury Lane will not open 'till Christmas. It is possible, however, that he might be enabled to employ you sooner. I don't know how that may be just now. As soon as I can find out, I will.

## *To* THOMAS MITTON, 26 AUGUST [1841]

MS Huntington Library. *Date:* 26 Aug was Thursday in 1841; Broadstairs address and proposed visit to Chapman and Hall support that year.

Broadstairs | Thursday August Twenty Sixth

My Dear Mitton.

I think it *possible* that I may have to see Chapman and Hall tomorrow evening. As I shall do well to hold myself disengaged, *in case*, I will alter our appointment, if you please, and come to you directly I arrive in town tomorrow,[1] which will be, I have no doubt, between 3 and 4. That will leave me the evening free.

In haste | Faithfully Yours always<br>CD.

## *To* LORD NUGENT, 26 AUGUST 1841*

MS Private.

Broadstairs, Kent<br>Thursday Evening | Twenty Sixth August 1841

My Dear Lord Nugent.

I write to you from the place where I am staying for the Autumn; for a most extraordinary and unheard-of purpose. I am an author—yet I want

---

[1] CD was in London 27–29 Aug.

to recommend a Publishing firm to your favorable notice, and to give them a high character!

You are one of the Committee of the Society for the Diffusion of Useful Knowledge.[1] I understand the Society are in want of a Publisher; and further that my publishers, Messrs. Chapman and Hall of the Strand, aspire to that office.[2] If you take any interest in the matter, I think my recommendation will have its weight with you when I tell you, after long dealings of very considerable magnitude with these gentlemen, that I respect them highly—that I have unbounded confidence in their honor, integrity, and first-rate business qualities—and that I *am certain* there is not a House in London that would better answer the Society's purpose.

Mrs. Dickens begs her compliments to Lady Nugent.[3] I take leave to add mine—and am, Dear Lord Nugent,

Faithfully Yours

The Lord Nugent.  CHARLES DICKENS

## *To* DANIEL MACLISE, [28 AUGUST 1841]*

MS Private. *Date:* Clearly refers to the Wilkie meeting on 28 Aug at which CD was in fact present (see *fn*), perhaps as a result of persuasion by Maclise.

In haste—Saturday Morning.

My Dear Mac

Occupations[4] too tremendous to admit of my going to the Wilkie Meeting[5]—Come here *as soon as it is over*—The carriage shall be ready at

---

[1] Founded by Lord Brougham in 1827. Its first Committee, almost half of them Whig MPs, included J. S. Mill, Lord Denman, Matthew Davenport Hill and eight Fellows of the Royal Society; Brougham was elected Chairman annually, and Lord John Russell Vice-Chairman. It suspended operations in 1846 owing to losses on its *Biographical Dictionary*. For accounts of the Society's cheap publications and the important part it played in the movement for popular education, see R. D. Altick, *The English Common Reader*, Chicago, 1957, pp. 269–73, and Chester W. New, *The Life of Lord Brougham to 1830*, Oxford, 1961, pp. 347–57.

[2] Charles Knight published for the Society 1829–46. But CD's recommendation—made also to Brougham on 2 Sep—seems to have been at least partially successful. In Oct 41 Chapman & Hall announced their appointment as agents for the sale of the

Society's monthly publications, and the Society's maps of 1841 and 1844 carry their imprint.

[3] Anne Lucy, daughter of Gen. the Hon. Vere Poulett. She married Lord Nugent in 1813.

[4] Presumably he was seeing Chapman and Hall that morning instead of the evening before (when he had merely held himself disengaged "in case").

[5] A meeting to discuss a monument to Wilkie, with Peel in the chair, held at the Thatched House Tavern, St James's Street. Macready describes it at some length, protesting at "the *servile*, crouching attitude" of the artists in allowing the lead to be taken by men of rank (the Duke of Sutherland, Lord John Russell, &c). As they left, CD asked Macready: "Did you ever hear such miserable commonplace—such a mere set of words without one idea?" (*Diaries*, II, 141, 142). Samuel Joseph was later selected to execute a statue (see *To* Hall, ?31 Mar, *fn*).

2; and I will wait for you—Forster will be at the Parthenon, of course, as
we agreed.

Faithfully Ever

CD.

## *To* WILLIAM SHOBERL, 29 AUGUST 1841

Extract in Sotheby's catalogue, July 1912; *MS* 1½ pp.; dated Broadstairs,
29 Aug 41.

My experience of Magazine editing, however, has been by no means a
pleasant one, and I have resolved not to connect myself, even in name, with
such duties any more,[1]

## *To* THOMAS MITTON, 30 AUGUST [1841]

MS Mr Alfred C. Berol. *Date:* The negotiations with Chapman & Hall and
death of Hook show year to have been 1841. *Address:* Thomas Mitton
Esquire | 23 Southampton Buildings | Chancery Lane | London.

Broadstairs | Monday Thirtieth August.

My Dear Mitton

I was up and down—here and there—torn to pieces—until dinner time
on Saturday, which was after you left town. The result was, that I made
them a proposition (to which I feel pretty sure they will accede) which I
am certain is the best I could make, and which I think you will look upon
in that light, also. It involves[2] the pause for a year—the breaking[2]
ground then, with a new work in monthly parts *instead* of a Novel[3] (which gives me,
of course, a much longer rest)—the payment of £150 a month all through
the year—the doing anything else, if I choose[4]—and secures such a share
of the profits to me,[5] as promises to enable me to repay the money advanced,
with great expedition. As soon as I have the figures and calculations

[1] Colburn had sent "people" to CD
to offer him the editorship of the *New
Monthly*, Hook having died 24 Aug (see
next). On CD's declining it, Shoberl
was dispatched (31 Aug) to make the
offer to Hood, who accepted it (at £300
*p.a.*)—his wife rejoicing at their "better
prospects" (see *Memorials of Thomas
Hood*, 1860, II, 120–3).

[2] Miswritten, but no real doubt of
CD's intention.

[3] Cf. *To* Mitton, 23 Aug, where CD
was envisaging (and Chapman & Hall
had agreed to) a three volume novel.

[4] This must have given CD a great
sense of freedom, after Bentley's

attempts to limit his activities. But
Forster saw it as the one drawback in
the new arrangement (F, II, xii, 194),
presumably fearing that, with so much
leisure and complete freedom, CD's
restless nature would drive him to em-
bark on some other project.

[5] Besides £200 for each monthly part,
he was to have three-fourths of the
profits until six months before completion of the book, when—after Chapman & Hall had paid him a fourth of
the value of all existing stock—he and
they were to divide the profits equally
(F, *ibid*).

(which I left with them, while they considered) I will send them to you, and you will then have the whole proceeding at your fingers' ends.[1]

In haste | Always Faithfully Yours
CHARLES DICKENS

Colburn sent people to me on Saturday night, and *before 7 on Sunday Morning* to negociate for my taking the New Monthly, now Hook is dead.[2] I declined, of course.

## *To* THOMAS MITTON, 1 SEPTEMBER 1841

MS Chas. J. Sawyer Ltd.

Broadstairs | First September 1841.

My Dear Mitton

I am sorry to say that *this* week, we are full—and I am afraid you would not get a comfortable bed out of the house, by reason that we have two already—one for Fred, and one for Fanny's servant. She and Burnett are still here; and Maclise came down yesterday.

Now, I am coming up next Tuesday, and intend to return on Wednesday. Why can't you come back with me on that day?[3] We shall then have plenty of room, and surely you are not so very strong and special in your engagements, but that you can spare a few days next week, as well as this.

Write and say *Yes*.[4]

Chapman and Hall have agreed to my terms; and for a year I am a free man. They are, I think, as fair as *could* be expected, and very promising indeed. More of this, when I come to town.

Faithfully Yours always
Thomas Mitton Esquire                                    CHARLES DICKENS

Write me by return.

## *To* LORD BROUGHAM,[5] 2 SEPTEMBER 1841*

MS Brotherton Library, Leeds.

Broadstairs, Kent. | Second September 1841.

My Lord.

I should apologize with becoming humility for the extraordinary liberty I take in writing to you; but that I hope the uncommon purpose of my

[1] See *To* Mitton, 3 Sep and *fn*.
[2] Hook had been editor of the *New Monthly* since 1836. For the plight of his family, see *To* Irving, 28 Sep and *fn*.
[3] An additional reason for postponing Mitton's visit may well have been that it was Forster who was to draw up the Agreement signed the following Tues-

day (*To* Mitton, 3 Sep and *fn*), and to see Mitton in the meantime would be awkward.
[4] Underlined twice.
[5] Henry Peter, Baron Brougham and Vaux (1778–1868; *DNB*), Lord Chancellor 1830–4. The impact he had made on the country by Oct 39 was shown in

communication may in itself be some excuse. I am an author; and I wish to recommend a publishing firm to your favorable consideration.

I learn that the Society for the Diffusion of Useful Knowledge are in want of a Publisher, and that my publishers, Messrs. Chapman and Hall of the Strand, aspire to that distinction.[1] I do assure you, My Lord, that there are not in London two persons so well calculated by their high respectability, their perfect integrity, and thorough knowledge of their business, for such a situation. I bear testimony to their fitness for it, after a connexion of some years and of great extent; and I do so, most earnestly, and with the strongest possible impression of their being the very people the Society need.

If I were less convinced of this, My Lord, I would not venture to trouble you. But as I know how truly you are interested in the cause of Education from which your name will always be inseparable; and how important even the humblest means are, in furthering its ends; I take the liberty of addressing this recommendation to you, and even of hoping that you will not be displeased by my intrusion.

I beg you to ascribe it, in any case, to my interest in all that concerns an Association which has such noble ends in view, and has done so much—and to the sincere respect and esteem with which I am

My Lord | Your faithful Servant.

CHARLES DICKENS

The Right Honorable | The Lord Brougham.

---

obituaries, diary-entries, and letters following reports of his death in a carriage accident—and the subsequent discovery that a hoax had been perpetrated (by himself—though this he strongly denied). The main editorial of the *Morning Post*, 22 Oct ended: "The most wonderful genius that belonged to public life is no more, and we, as belonging to the public, are grief-stricken mourners over his untimely grave"; Crabb Robinson recorded that he had "never remarked a more general sentiment of terror. Such power extinguished at once!" (*Diary, Reminiscences, and Correspondence*, ed. T. Sadler, III, 181); while Macready, believing him dead, summed him up as "a man who betrayed and deserted every great cause" (*Diaries*, II, 28); and Sydney Smith, on hearing of the hoax, wrote to Lady Grey: "Can anything be more silly? He sinks lower every Week" (*Letters of Sydney Smith*, ed. Nowell C. Smith, 1953, II, 694). Impressive as Brougham had been—as a prolific contributor to the *Edinburgh* from 1802, over an enormous range of subjects; as a supporter in Parliament of the abolition of slavery, Catholic emancipation, and popular education; as defender of Queen Caroline, thereby winning immense popularity; and as a Chancellor who brought in important legal reforms —yet, by 1834, not even his own party trusted him: vain, vindictive and unbalanced, capable of great folly and extreme disingenuousness, he never held office again. In Dec 37 Greville bemoaned "the depth of his fall, from the loftiest summit of influence, power, and fame to the lowest abyss of political degradation", adding: "one cannot help feeling regret and compassion at the sight of such a noble wreck and of so much glory obscured" (*The Greville Memoirs*, Second Part, I, 34). He was one of Peacock's chief butts in *Crotchet Castle* and *Gryll Grange*.

[1] See *To* Nugent, 26 Aug, *fn*.

### *To* ALFRED DICKENS, [3 SEPTEMBER 1841]

Mention in next two letters.

### *To* HENRY AUSTIN, 3 SEPTEMBER 1841*

MS Morgan Library.

Broadstairs. | Friday Third September 1841.

My Dear Henry.

We are coming to town on Tuesday, and return on Wednesday morning. Hadn't you and Letitia better come back with us? If so, let us meet on board the boat. All you have to do, is to go down to London Bridge Wharf, and go on board the *Ramsgate*[1] boat. You can make no mistake concerning it, as there is but one. She starts at 9, but the better plan is to be on board by a quarter before. I believe Mitton the Brilliant, returns with us also. I shall conclude that this is a bargain, unless I hear from you to[2]

P.S. The matter of Alfred, is a difficult one.[3] I have written, and told him exactly how the matter stands; and said that if he likes to renew his application, I don't object. But I have laid great stress on his saying nothing about it, and not leaving his present occupation for so much as a day.

### *To* THOMAS MITTON, 3 SEPTEMBER 1841

MS Huntington Library.

Broadstairs | Third September 1841.

My Dear Mitton.

Either I made a mistake in my last, or you have read it wrong. I don't [come][4] to town 'till Tuesday—and return [next mo]rning[5]—Wednesday.

I made a stipulation—to prevent [any][6] interference from Rufus;[7] which I expressly prohibited—that our agreement should be copied, in its phraseology and provisions, by Forster, from your Clock one.[8] As I shall have to look it over carefully, I shall be occupied, I think, every minute of the Tuesday afternoon, and until pretty late in the evening.[9] Will you

[1] Underlined twice.

[2] Letter was written on a sheet folded to make 4 pages, and must have ended on p. 3 or 4; but only the first page, with the postscript on the back of it, has survived.

[3] See *To* the Directors of the New Zealand Co., 4 Mar 41, *fns*.

[4] A triangular tear at vertical fold of the MS has removed several words or parts of words. Here a word of about 4 letters is lost.

[5] About 7 letters missing.

[6] Short word (2–3 letters) missing.

[7] No doubt William Chapman, the supposed villain of the dispute about the Deed, the "bad" brother of "Mr. Chapman of the Strand" (*To* Chapman & Hall, ?3 Aug).

[8] N mistakenly reads "from your draft only".

[9] On the evening of Tues 7 Sep the Agreement with Chapman & Hall (entirely in Forster's hand) was signed in Forster's chambers (F, II, xii, 194). See Appx, pp. 478–81.

engage to meet us on board the *Ramsgate*[1] boat at London Bridge Wharf on Wednesday morning? I believe the Austins are going back with us, too; —when I say "us", I mean Kate and myself.

I had a letter from Henry this morning saying that Beadnell[2] had called to tell him that the New Zealand people[3] want more assistants, and that Alfred might apply [to him].[4] I have written Alfred that he [?may do][5] so, if he likes; but have cautioned [hi]m[6] against coming to town for the purpose.

Faithfully Yours always

Thomas Mitton Esquire                                   CHARLES DICKENS

## *To* LORD BROUGHAM, 5 SEPTEMBER 1841*

MS Brotherton Library, Leeds.

Broadstairs | Fifth September 1841.

Mr. Charles Dickens presents his compliments to Lord Brougham, and is exceedingly obliged to him for his very kind letter and for the gratifying terms in which it is couched. Mr. Dickens need scarcely add, that immediately on his return to town (which will be early next month) he will gladly do himself the pleasure of calling on Lord Brougham; and that he feels much honored by Lord Brougham's request.

## *To* JOHN FORSTER, [9 SEPTEMBER 1841]

Extract in F, II, xii, 194n. *Date:* 9 Sep according to Forster. *From* Broadstairs.

M.[7] was quite aghast last night at the brilliancy of the C. & H. arrangement:[8] which is worth noting[9] perhaps.

---

[1] Underlined twice.
[2] George Beadnell (1773–1862): see Vol. I, p. 2.
[3] See 4 Mar 41.
[4] About 6 letters missing: what may be top of "h", dot of "i" and end of "m" are visible.
[5] 6 or 7 letters missing.

[6] About 2 letters missing; dot of "i" visible.
[7] Mitton, who had come to Broadstairs with CD the day before.
[8] The terms of the Agreement signed on 7 Sep (see *To* Mitton, 30 Aug, *fn*).
[9] Thus in F, 1872–4; misprinted "nothing" in F, II, xii, 194n.

## *To* THE SWEDENBORG SOCIETY,[1] 9 SEPTEMBER 1841*

MS The Swedenborg Society.

Broadstairs, Kent. | September The Ninth 1841.

Mr. Charles Dickens presents his Compliments to the Society for printing and publishing the writings of Emanuel Swedenborg; and begs to thank them cordially for their obliging communication, and for the copy of the work on Heaven and Hell,[2] accompanying it. He begs to assure the Society that he will not "reject the book unexamined", (he is at present quite unacquainted with it, save from their description)—and that it shall have his most careful and attentive consideration.

## *To* JOHN PAUL,[3] 9 SEPTEMBER 1841

Extract in N, I, 349, from catalogue source; *MS* 2 pp.; dated Broadstairs, 9 Sep 41.

I do not know at what precise time I shall be in Glasgow. . . . I received a letter, begging to know which would be the most convenient time for me to visit the city.[4]

## *To* JOHN FORSTER, [11 SEPTEMBER 1841]

Extract in F, II, ix, 169. *Date:* 11 Sep according to Forster. *From* Broadstairs.

I have just burnt into Newgate,[5] and am going in the next number to tear the prisoners out by the hair of their heads. The number which gets into the jail[6] you'll have in proof by Tuesday.

---

[1] The Society, founded in London 1810, published Swedenborg's works in 49 vols, 1834–60.

[2] Swedenborg's *De Coelo . . . et de Inferno*, 1758, translated as *A Treatise concerning Heaven and Hell*, by W. Cookworthy, 1778. Possibly CD had been sent the most recent translation, published by Newbery, 1839. He later possessed Swedenborg's *Life and Writings*, 2 vols, 1867 (*Catalogue of the Library of CD*, ed. J. H. Stonehouse, p. 106).

[3] Probably one of several newspaper reporters named Paul. Possibly the Paul who was a colleague of CD's on the *Mirror of Parliament* in the 1830s. Robert Paul, on the *Glasgow Herald* in 1882, may have been a relative.

[4] Cf. *To* Forster, 12 July and *fn.*

[5] I.e. he had finished No. 78 (Chs 63 and 64). This was only a fortnight ahead of publication (25 Sep), as against his three and a half weeks ahead for No. 75 (see *To* Forster, 11 Aug). But his two week-end visits to London had delayed him.

[6] Presumably No. 77 (Chs 61 and 62, published 18 Sep), in which Rudge is committed to Newgate and there meets Barnaby.

## *To* GEORGE CATTERMOLE, 12 SEPTEMBER 1841

MS Doheny Memorial Library, Camarillo, California.

Broadstairs | Sunday Twelfth September 1841.

My Dear George.

Here is a business letter, written in a scramble just before post time. Whereby, I dispose of loves to Cousin, in a line.

Firstly. Will you design upon a block of wood, Lord George Gordon, alone and very solitary, in his prison in the tower?—The chamber as ancient as you please, and after your own fancy.[1] *The time evening. The season, Summer.*

Secondly. Will you ditto upon a ditto, a sword duel between Mr. Haredale and Mr. Chester, in a grove of trees? No one else by. Mr. Haredale has just pinked his adversary who has fallen, dying, on the grass. He (that is, Chester) tries to staunch the wound in his breast, with his handkerchief—has his snuffbox on the earth beside him—and looks at Mr. Haredale (who stands with his sword in his hand, looking down on him) with most supercilious hatred—but polite to the last. Mr. Haredale is more sorry, than triumphant.[2] Thirdly. Will you conceive and execute after your own fashion, a frontispiece for Barnaby.[3]

Fourthly. Will you devise a subject representing Master Humphrey's clock as stopped—his chair by the fireside empty—his crutch against the wall—his slippers on the cold hearth—his hat upon the chair back—the MSS of Barnaby and the Curiosity Shop, heaped upon the table—and the flowers you introduced in the first subject of all, withered and dead?[4] *Master Humphrey being supposed to be no more.*

I have a fifthly, sixthly, seventhly, and eighthly—for I sorely want you,

---

[1] Cattermole's "Lord George in his cell" appeared in No. 83 (Ch. 73), published 30 Oct.

*aa* Squeezed in as an afterthought.

[2] In Cattermole's "Death of Sir John" (Ch. 81), which appeared in the final No. of *Barnaby*, published 27 Nov, Mr Haredale looks at his sword while he wipes it—not down at Chester as CD had instructed. Perhaps for this reason, in CD's text their eyes meet and are "on each other" at the more dramatic moment when Haredale has "plunged his sword through his opponent's body to the hilt" and is drawing it out again.

[3] Done by Browne—because, according to Kitton (*CD and his Illustrators*, p. 132), Cattermole was ill.

[4] This illustration ("Master Humphrey's room deserted", tailpiece to the last chapter of the book) is attributed by Hatton (see 13 Jan 40, *fn*) to Browne. But the style—for instance, the chairlegs, and the fireplace (with date 1581 in the shield at its apex—an antiquarian touch)—seems undoubtedly Cattermole's. CD's instructions are mostly followed, though the crutch and slippers are differently placed and the MS of only *Barnaby* is distinguishable on the table—with *Old Curiosity Shop* perhaps suggested by one of the carvings on the clock having become a Nell-like figure looking down on the room. For no obvious reason—except perhaps fun—the picture over the fireplace of Christ blessing the children has changed since No. 3 to a recumbent full-breasted nude.

*bb* Squeezed in as an afterthought.

as I approach the close of the Tale—but I won't frighten you, so will take breath.

Always My Dear Cattermole
Heartily Yours

George Cattermole Esquire.                    CHARLES DICKENS

P.S.  I have been waiting until I got to subjects of this nature; thinking you would like them best.[1]

## *To* FREDERICK DICKENS, 12 SEPTEMBER 1841

MS University of Texas. *Address:* Frederick Dickens Esquire | Commissariat | Treasury | Whitehall.

Broadstairs | Sunday September Twelfth 1841.

My Dear Fred.

The wording of the Minute[2] is certainly discouraging.  If I saw any way of helping you by coming up to town, I would do so, immediately.  But I cannot possibly apply to the Tories for *anything*.[3]  I dare say they would be glad enough if I would; but I cannot with any regard to honor, consistency or Truth, ask any favor of people whom, politically, I despise and abhor.  It would tie my hands, seal my lips, rob my pen of its honesty, and bind me neck and heels in most discreditable fetters.

*Is* Archer[4] in town?  If so, have you spoken to him?  If not, when is he coming?  You should speak to him, certainly.  I have told you before, that I am very much afraid you have not treated him with that show of respect, which he has a right to claim.  Why in the name of God should he have a personal dislike to you, but for some such reason as this?

If you think—and I see no objection to your asking Mr. Archer the question, that without doing anything improper, you might memorialize the Lords of the Treasury, I will draw a memorial for you.[5]  If you have reason to think this would be unofficial and ill-advised, I know of nothing better than waiting and hoping.

I should be as sorry as you, if you were to lose this step.  Let me hear from you by Return.

Affectionately Always
CD.

[1] Of the 11 illustrations preceding "Lord George in his cell", Browne had done ten.

[2] Concerning his application for promotion at the Treasury.

[3] Fred had obtained his junior clerkship at the Treasury through a Whig—E. J. Stanley, Patronage Secretary to the Treasury in Melbourne's Ministry (*To* Mitton, ?26 Mar 39; I, 533).

[4] Thomas Archer (?1782–1855), principal clerk in the Foreign Branch of the Commissary-in-Chief's office and in the Commissariat Dept of the Treasury; afterwards principal of the Dept.  His salary as principal clerk was increased from £900 to £1000 *p.a.* in 1844 in recognition of his long and laborious services.

[5] See 19 Sep.

## *To* JOHN FORSTER, [13 SEPTEMBER 1841]

Extract in F, II, xii, 194. *Date:* 13 Sep according to Forster. *From* Broadstairs.

There's no news since my last. We are going to dine with Rogers[1] to-day and with Lady Essex,[2] who is also here. Rogers is much pleased with Lord Ashley,[3] who was offered by Peel a post in the government, but resolutely refused to take office unless Peel pledged himself to factory improvement.[4] Peel "hadn't made up his mind"; and Lord Ashley was deaf to all other inducements, though they must have been very tempting.[5] Much do I honour him for it.[6] I am in an exquisitely lazy state, bathing, walking, reading, lying in the sun, doing everything but working. This frame of mind is superinduced by the prospect of rest, and the promising arrangements which I owe to you. I am still haunted by visions of America,[7] night and day. To miss this opportunity would be a sad thing.

[1] Who frequently stayed at Broadstairs in the summer. This year he left on 7 Oct (Clayden, *Rogers and his Contemporaries*, II, 202).

[2] Catherine Stephens, Countess of Essex (1794–1882; *DNB*), opera singer and actress; aunt of the Miss Smiths who sang in *The Village Coquettes*. Her soprano voice was highly praised by Hazlitt, Leigh Hunt and Talfourd, but George IV was not impressed by it. Retired in 1835, becoming in 1838 the second wife of the octogenarian 5th Earl of Essex, who died the following year. A story, "Narrative of an Expedition down the Thames, from the Euston Hotel, London, to the Albion Hotel, Broadstairs", in *Bentley's Miscellany*, XII (1842), 21–30, associates Rogers, CD, Lady Essex and Broadstairs. Travelling by boat to Ramsgate with her husband, Mrs Brown (a plebeian) scrapes acquaintance with a woman she believes to be the "Dowager Lady Essex" (but is in fact her lady's maid) and is told by her that Broadstairs is "the only place in these parts fit for *decent* people to be seen at". The Browns therefore go on to Broadstairs by omnibus and are received at the Albion "by Mr. Ballard himself, the civil, attentive, obliging young landlord". Mrs Brown is disappointed to find the hotel not the "fine large" place she expected: Ballard even waits at table himself. But when she discovers that Rogers is in the next room; that the voices she hears through the wall are those of Rogers and Dickens; that a man she had spoken to in the omnibus was Dickens; and, later, that a woman she has stared at in the hall is "the real Dowager Lady Essex", come to the hotel to drink tea with Rogers, she is content.

[3] Ashley had been staying at Broadstairs with his family during part of July and Aug, and had possibly been in touch with Rogers there.

[4] For Ashley's interesting CD in the subject, see *To* Southwood Smith, 15 Dec 40 and *fns*.

[5] On 30 Aug Peel had offered him the post of Treasurer to the Royal Household, but Ashley indignantly saw it as an attempt to put him "out of the way into the Palace" (E. Hodder, *The Life and Work of the Seventh Earl of Shaftesbury*, 1886, I, 351), and on 2 Sep refused it. As he had a large family and was not well off, it was a sacrifice.

[6] Commendation of his step came in from all quarters, and he wrote: "My pen would blush were I to detail the lofty, glowing, grateful praises I have received". On 17 Sep he accepted Peel's offer of a post on the Ecclesiastical Commission, on the grounds that it brought "no salary" and therefore "no official restraint" (*op. cit.*, I, 358 and 361).

[7] First thought of in July 39 when he was envisaging *Master Humphrey* as a serial publication to which others besides himself would contribute (see Vol. I, p. 564). The idea had been revived,

Kate cries dismally if I mention the subject. But, God willing, I think it *must* be managed somehow!

### *To* J. H. KUENZEL,[1] 13 SEPTEMBER 1841

MS Milwaukee Public Library.

Broadstairs, Kent. | Monday Thirteenth September 1841.
My Dear Sir.

I should have answered your letter immediately after its date; but I generally come to this part of England to pass the Autumn, and did not receive it until yesterday.

Accept my best thanks, I beg you, for your welcome letter; and assure the gentleman who so kindly and flatteringly remembers me in the present I received, at the same time through your hands, that I am warmly obliged to him, and feel honored by his approval.

In regard to the Britannia,[2] what can I say? That my best wishes are yours, that my most cordial sympathy and interest are with you? You know it already.

Believe me, my dear Sir—and I say it most unaffectedly—that next to the favor and good opinion of my own countrymen, I value, above all price, the esteem of the German people. I honor and admire them past all expression. I know them to be, in their great mental endowments and cultivation, the chosen people of the Earth; and I never was more proud or more happy than when I first began to know that my writings found favor in their eyes.

I can be indifferent to nothing which connects English Literature with Germany. The object of your new paper is my object, and that of every Englishman who has an interest or delight in the progress of human thought. God prosper it, and you! I wish to Heaven I could speak German, though never so badly. If I could, I would be among you in six months.

My Dear Sir | Faithfully Yours always
CHARLES DICKENS[3]

according to Forster (F, III, i, 196), by Irving's letter of 25 May 41 (see 21 Apr, *fn*).

[1] Dr Johann Heinrich Kuenzel (1810–1873: see Vol. I, p. 411*n*.

[2] *Britannia—eine Wochenschrift für englische Literatur und englische Gesamtleben*, a weekly periodical dealing with English life and literature which Kuenzel, in 1841, was planning to publish in Germany. Only one specimen-number was printed.

[3] This letter was first published, in a German translation, in the *Magazin für die Literatur des Auslandes*, No. 8, 19 Jan 1842; another German translation appeared in the *Tägliche Rundschau*, 26 Feb 1915. It appeared in English (with some inaccuracies) in Walther Fischer, "Des Darmstädter Schriftstellers Johann Heinrich Kuenzel", *Giessener Beiträge zur deutschen Philologie*, LXVII (1939), 26.

## *To* JOHN SCOTT, 13 SEPTEMBER 1841

Photograph New York Public Library. *Address* (wrapper, MS Auckland
Public Library): Carriage Paid | John Scott Esquire | 120 Camden Road
Villas | Camden New Town | London. | By Coach | Monday Sept. 13 | 1841.

Private
                                Broadstairs. | Monday Thirteenth September | 1841.

My Dear Sir.

I have been much struck by some passages in the latter portion of the
Tragedy,[1] which are very good indeed, and eminently dramatic.

But it is very unequal; and I fear would never, on the stage, get through
the first two acts. Besides that the verse halts woefully, and is often made
up of expressions so curiously inverted that it is difficult on first reading
them to understand their meaning, it has many most serious objections.
The author dead, they strike at the root of the whole composition, I fear.
If he were alive, I do think he could amend them, and make the play one
of great merit and promise.

I fear the characters of the two brothers, which afford a fine opportunity
for contrast, are not sufficiently played off: the one against the other.
Fadilla, appearing in that one love scene and never coming on the scene
again, would astonish an audience, unfavorably. Macrinus and Martialis
conducting their share of the plot in constant conversations with each
other, would—place yourself in imagination, in the pit, and you will feel
it—become insufferably tedious after their first entrance. And I very much
mistrust the mention of that African, who is exceedingly well introduced
at first, and whom one naturally expects to be of greater importance.
Further, I doubt whether Macrinus says or does anything good enough to
qualify him for killing the hero of the piece; and I doubt whether the hero
could ever raise himself in the estimation of the people, after his scene with
Fadilla. The mother, on the other hand, is a tragic conception; and in the
latter part of the play, would have a great effect.

I do not feel justified, under these circumstances, in exposing Mr.
Macready to the pain and vexation which I know he would feel, if he felt it
necessary to decline a play which I recommended to him. But I still think
he ought to see the Tragedy; for while I know that he has many better
plays upon his desk at this moment, I know equally well that he has
many which will bear no comparison with it.

If I may suggest to you the course you would do best to pursue, I would
advise you to send it to his house (No 5 Clarence Terrace, Regents Park)
with a short note to the effect that the author is no more; and that you, who
are doing your best for his widow and family, beg him to peruse it.[2] I

---

[1] According to a MS note on the letter, "Caracalla & Geta" by William Lemaitre (1802–39), a former colleague of CD's on the *Morning Chronicle* (see Vol. I, p. 122*n*).

[2] The play is not mentioned in Macready's *Diaries*.

think I would add a special allusion to its rising greatly in the last three acts, *in case* he should feel disposed to stop at the end of the second.

As I am not coming to town very soon, and have no one with me who is bound for London, I send you the MS by coach. Will you acknowledge, in one line, its safe receipt?

My Dear Sir | Faithfully Yours
John Scott Esquire. CHARLES DICKENS

## *To* WILLIAM HALL, 14 SEPTEMBER 1841†

MS Berg Collection.

Broadstairs. | Tuesday Fourteenth Septr. 1841.

My Dear Sir.

[1].—Gate of Newgate in 78; not in 79. I don't want Barnaby in the subject,[2] but feared he might be there.

I plainly see that it's all up with the mechanical genius.[3]—Don't trust him with anything; keep an eye on the till; restrain him from making any entries in the books; and un-confuse Mr. Cattermole whom I clearly perceive he will distract with wrong instructions.

*I am hideously lazy—always bathing, lying in the sun, or walking about. I write a No. when the time comes, and dream about it beforehand on cliffs and sands—but as to getting in advance—! where's the use, too, as we so soon leave off!—*

It would be a good thing, wouldn't it, if I ran over to America about the end of February, and came back, after four or five months, with a One Volume book—such as a ten and sixpenny touch? *I can't persuade Mrs. Dickens to go, and leave the children at home; or to let me go alone. I wish you'd take an opportunity one of these days, of asking all about the Fares—what a single fare is—what a double fare—what a cabin with child-stowage. I can depend on you, and am afraid to make any enquiries myself, lest it should get blabbed about, before I had quite resolved.*

Washington Irving writes me that if I went, it would be such a triumph from one end of the States to the other, as was never known in any Nation.[4] *Don't you conceive that it would be, on every account, an excellent employment of a part of the interval? I should like to hear.*

When you g[e]t[5] the riot-block,[6] will you sen[d][7] me a proof of it?

Faithfully Yours always
William Hall Esquire CHARLES DICKENS

[1] "Quite right" cancelled here, presumably by CD, but the punctuation after the words remains.

[2] The gate of Newgate is the background to "Mr Varden and the mob", by Browne (*Barnaby*, Ch. 64, No. 78, published 25 Sep). Barnaby was in Newgate at the time, but CD does not mention him during the burning of the prison or freeing of the prisoners (in Ch. 62 he is in the prison yard with his father; in Ch. 68 they reappear in Smithfield, free). But there is a reminder of him within the initial letter of Ch. 65: see next.

[3] Edward Chapman, no doubt: see next and *fn.*

*aa, bb, cc* Not previously published.

[4] Letter not traced.

[5] MS reads "got".

## *To* [EDWARD CHAPMAN], 16 SEPTEMBER 1841

MS Berg Collection. *Address:* clearly written not to Hall but to Chapman who was shortly to be married (see *fn*).

Broadstairs. | Thursday Sixteenth September 1841.

My Dear Sir.

Know for your utter confusion, and to your lasting shame and ignominy, that the initial letter *has been*[1] purwided—that it was furnished to the artist at the same time as the subject[2]—and that it is a

D[3]

—which stands for Double—Demnible—Doubtful—Dangerous—Doleful—Disastrous—Dreadful—Deuced—Dark—Divorce—and Drop —all applicable to the Precipice on which you stand.[4]

Farewell! If you did but know—and would pause, even at this late period—better an action for breach than—but we buy experience. Excuse my agitation. I scarcely know what I write.—To see a fellow creature—and one who has so long withstood[5]—still if—Will *nothing* warn you—

[a]In extreme excitement<br>C D<br>My hand fails me

P.S.                                   Pause.                                   Over

Put it off<br>P.P.S.<br>Emigrate<br>P.P.P.S —<br>And leave me<br>the business ——<br>I mean the Strand<br>one.[a]

## *To* HENRY ROBERTSON,[6] 17 SEPTEMBER 1841*

MS Rosenbach Foundation.

Broadstairs, Kent.
Saturday Seventeenth September | 1841.

My Dear Sir.

As I am staying here for the Autumn, I have only just received your

---

[6] Presumably Browne's "The rioters at Moorfields" (*Barnaby*, Ch. 66, No. 79, published 2 Oct).

[7] MS reads "sent".

[1] Each word underlined three times.

[2] "The Hangman", Browne's headpiece to *Barnaby*, Ch. 65 (No. 79).

[3] An enormous "D", the height of three lines of writing. Within Browne's "D"—the initial letter of Ch. 65—Barnaby and his father await liberation.

[4] On 22 Sep Chapman married Mary Whiting, of Hitchin, Herts. Her strict Quaker family disapproved of her marrying a non-Quaker; she was disowned by the Society; and the wedding took place in Leeds, the home of one of her brothers (see Arthur Waugh, *A Hundred Years of Publishing*, 1930, pp. 7–9). The marriage seems to have been a very happy one.

[5] Chapman was 37.

[aa] From here to the end is written as in a hand trembling with emotion.

circular note, acquainting me that my name (and that of Mrs. Dickens) is continued on the Free List of Covent Garden Theatre.

May I beg you to present my compliments and thanks to Mr.[1] and Mrs. Mathews?[2] I have no doubt they intend to pay me a compliment and do me an act of courtesy; although upon the first—and I need scarcely add, the only—occasion of my seeking to use this Privilege last season, I was refused admittance at the door.

Faithfully Yours

Henry Robertson Esquire.                          CHARLES DICKENS

## *To* JOHN FORSTER, [18 SEPTEMBER 1841]

Extract in F, II, ix, 169. *Date:* "a week later" than letter of 11 Sep according to Forster. *From* Broadstairs.

I have let all the prisoners out of Newgate, burnt down Lord Mansfield's,[3] and played the very devil.[4] Another number will finish the fires, and help us on towards the end. I feel quite smoky when I am at work. I want elbow-room terribly.

## *To* FREDERICK DICKENS, 19 SEPTEMBER 1841

Text from N, I, 353.

Broadstairs | Sunday Nineteenth September 1841

My dear Fred,

As a matter of composition, or in respect of brevity or plainness, you

---

[6] Henry Robertson was on the business staff of Covent Garden, in charge of its finances. For Macready's dealings with him during his contract there 1837–9 and his final clash with him as representative of the proprietors, see *Diaries*, Vol. I.

[1] Charles James Mathews (1803–78; *DNB*), actor and dramatist, son of Charles Mathews (see *To* Bartley, ?Mar 32, *fn*). Originally an architect—and as such spent a year (1823–4) in Italy with the Blessingtons and D'Orsay, ostensibly so that he might design under Lord Blessington's own eye a new house for him (never in fact built) in Ireland. But on the death of his father (1835) followed him briefly as manager of the Adelphi with Yates; then made his professional début as an actor at the Olympic, under Madame Vestris (see below) whom he married 1838. With her managed Covent Garden 1839–42, when he went bankrupt. Both were engaged by Macready for Drury Lane Oct 42, but after an immediate quarrel transferred to the Haymarket. His *Life* was edited, 1879, by the younger Charles Dickens.

[2] Lucia Elizabeth Mathews (1797–1856; *DNB*), generally known as Madame Vestris; a singing actress with a great reputation. As manager of the Olympic 1831–9 transformed the theatre and had a great success with burlesque extravaganzas beautifully dressed and mounted, Planché assisting.

[3] William Murray, first Earl of Mansfield (1705–93; *DNB*), judge. His support of the Roman Catholic Relief Bill led to the total destruction of his house and possessions by the Gordon rioters, 7 June 1780.

[4] I.e. he had finished No. 79 (Chs 65 and 66), published 2 Oct.

have not improved my draft[1] by altering it. I shall be very anxious to hear your further news.

I knew the German Doctor[2] had left town, but I thought he might have left his address also.

Will you take the enclosed[3] (but don't delay) to Mr Schloss,[4] bookseller, Dover Street—the publisher of the [Tiny][5] Almanac and Quizzing Glass.[6] If he can forward it, ask him to do so. If not, ask him to put the address upon it—and then put it in the post for me, will you? You must pay the postage; or the letter, being foreign, won't go.

Faithfully yours always<br>[CHARLES DICKENS]

Will you send me the amount of the inclosed cheque by return?

## *To* JOHN FORSTER, [19 SEPTEMBER 1841]

Extracts and summaries in F, III, i, 196–7. *Date:* 19 Sep according to Forster. *From* Broadstairs.

*A letter about many unimportant things; then, near the end, announcing:*

Now to astonish you. After balancing, considering, and weighing the matter in every point of view, *[a]*I HAVE MADE UP MY MIND (WITH GOD'S LEAVE) TO GO TO AMERICA—AND TO START AS SOON AFTER CHRISTMAS AS IT WILL BE SAFE TO GO.*[a7]*

*He promises further information immediately, and a request follows:*

On the ninth of October we leave here. It's a Saturday. If it should be fine dry weather, or anything like it, will you meet us at Rochester, and stop there two or three days to see all the lions[8] in the surrounding country?

---

[1] Presumably of the memorial mentioned in *To* Fred Dickens, 12 Sep.

[2] Kuenzel.

[3] Perhaps *To* Kuenzel, 13 Sep.

[4] Albert Schloss, a German publisher, bookseller and picture-dealer; in Holborn 1832–4, Great Russell Street 1835–8, and later in Berners Street. Best known for his publication *Schloss's English Bijou Almanac* 1836–43 (his "leetle Bijoux" as he called it in writing to Cruikshank 1835: L. W. Bondy catalogue, 1966). The *Almanac* for 1836 (published 1835)—the smallest of all, measuring $\frac{11}{16}$ by $\frac{1}{2}$ an inch—was "poetically illustrated" by L. E. L. and contained engraved portraits of Mrs Hemans, Byron, and others; the issue for 1842, "poetically illustrated" by Mrs Norton, included engraved portraits of CD and Rachel. An album of Schloss's, recently in the possession of

Winifred A. Myers (Autographs) Ltd, contains MS contributions by L. E. L., S. C. Hall, Knowles, Harley, Macready, Rogers, Landseer, Tenniel, Leech (a sketch of Scrooge), and numerous musicians; also the Tiny Tim quotation in CD's hand, dated 22 Jan 44 and the signature of George Hogarth followed by the words: "I am unworthy of such Distinguished Company, but my friend Mr. Schloss will have it so" (1846).

[5] N reads "Tring", surely a misreading of "Tiny".

[6] The magnifying glass sold with each almanac.

[a] F's capitals; passage underlined twice according to Forster.

[7] "The decision once taken," says Forster, "he was in his usual fever until its difficulties were disposed of" (F, III, i, 196).

[8] Sights, things of note (*OED*).

Think of this.[1] ... If you'll arrange to come, I'll have the carriage down, and Topping; and, supposing news from Glasgow[2] don't interfere with us, which I fervently hope it will not, I will ensure that we have much enjoyment.

## *To* GEORGE CATTERMOLE, 21 SEPTEMBER 1841

Text from MDGH, I, 51.

Broadstairs, September 21st, 1841.

My dear George,

Will you, before you go on with the other subjects I gave you,[3] do one of Hugh, bareheaded, bound, tied on a horse, and escorted by horse-soldiers to jail?[4] If you can add an indication of old Fleet Market, and bodies of foot soldiers firing at people who have taken refuge on the tops of stalls, bulkheads, etc., it will be all the better.[5]

Faithfully yours always

[CHARLES DICKENS]

## *To* W. C. MACREADY, 21 SEPTEMBER 1841*

MS Morgan Library.

Broadstairs. | Tuesday Twenty First September 1841.

My Dear Macready.

Forster tells me you are at Drury Lane at all unseasonable hours—are finding out all manner of small delinquencies—making all kinds of dim and distant preparations—and, in a word, justifying that stir and bustle of anticipation which is constantly fermenting within me.

I want to ask your advice—I would, as you know, take no man's so readily as yours, on any subject. On that which I have in mind, you have, from your experience and affections the best right to tutor me.

I am going to America—I think next February. If I go without our dear children, I shall stay Three Months. If I took them with me, I should stay six. What would you do, if you were me?

[1] This plan was carried out, but a week earlier (possibly owing to symptoms of CD's coming illness). Forster met CD at Rochester (almost certainly on Sat 2 Oct), and they "passed a day and night there; a day and night in Cobham and its neighbourhood, sleeping at the Leather-bottle; and a day and night at Gravesend" (F, III, i, 198). Catherine was presumably with them, but is not mentioned by Forster. They were "hardly returned", says Forster, before CD (on 5 Oct) fell ill.

[2] See *To* Forster, 12 July, and *To* Paul, 9 Sep.

[3] Subjects for Nos 83, 87, 88, and the frontispiece to Vol. III, given in *To* Cattermole, 12 Sep.

[4] "Hugh guarded by cavalry" appeared in *Barnaby* No. 81 (Ch. 69), published 16 Oct.

[5] Cattermole sketched these details very lightly into the background.

Kate is averse to taking them—fearing sickness might make them ill. At the same time she naturally finds it difficult to contemplate a subject which is so new to her and so startling, in any very reasonable light. I could take them all, and one servant, for a hundred and fifty pounds each way. I do not—and I almost think one should not, in such a case—make expence a consideration, on either side the question.

Now, here's the question. My dear Macready if you were I, what would you do.[1]

When I have once made up my mind to anything, I can keep it as much at ease as though the thing were done. But I can't make it up in this case, and am sorely tossed and tumbled on a moral ocean in this early stage of my design.

Our best loves to all.

Ever Your faithful friend

W. C. Macready Esquire.                                           CHARLES DICKENS

## *To* JOHN FORSTER, [?22 SEPTEMBER 1841]

Extract in F, III, i, 197. *Date:* "three days later" than letter of 19 Sep according to Forster, and clearly written before CD received (23 Sep) Macready's advice not to take the children to America (see 21 Sep, *fn*). But if written on the 22nd letter possibly did not leave Broadstairs until the 23rd; for Forster was reading it on the 24th when a note from Devonshire Terrace (clearly written that day and delivered by hand) announced to him that CD was on his way to share his breakfast (F, III, i, 196).

I wrote to Chapman and Hall[2] asking them what they thought of it, and saying I meant to keep a note-book, and publish it for half a guinea or thereabouts, on my return. They instantly sent the warmest possible reply, and said they had taken it for granted I would go, and had been speaking of it only the day before. I have begged them to make every enquiry about the fares, cabins, berths, and times of sailing; and I shall make a great effort to take Kate *and* the children. In that case I shall try to let the house furnished, for six months (for I shall remain that time in America); and if I succeed, the rent will nearly pay the expenses out, and home. I have heard of family cabins at £100; and I think one of these is large enough to hold us all. A single fare, I think, is forty guineas. I fear I could not be happy if we had the Atlantic between us; but leaving them in New York while I ran off a thousand miles or so, would be quite another thing. If I can arrange all my plans before publishing the *Clock* address, I shall state

[1] Macready was the friend consulted because he had himself been to America and was also a father of many children. On his first visit (1826), shortly after his marriage, Catherine Macready and his sister Letitia went with him. On his next visit (1843) he went alone. Receiving CD's letter on 22 Sep, Macready "answered him on the instant, recommending him not to take [the children] with him" (*Diaries*, II, 143). When CD read this on the 23rd, he decided to come up to London immediately to consult Macready further (see 23 Sep).

[2] See *To* Hall, 14 Sep.

therein that I am going: which will be no unimportant consideration, as affording the best possible reason for a long delay.[1] How I am to get on without you for seven or eight months, I cannot, upon my soul, conceive. I dread to think of breaking up all our old happy habits, for so long a time. The advantages of going, however, appear by steady looking-at so great, that I have come to persuade myself it is a matter of imperative necessity. Kate weeps whenever it is spoken of. Washington Irving has got a nasty low fever. I heard from him a day or two ago.

### *To* THOMAS MITTON, 22 SEPTEMBER 1841

*Photograph New York Public Library. Address:* Thomas Mitton Esquire | 23 Southampton Buildings.

Broadstairs | September The Twenty Second | 1841.
My Dear Mitton.
    The fruit arrived safely, and in great perfection. I should have acknowledged its receipt, but I knew you were cruising about, and thought a note

---

[1] For the MS draft and corrected proof of his address of Aug 41 "To the Readers of *Master Humphrey's Clock*", see *To* Mitton, 23 Aug and *fn.* Having cancelled in that proof the statement that he would begin his next book on 31 Mar 42, CD seems to have let the matter rest for a month; for no draft announcing his original intention of having a year's rest (*To* Mitton, 23 and 30 Aug) is known. Possibly he was unsure how to explain it to his readers. But now—as this letter says—the American decision afforded "the best possible reason for a long delay". A second proof, dated Sep 41 (Forster Collection, V & A), was therefore run off, with three new paragraphs added. One of them announced his decision to leave for America "early in the spring of next year" (later changed to "January next" by Forster). The next announced that he would start his new novel in monthly parts on 1 Nov 42 (in fact *Martin Chuzzlewit* began in Jan 43). The third, a paragraph coming before the American announcement and leading up to it, was cancelled in proof— probably by Forster. It read: "And now I come to an announcement which gives me mingled pain and pleasure; pain, because it separates me, for a time, from many thousands of my countrymen who have given my writings, as they were myself, a corner in their hearts and homes, and a place among their house-hold gods; pleasure because it leads me to the gratification of a darling wish, and opens to me a new scene of interest and wonder." As substitute for this, Forster added, to the paragraph which follows, the more modest sentence: "The pleasure I anticipate from this realization of a wish I have long entertained, and long hoped to gratify, is subdued by the reflection that it must separate us for a longer time than other circumstances would have rendered necessary." (The address, as printed in *Master Humphrey* No. 80, 9 Oct, is reprinted in J. Butt and K. Tillotson, *Dickens at Work*, 1957, pp. 88–9.) Some of the sentiments of the cancelled passage appeared six weeks later in a "Postscript" dated Nov 41 (added to the address of Sep in *Master Humphrey* No. 87, 27 Nov), in which CD thanked those who had written to him since the appearance of his address; pronounced himself happy if he had left anything by which he might be "associated in spirit" with his readers' "firesides, homes and blameless pleasures"; and promised "another tale of English life and manners" on his return from America.

might run after you for a week or two, and follow you home at last—which, very possibly, will be the fate of this.

I am not getting on with my work at all; being deliciously lazy, and walking about, all day long. Indeed I don't much care to get on; being so near my resting place.[1]

Fred will have his Promotion this week.[2] I am as glad of it, as though anyone had given me five hundred pounds.

Are you surprised to learn that I have made up my mind to go to America—that I have got all the information needful, about the Packets— that I shall sail, please God, in February, if the latter part of the Winter be not too immoderately severe—and that I am going to announce my intention in the Clock?—There.

I have sent the Alphingtonian notice to day.[3] I address this to the office, as your people will most likely know where to forward it.

A pleasant trip to you—I shall see you, of course, as soon as I return to town.

Faithfully Yours always

Thomas Mitton Esquire                                   CHARLES DICKENS


## *To* W. C. MACREADY, [23 SEPTEMBER 1841]

MS Morgan Library. *Date:* clearly Thurs 23 Sep, under which date Macready recorded in his diary: "As I was going to bed Dickens called in, having sent a note first" (*Diaries*, II, 143). *Address:* W. C. Macready Esquire.

Devonshire Terrace | Thursday Night.

My Dear Macready

If you are at home and *up*, I should like to have five minutes talk with you,[4] as I have just come to town, and want to go away by the Morning Boat.

Send me a word—In bed—or out?

Affecy. always
CD.

[1] CD had probably started No. 80, and had eight more numbers to do.

[2] He had it by 26 Sep (*To* Forster, that day).

[3] Presumably to his father, telling him that he was going to America.

[4] Macready's diary-entry for 23 Sep continues: "[CD] sat with me some time canvassing his contemplated voyage to the United States. He spoke of Mrs. Dickens's reluctance and regret, and wished me to write to her and state my views, putting them strongly before her. When he was gone, I wrote to her, enclosing the note to him" (*Diaries*, II, 143). In his covering letter to CD Macready wrote: "I have written what I truly and strongly feel to your wife, but not to convey, I fear, the full conviction (that is to my mind as rooted as the consciousness of my own existence) of what *is a duty* and *must be a source of happiness to her*—in sufficiently impressive terms.—You cannot therefore state too forcibly my impressions on the subject—nor explain to her too strongly how very anxious we shall be to fulfil in the strictest sense every duty of friendship in our care for and attention to your children. I am very anxious she should

## *To* JOHN FORSTER, [24 SEPTEMBER 1841]

Extract in F, III, i, 197. *Date:* written from Devonshire Terrace on the morning after seeing Macready (see last).

This is to give you notice that I am coming to breakfast with you this morning on my way to Broadstairs. I repeat it, sir,—on my way *to* Broadstairs. For, directly I got Macready's note yesterday I went to Canterbury, and came on by day-coach for the express purpose of talking with him; which I did between 11 and 12 last night in Clarence-terrace. The American preliminaries are necessarily startling, and, to a gentleman of my temperament, destroy rest, sleep, appetite, and work, unless definitely arranged. Macready has quite decided me in respect of time and so forth. The instant I have wrung a reluctant consent from Kate,[1] I shall take our joint passage in the mail-packet for next January. I never loved my friends so well as now.

## *To* FREDERICK DICKENS, 26 SEPTEMBER 1841*

MS Benoliel Collection.

Broadstairs | Sunday Twenty Sixth September | 1841.
My Dear Fred.

Unless you have *strong* reason for changing your mind, write and tell Mr. Percy,[2] when you hear from him, that I entertained strong doubts whether his case was one which called for such relief as I could afford; and

view this matter in its proper light, and that she should make all so much happier by the face she puts upon it. I hope and trust it will be a smiling one—and that the emotions of pain may be made as few as possible. God bless you, my dear Dickens | Your faithful and affectionate friend | W. C. Macready. | P.S. I have said nothing of the great delight and enjoyment that lies before her in that grand country, because I did not choose to use so selfish an argument:—but the reasons overbear one—She *must* [*underlined twice*] make herself happy in the thought of being able to *make such a tour in such a way ! !* It is like 'a tempting of Providence' not to do so" (MS Huntington). Edgar Johnson (*CD, his Tragedy and Triumph*, 1953, I, 358) gives a misleading impression by quoting from this letter as if it were Macready's to Catherine (though listing the letter as Macready *to* CD in a note at end of the book). Undoubtedly

Macready's tone in writing to Catherine must have been far gentler—eliciting from her, as it did, such a grateful reply (see *To* Macready, 29 Sep, *fn*).

[1] An easier task than CD expected. It was while she was still uncertain whether to take her three small children and baby with her or leave them behind (for her fluctuations see *To* Hall, 14 Sep, and *To* Macready, 21 Sep) that she wept whenever the American trip was spoken of (*To* Forster, 13 and 22 Sep). Edgar Johnson implies (*ibid*) that on Macready's counselling that they should remain at home she "rained more tears than ever", in spite of his offer of care for them. But in fact she received and acted upon his letter "with a perfect response", and on the day after receiving it could talk of the American adventure "quite gaily" (*To* Forster, 26 Sep).

[2] Name not clearly written; probably "Percy".

that you cannot make any report to me which will alter that impression. I think he's a damned rascal, but *that* you needn't tell him.

You have got your promotion on very handsome terms, and I am heartily rejoiced.—In the matter of Collinson,[1] Beard told me of Easthope's intention when he was here. Therefore I am not surprised.

Kate and I are going to America for five or six months (but I don't tell her how long)—and we sail on the Fourth of January. We must, I grieve to say (for everyone advises me to do so) leave the darlings behind us, which will be a very severe trial.

If I don't let the house,—and I don't think, at present, I shall try to do so,—I shall ask you to take up your residence there, and to board, and lodge, and keep the Cellar key 'till we return.[2] It will be a great comfort to us to know that you see them every day; and I hope you will dine there, for our peace and happiness, every Sunday, and have them down after dinner. Of course you can always have whom you like, to dine with you. This is our earnest desire, and I trust you will think of us, and be very careful of our dear children.

I announce my intention in the Clock,[3] next Saturday Week. Until then, it will be best not to talk of it. All our arrangements are made, and we go to Boston by the British and North American Mail Packet,[4] from Liverpool.

It makes me very down-hearted when I think of the parting. But the conviction that it will be a great thing to do, and the knowledge that I do it for their advantage, brings me up again.

Always Affectionately Yours

Frederick Dickens Esquire.                          CHARLES DICKENS

Over

Anne[5] goes with us.—Will you get the inclosed cheque in one note, and let me have it, half by the next post, and half by the next after.

## *To* JOHN FORSTER, [26 SEPTEMBER 1841]

Extract in F, III, i, 198. *Date:* two days after letter of 24 Sep according to Forster. *From* Broadstairs.

Only a word. Kate is quite reconciled. Anne goes, and is amazingly

---

[1] Presumably this was the Collinson whose name had been used to disguise Talfourd's authorship of *Glencoe* (see *To* Macready, 16 May 40, *fn*), and who had dined with CD on 1 Jan 40 (Diary entry: see Appx, p. 461), and on 23 Aug 40 in the company of Forster, Macready, Maclise, Angus Fletcher and Fanny Burnett (Macready, *Diaries*, II, 75).

[2] CD in fact let 1 Devonshire Terrace to General Sir John Wilson, and took lodgings for Fred and the children in Osnaburgh Street, near the Macreadys.

[3] See *To* Forster, 22 Sep, *fn*.

[4] See *To* Fletcher, 16 Nov, *fn*.

[5] Anne Brown, Catherine's maid, who was with the family until her marriage 1855; returned (as Mrs Cornelius) two years later; and stayed on at Tavistock House after CD and Catherine had separated.

cheerful and light of heart upon it. And I think, at present, that it's a greater trial to me than anybody. The 4th of January is the day. Macready's note to Kate was received and acted upon with a perfect response.[1] She talks about it quite gaily, and is satisfied to have nobody in the house but Fred, of whom, as you know, they are all fond. He has got his promotion, and they give him the increased salary from the day on which the minute was made by Baring.[2] I feel so amiable, so meek, so fond of people, so full of gratitudes and reliances, that I am like a sick man. And I am already counting the days between this and coming home again.

### *To* JOHN OVERS, 26 SEPTEMBER 1841*

MS Morgan Library.

Broadstairs. | Sunday Twenty Sixth September 1841.
Dear Mr. Overs.

I inclose you a cheque for Five Pounds. Please let me know that it has reached you safely.

I am delighted, truly delighted, to hear that you are getting so much better, and are enjoying such good and worthy relaxation. I hope you will have no need of Mr. Wood;[3] but if you should have any, you will like him very much.

The eleventh or twelfth of next month will find me, I hope, in town. I shall be glad to see you then, for many reasons—and not least among them, for one you will see stated in the Clock next Saturday week.

Faithfully Yours
Mr. J. A. Overs.                                        CHARLES DICKENS

### *To* LEWIS GAYLORD CLARK, 28 SEPTEMBER 1841

Text from Philadelphia *Saturday Evening Post*, 13 Nov 41, quoting the *New York Courier;* date and salutation from MDGH, III, 19. *From* Broadstairs (see *fn* to next).

September 28th, 1841.
My dear Sir,

I condole with you, from my heart, on the loss you have sustained;[4] and

---

[1] Part of her response was to write to Maclise asking him if he would make a drawing of the children for her to take to America. He replied on Mon [27 Sep]: "*With all my heart* I will do what you wish", and asked if she would like him to come to Broadstairs for the purpose, or wait till their return to London; yes, he went on, he had heard of their project, and thought of it "with a thrill now and then". He ended: "Give my best love to [Charles] and take my best love to yourself—I hope this is not saying too much—and embrace Charley and May and Katy, and hang me if I

believe you have named the younger yet—but kiss the little unknown too—we must include him in our projected group if it is only three dots and a line. [*sketch of baby's face here*]" (MS Morgan). He included the raven too. For a reproduction of his drawing, see Edgar Johnson, *CD, his Tragedy and Triumph*, I, plate 30.

[2] Henry Bingham Baring (1804–69), MP for Marlborough 1832–68; a Lord of the Treasury Sep 41–July 46.

[3] See *To* Macready, 24 Aug, *fn*.

[4] The death on 12 June 41 of Clark's twin-brother Willis Gaylord Clark

I feel proud of your permitting me to sympathise with your affliction. It is a great satisfaction to me to have been addressed under similar circumstances by many of your countrymen, since the "Curiosity Shop" came to a close. Some simple and honest hearts in the remote wilds of America, have written me letters on the loss of their children; so numbering my little book, or rather heroine, with their household gods, and so pouring out their trials and sources of comfort in them, before me as a friend, that I have been inexpressibly moved—and am, whenever I think of them—I do assure you.[1] ... You have already all the comfort that I could lay before you—all, I hope, that the affectionate spirit of your brother, now in happiness, can shed into your soul. The peaceful memory of the dead be with you!

I am going to *bring* you an article for good old Diedrick.[2] For on the fourth of next January, if it pleases God, I am coming, with my wife, on a three or four months' visit to America. The British and North American Steam Packet will bring me, I hope, to Boston, and enable me in the third week of the New Year to set my foot upon the soil I have trodden in my day-dreams many times, and whose sons (and daughters) I yearn to know and be among.

I hope you are surprised—and I hope not unpleasantly.

Ever faithfully yours,

CHARLES DICKENS

## To WASHINGTON IRVING, 28 SEPTEMBER 1841

Text from W. L. Andrews, *A Stray Leaf from the Correspondence of Washington Irving and CD*, privately printed, New York, 1894, p. 32.

1 Devonshire Terrace, York Gate, Regent's Park, London[3]

Twenty-eighth September, 1841

My dear Washington Irving

    I was very sorry to hear t'other day from Mr Clark, of the Knickerbocker

---

(1808–41; *DAB*), poet and editor of *Relf's Philadelphia Gazette*; one of the *Knickerbocker's* chief contributors, and assistant-editor 1834–41. The first American to advocate in print a law of international copyright. His brother wrote a memoir of him in the *Knickerbocker Magazine*, Apr 42, and edited his *Literary Remains*, 1844.

    [1] John Tomlin had written from "the backwoods of America" (see 23 Feb 41), though apparently not because he had lost a child. No other letter from the "remote wilds" is known. In his first public speech in America (Boston, 1 Feb 42) CD referred again to the letters he had received "from the dwellers in log-houses among the morasses, and swamps, and densest forests", from

"many a sturdy hand, hard with the axe and spade, and browned by the summer's sun", from bereaved mothers, whom he could reckon now "by dozens, not by units"; and it was these letters, he said, that decided him, at a time when he was wondering "whether or not to wind up [his] Clock", that to come to America and see his friends was "a positive duty" (see *Speeches*, ed. K. J. Fielding, pp. 20–1).

    [2] I.e. the *Knickerbocker*, so named after Irving's book (see 21 Apr).

    [3] Although headed with this address, letter was almost certainly written at Broadstairs, where next day CD told Macready it had been blowing a gale "for two days and nights".

and New York, that you were unwell. I hope you are better; and further-more that in proof of your being so, you will write me one line by the next Packet, to certify the fact.

I told Leslie[1] what you had written about him,[2] and he was much pleased. I know him, but have not known him long or intimately—I needn't tell you that London keeps a great many people apart, who incline strongly towards each other. His great abilities and uncommon gift of humour, with his pencil (a kind of Charles Lamb-like humour of the best quality) I have always doted on. We agreed that in your honor we would dine together instantly, and that we would be constant associates for ever-more.

It has been a toss up for some weeks, whether I should write you a long letter, or a short one. I am happy to say the latter carries it. For why should I inflict four sides of paper on you, when I am coming to see you? And are there not at this moment in the books of the British and North American Mail Packet Company, the words—"fourth of January eighteen hundred and forty two, Mr and Mrs Charles Dickens—for Boston"?

I look forward to shaking hands with you, with an interest I cannot (and would not, if I could) describe. You *can* imagine, I dare say, something of the feelings with which I look forward to being in America. I can hardly believe I am coming.

[Rogers][3] had been in great distress and desolation at having missed

---

[1] Charles Robert Leslie (1794–1859; *DNB, DAB*), painter. Son of a Phila-delphia clock-maker, but born in Lon-don and spent most of his life in England. Studied at the RA under Benjamin West. RA 1826. Through his friend Washington Allston met Coleridge, whom he sketched for the *New Monthly Magazine*, Apr 1819; was an intimate friend of Constable (whose memoirs he later published). Illus-trated Irving's *Knickerbocker's History of New York* and *Sketch-Book*, and was one of the illustrators of the Waverley Novels 1824–6. Made his reputation with paintings of humorous scenes from literature. *The Queen receiving the Sacrament at her Coronation*, 1838, and *The Christening of the Princess Royal*, 1841, were among his numerous port-raits; he painted CD as Bobadil in 1846.

[2] On 26 May 41 Irving had written of Leslie to CD: "I wish you would get acquainted with him. You would like one another. He is full of talent and right feeling. He was one of my choice and intimate companions during my literary sojourn in London. . . . We sympathised in tastes and feelings and

used to explore London together; and visit the neighboring villages, and occasionally extend our researches into different parts of the country. He is one of the purest and best of men; with a fine eye for nature and character, and a truly Addisonian humor" (MS Hunt-ington).

[3] Andrews reads "Bogus"; *D*, XII (1916), 247 follows; N, taking its text from *D*, silently changes to "Bogue". But undoubtedly what CD wrote, with his idiosyncratic "R", was "Rogers". In his letter of 26 May Irving had written: "By the way I see by the dedi-cation of your last work that you properly appreciate the character of Rogers; intrinsically a most benevolent man, full of sympathy for the poor mans joys and sorrows; and, as a lady of my acquaintance once beautifully said of him 'so kind to those in affliction'. He was one of the last persons I saw in London. I breakfasted with him. On taking leave he followed me to the street door; pressed my hand, and bade me farewell with a warmth and kind-ness that I shall never forget."

your niece.¹ He was with us last night, and bewailed his affliction in very moving terms. He begged me to say as much to you, and to remember him heartily—though I am not clear whether it is a recent occurrence, or whether my projected voyage reminded him of it.

*a*Did you know poor [Hook] ?² He has left a widow (poor creature, she was not married to him, but there is mourning out of matrimony, and it is no disparagement to the word) with four illegitimate daughters—I am not sure whether I should not have written, five.³ I heard yesterday at the Athenæum, that the King of [Hanover]⁴ has sent them five hundred pounds. It is a good thing to find gratitude in Kings, and better when the King is a bad one, so I hope it's true. J . . .⁵ declined to join in a subscription for rescuing these girls from poverty—it may be, from the very streets —because they were not born in wedlock. I hardly know what your politics are; remembering the Squire in Bracebridge Hall and the radical.⁶ —But I am sure this is not your creed.*a*

Murray has just re-published in a new form, Lockhart's translation of

---

¹ Sarah Sanders Paris (1813–85), daughter of Irving's sister Catherine and his favourite niece. She had married Thomas Wentworth Storrow, Jnr, in Mar 41 and had left America for Paris with her husband on 1 May. Irving wrote to her frequently and affectionately until his death.

*aa* Omitted in *D* and N.

² Name omitted in W. L. Andrews, *op. cit.*; but clearly Theodore Hook (see Vol. 1, p. 209*n*), who had died on 24 Aug.

³ In fact, two sons and three daughters (R. H. D. Barham, *Life and Remains of Theodore Edward Hook*, revised edition, 1877, p. 243). To relieve them from immediate want, four of Hook's "true friends" each gave £100; Marjoribanks was already providing for one of the sons (*ibid* and *n*). The whole of Hook's effects had been seized by the Crown on his death, in liquidation of the Mauritius debt for which he had been held responsible since 1817.

⁴ Name omitted by Andrews. But see R. H. D. Barham (*op. cit.*, p. 244): "The King of Hanover generously gave 500*l*. With that splendid exception, the names appearing on the list are mostly those of men in moderate circumstances, and of his own rank in life,—more than one of his nobler acquaintances declining, on the score, we believe, of a nice morality, to contribute to the undertaking." The subscription realized less

than £3000. For many years, says Barham, Hook had been courted by "princes of the blood" and the "Pride of Westminster" for the wit and charm of his conversation and his amazing powers of improvisation; but, like Sheridan, he met with "*fêtes*, flattery, and forgetfulness" (*op. cit.*, pp. 250, 254).

⁵ Possibly Jeffrey, who had "made his house like a home" to Irving during his visit to Scotland 1817 (*Life and Letters of Washington Irving*, ed. P. M. Irving, 1862, 1, 321) and seen more of him in London 1829–32—although in other contexts he was known to be generous.

⁶ The radical ("A Village Politician", in *Bracebridge Hall*) is a "meagre", "bilious" fellow with doctrines threatening the village's idyllic life under its kind-hearted Squire. Presumably CD had been uncertain how to interpret the irony of his routing by that "tough arguer", the old yeoman Jack Tibbets, who neither read nor believed in newspapers. Americans themselves were in no doubt as to Irving's politics, but felt so much pride in the admiration his work had won in England, particularly Scott's and Byron's, that "those who cared most for American principles forgave the author his Tory tastes, for he was so remote from politics" (Van Wyck Brooks, *The World of Washington Irving*, 1944, p. 160).

the Spanish and Moorish ballads, with all manner of gold and silver borders, and variegated colours. He is said to be making rather a desperate stake with it,[1] having suffered from recent failures in the trade. It looks tawdry and poor; and I fear will not do.

You knew Wilkie, I think, in Spain.[2] A very handsome subscription has been already made for raising a monument to him in London. They are going to raise another, in Edinburgh.[3] Poor fellow! He gave me a little picture of his painting, shortly before he went away,[4] and I little thought I had seen him for the last time. His sister is so sadly changed by grief for his loss, that she is hardly to be recognized for the person she used to be.[5] She had dressed herself as gaily as a bride, and was waiting for his coming home, when they had to tell her that he lay under the blue waters of the Mediterranean.

Believe me, always | Faithfully Yours

Washington Irving Esquire CHARLES DICKENS

## *To* W. C. MACREADY, 29 SEPTEMBER 1841*

MS Morgan Library.

Broadstairs. | Twenty Ninth September 1841.

My Dear Macready.

I take it very ill of you that you didn't say "Come up to the Council, Dickens"; and furthermore that you didn't tell me at what time the

---

[1] *Ancient Spanish Ballads, Historical and Romantic,* originally published by Blackwood & Cadell, Edinburgh, 1823. In Murray's lavish revised edn, 1841, William Allan heads a list of six illustrators; "the coloured titles, borders, and ornamental letters and vignettes" were by "Owen Jones, Architect". The *Examiner* reviewer, 25 Sep, treating it as a curiosity, commented: "The modern and not very correct taste for illustrated books, is here carried to its most gorgeous pitch. Every page of the volume is a framed picture."

[2] Irving and Wilkie had become close friends in Spain, visiting picture-galleries in Madrid together in the autumn of 1827 and exploring Seville the following spring (see S. T. Williams, *Life of Washington Irving,* especially I, 325, 333–6). Irving dedicated *The Alhambra* to Wilkie and wrote an unpublished essay on him (MS Yale: see Williams, *op. cit.,* I, 327, 482).

[3] This plan was apparently not carried out.

[4] On 30 Mar 40 Wilkie wrote to CD from Vicarage Place, Kensington: "My dear Sir | May I beg to present for the kind acceptance of Mrs. Dickens one of my Drawings, made of a Mother and child for the picture belonging to Mr. Moon, of the Cotter's Saturday Night, and which I shall be most glad if she will place in her room in token of the most humble respect and regard of | My dear Sir | Your most faithful and devoted Servant" (MS Huntington). Although explicitly intended for Catherine, the picture was at Gad's Hill on CD's death.

[5] Wilkie's sister Helen had lived with him since 1813. His last letter, of 26 May, was written to her (Allan Cunningham, *Life of Sir David Wilkie,* 1843, III, 469–71).

Cardinals meet.[1] I am in a whirl of doubt whether, coming by the Steam boat, I could arrive in time. If Forster don't write and tell me tomorrow morning, I'll disinherit him.

I think the address is in a manly honest tone, and of *the right* kind, and like you.[2] I have made a few slight suggestions, which occur to me.[3] About the prices, I am so thoroughly, entirely, and unalterably convinced, that if the Cardinals go to the Vote, I beg Dickens may be recorded as 12,[4] in consequence of the supernatural obstinacy of his convictions.

I should have written to thank you, My Dear Macready, for that letter,[5]

[1] In a letter to CD of 28 Sep Macready had enclosed a draft of his address to the public, outlining his forthcoming policy as manager of Drury Lane, and said: "I want you to make yourself one of the Public, and as that respectable individual read the enclosed—mark what you may not like —score down what you think better— but let me have your *mind & feeling* on it.—I do not engage to be guided by it; but I will fairly lay it before the Cardinals who meet in Conclave upon this document . . .—I had thought of requesting you to come up for this mighty business, but a little reflection has shown, that this mode will answer every purpose. | *Do not fail to send it back by return of Post* [underlined *twice*]—We meet on *Thursday*" (MS Huntington). The "Cardinals" were a committee consisting of Talfourd, Fox, H. P. Smith, Kenney, Forster, Maclise, Stanfield, Brydone and Serle (*Diaries*, II, 144).

[2] Macready's address was published in full in the newspapers of 4 Oct. His intention, he said, was to restore to Drury Lane "its legitimate dramatic representations"; and to advance the drama—as he had tried to do at Covent Garden—"as a branch of national literature and art". Shakespeare's plays would be "illustrated with uniform correctness, and as far as possible ... produced in strict fidelity to the poet's text with all needful appliances of scenic illusion"; while living dramatists would be strongly encouraged. Music would be associated with "aids of the picturesque in scenery and action" and "the utmost attention and encouragement given, to improve, in genuine English Opera, a School of Art". Arrangements would be made to restore to "the respectable frequenters of the Theatre . . . an agreeable resort for promenading and refreshment without danger of offence to propriety or delicacy"—such as had become a "national reproach"; the pit would be extended and improved; the lowest admission-prices possible charged. The principle adopted throughout would be "to demonstrate that the exclusive patent of a Theatre is a delegated trust for the interest of the Drama, and the advantage of the public" (*Morning Chronicle*).

[3] Macready replied on 1 Oct: "We had a long debate yesterday—I had altered in some respects what I sent you but I submitted all—both copies— your emendation &c &c—and from the stirring up (and there was a good deal of stirring) the paper which you will see in Monday's journals was decocted" (MS Huntington).

[4] Macready added a postscript to his letter of 1 Oct: "Your twelve votes were disputed by the revising barrister" (Talfourd, presumably).

[5] No doubt Macready's letter to Catherine of 23 Sep (see *To* Macready, that day, *fn*). On 27 Sep Macready noted having received "a very fervent and grateful letter from Mrs. Dickens . . . acquiescing in all I urged upon her" (*Diaries*, II, 144); and in his letter of 28 Sep he wrote: "Pray tell your good wife, that she made me very happy in the very sweet & amiable letter she sent me, and that she cannot gratify me more than by calling, and believing me her true friend:—this with all kindest regards from me, and all sympathising loves & greetings from all about me". The letter ended: "Forster told me you were 'bien content' with my freedom with your good little wife—I am so

but I had hardly the heart to do it. And even now, I can only say to you—not that I am more your friend than ever, for that I could not be—but that my warmest affection and love are yours always.

I wonder, can you imagine how often I shall think of Drury Lane when I am away; and how strange it seems to me, and how full of regrets I am, to be going away from such a source of interest and delight. No, I am sure you can't, in the full extent.

Kate sends her love to you, and all. We are in great force, and talk about it often, in the liveliest way possible. It has been blowing a smart gale here for two days and nights.—I have seen her *looking* (very hard) at the Sea, but she has *said* nothing.

She has been much comforted by a stout note from Fred, who is to live with the children. The girl who is going with us, is a moral cork jacket, too, and gives great confidence.

Always My Dear Macready
Your faithful friend
W. C. Macready Esquire                                                         CD.


## *To* CHARLES LEVER,[1] [?EARLY OCTOBER 1841]

Mention in Lever *to* CD, 11 Oct 41 (see *fn*). *Address* (envelope, MS Walter T. Spencer)*:* Favored by Hablot Browne Esquire | Dr. Lever. Signed by CD, in full.[2]

*Refusing an invitation, and protesting angrily at Lever's publisher's use of a comparison of his work with Lever's in advertisements.*[3]

delighted" (MS Huntington). On 1 Oct he wrote: "*You know* [*underlined twice*], that it makes me really happy to be assured of your content and comfort—deeply so.—You will soon be with us, and we shall talk over all the ways and means to make every item of additional confidence & comfort that we can" (MS Huntington).

[1] Charles James Lever (1806–72; *DNB*), novelist. Born in Dublin, of English ancestry. MB, Trinity College, Dublin 1831. Practised medicine until 1842, first in Ireland, then 1840–2 in Brussels. Both *The Confessions of Harry Lorrequer*, 1837–40, and *Charles O'Malley*, 1840–3, were published with great success in the *Dublin University Magazine* which he edited 1842–5; four more novels of Irish or military life followed 1843–5. He returned to Brussels 1845, and lived thereafter on the Continent, writing continuously. For his friendship with CD, from 1846, see later vols.

[2] No doubt the envelope contained CD's "angry" letter and was taken to Brussels by Browne (probably on Sun 3 Oct).

[3] On 11 Oct 41 Lever replied from Brussels: "I regret much, that circumstances should have prevented my seeing you here, & particularly so, as I find from your Note, that the unfavorable impression of me, certain misdeeds of my publisher has [*thus*] called down, should have made our acquaintanceship a matter only desired on one side. | I trust I need not assure you, that I neither abetted nor concurred in the 'Tactique' which could exhalt [*thus*] my very humble reputation by any depreciation of your very exhalted one—Living at a distance from the place of publication, —ignorant of—& indifferent to, the stratagems of the trade, I neither possessed the influence, nor the ability, to direct my publishers in a course which I believed as essentially *their* province,

## *To* HUGH TILSLEY,[1] 1 OCTOBER 1841

MS Walter T. Spencer. *Address:* Hugh Tilsley Esquire | Stamp Office | Somerset House | London.

Broadstairs, Kent. | October The First 1841.

Mr. Charles Dickens presents his compliments to Mr. Tilsley, and begs to thank him for his obliging letter, relative to the real name of the Keeper of Newgate, at the time of Lord George Gordon's riots—though Mr. Dickens is not aware that he will have any further occasion to mention it, or any opportunity, therefore, of correcting his mistake.[2]

It is singular that the various accounts of the trial (which agree in nothing else) unite in calling this gentleman Akerman.[3] Perhaps, however, the circumstance is most satisfactorily accounted for, by the fact that that is not his proper name.[4]

as scribbling my Manuscript was *mine.* | In conclusion, I can only add, that they who know me best, know me as your most warm—enthusiastic Admirer—one who felt your success, & popularity, as reflecting credit upon the whole world of Letters, & who so far from covetting [*thus*] comparison which could only injure himself—esteemed the critic ever kindest, who discussed his writings without reference to those he felt so immeasurably superior—. | But I know, you must ere this have acquitted me, of what I feel a heavy charge—& shall only repeat my constant desire to be personally known to you, & assure you how much I feel sincerely yours" (MS Huntington). The "misdeeds" of Lever's publishers, William Curry Junior & Co., of Dublin, had been their quoting, in advertisements of *Harry Lorrequer*, the following from a review in the *United Service Gazette*: "We would rather be the author of this work, than of all the 'Pickwicks' and 'Nickle-bys' in the world. It is full to overflow-ing of humour of a very high order; and as for incident, it contains enough to supply stock for half a score of modern novels" (an advertisement which was repeated, somewhat curiously, on the back cover of the monthly part of *Master Humphrey*, Nov 41). According to W. J. Fitzpatrick (*Life of Charles Lever*, 1879, I, 228*n*), CD, much annoyed, "at last, responded angrily to a civil letter of Lever's" (presumably the letter inviting him to Brussels):

hence Lever's letter of 11 Oct. Lever's original idea may have been that CD's visit should coincide with one already arranged with Browne—who, in a letter dated "Monday — Sept", had written to CD: "Can you conveniently send me the subject or subjects for next week by Thursday or Friday? as I wish if practicable, to start for Bruxelles by the Sunday's Boat—a word in reply will oblige | Yrs. truly | Hablot K. Browne. | P.S.—Upon second thoughts I send you the enclosed epistle—(if you read it, you will find out why)—the writer thereof is 'Harry Lorrequer' alias 'Charles O'Malley'—to whose house I am going" (MS Huntington). Browne's illustrations of Lever may have been an additional thorn in CD's flesh. Lever himself, after seeing the illustration to *Harry Lorrequer* No. 2 ("The Supper Scene"), had urged Browne not to make Lorrequer so like Nicholas Nickleby (*op. cit.*, I, 225).

[1] Hugh Tilsley (?1796–1863), later Assistant Solicitor of Inland Revenue. Author of *A Treatise on the Stamp Laws in Great Britain and Ireland*, 1847, and other works on the Stamp Acts.

[2] He appears, as Akerman, in *Barnaby*, Ch. 64—correctly (see below).

[3] He is Akerman in Holcroft's *Narrative* (CD's main source for the riots); in the *Annual Register*, 1780; in the accounts in the newspapers mentioned in *Barnaby*, Ch. 39; and elsewhere. No other name for the Keeper of Newgate has been found.

## *To* THOMAS BEARD, [12 OCTOBER 1841]

MS Dickens House. *Date:* PM 12 Oct 41. *Address:* Free | Thomas Beard Esq | 42 Portman Place | Edgeware Road.

1 Devonshire Terrace | Tuesday Morning

My dear Beard.

You will hardly believe it I dare say, for I cant,[1] but I have been very ill for a week,[2] and last Friday Morning was obliged to submit to a cruel operation, and the cutting out root and branch of a disease caused by working over much which has been gathering it seems for years.[3] Thank God it's all over and I am on the Sofa again—rather lean but filling the Doctor with boundless astonishment notwithstanding.[4]

Kate to whom I dictate this sends all kinds of loves. When you have time come and see me.

Faithfully yours always
CHARLES DICKENS[5]

[4] Two real mistakes in *Barnaby* were pointed out, many years later, in a letter to CD from the Rev. G. W. Brameld—according to Brameld *to* Forster, 5 Nov 72 (MS University of California, Los Angeles). One was that he had made Stagg arrive at the widow's cottage in June; yet, though Mrs Rudge and Barnaby then spend a week on their way to London, they arrive there on 2 June. The second, that CD put the total loss through damage done by the rioters at £150,000 or £125,000—of which the destruction of Langdale's house and stock was estimated at £50,000; yet surely the remaining £100,000 or £75,000 could not cover the destruction of 70 private houses and four prisons (including the recently rebuilt Newgate).

[1] Thus in MS.

[2] I.e. since 5 Oct, the day—almost certainly—of his return to London (see *To* Forster, 19 Sep, *fn*).

[3] Fistula. The operation was performed by Frederick Salmon (see *To* Mitton, 17 Oct, *fn*) on Fri 8 Oct. Macready called on him the same evening and recorded in his diary: "I suffered *agonies*, as they related all to me, and did violence to myself in keeping myself

to my seat. I could scarcely bear it" (*Diaries*, II, 145). The operation would have been performed without an anaesthetic.

[4] On 11 Oct Macready and Browning called on CD, and found him "going on very comfortably" (Macready, *Diaries*, II, 145). In a letter dated "Thursday Mg." (presumably the day before CD's operation) Browning had written: "Dear Dickens, | I am far luckier than the rest of your friends in having heard of your illness no sooner than of its partial abatement. Pray get well, and keep so, for all our sakes. | Forster tells me you don't absolutely reject an apple, roasted or otherwise! May I offer you two or three?—no more, because the Scripture blessing of the good man in 'his basket and his store'—has only been half-accomplished with us here—the only remains of the best article we can muster for the moment being spectrally true to one's notion of 'Osier's Ghost'! [*see Richard Glover's ballad "Admiral Hosier's Ghost" (included in Percy's Reliques): the ghosts of the sailors were "wasted with disease"*] | Ever yours faithfully" (MS Huntington).

[5] The whole letter, including the signature, is in Catherine's hand.

## *To* ANDREW BELL, 12 OCTOBER 1841\*

MS Rosenbach Foundation. *Address:* Free | Mr. Andrew Bell | Bradbury and Evans | Printers Whitefriars | Fleet Street.

1 Devonshire Terrace | 12th. October 1841.

My dear Sir

I am obliged to dictate this letter to you for I have been very unwell, having indeed undergone an extremely painful operation, which leaves me weak though I am recovering fast.

I thank you very much for your book[1] which I have read with great amusement and pleasure.

I think you are rather hard on the Americans and that your dedication[2] like Mrs Trolloppe's[3] preface[4] seems to denote a foregone conclusion.[5] It is much better however to be hard in such a case, than soft which you certainly are not[6]— for your descriptions are all exceedingly life like and bring their subjects before my eyes distinctly.[7] My notion is that in going to a New World one must for the time utterly forget, and put out of sight the Old one and bring none of its customs or observances into the comparison—Or if you do compare remember how much brutality you may see (if you choose) in the common streets and public places of London. I

[1] *Men and Things in America* (see *To* Bell, 7 Apr, *fn*).

[2] To Peel, "with Reverent Respect, ... by One of the Humblest of his Numberless Admirers".

[3] (Mis-spelt thus.) Frances Trollope (1780–1863; *DNB*): see Vol. 1, p. 499*n*. She was now publishing two or three books a year—her work-habits anticipating her son Anthony's: "I get up at half-past four every morning, and get nearly the whole of my day's task accomplished before breakfast" (letter of Autumn 40, quoted in F. E. Trollope, *Frances Trollope: her Life and Literary Work*, 1895, I, 320).

[4] To *Domestic Manners of the Americans*, 1832. In it she stated that in describing ordinary American life she had "endeavoured to show how greatly the advantage is on the side of those who are governed by the few, instead of the many"; should her countrymen forgo the blessings of their established constitution, they must be prepared for the "jarring tumult and universal degradation which invariably follow the wild scheme of placing all the power of the State in the hands of the populace."

[5] I.e. that he was a Tory, and would show himself as hostile to Republicanism as any of the English Tory travellers (Marryat, Hall, Capt. Thomas Hamilton and Mrs Trollope) whose books the Americans so bitterly resented.

[6] Bell had spent a year in America 1835–6, apparently hoping to find work (see 7 Apr, *fn*). Though calling himself a radical by upbringing, he looked at both small and great things in the country with a very jaundiced eye: the Bowery theatre was tawdry; the Americans did not know how to build houses; their maps were incorrect; their art and architecture were bad; the unemployment was shocking; they were not even hospitable (which could be accounted for by his admission elsewhere that he was "not of the gayest turn of mind" himself). His strongest criticisms were of "the pretended absence of poverty in America" and the treatment of the Negroes in Philadelphia.

[7] There are vivid descriptions of steamboat travel on the Hudson, a coach journey in a storm, the enjoyment shown by people at New Lebanon Springs; and he describes with admiration the New Lebanon Shakers (usually derided).

have often seen a boy, and more than once a Woman, quite as roughly used as your Negro in the Oyster room and either you or I rising from our desk and walking out, could find in the next street (always supposing that we were bent on looking for him) the counterpart of your Yankee swaggerer.[1]

Faithfully Yours

Mr Andrew Bell CHARLES DICKENS[2]


## *To* JOHN OVERS, 12 OCTOBER 1841

MS Dickens House.

1 Devonshire Terrace | 12th. October 1841

Dear Mr. Overs.

I dictate this letter to you because I have not been well and am yet lying on the Sofa, after being some days in bed. I have had to undergo a painful operation, and am only just recovering.

Thank you for the verses, which are very good.

I shall be very glad to hear what has passed between you and Mr. Macready and how you like the situation. That gentleman comes to me every day, but I think it better not to ask him.

Faithfully yours

CHARLES DICKENS[2]


## *To* R. S. HORRELL, 12 OCTOBER 1841

MS Public Library of Victoria, Melbourne.

1 Devonshire Terrace | 12th. October 1841

Dear Sir

I am obliged to dictate this brief letter to you, in consequence of having had to undergo a painful operation which leaves me weak, though recovering with great rapidity. As soon as I get about again and have disposed of such arrears as my compulsory retirement will have engendered, I will not fail to read your poem and write to you myself.

Faithfully yours

CHARLES DICKENS[2]


## *To* GEORGE REYNOLDS,[3] 13 OCTOBER 1841

Mention in Sotheby's catalogue, July 1910; *MS* 1 p.; dated Devonshire Terrace, 13 Oct 41.

---

[1] An incident in which a white American abuses and insults a Negro waiter in a New York oyster-cellar (pp. 181–2).

[2] The whole letter, including the signature, is in Catherine's hand.

[3] Unidentified.

## *To* THOMAS MITTON, 17 OCTOBER 1841

MS Huntington Library.

1 Devonshire Terrace | 17th. October 1841

My dear Mitton

Kate writes this note at my dictation because I find that the act of writing on the Sofa [is][1] very irksome indeed.

I asked the advice of a great City man,[2] whose name I must not repeat, but who is perfectly acquainted with the whole monied concerns, and monied people of London, relative to my life Insurances. He tells me that both the Argus and the Brittania are such *very* doubtful offices,[3] that if I can effect an insurance in any good one, of long standing, I had better get rid of those policies for any little money they may fetch, and put up with the loss.[4]

This is pleasant.

I must not go out till Tuesday. When I have been to Salmon[5] I will see this gentleman and come on to you. It will be nearly twelve before I reach your Office.

Faithfully yours always

Thomas Mitton Esquire                    CHARLES DICKENS[6]

---

[1] Word omitted in MS.

[2] Probably Sir John Wilson, KCB (1780–1856; *DNB*), Director of the Eagle Insurance Co. since 1827, who rented 1 Devonshire Terrace while CD was in America—possibly through H. P. Smith's intermediacy. In the course of a distinguished military career he was twice wounded and highly commended by Wellington for service in the Peninsula; knighted 1814; placed on half-pay 1816; Major-General 1825; Lieut.-General 1838; General 1854.

[3] The Argus (established 1833) and the Britannia (1837) were not among the many recently-founded Life Assurance Companies which collapsed during the next 25 years; but the Annual General Meeting of the Argus in Apr 41 shows it was going through an anxious phase (*The Times*, 7 Apr). The Britannia, with which CD had been insured for £999 since 17 July 38 (Policy, Mr C. C. Dickens), was merged in the Briton Medical and General Life Association in 1865.

[4] Before going to America CD insured himself with the Eagle (*To* Mitton, 18 Nov), but did not give up his Argus and Britannia policies (see *To* Mitton, 29 Oct).

[5] Frederick Salmon (1796–1868),

LSA 1817, MRCS 1818, LAC 1827; the surgeon who had operated on CD for fistula on 8 Oct. Appointed surgeon to the General Dispensary, Aldersgate Street, 1827; acquired the premises despite professional opposition, and opened the "Infirmary for the Relief of the Poor afflicted with Fistula and other Diseases of the Rectum" 1835. The Infirmary moved to Charterhouse Square 1838, and to City Road 1854— renamed St Mark's Hospital. Salmon worked for over 20 years almost single-handed, carrying out more than 3500 operations without a fatal result. He retired from the staff 1859. He also practised at 12 Old Broad Street 1836– 1864. Published *A Practical Essay on Stricture of the Rectum*, 1828 (containing graphic descriptions of contemporary surgery), other medical papers and *Oration on the Necessity for an Entire Change in the Constitution and Government of the Royal College of Surgeons*, 1833. His portrait, presented to him on retirement, now hangs in St Mark's Hospital. (Information kindly supplied by Dr Basil Morson of St Mark's Hospital.)

[6] The whole letter, including the signature, is in Catherine's hand. Hence, no doubt, the mis-spelling "Brittania".

## *To* MACVEY NAPIER, 21 OCTOBER 1841

MS British Museum.

1 Devonshire Terrace | 21st October 1841.

My dear Sir. If you had asked me three weeks ago, whether you might have reckoned upon me, for January,[1] I should have written you back, an emphatic "Yes", but within that short space, I have found out, that I laboured under the complaint called Fistula the consequence of too much sitting at my desk, and have undergone a painful operation. Now although I am Thank God, recovering so rapidly, that I am in possession of my usual appetite and spirits, and can already go out for a daily drive, I am so thrown back, in respect of my "Clock" and my American preparations, for I am going, that it will be as much as I can do, within any reasonable regard to my health, to come out punctually every week until the end of November, and then lay down my pen, for eight months at least. We sail (Mrs Dickens goes with me) on the 4th of January, and purpose to return in June. I don't go with any idea of pressing the Americans into my service. In my next fiction, and in all others I hope, I shall stand staunchly by John.[2] I *may* write an account of my trip—but that is another matter.

I had laid myself out, to redeem my promise to you—had considered the subject in various ways—and looked forward to its fullfillment[3] with great pleasure. I hope you will consider its redemption only postponed—I need not say, by a circumstance over which I had no control, and which I would most gladly have avoided.

In common with every body else, I have been perfectly charmed with the last number of the Review.[4] Believe me that I do anxiously look forward, to being among its contributors. If wars or rumours of wars,[5] should keep me at home, I will not fail to give you timely notice.

[1] The date he had suggested for publication in the *Edinburgh* of his proposed article on children's employment (see *To* Napier, 8 Aug).

[2] John Bull—an intention implicit in his "Postcript" to *Master Humphrey* of Nov 41 (see *To* Forster, 22 Sep, *fn*), but from which he departed in taking Martin Chuzzlewit to America.

[3] Thus in MS. He in fact never fulfilled this promise.

[4] Among the articles in the *Edinburgh Review*, Oct 41, which might have particularly appealed to CD were George Borrow's "The Zincali; or, an Account of the Gypsies of Spain"; "The Life, Journal, and Correspondence of Samuel Pepys . . . including a Narrative of his Voyage to Tangier"; and "Memoirs of the Life of Warren Hastings", compiled by G. R. Gleig.

[5] The threat of war with America over the long-vexed Canadian boundary question. Relations had been particularly strained since Dec 37 owing to the affair of the *Caroline*, an American ship carrying guns and supplies to the Canadian rebels, which had been attacked by a party of Canadian volunteers while anchored on the American side of the Niagara River. (Marryat, while in Toronto Apr 38, did not improve matters by drinking the health of "those who cut out the *Caroline*"—for which "insolence" newspapers carried reports that he had been burnt in effigy, and all his procurable novels with him: see Florence Marryat, *Life and Letters of Captain Marryat*, 1872, II, 36–8.) Feelings had recently been further inflamed by the trial in New York (and acquittal 12 Oct 41) of Alexander

I find it so irksome, lying on the Sofa to write my weekly matter, that I dictate my correspondence,[1] but I hope you will be able, to make this letter out, and to recognize my whole heart in it, though my pen is wanting.

A gentleman of your name[2] called here two days ago. I hoped it was you, and was about writing to you in Cecil Street, where the unknown gave his address, when your letter undeceived me.[3]

My dear Sir | Faithfully yours
CHARLES DICKENS

## To JOHN FORSTER, [22 OCTOBER 1841]

Extract in F, II, ix, 169. *Date:* written in his sickroom on 22 Oct according to Forster.

I hope I shan't leave off any more, now, until I have finished *Barnaby*.

## To JOHN OVERS, 22 OCTOBER 1841*

MS Morgan Library.

Devonshire Terrace | Twenty Second October 1841.
Dear Mr. Overs.

I find it such a very slow process to be obliged to write, lying on the sofa,

McLeod for the murder of a member of the *Caroline*'s crew. An anti-American article in *The Times*, 12 Oct, was headed "Our relations with the United States, and the manner of making war, if war be the unhappy result of our present negotiations". The *Morning Chronicle*, 18 Oct, contained a report that armed associations of Americans were ready to make incursions into Canada.

[1] The whole letter, including the signature, is in Catherine's hand.

[2] Macvey Napier (*d.* 1893), son of the elder Napier, and editor of his correspondence, 1879. On learning that CD and his father had met in Edinburgh, he had "expressed a great desire to *see* [CD], presuming on his having, as he said, danced *jigs* or *other things* with Mrs. D. when at School" (Napier *to* CD, 26 Oct 41: see below).

[3] Napier replied at length from Edinburgh on 26 Oct, devoting 12 out of 14 pages to sympathy with CD's sufferings and to advice: he had had the same operation himself three times (twice "bungled", the third time successfully), and his "flesh still [crept] at the recollection". He warned CD against ever

sitting on "*stone* or *turf*", urged him to use a sofa not a chair for many months ahead, advised "careful ablution, with cold water, at least thrice a day", and strongly urged that he should postpone his voyage to America until the following summer at earliest. CD might laugh at "this long, perhaps impertinent piece of old aunt like sermonizing", but Napier hoped it would also show him the "strong interest" he had in his welfare. He went on: "I shall say nothing of the promised Article, save that I shall hope you will go on with it, if you should find reason to make any change in your plans . . . and shall be quite satisfied if you could be ready by March for the April Number. . . . I think it would not do you any harm to be known as an *occasional* Contributor to the Review; and I shall hope for the time when you shall in reality appear in that character. By the way, supposing you should go to America, could not you turn the visit so far to account, as to write an Article or two, on some detached American subject—manners, literary habits &c. &c." (MS Huntington).

that I have not been able to read your papers yet. Defer your visit, therefore, until you hear from me again.

I am recovering with the greatest possible rapidity, thank God; and already go out for a drive every day.

Faithfully Yours

Mr. Overs.                                                              CHARLES DICKENS

## *To* JOHN OVERS, 22 OCTOBER 1841*

MS Morgan Library.

Devonshire Terrace<br>Friday Night Twenty Second October | 1841

Dear Mr. Overs.

I have had your letter read to me,[1] and I have read it myself; and I strongly disapprove of it, for three reasons.

In the first place, I think it rather inconsiderate to address three sides of foolscap, on such a subject, to a gentleman who receives three or four score letters every day, and has every moment of his time occupied by important business.

In the second place, I think you seem to vaunt your independence too much, and to flourish it rather unnecessarily in the eyes of a stranger; who might be apt to think (*being* a stranger to you) that a stream so very noisy is not very deep.

In the third place, I consider—even I—that the whole of that paragraph about the wives and children, and the wet and cold, is presumptuous and impertinent. You have no right to constitute yourself a judge of the regulations which Mr. Macready—for the security of his property, and the comfort of those about him when the Theatre is open—sees fit to establish.[2] That they are contrary to the custom of a place, bankrupt for many years—the lounge of vagabonds—and chosen resort of the worst hangers-on to the very worst haunts—is extremely possible. I hope they are, or Mr. Macready would not be the friend of mine he is.

I write to you directly, because it seems to me that tomorrow being Saturday, you have a very plain course to take. Nothing is easier than to tell Mr. Bryden[3] the post does not suit you—and that you wish to leave the Theatre, as soon as your services can be dispensed with.

I distinctly recognize, and always do in the case of every person about me, the right of every man to do his best for himself. I do not therefore quarrel with you at all for leaving this situation, but I do not hesitate to tell you that your letter is in execrable taste, and not at all becoming. This

---

[1] Clearly a letter from Overs to Macready, sent first to CD for his approval.

[2] In his reorganization of Drury Lane, Macready was screening off the saloon for the use of "the respectable frequenters of the Theatre" (see *To* Macready, 29 Sep, *fn*; also 28 Dec and *fn*).

[3] CD's mis-spelling, apparently, of Brydone (see ?23 May 40, *fn*).

is so obvious to my sense of what is right and proper, that I look upon it as a fact, and not a matter of opinion.

It is so much a custom with me to try to understand what people *think* when they are talking to me, that I saw in five minutes the other night (and said when you had left me) that you would not stay at the Theatre a month. I am therefore not at all surprised at your decision. But I am a little surprised at your working your ideas of Mr. Macready's character out of the wretched materials presented to your view, which would be well enough in a man who could neither read nor write, but is quite beneath you.

Faithfully Yours<br>CHARLES DICKENS

## *To* MRS GEORGE HOGARTH, 24 OCTOBER 1841

Photograph New York Public Library. *Address:* Mrs. Hogarth.

Devonshire Terrace<br>Sunday October Twenty Fourth 1841.

My Dear Mrs. Hogarth.

For God's sake be comforted, and bear this well, for the love of your remaining children.[1]

I had always intended to keep poor Mary's grave for us and our dear children, and for you. But if it will be any comfort to you to have poor George buried there, I will cheerfully arrange to place the ground at your entire disposal. Do not consider me in any way. Consult only your own heart. Mine seems to tell me that as they both died so young and so suddenly, they ought both to be buried together.[2]

Try—do try—to think that they have but preceded you to happiness, and will meet you with joy in Heaven. There *is*[3] consolation in the knowledge that you have treasure there, and that while you live on earth, there are creatures among the Angels, who owed their being to you.

Always Yours with true affection<br>CHARLES DICKENS

## *To* FREDERICK SALMON, 25 OCTOBER 1841

Extract in Parke-Bernet Galleries catalogue, 17 Nov 1953; dated 25 Oct 41.

I don't wait[4] to beg your acceptance of the enclosed, until you [finally][5] dismiss me, because I don't want to give any appearance of ceremony[4] to

---

[1] Mrs Hogarth's son, George Thomson Hogarth (*b.* 26 Apr 1821), had died suddenly in London on 24 Oct.

[2] George Hogarth was buried in Mary's grave—as were their father and mother.

[3] Underlined twice.

[4] Same extract in N, also from a catalogue source, reads (surely mistakenly) "write" for "wait", "crowing" for "ceremony".

[5] N's reading, which seems likelier than catalogue's "formally".

what is a spontaneous and most heartfelt emotion—though a very poor token—of gratitude. Put these books[1] upon some spare shelf for my sake—and let it be upon some shelf which has room for all I may write hereafter ... You once told me that Mrs. Salmon laughed too much at my books. I hope she will find some passages in the Old Curiosity Shop to make her cry,—without making her less happy or less charitable than they found her.


## *To* JOHN OVERS, [?25 OCTOBER 1841]

Mention in *To* Mrs Macready, ?25 Oct.


## *To* WILLIAM [BRYDONE],[2] [?25 OCTOBER 1841]*

MS Morgan Library. *Date:* presumably the Monday after CD had advised Overs to call on Brydone (see 22 Oct).

Devonshire Terrace. | Monday

My Dear Sir

I have told Mr. Overs—that is,[3] the person's name—to call on you at the *Theatre* tomorrow, at one. I am not sure whether I ought to have said the Theatre, or your house.

Faithfully Yours

William Bryden Esquire        CHARLES DICKENS


## *To* MRS MACREADY [?25 OCTOBER 1841]*

MS Morgan Library. *Date:* clearly same day as last.

Devonshire Terrace. | Monday Evening | ½ past 9.

My Dear Mrs. Macready

I have only this moment come home; having been out, all day. I wrote to Mr. Overs this morning—in consequence of what Mr. Bryden sd. to me last night—appointing him to be at the Theatre tomorrow at *One*. I also wrote to Mr. Bryden, telling him that I had done so. He lives in the remotest fastnesses of Islington, and I fear (as he will be long 'ere this in bed) it is too late to alter this state of things for the better.

My heartiest regards to all<br>Faithfully Yours ever<br>C.D.

---

[1] Inscribed copies of *Pickwick, Nickleby, Oliver,* 1841 (now in the Widener Collection, Harvard), and *Master Humphrey,* Vols I and II, bound in one vol. (Parke-Bernet Galleries catalogue, 4 Jan 1940).

[2] See 23 May 40, *fn.*

[3] Thus in MS.

## *To* JOHN FORSTER, [25 OCTOBER 1841]

Extract in F, III, i, 198. *Date:* 25 Oct according to Forster.

As no steps had been taken towards the funeral, I thought it best at once to bestir myself; and not even you could have saved my going to the cemetery. It is a great trial to me to give up Mary's grave; greater than I can possibly express. I thought of moving her to the catacombs, and saying nothing about it; but then I remembered that the poor old lady[1] is buried next her at her own desire, and could not find it in my heart, directly she is laid in the earth, to take her grandchild away. The desire to be buried next her is as strong upon me now, as it was five years ago; and I *know* (for I don't think there ever was love like that I bear her) that it will never diminish. I fear I can do nothing. Do you think I can? They would move her on Wednesday, if I resolved to have it done. I cannot bear the thought of being excluded from her dust; and yet I feel that her brothers and sisters, and her mother, have a better right than I to be placed beside her. It is but an idea. I neither think nor hope (God forbid) that our spirits would ever mingle *there*. I ought to get the better of it, but it is very hard. I never contemplated this—and coming so suddenly, and after being ill, it disturbs me more than it ought. It seems like losing her a second time.

## *To* JOHN FORSTER, [26 OCTOBER 1841]

Extract in F, III, i, 199. *Date:* the morning after last, according to Forster.

No, I tried that. No,[2] there is no ground on either side to be had. I must give it up. I shall drive over there, please God, on Thursday morning, before they get there; and look at her coffin.

## *To* JOHN FORSTER, [?OCTOBER 1841]

Extract in F, IX, i, 720. *Date:* written, says Forster, when CD "was under the greatest trial of his life, and illness and sorrow were contending for the mastery over him". The only time in CD's life when illness, sorrow, and the writing of a novel coincided seems to have been Oct 41.[3]

Of my distress I will say no more than that it has borne a terrible,

---

[1] Mrs George Thomson, Mrs Hogarth's mother (see Vol. 1, p. 134*n*), who had died on 13 Oct at her home, 7 Pelham Place, Brompton (not while on a visit to the Hogarths, as in F, III, i, 198). For the epitaph CD wrote for her tombstone, see 26 Nov, *fn*.

[2] This second "No" seems stylistically Forster's. Cf. the repetition of negatives in his version of letter of 6 or 13 Oct 38 (Vol. 1, p. 441 and *n*).

[3] Touched then "to the depths of the greatest sorrow of his life" (i.e. Mary Hogarth's death in 1837), he suffered "more than he let any one perceive, and was obliged again to keep his room for some days", says Forster (F, III, i, 198 and 199). Cf. reference to his illness as well as distress in *To* Forster, 25 Oct. This letter may be another part of *To* Forster, 26 Oct.

frightful, horrible proportion to the quickness of the gifts you remind me of. But may I not be forgiven for thinking it a wonderful testimony to my being made for my art, that when, in the midst of this trouble and pain, I sit down to my book, some beneficent power shows it all to me, and tempts me to be interested, and I don't invent it—really do not—*but see it*, and write it down.[1] ... It is only when it all fades away and is gone, that I begin to suspect that its momentary relief has cost me something.

## *To* MISS BURDETT COUTTS, 27 OCTOBER 1841

MS Morgan Library.

Devonshire Terrace. | Twenty Seventh October 1841.
Dear Miss Coutts.

Let me thank you for your kind recollection of me, yesterday. I was greatly pleased to hear from you once more, I assure you.[2]

I should have called in Stratton Street immediately on my return to town, but I have been exceedingly unwell. It is scarcely three weeks, since I was obliged to submit to a painful surgical operation (for which agreeable change I left the seaside) and although I have recovered with a rapidity whereat the Doctors are astounded, I have only just begun to feel my legs at all steady under my diminished weight. I almost thought, at first, that I was about to go through life on Two pillars of jelly, or tremulous Italian cream,—but I am happy to say that I am again conscious of floors and pavements.

They tell me that in two or three days I may go to Windsor, and set up for myself as one who has no need of the Faculty. I shall not be there, I

[1] Forster quotes this extract in Vol. III of the *Life* (1874), in his indignant and scornful attack on G. H. Lewes's article "Dickens in Relation to Criticism" in the *Fortnightly Review*, Feb 1872. Lewes had dwelt at length on the defects in CD's work apparent to "fastidious" and "cultivated" minds, and satisfied himself that the explanation of the vividness and power of CD's imagination lay in "the phenomena of hallucination". CD had once told him, he declared, "that every word said by his characters was distinctly *heard* by him". Forster caps this with the extract above, but insists that "all writers of genius to whom their art has become as a second nature, will be found capable of doing upon occasion what the vulgar may think to be 'hallucination', but hallucination will never account for" (and he instances Scott writing *The Bride of Lammermoor*). "The vulgar" was Forster's retaliation for the sneers of Lewes, whose "drift"—a comparison of CD with George Eliot, exemplar of the novelist with a cultivated mind—he saw clearly.

[2] Miss Coutts had written on 26 Oct: "Will you do me the favour to accept of the Game which accompanies this.— Should you ever be passing any where near Roehampton, I hope you will pay me a visit as I have a house there for a short time & I so much wish to ask you what you intend to do during the next year, for I assure you we have been much discomposed since your Address appeared in Barnaby Rudge; however we may regret, though, this cessation of our usual pleasure, I hope your excursion will be attended with all the gratification you anticipate" (MS Huntington).

hope, more than a fortnight at the utmost, and on my return I shall be only too well pleased to present myself at Roehampton, or, if you should have left there, at your house in town. I defer all particulars about America, until then.

Some friends in Yorkshire[1] have sent me a raven, before whom *the* Raven (the dead one) sinks into insignificance. He can say anything—and he has a power of swallowing door-keys and reproducing them at pleasure, which fills all beholders with mingled sensations of horror and satisfaction —if I may [say] so;[2] with a kind of awful delight. His infancy and youth have been passed at a country public house, and I am told that the sight of a drunken man calls forth his utmost powers. My groom is unfortunately sober, and I have had no opportunity of testing this effect,—but I have told him to "provide himself" elsewhere, and am looking out for another who can have a dissolute character from his last master.

With best regards to Miss Meredith, I am always Dear Miss Coutts

Most Faithfully Yours

CHARLES DICKENS

## *To* JOHN OVERS, 27 OCTOBER 1841*

MS Morgan Library.

Devonshire Terrace. | Twenty Seventh October 1841.

Dear Mr. Overs.

There can be no doubt that you should send *all* the songs to Mr. Tait.[3] I shall do nothing with February.[4]

Mr. Cruikshank called here on Sunday to say that your paper[5] could not appear next month (on account of press of matter) but that it would certainly be published in the No. following, and that he would send the money for it here, as though it appeared now. When he does so, it shall be forwarded to you. It is open to you, of course, to send any other papers there, you may think likely to suit the Omnibus.[6]

---

[1] The Smithsons.

[2] MS reads "if I may so".

[3] William Tait (1793–1864; *DNB*), publisher; founder and first editor (from 1834 co-editor with Mrs C. I. Johnstone) of *Tait's Edinburgh Magazine* (1832–61)—a magazine, wrote William Blackwood (2 Sep 33), "by way of rival to mine, . . . as much Radical as we are Tory" (Mrs Oliphant, *William Blackwood and his Sons*, II, 109). His contributors included Leigh Hunt, Harriet Martineau, J. S. Mill, Cobden and Bright, as well as the Tory De Quincey. A well-known Edinburgh figure, his shop was a meeting-ground for men of letters.

[4] Overs's 12 "Songs of the Months" appeared in *Tait's Edinburgh Magazine*, Jan–Dec 42. "The Song of February" (IX, 74–5), two 20-line stanzas, begins:
"Weave, weave me a chaplet that's
    meet for my tears.
Woe is me—woe is me—woe is me!
Weave, weave me a chaplet. The
    Vernal sprite hears:
The snow-drop, the crocus, the
    starwort appears . . ."

[5] "The Postilion" (see 8 Aug, *fn*).

[6] No others were published in *Cruikshank's Omnibus*.

I cannot read the inclosed, being ordered out of town in a few days, and having my attention engaged by a severe affliction in Mrs. Dickens's family. You had better, in future, consult your own judgment.

Faithfully Yours

Mr. J. A. Overs.                                    CHARLES DICKENS

## *To* C. HUNTON,[1] 27 OCTOBER 1841*

MS Chicago Historical Society.

1 Devonshire Terrace | York Gate Regents Park
Twenty Seventh October 1841.

My Dear Sir

The basket of game (No. 2)[2] arrived safely. I assure you I enjoyed it heartily; and that I am very much obliged to you.

I am happy to say that I am greatly better, and have the appetite of a mountaineer, with the spirits that usually belong to me.

With many thanks to you, I am Dear Sir

Faithfully Yours

C. Hunton Esquire.                                 CHARLES DICKENS

## *To* MRS HURNALL, 27 OCTOBER 1841

Mention in Sotheby's catalogue, Mar 1903; *MS*[3] 2 pp.; dated 1 Devonshire Terrace, 27 Oct 41.

*Containing an amusing reference to the numerous applications he receives for a lock of hair.*[4]

## *To* DANIEL MACLISE, 28 OCTOBER 1841

Mention in Sotheby's catalogue, July 1950; dated 28 Oct 41.

---

[1] Unidentified.

[2] On 21 Oct Catherine had written to Hunton: "Dear Sir. I am requested by Mr. Dickens, to thank you very much for the basket of game you had the kindness to send, and to say, in reply to your note that he will be *exceedingly glad* to 'hear from you again'. Mr. Dickens begs me to add that he is recovering with great rapidity, and that he would have written to you himself but that he is still obliged to be on the Sofa and finding it no very easy matter to use his pen in that position (though he is obliged to do so several hours a day) deputes his correspondence to me" (MS Chicago Historical Society).

[3] In a "female" hand, but signed by CD, according to catalogue.

[4] Cf. *To* Lester, 19 July 40 and *fn.*

## *To* THOMAS MITTON, 29 OCTOBER [1841]*

MS University of Texas. *Date:* clearly 1841 since concerned with the visit to America; handwriting supports. *Address:* Wait. | Thomas Mitton Esquire | 23 Southampton Buildings.

Devonshire Terrace. | Friday October Twenty Nine

My Dear Mitton

The Britannia southern charge is very preposterous in its proportion to the Northern; and comes, I suppose, of their scrambling way of doing business. There is no help for it, of course.[1] I should like the Board to know that I shall not be away more than six months altogether—and not South of New York for more than eight weeks. With regard to the Medical officers it will be best to say that I am going out of town—that I shall be back in the course of November—and that I will wait on them when I return.

I have been thinking about the Argus Policy. It will certainly be necessary for *my*[2] protection (not Smithson's; I am not particular about that;) that you shod. pay the extra rates. I am sorry to put you to the expence,—but you must look upon it as a consequence of purchasing the business,[3]—and make the best of it.

Going into the city every morning plays the Deuce with my work. I *hope* to be ordered off to Windsor, about next Monday week. Before then I will call upon you; and I will write to you the day before I do so.

Faithfully Yours

CD.

## *To* JOHN HUDSON, 30 OCTOBER 1841

MS Mr H. E. Quick.

1 Devonshire Terrace | York Gate Regents Park.
October The Thirtieth 1841.

Sir.

In answer to your obliging enquiries, I beg to tell you that I have, for the last three weeks, been confined to a sofa and a carriage; having undergone a surgical operation, which rendered those restrictions necessary in its after-treatment.

---

[1] On 4 Jan 42 CD's original Britannia policy (MS Mr C. C. Dickens) was endorsed, to cover his American visit: "In consequence of the additional premium of Thirty pounds paid this day, it is hereby agreed that the within named Charles Dickens, shall be at liberty to proceed to and reside in any part or parts of British North America, or the United States of North America not further South than Charleston in South Carolina, for a term not exceeding Twelve Calendar Months".

[2] Underlined three times.

[3] For business disagreements between Smithson and Mitton see *To* Mitton, 16 June 40.

If no wars or rumours of wars,[1] occur to prevent me, I am going, in January, to America for Six Months. I need scarcely add that I am going for any other reason than on account of illness, as Doctors do not commonly recommend sick people to make a voyage across the Atlantic, in the severest season of the year.

I shall be happy to receive the Pheasants you speak of—and to eat them with the appetite of a Hunter.

Faithfully Yours

Mr. John Hudson.                                        CHARLES DICKENS

### *To* JOHN FORSTER, [2 NOVEMBER 1841]

Summary in F, III, i, 199. *Date:* 2 Nov according to Forster.

*Reporting himself as progressing and ordered to Richmond.*[2]

### *To* JOSEPH LUNN,[3] 2 NOVEMBER 1841*

MS Huntington Library.

1 Devonshire Terrace | York Gate Regents Park<br>Second November 1841.

My Dear Sir.

Three weeks ago last Friday, I was obliged to submit to a painful operation, and I have been confined to a sofa and a carriage ever since.

I am now, thank God, going out of town for a little change of air; having made a very quick and famous recovery. In Three Weeks I shall be at home again. Directly I return, I will not fail to write to you, and appoint an hour for seeing you.

If, in the meanwhile, you should desire to write me, I shall be very happy to hear from you, and to pay immediate attention to your letter. Address to me here, and it will be forwarded without loss of time.

Faithfully Yours

Joseph Lunn Esquire.                            CHARLES DICKENS

---

[1] Cf. *To* Napier, 21 Oct 41 and *fn.*

[2] Forster adds that after a week or so at Richmond, CD, with Catherine and her sister Georgina, moved on to the White Hart at Windsor, where Forster joined them for a few days. But he is mistaken: CD spent the entire fortnight 6–20 Nov at Windsor.

[3] Joseph Lunn (1784–1863; *DNB*), dramatist. Wrote comedies and farces, mainly, many of them published in contemporary collections of plays; also adapted several plays from the French. An original member of the Dramatic Authors' Society. N misreads his name "Gunn", both here and in letters of 15 and 22 Nov.

## *To* GEORGE FLETCHER,[1] 2 NOVEMBER 1841*

MS University of Texas.

Private                                    1 Devonshire Terrace | York Gate Regents Park
                                                    Second November, 1841.
Sir.

It is no less painful to me to refuse, than it is to you to ask. Let me do so, briefly.

Nearly every day of my life, I receive letters akin to that which you have sent me. My inclination is, God knows, never to send an applicant away, empty-handed. But if I were the richest man in England, I should have to disappoint, almost as often as I helped. Judge then, being what I am, how frequently I am forced to hold my hand.

Fame's Trumpet should blow a little more of the wealth arising from the circulation of my works, into the Booksellers' pockets, and less into my own.[2] With a hundred claims upon my superfluity, I cannot render more than sympathy to such a case as yours. *If I could, I would.*

Mr. George Fletcher.                                      CHARLES DICKENS


## *To* W. C. MACREADY, 3 NOVEMBER 1841*

MS Morgan Library.

                                          Devonshire Terrace. | Third November 1841
My Dear Macready

Salmon don't agree with me—by which I mean that the Surgeon of that name, orders me to Windsor next Saturday, and won't let me dine with you on Sunday; objecting to chairs for another week; and laying stress on sofas. What can I do but say with the good Mussulmen—"to hear is to obey? Upon my (not exactly, eyes, but you can supply the term) be it."

You know that there are not many things I have a greater delight in than your society. So I will not add another word.

I was at Nina Sforza the other night—in spirit.[3]

                                                    Affectionately Yours Ever
                                                                      CD.

[1] Probably George Fletcher, of Birmingham, author of *The Provincialist: a Series of Tales, Essays, and Stanzas*, Birmingham, 1857—whom in 1843 and 1858 CD thanked for books he had sent.

[2] I.e. common report should make clear how much went into his publishers' pockets, how little into his own. CD used the same image rather differently in his speech at Hartford, 7 Feb 42. He did not see, he confessed, "why fame, besides playing that delightful *reveille* for which she is so justly celebrated, should not blow out of her trumpet a few notes of a different kind from those with which she [had] hitherto contented herself" (*Speeches*, ed. K. J. Fielding, p. 25).

[3] Zouch Troughton's tragedy *Nina Sforza* was first performed at the Haymarket on 1 Nov. See *To* Macready, 23 Nov and *fn*.

## *To* JOHN LANDSEER,[1] 5 NOVEMBER 1841

MS Victoria & Albert Museum.

1 Devonshire Terrace | York Gate Regents Park
Fifth November 1841.

My Dear Sir.

Let me thank you, both for your call and your note—and let me add that it affords me real pleasure to communicate with you in any way.

You are quite right in considering it very remarkable and worthy of notice, that Wilkes should have been the active magistrate in the suppression of the Gordon Riots.[2] I determined however, after some consideration, not to notice it in Barnaby, for this reason.—It is almost indispensable in a work of fiction that the characters who bring the catastrophes about, and play important parts, should belong to the Machinery of the Tale,—and the introduction towards the end of a story where there is always a great deal to do, of new actors until then unheard of, is a thing to be avoided, if possible, in every case. Now, if I had talked about Wilkes, it would have been necessary for me to glance at his career and previous position[3] (for in that lies the singularity you speak of)[4]—and if I had stopped to do that, I should have stopped the riots which must go on to the end headlong, pell mell, or they lose their effect. I therefore resolved to defer that point, with some others of equal curiosity and interest, until the appearance of another Edition would afford me an opportunity of relating them in *Notes*, where they would not stem the current of the Tale, or embarrass the action.

I need not tell you who are so well acquainted with "Art" in all its

---

[1] John Landseer (1769–1852; *DNB*), painter, engraver and author; ARA, FSA; engraver to King William IV. Campaigned, unsuccessfully, for full recognition of the profession of engraving. Father of Thomas, Charles, and Edwin. According to W. P. Frith (*My Autobiography and Reminiscences*, 1887–1888, I, 60–1), on one occasion rebuked Edwin, then visiting teacher at the RA life school, for reading *Oliver Twist* ("some of Dickens's nonsense") in front of his pupils.

[2] John Wilkes (1727–97; *DNB*) was City Chamberlain and magistrate at the time of the riots. While other City magistrates were—as in *Barnaby*—timid and inactive, he forced Kennett, the Lord Mayor, to call out the armed inhabitants of the Wards; raised his own patrols; helped to defend the Bank of England, killing two rioters himself; dispersed a large mob in Fleet Street; and examined prisoners in the Guildhall, committing the publisher of two treasonable newspapers to prison. Many of these details CD could have read in *Letters . . . of John Wilkes, Addressed to his Daughter*, 1804, II, 212–14.

[3] After satirizing George III and the Govt in his *North Briton* 1762–3, Wilkes had been briefly imprisoned in the Tower for seditious libel 1763 and expelled from the House of Commons 1764. His subsequent arrest and committal to the King's Bench prison 1768 led to the gathering of a great mob to demand his release, and to the "massacre" of St George's Fields.

[4] The "singularity" or irony of Wilkes's actions during the riots was not lost on his old enemy Samuel Johnson, who wrote to Mrs Thrale on 12 June 1780: "Jack, who was always zealous for order and decency, declares, that if he be trusted with power, he will not leave a rioter alive" (*Letters of Samuel Johnson*, ed. R. W. Chapman, Oxford, 1952, II, 370).

forms, that in the description of such scenes, a broad, bold, hurried effect must be produced, or the reader instead of being forced and driven along by imaginary crowds will find himself dawdling very uncomfortably through the town, and greatly wondering what may be the matter. In this kind of work the object is,—not to tell everything, but to select the striking points and beat them into the page with a sledge-hammer. And herein lies the difficulty. No man in the crowd who was pressed and trodden here and there, saw Wilkes. No looker-on from a window at the struggle in the street, beheld an Individual, or anything but a great mass of magistrates, rioters, and soldiery, all mixed up together. Being always in one or other of these positions, my object has been to convey an idea of multitudes, violence, and fury; and even to lose my own dramatis personae in the throng, or only see them dimly, through the fire and smoke.

Until I received your second note last evening, I did not observe the slip of the pen to which it alluded. Even if I had done so, I should have understood, of course, what you had intended to write.

Believe me | My Dear Sir<br>Faithfully Yours

J. Landseer Esquire                                          CHARLES DICKENS

---

### *To* MR LOFT,[1] 6 NOVEMBER 1841

Mention in N, I, 361.

---

### *To* LORD JEFFREY, [?EARLY NOVEMBER 1841]

Mention in Jeffrey *to* CD, 26 [Nov 41]. *Date:* presumably shortly after receiving Jeffrey's letter of 4 Nov.[2]

---

[1] Perhaps of James Loft & Co., sculptors and plaster cast manufacturers, of Soho, to whom he had paid £3.4.0 in Oct 38 (see Vol. I, p. 644).

[2] Jeffrey had written from East India College, Hertford, on 4 Nov: "My Very Dear Dickens—Tho' my own health has been for many months, in a miserable, and, for a good part of the time, almost a *hopeless* state, I have been more moved than I can tell you, by hearing (very lately) of the severe and painful malady with which *You* have been afflicted—At my time of life, and with the many warnings which late years have furnished of my fragility, no intimation of mortality ought to give a great shock, either to myself, or my friends—My life's work is substantially concluded—and my course, of enjoyment or suffering—of error or innocence, pretty fairly over—But for *You* . . . to be struck down, or even for a time disabled by pain and infirmity, does strike me as a cruel, and almost unnatural dispensation—and I must tell you that I feel it the more, from having been in the habit, during my languid and suffering hours, of cheering my weary vigils, by images and recollections of your beaming and happy eye, boundless activity, and unspoiled domestic enjoyment. I trust however that the cloud has now passed finally away from that bright prospect— . . . But I cannot help most earnestly exhorting you to expose yourself to no shadow of risk, while you are *in any degree* tender or weak . . .—Your notice of a projected *Regina* [?*Royal Progress*] to America—came upon me by surprise, on opening a No. of Barnaby . . . and even yet, I have not got over the kind of

## *To* FREDERICK SALMON, 7 NOVEMBER 1841

MS Comtesse de Suzannet.

White Hart Hotel Windsor.
Sunday Seventh November 1841.

My Dear Salmon.

I don't know whether it was because I had caught my wife's cold; or because of my being weak, and having stood too long, finishing Barnaby;[1] but yesterday and the evening before, all manner of queer pains were floating about my illustrious person: now twitching at the calves of my legs—now sticking shadowy pins into the soles of my feet—now entertaining themselves with my knees—now (but not often) shooting through that region which you have made as tender as my heart—and now settling in the small of my back; but particularly favoring the back; and the calves before mentioned. I had an odd sort of nervousness about me besides, and if it had not fortunately been the day for coming down here, should have felt quite ill.[2] The change, however, did me a world of good in the first half hour. And this morning, this uneasiness has greatly abated, and I have taken a breakfast to which no pen can do justice. In a word, I feel *immeasurably better*.

I think it best, however, remembering your injunctions, to send my servant up with this, to know whether I shall come to you tomorrow, instead of Tuesday; or whether there is anything you wish me to do in the meanwhile. I parboiled my feet last night in hot water with plenty of salt in it, and rubbed my back with camphor liniment.

Don't mind how brief your answer is—and forgive my troubling you on your day of rest.

Always Faithfully Yours
Frederick Salmon Esquire                      CHARLES DICKENS

shock I received from it— . . . If it will not be much trouble to you, do let me have a line saying how you now are" (MS Huntington).

In Jeffrey's next letter, dated 4 Berkeley Street, Friday 26 [clearly Nov 41], he wrote: "A thousand thanks for your kind, cheerful, and sweet tempered letter—I have been here, in your neighbourhood, for a week. But my Doctors insist that I shall (substantially) see no visitors, but themselves—or at all events, only such as will engage to take *all the talk to themselves*—and leave me to enact the part of *Audience* only . . . As I *must* see you, you know, I hope you will not object to these conditions—which are anything but disagreeable to me—since I am always best pleased to play the hearer—

when it pleases you—(on compulsion or otherwise) to be the Speaker. . . . With kindest remembrances to Mrs. Dickens, who must have been sadly shocked by this sudden catastrophe of her brother—and all kinds of blessings and good wishes to you | Ever very Faithfully Yours" (MS Huntington).

[1] Presumably No. 87 (Ch. 81 and "Chapter the Last"), published 27 Nov.

[2] After finishing *Barnaby*, 5 Nov, CD probably went on to compose the Preface (published in the final No. of *Master Humphrey*, 4 Dec). His feeling ill would account for his asking Catherine's help: the MS is in her hand, except for the heading, "Ginevra" quotation (see *To* Rogers, Sep 40, *fn*), address, date, and a few minor alterations (Forster Collection, V & A).

## *To* JOHN FORSTER, [?13 NOVEMBER 1841]

Forster's summary of letter, made before destruction, with two words quoted, MS Victoria & Albert Museum (FC). *Date:* Nov 41 since "from Windsor" according to Forster; possibly "tomorrow" was Sun 14 Nov, when Forster and CD met (see Forster's answers to the Eagle Life Assurance Co.'s questions of 13 Nov, Appx, p. 494); "saner" probably referred to the Company's enquiry about the "mad story"—possibly made in a confidential letter of the same date (see *To* Mitton, 18 Nov).

*As to Insurance for America. Will be* sapient saner *tomorrow.*

## *To* JOSEPH LUNN, 15 NOVEMBER 1841

MS Huntington Library.

*Private.*[1]

Windsor | November Fifteenth 1841.

My Dear Sir.

Your note has but just now reached me. I hasten to answer it.

I long ago found it necessary and just, to lay down with reference to Chapman and Hall, this position:—"I am every day asked to recommend works to you, and sometimes I am, in a manner, forced to do so. Understand that whenever I introduce any writer to you (which I never will, save when I cannot help it) I leave you to your own unfettered discretion in the acceptance or rejection of his work. You will never displease me by consulting your own inclinations; and I never require you to follow mine".

They thanked me, and said they would act upon this understanding—which they have always done. Last summer I was very anxious that they should publish a novel by a young lady of considerable ability,[2] to whose book Mrs. Norton,[3] from a strong interest in her, would have put her name as Editress. They declined it, notwithstanding, and I was not offended.

I cannot therefore introduce the author of Jest and Earnest[4] to them, "in a manner which will induce them to purchase and publish his second work".[5] But I will introduce him and his desire, gladly. And I will add (which is perfectly true) that I think very highly of his little book.[6] Beyond this, I cannot go. I shall be in town on Saturday. If you will let me know by that time that your son has no objection to this mode of introduction, I will *say* all I can to them,—which is better than writing it.

Let me assure you, and your son, most unfeignedly that I write this with a real interest in the author of Jest and Earnest, and a real desire for

[1] Underlined twice.

[2] Unidentified.

[3] Mrs Caroline Norton (1808–77; *DNB*): see Vol. I, p. 302*n*.

[4] Joseph Lunn's son, William Arthur Brown Lunn (*d.* 1879), musician and miscellaneous writer. His *Jest and Earnest*, published anonymously by H. Cunningham, 1840, was reprinted, with other tales, in *Miscellanies; Consisting of*

*Jest and Earnest* . . ., 1851, under his own name. Author (under the pseudonym Arthur Wallbridge) of *The Sequential System of Musical Notation*, 1844.

[5] Presumably *Bizarre Fables*, published, under the pseudonym Arthur Wallbridge, by Orr & Co., 1842.

[6] It consisted of 20 slight social sketches, each with a pointed "moral" in the style of Æsop.

his success. These publishers, however, are not speculative or inclined to launch out upon ventures; and I have very little confidence in the weight of my recommendation. I have always found, as yet, that however much "the Trade" may care for my writings, they are by no means deferential to my opinion of other mens'[1]—indeed that they rather doubt, and look with distrust upon it; possibly having in their minds' eye, the example of Scott and *his* publishers.[2]

The Editor of the Albion,[3] is as cool a gentleman as I ever encountered. I owe to him and such as him[4] the having used my best endeavours to advance the passing of an International Copyright Bill on this side of the water—the being staved off, now that it *is* passed, with promises deferred, from day to day—and the exquisite justice of never deriving sixpence from an enormous American sale of all my books.[5]

Do not suppose that I am ignorant of your claims as a brother. I am

---

[1] Thus in MS.

[2] As partner in John Ballantyne and Company during the firm's existence 1809–13, Scott—easily misled by his own antiquarian interests—had backed such total failures as Jamieson's *An Historical Account of the Culdees of Iona*, Weber and Jamieson's *Northern Antiquities*, Grahame's *British Georgics*, Singer's *General View of the Agriculture . . . in the County of Dumfries*, Anna Seward's *Poetical Works* (in three vols), and the *Edinburgh Annual Register*. The unsold stock had to be cheaply disposed of to Constable or sold to Constable and Longmans as part of the condition of their publishing Scott's novels; and Constable is recorded as saying: "I like well Scott's *ain bairns*,—but heaven preserve me from those of his fathering!" (J. G. Lockhart, *Memoirs of the Life of Sir Walter Scott, Bart*, Edinburgh, 1837–8, II, 174).

[3] John Sherren Bartlett (1790–1863; *DAB*), an English naval surgeon who, after capture by the Americans during the Anglo-American War of 1812, settled in Boston 1814. Founded the *Albion, or British, Colonial, and Foreign Weekly Gazette* (a paper containing English news, designed "to preserve the peace and good understanding between the United States and Great Britain") in New York 1822; and edited it until 1848. In 1840 founded the *European*, a periodical printed in Liverpool and taken to America by the Cunard Line. Wrote pamphlets urging the introduction of Indian corn into England as a cheap food. For a short time in 1857 was Acting British Consul in Baltimore.

[4] The *Albion* had printed six of CD's first seven Sketches, without acknowledgment, between 29 Mar and 15 Nov 34. With the *New-Yorker*, which published "Horatio Sparkins" 29 Mar 34, acknowledging the *Monthly Magazine* as its source, it shared the distinction of being the first paper in America to pirate CD. (See *D*, xxxv [1938–9], 47; LV [1959], 55–6.)

[5] An "Act for securing to authors, in certain cases, the benefit of International Copyright" (prepared by Mr Poulett Thomson and Lord John Russell) had been passed in England July 38. It gave the author of a book first published in a foreign country copyright in the United Kingdom, provided that that country conferred similar privileges on English authors. Lack of American reciprocity was CD's main grievance in 1842. "England has done her part", he said at the Boston Dinner, 1 Feb 42, "and I am confident that the time is not far distant when America will do hers" (*Speeches*, ed. K. J. Fielding, p. 21). How CD had used his "best endeavours" to advance the Bill is not known. Perhaps he signed the petition from "Authors of published Books" of 11 May 38; or the petition from Lardner, Thomas Campbell, Saunders & Otley, and "Authors of several published works", of 21 May 38.

well acquainted with them, and happy, I assure you, to respond to them with all my heart.

Believe me | My Dear Sir | Faithfully Yours

J. Lunn[1] Esquire.                                          CHARLES DICKENS


## *To* [ANGUS FLETCHER], 16 NOVEMBER 1841

Text from unidentified bookseller's catalogue, Dickens House. *Address:* clearly to Angus Fletcher; in *To* Fred Dickens, 3 Jan 42, from Liverpool, CD reports Fletcher "here".

Windsor, 16 Nov., 1841

My dear F—

Here's a short note, but to the purpose. I thank God I am getting stout and hearty, and can walk about the Parks here like a giant with his seven-leaguers on, and eat like the same with his knife and fork in hand, and sleep like the same with a hogshead of old crusted under his waistcoat.

We shall be *delighted* to shake hands with you at Liverpool. We shall be there at the latest the morning before the packet sails, unless some change is made in the arrangements. She will sail on the 4th of January. I think it will be the Britannia, but whatever her name may be she will be the British and North American Mail Steamer.[2] Mind—at the Adelphi Hotel.

Kate's best regards—all well.

Faithfully yours always,<br>CHARLES DICKENS


## *To* JOHN MURRAY,[3] 17 NOVEMBER 1841*

MS Carl and Lily Pforzheimer Foundation.

Windsor | Seventeenth November 1841.

My Dear Sir.

Your kind note only reached me here, last night.

If I had been in town I am not quite sure that I should have had

---

[1] Misread as "Quinn" in "Additions to the Nonesuch Edition of Dickens' Letters", *Huntington Library Quarterly*, V (1941), 118.

[2] It was the *Britannia*. A wooden paddle-steamer of 1135 tons and 440 h.p., with engines by Robert Napier and accommodation for 115 passengers, she had made her maiden voyage to America in July 40, taking 14 days 8 hours, at an average speed of $8\frac{1}{2}$ knots and fuel consumption of 38 tons a day. The first of the four mail boats with which the Cunard Line originated, she was only the third English steamer to cross the Atlantic (following maiden-crossings in 1838 by the *Sirius* and Brunel's *Great Western*). Stanfield's drawing of her (engraved for the first cheap edn of *American Notes*, 1855) was in the Gad's Hill library at CD's death.

[3] John Murray III (1808–92; *DNB*): see Vol. I, p. 543*n*. His chief contribution to the firm, before succeeding his father in 1843, was probably the initiation of Murray's Handbooks for Travellers, of which he wrote the first four himself: *Holland, Belgium, and the Rhine*, 1836; *France; South Germany;* and *Switzerland*, 1837–38.

philosophy enough to deny myself the pleasure of dining with you—though I am advised to dine at home for another week or so. Therefore I console myself under this tardy receipt of your invitation with the reflection that "it's all for the best".

Believe me | Faithfully Yours

John Murray Esquire.            CHARLES DICKENS

## *To* GEORGE SHURY, 17 NOVEMBER 1841*

MS Free Library of Philadelphia. *Address:* Free | G. Shury Esquire | George Street | Euston Square | London.[1]

Windsor | Seventeenth November 1841.

Sir.

I beg to acknowledge the receipt of your letter. I am staying here for a few days, and it has been forwarded to me.

You will no doubt perceive that by this time I am *past* all further information on the subject of the Gordon Riots; and you will readily understand that in using them for purposes of fiction, it has been necessary—quite indispensable to the Progress of the Story—to reject many circumstances growing out of them, though in themselves sufficiently amusing and characteristic. Your anecdotes are of this kind; but I am not the less obliged to you for doing me the favor to communicate them, or less entertained by the story of the chimney-sweeper, which is very quaint and whimsical.

Pray accept my thanks; both on this score, and for the obliging tenor of your expressions.

Faithfully Yours

G. Shury Esquire.            CHARLES DICKENS

## *To* [?JOHN] DE GEX,[2] 18 NOVEMBER 1841*

MS Eastgate House, Rochester. *Address:* probably John De Gex, of whom CD saw more than of his brother Edward;[3] but he was friendly with both.

White Hart Windsor. | Eighteenth November 1841.

My Dear De Gex.

Where on earth were[4] you and Frank[5] today.—I had a dinner ready, the

---

[1] At this address 1835–46.

[2] John Peter de Gex (1809–87), barrister of Lincoln's Inn; called to the Bar 1835; QC and Bencher of his Inn 1865; Treasurer and knighted 1882. In addition to an extensive bankruptcy practice, published many volumes of reports on cases in bankruptcy and in Chancery. CD had probably met him and his brothers through the Rosses.

[3] Edward Peter De Gex (1812–79);

after the death of his father (see Vol. 1, p. 325*n*) 1838, carried on the business at the Prince of Wales Hotel, 10 Leicester Place, with his mother until 1845. Admitted a solicitor 1851, and became partner (1852) in the firm Austen & De Gex, solicitors, of 4 Raymond Buildings, Gray's Inn.

[4] MS reads "where".

[5] Probably Frank Ross (see *To* Ross, 1 Dec).

particulars of which would madden you both. We return to Town on Saturday.[1]


## *To* THOMAS MITTON, 18 NOVEMBER 1841

MS Huntington Library.

White Hart—Windsor | Eighteenth November 1841.

My Dear Mitton

You will be very glad, I am certain, to hear that they have insured me at the Eagle for £5,000 at the ordinary Rate.[2] They were very particular in requiring an emphatic contradiction of the mad story,[3] but they stuck at nothing else—having Salmon's report, of course.

You cannot think what a comfort this is to my mind, or, if I *should* get into any danger in my Travels, how pleasant it will be to reflect that my darlings are well provided for.

I shall see you on Monday.

Always Faithfully Yours

Thomas Mitton Esquire.                               CHARLES DICKENS


## *To* DANIEL MACLISE, [18] NOVEMBER 1841*

MS Mr Horace G. Commin. *Date:* 19 Nov 41 was Friday; presumably CD was writing on Thurs 18th, or he would have said "We come home to-morrow".

White Hart, Windsor<br>Thursday Nineteenth November 1841.

My Dear Mac.

We come home on Saturday. Dine with us on Sunday at five, and behold the once more vigorous, hearty, blooming, grateful,

Boz.

Daniel Maclise Esquire

R. A.[4]

---

[1] End of letter missing.

[2] CD had given Forster as a reference. For Forster's answers to the Eagle Life Assurance Company's questions, see Appx, pp. 494–5.

[3] See *To* Forster, 6 Sep 40. Since mental health was not specifically mentioned in the Company's printed enquiry, presumably the secretary, H. P. Smith, accompanied it with a confidential letter.

[4] Written very large, clearly as a joke. Perhaps connected with the Art Union Exhibition at the Suffolk Street Gallery at which Maclise, who had won the highest Art Union prize of the year, exhibited his prize-winning picture, *The Sleeping Beauty*. In the first of two notices of the Exhibition in *Punch* (12 Sep 41), Maclise is referred to throughout as "D. Maclise, R.A.", obviously sarcastically, and visitors to the Exhibition are warned against supposing that the highest prize had "commanded the best picture".

## *To* JOSEPH LUNN, 22 NOVEMBER 1841

Extract in Maggs Bros catalogue No. 399 (1920); *MS* 1 p.; dated Devonshire Terrace, 22 Nov 41.

I shall see Chapman & Hall tomorrow, and will write to you in the evening.

## *To* MESSRS LEA & BLANCHARD, 23 NOVEMBER 1841

MS Messrs Lea & Febiger.

> 1 Devonshire Terrace. | York Gate Regents Park.
> Tuesday November Twenty Third | 1841.

Dear Sirs.

I have had the pleasure of receiving your welcome letter of the Thirtieth of last month—and thank you cordially for its obliging tenor.

I shall only be six months in America, altogether; and my present purpose is to land at Boston: go from thence to New York; and thence into the South. Of course I shall visit Philadelphia at some time or other in the half year; and when I do, I shall not fail to see you immediately. It is scarcely possible until one is on your side of the Atlantic, to be at all certain as to dates and seasons; but as soon as I arrive, and have shaped my course minutely, I will write to you again.

In the meanwhile, accept my thanks for your polite attention; and the assurance that I am

> Dear Sirs | Faithfully Yours

Messrs. Lea and Blanchard.                                    CHARLES DICKENS

## *To* THE COUNTESS OF BLESSINGTON, 23 NOVEMBER 1841\*

MS Benoliel Collection.

> Devonshire Terrace.
> Twenty Third November 1841.

My Dear Lady Blessington.

If a very distressing illness from which I am but just now recovering, and the preparations for my half year's expedition to America, leave me but two mornings to devote to your service, believe me that I *will* redeem my pledge.[1] Indeed I should have done so by this time, but the Surgeon's knife is a bad sharpener of the pen; and I have been acutely nibbed, I do assure you.

Whether I appear before you with a contrite heart and a sorrowful face, or in the modest triumph of having been as good as my word, I shall see

---

[1] To write something for her *Book of Beauty* or *Keepsake* (see 16 Apr 40 and 2 June 41); a promise not kept until July 43.

you, please God, between this and Christmas.[1] At the worst, I hope I shall not come *quite* empty-handed.

I should have answered your note before, but I have been at Windsor for change of air, and have but just returned.[2]

Believe me | Dear Lady Blessington

Faithfully Yours

The | Countess of Blessington                                        CHARLES DICKENS

## *To* JOHN BRADFORD,[3] 23 NOVEMBER 1841

Extracts from American Art Association and Anderson Galleries catalogue No. 3976, Carnegie Book Shop catalogue No. 36 (*aa*) and N, I, 363; *MS* 2 pp.; dated 1 Devonshire Terrace, 23 Nov 41.

I have read your little book.[4] . . . It has pleased me very much*ᵃ*—very much—and does you infinite credit.*ᵃ* . . . I entertain a very strong objection to seeing my opinion of any Book in print, as it does seem a kind of presumption and a dictating to people's taste. It is my invariable custom to request that any communication of this nature may be considered private.[5]

---

[1] He visited Gore House at least once in December. On 11 Dec D'Orsay wrote: "My Dear Dickens | I am so dissatisfied with the Sketch I have made of you [*when is not known*], that I am most anxious to try my pencil again— Knowing how busily occupied your Mornings are, it will perhaps be more convenient to you, and certainly more agreeable to us, if you will name a day to dine at Gore House.—I have set my heart on giving the representation of the outside of a head, the inside of which, has furnished delight to countless Thousands so you must forgive me if I take up so much of your time— | I have just received some warm Neck wrappery from Paris. Will you accept the one I send which may when you are pacing the deck when crossing the Atlantic remind you of your affectionate & sincere | A. D'Orsay | P.S. Name your day. I will ask Elliotson, Foster & Mac Clise [*both names thus*]" (MS Huntington). For CD's reply see *Addenda*, p. 497. On 13 Dec D'Orsay wrote: "Any day this week at two o'clock you will find me" (MS Huntington). CD sat for him on 16 Dec. For this portrait (dated), in profile looking to the left (like the majority of D'Orsay's portraits) and tinted, see F. G. Kitton,

*CD by Pen and Pencil*, I, facing p. 35).

[2] Lady Blessington had written on 17 Nov: "My dear Mr. Dickens | Will you pardon me if I venture to remind you of a promise, the fulfillment [*thus*] of which before you leave England, would confer a lasting sense of obligation on me. If I thought less highly of your writings, I should not thus torment you, so you must consider this letter as one of the many unpleasant results brought on you by a Genius of which no one is a more sincere admirer, than My dear Mr Dickens's | obliged | Marguerite Blessington" (MS Berg).

[3] John Bradford, of Pavilion Place, Newton Abbot; author of *Tales of the Moor*, 1841, and *Songs of Devon, and Miscellaneous Poems*, 1843, both published under the pseudonym Josias Homely; also of a novel, *Roger Whatmough's Will*, 1864.

[4] *Tales of the Moor*, two long stories interspersed with verses. "The chief object of these Tales", Bradford wrote in his Dedication, "is to inculcate principles of Christian charity and general benevolence."

[5] N and catalogues read "privately"; almost certainly through misreading CD's long final "e".

But I am not proof against your solicitation and the tone of your last note and cannot find it in my heart to lay upon you the injunction which my inclination leads me to impose. If you must, however, include my opinion ... do me the favor to say generally that I have expressed myself much pleased with your production, and do not quote me.[1]

## *To* JOHN OVERS, 23 NOVEMBER 1841*

MS Morgan Library.

Devonshire Terrace. | Twenty Third November 1841

Dear Mr. Overs.

I will tell you why the interest I had in you, has undergone a change. I need scarcely look for a better text than your last note, which informs me that you can much more easily imagine my having been unjust, irascible, and everything which you ought to know I am not, than you can entertain the idea of your having committed a fault.

I think in this, and in all you have written and done since I first mentioned you to Mr. Macready, you have shewn a deficiency of that moral sense which I believed you to possess; and that you have lost sight of your true position in regard to that gentleman, and all other gentlemen with whom you have come in contact.

I spoke of you to Mr. Macready (as you know) as one who was incapacitated by illness from pursuing his usual occupation, or devoting himself to any labour. Mr. Macready accordingly engaged you, in the only capacity about the Theatre, then unfilled, in which such a man *could* be employed. If I could have recommended you as a stage carpenter, you would have been engaged as one, and paid as one. If I could have recommended you as a scene painter, you would have entered the Theatre on the footing of a scene painter, and at a scene painter's pay. But you went there, emphatically a disabled man. Nobody supposed that you were to remain so all your life, but you went there invalided, and unfit for work. The first thing you do, before you have been there a fortnight, is to write a letter to Mr. Macready, measuring your salary, by that of the different artizans employed in the house, every man working at his own craft, and in the full possession of its cunning, such as it may be, and of his bodily powers!

Further than this, you ask me how I think Mr. Macready would like your situation. You take the case of a man who by long study, liberal education, incessant application and constant self denial, combined with divers physical and mental gifts, has raised himself, slowly and in the course of years, to the summit of an art in which very few attain to excellence. You set him beside yourself—measure, head to head, and heel to heel—and seem to recognize no difference between the two.

[1] CD's name heads the "Literary Patrons" at the end of the book, but his opinion of it was omitted.

This not being enough, you go on to lecture this gentleman—with certain flourishes of which I will say no more than that they were very preposterous—upon his government of his own establishment (of which you know nothing at all)—tell him plainly, that your feelings are much finer than his—and that he must get a less sensitive man to carry into effect his ogre-like commands. And in the very first instance you go to him with a kind of malice prepense; for not having seen Mr. Bryden in one or two calls, you write me like an ill-used, suffering person, in a tone which hurts and surprises me beyond expression. For I can remember the time, without any violent effort, when I, wanting employment in my path of life, had to call a dozen times upon a busy man,[1] and yet bore it with a Christian fortitude—though conscious of my own deserts, as most men are.

I have already told you (although you suppressed this Truth from Doctor Elliotson) that I distinctly recognize your right to leave the situation when you found it did not suit you. Your manner of leaving it, and your whole course of reflection upon the subject, is what I quarrel with; and it is this which leads me to the conclusion that Mr. Macready and Mr. Bryden treated you with a delicacy and a consideration which you did not deserve at their hands; and renders me very sorry that I ever recommended you.

Surely this same deficiency of which I have spoken, is apparent in your believing that my "zeal" for my friend, led me to write you a reproof which you had not merited.[2] You ought to know that zeal for my friend would have induced me to laugh at the whole business. It is not because I am anxious to defend Mr. Macready from *your* censures, that I am warm with you; but because your conduct has disappointed me, and has shewn me that you were not the sort of man I took you for. In anybody else the supposition that I was unjust because I was ill, or because I had a strong attachment to an intimate friend, would have been extremely insulting. Coming from you, it only confirms me in the impression that there is something wanting in you, which I believed you to possess.

As between you and me, it is no matter whether Mr. Macready had or had not the letter which you wrote. *I* had it, and you wrote it. That is enough.

I repeat, that in this matter I am disappointed in you. I am changed in no other respect. Disappointment, of course, slackens my zeal to serve ·you; but I still entertain the desire; and I would do so, if I had the opportunity.

                                        Faithfully Yours
Mr. J. A. Overs.                        CHARLES DICKENS

---

[1] Easthope, presumably (see Vol. I, pp. 149 and 196).   [2] See second letter of 22 Oct 41.

## *To* W. C. MACREADY, 23 NOVEMBER [1841]*

MS Morgan Library. *Date:* 23 Nov was Tuesday in 1841 and 1847; handwriting points unmistakably to 1841. *Address:* W. C. Macready Esquire | Clarence Terrace.

Devonshire Terrace. | Tuesday. November Twenty Third.

My Dear Macready.

Please to be an out and out villain, *to night*.[1]

Faithfully Yours always

W. C. Macready Esquire                          CHARLES DICKENS

## *To* HENRY VINCENT,[2] 23 NOVEMBER 1841

MS Widener Collection, Harvard.

Faithfully Yours<br>CHARLES DICKENS

1 Devonshire Terrace. | York Gate Regents Park.<br>Twenty Third November 1841.

Henry Vincent Esquire
With Mr. Charles Dickens' Compts.[3]

## *To* JOSEPH LUNN, 24 NOVEMBER 1841*

MS Free Library of Philadelphia.

Devonshire Terrace | Twenty Fourth November 1841.

My Dear Sir.

I have spoken to Chapman and Hall; and left them Jest and Earnest to look at. All I can do, I have done.

---

[1] When CD, who had missed the first night of *Nina Sforza* I (Nov), was to be present, in a private box (ticket sent with a note by Webster on 22 Nov: MS Huntington). Macready played the villain, Spinola—described by *Punch* (6 Nov) as "a regular thorough-paced *Mephistopheles* of the Surrey or Sadler's Wells genus". The *Examiner* (6 Nov) commented: "We never saw what may be called such *gusto* of the villainous"; and on the day after the performance of 23 Nov Macready recorded in his diary —far from pleased—a remark made by one of the audience: "That he was sure I should end my days on a scaffold!" (*Diaries*, II, 147).

[2] Henry Vincent (1813–78; *DNB*), Chartist. Had been sentenced to 12 months' imprisonment at Monmouth Assizes in Aug 39 for attending a "riotous assemblage" in Newport; and to another 12 months in Mar 40, following a rising designed to free him. Talfourd, who had prosecuted in both trials, presented a petition to the Commons, calling attention to the injustice being done him, and his "unspotted character"—which led to his release Jan 41. Contested Banbury as a Radical in July 41, Ipswich in 1842, and other constituencies 1843–52, but was never elected. Co-founder with Joseph Sturge of the Complete Suffrage Union 1842. Had great success, from 1841 until his death, as a public lecturer in both England and, later, America. If CD ever met him, it would doubtless have been through Talfourd.

[3] Written on a loose sheet of letterpaper, preserved in a copy of *The Pic Nic Papers*.

If your son will call upon them in the course of the week—say on Saturday—they will tell him, I have no doubt, at what conclusion they have arrived.

Pray make my compliments to him. And believe me

Faithfully Yours

J. Lunn Esquire.                                        CHARLES DICKENS


## *To* [EDWARD] JESSE,[1] 24 NOVEMBER 1841

Text from N, I, 364. *Address:* N gives christian name as "Edmund", clearly a mistake for Edward (see *fn*).

1 Devonshire Terrace, York Gate, Regents Park

November Twenty-Fourth 1841

My Dear Sir,

I have been very anxious to write you before, but my engagements have been rendered so very uncertain by a variety of avocations, that I have been disabled from communicating with you until now.

If to-morrow week will suit you, and the weather should be at all fine, we should be delighted to avail ourselves of your kind offer,[2] and to meet you at Hampton Court.

Believe me, | Faithfully yours

[CHARLES DICKENS]

## *To* MISS BURDETT COUTTS, 24 NOVEMBER 1841

MS Morgan Library. *Address:* Miss Coutts | Roehampton | Surrey.

1 Devonshire Terrace. York Gate.

Thursday Twenty Fourth November 1841.

Dear Miss Coutts.

I beg to report myself quite well, and contemplating a descent upon

---

[1] Edward Jesse (1780–1868; *DNB*), Surveyor of Royal Parks and Palaces since *c*. 1830. Author of *Gleanings in Natural History*, 1832–5, *A Summer's Day at Hampton Court*, 1839, *A Summer's Day at Windsor, and a Visit to Eton*, 1841, and other books. A footnote in the 1st edn of *Pickwick*, Ch. 2, to Jingle's story about his dog, runs: ". . . The stranger's anecdote is not one quarter so wonderful as some of Mr. Jesse's 'Gleanings'. Ponto sinks into utter insignificance before the dogs whose actions he records.—Ed." Thirty pages of *Gleanings*, 1835, had been devoted to anecdotes of "the sagacity of dogs"—which CD was clearly burlesquing: see Kathleen Tillotson, " 'Pickwick' and Edward Jesse", *Times Literary Supplement*, 1 Apr 1960. See also her suggestions that the Theory of Tittlebats in *Pickwick* may have been inspired by Jesse's "observations on eels" (*Gleanings*, 1832 and 1834), and that Seymour —who had illustrated *Maxims and Hints for an Angler* (see Vol. I, p. 136*n*), first published, in a shorter version, in *Gleanings*, 1832—may have based his original idea of Mr Pickwick as "a long thin man" on Jesse's own figure.

[2] Probably made during CD's fortnight at Windsor earlier in Nov.

Roehampton, where—I learn on enquiry at your house in town—you still
are.

My domestic peace is so disturbed by rumours of Adelaide Kemble,[1]
and my hearth is rendered so very desolate by the incursions of those who
have heard her, that I can never hope for peace of mind until I have carried
Mrs. Dickens to Covent Garden Theatre. If, to this end, you can let me
have your box any night next week,[2] you will eternally oblige me, and do
much to smooth my passage from my Native Shores.

I heartily wish I had been to America and had come home again. I am
told that getting up in the morning *there* in the winter time, is beyond Miss
Meredith's conception.[3]

I beg my compliments to her, and am with sincerity

Always Faithfully Yours

Miss Coutts.                                              CHARLES DICKENS


## *To* WALTER SAVAGE LANDOR, [LATE NOVEMBER 1841]

Mention in Landor *to* CD, [Nov 41].[4] *Date:* clearly after CD's return on 20
Nov from his convalescence at Windsor. The invitation for "Saturday
week" must have been to the christening of Landor's godson Walter
Landor Dickens on Sat 4 Dec;[5] Landor was therefore replying not later than
Fri 26 Nov to a letter written shortly before.


[1] Adelaide Kemble (?1814–79;
*DNB*), soprano; younger daughter of
Charles Kemble and sister of Fanny
Kemble; had trained and sung in Italy.
Since 2 Nov had been appearing at
Covent Garden as Norma with great
success. *Punch* (6 Nov) hailed her performance with: "Let every amateur,
professor, and enthusiastic raver concerning 'native talent' go down on his
knees, and . . . return thanksgiving unto
Apollo for having at last sent us a singer
who knows her business!" She retired
from the stage 23 Dec 42 and married
Edward John Sartoris 1843. They lived
much in Italy.

[2] CD went on 30 Nov (see *To* Maclise, 29 Nov and *fn*).

[3] Cf. *To* Miss Coutts, 16 Aug 41 and
*fn*.

[4] Landor had written: "This delights
me, that you are well again. Thank God
for it. On Saturday week I will be with
you. Do not think of beds. Lady B.
will give me one—for I must leave you
about ten. | With kindest regards to my
godson (to whom you need say nothing
about them—especially if he is asleep)
and to his Mama, I remain ever, My
dear Dickens Yours sincerely" (MS
Huntington). Landor then wrote to
tell Lady Blessington that she might
expect him on 3 Dec if it would be convenient for her (R. H. Super, *W. S.
Landor*, p. 331). But possibly he stayed
with CD after all: see references in *To*
Landor, 22 Nov 46 (N, I, 814), to his
piercing snore on some earlier occasion.

[5] At St Marylebone parish church,
by the Rev. G. H. Thompson.

## *To* GEORGE THOMSON,[1] 26 NOVEMBER 1841

Facsimile in *D*, x (1914), 235.

Devonshire Terrace.
Friday November Twenty Sixth 1841.

My Dear Sir.

I hope you may like the inclosed,[2] but if you do not, pray have no hesitation in saying so. It is very difficult to write such a piece properly, unless in the first freshness and fulness of grief.

Believe that I would not have delayed doing this, if I had not been ill.

Faithfully Yours always

George Thomson Esquire.                                        CHARLES DICKENS


## *To* JOHN PAYNE COLLIER,[3] 27 NOVEMBER 1841*

MS Folger Shakespeare Library.

1 Devonshire Terrace | York Gate Regents Park.
Twenty Seventh November 1841.

My Dear Collier.

Many thanks for your pleasant and welcome recollection of me.

Oddly enough, I was talking about your pamphlet,[4] at the very moment when a very small boy, in a very large coat and a very glazed hat, was heard to proclaim at the Street Door in a very shrill voice, that he belonged to the Parcels Delivery Company. As I happened to be holding forth with

---

[1] George Thomson (1757–1851; *DNB*), Catherine's grandfather: see Vol. 1, p. 134*n*. On 4 May 41 Jeffrey wrote to Lord Cockburn of his "pilgrimage" to "the new abode of old George Thomson" (7 Pelham Place, Fulham Road), whom he found "marvellously entire, though affecting to regret his too late transplantation from Edinburgh" (Cockburn, *Life of Lord Jeffrey*, 2nd edn, 1852, II, 338). After his arrival in London, published Vol. VI of *The Melodies of Scotland*, [1841].

[2] An epitaph, in CD's hand, for George Thomson's wife Katherine (see *To* Forster, 25 Oct and *fn*). It reads: "Sacred to the Ashes | of | Katherine Thomson, | For Sixty Years | The dear Wife | of | George Thomson | Of Edinburgh. | She died at Brompton | on The Thirteenth of October 1841; | Closing, | At the age of Seventy Five, | A life | of affectionate devotion | And domestic excellence. | Reader! | The adjoining grave | Is that of her Grandchild | who

died | In the early bloom | of womanhood. | This | Is the resting-place | of one | whose honored head | Was gray. | It is hard to lose | Those whom we fondly love | at any time; | But it is a happy thing | To believe | That in Eternity | There is perpetual youth | And happiness | For all. | The will of God be done!" (Facsimile, *D*, x [1914], 237). CD intended this for Mrs Thomson's tombstone in Kensal Green Cemetery, but it was not in fact used. W. Forbes Gray (in *D*, XXII [1926], 220–1) quotes the inscription engraved on the stone on Thomson's own death, 1851, for him and his wife, saying that it also was composed by CD.

[3] John Payne Collier (1789–1883: *DNB*), see Vol. 1, p. 31*n*.

[4] *Reasons for a New Edition of Shakespeare's Works*, 1841. A copy inscribed "with the best Remembrances of the Author" was in the Gad's Hill library at CD's death (*Catalogue of the Library of CD*, ed. J. H. Stonehouse, p. 87).

great effect on your side of the question (although I am the proprietor of a Boswell's Malone),[1] and as I happened to be doing so without knowing much about it, I went to work and read you straightway.

I think you make out a very good case; and that Whittakers[2] will make out another very good case in *their* way, if they allow a reasonable time for doing so. I heartily and cordially wish you "well through it"—as the monthly nurses say—and shall have my eye on you, please God.

Always Believe me | Faithfully Yours

John Payne Collier Esquire.          CHARLES DICKENS

## *To* DANIEL MACLISE, 29 NOVEMBER [1841]*

MS Benoliel Collection. *Date:* 29 Nov was Monday in 1841; handwriting supports that year.

Devonshire T. | Monday Twenty Ninth November.

My Dear Mac

dine[3] with us tomorrow at *half past four*, as a preparation for the classic Addle Head.[4]

My soul is filled with Grattan.[5]

Yours Miserably.
Her[6] Maddened adorer.[7]

Who is *he*[8]—her husband[9]—that he should possess that Being—Tell me—What has he done, to be so blest—Would nothing less satisfy his craving lust—Are there no legs but these—Is the world so narrow that he could find no other Wife!—

[1] The "third variorum" edn of Shakespeare, 21 vols, 1821, based on materials left by Edmund Malone to James Boswell the younger (1778–1822), who did the final editing. CD acquired it at the Hill sale. Collier had criticized various passages from the Malone text in his pamphlet.

[2] Whittaker & Co., of Ave Maria Lane, publishers of Collier's eight-vol. edn of Shakespeare's *Works*, 1842–4.

[3] Thus, with small "d", in MS.

[4] I.e. Adelaide. This must have been the night on which Miss Coutts had lent CD her box at Covent Garden to hear Adelaide Kemble in *Norma*.

[5] Probably Mrs Henry Plunkett Grattan (1811–76), actress, and referring to her performance in *Die Hexen am Rhein*, a romantic burletta with spectacular water-effects, which had been running at the Adelphi since 4 Oct. She had acted in America *c.* 1836–1840 and returned there *c.* 1850.

[6] Written large.

[7] This was presumably CD's answer to a letter from Maclise asking: "Is it for Tuesday or Thursday you have got The Box at Convent Gardin—and did I hear you aright in asking me to a chop on the same day—or is it but a delusion —The fact is my senses have been steeped in forgetfulness ever since, of all things but the blessed memory of Grattan, who I learn is the daughter of my Lord Byron—and 'no relation to Colley Grattan of High ways and bye ways notoriety'" (MS Huntington).

[8] Underlined twice.

[9] Mrs Grattan's husband was Henry Willoughby Grattan Plunkett (1808–89), actor, producer and dramatist, who performed under the name Henry Plunkett Grattan. He contributed to *Punch* 1841; edited the *Squib Annual* June–Dec 42. Spent 23 years in America.

## *To* MISS HANNAH MEREDITH, [30 NOVEMBER 1841]*

MS Morgan Library. *Date:* clearly the day of his visit to Covent Garden
to see Adelaide Kemble; handwriting supports.

Devonshire Terrace. | Tuesday Evening

My Dear Miss Meredith.

Pray make my compliments to Miss Coutts, and say that I shall be *most
happy* to dine at Roehampton on Thursday, when I will duly and conscientiously report, concerning Adelaide Kemble.[1] I will return home at
night—I should say, *must*—having a bore of German extraction,[2] to breakfast with me in the morning. The way is very short, and the road very
pleasant, though not so pleasant as remaining; which my inclination would
lead me to prefer.

Always Believe me
(with much to say, about your note)
Faithfully Yours

Miss Meredith CHARLES DICKENS

## *To* JOHN OVERS, 30 NOVEMBER 1841*

MS Morgan Library.

Devonshire Terrace. | Thirtieth November 1841.

Dear Mr. Overs.

Before I answer your last, I have something to say which may be disposed of in a very few words.

Doctor Elliotson renders it quite clear to me that when you spoke to him
about your having left the Theatre, you felt doubtful of having done quite
right in your *way* of proceeding, and wanted the moral courage to tell him
the whole Truth. What you did tell him was the Truth, I have no doubt,
but you did not tell him *all*. Another time tell all, and you will find it best
in the end.

I have no desire or intention to speak harshly upon this point, for I do
not look upon it as a very serious or unnatural proceeding, and found upon
it no accusation against you. Having noticed it, I have done with it.

I don't know where you discovered in my last note that I looked upon
you as the subject of a moral deficiency which rendered you unfit to
associate with gentlemen. Do you not think it probable that if I entertained any such opinion, I should have abstained from writing to you?

I have no quarrel with you, and want no submission from you. I hate it;
have no right to exact it; and am, in my nature, repugnant to it. All I want
is that for your own welfare and happiness, you should submit yourself, if I
may use the expression, *to* yourself, and feel that you have acted foolishly.
It is because I wish you to maintain a worthy independence, and because
I respect the quality, that I am vexed when you mistake a wrong-headed,

---

[1] For CD's view of her, see *To* [2] Unidentified.
Burnett, ?Dec 41 (*Addenda*, p. 497).

loud-tongued, vaunting demonstration, for a virtue which shrinks from such display, and lives in a man's heart; not upon his lips or the nib of his pen. There is a farce[1] in which a stage-stricken footman breaks a plate or two at dinner time, and throwing himself into an attitude cries "I acknowledge it—I will pay the forfeit of my crime—lead me to the Scaffold!" That man might have written your letter to Mr. Macready, and no doubt would have assassinated Mr. Bryden for not being at home when he called upon him.

If you wish to see me before I go away, you can do so any Sunday but next Sunday, between Twelve and One. Let this matter rest where it is. It has been quite enough discussed, and had better be left alone for the future.[2]

Faithfully Yours<br>CHARLES DICKENS

Mr. J. A. Overs.

## *To* MISS MYERS,[3] 30 NOVEMBER 1841*

MS Huntington Library.

1 Devonshire Terrace | York Gate Regents Park<br>Thirtieth November 1841.

Mr. Charles Dickens presents his compliments to Miss Myers, and begs to inform her that Mr. Mantalini's companion in the cellar is certainly not his wife. The exact position she holds in relation to that gentleman, Mr. Dickens can only suspect.[4]

## *To* JOHN FORSTER, [LATE NOVEMBER 1841]

Summary and extract in F, III, i, 199. *Date:* near the close of November according to Forster.

*Describing himself as thoroughly on his legs again, in the ordinary state on which he was wont to pride himself, bolt upright, staunch at the knees, a deep sleeper, a hearty eater, a good laugher; and nowhere a bit the worse,* 'bating a little weakness now and then, and a slight nervousness at times.

---

[1] Unidentified.

[2] None of Overs's letters to CD have been traced. If CD did not himself destroy them, probably Georgina did (see Preface, p. vii).

[3] Unidentified.

[4] This was CD's answer to the following note: "Strond St. D[over] Kent | Novr. 1841 | To decide an important wager would Mr. Charles Dickens kindly favour Miss Myers by answering the following Question? | 'Is the washerwoman in the Cellar Mr. Mantalini's wife *or not*' ". Beneath it is written in the same hand: "The young Lady who wrote the above, is Madame Waldow Cohen of this City" (MS Huntington). For CD's answer to a similar question, asked by Dr J. H. Hutton in 1839, see Vol. I, p. 590.

## *To* FRANCIS ROSS,[1] 1 DECEMBER 1841

Extract in Anderson Galleries catalogue No. 1628 (1922); *MS* 1 p.; dated
Devonshire Terrace, 1 Dec 41.

*Postponing a trip for a week on account of the* particularly national
*weather.*[2]

## *To* W. C. MACREADY, 2 DECEMBER 1841*

MS Morgan Library

Devonshire Terrace.
Thursday Second December | 1841.

My Dear Macready.

I have not answered your kind note of last Sunday, really because I have
not known how. I have so much pleasure and delight in your sympathy
and approval, that I *can't* be warm enough on paper, and that's the Truth.[3]

I should not write to you now, but to congratulate you most heartily upon
your release from the fangs of Webster;[4] not because I shall be able to see

[1] Francis Ross (*b.* 1804): see Vol. 1, p. 85*n.* Editor of the *London Saturday Journal* from its inception in Jan 39 to Jan 41, when James Grant became joint editor with him. By Dec 41 Grant was editing it alone. The magazine was advertised on the wrapper of *Master Humphrey*, Part 15 (June 41).

[2] Perhaps the excursion to Hampton Court planned for 2 Dec, if the weather should be fine (*To* Jesse, 24 Nov).

[3] The final No. of *Barnaby* was published on 27 Nov, and on the 28th Macready had written to CD: "I have just called at your house:—it was only to say how d'ye do to you, and add my thanks with my farewell to poor dear Barnaby. | I do not like to part with what has given me so much delight— what has made me think and feel so much—has wrung my heart with its fictitious griefs, and solaced and soothed it under sufferings of its own without one word.—In my thank you and God bless you, dear Dickens, imagine language that might read far better, but would not comprehend so much.—With all that is affectionate to all around you I am ever your most faithful & attached friend" (MS Huntington).

[4] Macready had entered on the lease and management of Drury Lane on 4 Oct, but his engagement under Webster at the Haymarket had not yet ended. On 28 Nov he learnt with great indignation that the Lord Chamberlain had extended Webster's license for two months, and probably feared that he might be involved in the extension. However, this was not so, and on 7 Dec—with a performance of Bulwer's *The Lady of Lyons*—his engagement under Webster came to an end, no doubt with feelings of relief on both sides. It could not have been easy to be Macready's manager if uninfected by his high ambitions for a dramatic renaissance: see the various protests in Webster's letter to him of 30 Sep 40 (quoted in A. S. Downer, *The Eminent Tragedian*, pp. 199–200), culminating in: "Unless we can work amicably and zealously together . . . it would be far better for me to jog on comfortably in my old & humble but profitable way, than to endure this continued scene of splendid misery which will probably end in loss." Their relations continued to be strained, in spite of the success of *Money*; and in Nov 41 Macready summed Webster up as "merely contemptible" (*Diaries*, II, 147). But CD was on very friendly terms with him later.

you in your proper sphere again before I go, or for any selfish reason, but because the only point that anxious friendship could have twisted into a doubt of your triumph from the first, is now removed. I fully and entirely believe that you will take the people up exactly where you left them when you closed Covent Garden, and that you will have no check or obstacle from the outset.

I tell you what I soberly believe—not what I wish. There is no sobriety in my wishes for you and yours, which are as boundless as my interest and affection.

Ever My Dear Macready<br>Your faithful friend

W. C. Macready Esquire.                              CHARLES DICKENS


## *To* JAMES ANDERSON,[1] 2 DECEMBER 1841*

MS Library of Congress.

1 Devonshire Terrace. | York Gate Regents Park.<br>Second December 1841.

My Dear Anderson

Will you give me the pleasure of your company at Dinner on Sunday Week, the Twelfth, at a quarter past Six o'Clock? Pray do not imagine from this length of notice that we have a formal party; for I hold such things in unspeakable abhorrence.

Faithfully Yours

J— Anderson Esquire.                              CHARLES DICKENS


## *To* MRS S. C. HALL,[2] 2 DECEMBER 1841

MS Brotherton Library, Leeds.

Devonshire Terrace.<br>Thursday Second December 1841.

My Dear Mrs. Hall.

I am exceedingly sorry to hear of your good husband's illness, and almost as sorry that you should think it necessary to apologize to me for any delay in sending Catlin,[3] under such anxious circumstances.

---

[1] James Robertson Anderson (1811–1895; *DNB*), actor: see Vol. I, p. 475*n*. The first actor Macready sounded (14 Feb 41) on his willingness to come to Drury Lane, promising him an official situation and the prospect of being his successor in course of time. Anderson, who had lacked opportunities of playing tragedy during his two seasons at Covent Garden under Madame Vestris, accepted gladly. He became—under

Serle—stage-manager, and played many leading roles (e.g. Othello to Macready's Iago May 42), at a salary of £16 a week. Besides having on many occasions met CD through Macready he had often, he says, been fellow-guest with him at Talfourd's parties (*An Actor's Life*, 1902, p. 90).

[2] Anna Maria Hall (1800–81; *DNB*): see Vol. I, p. 481*n*.

[3] I.e. Catlin's *Letters and Notes on the*

I am greatly taken with him, and strongly interested in his descriptions. He is an honest, hearty, famous fellow; and I shake hands with him in every page.

Pray make my best remembrances to your spouse, and give him my earnest wishes for his speedy recovery.

Be careful in your choice of a Raven. Have an undeniable character with him from his last place. I have one, now, whose intelligence is scarcely beyond a fowl's. I have another, whose infancy and early youth were passed at a village alehouse in Yorkshire, who is a wonder—a paragon.[1] I could tell you such things of him, as would make your hair stand on end. Nothing delights him so much as a drunken man—he loves to see human Nature in a state of degradation, and to have the superiority[2] of Ravens asserted. At such time he is *fearful* in his Mephistophelean humour.

Always Faithfully Yours

Mrs. Hall.                                                CHARLES DICKENS

## *To* FRANCIS ALEXANDER,[3] [?3] DECEMBER 1841

MS Comtesse de Suzannet. *Date:* 2 Dec 41 was Thursday; CD was probably writing on Fri 3rd.

1 Devonshire Terrace | York Gate, Regents Park, London.<br>Friday Second December 1841.

Dear Sir.

I answer your letter immediately, that it may be conveyed to you by the next packet; and briefly, because I hope to see you very soon.

*Manners, Customs, and Condition of the North American Indians,* with Four Hundred Illustrations, engraved from his Original Paintings, 2 vols, 1841. George Catlin (1796–1872; *DAB*) had spent eight years in visiting about 50 Indian tribes. He had avoided the frontier tribes—weakened by disease and drunkenness through contact with the white man—and wandered on until he came on the few uncontaminated remnants of tribes in their natural state; with them he lived as one of themselves, sketching and noting what he saw and transmitting his notes and sketches to the New York *Daily Commercial Advertizer* 1832–9. His Indian Collection—consisting of his own oil paintings, together with specimens of Indian dress, manufactures, arts, and weapons, with live Indians performing war-dances or smoking in a wigwam, and Catlin himself explaining—after being shown in various Eastern cities of America, was exhibited 1840–4 in the Egyptian Hall, Piccadilly, with tremendous success. (The collection is now in the United States National Museum, Washington.) For evidence that CD visited Catlin's "Indian Gallery" with Forster, see *To* Forster, 16 Apr 42 (F, III, vi, 264). It is conceivable that *To* Maclise, 31 Oct 40 refers to a second visit to it; and on 10 Apr 41 Cruikshank wrote that two tickets had been reserved "for the dinner in the Egyptian Hall" for himself and CD, in case they would like to see "the affair". "*I* have not seen it—have you", he asked (MS Huntington).

[1] The raven given him by Smithson. The other raven CD presumably bought himself after the death of Grip.

[2] Written above "intelligence" cancelled.

[3] Francis Alexander (1800–?81; *DAB*), portrait-painter and litho-

My stay in Boston will be but a short one, as I am going on into the South. I shall be most happy to sit to you, however, and hold myself engaged to do so, directly on my arrival.[1] I leave Liverpool on the Fourth of next month by the Britannia Steam Packet.

Your welcome communication, and all the other letters I have received from America, fill me with glad and cheerful anticipation. Trust me, that my heart warms towards the land, and that for every hearty greeting, I have as hearty a response.

There is no such clock![2] If there were, I should be its owner. You and I and Mrs. Alexander have the same silent sorrow in not being able to possess it.

I thank you cordially for your frank and genial favor; and am

My Dear Sir | Faithfully Yours

Francis Alexander Esquire.                                      CHARLES DICKENS

## *To* DANIEL MACLISE, [5] DECEMBER 1841*

MS Private; seen before partial destruction in Prestwick air-crash, Dec 1954; MS fragment (*aa*) Colonel Richard Gimbel. *Date:* 4 Dec 41 was Saturday; clearly CD was writing on the 5th (see *fns*).

Sunday | Fourth December 1841

My Dear Mac

You have *her*[3] in your mind this morning? Is she lovely, or no? Do you dine there?[4] If you don't will you dine here? Are you disposed to walk? Shall I call on you?

*a*Weren't you closely stowed (oh happy stowage!) in the Talfourdian car, last night?[5]

Answer these interrogations.

Ever Yours

GRATTAN*a*[6]

grapher. Son of a Connecticut farmer. Studied at the Academy of Fine Arts, New York, *c.* 1820. After painting in Providence and Boston, travelled in Italy 1851–2. Became a successful portrait-painter in Boston on his return, his sitters including Daniel Webster and his wife. In later years retired to Florence. See Vol. III.

[1] This disposes of the story told by H. W. French (*Art and Artists in Connecticut*, 1879, p. 63), that Alexander, on meeting the boat, "at once" asked for a sitting, and that CD, though acquiescing, later remarked: "The impertinence of the thing was without limit; but the enterprise was most astonishing and deserved any kind of reward demanded."

[2] As the one drawn by Cattermole, presumably. Cf. *To* Humphreys, Jan 40 and *fn*.

[3] Underlined with about 50 little strokes which curl downwards and then up, forming a waving tail which finally runs off the top right-hand corner of the paper. Doubtless the reference is to Marion Ely, Mrs Talfourd's niece.

[4] At the Talfourds': see Macready's diary entry for 5 Dec 41. The Talfourds' guests at dinner that night included Maclise, Forster, Stanfield, Ainsworth, "etc" (*Diaries*, II, 149).

[5] On Sat 4 Dec, CD himself entertained Maclise, the Talfourds, Landor, Macready, Elliotson, Quin and Stanfield. "The Talfourds *extremely disagreeable*", Macready recorded (*op. cit.,*

## *To* D. M. MOIR,[1] 6 DECEMBER 1841†

MS Doheny Memorial Library, Camarillo, California.

1 Devonshire Terrace | York Gate Regents Park
Monday Sixth December 1841.

My Dear Sir.

I have been greatly pleased to hear from you; and am very proud to be ranked among that class of your admirers who are your private friends.

Let me thank you for the copy you have sent me of your very interesting and elegant Memoir of poor Galt.[2] I have read it through; and it has impressed me very much.[3]

For your hearty and cordial wishes, I thank you no less. I reciprocate them, I assure you, with unaffected sincerity and warmth of heart; and shake the hand you autographically extend to me, with a most emphatic squeeze.

*a*I am exceedingly sorry to leave home, for my household Gods, like Charles Lambs[4], "take a terrible deep root".[5] But I look forward with a pleasure it would be hard to express, to seeing Washington Irving—So would you if you were going, I am sure. As I write his name and Lamb's, a crowd of passages from your books come flocking upon me, very much akin to both;[6] and I feel, directly, that you love them as well as I do.

---

II, 148). CD had also invited Cruikshank, who replied on 1 Dec that his wife had been dangerously ill, but was going on well, and ended: "as I hope she will continue to go on in the same way—why in that case, at half past six on Saturday next you will see (no great sight) | Yours truly" (MS Huntington).

[6] For this joke, see *To* Maclise, 29 Nov, *fn.*

[1] David Macbeth Moir (1798–1851; *DNB*), physician and author; contributed to *Blackwood's*, over the signature "Delta", nearly 400 prose and verse pieces; also a novel, *The Autobiography of Mansie Wauch, Taylor in Dalkeith* (republished in book form 1828). Contributed to *Fraser's* and the *Edinburgh Literary Gazette*; and wrote on medical subjects. He had been present at the Edinburgh dinner of 25 June, when CD's naming him as in the foremost rank of Scottish men of letters was greeted with loud cheers.

[2] John Galt (1779–1839; *DNB*), novelist. Wrote several plays, historical novels and biographies, and edited the *New British Theatre*, 1814–15; but is remembered now chiefly for his novels of Scottish country life, especially *Annals of the Parish* and *The Ayrshire Legatees*, 1821. Visited Canada as Secretary of the Canada Company 1824 and 1826, and founded the town of Guelph; but was imprisoned for debt on his return 1829. Spent his last years in Greenock, where he had lived as a child—poor and paralysed, but still writing. Published his *Autobiography*, 1833, and his *Literary Life*, 1834.

[3] The *Memoir* was prefixed to a reprint of *Annals of the Parish* and *The Ayrshire Legatees* (Vol. I of Blackwood's Standard Novels), 1841. Moir and Galt had been intimate friends since 1823.

*aa* Given in N, I, 366, from catalogue source; letter otherwise unpublished.

[4] Thus in MS.

[5] CD misquotes, from memory, from "New Year's Eve" in *Essays of Elia*: "My household-gods plant a terrible fixed foot, and are not rooted up without blood".

[6] Moir's good-natured enjoyment of humble people and local customs was an obvious link with Lamb and Irving. Mrs Oliphant (*Annals of a Publishing House*, I, 315–16) refers to him as "the gentle 'Delta' of Blackwood, the well-beloved physician, whom everybody

I shall only be six months gone, please God.*a* My other halfyear of rest I mean to pass in England. There may be some railroad then—Heaven knows—which will tempt you to London.[1] If I hear of it, I will subscribe my mite, that I may see you here. A very pleasant recollection of a very unpleasant night when we rode from Blackwood's to Edinburgh[2] inclines me to believe that we could be quite happy together for a whole day,—even though it were the Twenty First of June.

Mrs. Dickens begs me to send a great many Scottish remembrances to yourself and Mrs. Moir.[3] Adding as many more of my own, I am

My Dear Sir | Faithfully Yours always

D. M. Moir Esquire. CHARLES DICKENS

## *To* W. C. MACREADY, 7 DECEMBER 1841*

MS Morgan Library.

Devonshire Terrace | Seventh Decr. 1841.

My Dear Macready.

Now that you are a Manager again, I shall write you epigrammatic notes.

Firstly. Will you dine with me next Saturday week, at a quarter past 6?

Secondly. Will you allow my brother Fred, to represent me in my free admission, while I am away? He is a very good fellow, and I should be glad to give him that great pleasure, and keep him out of harm's way at the same time.

Thirdly. Will you call for me one morning, as you go down to the Theatre. I feel its[4] time I saw the Pit.[5]

Affectionately Yours Ever

W. C. Macready Esquire

CD.[6]

delighted to honour". But the broadly comic style of *Mansie Wauch* is nearer to *Pickwick*.

[1] It was not possible to do the whole journey from Edinburgh to London by rail until Oct 48, 15 months after the opening of the Berwick–Newcastle line.

[2] CD had dined with the Blackwoods on 30 June (*To* Forster, that day).

[3] *Née* Catherine E. Bell, of Leith. She married Moir in 1828.

[4] Thus in MS.

[5] Before Macready's opening night (27 Dec), the interior of Drury Lane had, says Thomas Marshall (*Lives of the Most Celebrated Actors and Actresses*, [1847], p. 32), "undergone a thorough renovation, and presented an entirely new appearance. . . . The private boxes, formerly on a level with the pit, were, with the exception of that belonging to Miss Angelina [*thus*] Burdett Coutts, and one opposite, entirely removed, and the space added to the pit, making an additional number of seats for 106 persons. The pit seats were covered with handsome red cloth, with backs stuffed and covered with crimson; each person sitting in a separate stall, in the centre of which was an opening, enabling the spectator to quit and return to his or her seat without inconvenience."

[6] In a letter dated "Tuesday Night", clearly 7 Dec, Macready replied: "I must write winged words. You know it is a happiness to me to gratify a wish of yours:—Your brother Fred. shall not be forgotten.—We dine on a particular occasion with Hor. Twiss on the 18th. —ergo—.— As I am down every day, you can choose your own, & I will call for you; but defer it for some days, for

## *To* LORD JEFFREY, [?8 DECEMBER 1841]*

MS Mr D. Cleghorn Thomson. *Date:* clearly CD's reply to the letter from Jeffrey asking if he was "surfeited with idleness yet", dated "Wedy."[1] (probably 8 Dec, the first Wednesday after publication of the final No. of *Master Humphrey*).

[2]I am not at all tired with idleness. It is delicious—if I can call that idleness which is full of busy preparation.[3] I have not written a line since I penned the words "Master Humphrey's Clock has stopped for ever".[4] I have had a few visions of things to be done, and they have been very pleasant. Otherwise I have done nothing but walk, and lounge about, and read drowsily, all day long.—What do you think of my reading the Curiosity Shop, *all through*?[5] It deserves a note of interrogation as large as a lamp-post.

Always My Dear Lord Jeffrey
Yours affectionately and attached
CHARLES DICKENS

## *To* EDWARD MARJORIBANKS, 11 DECEMBER [1841]

MS Brotherton Library, Leeds. *Date:* clearly 11 Dec 41 (a Saturday).

Devonshire Terrace. | Saturday Eleventh December.

My Dear Sir
    I am sincerely obliged to you for so kindly thinking of me; and will call on you at the Banking House on Tuesday, at Three o'Clock. As I have a most dove-like innocence on the subject of American roads; and as my

as yet it is only Chaos:—the pit is like an angel, bottomless. | I have had a very delightful letter from—let me say *our* friend Colden—in which you are mentioned—I send it to you.—You will be *very happy* [*underlined twice*] in your visit—tell Mrs Dickens I will give bail for the issue" (MS Huntington).

[1] Jeffrey had written from 4 Lower Berkeley Street: "I had hoped to have seen you again before this time—When will you come? Remember that your days here are numbered—and that the number of mine may not stretch out till your return!—are you surfeited with idleness yet? or are you *privately* solacing yourself with occupations of which the public may hear, one day? | If I were to come to your door any day about 12 o'clock—(for I now generally *walk* out a little at that time) should I have a chance of seeing you and Mrs. Dickens?" (MS Huntington).

[2] Beginning of letter is missing.
[3] John D. Sherwood, a New York journalist, called on CD at about this time and found him "cramming himself with all sorts of information", his study piled "with Marryatt's [*thus*], Trollope's, Fidler's, Hall's", and blazing "with highly-colored maps of the United States, whose staring blues, reds, and yellows, so much in contrast with the colorless maps of Europe, greatly amused him" (Sherwood, "Visits to the Homes of Authors", *Hours at Home*, New York, July 1867; quoted in F. G. Kitton, *CD by Pen and Pencil*, I, 36).
[4] The concluding words of "Master Humphrey from his Clock-Side in the Chimney Corner" (in No. 88, published 4 Dec)—the final number.
[5] Question-mark written large.

course may depend in many material respects upon the severity of the season; I think the best and shortest plan will be for me to have a Letter of credit on your correspondent at New York for eight hundred pounds. That will be a good central point, and if I should want to have any sum or sums lodged elsewhere, I presume they can readily arrange for me.

This is all subject to your opinion and kind advice, of which I shall have the benefit on Tuesday.

Meanwhile and always—with best remembrances to your family—believe me My Dear Sir

Faithfully Yours

Edward Marjoribanks Esquire                 CHARLES DICKENS

## *To* JOHN FORSTER, [?13 DECEMBER 1841]*

MS Mr Frederick J. Macartney. *Date:* probably the day before the appointment made with Marjoribanks in last; handwriting supports. *Address:* John Forster Esquire.

Devonshire T. | Monday Night.

My Dear Forster.

I overlooked this morning an appointment with Marjoribanks to-morrow at 3. When I leave him, I will call on you. Perhaps you'll dine here?

Faithfully Yours Ever

CD

## *To* MISS BURDETT COUTTS, 14 DECEMBER 1841

MS Morgan Library. *Address:* Free | Miss Coutts | Roehampton | Surrey.

Devonshire Terrace | December Fourteenth 1841.

Dear Miss Coutts.

I am sincerely obliged to you for your kind Invitation,[1] but I am obliged, most reluctantly, to deny myself the pleasure of accepting it.

Every day this week I am engaged. As I shall have only a fortnight more when next Sunday comes, I have "registered a vow" (in imitation of Mr. O Connell)[2] to pass those fourteen days at home, and not to be

[1] Miss Coutts had written on 13 Dec: "If you are disengaged will you come & dine with us & remain till Saturday; Prince Ernest of Hesse Philippsthal dines with us Wednesday & the Nugents are staying with me; if you cannot come on Wednesday will you be able to do so any of the following days but I hope you will come one of them & stay with us as long as you can" (MS Huntington).

[2] Thus in MS. On killing J. N.

D'Esterre in a duel 1815 O'Connell had made a vow never to fight again. After refusing a challenge from Sir Henry Hardinge 1830, was taunted in Parliament, and according to Michael Macdonagh (*The Life of Daniel O'Connell*, 1903, pp. 212–13) replied: " 'There is blood upon this hand', . . . raising his right hand, which was covered with a black glove. 'I regret it deeply; and the honourable and learned gentleman, the

tempted forth. Having withstood your note and acted so manfully in this trying situation, which is a kind of reversal of Eve and the Serpent, I feel that I can be adamant to everybody else. This is the only comfort I have in the penmanship of these words.

You will allow me, notwithstanding, to call upon you one morning before I go, to say good by'e, and to take your orders for any article of a portable nature in my new line of business—such as a phial of Niagara water,[1] a neat tomahawk, or a few scales of the celebrated Sea Serpent,[2] which would perhaps be an improvement on writing paper, for Miss Meredith's pillows.[3]

I beg my compliments to her, and am sincerely

And Faithfully Yours

Miss Coutts.                                                        CHARLES DICKENS

## *To* [MURDO] YOUNG,[4] 14 DECEMBER 1841

Extract in George D. Smith catalogue No. 165; *MS* 1 p.; dated Devonshire Terrace, 14 Dec 41. *Address:* "Micado" Young in catalogue; obviously a misreading of Murdo.

*Thanking him for* the beautiful copy you have sent me of your Tragedy.[5] ... I am living just now in a perpetual state of Weighing Anchor.

Solicitor-General for Ireland, knows it. He knows that I have made a vow to Heaven, else he would never venture to . . . use those taunts which in this House he has safely resorted to.' " O'Connell also vowed to the Anti-Union Association 1831 that he would wear deep mourning until the Irish Coercion Act was repealed.

[1] On his return from America CD brought Miss Coutts a rocking chair, her mother a small piece of rock from the Niagara Falls and some Virginia marble, and Miss Meredith an eagle's feather, also from Niagara.

[2] "The American sea-serpent", frequently alleged to have been seen off the American coast during the early 19th century. It was most recently reported as a monster 100 metres long, seen by a French captain on 21 Apr 40 in the Gulf of Mexico (*Zoologist*, v [1847], 1715). T. C. Grattan (see Vol. III) describes its arrival in Massachusetts Bay, Aug 39 (*Civilised America*, 1859, I, 53–5).

[3] Both Miss Meredith and Miss Coutts used to stuff pillows with finely

cut up pieces of paper and send them to hospitals and other institutions (*Letters from CD to Angela Burdett-Coutts*, ed. Edgar Johnson, 1955, p. 34*n*).

[4] Murdo Young (?1791–1870), proprietor of the *Sun* for more than 30 years; had succeeded Patrick Grant (see Vol. I, p. 6*n*) as editor 1829. Described by Charles Mackay, who worked under him *c.* 1834, as "a sound Whig with a leaning towards Radicalism" (*Through the Long Day*, 1887, I, 53). Credited with being the first organizer of the system of newspaper expresses (*Reporters' Magazine*, I [1880], 18). In 1853 became father-in-law of W. C. Kent—later a friend of CD's. The *Sun* had reviewed CD's novels very favourably (see, for instance, Vol. I, p. 562*n*).

[5] *Wallace; an Historical Tragedy*, in Five Acts, 1837. A prefatory note to the 2nd edn, 1838, described it as written about 18 years earlier, in six days; "and like the Patriot whose memory it attempts to honour, it was 'conceived in sorrow, and born to misfortune'."

## *To* LEWIS GAYLORD CLARK, [MID-DECEMBER 1841]

Extract in *New York Evening Post*, 4 Jan 42. *Date:* According to the *New York Evening Post*, Clark had received the letter "by the last steamer"; it therefore presumably went either on the *Garrick*, which left Liverpool for New York 14 Dec, or—more probably—on the *Royal Sovereign*, which left for New York 16 Dec.

*Saying that after a few days in Boston he will be visiting New York.* My design is to spend but little time in these two cities, but to proceed to the south, as far as Charleston. Our stay will be six months; during which time, I must see as much as can be seen in such a space, of the country and the people.

You make me very proud and happy by anticipation, in thinking of the number of friends I shall find; but I cannot describe to you the glow into which I rise, when I think of the wonders that await us, and all the interest I am sure I shall have in your mighty land.

## *To* JOHN FORSTER, 15 DECEMBER 1841

Letter summarized by Forster before destruction, MS Victoria & Albert Museum (FC); dated Devonshire Terrace, 15 Dec 41.

*Mentioning a letter from Spencer Hall[1] about* The Glory and Shame of England[2] *not being by an American.*

## *To* SAMUEL JOSEPH, 15 DECEMBER 1841*

MS Morgan Library.

1 Devonshire Terrace | York Gate Regents Park
Fifteenth December 1841.

Dear Sir

I have not, as you may suppose, much time to spare just now; but rather than put you to any serious inconvenience, I will sit to you *three times* next week.[3] And unless I hear from you to the contrary, I will come to you on Monday at Twelve o'Clock.

Faithfully Yours

— Joseph Esquire.                          CHARLES DICKENS

[1] Brother of William Hall and Librarian of the Athenæum (see Vol. 1, p. 399*n*).

[2] The author, C. E. Lester (see *To* Lester, 19 July 40 and *fn*), was in fact an American.

[3] For the bust commissioned by Basil Hall, see ?31 Mar. Samuel Haydon, a friend of John Dickens and the family, saw the bust at the time CD was sitting for it ("always accompanied by some friend") and considered it admirable, "full of life" (F. G. Kitton, *CD by Pen and Pencil*, I, 20). But Hall, presumably because of his breakdown in 1842, failed to buy it; and in July 48 Joseph, then bankrupt, was still seeking a purchaser. CD admired the bust, but declined buying it himself. The clay model, never even cast into plaster, was later destroyed (F. G. Kitton, *ibid*).

## *To* MARY TALFOURD,[1] 16 DECEMBER 1841

MS Berg Collection.

Devonshire Terrace | Sixteenth December 1841.

My Dear Mary.

I should be delighted to come and dine with you on your birthday, and to be as merry as I wish you to be always; but as I am going, within a very few days afterwards, a very long distance from home, and shall not see any of my children for six long months, I have made up my mind to pass all that week at home for their sakes—just as you would like your Papa and Mamma to spend all the time they could possibly spare, with you, if they were about to make a dreary voyage to America; which is what I am going to do myself.

But although I cannot come to see you on that day, you may be sure I shall not forget that it is your birth day; and that I shall drink your health and many happy returns, in a glass of wine filled as full as it will hold. And I shall dine at half past five myself, so that we may both be drinking our wine at the same time, and I shall tell *my* Mary (for I have got a daughter of that name—but she is a very small one as yet) to drink your health too; and we shall try and make believe that you are here, or that we are in Russell Square, which is the best thing we can do, I think, under the circumstances.

You are growing up so fast, that by the time I come home again, I expect you will be almost a woman; and in a very few years we shall be saying to each other, "don't you remember what the birthdays used to be in Russell Square?"—and "how strange it seems"—and "how quickly Time passes" —and all that sort of thing, you know. But I shall always be very glad to be asked on your birthday, and to come if you'll let me, and to send my love to you and to wish that you may live to be very old and very happy, which I do now, with all my heart.

Being always | My Dear Mary

Yours affectionately

Miss Talfourd.                                          CHARLES DICKENS

## *To* LORD BROUGHAM, 17 DECEMBER [1841]*

MS Brotherton Library, Leeds. *Date:* endorsed "1841 Mr. C. Dickens".

1 Devonshire Terrace | York Gate Regents Park
Friday Evening | Seventeenth December[2]

Mr. Charles Dickens presents his compliments to Lord Brougham, and begs to say that he is disengaged next Monday, or any day in the *following*

---

[1] One of Talfourd's two daughters, later Mrs William Wreford Major (see later vols).

[2] Word confused; must be "December", written on top of "September".

week (that is, the week after Christmas Day) that may suit Lord Brougham's convenience.¹

## *To* LADY HOLLAND, [?17 DECEMBER 1841]

Mention in Lady Holland *to* CD, 25 Dec 41 (see *fn*). *Date:* probably early in the same week.

*Saying that he could not come to see her on the following Wednesday evening [22 Dec] but hoped he might call some other day, and asking for an introduction to Lord Morpeth.*²

## *To* JOHN ROSS,³ 20 DECEMBER 1841\*

MS Birthplace Museum, Portsmouth.

Devonshire Terrace. | Twentieth December 1841.
Dear John Ross.

I had an appointment of some duration, so early this morning, that I was obliged to go out and come home again, before I could answer your note. Will the inclosed do? If not, I shall be at home between half past ten and half past eleven tomorrow morning, and from four to half past

---

¹ Brougham replied: "Dear Sir | Monday next will be perfectly convenient. You will meet no one but the Chancr. [*Lord Lyndhurst*] & the Chief Justice [*Lord Denman*]. | Yrs ever truly | H. Brougham | ½ before 7 exact" (MS Huntington). During the visit Brougham entrusted CD with a letter and pamphlet for Joseph Story (1779–1845; *DAB*), the distinguished American judge and jurist.

² George Howard, later 7th Earl of Carlisle (1802–64; *DNB*), who had been defeated in the General Election and was now in America. Lady Holland had written (in a letter dated "Thursday", probably 16 Dec): "It would give me much concern were you to leave England without giving me the opportunity of again enjoying your society before your departure, I owe you so much for having beguiled many tedious painful hours that it would be a satisfaction to testify my gratitude—can you give me a day? and the sooner the better, Mr. Rogers will be with me on Wednesday,

would that day suit you? be kind enough to let me know—my hour is ½6" (MS Huntington). After receiving CD's reply, she wrote again: "It will give me pleasure to see you any day—I am always to be found from 11 to one; or *after* 4 o'clock—You flatter me much by asking a letter of introduction to Ld. Morpeth. *Your* own name is sufficient God knows, but I shall not resist having mine coupled with it to Ld. Morpeth. | Yrs. with admiration | & true regard | E  V  HOLLAND | S[outh]  St.—Xmas day" (MS Huntington). She wrote afterwards to Lady Augusta Fox: "Mr Dickens has just been to take leave of me. . . . He is resolved to go into the slave districts, determined to ascertain by personal inspection the condition of the poor slaves. He should not divulge this on the other side of the Atlantic: his life might be endangered" (*Elizabeth, Lady Holland to her Son, 1821–1845*, ed. Lord Ilchester, 1946, p. 196).

³ John Ross (1808–85): see Vol. I, p. 248*n*.

four in the afternoon; and shall be delighted to amend it in any manner
you may point out.

Faithfully Yours

John Ross Esquire.                                              CHARLES DICKENS


## *To* JOHN ROSS, 20 DECEMBER 1841*

MS Birthplace Museum, Portsmouth.

1 Devonshire Terrace. | York Gate Regents Park
Twentieth December 1841.

My Dear Ross.

I wish I had been at home when you called yesterday; and I wish you
had mentioned in the note you sent afterwards, what country paper it is
of which you desire to become the Editor,[1] and who are the proprietors;
as I should have then been enabled to address them personally on your
behalf. Believe me that any recommendation I can possibly make to them,
is as heartily at your service as it is thoroughly deserved by you.

It is needless for me to tell you that I know you to be a man, of all others
qualified for such an office, by your long newspaper experience, your
education, conduct, abilities, and position in society. Only let me know
how I can best convey this information, and much more, to the gentlemen
whom you seek to propitiate, and I will do so in the most earnest words I
can possibly employ. I cannot do more than justice to my earnest feeling
in the matter, and my strong conviction that you are the person they want.

Point out any way in which I can serve you in your endeavour to attain
your object; and I will promptly exert myself. And believe me that I am
warmly interested in your success, and ready to promote it, heart and
hand; not merely for the love of you, but for the love of the right cause[2]
which I know you will serve well (no man better) if you get this opportunity.

Always My Dear Ross | Faithfully Yours

John Ross Esquire                                              CHARLES DICKENS


## *To* CHARLES SMITHSON, 20 DECEMBER 1841

MS Huntington Library.

Devonshire Terrace. | Twentieth December 1841.

My Dear Smithson.

The Pie was no sooner brought into my room yesterday evening, than
I fainted away.

---

[1] No record has been found of any
country paper edited by Ross. He spent
most of his working life on the parliamentary staff of *The Times*.

[2] The Radical cause.

Topping put his shoulder out, in carrying it from the waggon to the hall-door; and John is in the hospital with a damaged spine—having rashly attempted to lift it.

There never *was* such a Pie! We are mad to know what it's made of, but haven't the courage to cut it. Indeed we haven't a knife large enough for the purpose. We think of hiring Fletcher to eat it. We sit and stare at it in a dull astonishment, and grow dizzy in the contemplation of its enormous magnitude.

It prevents my writing at any length, as my faculties are absorbed in crust. I have a shadowy recollection that I owe Mrs. Smithson a large sum of money,[1] and that it preys upon my mind. Fred was to have told me the amount, but he forgot it on his way home. I seem to remember, too, that you paid for **THE** Raven[2]—Good God!—if you could only hear him talk, and see him break the windows!

You will be glad to hear—I can only hint at his perfections—that he disturbs the church service, and that his life is threatened by the Beadle. Maclise says he *knows* he can read and write. I quite believe it; and I go so far as to place implicit reliance on his powers of cyphering.

Ease my mind, or ask Mrs. Smithson to ease it, on the subject of my liabilities. I am going to send her two books,[3] and will remit (if you or she will put me in a condition to do so) at the same time.

Kate joins me in hearty wishes that you and yours (including "beauteous Bill")[4] may enjoy very many happy Christmases, and New Years.

---

[a]Since writing the above, I have looked at the Pie, and[5]—I am very weak

my

┼ Mark[a]

## *To* THE COUNTESS OF BLESSINGTON,<br>[22] DECEMBER 1841

Envelope only, MS Berg Collection. *Address:* The | Countess of Blessington | Gore House | Kensington. PM 22 Dec 41.

[1] Probably she had paid for CD's and Catherine's carriage to or from Malton (see *To* Smithson, 13 June).

[2] It was a gift from Smithson.

[3] No doubt *Old Curiosity Shop* and *Barnaby*, detached from *Master Humph-* rey: see *To* Macready, 27 Dec, *fn.* He sent them on 1 Jan.

[4] Amelia Thompson.

[aa] In very quavery writing.

[5] Crossed through but intended to be read as part of the weakness-joke.

## *To* SAMUEL ROGERS, 23 DECEMBER 1841*

MS Colonel Richard Gimbel.

1 Devonshire Terrace | Twenty Third December 1841.

Do you remember that you promised me a letter to Sir Charles Bagot?[1] And will you let me have it, before the end of next week? And will you let me know your movements; and whether I am to shake hands with you before I leave England on the second day of the New Year, in the Flesh, or in the Spirit?

Affectionately Yours always

Samuel Rogers Esquire.                           CHARLES DICKENS

## *To* MISS BURDETT COUTTS, 23 DECEMBER 1841*

MS Morgan Library. *Address:* Free | Miss Coutts | Stratton Street | Piccadilly.

Devonshire Terrace
Thursday Twenty Third December | 1841.

Dear Miss Coutts.

I am truly indebted to you for your kind note.[2] I had intended coming to Roehampton on Sunday; but having this timely information of your movements, I will call in Stratton Street on that day, shortly after Two o'Clock, to say good by'e.[3]

As you make no mention of your cold, I hope and conclude it is better. With much pleasure in the sight of your hand writing, I am always

Faithfully Yours

Miss Coutts.                                     CHARLES DICKENS

## *To* GEORGE HOGARTH, 23 DECEMBER 1841*

MS Dickens House.

Devonshire Terrace. | Twenty Third December 1841.

My Dear Hogarth

I don't know how I came to make the mistake; but in my last to you, I proceeded on the notion that tomorrow would be Christmas Day. Now as

[1] Sir Charles Bagot (1781–1843; *DNB*), newly-appointed Governor-General of Canada. Conservative MP and Under-Secretary for Foreign Affairs 1807; diplomat 1814–35. As minister to United States 1815–20, was responsible for the Bagot-Rush Treaty of 1818. Took up office in Kingston 12 Jan 42. CD dined with him there on 8 May 42.

[2] Miss Coutts had written on 22 Dec saying that she hoped CD would call to say goodbye at either Roehampton or Stratton Street (MS Huntington).

[3] After his visit on Sun 26 Dec, Miss Coutts wrote again saying it had just occurred to her that he might like her box at Drury Lane for the following evening (Macready's opening night), and enclosing the ticket for him to keep or return (MS Huntington).

it is not, and I shall see Chapman and Hall tonight,[1] I think it will be best for you to come here (if you can) *very soon* after the receipt of this to-morrow morning.

Affecy. always

CD.

## *To* MISS CATHERINE HUTTON, 23 DECEMBER 1841

MS Mr Robert K. Black.

London. 1 Devonshire Terrace | York Gate Regents Park.

Twenty Third December 1841

My Dear Miss Hutton.

I don't know why your last letter to me should have caused you any uneasiness, but I *do* know that it gave me much pleasure; and I am very glad to have this opportunity of telling you so.

Thank you, heartily, for the Purse.[2] I had been debating within myself whether I should carry one in America (I never do in England) when the opportune arrival of your pretty present, carried the question by an enormous majority.

The merriest of Christmases and the happiest of New Years to you! I hope to carry you easily through a dozen New stories, at least.[3]

Always Believe me

With true regard | Faithfully Yours

Miss Catherine Hutton.                               CHARLES DICKENS

## *To* ROBERT OWEN,[4] 27 DECEMBER 1841*

MS Dr De Coursey Fales.

Devonshire Terrace | Twenty Seventh December 1841.

My Dear Sir.

Some time ago, you sent me an interesting book of which you are the

---

[1] He must therefore have refused an invitation to himself and Catherine, dated "Saturday 18th" (almost certainly 18 Dec 41), to dine with the Stanfields on the 23rd (MS Huntington). The letter also asked him to write his name in a book Stanfield was sending—probably *Master Humphrey*, Vol. III, published 15 Dec.

[2] Listing at the age of 88 her life's activities, Catherine Hutton wrote that she had "netted upwards of one hundred wallet purses, in combined colours, and in patterns of my own invention. I net much still" (*Reminiscences of a Gentlewoman of the Last Century*, ed.

Mrs C. H. Beale, Birmingham, 1891, p. 213). In Nov 1838, aged 82, she had sent the future Napoleon III a purse, when asking for his autograph (*op. cit.*, p. 207).

[3] On 18 Jan 42, when Catherine Hutton was 85, she copied out this sentence in a note recording CD's departure for America, and ended it: "Dear Boz, | 'Its Oh! in my heart I wish him safe at home!'" (MS Mr W. J. Carlton).

[4] Robert Owen (1771–1858; *DNB*), socialist, philanthropist, creator of the New Lanark Mills model community and schools (1816–28), and virtual

Author.[1] I forgot to thank you for it; and I take shame to myself for having done so. Accept this tardy ackowledgement, and believe me

Faithfully Yours

Robert Owen Esquire.                                   CHARLES DICKENS


## *To* SAMUEL JOSEPH, 27 DECEMBER 1841*

MS Messrs Young & Sossen Inc.

Devonshire Terrace | Twenty Seventh December 1841

My Dear Sir.

I regret to say—and I would not say it unless I were *forced*—that I cannot sit to you any more before I leave England. I have made a list of my indispensable engagements, this morning; and I find that every hour of my time, this week, is fully occupied.

Faithfully Yours

—Joseph Esquire                                       CHARLES DICKENS


## *To* FRANCIS ROSS, 27 DECEMBER 1841

Mention in Anderson Galleries catalogue, Feb 1922; *MS* 1 p.; dated Devonshire Terrace, 27 Dec 41.

*Making an appointment.*


## *To* LORD BROUGHAM, 27 DECEMBER 1841*

MS Brotherton Library, Leeds.

1 Devonshire Terrace | York Gate Regents Park.<br>Twenty Seventh December | 1841.

Dear Lord Brougham.

I shall be at home on Friday Morning, from twelve o'Clock until Two. If it should be inconvenient to you to leave home at that time, I shall be happy to come to you. Pray have no delicacy in requesting me to do so, as it would not put me out of the way at all.

Always | Yours faithfully and obliged

CHARLES DICKENS

The Right Honorable | The Lord Brougham.

---

founder of the English Trade Union movement. Since 1834 he and his disciples had propagated his plan for the "New Moral World". He published *The Book of the New Moral World*, in 7 Parts, 1836–42. For the violent controversies it stirred up, and CD's reactions, see *To* Overs, 13 July 40 and *fn.* CD later knew his son, Robert Dale Owen.

[1] Possibly *Socialism, or the Rational System of Society*, 1840, Owen's latest book.

### *To* W. C. MACREADY, 27 DECEMBER [1841]*

MS Morgan Library. *Date:* 27 Dec was Monday in 1841; handwriting supports that year.

Devonshire Terrace.<br>Monday Twenty Seventh December

My Dear Macready.

God bless you and yours, and all you do. Health and happiness for many years, and all the merriment and peace I wish you.

You are at the head of *my* audience, as you know. Here are my latest pieces.[1]

Ever Your affectionate friend

W. C. Macready Esquire            CHARLES DICKENS

I am so excited about tonight, that I can do nothing.[2]

---

[1] Inscribed copies of *Old Curiosity Shop* and *Barnaby*, 1841 (Parke Bernet Galleries catalogues 17 Nov 1953 and No. 1468), published 15 Dec—each in one vol., detached from *Master Humphrey*. Because of the omission from *Old Curiosity Shop* of the "Master Humphrey" sections in the first nine Nos of the original work, new matter had been added and the text reset at some of the junctions (see, e.g., *To* Hood, ?Feb or Mar 41, *fn*). The paging betrays the omissions: p. 2, for instance, is numbered "2–38" and the following page "39"; a later page is "47–79", followed by "80". In *Barnaby*, on a page between the title and two-page Preface, the following advertisement appeared (though not in all copies): "This Tale is now reprinted, for the reader's greater convenience, from the stereotype plates of '*Master Humphrey's Clock*,' and is here presented, complete, in one volume. As it began to appear in the second volume of that publication, the numbering of the pages in the present Edition will occasionally be found to be defective." On receiving CD's letter and the books, Macready replied (clearly the next day): "You do not want words from me to know how valuable and how affectionately cherished are any remembrances of you.—I thank you in one short but hearty acknowledgement for your present, and go to work the more sprightly for it. | God bless you—is the earnest & constant prayer of your sincere friend | W. C. Macready | P.S. I wanted to catch you for a few words—can you come round after the play tonight?" (MS Huntington).

[2] That night Drury Lane opened under Macready's management with *The Merchant of Venice*, followed by the new Christmas pantomime *Harlequin and Duke Humphrey's Dinner; or, Jack Cade, the Lord of London Stone*. Macready, playing Shylock, was called for as the play began—the whole audience rising to greet him with "loud and long-continued acclamations" (*Morning Chronicle*, 28 Dec). "This second management", says Thomas Marshall, "was, in spirit, a prolongation of the first. The same Shaksperian splendour . . . ; the same reversion to the genuine text, and careful regard for the poetical idea of each drama . . . ; the same abundant success in public enthusiasm; and the same abrupt termination [in June 43]"—with a very substantial financial loss (*Lives of the Most Celebrated Actors and Actresses*, p. 33).

## *To* W. C. MACREADY, 28 DECEMBER 1841

MS Morgan Library.

Devonshire Terrace
Tuesday Twenty Eighth December | 1841.

My Dear Macready.

This note is about the saloon. I make it as brief as possible. Read it when you have time. As we were the *first* experimentalists last night, you will be glad to know what it wants.[1]

1st. The refreshments are preposterously dear. A glass of wine is a shilling, and it ought to be sixpence.

2ndly. They are served out by the wrong sort of people—two most uncomfortable drabs of women, and a dirty man with his hat on.

3rdly. There ought to be a boxkeeper to ring a bell or give some other notice of the commencement of the overture to the afterpiece. The promenaders were in a perpetual fret and worry to get back again.

And fourthly and most important of all:— *if the plan is ever to succeed*, you must have some notice up to the effect that as it is now a place of resort for ladies, gentlemen are requested not to lounge there in their hats and great coats. No ladies will go there, though the conveniences should be ten thousand times greater, while the *sort* of swells who have been used to kick their heels there, do so in the old sort of way. I saw this expressed last night, more strongly than I can tell you.

Hearty congratulations on the brilliant triumph.—I have always expected one, as you know, but nobody could have imagined the reality.

Always My Dear Macready
Affectionately Yours

W. C. Macready Esquire                                              CD.

---

[1] Macready had gone to great lengths to civilize the saloon. *The Times* and *Morning Chronicle* of 28 Dec praised not only the sumptuous new *décor* but also the provision of a special staircase to the upper circles for use by women of the town, to preclude their use of the saloon. Thus "The crying evil, the long-inflicted disgrace, that the eyes and ears of innocence were insulted, and the minds of youth corrupted by the shameless scenes within its walls, was abolished. A noble example in managerial reform" (Thomas Marshall, *Lives of the Most Celebrated Actors and Actresses*, p. 32). But on 15 Jan 42 *John Bull* protested at the use of the staircase by "those unfortunate women whom we had supposed to be excluded from this theatre" yet were admitted along with respectable members of the audience "from the second circle upwards". A reply from Macready (written by Forster) appeared in *The Times* on 31 Jan (see *Diaries*, II, 155), stating that these women were admitted only to the gallery, and by a separate box-office; and on 1 Feb *The Times's* third leader gave Macready its unqualified support (see A. S. Downer, *The Eminent Tragedian*, p. 210).

### *To* W. C. MACREADY, [28 DECEMBER 1841]*

MS Morgan Library. *Date:* clearly same day as last—CD having in the meantime received Macready's note of 28 Dec (see *To* Macready, 27 Dec, *fn*).

Devonshire Terrace

My Dear Macready.

Hurrah—ah—ah—ah—ah ! ! !

I will come round after the comedy.[1]—I have already despatched a letter to you at Drury Lane, per post, concerning the Saloon. The suggestions, such as they are (they *are* very few) are all important to its success.

Ever Your affectionate friend

W. C. Macready Esquire

CHARLES DICKENS

### *To* DANIEL MACLISE, 28 DECEMBER 1841*

MS Benoliel Collection. *Address:* Daniel Maclise Esquire.

Twenty Eighth[2] Decr. 1841.

My Dear Mac

Call at the Parthenon for me, not later than five and twenty Minutes afore 7.

Faithfully Yours always

CD

### *To* ROBERT KEELEY, [?29 DECEMBER 1841]

Mention in Keeley *to* CD, Dec 41 (see *fn*). *Date:* shortly before CD's departure for America; possibly the day after Keeley's and his wife's appearance together in *Every One Has his Fault*, Drury Lane, 28 Dec.

*Praising the Keeleys' talents;[3] mentioning that he had been ill, and was shortly leaving for America.[4]*

[1] Mrs Inchbald's *Every One Has his Fault.*

[2] Written "Eigth".

[3] CD had seen Mrs Keeley play Nerissa on Macready's opening night. For his admiration of Keeley as one of the "most touching, as well as the drollest" of low comedy actors, see "Robert Keeley", *All the Year Round*, New Series, I (1869), 438–41. CD compares him with Harley—"an excellent artist in his way; but . . . always full of his own humour, and showed it, as much as to say, 'See how funny I am!'" But "Keeley's was the truer art"; his

acting was subtle "in the highest degree"; he was a "master of pathos"; and excelled in those of Shakespeare's clowns who are "unconscious or saddened humorists".

[4] Keeley replied from 5 Ampthill Place, Brixton: "Thank you for your note. We are very proud of your estimation of our talents, the more especially as we receive it from one, to whom, without affectation, we can return it seven-fold. | You have chosen a cold time o'year for your voyage. I should recommend you by all means, the instant you arrive, to get Southward with

## *To* FREDERICK SALMON, 30 DECEMBER 1841*

Text from transcript by Walter Dexter.

Devonshire Terrace
Thursday Night December Thirtieth 1841

My Dear Salmon.

Here are two books which complete your set, so far.[1] I was sorry to miss you to-day, and will come down to-morrow morning at half-past ten.

Faithfully Yours always

Frederick Salmon Esquire　　　　　CHARLES DICKENS

all possible haste.—If you are annoyed with any chronic disorder, you will find the climate a marvellous physician. I lost a rheumatic affection of ten years standing by wintering in New Orleans and Mobile; and received the advantage of seeing more of the people of the South and West, by returning to Philadelphia up the Mississippi and Ohio rivers and over the Alleghany mountains, than I could by any other means have attained.—Of course, this advice applies only to the remaining winter months." He also enclosed a letter of introduction to the Philadelphia painter, Thomas Sully (MS Huntington).

[1] One of them was the first independent edn of *Barnaby*, with an inscription to Salmon dated 30 Dec 41 (now in the possession of Col. Richard Gimbel). The other, completing Salmon's "set" (for what he already had, see 25 Oct, *fn*), was no doubt *Master Humphrey*, Vol. III; for Salmon kept this letter in *Master Humphrey*, Vol. I. Other books given to friends at about this time (and now in the Widener Collection, Harvard) were *Master Humphrey*, Vols II and III, on 29 Dec, to Harley (who had written to him 16 Dec, inviting him and Catherine to dinner on 28 or 30 Dec: MS Huntington); and the first edn of *Barnaby* to Jeffrey, inscribed: "Lord Jeffrey From his affectionate friend Charles Dickens. New Year's Night 1842". Jeffrey wrote on the same day, asking CD to deliver two notes in America; saying he hoped to see him again before he left; and echoing Brutus's farewell to Cassius: "If we shall meet again, why we shall smile—if not, our last parting was well made" (Anderson Galleries catalogue, March 1916). To Landor CD gave *Barnaby* (now in the possession of Col. Richard Gimbel); Talfourd wrote on 30 Dec saying how dearly he would prize the volumes he had received from CD the night before (MS Huntington); Rogers had written on 6 Dec: "I shall hope to [see] you *all* on Friday at 6½" (MS Huntington)—presumably to say goodbye; and Hood wrote on "Saturday [?26 Dec]": "As you are going to America, and have kindly offered to execute any little commission for me—pray, if it be not too much trouble, try to get me an Autograph of Sandy Hook's [*a town in New York Bay*]. I have Theodore's" (MS Huntington). At about this time, Hood must have written his review of *Barnaby* for the *Athenæum* (22 Jan 42)—praising the workmanship, delighting in Miggs ("one of the jewels of the book"), seeing Dennis's hanging as "a fine moral lesson", and finding the book "particularly well-timed", since there was now a "worse fanatical demon abroad", a "growing spirit . . . setting itself against Art, Science, Literature, the Drama, and all public amusements" (i.e. Evangelicalism).

## *To* UNKNOWN CORRESPONDENT,
## [? DECEMBER 1841]*

MS (fragment only) *Private. Date:* probably shortly before leaving for America.

Let me thank you for your note, and your kind wishes. Be assured that I shall endeavour to deserve them, by doing all in my power to come home in safety.

Believe me | Faithfully Yours
CHARLES DICKENS

## *To* HENRY AUSTIN, 1841

Extract in George D. Smith catalogue, 1901; *MS* 1 p.; dated London, 1841.

*Concerning Yorkshire dialect.*

If you could send me the dirty scrap of print[1] back tonight you would oblige me heartily.

## *To* JOSEPH [HAYDN],[2] [?1841]

Text from N, I, 363. *Date:* CD's imprecise "Monday Night" (written to a stranger) suggests not later than 1841. *Address:* N's "Haydon" is almost certainly a mistake.

Devonshire Terrace | Monday Night

My dear Sir,

Will you allow me to appoint *next Wednesday Morning* at the hour you name? I shall not be disengaged in the morning until then.[3]

Very faithfully yours
[CHARLES DICKENS]

---

[1] Perhaps some belated review of *Nickleby*,commenting on John Browdie's broad Yorkshire.

[2] Joseph Timothy Haydn (?1786–1856; *DNB*), compiler of reference books. Born in Ireland. Founded and edited the Dublin *Evening Mail* 1823 and *Statesman and Patriot* 1828. Employed in the records department of the Admiralty until his death. Besides compiling his *Dictionary of Dates,* 1841, edited Samuel Lewis's Topographical Dictionaries and Atlases, 1831–42.

[3] Whether this meeting took place is doubtful; for on 13 Jan 50 CD wrote to Haydn saying how glad he would be to "commence a personal knowledge" of him.

# APPENDIXES

# A. DICKENS'S DIARY[1]

*Wednesday, January 1, 1840*
Laus Deo.[2]

Dinner party at home—Tom Hill, Blanchard,[3] Stone,[4] Thompson, Collinson, Hullah[5] and wife,[6] Maclise, Forster, Kate, and I.

*Wednesday, January 8, 1840*
Dine at Chapman and Hall's—5 punctually.
Thinking of title for new work this morning.

*Thursday, January 9, 1840*
At home all day and evening—correcting proofs of Young Couples, and considering new work in all possible ways.
qy. Title
    Old Humphrey's Clock
    Master Humphrey's Clock.

*Friday, February 28, 1840*
Mr. Prevost[7]
    25 New Street
    Dorset Square

*Saturday, April 25, 1840*
At 2. Meeting of Committee for Dowton's[8] retiring benefit,[9] in the Committee Room of C.G.T.

[1] Kept in *The Law and Commercial Daily Remembrancer* (MS Forster Collection, V & A): see Vol. I, p. 629.

[2] Written very large.

[3] Samuel Laman Blanchard (1804–1845; *DNB*): see Vol. I, p. 290*n*.

[4] Frank Stone (1800–59; *DNB*): see Vol. I, p. 487*n*.

[5] John Pyke Hullah (1812–84; *DNB*): see Vol. I, p. 113*n*.

[6] Caroline Hullah, *née* Foster: see Vol. I, p. 445*n*.

[7] Louis Augustin Prévost (1790–1858; *DNB*), linguist. Born at Troyes; settled in England 1823; taught languages 1823–43; and served on the British Museum staff 1843–55, where he catalogued the collection of Chinese books. He mastered over 40 languages. He is referred to in the *Critic*, XVII

(1858), 220, and in Robert Cowtan, *Memories of the British Museum*, 1872, p. 360, as CD's French tutor; and this is supported by payments to him of £2.7.6 on 8 Dec 37, £3.3 on 1 Feb and £2.16 on 28 Feb 40, recorded in CD's account-book (MS Messrs Coutts). W. J. Carlton suggests that he may have been the French master at Wellington House, described in "Our School" (*Household Words*, 11 Oct 51, IV, 51): see "Dickens Studies French", *D*, LIX, (1963), 21–7.

[8] William Dowton (1764–1851; *DNB*), actor. Played at Drury Lane 1796–1834, excelling in comic parts. A proposal by Macready to give him a complimentary dinner in 1834 was turned down (*Diaries*, I, 106).

[9] At Her Majesty's Theatre 8 June. He

*Saturday, August 29, 1840*

Entered upon house at Broadstairs for five weeks.

*Thursday, September 3, 1840*

Put down names at the libraries.[1]

*Thursday, December 31, 1840*

Mems.

To answer Harness invitation for 7th. January—19 Heathcote St.
Do. case of distress Agnes Turner 102 New Road Chelsea
Subscription £1 Shakespeare Society[2]
Do. London Library £5 Messrs. Bouverie & Co. 11 Haymarket
1st annual subn. (£2) 1st. May 1841
W. H. Harrison Crown Life Office 33 New Bridge Street—concerning
his paper for Mrs. Macrone's book.[3]

*Occasional Memorandum, June* [1840][4]

6th. Promissory note to Macfarlane[5] at 4 months, due 9th. October
57.7.3.

*Saturday, January 16, 1841*

3–18 gal casks of beer received. The first fit to tap in one month from
this day.

*Tuesday, January 26, 1841*

Forster at half past five.

*Wednesday, January 27, 1841*

Stanfield at 6.

played Sir Robert Bramble in Colman's *Poor Gentleman*, and Knowles delivered a verse-address. The proceeds saved Dowton from threatened destitution. An entry in CD's account-book (MS Messrs Coutts) reads: "Mr Dowton's subscription [£]5.5."

[1] I.e. the Royal Kent Library (attached to the Assembly Rooms) in Albion Street; and, presumably, Barnes's Library (see *To* Mitton, ?31 May 40, *fn*), also in Albion Street. For a facsimile of the page on which CD entered his name, Sep 40, in the Royal Kent Library's subscribers' book, see *D*, IV (1908), 150.

[2] Founded 1840. J. P. Collier was Director; Ayrton, Dilke, Dyce, Harness, Jerrold, Macready and Talfourd on its first Council; among other members were John Black, Browning, W. J. Fox, Hook, Horne and Archer Shee. Its object was "to print and distribute to the Subscribers books illustrative of Shakespeare and of the Literature of his time"—which they received at cost price. The Society's 48 publications 1841–53 included 21 by Collier.

[3] See *To* Harrison, 14 Mar 40, *fn*.

[4] Entry at end of volume.

[5] Cf. similar promissory note to Macfarlane in CD's Diary-entry for 14 Aug 39 (Vol. I, p. 641 and *n*).

*Friday, January 29, 1841*

Harness at ¼ before 7.
Evening party at Miss Coutts's.

*Saturday, January 30, 1841*

Miss Coutts at half past 6—changed to Tuesday, same hour.

*Sunday, January 31, 1841*

Rogers at[1]

*Tuesday, February 2, 1841*

Miss Coutts at Half past Six.
Parthenon Committee at 3.

*Wednesday, February 3, 1841*

Dr. Smith at 6 o'Clock.

*Thursday, February 4, 1841*

Ainsworth at 6.

*Saturday, February 6, 1841*

Cattermole at the Athenæum at 6.

*Tuesday, June 15, 1841*

To give mother £4 at the end of the Month.[2]
To mention allowance,—he to pay it.
Can he let her have £4 now? Mitton to pay you.[3]

*Thursday, June 17, 1841*

Upcott. Books.
Harley Clock.

*Saturday, December 11, 1841*

Talfourd's—at ¼ before 7.

*Saturday, December 18, 1841*

Talfourds with us at ¼ past 6.

*Thursday, December 23, 1841*

Chapman's at 6 o'Clock.

---

[1] Time not written in.
[2] These entries were probably notes for a letter CD intended to write John Dickens, instructing him to pay his wife £4 out of his allowance (see *To Mitton*, 6 Mar 41, *fn*).
[3] CD's accounts show a payment to "Alphington" of £4 on 29 June.

# B. AGREEMENTS WITH PUBLISHERS
## AGREEMENT WITH CHAPMAN & HALL FOR
## *MASTER HUMPHREY'S CLOCK*, 31 MARCH 1840

MS Widener Collection, Harvard.

Articles of Agreement made and entered into this thirty first day of March One thousand eight hundred and forty Between CHARLES DICKENS[1] of Devonshire Terrace in the Parish of St Marylebone in the County of Middlesex Esquire of the one part and EDWARD CHAPMAN and WILLIAM HALL of the Strand in the same County Publishers of the other part. WHEREAS the said Charles Dickens intends to write and compose a certain periodical Literary Work to be published at weekly intervals and hath proposed to the said Edward Chapman and William Hall to become the Publishers thereof And it hath accordingly been agreed that the same shall be so written printed and published by the said parties hereto respectively upon the terms and conditions hereinafter mentioned and declared Now THESE PRESENTS WITNESS And the said Charles Dickens doth hereby for himself his heirs executors and administrators in consideration of the several payments hereinafter stipulated to be made to him by the said Edward Chapman and William Hall their executors and administrators and of the Covenants and Agreements on their part hereinafter contained covenant promise and agree with and to the said Edward Chapman and William Hall their executors and administrators That he the said Charles Dickens shall and will compose and write a new Work the Title whereof shall be "MASTER HUMPHREY'S CLOCK". And that the said New Work shall consist of parts or numbers each of which shall contain one Sheet in Royal Octavo forming sixteen pages of which twelve pages shall be original Literary Matter to be contributed and furnished by the said Charles Dickens and four pages shall be devoted to the Title and Advertisements And that the said Work shall be continued for an indefinite period of time as hereinafter mentioned but subject to the provisions hereinafter contained for determining the same And that he the said Charles Dickens shall and will write and deliver to the said Edward Chapman and William Hall their executors and administrators the Manuscript of the several and respective parts of the same work in regular succession on a day which shall be at least thirty days previous to the day on which the same Number or part is intended to appear, so that the said intended New work and the respective parts or numbers thereof from the first part or number thereof may be regularly published by the said Edward Chapman and William Hall on Saturday in every Week commencing on the fourth day of April next AND THESE PRESENTS FURTHER WITNESS that the said Edward Chapman and William Hall do hereby for themselves their heirs executors

[1] Words and phrases given here in capitals represent small letters written bold, as in the text printed in A. S. W. Rosenbach, *A Catalogue of the Writings* of CD in the Library of Harry Elkins *Widener*, privately printed, Philadelphia, 1918, pp. 47–56.

and administrators in consideration of the right or licence hereby granted to them and of the covenants and agreements on the part of the said Charles Dickens his heirs executors and administrators herein contained covenant promise and agree with and to the said Charles Dickens his executors administrators and assigns That they the said Edward Chapman and William Hall their executors or administrators shall and will at their own costs and risk print and publish the said intended New Work and the respective parts or Numbers thereof in the manner and style herein more particularly mentioned And that they shall and will also procure to be designed engraved printed and published therewith such Engravings on Wood as the said Charles Dickens his executors or administrators and they the said Edward Chapman and William Hall their executors or administrators may think advisable to illustrate the said Numbers or parts with And that they the said Edward Chapman and William Hall shall and will at their own proper charges defray and pay all costs and expenses attendant upon or incidental to the designing engraving printing publishing advertising and selling the said New Work and the respective parts or numbers thereof and each and every of them And shall and will duly and regularly print and publish the said intended New Work and the respective parts or numbers thereof on Saturday the fourth day of April now next and on the Saturday of every succeeding Week in due and regular succession AND ALSO shall and will pay unto the said Charles Dickens his executors or administrators the sum of Fifty pounds Sterling on the delivery of the Manuscript of the fifth and every other of the parts or numbers of the said intended New Work respectively; the sum of Two hundred pounds having been already paid for the first four Numbers thereof AND that they the said Edward Chapman and William Hall their executors or administrators shall and will print publish and carry on the said Work upon the Terms and Conditions hereinbefore and hereinafter contained for a period of twelve calendar months from the day of the publication of the first part or number thereof and thereafter until the same shall be discontinued in manner hereinafter mentioned AND IT IS HEREBY MUTUALLY AGREED by and between the parties hereto That the said New Work shall be published at the price to the public of Three pence a number And that all numbers sold shall be accounted for by the said Edward Chapman and William Hall their executors or administrators to the said Charles Dickens his executors or administrators at the rate of Two pence each allowing thirteen numbers as twelve And that the said Edward Chapman and William Hall shall charge the Work with Five pounds per Cent upon the Total amounts sold as a recompence for their care and trouble in the management thereof and also with all Commissions and Charges which they may pay or allow to the Agents for the Sale of the said work And that the entire management of the publication and sale of the said Work shall be vested in the said Edward Chapman and William Hall their executors or administrators but the said Work or any part or Number thereof shall not be published in any other manner or form than herein expressed without the previous consent in writing of the said Charles Dickens his executors or administrators AND IT IS FURTHER AGREED that all advertisements to be inserted in the said Work shall be accounted for by the said Edward Chapman and William Hall their executors and administrators at the rate of Six pounds a page and not by the advertisements separately provided that in case there should at any time be a deficiency in the number of advertisements requisite for any part or number of the said Work and the said Edward Chapman and William Hall their executors and administrators should find it necessary to insert their own advertisements to complete the requisite number of advertisements, then no charge shall be made to them for such their advertisements but that the page or pages or proportionate part or parts of page or pages only which shall be occupied by advertisements other than those of the said Edward Chapman and William Hall shall be accounted for by them to the said Charles Dickens his executors and administrators at the rate aforesaid AND IT IS FURTHER AGREED that out of or from the monies received by the said Edward Chapman and William Hall their executors or administrators by for or on account of the sale and publication of each part or number of the said Work and out of or from the money which they shall be liable to account for in respect of the paid for advertisements contained in each such part or number there shall be paid or deducted in the first place all expenses of printing and illustrating the part or number in respect whereof such monies shall be received or accountable for and also all expenses of advertising which shall from time to time be incurred and also all expenses of Insuring the Stock of the said Work and the several drawings and engravings to illustrate the same from loss or damage by fire and all such sale or management and agency charges in respect of the same part or number as are hereinbefore mentioned and also the sum of Fifty pounds which shall have been paid to the said Charles Dickens for such part or number at the time and in the manner aforesaid and that the residue or surplus of the monies so received and accountable for by the said Edward Chapman and William Hall their executors or administrators for or in respect of each such part or number shall forthwith after the auditing and signing the Accounts as hereinafter mentioned be divided into two equal moieties one whereof shall be paid by the said Edward Chapman and William Hall their executors or administrators to the said Charles Dickens his executors or administrators and the other retained by the said Edward Chapman and William Hall their executors and administrators to and for their own proper use PROVIDED ALWAYS and these Presents are made upon this express condition and understanding That the sum of Fifty pounds for each and every number of the said Work is to be paid by the said Edward Chapman and William Hall their executors or administrators to the said Charles Dickens his executors or administrators at the time and times and in the manner in that behalf aforesaid absolutely and is to be kept and retained by the said Charles Dickens his executors or administrators to and for his or their sole or separate use without reference to the said residue or surplus or any other matter or matters herein contained [a]And that the Account of the receipts or charges in respect of each part or number shall be considered wholly distinct from the accounts of the receipts or charges in respect of any other part or number or parts or numbers of the said Work so that if the receipts in respect of any one of the said parts or numbers shall be less than the amount together of the expenses and charges incurred on account thereof and the sum of Fifty pounds paid to the said Charles Dickens his executors or administrators for the same such deficiency shall be borne wholly by the said Edward Chapman and William Hall their executors or administrators without any right on their part to have such deficiency made good out of the gains or profits of any other part or number of the said work or otherwise howsoever [ab]But it is nevertheless agreed by and between the parties hereto that all charges for advertising and other expenses not specifically incurred for or in respect of any one particular number during any one half year shall be distributed over the whole of the numbers or parts published in such half years respectively in equal proportions[b] AND IT IS FURTHER AGREED that true and particular accounts in writing shewing as well all sums of money received on account of the said Work and accountable for in respect of the Advertisements inserted therein as all expenses charges and allowances fairly attending the same or necessarily incurred in respect thereof shall be kept by the said Edward Chapman and William Hall their executors or administrators which Accounts together with all vouchers relating thereto shall at all reasonable times be open to the inspection of the said Charles Dickens his executors or administrators or his or their Solicitor for the time being with power to take copies or extracts therefrom respectively And that a true and particular account in writing shewing all such sums of money expenses charges and allowances as last aforesaid in respect of the parts or numbers of the said Work which shall have been from time to time published up to the thirtieth day of June and the thirty first day of December in every year and of which no such Account shall have been previously made up stated and delivered, shall be made up stated and delivered by the said Edward Chapman and William Hall their executors or administrators to the said Charles Dickens his executors or administrators within three calendar months next following the thirtieth day of June and the thirty first day of December in each and every year And that after the delivery thereof the said Accounts shall forthwith be audited and signed by the said Parties hereto as correct unless it shall then appear that there is any inaccuracy therein which if found shall be immediately corrected and the Account so corrected signed as aforesaid And within seven days after the signature of each such Account by the said Charles Dickens his executors or administrators the said Edward

---

[aa] Among the many additions Smithson & Mitton made to William Chapman's draft of this Agreement (MS Mr C. C. Dickens), this was the only one disputed by Chapman, who at first cancelled but later stetted it (see *To Chapman & Hall, 27 Mar 40, fn*).

[bb] Added to the draft by Chapman when finally accepting the previous clause.

Chapman and William Hall their executors or administrators shall and will pay to him the said Charles Dickens his executors or administrators the equal moiety of the balance of every such account to which he or they shall be entitled under the agreement in that behalf hereinbefore contained And that each account so to be rendered as aforesaid shall unless in the meantime so corrected and in that case the same so corrected be considered and admitted to be correct at the expiration of six calendar months next after the time to which each such account shall have been so made up as aforesaid And shall not be thereafter opened or questioned by either of the said parties hereto (except for manifest error appearing upon the face thereof) AND IT IS HEREBY FURTHER AGREED that if upon the making up of any such half yearly account as aforesaid it shall be ascertained that the monies received by the said Edward Chapman and William Hall their executors or administrators or for which they or either or any of them shall be liable to account in manner aforesaid shall be less than the amount of all the expenses and charges necessarily incurred in respect of the said Work as aforesaid within the half year to which such account shall relate then and in every such case the whole of such deficiency shall be borne and defrayed by the said Edward Chapman and William Hall their executors or administrators and the said Charles Dickens his executors or administrators shall not in any event or on any account or pretence whatsoever be personally charged with or liable for such deficiency or any part thereof AND IT IS HEREBY FURTHER AGREED and especially the said Charles Dickens for himself his heirs executors and administrators doth hereby further covenant promise and agree with and to the said Edward Chapman and William Hall their executors and administrators that the Copyright of and in the said Work and of the successive numbers or parts thereof as they shall from time to time appear shall from thenceforth become and be the property of the said Charles Dickens as to one equal moiety thereof and the property of the said Edward Chapman and William Hall as to the other equal moiety thereof AND for the purposes of this Agreement and subject thereto the said Charles Dickens doth hereby give and grant to the said Edward Chapman and William Hall their executors and administrators full licence and the sole and exclusive right of printing publishing and selling the said intended New work and all the numbers or parts thereof And doth hereby covenant promise and agree with and to them the said Edward Chapman and William Hall their executors and administrators That he the said Charles Dickens his executors and administrators shall and will from time to time and as often as he may be required so to do after the publication of any part or number or parts or numbers of the said intended Work by proper and valid Assignment or Assignments in the Law to be prepared by and at the expense of the said Edward Chapman and William Hall their executors or administrators assign transfer and make over one equal moiety of the copyright of and in all and every such part or number or parts or numbers as may be then published unto the said Edward Chapman and William Hall their executors and administrators to be held by them subject nevertheless to all the stipulations and agreements herein contained And in every such Assignment there shall be contained a Covenant on the part of the said Edward Chapman and William Hall their executors or administrators for securing to the said Charles Dickens his executors administrators and assigns the right of purchasing the share and interest of the said Edward Chapman and William Hall their executors or administrators of and in the copyright of the said work upon the same terms as are hereinafter expressed in relation to either of the parties hereto who shall be desirous of selling or disposing of his or their share and interest of and in the said Copyright AND IT IS HEREBY FURTHER MUTUALLY COVENANTED AND AGREED by and between the said several parties hereto that in case it shall be thought advisable by the said parties hereto to publish at any time any portion or portions of the said Work in a separate and distinct form the same allowance[s] for expenses management and agency as are herein before mentioned and provided for shall be made and allowed to the said Edward Chapman and William Hall their executors and administrators in respect of such separate publication or publications And that subject thereto all subsequent profits arising therefrom shall be divided in like manner and be subject to the like regulations and provisions as is and are herein expressed and contained in relation to the said work as published in the form hereby agreed upon AND IT IS HEREBY FURTHER COVENANTED AND AGREED that if either of the parties hereto his or their respective executors or administrators shall be desirous of selling or disposing of his or their share and interest of and in the Copyright of the said intended New Work or any part thereof then he or they shall in the first instance offer to transfer and relinquish the share or interest which he or they shall so desire to sell or dispose of to the other of the said parties hereto his or their executors or administrators and shall not sell dispose of or transfer such share and interest of and in the said Copyright or any part thereof to any other person or persons unless and until the party hereto to whom the same shall have been so offered shall have declined to purchase the same at a price to be fixed on (in case the parties cannot agree) by two indifferent persons one to be chosen by the said Charles Dickens his executors or administrators and the other to be chosen by the said Edward Chapman and William Hall their executors or administrators or if such two persons differ then at a price to be fixed by a third person or umpire to be chosen by the two Persons first appointed or unless or until the party to whom the same shall have been so offered shall have refused or neglected to name one of the said two persons for the space of seven days after he or they shall have been requested in writing so to do by the other of them or unless and until the party to whom the same shall have been so offered shall have neglected to pay the said price for fourteen days after the same shall have been so agreed on or fixed PROVIDED ALWAYS that it shall and may be lawful for the said Edward Chapman and William Hall their executors or administrators by giving three calendar months Notice in writing to the said Charles Dickens his executors or administrators to declare that at any time after the expiration of twelve calendar months from the publication of the first number of the said New Work the same shall thenceforth so far as they are concerned cease and be discontinued and thereupon this Agreement shall as to all clauses and liabilities relating to any other future number or numbers of the said Work become void and of none effect And in like manner it shall and may be lawful for the said Charles Dickens his executors or administrators by giving the like notice in writing to the said Edward Chapman and William Hall their executors or administrators to declare that at any time after the expiration of five years from the publication of the said first Number of the said New Work the same shall thenceforth cease and be discontinued and thereupon in like manner this Agreement shall as to all clauses and liabilities for the future cease and become utterly void and of none effect PROVIDED ALSO that if at any time hereafter while the said New Work shall continue to be published both of them the said Edward Chapman and William Hall should die or any other event or events should happen in consequence whereof the publication of the said New Work can no longer be continued by them the said Edward Chapman and William Hall or one of them personally at their or his own costs and risk and for their or his own personal benefit then and in either of such events this Agreement shall for the future cease and become utterly void and of none effect PROVIDED ALSO AND IT IS HEREBY DECLARED that after this Agreement shall have ceased under any of the provisions for that purpose hereinbefore contained it shall be lawful for the said Charles Dickens his executors or administrators to continue the publication of the said Work for his or their exclusive benefit (except as regards the parts or numbers thereof which shall have been published prior to the ceasing of this Agreement) in such manner in all respects as he or they shall think fit and for that purpose to use the name or title under which the said Work shall have been published at the ceasing of this Agreement or any time prior thereto AND IT IS HEREBY FURTHER AGREED that if at any time hereafter any dispute doubt or question shall arise between the said parties hereto or their respective executors or administrators under or in relation to these presents then every such dispute doubt or question shall be reduced into writing and referred to the arbitration of two indifferent persons one to be named by the said Charles Dickens his executors or administrators and the other to be named by the said Edward Chapman and William Hall their executors or administrators or in case either of the parties in dispute shall refuse to join in such nomination then both of the said Arbitrators to be named by the other of the said parties And in case such Referees cannot agree upon an Award then the said dispute doubt or question shall stand referred to the umpirage or arbitration of such one person as the said two Referees shall by writing under their hands appoint so that every such reference shall be made within forty days next after such dispute doubt or question shall arise And the Award or determination which shall be made by the said two referees or by their Umpire concerning the premises shall be final and conclusive on the parties respectively and their respective heirs executors and administrators so as such referees shall make their Award in writing under their hands or appoint an Umpire within forty days after the references to them And so as such Umpire shall make his determination in writing under his hand within twenty days after the time appointed for making the Award of the said Referees shall be expired And that this submission to Reference shall be made a Rule of Her Majesty's Court of Queen's Bench at Westminster on the application of either of the parties to the Reference And also that no Suit at Law or in Equity shall be commenced or prosecuted against the Referees or their Umpire concerning any of the matters or things so to be referred to them or him as aforesaid or concerning their or his Award or determination And that the several and respective parties to such Reference shall submit to be examined by the said Referees or their Umpire upon oath or affirmation or Declaration by way of oath for the discovery of any of the dealings or transactions relating to the matters to be referred as aforesaid and shall produce all Books papers and writings in their or his custody or power touching the matters to be referred unto the said Referees or their Umpire And that no Suit at Law or in Equity shall be commenced or instituted by either of the said parties hereto his or their executors or administrators touching the matters in dispute before the person or persons his or their executors or administrators to be made Defendant or Defendants to such suit or suits shall have refused or neglected to refer the matter in difference to arbitration pursuant to the Agreement hereinbefore contained or unless the time limited for making such Award or determination shall have elapsed or expired without any such Award or Determination having been made IN WITNESS whereof the said parties to these presents have hereunto set their hands and seals the day and year first above written.

| | |
|---|---|
| Signed sealed and delivered by the within named Charles Dickens — Edward Chapman and William Hall in the presence of — | CHARLES DICKENS |
| | EDWARD CHAPMAN |
| WM. CHAPMAN<br>  Sol. Richmond<br>CHAS. SMITHSON<br>  Solr. 23 Southampton Buildings | WILLIAM HALL |

## FINAL AGREEMENT WITH RICHARD BENTLEY, 2 JULY 1840

MS (Copy) Mr C. C. Dickens.

Articles of Agreement, made the second day of July One thousand eight hundred and forty, Between Charles Dickens of Devonshire Terrace

Esquire of the one part and Richard Bentley of New Burlington Street, Publisher of the other part.—

Whereas by an Agreement under the respective hands of the above named Charles Dickens and Richard Bentley bearing date the twenty seventh of February One thousand eight hundred and thirty nine, the said Charles Dickens for the considerations therein stated to be paid to him by the said Richard Bentley did agree with the said Richard Bentley for the sale to him of the Copyright of a certain Work which he then intended to write to be entitled "Barnaby Rudge or a Tale of the Great Riots". And whereas by certain other Articles of Agreement under the hands and seals of the said Charles Dickens and the said Richard Bentley bearing even date with the last recited Agreement. It was agreed that the said Charles Dickens should from a certain day therein limited discontinue his Editorship of a certain work of which he had theretofore been the Editor for the said Richard Bentley under the title of "Bentley's Miscellany" that the said Charles Dickens should be entitled to a certain sum on all Numbers of such Miscellany containing any Article written by him the sale of which should reach or exceed six thousand Copies the same to be accounted for as therein mentioned that subject to certain stipulations therein contained in relation to a certain work under the title of "Oliver Twist" the sole copyright of all other works written by the said Charles Dickens which had theretofore appeared in the Miscellany so far as respected the printing and publishing the same works detached from the said Miscellany should from a period of three years to be computed from their appearance in the said Miscellany become the property of the said Charles Dickens and Richard Bentley as Tenants in Common in equal moieties that in consideration of the sum of Five hundred pounds paid by the said Richard Bentley to the said Charles Dickens the said Charles Dickens would if required assign to the said Richard Bentley the sole and exclusive Copyright of and in the said Work entitled "Oliver Twist" for three years from the twentieth of October then last with certain stipulations as to the mode of publication that at the expiration of said period of three years the said Copyright should become the property of the said Charles Dickens and Richard Bentley as tenants in common in equal moieties to which [were][1] added clauses for the said Charles Dickens if he should think fit at the expiration of the said period of three years to take a moiety of the unsold printed Copies together with the engravings etchings &c. published therewith at the cost price thereof That the said Richard Bentley should be at liberty to charge the said Work with certain expences during the period same should be published on the joint account of himself and said Charles Dickens with power for either party to purchase the share of the other in the event of his being desirous of disposing of his interest therein. A stipulation that at no time should the Work be published in any other manner or form than that prescribed and a power for the said Charles Dickens to put an end to the now reciting Agreement in the event of the said

[1] MS reads "was".

Richard Bentley neglecting to perform his portion of its condition and concluded with mutual Releases of all claims which either of them might have against the other under or by virtue of an Indenture of the twenty second of September then last.—And whereas up to the present time no request has been made by the said Richard Bentley to the said Charles Dickens to assign to him for a period of three years the Copyright of the said Work entitled "Oliver Twist" in pursuance of the provisions of the last recited Agreement but the said Richard Bentley has been permitted to continue the publication thereof and at the present time there are now remaining unsold One thousand and two Copies of the said entire work in three Volumes together with the plates and illustrat[ions][1] thereof. And whereas the said Charles Dickens hath contracted with the said Richard Bentley for all the residue of his right and interest under and by virtue of the aforesaid two several recited Agreements and for the said instruments to be given up to him the said Charles Dickens (without prejudice to the said Richard Bentley being at liberty to reprint publish and sell any Number of the aforesaid Miscellany which shall have originally contained any Article written by the said Charles Dickens and for liberty to do which the said Charles Dickens hereby gives and grants to the said Richard Bentley full licence so to do and agrees to execute a proper and more formal deed or instrument to effectuate such purpose the same to be prepared by and at the expence of the said Richard Bentley) in case he shall require it. And hath agreed to pay the said Richard Bentley on the signing of this Agreement the sum of Two thousand two hundred and fifty Pounds. And the said Richard Bentley hath agreed to deliver the aforesaid One thousand and two Copies of the said entire work called "Oliver Twist" in a perfect and complete state in quires (not bound) fit for Sale with the illustrations to accompany same as also the original plates from which the same every and any of them may have been struck off unto Messrs. Chapman & Hall of the Strand Publishers on his the said Charles Dickens behalf and the said Charles Dickens hath agreed to cause to be delivered to the said Richard Bentley at any time or times within a reasonable time after having been required so to do any number of copies to be struck from the said plates so given up as aforesaid on receiving from the said Richard Bentley the sum of Four shillings per hundred being the expence of the paper and striking off the same. And doth also give up to the said Richard Bentley all right and interest of him the said [Charles Dickens][2] in or to any portion of the Profit which would have otherwise accrued or might hereafter accrue to him for and by reason of the sale of any number of the Miscellany in which any portion of his works originally appeared having reached or exceeded a Sale of six thousand Copies. Now this Agreement Witnesseth and the said Richard Bentley in consideration of the sum of Two thousand two hundred and fifty pounds to him paid by the said Charles Dickens at or before the execution of this Agreement and of the said Charles Dickens

[1] MS reads "illustrative".  [2] MS reads "Richard Bentley", but clearly should be CD.

having consented to forego for his benefit all share and interest which could or might at any time have arisen by the sale of any part of the said Miscellany to the extent hereinbefore mentioned and in consideration of the grant or licence hereinbefore contained on the part of the said Charles Dickens to reprint publish and sell any number of the said Miscellany which hath heretofore contained any article written by the said Charles Dickens doth hereby agree with and to the said Charles Dickens at any time hereafter when thereunto requested to assign and make over all the right and interest of him the said Richard Bentley of and in the aforesaid two several recited Agreements of the twenty seventh of February One thousand eight hundred and thirty nine (with the exceptions before stipulated) and hath on the execution of this Agreement in pursuance thereof delivered up to the said Charles Dickens the said two original Agreements and also the said One thousand and two Copies of the said entire work entitled "Oliver Twist" together with the plates etchings &c. used in the getting up of the said Work and hereby undertakes to execute any instrument by way of Release (to be prepared by and at the expence of the said Charles Dickens) of all claims and demands which he has or could or might have against the said Charles Dickens for or in respect thereof which said Deed or Instrument shall contain a Covenant on the part of the said Richard Bentley not to advertize or publish any numbers of the said Miscellany in which any portion of the said work entitled "Oliver Twist" shall have originally appeared in any other manner or form than as the same has heretofore been published And the said Charles Dickens on his part hath at or immediately before the execution of this Agreement paid to the said Richard Bentley the sum of Two thousand two hundred and fifty pounds and doth hereby agree to give and grant to the said Richard Bentley (by a proper Instrument to be prepared by and at the expence of the said Richard Bentley) liberty to print publish and sell in any reprint of the parts or numbers of the said Miscellany in which portion of the aforesaid work entitled "Oliver Twist" originally appeared in the same manner and form and to a like extent as the same did so originally appear but the licence so to be given by the said Charles Dickens to the said Richard Bentley to cease in the event of the said Richard Bentley causing to be reprinted in any greater quantity in any one part or number the said work entitled "Oliver Twist" than[1] originally appeared in each monthly part or number or on the said Richard Bentley advertizing the said work in any other form than is hitherto advertized. And further that he the said Charles Dickens will assign unto the said Richard Bentley all interest which could or might arise to him for or by reason of the sale of any monthly part or number of the said Miscellany in which any portion of his works shall have originally appeared reaching and exceeding six thousand copies and also will release and discharge the said Richard Bentley from any liability in respect of any covenants or conditions in the said Agreement or Indenture bearing date

---

[1] MS reads "then".

the twenty seventh day of February One thousand eight hundred and thirty nine, As witness [our hands][1] the day and year first above written.—

Witness to the Signature of the parties— } Charles Dickens.
Richard Bentley.

John S Gregory—Bedford Row
Thos. Mitton 23, Southampton Buildings.

Received the day and year first above written by me the undersigned Richard Bentley the sum of two thousand two hundred and fifty pounds from the within named Charles Dickens being the consideration Money expressed to be paid by him to me ............................ } £2250.

Richard Bentley

Witness to the signature of the said Richard Bentley—

Thos. Mitton.


## AGREEMENT WITH CHAPMAN & HALL FOR *BARNABY RUDGE*, [JULY] 1840[2]

MS (Copy) Mr C. C. Dickens.

Articles of Agreement made and entered into this [     ] day of [     ] 1840 Between Charles Dickens of Devonshire Terrace in the Parish of Saint Mary le bone in the County of Middlesex Esquire of the one part and Edward Chapman and William Hall of the Strand in the same County Publishers of the other part.

Whereas the said Charles Dickens intends to write and compose a certain Literary Work of the nature more particularly mentioned and hath proposed to sell and assign the Copyright and sole right of printing and publishing the same to the said Edward Chapman and William Hall for the term and upon the conditions hereinafter contained to which they have agreed And whereas two Chapters of the said proposed New Work have been written by the said Charles Dickens and delivered to the said Edward Chapman and William Hall as they do hereby acknowledge—Now these Presents witness And the said Charles Dickens doth hereby for himself his heirs Executors and Administrators in consideration of the said Agreement and of the sum of money hereinafter agreed to be paid to him by the

---

[1] MS reads "my hand". Here, as for earlier mistakes in this Agreement, copyist has added "sic" in the margin.

[2] On 25 July 40 William Chapman sent Smithson & Mitton a draft of the Agreement (see *To* Chapman & Hall, 2 July 40, *fn*). It was probably signed not long after.

said Edward Chapman and William Hall their Executors and Administrators and of the Covenants and Agreements on their part hereinafter
contained covenant promise and agree with and to the said Edward Chapman and William Hall their Executors Administrators and Assigns that he
the said Charles Dickens shall and will compose and write a New Work the
Title whereof shall be "Barnaby Rudge" And that the said New Work
shall contain literary matter or composition which shall be equal to ten
numbers each containing two Sheets of letter press of the same kind and
size and in all respects equal to two former works written by the said
Charles Dickens and published by the said Edward Chapman and William
Hall and called "The Posthumous Papers of the Pickwick Club" and "The
Life and Adventures of Nicholas Nickleby"—And that he the said Charles
Dickens shall and will write and compose the said Work and deliver the
manuscript thereof to the said Edward Chapman and William Hall their
Executors Administrators and Assigns at such one time or at such periodi-
cal times but not to exceed in the whole the space or time of Five years from
the day of the date of these presents and either complete or in such periodicals parts and proportions as they the said Charles Dickens and the said
Edward Chapman and William Hall their Executors Administrators or
Assigns may hereafter agree appoint and determine And further that the
Copyright of and in the said Work and of every part thereof shall from the
time of writing and composing the same thenceforth become and be the
property of the said Edward Chapman and William Hall their Executors
Administrators and Assigns And the said Charles Dickens doth hereby give
and grant to the said Edward Chapman and William Hall their Executors
Administrators and Assigns full licence and the sole and exclusive right
of printing publishing and selling the said intended New Work and every
part and portion thereof for such period and space of time as may be
occupied in the publication thereof in numbers at Monthly intervals (but
so that the same shall not be divided into more than fifteen monthly parts
or numbers) and for the space or time of Six Calendar Months next after
the publication of the last monthly number thereof And further that he
the said Charles Dickens his Executors or Administrators shall and will
from time to time and as often as he may be required to do so by the said
Edward Chapman and William Hall their Executors Administrators and
Assigns after the publication of any part or number of the said intended
new work, by proper and valid assignments in the law to be prepared by
and at the expence of the said Edward Chapman and William Hall their
Executors Administrators and Assigns assign transfer and make over the
Copyright of and in all and every such part or number or parts or numbers
and at the completion thereof of the whole of the said New Work unto the
said Edward Chapman and William Hall their Executors Administrators
and Assigns to be held by them for their own use and benefit from thenceforth for the term of Six Calendar Months to be computed from the day of
the publication of the last part thereof as aforesaid And the said Edward
Chapman and William Hall in consideration of the Covenants and Agree-

ments hereinbefore contained on the part of the said Charles Dickens his heirs Executors and Administrators do hereby covenant promise and agree with and to the said Charles Dickens his Executors Administrators and Assigns that they the said Edward Chapman and William Hall their Executors Administrators and Assigns shall and will well and truly pay or cause to be paid to the said Charles Dickens his Executors Administrators or Assigns the sum of £3000 of lawful British Money as the consideration for the purchase of the said Copyright as hereinbefore is mentioned the same to be paid and payable to the said Charles Dickens his Executors Administrators and Assigns at the time when the said Work shall be completed and the Manuscript of the whole thereof delivered to the said Edward Chapman and William Hall their Executors Administrators or Assigns as aforesaid or at such other time and times and in such parts and proportions as may be mutually agreed upon between the said parties hereto And it is hereby declared and agreed by and between the said parties hereto that the said Work may be published by the said Edward Chapman and William Hall their Executors Administrators or assigns either in ten or fifteen Monthly Numbers as they may think fit—And it is further agreed and particularly the said Charles Dickens for himself his Heirs Executors and Administrators doth covenant promise and agree with and to the said Edward Chapman and William Hall that in case it shall be determined to commence the publication of the said Work in parts before the whole of it is written and delivered to the said Edward Chapman and William Hall their Executors Administrators or Assigns the said Charles Dickens shall in that case duly and regularly write compose and deliver to the said Edward Chapman and William Hall their Executors Administrators and Assigns a sufficient part of the said Manuscript of the said Work from time to time so that they may always have and possess the Manuscript of any forthcoming or future portion of the said Work at least thirty days before the day on which it is intended that the same shall be published—Provided always And these presents are upon this express condition nevertheless that notwithstanding the Covenants hereinbefore contained on the part of the said Edward Chapman and William Hall for payment of the said sum of £3000 to the said Charles Dickens his Executors Administrators and Assigns the said Edward Chapman and William Hall their Executors or Administrators shall not be liable or called upon to pay the same until the said Charles Dickens his Executors Administrators or Assigns shall have first paid or allowed in account thereout to the said Edward Chapman and William Hall their Executors Administrators or Assigns the sum of £2250 and such further sum or sums as are mentioned in and secured by a certain Indenture of Assignment bearing even date with these presents and made between the said parties hereto or so much as may be then due upon or by virtue of the same.

## MEMORANDUM OF AN AGREEMENT WITH
## CHAPMAN & HALL FOR [*MARTIN CHUZZLEWIT*],[1]
## 7 SEPTEMBER 1841

MS Widener Collection, Harvard.

Memorandum of an agreement entered into this 7th. day of September 1841, between Charles Dickens Esqre and Messrs Chapman and Hall of the Strand.

Mr. Dickens agrees to write, and Messrs Chapman and Hall to publish, a new periodical work, on the following terms and conditions:

That, with the close of the story at present going on in the publication called Master Humphrey's Clock, the further Continuance of that publication shall, by mutual consent, determine and cease. The properties in the copyright, existing stock, plates &c, and all conditions relative to the delivery of accounts and payment of proceeds excepting as hereinafter specified, to remain as secured by the articles of agreement between the same parties, dated the 31st of March 1840.

That the new work shall be, in form size and price, precisely similar to the Pickwick Papers and Nicholas Nickleby; that it shall be published in twenty numbers at one shilling each; and that the publication of the first number shall take place on the first of November 1842.

That Messrs Chapman and Hall will, for the consideration here after mentioned, undertake, at their sole cost and risk, all the charges and expenses of this work: the printing, paper, illustration by such engravings as may be mutually agreed, advertising, binding, selling: indeed, everything incident to its due and regular publication on the first of every month for the space of twenty months: and will further pay to Mr. Dickens, on the first day of every month during such publication, the sum of £200[2] sterling: Mr. Dickens undertaking to furnish the manuscript of each number in time for its appearance as above stipulated.

That, in the sale of the work in monthly shilling numbers as before specified, Messrs Chapman and Hall shall account for all numbers sold at the rate of 8s. per dozen, counting 13 numbers as 12; and shall charge the work with £5 per cent upon the total amounts sold as a recompense for their trouble as booksellers, and also with all commissions or charges allowed to the agents for the sale of the work: it being understood that they bear all losses arising from bad debts: and that, while the entire management of the publication and sale of the work is entrusted to them, they shall not be allowed to print or publish it, or any part of it, in any other form than is specified herein, without the consent in writing of Mr. Dickens.

That, for all the advertisements inserted in the three pages of the wrapper of the work, Messrs Chapman and Hall shall account to the work

---

[1] Not yet given a title.

[2] "£" written after numerals here and elsewhere in the Agreement—though not consistently. We have given "£" before the amount throughout.

without the charge of anything for collecting: that the price of each advertisement so inserted (deducting only the government duty) shall be allowed: Messrs Chapman and Hall undertaking that the return from such advertising in each number shall in no case be less than £10: but that, in each number, they shall be allowed to insert an advertising sheet of their own, all the profits arising from which, as well as all the expenses incurred, to belong exclusively to them.

That out of all monies received by Messrs Chapman and Hall, by, for, or on account of, the sale and publication of each number of this work, and out of the money received from the advertisements on the three pages of wrapper, there shall first be paid or deducted all expenses of printing, paper, and illustration of the said number; also a proportionate share, due upon each number, of all the expenses of advertising from time to time incurred, and of the expenses of insuring the stock and engravings of the work from loss or damage by fire; also, all such sale and agency charges upon each number as were before specified; also, the sum of £200 paid to Mr. Dickens, as before mentioned, for each number:—and that, when these respective deductions have been made, the residue of the monies so received by Messrs Chapman and Hall in respect of each number, shall, after the delivery of proper accounts at periods to be hereafter mentioned, be thus apportioned: Mr. Dickens shall receive three fourths of the whole residue, and Messrs Chapman and Hall one fourth.

That in no case, however, shall the payment to be absolutely made to, and retained by, Mr. Dickens, of £200 upon each number, be considered as in any way dependant on such residue or surplus of each number. The accounts of the receipts or charges in respect of each number, are to be considered wholly distinct from the accounts of the receipts or charges in respect of any other number (excepting only the charges for advertising and other expenses not specifically incurred for one particular number, which are to be distributed, in equal portions to each number, over the space of time for which each account is rendered); so that, if the receipts upon that number should fall short of the necessary expenses, and of the £200 payable to Mr. Dickens upon it, the deficiency shall be wholly borne by Messrs Chapman and Hall. And in like manner it is agreed that if, upon the making up of the accounts to be hereafter stated, it is ascertained that all the monies received by Messrs Chapman and Hall or for which they shall be liable to account, during the six months for which the account runs, shall have fallen short of the expenses incurred in that half year, then Messrs Chapman & Hall are to bear & defray the whole of such deficiency.

That accounts in writing are to be made up and rendered to Mr. Dickens by Messrs Chapman and Hall, as soon as possible after each Christmas and Midsummer: in the manner and with the stipulations described in the agreement between the parties on account of Master Humphrey's Clock, dated the 31st. of March 1840.

That, after the last number of the work shall have appeared, and for six months afterwards, namely, to the 31st of Decr. 1844 Mr. Dickens shall be entitled to receive, out of the residue or surplus of each number, or out of the residue or surplus arising upon the collected sale when the work appears in one volume (as in the instances of Pickwick and Nickleby), the amount of three fourths of the whole sum, Messrs Chapman & Hall receiving one fourth; but that, on the expiration of those six months, namely on the 31st day of Decr. 1844 just mentioned, Mr. Dickens agrees to assign and make over to Messrs Chapman and Hall, the interest in one full moiety of the profits and copyright of the various numbers of the work, and the collected volume: provided that, for and in respect of the stock of numbers or volumes that may then happen to remain on hand, Messrs Chapman and Hall pay over to Mr. Dickens the full amount of one fourth of the paper and print cost of the stock so remaining.

That Mr. Dickens will at any time, when requested so to do, and at the expense of Messrs Chapman and Hall, assign and secure to them the interest in the profits & copyright of the various numbers and collected volume of this work, to the amount of one fourth, as herein before stipulated, up to the 31st of December 1844, and, when that time shall have expired, and upon the fulfilment of the above named condition as to the existing stock, will further assign and secure to Messrs Chapman & Hall from the 31st of December 1844 an interest in the copyright and profits of the said work to the amount of a full moiety:—provided always, that with respect to any right of disposing of such interest or copyright, or of using it in any new form of publication, the conditions of the agreement of the 31st of March 1840, for and in respect of Master Humphrey's Clock, shall be in like manner binding on the parties, in respect of the present agreement. The same is also agreed to, with reference to any disputes that may arise: in which case the conditions of arbitration described in the agreement for Master Humphrey's Clock, shall be binding here also.

It is further agreed that, for the considerations mentioned, and subject to the conditions of this agreement, Messrs Chapman and Hall shall, in the interval of twelve months which will elapse between the publication of the last number of Master Humphrey's Clock and the first number of the new work herein specified, advance to Mr. Dickens the sum of £150 sterling on the first day of every month: making in all the sum of £1800: to be repaid to Messrs Chapman & Hall, with interest at the rate of £5 per cent, out of his share of ¾ths. of the surplus or profits as herein before secured to him, when the work shall have commenced: such rate of interest to be payable only on the time for which the separate portion of money is advanced—the first payment for twelve months, the last payment for one month—and, on the publication of the first number of the work, to cease altogether. Also, that such advances shall not in any way interfere with the monthly payments of £200 to Mr. Dickens as herein secured to him from the commencement to the close of the work, but shall, with the interest as above, be wholly paid and satisfied out of his ¾th. share of the surplus or profits in the following manner: one half of that surplus or profit on the whole work, to be appropriated by Messrs Chapman and Hall to the repayment of this advance till the whole shall be liquidated; the other one fourth, also due to Mr. Dickens, to be appropriated by Messrs Chapman and Hall in satisfaction of an existing debt (as acknowledged in a letter signed by Mr. Dickens and now in possession of Messrs Chapman & Hall, dated 31st of July 1841) until that also shall be paid.

Providing always, that if it shall be found,—when the accounts of the sale and proceeds of the first five numbers of the new work herein described, are ascertained—that the amount of one half of the surplus or profit so set apart as above, is not likely to liquidate the advance of £1800 within one month after the completion of the work—in that case, Messrs Chapman and Hall shall be allowed, with a view to the more speedy liquidation of the same, to appropriate to their use, on and after the publication of the sixth number, £50 a month from Mr. Dickens' monthly payments of £200.

And it is further understood that if the whole of this advance of £1800, with interest as above, is not repaid to Messrs Chapman & Hall on or before the 31st day of December 1844, then that one fourth of the surplus of the whole proceeds, due to Mr. Dickens, shall continue to be appropriated to its discharge; the remaining fourth, also due to him, being applied in payment of the debt subsisting under the letter of the date of the 31st of July 1841. But that if the whole advance of £1800, with interest as above, shall have been liquidated by or before that time, then, and in that case, the sum of one fourth of the whole surplus (being one half of what would be due to Mr. Dickens) shall continue to be paid in discharge of the same, and that only.

Finally it is agreed that after the accounts on the conclusion of the publication of Master Humphrey's Clock shall have been finally made up, and the surplus proceeds (including the subscription) paid to Mr. Dickens, under the agreement of the 31st. of March 1840, then, namely, from the 1st of January 1842, Messrs Chapman & Hall shall appropriate the whole of the various sums arising due to Mr. Dickens from his share in the profits of the continued sale of the numbers and volumes of Master Humphrey's Clock, in satisfaction of the existing debt acknowledged in the letter of the date of the 31st day of July 1841, until the whole shall be paid.

Signed this 7th day of September 1841, in the presence of }     CHARLES DICKENS

EDWARD CHAPMAN

JOHN FORSTER[1]     WILLIAM HALL

[1] The whole Agreement is in Forster's hand. In thus preventing any "interference" by William Chapman (see *To* Mitton, 3 Sep 41), CD excluded his own solicitors too.

# C. DOCUMENTS CONCERNING
# CHAPMAN & HALL'S LOANS TO DICKENS

## (1) *DEED DRAFTED BY WILLIAM CHAPMAN,*
## *DECLINED BY SMITHSON & MITTON,*
## *26 MAY 1841*

MS¹ Mr C. C. Dickens.

This Indenture made the [          ]² day of [          ] AD. 1841 Between
Charles Dickens of No 1 Devonshire Terrace in the Parish of St. Maryle-
bone in the County of Middlesex Esquire of the one part and Edward
Chapman and William Hall of the Strand in the said County of Middlesex
Booksellers and Publishers and Partners in Trade of the other part Whereas
the said Charles Dickens is justly indebted to the said Edward Chapman &
William Hall in the sum of £[          ] of lawful Money of Great Britain
And Whereas the said Charles Dickens is possessed of and entitled to one
third part or share of the entire Copyright of and in a certain Book or
Work entitled "The Posthumous Papers of the Pickwick Club" (subject to
the exclusive right of the said Edward Chapman & William Hall to publish
and sell the same for a term of five years from the 1st. day of December
1837) And the said Charles Dickens is also possessed of and entitled to the
entire Copyright of and in a certain other Book or Work entitled "The Life
and Adventures of Nicholas Nickleby" (subject to the exclusive right of
the said Edward Chapman and William Hall to publish and sell the same
for a term of five years from the 1st. day of November 1839) And the said
Charles Dickens is also possessed of and entitled to a certain *contingent* interest in One Moiety or equal half part of the Copyright of and in a certain
other Book or Work entitled "Sketches by Boz First and Second Series"
And the said Charles Dickens is also possessed of and entitled to the entire
Copyright of and in a certain other Book or Work entitled "Oliver Twist"
And certain printed Copies or Stock thereof now in the possession of the
said Edward Chapman and William Hall And the said Charles Dickens is
also possessed of and entitled to One Moiety or equal half part of the Copyright of and in a certain other Book or Work entitled "Master Humphrey's
Clock" now in course of publication under an Agreement bearing date the
[Thirty-first] day of [March]³ 1840 between the said Charles Dickens and
the said Edward Chapman and William Hall and of and in certain printed
Copies or Stock thereof and also to One Moiety or equal half part of and in
the Profits to be made and derived from the publication of the last mentioned Work after payment of certain Expenses Advertising the same and
in the manner stipulated and provided for by the last mentioned Agree-

---

¹ Legal abbreviations have been expanded throughout; and Christian
names, sometimes shortened, given in
full.

² Empty square brackets indicate
blank spaces in MS.
³ Date supplied from Agreement on
p. 464.

ment And Whereas the said Charles Dickens hath at the request of the said
Edward Chapman and William Hall Agreed that the Payment of the said
Debt or sum of £[         ] (but without interest thereon) shall be secured
by the Assignment of the said several Copyrights and Shares and otherwise
in the manner herein after expressed Now therefore this Indenture Witnesseth that in pursuance of the said Agreement and in consideration of the
said sum of £[         ] so as aforesaid owing to the said Edward Chapman
and William Hall by the said Charles Dickens and for securing the payment of such sum of £[         ] He the said Charles Dickens Hath granted
bargained sold and assigned and by these presents Doth grant bargain sell
and assign unto the said Edward Chapman and William Hall their Executors Administrators or Assigns All that the one third part or share of him
the said Charles Dickens of the entire Copyright of and in the said Book or
Work entitled "The Posthumous Papers of the Pickwick Club" (subject to
such right of publishing and selling the same for the term of five years from
the 1st. day of November 1837 as aforesaid) And also all that the entire
Copyright and interest of him the said Charles Dickens of and in the said
Book or Work entitled "The Life and Adventures of Nicholas Nickleby"
(subject to such right of Publishing and selling the same for the term of five
years from the 1st. day of November 1839 as aforesaid) And also all that
the share right and interest of him the said Charles Dickens of and in One
Moiety or equal half part of the said Copyright of and in the said other Book
or Work entitled "Sketches by Boz First and Second Series" And also all
that the entire Copyright of him the said Charles Dickens in the said
other Book or Work entitled "Oliver Twist" together with all the printed
Copies or Stock of the last mentioned Work now in the possession of the
said Edward Chapman and William Hall as hereinbefore is mentioned
And also all that the Moiety or equal half part or share of him the said
Charles Dickens of the said Copyright of and in the said Book or Work
entitled "Master Humphrey's Clock" and of and in all and every the
printed Copies or Stock of the last mentioned Work now printed or hereafter to be printed And also of and in all the profits and proceeds of and
arising from the Sales of the last mentioned Work and the said printed
Copies or Stock thereof after payment of such Expenses as herein in that
behalf are mentioned and referred to And also all the Shares right title interest trust possession property claim and demand whatever both at Law
and in Equity of him the said Charles Dickens in of or to the Copyrights
and shares of Copyrights and premises hereby assigned or expressed and
intended to be To have hold receive take and enjoy the several Copyrights
and shares of and interest in Copyrights and printed Copies and Stock
hereby assigned or expressed and intended so to be and all and every the
profits gains and proceeds to be made or derived from the publication and
sale thereof and of every of them (subject to the several Agreements heretofore entered into and now subsisting of and concerning the same respectively) and all other the premises hereby assigned or expressed and intended so to be unto the said Edward Chapman and William Hall their

Executors Administrators and Assigns absolutely and to and for their own use and benefit Upon the trusts following (that is to say) Upon trust that the said Edward Chapman and William Hall their Executors Administrators and Assigns do and shall (subject to the permission hereinafter contained respecting the said Work entitled "Master Humphrey's Clock") retain such part of the profits gains and proceeds to be made or claimed from the publication and sale of the hereafter mentioned books or works as shall be received by them under these presents in or towards payment of the said sum of £[       ] until such last mentioned sum shall be fully paid And after full payment of such sum of £[       ] do and shall account for and pay over the unapplied part of such profits gains and proceeds and assign the other or remaining parts of the same premises hereby assigned or intended so to be unto the said Charles Dickens his Executors Administrators or Assigns Provided always and it is hereby declared and agreed that the said Edward Chapman and William Hall their Executors Administrators and Assigns shall be entitled to an allowance or deduction of £5 per cent by way of Commission on the Sales of the printed Copies of the said Work entitled "Oliver Twist" now in the hands of the said Edward Chapman and William Hall and also to deduct all charges and expenses of Advertizing such last mentioned Book or Work and all such sums as shall be paid or allowed in respect of Foreign Commission thereon And the said Charles Dickens doth hereby for himself his Heirs Executors and Administrators Covenant with the said Edward Chapman and William Hall their Executors and Administrators in manner following that is to say that unless the Monies which under or by virtue of these presents shall have been received by the said Edward Chapman and William Hall their Executors Administrators or Assigns in or towards liquidation of the said sum of £[       ] on or before the [       ] day of [       ] 1846 shall have fully paid such last mentioned sum He the said Charles Dickens his Heirs Executors or Administrators shall and will immediately after the said [       ] day of [       ] 1846 pay unto the said Edward Chapman and William Hall their Executors Administrators or Assigns such a sum of Money as with the Monies which under or by virtue of these presents shall have been received by them towards liquidation of the said sum of £[       ] will make up the full amount of such sum of £[       ] And also that the said Charles Dickens is now lawfully rightfully and absolutely possessed of and entitled to the said several Copyrights and shares of Copyrights and interest of and in the said Books and Works hereinbefore mentioned and hereby assigned or expressed and intended so to be and to the said printed Copies or Stock of the said Works respectively hereinbefore mentioned and to the premises hereby assigned or intended so to be And that he now hath in himself full power and lawful and absolute authority to grant bargain sell and assign the same unto the said Edward Chapman and William Hall their Executors Administrators and Assigns in manner aforesaid and according to the true intent and meaning of these presents And Also that the said premises hereby assigned or intended so to be shall henceforth be and remain unto and be peaceably held and enjoyed by the said Edward Chapman and William Hall their Executors Administrators and Assigns without any interruption whatever And also that the said Charles Dickens his Executors Administrators and Assigns and every other person having or claiming any interest in the said premises hereby assigned or intended so to be shall and will at any time hereafter upon the request of the said Edward Chapman and William Hall their Executors Administrators or Assigns but at the Cost of the said Charles Dickens his Executors or Administrators make and execute or cause to be made and executed all such Acts and Assurances for better assigning the same premises unto the said Edward Chapman and William Hall their Executors Administrators or Assigns upon the trust hereinbefore declared and for otherwise effectuating the true intent of these presents as by the said Edward Chapman and William Hall their Executors Administrators or Assigns shall be required And the said Edward Chapman and William Hall do hereby for themselves their heirs Executors and Administrators Covenant promise and agree with and to the said Charles Dickens his Executors Administrators and Assigns in manner following that is to say that so long as the said several Copyrights and Shares of Copyrights or interest of the said Charles Dickens of and in the said several Works and other the premises hereby assigned or expressed and intended so to be shall remain vested in them the said Edward Chapman and William Hall their Executors Administrators or Assigns or any of them by virtue of these presents they the said Edward Chapman and William Hall their Executors Administrators or Assigns or any of them shall not nor will print Publish sell or use the same Books and Works or any or either of them or any part or parts number or numbers thereof or extract or extracts therefrom or of or from any or either of them in any new or other form than the form in which they severally and respectively are printed published sold and used at the present time and shall not nor will print publish sell use or deal with the same or any or either of them in any manner whatsoever so as to reduce or alter the prices or price at which the same or any or either of them are or is now sold without the consent in writing of the said Charles Dickens his Executors Administrators or Assigns signed by him or them in the presence of one or more Witness or Witnesses And also that they the said Edward Chapman and William Hall their Executors Administrators or Assigns shall and will keep and cause to be kept true and correct accounts of all Sales and Publications which shall be made and of all the gains and profits which shall be received by or become due to them or any of them in respect of such Sales and publications or otherwise under or by virtue of these presents and shall and will on the four usual Quarter days in each year henceforth and until the said [       ] day of [       ] 1846 or until the said sum of £[       ] shall have been paid off and discharged as is hereinafter mentioned make out and deliver to the said Charles Dickens his Executors and Administrators a true full and particular account in the nature of a Balance Sheet of all and every sums and sum of Money which

shall be or shall [have] been received by them or any or either of them
either from him the said Charles Dickens his Executors or Administrators
or by them the said Edward Chapman and William Hall their Executors
Administrators or Assigns in respect of the said Sales Publication and
premises under or by virtue of these presents or otherwise for or towards
the liquidation of the said sum of £[      ] And shall and will at all reasonable times produce the said Accounts and all Books Vouchers Papers and
documents relating thereto to the said Charles Dickens his Executors
Administrators or Assigns or his or their Solicitors or Agents when and as
they the said Edward Chapman and William Hall their Executors Administrators or Assigns shall be required so to do And that they the said
Edward Chapman and William Hall their Executors Administrators or
Assigns shall and will carry on and effect such Sales and Publications in
the best and most advantageous manner and according to the best of their
skill and ability in such manner as that the said sum of £[      ] may by
the ways and means aforesaid be liquidated as speedily as possible Provided
Always and it is hereby further agreed and declared between the parties
to these presents that a certain Agreement bearing date the [      ] day
of [      ] in the Year [      ] and made or expressed to be made between the said Edward Chapman and William Hall of the one part and the
said Charles Dickens of the other part and relating to the Sale and Publication of the said Book or Work entitled "Master Humphrey's Clock" and
the payments thereby agreed to be made and particularly the payment by
the said Edward Chapman and William Hall to the said Charles Dickens
of the sum of £50 for and in respect of each number of the last mentioned
Work shall notwithstanding these presents or anything therein contained
be and remain in full force and virtue and that the said Edward Chapman
and William Hall their Executors Administrators or Assigns or any or
either of them shall not be in any manner authorized or entitled to receive
or apply in or towards the liquidation of the said sum of £[      ] more
than one equal fourth part (being one half of the share of the said Charles
Dickens) of and in the clear profits to arise or be made from or by reason of
the Sale and publication of the last mentioned Work after all such payments
as are by the last mentioned Agreement stipulated and provided for shall
have been made But that one other equal fourth part (being the remaining
half of the share of the said Charles Dickens) of and in such last mentioned
clear profits together with the said sum of £50 for and in respect of each
number of the last mentioned Work shall continue to be paid to and received by the said Charles Dickens his Executors Administrators or
Assigns notwithstanding that the said sum of £[      ] or any part thereof
shall remain unpaid and that in the same manner as if these presents had
not been made  In Witness &c[1]

[1] At foot of last page is written: "Returned this Draft with letter declining
to entertain it the 26th. May 1841 [TM]."

## (2) *LETTERS FROM WILLIAM CHAPMAN TO SMITHSON & MITTON*

MSS Mr C. C. Dickens.

Richmond 4 June 1841

Dear Sirs,

### Dickens to Chapman & Hall

I was from home all last week & part of this, & on my return find that my brother is in the Country for a few days. Any reply to your proposal of the 25th. ult. must remain until he and Mr Hall can consult thereon. I shall also defer any comment on your letter except stating that I can by no means share your surprize[1] as to how Mr Bacon "came to hit upon the present mode"—which is but the necessary result of both Mr Dickens' Letter[2] & the arrangement entered into at our meeting at Mr Forsters.[3] I should have been surprised[1] if Mr Bacon as a man of business had hit upon any other mode.

I am Dear Sirs | Yours very truly

Messrs. Smithson & Mitton                     WM. CHAPMAN

Richmond 12 June 1841

Dear Sirs,

### Dickens to Chapman & Hall

My brother having returned to town, he & Mr Hall have taken your letter into consideration—and I am requested to say that if the mode of security first shadowed forth in Mr Dickens' letter of 2nd July last & put into shape by me in the drafts forwarded to you shortly afterwards—; if, again, the bodily form given by Mr Bacon to the understanding minuted down by Mr Forster at the Meeting at his Chambers on the 10th. Nov. last; are repugnant to Mr Dickens' feelings; they have that respect for and confidence in him that they would desire to consult his wishes in every respect—this is stated because they infer that the objections stated by you are entertained also by Mr Dickens—(not that it appears by your letter that he has been consulted on the subject, but that the objections are yours as matters of business)—Of course did they not presume Mr Dickens to coincide in those objections, the matter would be left as such matters usually are, to the decision of professional men; and in that case I must & should have maintained the propriety of the Deed proposed, as necessarily intended by the expression "a lien in the nature of a Mortgage" in Mr Forster's Memorandum—to the expressions in which I beg to call your attention.—Professional rules however must sometimes bend to the feelings of Clients, & therefore it is, that being relieved by their instructions from

[1] Thus in MS.                    [3] On 10 Nov 40: see next.
[2] Of 2 July 40.

all responsibility, I state Messrs. Chapman & Hall's desire to meet Mr Dickens' wishes—I would however just throw out for your consideration the following facts—that Mr Dickens' Letter of the 2nd July 1840 is virtually superseded by the new arrangement & that consequently my Clients possess no document stating the terms upon which they are to have a lien upon the Copyrights & Stock—that the £2250 was the purchase money (partly) of "Barnaby Rudge"—that "Barnaby Rudge" being published in "the Clock" is in fact being paid for twice over, unless the £2250 & about £1000 subsequently advanced are in some manner secured—that Messrs. Chapman & Hall consented to sacrifice the profits they expected to derive from the proposed publication of "Barnaby Rudge" on the undertaking made to them by Mr Forster, that in consideration of their giving up to Mr Dickens his Agreement for that work, he would no longer object to legal assignments of the Copyrights as Security—which understanding they consider is clearly expressed in Mr Forster's Memorandum which was read & agreed upon in the presence of Mr Mitton who was a consenting party thereto. It was also proposed by the letter of July that Mr Dickens should assign a Life Policy which he had effected—You now offer to suggest that Mr Dickens should give a Bond for every thing which is due— "and they will then have legal & equitable Security combined". These words necessarily imply that you consider the letter of July as subsisting— but as the terms mentioned in that letter are now so materially varied, would it not be better that Mr Dickens should write a fresh letter of similar import in accordance with the altered state of things—which letter, with the Bond & the Policy would be what I presume Mr Dickens intends Messrs. Chapman & Hall to have.

I beg to [be] favored with an early answer, & to repeat that this concession is made entirely by Messrs. Chapman & Hall out of deference to Mr Dickens' wishes—and that I am to be considered as in no degree qualifying my opinion as to the propriety of either the Deed I first prepared, or of that subsequently prepared by Mr Bacon.

I am Dear Sirs | Yours very obedy.

Messrs. Smithson & Mitton                                    WM. CHAPMAN


Richmond 10 July 1841

Dear Sirs,

### Dickens to Chapman & Hall

Various causes, principally absence of my Clients & myself from home have caused me to delay until now any further communication—I would now remark only on that part of your last letter (of the 15th. June) which refers to Mr Dickens' Letter of the 2nd July 1840—you state that that letter "so far as respects his other Copyrights is altogether untouched by what has taken place since that letter was written" and you add—"if the Bond is to be given we should think the old letter would very well suffice for all purposes"—My opinion is that the old letter is totally inapplicable to existing circumstances—but as I wish as far as possible to adhere to Mr Dickens' own words—I inclose a Copy of that letter altered in red ink, shewing what part is useless, and adding such words as serve to explain the existing state of things—I trust that no objection will be raised to this to accompany the Bond you offer and in that case Mr Dickens need on his return have little trouble in the matter.

I am Dear Sirs | Yours very truly

Messrs. Smithson & Mitton                                    WM. CHAPMAN

## (3) *BOND BETWEEN DICKENS AND CHAPMAN & HALL, 31 JULY 1841*

MS (copy) Mr C. C. Dickens.

Know All Men by these Presents that I Charles Dickens of Devonshire Terrace in the Parish of St. Marylebone in the County of Middlesex Esquire am held and firmly bound to Edward Chapman & William Hall of the Strand in the Liberty of Westminster Publishers in the penal sum of £6000 of lawful money of Great Britain to be paid to them the said Edward Chapman and William Hall or their certain Attorneys Executors Administrators or Assigns for which payment to be well and truly made I bind myself my heirs executors and administrators firmly by these presents Sealed with my Seal.—Dated this 31st. day of July A.D. 1841.—

Whereas the said Charles Dickens on the 2nd. day of July 1840 having occasion to borrow the sum of £2250 the said Edward Chapman and William Hall on that day advanced and lent him the same as he the said Charles Dickens doth hereby admit and acknowledge. And the said Charles Dickens is also indebted to the said Edward Chapman and William Hall in a further sum of money for advances made by the said Edward Chapman and William Hall for him And whereas by a Settlement of Accounts made between the said parties up to the 31st. day of December 1840 there appeared then due and owing by the said Charles Dickens to the said Edward Chapman and William Hall the sum of £3019..9..5 including the said sum of £2250.—And whereas it has been agreed that the said Edward Chapman and William Hall shall not call in nor compel payment of the said sum of £3019..9..5. before the 2nd. day of July which will be in the year 1845 and that the same shall not bear interest in the meantime but that nevertheless the same shall be subject to reduction in manner hereinafter mentioned that is to say that the said Edward Chapman and William Hall shall be at liberty to retain to themselves one half part of all such profits as may arise and accrue to the said Charles Dickens (over and above the sum of £50 agreed to be paid to him weekly) from and out of a periodical work now in course of publication entitled "Master Humphrey's Clock" and also to retain to themselves all such sum and sums of money as may arise by the Sale of the Printed Stock and copies of a certain work called "Oliver Twist" after deducting the sum of £5 per Cent as Commission on the Sale thereof and all charges of advertizing and foreign Commission. Now the Condition of the above written Obligation is such that if the said Charles Dickens his heirs executors or administrators some or one of them do and shall on the 2nd. day of July which will be in the year 1845 well and truly pay or cause to be paid unto the said Edward Chapman and William Hall their executors administrators or assigns the full sum of £3019..9..5 or so much thereof as according to the agreement hereinbefore mentioned may be then justly due and owing to the said Edward Chapman and William Hall then the above written obligation to be void otherwise to be and remain in full force and virtue.

# D. MISCELLANEOUS

## LETTER FROM "A TEMPLAR" TO THE EDITOR OF THE MORNING CHRONICLE, 23 JUNE 1840[1]

Middle Temple, June 23.

Sir,

A letter upon this subject, signed "Manlius", appears in your paper this day, which, as it involves a principle of the very highest importance, and is well calculated to mislead many well-meaning persons (more, however, on account of the prominent position which you have assigned to it than on account of the intrinsic force of the arguments contained in it), ought not, in my opinion, to be allowed to pass without notice.

The doctrine which "Manlius" has been attempting covertly to argue —however he may attempt to disguise it—is simply this, that a counsel ought not to defend a prisoner of whose guilt he is either absolutely certain, or entertains a strong suspicion.

From this doctrine I entirely dissent. In my opinion, in no case whatsoever would a counsel be justified, merely on account of any knowledge that he may have acquired, or of any suspicion that he may entertain of the prisoner's guilt, in refusing to defend a prisoner, or, having undertaken that defence, in neglecting to exert, to the utmost of his power, all his talents and abilities to procure his acquittal. One great error seems to pervade the whole of "Manlius's" letter, and to be the sole prompter of all his questions; it is this—"Manlius" seems to imagine that the whole question which the jury had to try upon the late trial of Courvoisier, was whether or not the prisoner was guilty.

No opinion can be more fallacious—none can be more unconstitutional. The question which the jury had to try was, not whether or not Courvoisier was guilty, but whether, upon the evidence produced before them, they could conscientiously pronounce that awful word which was to deprive a fellow-creature of his life. Though a juryman may be morally certain of the guilt of a prisoner, yet, unless he is convinced that the evidence produced before him is such as not to leave any reasonable doubt of his guilt, he not only is not justified in bringing in a verdict of guilty, but, on the contrary, he would, if he did so, be acting contrary to law—he would be guilty of a violation of his oath, and (in the case of life and death) he would be guilty of the murder of a fellow-creature. Such at least is the theory of our law. The maxim that "No man is to be esteemed guilty until he is proven so to be," is one which has ever been acted on in our courts, and is, in fact, the very corner stone of our criminal jurisprudence.

This error being cleared away, the question next comes to be considered, What is the duty of the prisoner's counsel? I hold that his first duty is to endeavour to procure, by every means in his power, the acquittal of his client; and if he cannot do that, at least to see that he is legally convicted.

[1] Replying to *To* the Editor of the *Morning Chronicle*, ?21 June 40, and replied to on 26 June (see pp. 86 and 90).

L.C.D.—R

Though a man be guilty, that is no reason that he should be convicted contrary to law. To warrant a conviction a man must not only be guilty, but his guilt must be legally proved; if that is not done, and yet, nevertheless, the man be convicted, he is as equally murdered as if he were perfectly innocent. If, then, the counsel for the prisoner is unable to procure his client's acquittal, he should at least endeavour to see that he is not convicted contrary to law. It is therefore his bounden duty to point out to the jury any contradictions, inaccuracies, or omissions that may appear to him in the evidence produced by the prosecutors; and if, through any maudlin sentimentality, or through any fear of inculpating others, he should neglect to do so, he would be guilty of a gross violation of duty, and would deserve to have his gown stripped off his back.

If, then, we admit this to be the duty of the prisoner's counsel, we can easily judge whether Mr. Phillips exceeded his duty upon Courvoisier's trial. In my opinion he certainly did not. He was fully justified in adopting the course which he did.

Some of the questions asked by "Manlius" have greatly surprised me. He surely must be one of those "practical men" who, in addition to their other qualifications, treat the rules of logic with the most sovereign contempt. Because Courvoisier was guilty, it follows as a matter of course that he could be legally convicted, and therefore the idea of a conspiracy to convict him in a legal manner was perfectly absurd! Because Courvoisier was guilty, his fellow-servant could not by possibility have a foreknowledge of the murder; nor could the articles found in his box have been deposited there by the police! Because Courvoisier was guilty, Mr. Phillips was not justified in exposing the startling equivocation of the landlady of the hotel[1] in Leicester-square, or in warning the jury that they would hazard their eternal salvation if they convicted the prisoner upon insufficient evidence!

Far be it from me to attempt for a moment to insinuate that the female servant was an accomplice in Courvoisier's crime, or that the police or any of the other witnesses for the prosecution did anything but their duty. All I mean to contend for is, that since, notwithstanding the guilt of Courvoisier, any of these circumstances might have taken place, Mr. Phillips was perfectly justified in the performance of his duty, namely, that of showing to the jury that upon the evidence produced before them they could not legally and satisfactorily convict his client, in alluding to any of these circumstances. And not only was he justified in so doing, but in my opinion he was absolutely bound to do so; for some of the circumstances—such, for instance, as the discovery of the blood-spotted gloves in the prisoner's box, four days after that box had been diligently searched, and the mysterious manner in which, at the eleventh hour, the missing plate was brought to light, were of such an extraordinary and mysterious nature that, had he failed to animadvert on them, he would have failed in the performance of his duty.

---

[1] "We wish our correspondent had pointed out the startling equivocation" (Editorial note in *Chronicle*).

As for the murder for which Courvoisier was tried being a most "savage, barbarous, and inhuman murder," as "Manlius" stigmatises it, that circumstance only rendered the duty of pointing out the deficiencies and inconsistencies in the evidence produced for the prosecution more incumbent upon Mr. Phillips, in order to prevent the jury being so hurried away by their feelings as illegally to convict the prisoner.

For the language employed by Mr. Phillips, in speaking of the police, and which is condemned by "Manlius" as "wild flowers, which have a rank and foul smell in the nostrils of honest men," I do not think that I am called upon to apologise. At present I am not speaking for Mr. Phillips; I am only speaking for myself; and it is the principle alone that is involved in the letter of "Manlius" that has called forth these remarks.

I am greatly afraid, that in making the remarks that I have done, I have trespassed too long upon your valuable columns. The importance of the subject must be my excuse. "Manlius's" letter, in my opinion, is calculated to do much mischief if suffered to pass without notice; for, as it is likely to meet with approval among overscrupulous persons, and as such persons are neither few nor powerless (such mawkish scrupulosity being, I am sorry to say, even to be found among a few of the bar and the bench), the letter if not replied to may go far to create a false tone of public opinion which would be productive of the most grievous consequences.

I cannot, perhaps, better conclude this rather long letter, than by citing for the benefit of "Manlius," and all the other "plain," "practical," and overscrupulous Manlii, the opinion expressed by Lord Erskine upon the question, whether or not a counsel ought to refuse to defend a prisoner—a question, which, though not in words, is yet in effect the same as that put covertly by "Manlius;" for if a counsel should defend a prisoner, surely he should defend him to the best of his ability and power. Lord Erskine had been much blamed for undertaking the defence of Paine when prosecuted for a libel. In his speech, therefore, upon the trial he took occasion to notice these accusations, and then continued by saying, "I will for ever, and at all hazards, assert and maintain the dignity, independence, and integrity of the English bar, without which, substantial justice, the most valuable part of the English constitution, can have no existence. From the moment that an advocate can be permitted to say that he will or will not stand between the Crown and the subject arraigned in the court where he daily sits to practise, from that moment the liberties of England are at an end. If the advocate refuses to defend from what he may think of the charge or of the defence, he assumes the character of a judge—nay, he assumes it before the hour of judgment—and, in proportion to his rank and his reputation, puts the heavy influence of perhaps a mistaken opinion into the scale against the accused, in whose favour the benevolent principle of English law makes all presumptions, and which commands the very judge to be his counsel."

A TEMPLAR.

### PRINTED ENQUIRY CONCERNING DICKENS'S HEALTH, FROM EAGLE LIFE ASSURANCE COMPANY, WITH FORSTER'S MS ANSWERS

Facsimile in A. F. Shepherd, *Links with the Past: a Brief Chronicle of the Public Service of a Notable Institution*, 1917, p. 124.

Eagle Life Assurance Office.<br>
Novr. 13 1841

Sir,

Having been referred to you for an account of the health and habits of Charles Dickens Esquire 1 Devonshire Terrace Marylebone I request the favor of a reply to the following Questions.

On your answer, which shall be considered as strictly confidential, the validity of the proposed Assurance must, in a great degree, rest; you will therefore, pardon me for reminding you of the importance of a full and deliberate statement.

I have the honour to be,<br>
Sir,<br>
Your most obedient, humble Servant,<br>
HENRY P. SMITH, Actuary.

How long have you been acquainted with C Dickens Esq — Five years—or more—most intimately.

How often are you in the habit of seeing him? When did you see him last? — I see him—generally—every day. We were together this morning.

In what state of health was he when you saw him last? .............. — In perfectly good health.

What is his general state of health? — I should say—extremely good.

Are you acquainted with his ever having been afflicted with a rupture, gout, dropsy, asthma, consumption, vertigo, fits, hemorrhage of any kind, cancer, insanity, or other disease, or of his having any symptoms of any disease? ...................... — I know that he has never had any of the diseases named. But, of late, for a short period, he has been under the care of Mr. Salmon, of Broad Street.

Do you believe he is now quite free from any disease, or symptom of disease, and in perfect health? ...... — He is now, I believe, quite free from every such symptom, and in excellent health.

Is he active or sedentary? ........ — His pursuits are sedentary; but he has great opportunities of leisure, and in these is always active. His tastes are very much so; and his habits remarkably sober & temperate.

Are his habits perfectly sober and temperate? ....................

| | |
|---|---|
| Has his Life ever, to your knowledge, been refused at any Insurance Office? | I recollect hearing some four years ago with some surprise, that he had been refused at the Sun Insurance Office. However, I know him to be already insured. |
| Did any member of his family die of pulmonary or hereditary disease of any kind? ..................... | His family are all alive, and all very strong hearty people. |
| Are you acquainted with any circumstances having a tendency to the shortening of his life, or which can make an insurance upon his life more than usually hazardous? ......... | I am acquainted with no such circumstances as the last two questions refer to. |

Are there any other circumstances within your knowledge which the Directors ought to be acquainted with?[1]........................

Signed   JOHN FORSTER
Dated    November 14th. 1841

---

[1] In an accompanying note Forster wrote: "I have really answered the questions in a most conscientious spirit to the best of my knowledge and belief. Macready, who has known Dickens also intimately for four years and upwards, would, I am sure, give you an equally good report. I wish that, if you thought it advisable to get all the information, you would send the questions to him as well" (A. F. Shepherd, *op. cit.*, p. 121). Smith sent the questions to Macready the next day, and received from him the following answers:

"Between 4 and 5 years.

once—twice—thrice—four or five times a week, as it may happen—very frequently. *On 31st. Octr.*

very good general health.

—as far as I know it, *very good.*

none, except that from which he has lately & so rapidly recovered.

I believe & trust so.

I should say, inclining to activity, but from occupation rather sedentary.

perfectly.

No.

Not that I know of.

*Certainly not*—to the *best of my judgment.*

*Not* that I can think of.
W. C. MACREADY
November 15th. 1841.
5 Clarence Terrace"
(Facsimile in A. F. Shepherd, *op. cit.*, p. 120).

# ADDENDA

## To COUNT D'ORSAY, 1 APRIL 1840*

MS Comte de Gramont.

Devonshire Terrace | April 1st. 1840.

Dear Count D'Orsay

I have a dim idea of lighting my small torch at the nightly fires of Wolverhampton[1]—and I cannot tell you how sorry I am that I have arranged to go to Birmingham with this view on Friday next, and to remain there or in the neighbourhood until the Monday following.

I am afraid you will be responsible if I look upon furnaces and coal pits with a jaundiced eye, for you put me out of humour with the expedition. Indeed if I had had your note one day earlier, I would have deferred it to another opportunity.

I beg my compliments to Lady Blessington, and am always

Faithfully Yours

CHARLES DICKENS

## To GEORGE BEADNELL, 26 JULY [1840]*

MS Douglas Library, Queen's University, Ontario. *Date:* 26 July was Sunday in 1840; handwriting supports that year.

Devonshire Terrace | Sunday 26th. July.

Dear Sir.

I go so very seldom to the Parthenon, and have so neglected my duties as a Member of the Committee (which I have never yet been able to attend) that I feel a great delicacy in proposing any candidates, and cannot therefore comply with your request.

Truly Yours

George Beadnell Esquire          CHARLES DICKENS

## To MESSRS CHAPMAN & HALL, 8 JULY 1841*

MS Bodleian Library.

Loch. Earn Head. | Thursday Eighth July 1841.

Dear Sirs.

With the view of having a whole day at Abbotsford and Dryburgh Abbey, I have altered my plan slightly, and arranged to be at Glasgow on

---

[1] Experience he stored up and used in *Old Curiosity Shop*, Ch. 44. See also *To* Forster, 4 Oct 40.

*Tuesday.* I write a hasty note to tell you this—that you may write to me accordingly. Copy and subjects by tomorrow's post.

Faithfully Yours always

Messrs. Chapman and Hall                              CHARLES DICKENS


## *To* COUNT D'ORSAY, 13 DECEMBER 1841*

MS Comte de Gramont.

     Devonshire Terrace. | Monday Thirteenth December | 1841. My Dear Count D'Orsay.

 I am sincerely obliged to you, both for your beautiful present[1] and your kind note; the latter has a most welcome and acceptable quality of heartiness which delights and does me good.

 I need hardly say that I shall be more than pleased to give you any opportunity you require for the completion of that likeness. I am sorry to say, though, that every day this week I am engaged to dinner; and as I shall only have a fortnight left when this week is over, I have "registered a vow"[2] to spend those fourteen days at home, both because I want to hold on tight by my household Gods to the last, and on account of my health which I am afraid may suffer from too much dining. Now, any morning this week, at any hour you name, I am wholly at your service, and on receiving due notice from you, will repair to Gore House and sit there as long as you like.[3]

 To save you further trouble in the matter of my head, I have directed my servant to wait for an answer to this. It shall be forwarded to you with care, and with the proper side upwards, whenever you may appoint.

 With a most sincere and unaffected pleasure in your cordiality and friendship, always believe me Dear Count D'Orsay.

Faithfully Yours

CHARLES DICKENS

## *To* HENRY BURNETT, [?DECEMBER 1841]

Extract quoted in Henry Burnett *to* F. G. Kitton, 19 Dec 88 (MS Huntington Library).[4] *Date:* probably between 30 Nov 41, when CD saw Adelaide Kemble in *Norma* (*To* Maclise, 29 Nov), and 4 Jan 42 when he sailed for America.

Adelaide Kemble is much talked about—I think her desperately unpleasant—almost repulsive.

[1] A piece of "warm Neck wrappery from Paris": see *To* Lady Blessington, 23 Nov 41, *fn.*

[2] Cf. *To* Miss Coutts, 14 Dec 41.

[3] CD sat for D'Orsay on 16 Dec: see *To* Lady Blessington, 23 Nov 41, *fn.*

[4] "Any thing I send you of CD's", wrote Burnett, "you are welcome to use. If you kindly post to me copies of letters I will promise not to pass my pencil over any thing but that which I believe Dickens would have wished to remain secret." He then quotes the above passage as an instance.

# INDEXES

# PUBLISHER'S NOTE

Not long after this Index was set up in proof its compiler, Mr. J. C. Thornton, died. The publishers wish to take this opportunity of expressing their appreciation of all that he contributed to making the contents of this volume and its predecessor readily accessible to the reader, and their sense of the loss which his death brings to scholarship in general as well as to this edition.

# INDEX OF CORRESPONDENTS

# INDEX OF NAMES AND PLACES

The index includes references to persons, publications, and places mentioned in the letters, the headnotes, the footnotes, the appendixes, and in the preface.

The index aims to be complete with the exception of the following items, which have been excluded: the sources from which letters have been obtained; references to standard works of reference, e.g. *DNB*; several place names and titles of works relevant to the subject of a biographical note and not mentioned elsewhere. The headnotes are only indexed when there is no corresponding item in the text of the relevant letter.

In the longer articles references are classified very broadly, e.g. 'social', 'CD, in relation to', and explanatory material is sometimes given in brackets after the page number. Sub-headings and any classification of sub-entries are arranged in alphabetical order except where a chronological order is followed.

Allusions and mention of a person or place otherwise than by name are included, sometimes with an indicative word in brackets after the page number, sometimes without explanation since this is usually to be found in the relevant footnote.

Holders of titles are generally indexed under the title, married women under their married names. Cross-references are given when likely to be helpful.

Books and writings are entered under the name of the author. If the author is little known, a cross-reference is usually given under the title. Writings of unknown authorship are indexed by title. Periodicals are also indexed by title. References to the characters in Dickens's novels are listed as a sub-section under the title of the novel within the article for DICKENS.

Localities, buildings, and streets are indexed under the name of the town or city to which they belong. If a separate entry is desirable, a cross-reference is given, e.g. DRURY LANE THEATRE, which has a cross-reference from LONDON: *Theatres*.

*Abbreviations and Symbols*

The letter 'D' stands for the name DICKENS, 'CD' exclusively for Charles Dickens. Initial letters are used to abbreviate most of the novels and writings by Dickens, e.g. *BR, MHC, OCS, S by B*, and are alphabetized as though spelt out.

The word 'and' is sometimes used to mean 'in relation to' or where the connection would otherwise require a lengthy explanation.

The word 'also' preceding a series of page numbers indicates that the references are minor and miscellaneous.

Footnotes are indicated by the letter 'n' (or 'nn') placed after the page number, headnotes by 'hn' similarly placed, thus 123n, 123 & n, 123hn.

If the footnote contains a person's main biographical particulars, the reference to it is placed first after the name in the index and distinguished by an asterisk.

All other abbreviations are those in common use.

As there is a separate Index of Correspondents, the article dealing with each correspondent in this index does not show which of the references are contained in letters to that correspondent. The names of the correspondents are, however, distinguished in the sequence of names by being printed in capitals.

The sign ∼ is used to show that the reference which follows it is linked with the preceding reference.

J. C. T.

Abbotsford 323, 496
Abercromby, Helen 252n
Abraham 368
*Actor's Life, An* see Anderson, J. R.
ADAMS, Henry Gardiner 11n*; as
editor of *The Kentish Coronal* 11 & n,
30, 81; Overs and 38, 65; also 452
Addison, Joseph: *Spectator* (quot.) 127n
Adelphi Theatre: dramatic version of
*OCS* at 146, 147 & n, 148 & n;
Forster to review pantomime at 10hn;
Forster suggests visit to 10n; Grat-
tan (Mrs) at 433n; *Jack Sheppard* at
11n, 21n, 148n; Mathews at 10n,
385n; Stirling's *The Fortunes of
Smike* at 37n; Yates's management
of 10n; also 311n, 331n, 332n
Adlington, Gregory, Faulkner & Follett,
solicitors 14 & n, 32n
'Admiral Hosier's Ghost', ballad 401n
Æsop 420n
*Age, The* 29n, 369 & n
AINSWORTH, William Harrison 14n*
CD, *relations with: BR*, on 212n
(letter to CD quot.); friendship, their
(*see also* Forster *below*) 14n; social
meetings: at Devonshire Terrace
169 & n, 463; ~ at Kensal Lodge,
birthday party 194 & n, 202, 203 & n,
204, 204–5n; ~ at Kensal Manor
House, housewarming 274 & n (letter
to CD quot.); ~ also 275n
*Forster, relations with:* their reconciliation 14n, 194 & n, 171 ('our
friend'), 171n, 204n
*Other references:* Athenæum, declined nomination to 14n; *Bentley's
Miscellany*, as editor of 14n, 47n,
151n; 'brighter ale' 204 & n; Cruikshank and 14n, 151n, 275n (letter to
CD quot.); Macready and 194n;
Overs and 19, 19–20n (letter to
Overs quot.); also viin, 7, 43n, 259n,
439n
*Works: Guy Fawkes* 14n, 151n;
*Jack Sheppard:* and *OT* 14n, 20–1, 20n,
21n; ~ dramatic version 2n, 10n, 11n,
21n, 87n, 148n; ~ Forster's review
of 171n; ~ also 19n; 'Old London
Merchant, The' 169n; *Old St Paul's*
151; *Stanley Thorn* 14n; *Tower of
London, The* 14n, 151n, 171n
*Ainsworth's Magazine:* 'A Few Words to
the Public about Richard Bentley'
14n; also 169n, 296n
Akerman, Keeper of Newgate 400 & n
Albert, Prince-Consort: allowance for
17 & n, 29n; birthday presents for
26n; father of 16n; Protestantism,
his 17 & n; verses on his marriage
16 & n; also 34n, 81n, 246n, 368

*Albion, or British, Colonial, and Foreign
Gazette* 421nn
Alderley see Stanley of Alderley
ALEXANDER, Francis 438n*; CD
promises to sit for 439 & n
Alexander, Mrs Francis 439
Alexis, magnetic boy see Didier, Alexis
Alison, William Pulteney 314n*; CD
meets 314, 316, 317n
*All the Year Round:* 'A Message from
the Sea' 52n; 'Robert Keeley' 455n;
'Some Recollections of Mortality' 9n,
10nn (quot.); also 34n
ALLAN, Miss 309, 321
Allan, William (later Sir William) 65n*;
appointment as queen's limner 66n,
317 & n; CD's party for 65, 68; with
CD in Edinburgh 308 & n, 314, 317 &
n, 321 ('iron uncle'); also 245n, 397n
Alleghany mountains 456n
Allen, John viin
Allen, Mrs Thomas see Lamert, Mrs M.
Allston, Washington 395n
Alphington, Devon: Mile End Cottage:
CD's visit (*Mar 39*) 214n; ~ (*July
40*) 106 & n, 107n, 109 ('doll's house')
& n, 113; proposed sale of 225; also
61, 78, 226n, 289n, 463n
Altick, Richard Daniel: *The English
Common Reader* 371n
Amberley, John Russell, Viscount 285n
Amburgh, Isaac van see Van Amburgh
America
CD's *proposed visit to:*
—— early thoughts of 52 & n,
267n, 380 & n
—— announced to friends, etc.:
Blessington (Countess of) 425; Brough-
ham (commission to CD) 447n; Chapman & Hall 383 (to Hall), 388; Clark
(L. G.) 394, 445; Coutts (Miss) 412,
431, 443–4 ('to take your orders'),
444n; Forster 386 & n, 388–9; Fred
D 392; Holland (Lady) 447 & n
(letter to CD quot.); Hood 456n
(his pun); Irving 395; Jeffrey 418 & n
(letter to CD quot.), 456n (commission to CD); Keeley 455 & n; Lea &
Blanchard 425; Macready 387; ~ his
advice sought 387–8, 388n, 390 & n,
391 & n; *MHC*, in 366n, 388–9, 389n;
Mitton 390 & nn; Napier, who
advised against 406n
—— preparations: whether to take
the children 383, 387–8, 388n, 390n,
391n, 392, 399; Kate reconciled 392;
Maclise to draw the children 393n;
'thrown back' by 405; 'rumours of
war' *ib.* & n, 415; insurance 346n,
414 & n, 420; anticipation (letters
from America) 439, 440; 'busy'

505

COUTTS, Angela Georgina Burdett, later Baroness Burdett-Coutts

*CD, relations with:* invitations to CD: accepted 95 (2), 100 ('going out') & n, 166, 184 ('library dinner') & n (*cf.* 189 CD prevented by cold), 194 & n (letter to CD quot.), 196, 201n, 434, 463; ~ declined 106, 121, 168, 358 (CD's 'daymare'), 359n (letter to CD quot.), 411 & n (letter to CD quot.), 443 & n (letter to CD quot.); CD to call on (at his request): meets Harness 182 & n (*cf.* 168); ~ at Roehampton 430; ~ to say good-bye 444 & n, 450 & n; Covent Garden, offers box to CD at 168 ('kindness') & n, 431, 433n; Drury Lane, offers box to CD at 265 & n, 450n; *MHC*, 'next' number of 192 & n (letter to CD quot.); *OCS*, receives presentation copy of 266, 283 & n (letter to CD quot.); Urania Cottage, in connection with 270n

*Other references:* Dunn and 207-8, 207n; Meredith (Miss) and 168n; pillows for hospitals stuffed by 444n; also vii, 178n, 181, 307n, 441n

Coutts, Sophia *see* Burdett, Lady

Coutts & Co., also mentioned as 'my bankers': CD's account with 3hn, 5 & n, 105n, 130n, 133 & n, 160n, 173n, 176n, 189n, 214, 215n, 226n, 253n, 279n, 312, 341n, 461n, 462n, 463n; John D and 207n, 289n; also viin, 3n, 442n

Covent Garden Theatre: CD on free list 385; Harley at 45n, 169n; Hunt's *A Legend of Florence* at 14n; Kemble (Adelaide) at 431 & n, 433n; Macready and 398n, 437; *Merry Wives of Windsor* at 168n; monopoly 21n; pantomime (*1840*) 239n; Passion Week, closed in 250nn; Vestris's (Mme) management of 14n, 21n, 45n, 71n, 385n, 437n; also 114 ('shut up'), 137, 265n, 309n, 311n, 385n, 461n

Cowper, Countess (Hon. Emily Mary Lamb, later Lady Palmerston) 25n, 28n (Melbourne's sister)

Cowper, Lady Frances Elizabeth (later Lady Jocelyn) 28n*; 23n, 28

Cowper, Leopold Louis Francis, 5th Earl 28n

Cowper, William: *John Gilpin* (quot.) 163 & n; translation of Homer 229n

Cowtan, Robert: *Memories of the British Museum* 461n

Cox (J. L.) & Sons, printers 259 & n

Craigcrook, West Lothian 305n, 316 ('a beautiful place'), 319, 320

Craigforth House, Stirlingshire 335n

Crewe Hall, Shropshire 104n

Critchley, Miss 342n

*Critic, The* 461n

Croker, John Wilson 225n

Croker, Thomas Crofton 330n

Crowe, Mrs (Catherine Ann Stevens): *Adventures of Susan Hopley* 256 & n; also 320n

Crown Life Assurance Co. 462

CRUIKSHANK, George

*CD, relations with* (see also *Pic Nic Papers* below): *BR* and 151nn; collaboration over an Annual proposed by CD 151n, 213nn; meetings 162, 169 (New Year's Eve party), 183 (2), 213n, 438n (at Egyptian Hall), 440n (letter to CD quot.)

*Illustrator, as:* Ainsworth's Magazine 14n; Bentley's Miscellany see *OT* below; *Comic Almanack* 162n; *Comic Annual* 151n, 220n; *Jack Sheppard* 20n; *OT ib.*, 85n, 277n; *Pic Nic Papers* 151 & n, 169n, 273 & n, 282 & n (letter to CD quot.), 287 (2)

*Other references:* Ainsworth and 151n; Bentley, quarrels with 13, 14n; Grant and 276 & nn; illness 162n; Lindsey (Lord) and 216 & n (letter to CD quot.); *Omnibus* (see also *George Cruikshank's Omnibus*): projected 213n (letter to CD quot.); ~ CD's praise of 276; Overs and (as contributor to *George Cruikshank's Omnibus*) 283 & n, 340 & n, 341, 354 & n (letter to CD quot.), 363, 412; also 386n

Cruikshank, Mrs George 440n

Cubitt, Lewis 263n

*Cultivator, The* 52n

Cunard Line, The 421n, 422n

Cunningham, Allan: *Life of Sir David Wilkie* 397n

Cunningham, H., publisher 420n

Curling, Jonathan: *Janus Weathercock* 252n

Curry (William) Junior & Co. 400n

Curtis & Son, printers 47n

Czarnowski, O. von 7n

Daguerre, Louis Jacques 284n

*Daily Commercial Advertiser* 438n

*Daily News, The:* CD's letters in 81n, 86n, 87n

Dalmally, Argyllshire 326

Dalmeny, West Lothian 320n, 321n

Dalrymple, A. 321n

Dalrymple, Mrs A. *see* Liston, Anne

DALTON, John Stuart 96n*; 96 ('a mutual admirer'); letter to *ib.*

Dalziel, George 135n

Dalziel Brothers, the 9n, 45n

*Dance of Death, The,* ed. Douce 229n

Dante Alighieri 149n

Tillotson, Kathleen (cont.)
84n; ed. *Oliver Twist* 44n, 84nn, 102n, 103n, 253n; ' "Pickwick" and Edward Jesse' 430n
TILSLEY, Hugh 400n*; 400
Tilt, Charles 151n, 213n
*Times, The:* anti-American article in (quot.) 406n; *BR* advertised and controversy discussed in 31 & nn, 32n; Drury Lane, on 454n; Elliotson, on 368n; Macready's letter to 454n; staff 101n, 448n; also 266n (quot.), 275n, 369 & n, 404n
*Times Literary Supplement, The* 18n, 430n
Todd, Rev. Henry John: ed. Spenser's *Works* 229n
Tom, servant to CD 322 & n, 327
TOMLIN, John 217n*; 217-18, 394n
Tonson, Jacob 273n
Topping, William: Grip and 202 ('groom'), 231, 304; groom, duties as 62 (2), 76; Smithson's pie and 449; smoking chimney and 98; sobriety of 412 ('groom'); also 42 & n, 92, 95, 97, 146, 148, 224, 317, 348, 387
Toronto 405n
Torquay, Devon 109n
*Tory, S.S.* 222n
Tothill Fields Prison (Westminster Bridewell): CD's visits to 246 & n, 253n, 283 ('to view your charge'); Boy Jones in 246n; 'silent gruel' 281 & n
Touchet, Mrs 274n
Toulmin, Camilla: *Landmarks of a Literary Life* 309n
TOWNSHEND, Rev. Chauncey Hare 110n*; Bulwer and 110n (letter to Bulwer quot.); Coldbath Fields Prison visited with CD 283n (letter to CD quot.); *Facts in Mesmerism* 110n, 291n, 292nn; *GE* dedicated to 110n; magnetic boy (Didier) and 110n, 291 & nn; social 110, 297 & n (letter to CD quot.), 342 & n (letter to CD quot.); sonnet to CD 112 ('gentleman who leaves England'), 112n (quot.)
TRACEY, Augustus Frederick, Lieut. R.N. 270n*; humanity to prisoners 270-1, 270n, 273-4, 274n, 281; also 283
Tractarians, the 16n
Traill, Professor 315n
*Traveller, The* 79n
Travers, Benjamin 242 & n ('anonymous man')
Travers, Susanna *see* Lamert, Mrs M.
Trentham, Staffordshire 68n
*Tribune,* New York viin
Trollope, Anthony 7n, 402n
Trollope ('Trolloppe'), Frances (Mrs Thomas Anthony Trollope, *née*

Trollope, Frances (cont.)
Frances Milton) 402n*; *Domestic Manners of the Americans* 402 & nn (quot.); *Martin Armstrong,* advertisement for 6n; also 12n, 442n
Trollope, Frances Eleanor (Mrs Thomas Adolphus Trollope second, *née* Frances Ternan): *Frances Trollope: her Life and Literary Work* (quot.) 402n
Trollope, Mrs Thomas Adolphus (first, *née* Theodosia Garrow) 107n
Trollope, Mrs Thomas Adolphus *see* Trollope, Frances Eleanor
Trossachs, the 322-3
Troughton, Zouch: *Nina Sforza* 416 & n, 429 & n
Tucker, Judge Beverly 143n
Tuckett, Capt. Harvey 359n
Tull, E. M.: *Charles Dickens and Reading* 288nn, 300n
Turner, Agnes 462
Turner, Joseph Mallord William 103n
*Twa Drovers, The* ('*Two Drovers*') 316 & n
Twickenham, Middlesex: CD at Eel Pie House 65 & n, 66
Twiss, Horace 441n
Tyas, publisher 134n
Tyler, Wat 176 & n
Tyndrum, Perthshire 326, 335
Tytler, Patrick Fraser: *England under the Reigns of Edward VI and Mary* 229n

*United Service Gazette, The* (quot.) 400n
United States of America *see* America
University College, London 51n, 164n
University College Hospital 109n, 368n
UPCOTT, William 2n*; asks CD for autograph 7, 37-8, 37n; CD gets portrait of Gordon from 296 & n; also 1, 463
Urania Cottage 270n

Valentine *see Famous History of Valentine and Orson*
Van Amburgh, Isaac 21n, 103n
Van Diemens Land 358 & n
Vasey, engraver 9n
Vestris, Lucia Elizabeth (Mrs C. J. Mathews) 385n*; manages Covent Garden 14n, 21n, 45n, 71n, 385 & nn, 437n; also 265n
Victoria, Australia 135n
Victoria, Princess (Princess Royal) 201 & n
Victoria, Queen: attempted assassination of 81-2, 81n, 82n; bridal night, Greville on (quot.) 25n; CD sees wedding procession 22hn & n; CD's books read by 26n; joke about love for 23 & n, 24 & n, 25-7, 28-9, 34n;